Today Lord Sugar is the owner of Amshold Group Ltd
and the popular star of the award-winning BBC series
The Apprentice, and the more recent *The Junior Apprentice*.
He has two honorary Doctor of Science degrees, one awarded
by the City of London University in 1988, and the other
from Brunel University in 2005. He was knighted in 2000.
In 2008 he was appointed to the Government Business Council
by PM Gordon Brown, and in 2009 he led the government's
Apprenticeship advertising campaign and roadshow seminars.
In the same year the PM appointed him Enterprise Champion
to advise the government on small business and enterprise,
and he was also awarded a life peerage, becoming
Alan, Baron Sugar of Clapton in the
London Borough of Hackney.

Follow Alan Sugar on:

twitter.com/Lord_Sugar

facebook.com/LordSugar

youtube.com/amshold

ALAN SUGAR

What You See Is What You Get

MY AUTOBIOGRAPHY

PAN BOOKS

First published 2010 by Macmillan

This edition first published 2011 by Pan Books
an imprint of Pan Macmillan, a division of Macmillan Publishers Limited
Pan Macmillan, 20 New Wharf Road, London N1 9RR
Basingstoke and Oxford
Associated companies throughout the world
www.panmacmillan.com

ISBN 978-0-330-52047-8

7 9 8 6

A CIP catalogue record for this book is available from
the British Library.

Typeset by Ellipsis Digital Limited, Glasgow
Printed in the UK by CPI Mackays, Chatham ME5 8TD

This book is dedicated to my mum and dad,
Johnnie and Rita, and Harold Regal

And to some of those who served me so well at Amstrad
but are no longer with us:
Dickie Mould, Michael Davis, Bill Weidenauer,
Simon Angel, Jim Rice and Eric Shaw

And to two men who helped me flourish in business
but, sadly, are also no longer with us:
Nick Lightowler and Shigemasa Otake

Contents

1

The Lucky Mistake

Tar Blocks, Ginger Beer and Other Childhood Enterprises

1947–60

There are three reasons why you might never have got the opportunity to read this book. The first is that maybe I wasn't planned to be in this world, the second is that once I did arrive I was abandoned, and the third is that my mum – accidentally – nearly killed me! Being twelve years younger than my closest sibling twins, I often joke that I think (well, I'm sure) I was a 'mistake' – maybe the result of a good night out during the post-war euphoria.

In the late forties, it was normal for babies to be left outside shops in their prams while the mothers went inside. That in itself gives you a picture of what times were like back then – parents were not worried about weirdoes abducting babies. One day, my mum (who hadn't had a baby to think about for twelve years) went to Woolworths and parked me outside in my pram. She did her shopping, walked out and took the 106 bus from Stoke Newington back to Clapton. Only when she was halfway home did it dawn on her: 'I've left Alan outside Woolworths!'

Like all kids, I picked up various bugs and sniffles and occasionally had to be off school. My mum would tuck me up in her bed and nip down to the shops to buy me some comics – the *Beano* and the *Dandy*. I'd finish reading them in half an hour and be bored stiff. On one particular day, when I was about ten, I got up, went into the kitchen and sat at the table, watching her cooking.

My mother had no sense of smell at all – an extraordinary phenomenon. I guess in those days medical science wasn't sufficiently advanced to know the reason or come up with a cure. Anyway, as I sat in the kitchen, I started drifting off. I folded my arms on the table and laid my head down, unable to keep awake. I was lucky that around midday my sister Daphne came home from work for lunch. Mum had left one of the gas rings on, and because she couldn't smell, she had no idea that the whole kitchen had filled with gas. It was so bad, Daphne swears she could even smell the gas from outside the front door. You can imagine her horror when she saw me, head down on the table. She rushed to pick me up and took me out on to the balcony for some fresh air.

I sometimes wonder just how much gas was in the air that day. Mum was cooking on the other gas ring, which was lit, so I reckon it wouldn't have taken too long for the whole room to blow up. So there you have it. I may have entered the world by mistake, been abandoned and nearly killed, but I am here to tell my story.

This may have given you the wrong impression of my mum, Fay, who was the strong centre of the family. She was nearly forty when I was born on 24 March 1947 at Hackney Hospital and she had a difficult labour. To use her words, 'They were very worried about me – I was on the gates.' (On the gates of heaven, she meant.) In the end, I was born by Caesarean section, and was pulled out with a pair of tongs which grabbed me by my upper lip, according to Mum. Later in life, when I was at the swimming baths or at the seaside and came out of the water shivering with cold, two dark marks would appear on my upper lip. Mum would say, 'Look at Alan's upper lip. See those two blue marks? That's where they schlapped him out.' Is that an old wives' tale or what?!

My dad Nathan (Nat to everyone) was also nearly forty when I was born. My parents' relatively advanced age endorses my theory that I wasn't a planned arrival. I was always slightly embarrassed at school on parents' day because they looked much older than the other mums and dads – more like grandparents.

They were both born in the East End of London, my mum on 31 December 1907. She was one of twins, but sadly her twin sister died at birth. Mum was only fourteen when her mother died and, as the eldest of six children, she had the heavy task of running the home – cooking, cleaning and shopping for everyone. Her father, Aaron, had a horse and cart and his business was hauling stuff – I guess in modern-day terms he would be a man with a van. I never met my maternal grandfather, who died before I was born, but I was named after him, Alan being the anglicised version of the Hebrew name Aaron.

My dad was born on 3 August 1907, and was also one of six children. I'm told that his father, Simon, was a cobbler, and I think the whole family, as with so many other Jewish families, derived their income from the garment industry one way or another. Anyway, it's safe to say that my parents both came from ordinary, low-income, working-class families. Certainly there was no inheritance coming my way.

Mum and Dad married on 1 March 1931 at Philpot Street Synagogue. My eldest sister, Shirley, was born on 10 January 1932, ten months after Mum and Dad got married – they didn't hang about. The twins, Daphne and Derek, were born on 28 August 1934. In terms of appearance, Derek and Shirley take after Dad, and Daphne and I take after Mum.

My mum was short, around 5 ft 3 in., and stocky – not fat but strongly built and fit. She got her exercise humping two full shopping bags on and off buses, walking the long distance from the bus stop to our block of flats and then climbing the three flights of stairs up to our flat – and that was when she was in her forties and fifties. It makes me laugh these days how most housewives have cars and, if they can afford it, go down to the gym to keep fit by walking on a treadmill! My build is just like hers and fortunately I am blessed with her fitness. Dad was also stockily built and quite short, around 5 ft 6 in. Although he wasn't fat, he would go up and down in weight and have to cut back on what he ate from time to time and I inherited that tendency too.

By the way, to correct some of the snipers in the media who have in the past used some colourful language to describe me, including 'the short, stocky, 5 ft 6 in. midget', my official height is 5 ft 8 in. and has been since I was sixteen.

My parents' first married home was in Stepney. They moved to 16 Woolmer House, Upper Clapton – in the borough of Hackney – on 7 June 1942. At that time, people were being moved out of Stepney and the docks area, as it was a prime target for German bombing.

Woolmer House, where I was brought up, was part of a very large council estate on the main Upper Clapton Road. Our block was three storeys high, with no lift, and was situated in a cluster of about three other blocks, with what I called a playground in the middle which had some poles for the housewives to hang out their washing.

Our corner flat was on the top floor, and it was unusual because it had two levels. It had a toilet and separate bathroom, with a bath that doubled up as a table (you lifted up the hinged top when you wanted a bath), a kitchen, a lounge and one large bedroom on the first level, which was where Mum and Dad slept, while upstairs there were two more bedrooms for the kids.

I have no memories of my eldest sister Shirley when she lived at home, but I'm told that because I had a mop of curly blond hair she would call me Mopsy! I was a page boy at her wedding when I was five, and a day or so before the event I got hold of a pair of scissors and cut all my curls off. Everyone, including Shirley, went bananas. Why did they let a five-year-old near a pair of scissors, you may ask.

I also have only a vague recollection of Daphne and Derek living at home. Derek did his National Service in Singapore, and when he came back he worked in a garment factory as a machinist. He was very bright and these days would have gone to university, but back then there was no chance my parents would have been able to support him. While working in the factory he studied for the Knowledge, to become a London taxi driver. I'd sometimes help him study – I'd call out, 'Balls Pond Road to Piccadilly Circus' and he'd have to tell me the route.

As we lived at the top of a block of flats, I never had the chance to play with other kids of my age when I was very young. All I knew were teenagers and adults. It's not so much that I lacked confidence, but it was a definite shock to the system when Mum dropped me off on my first day at Northwold Road Primary School, as I didn't like the idea of going to school and not being with her. At breaktime, when they let us out into the playground, I saw my chance, escaped through the open gate and ran all the way home, crying my eyes out, with a member of staff chasing after me. When I got there, I was greeted by Daphne, who asked, 'What are you doing?' She could see I was upset and then she spotted an out-of-breath teacher, puffing and panting behind me.

Between them they calmed me down, and I went back to school like a good boy. I guess this nervousness at the first day of school is quite typical and it can't have taken me long to settle in, as the teachers were soon telling me to stop talking.

I got on like a house on fire with the other kids, who were all from the local area. There were quite a few Jewish kids, but the majority were non-Jewish. At that time, 1953–9, there were only a couple of Asian and black kids, who obviously stood out. I mention this because all of us kids were totally unaware of anything to do with race or religion. We behaved like all children do – joking, larking around, sometimes spiteful to each other, as you would expect. But one thing that was definitely, and pleasantly, missing was racism. It's wonderful to think back to, and I guess it's proof that it is adults who poison the minds of youngsters.

In my last year at Northwold Road Primary, when I was about eleven, we had an 'open day'. The event took place in the grand hall where the whole school met for assembly each morning. The hall was decked out with pupils' schoolwork, displayed for visiting dignitaries, parents and headteachers of secondary schools.

Typically, a member of each class would take the visitors through his or her class's work. I was chosen by my teacher to talk to the parents of the kids from our class. It came naturally to me, explaining in detail the work on show. Knowing me, I imagine I was offering *too much* detail and maybe repeating myself, especially if I thought the audience wasn't grasping what I was saying. I recall explaining to one parent why a conker tree is called a horse chestnut tree: if you break a leaf off a branch, at the base of its stem you'll see a series of dots in the shape of a horseshoe.

While I was talking, I could see people smiling and whispering to each other and I had no idea why. I know now they were smiling at this little kid who was nevertheless a good presenter. I must have been, because a couple of days later, the headmaster, Mr Kershaw, chose me to give a presentation on behalf of the whole school to an audience which included the Lord Mayor and an array of visiting secondary school headteachers (one of whom was Mr Harris, my future head-master at Joseph Priestley Secondary School). Clearly I was already set on the path to what I've been doing for the rest of my life: selling, presenting and marketing.

I wasn't one of the brainy ones at school. In those days, in your final year at primary school, everyone would sit the Eleven Plus exam. If you passed, you would get a place at a grammar school, somewhere like the prestigious Grocers in Hackney Downs. I got a 'marginal pass' in my Eleven Plus, a polite way of saying, 'You failed, but only just.' However, it did allow me to apply for one of the limited number of places the grammar schools would give at their discretion, known as 'governors' places'. You went along for interviews to see whether you could project yourself in such a manner that they would overlook the marginal failure of the Eleven Plus.

I remember going on one such visit to a school in Cambridge Heath Road, Bethnal Green. Throughout the thirty-minute ride on the 653 trolleybus, I was wondering whether I wanted to make this journey for the next five years of my life. With my motor-mouth, I passed the interview with flying colours and was offered a place at the school, but by a stroke of luck I never went there. The stroke of luck was down to my soon-to-be headmaster Mr Harris who, unbeknown to me, had been soliciting Mr Kershaw to recommend to my mum and dad that I should attend *his* school, Joseph Priestley, in Morning Lane. It was soon going to merge with another school, Upton House, to form what was to be known as Brooke House School, a very advanced and modern comprehensive – one of the first, I believe, to come into existence. Saying yes was the best move my parents made.

That school was a fantastic establishment, with such diversity – I performed in Shakespearian plays *and* learned bricklaying! There were science laboratories and handicraft workshops, and we were taught plumbing and metalwork, draftsmanship and technical drawing, the arts, economics – basically everything you could think of. I learned how to build a brick wall, operate a lathe, produce hydrogen in a laboratory, do calculus and to this day I can recite act one, scene one of *Twelfth Night*.

*

I can clearly remember the day I joined Joseph Priestley – 8 September 1958, the day after my brother Derek's wedding to Brenda Press. I was very nervous and dreaded the prospect of having to meet a whole new bunch of people. Thankfully, there were a few kids from my class at Northwold Road joining at the same time, so at least there would be some people I knew.

I remember my mum laying out the new school uniform for me and my arrival in the playground on the first day. I stood huddled together with my friends, observing the rather boisterous behaviour of the older pupils. Within minutes, I heard racial remarks about Jews.

'Hey, Charlie, tell that bloody Jew to get out my way – he ain't playing with us.'

'The fucking Yids are using the goalposts – tell 'em to piss off.'

While the comments weren't directed at me, it was still a total shock. It was the first time I'd heard the expression 'Yids' and I couldn't quite understand what was going on. When I went home that night, I described this to my mum and dad. I can't remember whether they gave me any good counselling on the subject, but I *was* traumatised. For the first time ever, I realised that I was, apparently, different. How could that be? We'd never heard anything like this at Northwold Road Primary.

The guys with whom I'd joined Joseph Priestley weren't Jewish, but as time went on they started to recognise the fact that I *was*, and regrettably some of them became racists. The point I am illustrating is that you could see how the innocent minds of kids coming from a school like Northwold Road were poisoned by others. One incident that sticks in my mind happened soon after I joined the new school. The Jewish holidays of Rosh Hashanah and Yom Kippur fell in September and, excused by a letter from Mum and Dad, I was allowed to take two days off for Rosh Hashanah and a day off the following week for Yom Kippur. When I returned there was a completely different atmosphere. I used to sit with a variety of my old friends from Northwold Road, but when I went to take my place on this particular day, the two kids near me were cold and distant. My absence had highlighted to them that I was a Jew – a matter that had never come up before, perhaps because I spoke like any other Cockney kid from Clapton and didn't look typically Jewish, being fair-haired and fair-skinned. Or perhaps these two mates *did* know I was Jewish but had thought I was just like them anyway.

At first I couldn't work out what was going on. I'd speak to them and get simple 'yes' and 'no' answers, and at breaktime they distanced themselves from me. There was no sign of friendship any more. And then, one day, one of them said something like, 'Well, you Jews are all the same.' From that point on, we never spoke again and I was isolated as a 'different' person. It was quite amazing, considering that a month or so earlier we had been the best of pals.

You have to understand that back then we kids from Northwold School, of all religions and races, knew nothing about the Holocaust or Nazis. Obviously we all knew about the Second World War. We'd learned how great Winston Churchill was and how Britain had won the war, but that's all we were ever taught there. The non-Jewish kids at Northwold Road did not have the opportunity to understand what went on in the Holocaust or form opinions on it. Who knows, if they had been made aware of it, they might have agreed with the Nazis – I'm pretty sure some of the parents did. How else could some of the kids at the new school be racist? It *must* have come from the parents.

*

At Woolmer House there were a few Jewish families, but the majority were non-Jewish, and the kids played together in the same way I'd experienced in Northwold Road. Next door to us on the top floor lived the Moores. Percy and Ivy Moore had eleven children and they were a real salt-of-the-earth English family. There was mutual respect between the Sugars and the Moores.

Life was hard in the late fifties – perhaps harder than I ever understood – but for some reason we had a telephone, which was deemed a luxury in those days. I suspect it was because my dad liked to place the odd bet with his bookmaker, though he kept this very close to his chest. He shouldn't really have been betting, considering how he complained about every single penny that had to be spent. In fact, the thought of being without money and not being able to put food on the table used to worry the hell out of him.

My father was also paranoid about running out of electricity. We'd feed the meter with shillings at the start of the week, but because the single-bar heater we had in the lounge consumed electricity at a rate of knots, the meter would sometimes run out by Thursday afternoon and there'd be no money to feed it. The Moores had the same problem. Often Ivy would pop in to borrow a shilling; sometimes Mum would borrow a shilling from her. The respective dads would come home with their pay-packets on Friday, so on Saturday morning the shillings would get thrown into the meter again.

Ted, the Co-op milkman, would come round daily. This poor sod used to climb the stairs in our block and deliver milk to every flat. He'd knock on the door at the end of the week to be paid. You'd have to give him your Co-op number (ours was 85 4 139 – how's that for memory?) and he'd hand over a little receipt. You built up points and eventually you were able to redeem them for stuff in the Co-op shops.

Then there was the rent man, who would come round monthly and pick up four weeks' rent at 8s 6d (eight shillings and sixpence) per week – that's around 42p in today's money. The fact that the Sugars and the Moores made sure that the rent was always paid on time shows the kind of discipline and decency that existed in those days.

My dad, who was a tailor, installed a sewing machine in my brother's old bedroom upstairs and called it his 'home workshop'. He wasn't the best tailor in the world – I recall him going to evening classes to improve his tailoring and machinist skills, to try to command better pay in the garment factories, and he'd occasionally knock up coats for relatives and friends.

It wasn't just Dad who sharpened his tailoring skills in his makeshift workshop. I used to watch him and over the years he taught me how to do various things, such as how to shorten a pair of trousers. I became a dab hand at what's known as cross-stitch. Later in life, I would buy a pair of trousers, bravely cut an inch or two off the legs, fold up the bottoms, execute my cross-stitching craft and press them into place. This ability is something which fascinates my wife Ann. I haven't done it for years, but she's always telling people how I can shorten trousers and even dresses. This skill was to play a part in a funny story you'll read about later.

I would also watch my mum cook. I was the talk of the flats when one day, around the age of eleven, for some mad reason, I decided I would make a ginger cake. I'd seen Mum make them many times and knew the ingredients off by heart. You can imagine my mum's surprise when she got home and I presented her with a still-warm cake.

'When did you make this?' she said.

'I've just taken it out of the oven.'

So far, so good. She had a smile on her face and she was nodding her head in happy surprise. Then suddenly it dawned on her that she didn't have any ginger or baking powder.

'How did you make it?' she asked.

I explained that Mrs Clark, a few doors away, had lent me some baking powder and that Mrs Cohen, a floor below, had lent me some ginger powder. And by the way, while I was at it, 'We've now run out of sugar, as I used the last lot.'

She went mad. 'You can't go asking people for things – tell me again who you asked.'

She ran off to Mrs Clark and Mrs Cohen to apologise, but came back with a smile on her face. It seems that Clarkie and Mrs Cohen were killing themselves laughing at my sheer cheek. They told Mum I'd explained to them I was making a ginger cake as a surprise for her and they just wanted to know if the cake had come out okay. In fact, it was perfect. I took them some when it had cooled down (best eaten a day after cooking). The ginger cake became a historic story in the family and a favourite amongst the neighbours for years after.

I've often wondered where my entrepreneurial spirit came from. It certainly didn't come from my father. He had a skill – making clothes – but he never exploited it. Employment wasn't secure in those days and he was constantly in and out of work. It was normal to be told on Friday night, 'Don't bother to come in on Monday, as there's no work.'

Often the out-of-work tailors would congregate in a huddle outside Black Lion Yard in Whitechapel Road. Sometimes, during school holidays, I would join him, standing around while the men exchanged stories. The conversation usually revolved around which factories might be getting work that week.

You would have thought that, having acquired the skill to make clothes, my father would have realised that by turning out one or two coats a week and selling them, he could make more than the pittance he was earning. He could even have taken it a stage further by advertising the fact that he was available to make coats. But my father was a cautious person, always careful to ensure nothing went so badly wrong that he'd be without money. I don't know why he had this fear; maybe growing up without money had left a scar. My brother Derek once told me that, shortly after the war, the family had the opportunity of buying a house in Dagenham for what sounds a ridiculously small amount of money today – around £400 – although in those days (1946–7) £400 was a fortune. Dad didn't have the foresight to do it. The story goes that he also had the opportunity of taking a small shop with a workshop at the back where he could make and sell clothes, but again he didn't go for it.

My mother's side of the family was a slightly different story. Her brother, Uncle John, was the rich uncle – every family has one. My mum's maiden name was Apple, so you can imagine the jokes when an Apple married a Sugar. Uncle John was a real character. He had a store, Apple's Hardware, in Victoria. People used to go there just to see the price tickets on his wares, on which he'd write stupid little quips. For example, a price ticket on a broom would say, 'This broom was used by a very tall girl by the name of Jean, so it's very hygienic.' Pathetic, I know, but if you can imagine the forecourt of his shop and the pavement lined with all these silly little jokes, you can see why he got himself quite a reputation. Apparently, he exploited the post-war boom and his hardware business enabled him to accumulate money and pick up some properties in the area.

Back at home, lack of money was always the main item on the agenda. We made the most of what we could afford, but we didn't have money for anything more than the basics one needed to live. Certainly there were no luxuries. This was brought into focus for me when I saw some of the more fortunate kids at school starting to amass possessions: a pair of football boots, a ball, a new Dinky toy car, roller skates. I couldn't have these things unless the family clubbed together for my birthday. My parents did their best, but not being able to have what I wanted made me determined to do something for myself – to be self-sufficient.

I had loads of enterprises on the go. Next to Woolmer House there was a rag-and-bone merchant who would go round collecting items such as old iron and other metal, clothing and material. He'd pay scrap value for the stuff. In his yard was a sign saying, 'Wool 5s per lb [five shillings per pound of weight], cotton 1s 6d per lb [one shilling and sixpence], brass and copper 2d per lb [tuppence].' Playing out in the street when I was eleven, I noticed people taking items in and getting money in exchange and I wondered if I could get hold of any stuff, so that I too could make some money. It was during one of my other ventures – car-cleaning – that I found something.

In the back streets of Clapton, some of the big Victorian houses were converted into small garment factories with rooms full of machinists. These factories would sub-contract for bigger manufacturers using 'outdoor workers' (the old name for sub-contractors). One day, while cleaning the factory boss's car, I saw in the front garden some open sacks of material trimmings, ready for the dustman to take away. When I went inside to collect my 1s 6d, I asked the boss what was in these sacks and he explained they were remnants of the material used to make the clothes. I asked him if I could take some and he said I could, but looked puzzled.

'What are you going to do with them?' he asked.

'Don't worry, leave it to me,' I replied. The sacks were bigger than I was, so I went back to the flats and borrowed a pram. I loaded on two sacks and took them round to the rag-and-bone man.

Here was my first experience of getting 'legged over'. Unbeknown to me, the sacks contained gold dust as far as the scrap merchant was concerned, as the material was wool. This bloke took one look at this eleven-year-old and said, 'What you've got in those sacks is rubbish.' He weighed the stuff on his scales and said, 'I'll give you half a crown [2s 6d] for the lot.' I took it. Naïve – stupid, you might say – but half a crown was a lot of money in those days.

The next week, after cleaning the boss's car, I asked him what kind of material was in those sacks. When he told me it was wool, I was furious – I should have got at least £1 10s for two sacks of wool. I took a scrap of the material to the rag-and-bone man and confronted him. 'I've just been told this is wool – you told me it was rubbish. I want some more money or I want the two sacks back,' I yelled at him angrily. I won't tell you what he said to me. He slung two shillings at me and told me to clear off.

'I can get loads more of this stuff and I'm going to find another rag-and-bone man to sell it to!'

He just laughed and virtually threw me out.

Another side of me came out now. I was wound up and angry. I wasn't frightened to speak up, but short of grabbing hold of him or kicking him, what could I do? He was a grown man and I was an eleven-year-old shnip. I went back home and told my mum and dad what had happened. They laughed, then my father asked, 'How much did you get in the end?'

'Four and six.' A sudden look of fear came over his face at the realisation that his eleven-year-old son had made 4s 6d.

'Where did you get this stuff from?' he said.

'I told you – from the factory down the road.'

'They let you take it? You sure you didn't take it without asking?'

'No. The boss gave it to me. He wanted to get rid of it. Normally the dustman takes it away.'

'Are you sure?'

I couldn't believe it. Instead of being complimented, I was being interrogated as if I'd done something wrong! It was a strange attitude, but one I'd become increasingly familiar with in later years. Many's the time I'd have to play down the success of my business activities because my father could not believe that someone so young could make so much money. To put things into perspective, his take-home pay at the time was £8 for working a forty-hour week. How could an eleven-year-old boy go out and make 4s 6d in just a couple of hours? Basically, I'd spotted some stuff in one place and seen another place to sell it. And what's more, I really enjoyed doing it.

At the numerous talks I give around the country these days, I often hear the term 'entrepreneurial spirit' bandied about. At these talks, there'll be a Q&A session and it never fails to annoy me when somebody stands up and says, 'Hello, I'm an entrepreneur . . .' It really winds me up. An entrepreneur is not a word to be used lightly and it's certainly not something you call *yourself*. It should be a term used by a person when describing another's abilities. I refer to *my* entrepreneurial spirit as I have been branded an entrepreneur so many times by so many people that I feel I've earned the right, and I can see what it takes to be labelled as such. I often say that it doesn't matter which business school you go to or what books you read, you can't go into Boots and buy a bottle of entrepreneurial juice. Entrepreneurial spirit is something you are born with, just like a concert pianist's talent. Stick me in a room with a piano teacher for a year and maybe I'll end up being able to give you a rendition of 'Roll Out the Barrel', but would I ever be a concert pianist playing at the Royal Albert Hall? Not in a million years. In the same way, you've either got entrepreneurial spirit or you haven't. It resides within you and it's sparked off by ideas that come about through the various situations you find yourself in.

One such story – where a situation sparked off an idea – started with the simple need to light a fire for warmth. In those days, before everyone had central heating, raw coal was used as fuel. In our case, it heated the boiler for the bath and we had a coal fireplace. There was also a fireplace in my bedroom, but it was never used and many a winter's morning I would get up and find the windows iced over. Sometimes the glass of water by my bed would be frozen solid.

The coalmen would arrive outside Woolmer House with their large flatbed lorry loaded with sacks of coal. These poor fellows would hump their sacks up three flights of stairs and empty them into the large coal box we had in the hall. They must have been very fit, but heaven knows what today's Health and Safety brigade would have made of their working conditions, especially as they breathed in the clouds of coal dust that filled the air each time a sack was emptied.

Lighting the fire was a specialised job. You could buy fire-lighter strips, but they were a waste of money. Instead, most people bought little bundles of wooden sticks which were packaged in rolls and sold by most general hardware shops, such as Uncle John's. Many's the time I was sent down to Mr Braham's or Mr Morris's shop to buy these sticks, which sold for sixpence a bundle. You would make a little wigwam out of them, put some paraffin on them and stuff a bit of newspaper inside. Then you'd arrange the coal around the sticks. To start the fire, you lit the paper, which in turn would set light to the sticks and then the coal. It took about ten minutes to get a fire going.

Why have I told you all this? Well, it relates to another of my cheeky childhood schemes, which stemmed from, of all things, road construction. In the late fifties the roads in Clapton were being resurfaced. I used to look out of the window and watch the workers with all their machinery, fascinated by the sights and sounds of it all – the plumes of fire and the clattering of pneumatic drills as they loosened the surface and dug it up. Nowadays, roadworks are performed quite quickly, but back then they went on for months. Sometimes I'd go down to the street and watch them more closely. I'd chat with the workers and ask what they were doing and I even started running back and forth to the café for them, getting them tea and sandwiches.

The removal of the old road surface uncovered a base layer of wooden blocks set into the ground in a herringbone pattern. New road construction techniques no longer required these blocks, so they were discarded. The workers showed me the blocks, which were impregnated with tar, and they chucked a couple onto their fire – they burned like a rocket. Bingo! It occurred to me that these discarded wooden blocks could be made into fire-lighting sticks. I could cut them up into bundles of sticks and flog them to Mr Braham and Mr Morris.

It was an education going into Morris's. This silver-haired little man, who spoke English with a high-pitched Polish accent, was renowned for his computer-like brain – he was a human checkout till. Customers would put their shopping on the counter, he would call out the items and their prices one by one, tot it all up in his head and declare the total. He was magic – faster than a calculator.

Out came the old pram and, with the permission of the workers, I loaded it up with the wooden blocks and took them back to the flats, stacking them in a corner of the playground. I went backwards and forwards collecting these blocks, and by the evening I'd amassed a big pile. Using a small axe we used to have at home – don't ask me why – I set to work chopping them up into sticks. The other kids in the flats thought this looked like fun and they too brought along various implements and helped me out, even though they didn't know why I was doing it.

My dad hoarded all manner of things, including old balls of string. I used some of it to tie the sticks into bundles and as soon as I had a few, I went round to Mr Braham and asked him if he wanted to buy some. He looked at me as if I were nuts. 'I've got enough of this stuff out in my back yard – why would I want any more?'

I knew he'd have a fire going in the back of his shop (as I once worked there on a Saturday before I jumped ship to the greengrocer's down the road) so I chucked on one of the sticks, which burst into flames. He looked at me and smiled, as if to say, 'You little sod – how did you do that?'

Threepence a bundle was the price he said he'd pay, and within two days I'd converted all the stuff and taken it to his yard. The other kids were on to this like a shot, but they didn't have my sales skills.

I wanted to go further afield and deliver to other shops, but this was virtually impossible, as the stuff was heavy and the pram could only hold a limited amount. One of the kids' dads had a van and I suggested to him that if he could get his dad to drive us around, we could widen the empire. I would, of course, share some of the proceeds with him. He got the green light and we made up a load of bundles and put them in the bike shed. Then we went on the road, so to speak.

The following week, as word about my venture spread throughout the flats, admiring neighbours would say, 'We heard about your sticks, Alan.' And, of course, my mum and dad got wind of it too. By now, my schemes were like water off a duck's back to my parents. The old man couldn't accuse me of any wrongdoing, as he'd seen the road being dug up. All the same, I never saw any signs of pride or heard any congratulations from them for my enterprises. I'm going to give them the benefit of the doubt about that, as maybe I've just forgotten. All I *do* remember is my mum laughing or tutting or shrugging her shoulders, and my father shaking his head.

There was, of course, a limit to how many of these blocks I could deal with. What I had stashed away was minute compared to what was available, so you can imagine my frustration when I saw my wooden gold being carted off in lorry-loads, just to be dumped somewhere.

Anyway, in the end, the bigger boys in the flats got in on the action. They started doing the same thing and sort of muscled me out. 'That's it, mate, it's over for you. Get out of the way, we're taking over.' You couldn't argue, as you felt you might get beaten up or something. I wasn't too sorry though, as it was a lot of hard and dirty work to make a relatively small amount of money.

Nevertheless, I learned an important lesson. I think it was Karl Marx who said, 'Catch a man a fish, you can sell it to him. Teach a man to fish, you ruin a wonderful business opportunity.' I'd discovered that as soon as any new business idea is born, up springs the competition. This truism would rear its head time and time again throughout my business life.

*

Not *all* my early enterprises made money or got me a pat on the back. At Brooke House, the English teacher, Mr Jones, decided the school should have its own monthly magazine. My brother-in-law Harold Regal (married to Shirley) was a printer, and sometimes in the school holidays I'd go along to the small printing company he owned in Clerkenwell. I'd play around with the printing equipment and watch the compositors line up lead letters in a block and put it on the printing press. As a result, I had the brainwave that the school should buy its own printing machine and, together with one of the other pupils, I would be responsible for producing the school magazine. This idea was put to the deputy headmaster and funds were made available.

I purchased a second-hand Adana printing machine on behalf of the school but, unfortunately, I had bitten off more than I could chew. Anyone in the business who can remember that far back will know it was a ridiculous venture. The Adana was good for printing business cards or invitations, but not a multi-page job like a magazine. The reality hit home when we attempted to do it – it took us about an hour to set one sentence! Despite this setback, the school magazine went ahead using the old-fashioned duplicator, and to compensate the school for their disappointment over the printing-machine investment, I took on the role of selling the magazine externally.

The council estate where I lived housed many of my fellow pupils and, like most kids, they never told their mums and dads what went on at school so I took it upon myself to knock on the doors of the kids' parents. My sales patter was that I was representing the school and would they like to buy the magazine for a shilling? After a couple of days' work, I had sold over a hundred copies!

I turned up at Mr Jones's English lesson with the news that I'd earned the school £5 from sales of the magazine, but that I'd run out of copies and needed some more. You would have thought he'd just won the lottery. The man was flabbergasted. He asked me how I'd done it and I told him, 'I just visited the parents of the kids in our flats.'

The story spread to the headmaster, the deputy head and the teaching staff. From that day on, I was known as the school's enterprise star, an accolade the headmaster never failed to bring up at open days.

The deputy head called me into the staffroom a few weeks later (I used to make the tea for the staff from time to time). He told me that while he was pleased with the school magazine enterprise, I had lumbered him with the Adana machine and it was up to me to sell it. I explained that to sell it I would need to advertise it in the *Exchange & Mart*, so if could he give me ten bob, I'd get the job done.

He turned to the other staff and said, 'Did you hear that? This boy has landed me with a fifteen-pound printing machine and now wants ten shillings to get rid of it for me!' He was seriously angry.

I shrugged my shoulders and politely suggested that if he had any other ideas, perhaps he should try to sell it himself. He told me to get on with it and I sold it for about £17, so he had nothing to complain about.

*

There is a perverse kind of cruelty that can be put upon children, unwittingly, by parents who are meaning to do so well for them. Like all secondary school kids, I was growing every year and at twelve I needed a new school uniform. A new uniform represented a significant financial outlay to a poor family like ours. What's more, by now the school had become Brooke House Comprehensive and the new regime was very hot on uniform compliance. The local school outfitters, of course, had a field day. All the boys' parents took them there and kitted them out in grey short trousers (for the junior school), black jackets with the statutory school badge affixed to the breast pocket and, of course, the school tie.

I don't know what was going through my father's mind at the time – perhaps he really *was* that skint – but he decided he would *make* me my school uniform. Unfortunately, in doing so, he made me stand out from the other kids – quite unintentionally, of course.

Bless him, he had this worry about money falling out of my pockets – I think this may have happened to me *once* when I went to the cinema with my cousin Denise – so, in his mind, I needed deep pockets. He made me a pair of short trousers with very deep pockets. So deep, in fact, that in order to accommodate them, the overall length of the trousers had to be somewhat longer than normal. Now picture the scene: me arriving at school wearing a pair of short trousers that were much longer than everybody else's. They looked like they were falling down, and this tempted the older lads to come up to me and try to pull them down.

As if that wasn't bad enough, in making the jacket, Dad decided to add some leather elbow patches, the sort you sometimes see on posh riding clothes. He reckoned that I, being a young lad, would lean on my elbows a lot and wear the material out. So the elbow patches were another object of ridicule. Thinking about it now, if felt-tip pens had been available in those days, he might have taken his old white wedding tie and tried to replicate the stripes of the official school tie. It must have killed him to actually have to pay for a real one.

Then there was the school badge. Instead of buying one and sewing it on, my Auntie Gertie, out of the kindness of her heart, embroidered one for me. This turned out to be slightly smaller than the official one. Luckily, to the untrained eyes of the other kids, it wasn't noticeable.

The point illustrated by this episode is that even with the best intentions in the world, some parents' actions can end up subjecting their children to ridicule. It also serves to highlight how kids innately want to conform, and how they will torment a child who is not in 'standard issue', making them feel inadequate. I complained about this to my father several times, but it just fell upon deaf ears.

Fortunately, the following year I went into long trousers, plus I needed a bigger jacket. I must have kicked up enough of a fuss that a standard uniform was purchased. Come to think of it, I may well have paid for it myself from the proceeds of one of my enterprises.

*

The necessity of supplementing my pocket money was of prime importance to me. Looking back, I now realise that none of the other kids I knew, at school or in the flats, had the sort of motivation I did. Some of the Moores' kids would have a paper round or milk round, but nothing beyond that. Naturally, I did those things too – for two shillings a day. And on Saturdays I had jobs at the baker's and green-grocer's – for half a crown a day. All of these were, to use a good old-fashioned East End expression, 'two bob jobs', but considering I was eleven or twelve years old, one couldn't complain.

It was at the greengrocer's, Charlton's in Clapton, where my famous beetroot-boiling story originated. On Saturday mornings I would get up early and turn up at Charlton's for a seven o'clock start and part of my job was to help set out the display of veg at the front.

Beetroot was rarely purchased in its raw form; customers wanted it ready-boiled and we would provide this service. My first duty on arrival on Saturday morning was to get a small metal bath and place it on the gas ring, half fill the bath with water and chuck in a sack of raw beetroot. I would then light the gas and get on with my next task, which was humping sacks of potatoes from the basement up the stairs.

After an hour or so, I had to call two sturdy men to lift the boiling bath of beetroot off the burner, walk it out to the yard, chuck out the water and then take the piping hot beetroots and put them out on dis-play at the front of the shop. For some reason, the press, when covering my business career, have latched on to the beetroot story and repeat it endlessly and inaccurately. 'He used to sell beetroot from the back of his minivan' or 'He sold beetroot on a market stall' are a couple of variations. Well, you've just read the *official* beetroot story. Never let it be distorted again!

Ginger beer manufacture was another of my ventures, after talking to a lady in our flats who said she had a ginger beer plant, although to me it looked like a load of sand or sediment in some water. She offered to give me some of it and told me that if I continued to feed it with two teaspoons of sugar a day, plus some ginger and this and that, it would continue to grow. More importantly, the pint of liquid it resided in would turn into concentrated ginger beer which, by adding more water, some lemon juice and sugar, could produce *ten pints* of ginger beer to drink. My entrepreneurial mind sprung into action again – after all, a large bottle of Tizer or R. Whites lemonade used to cost about 1s 3d in the shops.

In those days, there was no such thing as the disposable plastic bottle. Drinks bottles were made of glass and were quite valuable – they had a return value of a penny each. In one of my earlier ventures, I would scour the streets around our flats looking for empty bottles and I even asked some of the people living in the flats if they had any. I'd take any empties I collected round to the sweet shop and redeem them for cash to buy sweets. Now I had a dilemma: instead of returning the bottles for cash, I needed to use them for my own ginger beer production.

I used the fold-down table that went over the bath as my production bench, a plastic bucket to make the mass production quantity of mix and my mum's small funnel to pour it into the empty bottles. Then I started knocking on the neighbours' doors trying to flog them stuff again. They may have been thinking, 'Oh no, not him again,' but I'd have to say that there was always a smile on their faces.

I even tried to sell some ginger beer to the sweet shop downstairs. The owner agreed to take a few bottles on a sale-or-return basis and he did quite a good job trying to sell some, but with limited success. He explained to me that the presentation wasn't very professional, as the bottles didn't have labels.

Not one of my better ventures then. My mother, to say the least, was not happy with me using two teaspoons of sugar a day, not to mention the half a teaspoon of ginger. But, mothers being mothers, she never complained or charged me.

On reflection, I don't know how I fitted all this stuff in. On top of my more unusual activities, I always had time for the annual late-October tradition of making a Guy Fawkes out of my old clothes padded out with a load of newspapers. Armed with my Guy, I stood outside the flats on the main Upper Clapton Road asking passers-by for a 'penny for the Guy'. I'd use my takings to buy some fireworks for the various bonfire night parties on 5 November, mostly held on an old bombsite within the council estate.

There was no point asking my mum and dad for money to buy fireworks. To the old man it would have been like holding up a red rag to a bull – spending money on things that go up in flames. I recall comments like, 'Why do you want to waste your money on them? Why don't you just go and watch the other people letting off *their* fireworks?' I guess it was a good point, but you can't tell kids. Besides, there was a special excitement in lighting your own fireworks. In fact, if I remember rightly, my dad came down and took charge of letting off some of my rockets, launching them from an empty milk bottle.

*

Even with my money-making schemes, I couldn't afford to buy the kind of bicycle I wanted – a Pat Hanlon Special or a Condor Special. So when I was about thirteen I decided I would make one instead! It was amazing how people would throw away old frames, wheels, handlebars and so on, which I'd collect. My pals in the flats would teach me things like how to straighten spokes on wheels, how to assemble a chain and put the gears on – basically how to build bikes.

That knowledge hasn't left me, even today. I was in my local bike shop in Chigwell a while ago, having taken in my brand-new Italian Pinarello bike (sold to me by some American smoothie for the grand sum of $9,000). The bike was attracting a lot of attention from everyone in the shop. One of the customers, who must have been about my age, looked a bit sheepish as he recognised me as the bloke on the telly. He started speaking to me and I could see that he thought I was just one of those rich people who, now that biking was fashionable, had jumped on the bandwagon and bought the best bike available. Then I spotted an antique Pat Hanlon and mentioned that I used to go to her shop in Tottenham, and I reminisced about Condor, when it was situated in Balls Pond Road. Well, I've never seen an attitude change so quickly. You would have thought he'd met a long-lost friend from fifty years ago.

I still retain my bike-building skills, to the surprise of some of my friends, my wife and even my children. One of them would ask, 'Who fixed that puncture?'

'I did,' I'd say.

They'd look at me quizzically. 'How do you know how to fix punctures?'

'It's easy,' I'd shrug.

Not being aware of my childhood exploits, they'd be amazed that I was an expert at puncture repairs. In my youth, I used the back of a fork as a tyre lever, plus a bit of orange glue and some sandpaper.

*

In the flats opposite ours lived Manny Phillips, one of my brother Derek's pals. Manny's family was more well-to-do; they had quite a good business selling things in the markets. During the summer holidays I'd go with Manny to Oxford market and Chelmsford market, as well as Ridley Road, Dalston. Manny sold foam rubber bits and pieces which people would buy to make cushions. I'd help him load up the stall with the stuff, wrap it up for the customers and generally run back and forth to the café for him during the day. It was at Chelmsford where I first experienced the amazing salesmanship of some of these stall holders. The man on the stall next to Manny's sold towels and bedding and he attracted a crowd of people by piling his items one on top of another, creating a perception of value-for-money. He'd start his patter by letting the crowd know the high prices of these items in the shops.

I was fascinated by his spiel. 'There you are, two big bath towels, three hand towels, four flannels, five pillow cases, three sets of sheets. I'll throw in two pillows and, wait for it, a wonderful full-size blanket. Now, the lady over there – put your hand down, love – I don't want twenty-five pounds, forget twenty pounds, forget fifteen, don't even think about ten. The lady over there – put your money away, dear. Now, I want *five* – hands up – five pounds the lot.'

One day he was making his pitch, he had the audience all teed up, and just as he reached the crescendo and was about to announce the final punchline – I don't know what possessed me – suddenly I blurted it out.

If looks could kill, I'd have been stone dead there and then.

When the crowd dispersed he got hold of Manny and started shouting at him. 'What is this kid doing? Is he mad? Is he crazy? Tell him to shut up.'

I really got it in the neck from the guy and Manny. Mind you, Manny should have known I couldn't be relied on to keep quiet. When my brother and sisters came over on Friday nights for dinner, they'd inevitably end up playing cards and Manny would sometimes be in the card school. They'd play for pennies or shillings, but took it very seriously. I used to sit there watching studiously and sometimes I'd say something that disclosed one of the player's tactics. I'd quickly be told to keep my mouth shut.

Around Christmas time I worked with Manny and his father in Ridley Road market. At that time of year they changed their wares. They put their foam rubber into storage and decked out the stall with toys: dolls, Meccano sets, children's cars and prams, and so on.

Mr Phillips, Manny's father, was quite a tough person. I recall one day watching him sell a very large doll which came in a presentation box. I don't remember the exact price, but let's say it was £3. Shortly after he sold it, a lady came up to the stall and asked me how much the same doll was.

'Three pounds,' I said immediately.

Sharp as a needle, Mr Phillips jumped in. 'What are you talking about, you idiot – it's much more than three pounds.'

He then turned to the lady. 'I'm sorry, dear, he's made a terrible mistake – it's not three pounds, it's much more than that. I'm sorry, love.'

I was dumbfounded. Had I made a giant error? I didn't think so.

Mr Phillips continued: 'Okay, dear – look, we're honest traders down here. This stupid boy offered it to you for three pounds – what can I do? I'm gonna have to stick to it. Okay, love, you can have it for three quid if you want.'

The lady obviously felt she had a bargain. Meanwhile, I was still standing there gobsmacked.

When the lady had parted with her money and taken the doll, I said to Mr Phillips, 'I'm sorry I made a mistake.'

You would have thought he'd say, 'Don't worry, kid, I didn't mean it – *I* know you didn't make a mistake. I was just using a bit of salesmanship.'

But instead, he said, 'Well, you're not getting paid today – forget it.'

'What are you talking about?' I complained. 'I saw you sell that doll for three pounds no more than an hour ago. I thought I was doing the right thing.'

'No, you didn't. No, you didn't.' And he smiled and walked away.

Being only twelve, I genuinely believed I wasn't going to get paid that day. On the way home in the van, Manny and his father continued the charade and I was nearly in tears.

When we arrived back at the flats, they said, 'Here's your money – we were only joking.' Bastards.

This was one of life's lessons. The joke was cruel, of course, but at the same time I understood how astute Mr Phillips had been, making that customer feel she'd got a bargain.

Back to the man in Chelmsford market. Let me tell you, he is no different from the suited and booted executive with a fancy Power-Point presentation, trying to sell Rolls-Royce engines to Boeing. The commodity may be different, the environment may be different, but the presentation and selling skills are exactly the same – and don't let anyone tell you otherwise. Just as the suited and booted chap is fully conversant with the technicalities of his engines, the stallholder in Chelmsford market knows all about the cotton content of his towels and sheets. And at the end of the day, both people present their specifications and prices to the end customer.

*

During my schooldays, in spite of my sidelines and ventures, I still had time for recreation. This mainly centred around the local youth clubs, predominantly the Jewish ones. There was a club in Lea Bridge Road where I'd go with some of my friends from Northwold Road School and get up to all the usual shenanigans you'd expect at these places. The youth club also encouraged us to get involved in charitable work.

There is often talk of 'the school of hard knocks' – a way of toughening you up. In those days, people said that sending young men into the army to give them some backbone was a way of making the man. I don't want to undermine the tremendous devotion and bravery shown by our soldiers, both male and female, in all the campaigns they have served in for this country, but I will say, with the greatest respect, that the army doesn't hold the monopoly on toughening people up.

Some childhood incidents, which I can now laugh about, have stuck in my mind. I volunteered to do some work for Meals on Wheels, a charity service providing food to old people. I would assist the adult who drove the van, running up and down stairs to deliver the food.

In one particular case, I had to deliver to an old lady who lived on the sixth floor of a block of flats. The flats had a lift, but it smelt like Battersea Dogs' Home, so I used the stairs. Having climbed the six floors, I knocked on the door and this eighty-year-old Jewish lady opened it. She had grey hair, some whiskers growing from her chin and bloomers hanging down around her knees. Frightened enough by this sight, I handed over the meal. She ripped the top off and shouted at me, 'You call this meatballs?!'

When I think of this now, bloody hell, I could have been scarred for life – never mind being up to your neck in muck and bullets in the trenches. You don't want to know what she did with the milk-free ice-cream dessert.

My involvement with the Lea Bridge Road youth club had another, less amusing outcome after my Bar Mitzvah. In order to be Bar Mitzvah'd, at the age of thirteen, one has to learn all the Jewish laws and rules. It was a nightmare, but it was a way Jewish families conformed and was a strict discipline that my mother and father insisted upon.

From this, you might get the impression that my parents were fanatically religious Jews. In fact, the complete opposite is true. My mum had some very funny ways. Despite knowing the full monty about kashrus (Jewish dietary laws), she would buy all her meat from the kosher butcher's, but then serve it up followed by a dessert containing milk – a forbidden combination, as one of the rules of kashrus states that meat and milk may not be served in the same meal.

In my opinion, these crazy dietary laws were crafted by hypocrites.

Anyway, because of Mum's odd ways, we didn't conform, although my mum *would* delight in shutting down the kitchen on Yom Kippur – no one was allowed to eat, so she had a day off. When it came to observing the Jewish holidays, my dad would take me to the synagogue but we certainly weren't regular visitors. The only tradition Mum and Dad kept was to invite all our immediate family round every Friday night for dinner.

After my Bar Mitzvah, the many friends I had at the Lea Bridge Road youth club became distant for some reason. I can remember being rejected by one particular individual, a boy called Harvey, who made it plain I was no longer his friend. Before that, Harvey and I had been close pals, seeing each other as much as we could. He would come to my flat and I would go to his house. He came from a better background than mine. His mother once said to me, 'You don't speak very nicely.' I guess that was due to the people I mixed with in my flats or at school. I was a Cockney.

Certain people in the Jewish community wanted to elevate themselves. They sent their children to schools which had special elocution classes. This segregation created Jews who didn't want to be associated with normal Jews, which I think is strange. On reflection, I suppose that Harvey's mum leant on him and told him not to hang around with me any more. I often wondered what I might have done wrong, but, in all honesty, the only explanation I can find for Harvey's behaviour was that his family became aware I was from a much poorer background than theirs.

He wasn't the only friend I lost. Traditionally, Bar Mitzvah boys are thrown a lavish party to which all family and friends are invited. This was not the case with me, as my mother and father could not afford such an affair. Instead we had a small get-together at home. The boys at the youth club, however, thought that they'd not been invited to some glamorous Bar Mitzvah party. One prick by the name of Elkham Miller and his sidekick Michael Marsham actually spelled this out to me shortly afterwards. They said the reason they didn't talk to me any more was that they weren't invited to my Bar Mitzvah party. When I told them I hadn't had a party, they simply didn't believe it. It's strange how thirteen-year-olds can be damaged by the reactions of those who they thought were their friends.

Possibly the British Psychological Society will use extracts of this book as a new case study in their journals, explaining how this is a classic textbook case, how the inner damage caused gave rise to hidden personality swings that are exposed when certain events spark off memories. What a load of bollocks! Do you know, there's a whole industry in this! And some people *pay* for it! Have I missed out on that particular enterprise? Amspsych Ltd. No, it doesn't have a nice ring to it.

By the way, this is not an invitation for *Disturbed Weekly* to call me up for an in-depth interview, put me to sleep and take me back to when I was thirteen. Forget it! But cop the next chapter – any budding psych reading this will think they've won the lottery, because from that moment on I became a recluse. For about two years, I didn't want to socialise with anybody.

2

'Shame About the Spelling, Sugar'

School Days – 'Sugar's Got Rolls of Film for Three Bob'

1960–3

While my social life was non-existent, I still kept busy with work and my hobbies. Sometimes they combined, as with the Saturday job I took in a chemist's in Walthamstow High Street market. Having found that I enjoyed science and engineering at school (in contrast to some of the more boring subjects such as history and the arts), I thought pharmacy might be the way to go, and naïvely I figured I would learn about it on the job. The shop was owned by a very nice man called Michael Allen. When I told him I aspired to be a pharmacist, he taught me as much as he possibly could about drugs and that sort of stuff.

I spent most of my time in the front of the shop selling cough syrups and lozenges. Here I was, a young kid, being asked by punters what cough syrup they should take. Mr Allen taught me to ask if it was a chesty cough or a dry cough. For chesty, you got a bottle of Benylin; for dry, you got a bottle of Pholcodine Linctus.

Mr Allen was a bit of a boffin who knew all the technical pharmaceutical stuff, but in my opinion lacked a bit of business savvy. I introduced one of my marketing ideas to him and his staff. When asked by the customer for a bottle of, say, Milk of Magnesia, if you were to reply, 'Small or large?' most punters would say, 'Small.' Much better to ask, 'Do you want the small 1s 6d one or the extra-value 2s 6d one?' I applied this to lots of things in the shop, ranging from Old Spice aftershave to cough syrup, and it worked nine times out of ten.

There were exceptions to this rule. Packets of Durex, for example, came in both economy and bulk packs, but I wasn't going to ask a strapping six-foot-tall punter if he wanted the small pack – it could have been taken the wrong way.

Now, here's a bit of trivia you may find as surprising as I did: a large number of married women would buy contraceptives as part of their weekly shop, on behalf of their lazy husbands. At first, as a young lad of fifteen, I was a bit embarrassed when a woman asked me for them, but after a while it was like water off a duck's back. However, when it came to Tampax or sanitary towels, I certainly wasn't going to try my 'small or extra-value' scam. Instead, it was a case of: 'They're over there, madam, help yourself.' That was where I drew the line. After all, there was a limit on how far you'd go for the boss!

It was at Mr Allen's shop that I also developed my interest in photography, which was sparked by the cameras, film and developing paper he sold. I couldn't afford a good camera, but I soon picked up tips on which model was the most economic to buy. This information was going to be useful because another sideline I had in mind was to become a photographer. While I scraped together the money to buy a Halina camera, I was already working out what to say to my parents. I had visions of my father shaking his head in disapproval when I brought it home. 'Another waste of money,' he'd say, while my mother would shrug her shoulders and ask, 'How much was that?' All this despite the fact that I was paying for it myself!

It *was* difficult for me to justify laying out £12 for a camera when the old man got £8 for doing a week's work, so I tried to save his pride with answers such as, 'I'm paying off for it to Mr Allen,' which, to be fair, I did do when it came to my next camera – the Yashica, a poor man's Rolleiflex.

Not only did I buy the camera, but I also invested in an enlarger, a lens and developing equipment. Mum and Dad couldn't understand how I'd managed to buy them and the situation wasn't helped by my brother-in-law, Harold Regal, who said, 'This is very expensive stuff, Alan. How have you managed to afford all this?' I didn't need him winding the old man up.

My father was such a worrier. I swear he thought that one day there'd be a policeman knocking at our door – I don't know why. He just couldn't accept what this young lad was up to. My only criticism of him would be that he didn't support me in any of these activities and always seemed to think there was something wrong. I wouldn't say the same about my mother though; she was quite supportive.

Once I'd got the equipment and converted my dad's workshop (the spare bedroom) into a darkroom by putting a blanket across the window and shutting the door, I set about finding customers. It struck me that many of our neighbours had kids and grandchildren, so I decided to knock on people's doors and ask them if they'd like me to photograph the children on a 'no obligation' basis – a no-brainer, as you can imagine. 'Sure,' they invariably replied. I took the precaution of writing 'PROOF' on the corner of the photos in biro and presented them to the parents and grandparents who, of course, loved them.

'What's this word "proof"?' they would say. 'Can't I have one without that on it?'

'Well, that's a rough example. If you want a final, good-quality one, I'll print you off a large one for half a crown.'

That was it! I was at the races. It was pictures of children and grandchildren for the next few months.

At school, photography was becoming a fashionable hobby and we had a photographic society whose members included one of the more financially fortunate pupils, a posh kid who used to hold court. His dad owned a shop and everybody looked up to him as if his shit didn't stink.

When I showed my photographs, he'd sneer at them and look down on me as a second-class photographer. On one occasion, I showed him some negatives I'd developed myself. He observed some smear marks on them and announced haughtily, in front of the society, 'Oh, Sugar, it seems that you dry your negatives by farting on them.' You can imagine the laughter.

My next scheme wiped the smile off his face, in more ways than one. At that time, he used to be the supplier of photographic materials to the kids and the teachers. Now, at the rear of Mr Allen's shop there was a small film-processing factory. I'd occasionally go and see how the developing process worked and noticed that they discarded the empty 35mm cartridge cases. I wondered what could be done with these seemingly useless items, but at the time nothing came to mind.

Until one day I went into the ex-army shop on Chatsworth Road in Hackney. Ex-army stores originally sold second-hand uniforms, boots and other surplus army supplies, but the availability of this stuff diminished in the post-war years, so they extended their stock to *anything* surplus. I went to buy a pair of army boots (a fashion statement at that time) and noticed some large, round cans that looked like something you would store film in – the type of film you'd see on a cinema projector. I asked the fellow what was in the cans and he told me he'd bought a job lot of unexposed Ilford FP3 film, as used by film studios for the making of black-and-white movies. FP3 was also sold in photographic stores as black-and-white transparency film for around 5s 1d for a 20-exposure roll and 6s 10d for a 36-exposure roll. Now here I was in the ex-army store, with reels and reels of this stuff, each reel with hundreds of yards of film on it, the very same film you could buy in the photographic shops, but in bulk. The vision of the empty 35mm cartridges came out of my memory bank and I asked the man how much he wanted for a reel.

'What are you going to do with it?' he asked. 'Who do you think you are – Hitchcock?'

'Never mind that, mate, how much for a reel?' I persisted.

He was bright, because before he gave a price, he wanted to know what I had in mind for it, in case he was missing a trick. There must have been fifty cans there, so who knows how much he paid for them. I bet he bought them for the scrap value of the metal cans.

'How much do you want to pay?' he said.

I looked at the can. The label indicated 500 yards of film inside. I knew from watching the process at the development factory that a 36-exposure film, out of its cartridge, was about two yards long. If I sold the film to the punters and undercut the shops by, say, 50 per cent, it would mean that I'd have to charge about three bob for a 36-exposure film. I quickly worked out that 250 x 3s came to £37 10s.

'I'll give you five quid for one can,' I said. After a bit of haggling, the bloke accepted. He was intrigued about what I was going to do with it. Now I had to set up a production line. Although I'd converted my dad's workshop into a darkroom, there was still light coming around the edges of the blanket over the window and around the door frame. This was good enough for developing prints on photographic paper, but not good enough for playing with unexposed film.

My second darkroom was my bed. Under the bedcovers, I measured off and cut the film into two-yard lengths from the bulk reel. The whole operation was risky because if any light got in, I could expose the whole spool and that'd be a fiver down the drain. Once cut, I loaded the film into one of the discarded empty 35mm cartridges. I tried to be selective and take only those that had an original Ilford FP3 label on them, but I had to accept what was available. If I loaded the film into a cartridge with an FP3 label, it would be an easier sell; if I had to use an empty Kodak cartridge, you can imagine it would take a bit of explaining as to why the film inside was FP3.

In those days there were no inkjet printers or photocopiers to run off labels. Instead, I got some kid at school to use the library typewriter to type out 'ILFORD FP3 36 EXP' over and over on a sheet of A4 paper, cut the words out and glue them on to the non-Ilford cartridges using LePages glue. In exchange, I gave him some film, so he was happy as Larry.

Word spread like wildfire at school: 'Hey, Sugar's got 36 EXP FP3 for three bob!' At first, I had to overcome the suspicion that they'd fallen off the back of a lorry, a rumour put about by the posh tosser. That was easy to dispel because when you looked at the end product you could see it wasn't packaged in the same way as retail film. I was soon getting orders from the kids, the kids' parents and the teachers. Like all products, it was accepted with scepticism at first, but eventually they realised it was okay. In fact, my generous length of two yards gave them forty-odd exposures.

The posh tosser didn't give up. After his suggestion that the stuff was nicked had backfired, he then said the film was out-of-date and thus inferior. I killed that one off by offering a money-back guarantee.

This exercise had a twofold benefit. Firstly, I made some money and saw how cutting prices generates sales. But I also learned a valuable lesson about what happens when someone encroaches upon the territory of the so-called elite, be it disturbing their business or upsetting what they perceive to be their special rights. They go into arsehole mode and use rather sneaky and spiteful tactics.

I don't know what happened to this prat in later life. He's probably a *Daily Mail* journalist. From what I recall, he fits the criteria exactly: a pathetic loser who does nothing in life other than engage in spiteful sniping to cover up his own lack of achievement.

Having ruined the tosser's film business, I decided to rub it in a bit more by showing the photographic society how to get – in photographic terms – a real scoop. One sports day, I took pictures of the guys running around the track at Eton Manor Sports Centre at Hackney Marshes. I developed the photos overnight and delivered them next morning – something no one thought possible. Of course, nowadays, we can take pictures with a digital camera and print them instantly; in those days you took your film to a developer, it went away for processing and maybe a week to ten days later you'd get your pictures. Well, here's me: Eton Manor, three o'clock in the afternoon, snapping one of our champion runners, pictures on the desk next morning – scoop!

The tosser and his hangers-on assembled quickly at the noticeboard where I'd displayed the pictures. There were a few where the runners' arms were blurred, as I hadn't used a fast enough shutter speed, and the tosser was holding court, criticising. 'I say, Sugar, about time you got yourself a camera with a two-thousandth of a second shutter speed.'

His snipe was squashed when Mr Pollard, my form tutor and chemistry teacher, came up behind the assembled crowd and expressed his admiration for the blurred pictures from an artistic point of view – the way they portrayed a feeling of speed. He was so impressed he called over Mr Cannon, my housemaster. Instead of complimenting me, Mr Cannon said, 'You must have been up all night, Sugar – this must have taken you ages. You were supposed to be doing your homework. How are you going to pass your GCEs?'

'Screw him,' I thought to myself.

While on the subject of photography, one of the young lads I'd seen around was soon to be Bar Mitzvah'd and, as his mum and dad couldn't afford much, I offered to take the Bar Mitzvah photographs.

Bloody hell, what a risk that was! When I got to the venue, I found myself taking pictures of adults and doing group photos. Only then did it dawn on me: these people are expecting memorable photographs, pictures they'll frame and treasure for the rest of their lives. I thought to myself, 'What have I done? What am I doing here?' Thankfully, it came off quite well in the end. I can't remember what I charged but I certainly undercut the professional photographer.

Based on that event, I decided to professionalise myself. I went to a local printer's, Austin Press, who made me a rubber stamp: '*Photographed by* ALAN SUGAR – Phone: UPP 7875'. Even as I tell this story, I can see my mum smiling and shrugging her shoulders and my dad still shaking his head.

*

Along with photography I was fascinated by electronics. In Dalston Lane, Hackney, there was a shop called Tiny's Radio where we kids would go to buy things such as diodes, coils, resistors and variable capacitors. With these components, we could cobble together a 'crystal set' which could pick up radio stations. Having acquired a soldering iron and conferred with a few of the school boffs, I assembled my crystal set and plugged it into my tape recorder. Suddenly the sound of radio blasted out. My dad ran up the stairs and said, 'Where's the music coming from? How have you managed to do that?' I showed him this little crystal set and tried to explain what was going on. He seemed quite impressed, for once, with how I had managed to do it.

As I mentioned earlier, I became a recluse during this period. Because of this, my mum and dad allowed me to get involved in any kind of hobby I wanted, in order to keep me occupied. When I think back to those days, I never went anywhere other than to Dalston Lane or Tottenham Court Road – to buy electronic components – then back home again. My mum and dad were really worried – no question about it. So were my brother and sisters. It was a topic of much debate within the family. As we all know, the worst thing you can ever do in this situation is to try and fix someone up with a friend. My mother would 'find' me friends and force me to go round and visit them, but to no avail.

In the summer, my mum and dad went on holiday to Cliftonville in Kent and they dragged me along. To keep the cost down, the three of us shared one room in a small hotel. There were quite a few young people staying there and I got very friendly with them that week. My mum and dad were delighted, but of course the holiday came to an end, we all went back home, and the people I'd met didn't live in my vicinity – so back I went into my shell again.

I remember my dad saying to me, 'What's the matter with you? You enjoyed yourself while you were on holiday – why can't you go back to the youth clubs and find yourself friends again?'

And I remember thinking, 'Leave me alone – stop pushing,' and I just carried on in a very quiet way.

Monday to Friday there was no problem – school took up most of my time. But the highlight of the weekends was taking the 653 bus to Tottenham Court Road to buy a reel of solder.

Eventually, Daphne and my sister-in-law Brenda cornered me one Friday evening and tried, in a more caring manner, to address what was going on. They wanted to understand what the problem was and why I wouldn't socialise with other kids. Was it perhaps that I was mixing too much with adults and not getting the opportunity to meet youngsters? That, of course, was wrong because previously I *had* enjoyed a social life – with the ratbags who gave me the elbow.

In one of the pep talks that Daphne and Brenda gave me, Brenda said that her brother, Adrian Press, would gladly play host and take me around the youth clubs that he went to. 'You know Adrian,' Brenda said. 'You've played with him when you've been round my mum and dad's house. You were page boys together at our wedding. It's not like he's a stranger. Why don't you agree to meet up with him and let him introduce you to a bunch of pals?'

Reluctantly, I went along with this, simply on the basis that at least I knew Adrian as we'd met on a few occasions. First, Adrian took me to Brady Club, off the Mile End Road, where he introduced me to a bunch of guys. I was painfully shy. After the initial niceties and hellos, I ended up feeling like a wallflower as the evening went on.

This pattern continued for several weeks, if not months, either at Brady Club or Stamford Hill Club, up the road from me. When I think back, I feel a bit sorry for Adrian because I was like baggage he had to drag around with him. Eventually, he sat me down in the cafeteria of

Brady Club and told me very nicely that all *he* could do was introduce me to people. It was up to me if I wanted to take it further and do something about it – he couldn't keep trying to get me involved if I didn't want to participate. He wasn't being an arsehole; he was actually a really nice guy, as he still is to this day. Despite Adrian's pep talk, my social skills didn't improve. It was getting to the stage where I'd be making feeble excuses about why I couldn't meet up with him.

Inside me was this feeling of *wanting* to talk to people, *wanting* to join in with all the joking and larking around, but something was holding me back. I have no idea what it was – I can only put it down to shyness.

Among the group of friends that Adrian introduced me to were a couple of the boys he went to school with, Tony Kaye and Steve Pomeroy, as well as their friends Malcolm Cross and Geoff Salt. I'd met them quite a few times during various trips to Brady Club or Stamford Hill Club, but had not really taken it any further than the initial 'Hello, how are you?'

Then came an amazing breakthrough. We were at Stamford Hill Club when it started to rain and a load of us were invited back to somebody's flat nearby. They decided to play a game – it was something like imitating TV adverts or making up your own ones. And there I was, stuck, because they were going round, one by one, asking each person to come up with a funny TV advert. The only options for me at that moment were either to get up and run out of the room or finally talk.

It was soon my turn. There was silence while everyone looked at me in anticipation of what I was going to say – most of them had never heard me speak. The silence seemed to last an hour. Imagine standing on the end of the high diving-board at the swimming-pool when all your mates had jumped off – and now it was *your* turn.

Suddenly I spurted out some funny thing I came up with, associated with the advert for Surf washing powder that was running at the time, where housewives were asked what they thought of Surf. My comment was, 'I don't like it – it makes my face all scurfy.'

There was a moment of stunned silence – the kind where you think you've just dropped the biggest lead balloon of your life – then, a second later, the whole lot of them just rolled about in hysterics. They looked at me as if to say, 'Where did *you* come from? Where have *you* been?'

This gave me some encouragement and I continued to tell some funny stories. If I didn't know better, I would have said that my mum and dad had *paid* these people to laugh. It was very much a break-the-ice moment and though I couldn't see why I was so popular all of a sudden, I was.

I guess that in kids' circles it goes like that. Suddenly there's a new kid on the block who's quite funny and streetwise. There was no stopping me from then on, and I went from this quiet recluse to someone who never stopped talking and larking around.

Adrian knew something had changed. He said, 'Wow, what's happened to you? You seemed to really enjoy yourself there today.' I'm obviously grateful to him for persevering with me and introducing me to this bunch of friends. From that moment on, Steve Pomeroy, Tony Kaye, Geoff Salt and Malcolm Cross became my pals. They are still my good friends to this very day.

Steve Pomeroy's parents ran a lemonade factory in Hackney. It was a fascinating place, specialising in producing lemonade for pubs and for the kosher wedding market. The Pomeroys lived in a grand house in Osbaldeston Road in Clapton. I never really got to know Mr Pomeroy, as unfortunately he died shortly after Steve and I became friends. Steve's mother was a real character and later in life we had a lot of banter together at her factory.

Tony Kaye, and I'm sure he won't mind me saying this, was regarded as being from a rather well-to-do family. His father was an importer/trader in fancy goods. They lived in Dunsmure Road, Stamford Hill, considered to be a more opulent part of the neighbourhood.

Whenever Geoff and I were together, no one would believe his name was Salt and my name was Sugar. People would think we were taking the piss. Geoff lived at Finsbury Park. His father worked in the fashion industry and his mother was a rather lovely, dignified, serious lady. Geoff was considered a bit of a renegade by his parents, whereas his elder brother Steven was far more of a conformist. Geoff's father would often be giving him a load of stick and moaning at him.

Malcolm Cross lived in Hackney with his mum and dad and four brothers. I would say that his family was most like ours financially. Malcolm was a bit older than the rest of us and was the first to get his driving licence. Naturally, he became the chauffeur for the group.

The friendship blossomed amongst the five of us, and we spent most of our time at Stamford Hill Club and one another's houses. Tony Kaye's mum and dad used to have frequent holidays, thus freeing up their home for us to invade. We spent many a weekend there, playing cards and frolicking around.

This era, when I was in my mid-teens, seemed to last a lifetime. It was only a couple of years, but quite a lot was happening. I was growing at a fast rate of knots, not just physically, but also socially. I progressed from messing around at the youth club to going to nightclubs such as the Scene and Le Kilt, as well as various other establishments scattered around the West End. We weren't really into the mod scene – we all wore sharp suits and listened to the latest music, but we didn't take it as seriously as some who considered themselves to be the bee's knees in fashion and entertainment. There were 'tier one' people, the likes of whom used to hang around with characters such as Marc Bolan, who also came from our area. And then there was us – second division – who were not quite the top scene, if you get my drift. Nevertheless, we didn't do too badly.

*

While all this growing up was going on, I started studying for my GCE O Levels. English was my worst subject. Sure I could bunny off of scratch and was always called to host debates or enter into discussions, but when it came to the written word, my spelling was atrocious. I have no idea why; I still have this mental block as far as spelling is concerned. All I can say is, thank goodness for the spellchecker.

My father had a theory that my spelling was bad because I didn't read enough. But I have another theory: there's something in this brain of mine that will just not sign on to spelling or remembering a person's name. If you introduce me to a new person and say, 'This is Fred,' within five seconds I can't tell you their name. I have to meet a person and call them by their name loads of times before it sinks in.

Because of my poor spelling, any exam I took was immediately marked down, so I never excelled at English. By the fifth form, I was in the top stream (5-1) for maths, chemistry, physics, etc., but when it came to English I was relegated to 5-2. However, the bottom stream curriculum seemed to be a bit more interesting – less grammar and more practical lessons. One of the topics discussed was advertising, and for once I stopped looking out of the window and paid attention. We were asked to analyse the launch of a moisturiser called Cream of Cactus: why pick this name? What was the advertiser getting at in the copy?

It seemed obvious to me. The cactus is known to exist in the hot desert and remain moist inside. I explained the analogy and what the advertiser was up to and got full marks on my essay, albeit with the caveat 'Shame about the spelling, Sugar.'

The subjects I enjoyed most were science and engineering. Sometimes I would bump into Mr Harris, the headmaster, walking through the corridor. He would look up and say something like, 'Hello, Sugar. How are you doing in the commerce and economics division?'

'No, sir, I'm in science and engineering 5-1,' I'd say.

'No, no, no, surely you're in commerce and economics.'

'No, sir, science and engineering 5-1.'

'No, no, no, no, no . . .' And he would wander off, shaking his head.

It seemed that Mr Harris had it in his brain that that's where I should be, despite my passion for chemistry, physics, metalwork and technical drawing.

Mathematics, on the other hand, was not one of my greatest talents. It is now, but back then I wasn't interested. I used to muck about in class. We had a weirdo teacher we called Theta Grant because of the strange way he would say and write the Greek symbol theta on the blackboard. This made us all laugh, but this fellow was a bit of a nutter – he had a violent temper – so we made sure he didn't see us laugh at him. We only called him Theta behind his back.

He pulled no punches, this chap. If he thought you were a dunce, he'd sit you at the back of the class, while the bright kids sat in the front row. Needless to say, I was at the back, right by the window, watching the football outside. A total waste, when I think back.

Nowadays, I try to explain to young people that when you're at school, you may think you have the weight of the world on your shoulders, but you don't. Your biggest problem is whether you're going to get those new trainers or that your mobile or iPod needs charging. The reality is that you have no worries, nothing to concern yourself with. And one day, when you get into the real world of work and marriage and life in general, you might look back and remember the words of this old fart.

I then go on to say, 'The fact of the matter is, the law says you *have* to go to school. Well, while you're there, you might as well suck in every bit of information the teachers want to give you, as it's all free. Don't mess around like I did.'

Of course, this lecture falls on deaf ears. I've lost count of the number of times I have made this little speech during my various visits to schools and other institutions. But it is so true. I wasted my school days messing about, being uninterested, being a bit of a joker in class, only to cop on later in life. This was particularly true in French. I didn't bother with it at school, only to find myself, years later, sitting like a dummy in business meetings.

I wasn't considered a contender for a GCE pass in maths, but I knew I *had* to pass it to go forward to the next level of education – maths GCE was mandatory. To make matters worse, at mid-term we were going to have to step up a gear and move on to calculus, a very tough area of mathematics. I knew I would have absolutely no chance of passing the maths GCE unless I understood calculus.

Here's an annoying thing: to cut a long story short, I set my mind to it and, trust me when I tell you that this maths dummkopf, who'd been sitting at the back of the class for years, suddenly became the guru of calculus. Some of the boffs sitting in the front row couldn't keep up with me and, would you believe, would ask *me*, 'Sugar, can you tell me how to differentiate this quadratic equation? I'm getting a bit confused on the integral of this, that or the other.'

When I finally sat the GCE O Level, I passed! Not with a high grade, but a pass nonetheless. Theta Grant could not understand what had happened to me. When I returned to school the next term, he was over the moon. 'Congratulations, *Mister* Sugar,' he said. 'I cannot believe it. Wonderful.'

What's annoying about this is that I had had it in me all along, but had wasted years at school because I couldn't be bothered. Try telling this story to youngsters these days. The following term I went on to do applied maths. I sailed through that and got a good grade.

In trying to compensate for my shortcomings in English, there was a suggestion that taking English literature as one of my GCEs would be a good move. We had to study *Twelfth Night* and the school put on a production of the play, for which I auditioned. Stupidly, I applied for the part of Orsino – effectively the leading role. On reflection, I'm pleased I never got it.

I learned act one, scene one for the audition, but was upstaged by a budding Sir John Gielgud. As a consolation, I was given the part of Curio, assistant to the king. From what I remember, we performed in front of a load of visiting dignitaries in the school's grand hall, and it went down very well – not that my few lines had anything to do with that.

I also joined the school's Senior Science Society as the lower-sixth representative. The purpose of the society was to inform pupils throughout the school about the latest scientific innovations and developments. Unfortunately, the society's chairman was a pompous twit who turned out not to be the brightest star in the sky. He was clutching on to low grades in GCE chemistry and physics, trying to go on to achieve his A Levels, but if you listened to all his bullshit, you would think you were taking part in the Manhattan Project.

I found myself arguing with this chairman all the time, basically because he was a prat. Sorry, but there's no other way to explain it. You've probably got the impression that anybody whom I don't agree with I automatically call a tosser or a prat – I *know* that's how it may come across at the moment – but trust me, he *was* a double-barrelled prat. I could not take any more of him, so I duly resigned and left him to find a new recruit. Was this the first of many boardroom conflicts? Well, maybe.

*

My education took place twelve years after Daphne's and Derek's, so my parents were in a twelve-year time warp. They expected their children to start contributing financially to the running of the home when they reached an age suitable for employment. Just as soon as Shirley, Derek and Daphne were earning money, they had to part with some of it to go towards housekeeping. This was quite normal in those days.

Then I came along and was earning more money on the side with my various ventures than I would have done if I'd left school at fifteen and worked in a factory. I was deemed to be an *investment* by my parents. Nevertheless, there needed to be a justification for why I was staying on at school.

They'd ask, 'What are you going to be? What are you going to do? What do all these exams make you into? A doctor? A lawyer? An accountant?'

My answer was that I wanted to do something in the science professions. As far as my mother and father were concerned, that meant maybe a chemist or a pharmacist. They wouldn't have even thought about the job of a researcher (who doesn't actually work in a shop dispensing pills) or somebody inventing something in a high-technology industry.

You have to sympathise with their outlook on life and employment. Understandably, it came as a great disappointment to them when I told them, halfway through studying for A Levels, that I was going to jack it in. I made the decision shortly after my return from the summer holidays, a week or so into the upper-sixth. They wanted to know: 'Why did you bother to get these GCEs? What are you going to do now?'

This was further aggravated by Shirley's husband Harold, who had a weird sense of humour and would try to capitalise on the dilemma facing me and my parents over choosing a career. He famously interjected once by saying, 'Why are you bothering? Become a dustman – they pay them loads of money these days.' This little chant of Harold's was one he would repeat at certain milestones in my life – not in a nasty way, I hasten to add, but to remind himself of what he'd said so many years earlier.

My reason for leaving school was that my best friends were taking on jobs. Malcolm was working in a radio and TV store as a television engineer. Funnily enough this store was opposite Mr Allen's, and we'd often meet each other on Saturdays and discuss what we were getting up to that night. Geoff was trying to pursue a career in the fashion industry on the administration and sales side. Steve was working for his parents' firm, making lemonade. And Tony – well, sorry, but he was just a rich man's son. He was talking about going to Africa to do some goody-goody work, but if you ask me, it was to bunk off getting a real job. They all had cars except me. So, in summary, the reason for me leaving school was to get a job with wheels.

I went to see the headmaster to tell him about my decision. Mr Harris wasn't happy at all. He felt I had the potential to stay on and complete the A Level courses. Nevertheless, he accepted my decision and pointed me in the direction of the careers officer who informed me of the opportunities available in technology. Apparently, being a computer programmer was becoming very popular and he arranged for me to take IBM's aptitude test – a way of evaluating if a candidate had what it takes to be a programmer. Thinking of this now puts a smile on my face, having employed hundreds of computer programmers in my lifetime and watched them sitting around in their sandals and jeans flicking elastic bands at each other.

I went along to IBM's offices in Wigmore Street where the staff were very polite. Once we'd finished our exam papers, they sent us off to have lunch in the canteen while they marked them. They let the people who were clearly of no interest to them go and I was one of those people.

I also sat a similar exam at ICL in Putney. Once again, I got the Dear John letter. Obviously I wasn't cut out for computer programming.

Funny how things work out. Twenty-four years later I entered into a Licensing Agreement with IBM which resulted in me taking 30 per cent of the European personal computer market away from them. And, please excuse my boast, I now own IBM's European headquarters building on London's South Bank, which I bought for £112 million. Anyway, moving on . . .

News of my failure at both IBM and ICL filtered back to the school and I was summoned to Mr Harris's office. Again he told me that I should stay and pursue my A Levels in subjects more suitable to me, such as economics. I reminded him again that I was not in the economics division but in *science and engineering*, but he simply could not accept it. There was no moving him. I was equally adamant that I was going to leave school.

I didn't tell my mother and father about the IBM and ICL episodes, but intent on finding a job, I started to look in the vacancies columns of the national newspapers. I spotted an advert from the Ministry of Education and Science who required applicants with GCE passes to join their statistics division. Naïvely, the word 'science' attracted me. I had visions of being involved in scientific experiments – missiles, rockets and the like.

I went to the Ministry's Curzon Street building and was interviewed by a very high-ranking civil servant, Miss Mayer, HEO (Higher Executive Officer), a middle-aged lady with silver hair and a very posh accent. I'll never forget that interview because while we were talking she was fiddling around with a large pearl necklace. It broke, and suddenly all the pearls fell to the floor. She was terribly embarrassed, as was I. We scrambled around picking up pearls all over the place.

During the interview I'd thrown in a few buzzwords like 'digits' and 'data', which made me look like I knew what I was talking about, and I got the job. And because I had six GCE passes, I was given the level of CO (Clerical Officer) – one up on the pecking order from the ordinary plebs in the department.

The job paid £32 per month – £8 a week in East End terms – and they wanted to pay it directly into my bank account. We'd never had bank accounts in my family, but my sister Shirley explained to me what I needed to do. So, shortly after joining the Ministry, I walked out of Curzon Street into Berkeley Square and looked for a bank. There was one on the right-hand side – Lloyds. In I walked, armed with a letter confirming my employment at the Ministry, and asked to open a bank account. I've been with Lloyds ever since that day in 1963.

Remember the famous advert with Maureen Lipman as a Jewish grandmother on the phone to her grandson, telling him how clever he was with his 'ology'? Well, having reported to my mother and father that I was now working at the Ministry of Education and Science as a clerical officer, I was hailed as the first person in the family to have what was deemed a *professional* job. 'My son, the clerical officer in the Ministry.'

If they only knew!

3

The Man at the Ministry

And Leaving To Be 'A Bloody Salesman'

1963–6

Even though I was only sixteen, I wasn't at all nervous turning up on the first day. I was all suited and booted and raring to go. The Curzon Street office was in the heart of Mayfair. It was a very large and ugly block of grey concrete – exactly what you'd expect a government building to look like. I entered the building, stepped into the lift and the operator greeted me with 'Good morning, sir,' and took me up to my floor. I reported to an EO (Executive Officer), a woman in her thirties who showed me to my desk in a large open-plan office while the other people glanced up for a moment to suss out the new boy.

In a weak moment, I reported the lift operator calling me 'sir' to my family one Friday night. They were so proud. '*Sir*, they call him! Can you believe that?'

Anyway, this job turned out to be double brain damage. On the first day, a pile of papers was plonked in front of me and I was informed by my EO that I was working on something called the Plowden Report on Junior Education.

In case you care, Lord Plowden had promised to come up with a report on primary school education and the pile of papers was the result of manual surveys on individual pupils across a whole section of the country. My job was to go through each form and code the answers to enable the data to be entered into an IBM punch-card computer system. This would result in a print-out telling you how many little Johnnies drank their quarter-pints of milk every day at school. If that wasn't bad enough, many of the people surrounding me were a breed of robot, the likes of which I'd never come across before. To say they were boring would be too kind. The highlight of their day came during the tea break, when they'd debate the virtues of using Marvel powdered milk as opposed to conventional milk that might go off if you kept it for two or three days. Scintillating stuff, as you can imagine.

At first, I would sit quietly on my own. Like all new people joining an organisation, I had to go through that period when people stare at you and try to get the measure of what you're like. The employees around me weren't my cup of tea, so there wasn't much dialogue when I first started. Thankfully, after a few weeks, I found that some of the younger staff, particularly the girls doing the typing and clerical tasks, were more my kind of people. I struck up a working relationship with them, and a couple of the fellows, and we secretly laughed and joked about some of the weirdoes working in the organisation, as you do.

At the age of sixteen, I was eligible to pass a motorbike driving test and I decided to get a Lambretta scooter, a rather fashionable machine at that time of mods and rockers. It cost me fifty quid from some bloke in Edgware. I justified it to my mother and father by saying it would save me a lot of money on the bus fare to Curzon Street. Well, at least I had some wheels.

I did what everybody else did with their bikes: stripped it down and had the side panels chromium-plated and the main body sprayed – in my case, a luminescent mauve. I would proudly park this motorbike outside the offices in Curzon Street where its gleaming side panels were much admired by the younger members of staff in the department.

As a learner driver, you had to display L-plates, which wasn't very cool. I decided it would look better if I cut out the letter L from the white background and stuck it on the front and rear of the bike, only to be stopped one day by a copper who pulled me over and asked, 'What's that L for? L for love? L for luck? Get off that bike and go and buy yourself some proper L-plates.'

This was all rather embarrassing, considering I was in Oxford Street, suited and booted, on a Saturday night. I was in somewhat of a fix with the copper standing next to me. Where was I supposed to go at eight o'clock at night to get L-plates? I asked for dispensation so that I could at least drive the bike to another location where I could park it.

After a bit of negotiation, the copper reluctantly agreed, but told me I wasn't allowed to ride it back home until I had proper L-plates. Fortunately, he didn't hang around and after that evening's ventures I naughtily broke the law and drove the bike back to Clapton. I replaced the L-plates the following Monday. I passed my motorbike driving test in Walthamstow. My current licence still says I can ride a motorbike, although I haven't been on one since.

Back at the Ministry, for once there was a bit of excitement. Miss Mayer came storming into the department and asked me to step into her office. She was having a high-level meeting with a load of top-ranking officials. From what I could glean, the Plowden Report had gone tits-up and they wanted me to explain a few things. That's how bad it was there – they had to get a sixteen-year-old kid to explain to them what was going wrong.

It transpired that a bunch of punch-card operators had entered the data incorrectly, so they asked me to review the print-out and compare it with some of the forms that I had coded. There were thousands of these forms. I said if they gave me a couple of these clerks to sit with, I'd help them read the data, so they could input the whole lot again.

They agreed and, believe it or not, they put me in charge of five or six people, some of them my seniors by ten years or more. They'd be asking me, 'What's this, Alan? What's wrong with that? What shall I do with this? What does that mean?'

I got on really well with them and they soon started taking the mickey out of me. 'You're Miss Mayer's favourite,' they'd say. 'Miss Mayer's son.' But they respected the fact that I was one of them. I hadn't snitched or dropped them in it for the big cock-up first time around. Within a couple of days, I had them sorted out, and I was sitting at my desk with my feet up.

After about two weeks, we'd done the whole lot again. I guess the print-outs must have made some sense this time because Miss Mayer told me that I'd done a good job – I suppose the data suited what they wanted to see. However, there were no tips or bonuses going – let's face it, this was the government.

*

Eight quid a week was all well and good, but it wasn't enough for me to keep up with my mates. I saw the job at the Ministry as something of an investment, so that one day I would end up not having to worry about income. In the meantime, I needed to supplement my earnings. I'd kept my job at the chemist's shop plus a few other ventures, and it was a rather weird situation – I was earning less from my career than I was from my sidelines!

It was working with Mr Allen that once again prompted a new business venture. I'd become something of an expert in cosmetics and toiletries, as a result of selling them. Some of the girls at the youth club I went to in Stamford Hill were very impressed at my knowledge of Rimmel Coty, Yardley, Lancôme, Helena Rubinstein and Chanel, not to mention the full colour range of L'Oréal hair dyes. Yes, it *was* Walthamstow, but believe it or not they had the clientele for that stuff.

Thinking about the Cream of Cactus advertising campaign at school had sparked my interest in the cosmetics industry. I must have driven Mr Allen nuts, I was so inquisitive. At that time, a 'Flaming Red' Rimmel lipstick would sell for 1s 6d, but the Lancôme equivalent was 4s 6d – three times the price!

'Tell me, Mr Allen, these look the same to me – why is one 1s 6d and the other 4s 6d?'

'Advertising,' he said. 'They're both made of the same stuff. There *is* no technical justification, apart from a flasher wind-up case.'

As well as absorbing how people would buy stuff based on the prestige of the brand and the advertising, I was fascinated by what the cosmetic products were actually made of. Take hair lacquer, for example. It was effectively industrial alcohol with something called shellac dissolved into it, the theory being that as soon as it was sprayed onto a warmish surface, the alcohol would evaporate, leaving the shellac to hold the hair in place – quite simple, when you think about it.

A bit of trivia. Ladies may sometimes wonder why they get that cold sensation when the hair lacquer touches their neck. This is because the heat from the body evaporates the alcohol, giving the cooling effect. The same principle applies in an old army trick I once heard about: apparently, in Africa during the war, soldiers put their bottles of beer in a bowl of petrol and left it exposed in the baking sun. As the petrol evaporated, the effect was to take the heat out of the beer. Earth-shattering stuff, right?

I called a meeting with my friends Steve Pomeroy and Geoff Salt and told them that cosmetics was a bit of a mug's game, and that perhaps we should start a little business making shampoo and hair lacquer. Steve's family's business was lemonade, so they knew where to buy bottles and labels. I could source the ingredients to make the hair lacquer and the shampoo – a soap detergent with a little bit of perfume in it.

Having convinced the two lads we should enter into business, we slung fifty quid each into the pot and formed a brand name – Galsté – made up of our three names: Geoff, Alan and Steve.

I found a fellow by the name of Sidney Summers in Tottenham who was a wholesale supplier to hairdressing salons. From him, we bought gallon drums of shampoo, hair lacquer and some green, gooey setting lotion. Then we designed a small label that Steve had printed and we set up a bottling plant in the basement of Steve's house in Clapton.

Unfortunately, the bottle openings were rather small, so I had to make a sort of pipette to fill them up. On top of that, the setting lotion was so thick and gooey that we had a lot of trouble getting it into the bottles. I got lumbered with sorting out the technical problems, but after hours of sweating and cursing, I eventually succeeded.

Armed with three products in our range, the next task was to go off and sell them. Geoff, who claimed to be a good salesman, had the task of calling on chemist's shops and other general stores to see if he could get any orders. Steve was considered the expert on supplies and manufacture, but I was the one who had to sort out the filling of the bottles, so come to think of it, he wasn't really tasked with anything!

I asked Mr Allen to stock some of the bottles on a sale-or-return basis. He always chuckled when he heard about my ventures and was happy to agree. Naturally, when people came into the shop, I would recommend *my* shampoo and hair lacquer, and managed to persuade a few punters to part with their cash. Unfortunately, Geoff and Steve weren't as enterprising as I was, and after a couple of weeks or so they had zero sales.

One Saturday night when we were out, we discussed the project and decided we would try to sell the stuff in East Street market, off Walworth Road in south London. The next morning, Steve took his firm's van and we drove to the market, laden with all this gear. We found the market inspector – affectionately known by market traders as 'The Toby' – and asked him if we could take a stall on a casual basis, as we weren't licensed.

Eventually he found us a spot at the end of the market strip, as one of the traders hadn't bothered to turn up. I can picture it now: a large stall with just three products on it! It didn't look very inviting and was made worse by the fact that all three of us were manning such a sparsely populated stall. We didn't sell much that Sunday, and when the market closed just after lunchtime, we went home with our tails between our legs.

I persevered for two or three more weeks with little success. I decided to spruce the stall up a bit by selling other products. We turned to Steve's uncle, who used to make household cleaning materials such as bleach and pine disinfectant – similar to Dettol. We laid out the stall nicely, with all the products lined up beautifully, including the bottles of pine disinfectant, bleach and toilet cleaner. However, as these were not well-known brands, the move wasn't that successful.

One day, out of sheer frustration and laziness, I decided I wasn't going to bother spending time setting the stall up neatly, so we just chucked the whole lot on in one big pile. This created some excitement amongst the shoppers, who thought that there were bargains to be had. People delved in looking for buried treasure and the stuff started to sell like wildfire.

Messrs Salt and Pomeroy lost interest in getting up at six o'clock on Sunday mornings, so I ended up being the only one to go to the market. Having passed my car driving test by then, I'd borrow Malcolm Cross's van and take his brother Ronald along with me as a stall boy.

We'd chuck all the stuff on the stall and a crowd would gather round as usual. One lady stepped up and asked for six bottles of the shampoo. This was like manna from heaven to me.

'There you go, ladies and gentlemen,' I said. 'There's a lady who's bought our shampoo and now she's back. Look at that – you can't get a better testimony than that. Good stuff, isn't it, dear?'

'Oh,' she said, 'it's not for me – I use it to wash my dog!'

You've never seen so many people disperse so quickly. Ronald was in hysterics.

In the end, we dissolved the business because of the lack of interest of my two partners. I was left with a pile of unsold stock, which I kept in the bicycle shed I had at the flats.

Back at the Department of Science and Education, one of the topics of conversation was the impending death of Winston Churchill, who'd had a stroke. It had been dragging on for days, if not weeks, and we were hearing regular updates on the news. To liven up the office one day, I popped into the typing pool and, with a look of surprise on my face, said to the girls, 'Have you heard the latest news about Churchill?'

'No,' they said. 'What is it? Has he died?'

'No,' I said with a deadpan face. '*He's* all right, but his doctor's dead.' I cracked up laughing at this and they all joined in. It was most likely the highlight of their week – that's how boring it was there.

Sadly, Winston Churchill did die a few days later. I believe his funeral was a national holiday – any excuse for a day off at the Civil Service, right?

We also had a couple of days off when the department moved from Curzon Street to a new location at Richmond Terrace, roughly opposite Downing Street. While helping to settle in after the move, I decided to explore the new building. In certain areas, I found drawings pinned up on the wall which looked remarkably like aeroplanes or missiles. I'm not suggesting it was some Secret Service type of place, but it looked rather interesting to me. I asked Miss Mayer whether we were merging with the science part of the Department of Education and Science and, more to the point, whether I could get myself into a department where I could do something more interesting than compile educational statistics. 'Mind your own business,' was the reply. 'And get on and do what you're told to do.'

That was the final straw. I realised this place really wasn't for me. I looked around at some of the people there, particularly the older ones, and thought to myself that I didn't want to end up like these robots, pushing a load of boring paper around.

I started looking for another job and saw a promising newspaper advert for a trainee cost accountant with a statistics background. The firm was Richard Thomas & Baldwins, an iron and steel manufacturer located on the corner of Gower Street and Euston Road.

The first obstacle I had to overcome was telling my father I was leaving my Civil Service job. His mentality was that you didn't leave your job. You worked for a company and you got 'grandfathered in' – for ever. He wasn't happy that I was flipping jobs so quickly, but I brought him round by explaining that I'd now attained experience in statistics which, if I got this new job, would eventually allow me to become a qualified cost accountant.

I did get the job and the pay was a bit more, about £10 or £11 a week. I was planted in a small office with ten much older men, all of whom were either qualified or trying to qualify as cost accountants. These guys ended up doing me the biggest favour of my life, as I'll explain shortly.

The function of this department was to produce a weekly report on the output of the factory in Wales for the directors. My job was to get the daily output figures from the blast furnace and put this informa-tion into a format which would become part of the directors' report. Each day, a chap called Alun, who had a strong Welsh accent, used to phone me from the factory and read me the output figures.

The lads in the department warmed to me because I was forever messing around and telling a few jokes here and there. One of the things I did was put on a Welsh accent whenever I spoke to Alun at the plant. One day he called up and said, 'Hello, is that you, Alan?'

I replied in a Welsh accent, 'Yes, it is me, Alun – this is also Alan.'

'Where has that Welsh accent come from?' he asked.

I explained to him that when in Rome, you do as the Romans. I said it was to show my devotion to the firm, and that having dealt with so many Welsh people within the company, a bit of the accent had rubbed off on me. Anyway, I told him not to let it bother him and to carry on giving me the daily figures.

He was obviously a bit thick. 'Righto, Alan,' he said. 'Are you ready?'

'Yes.'

'Pig iron, 17.4 tons.'

'Righto, Alun. Pig iron, 17.4 tons.'

'Sinter, 2.6 tons.'

'Righto, 2.6 tons, sinter. Thank you, Alun,' I said. 'I'll speak to you tomorrow.'

'Hang on, don't you want to hear about the slag?'

I waited a moment, raised my voice and said, 'Alun, I'm fed up listening to you moan about your wife.'

As the words came out of my mouth, I knew I was in trouble.

He went bloody mad. 'How dare you talk about my wife like that? I'll have you know I've been married to Glynis for eight years. She's a wonderful lady. You have no right to call her that. Admittedly, we have no children at the moment . . .' and he carried on ranting and raving. 'I'm going to complain about you, speaking in a Welsh accent and insulting my wife . . .'

'It's a joke, it's a joke . . .'

'You London spivs, you're all the bloody same. You don't know what life is like down here in Wales . . .'

'Okay, son, okay, don't worry, speak to you tomorrow, see you.'

My little joke flew around the office. Unfortunately, it didn't take long for word to get back to the powers that be and I was bang in trouble. I was told that the chief accountant had received a complaint and I was to report to his office the next morning.

I prepared a little speech overnight explaining that it was just a joke and that we East End boys, well, we make jokes like this. It wasn't meant in any nasty way; it's just what we chirpy chappies do.

I knocked on the boss's door at nine o'clock and he told me to come in. It was a bit like standing in front of your dad and knowing he's going to tell you off for doing something naughty, but realising that he's struggling not to laugh. Such was the demeanour of Mr Jones, the chief accountant, and I suppose I must have picked up on this. The nervous feeling in my stomach subsided and I felt a bit more relaxed.

He said to me, 'Mr Sugar, I've had a complaint from the plant.'

Blow me down, I did it again. In the corner of his room was a large rubber plant. I pointed to it and said, 'Haven't you been watering it, sir?'

He was not amused and launched into a tirade. 'To get on in this firm, you have to stop being a joker. This is a serious business. You've upset one of the people down in the plant. You've got to understand that these people are different from Londoners. They take things very seriously down there and you've insulted the gentleman and his wife.'

'I'm very sorry,' I answered. 'What would you like me to do? All I can do is apologise. I'll write him a note; I'll do anything you want me to do.'

'Well, if you write him a note, we'll call the matter closed. But I don't want to hear any more complaints about you.'

The other guys in the office were eager to know what had happened. When I told them about the plant joke, they all put their heads in their hands. 'You didn't! You didn't say that, did you? You're a bloody nutter!'

Some of these fellows were in their thirties, already married with children, and there was a senior manager, Glen, who was in his forties. They all took a liking to me and when we chatted during the moments of boredom, they would often tell me that I was wasting my life in this job, doing what they're doing.

In a nice sort of way, they said, 'Look at us – we've got houses and mortgages and children, so we need the job. But you're young – you're at the time of your life when you have no responsibilities. You should be getting out there and doing other things. If *we* had our time over again, we'd be in sales.'

I think the management had concluded that I wasn't really cut out for the job, but as they liked me, rather than fire me, they kind of diplomatically suggested I look elsewhere. They said I was clearly a born salesman and should find myself a job in sales because this job was not for me. They were right. I could tell that my temperament was not the same as theirs. I was never going to be a bookworm, dealing in boring figures. In hindsight, it was a nice way of getting rid of me.

I noticed an advert in the *Evening Standard* for a travelling salesman. The firm was called Robuck Electrical, manufacturers of tape recorders and record-players. What with my interest in electronics as a kid, I thought this looked quite promising.

I went for an interview in Holloway Road and met a tall chap by the name of S. J. Robinson. He was the sales manager and, with his military moustache and tough demeanour, he was not the type you'd want to mess with. He explained to me that the owner, Sam Korobuck, wanted him to build a new sales team and that there were positions available for all parts of the country, including London.

I was seventeen years old, so one of the attractions of this job was that it came with a minivan. Well, beggars can't be choosers. I would need the van because I'd be carting around sample tape recorders and record-players.

I flew through the interview. Robinson was very impressed with me, although he was concerned that I was only seventeen and lacked experience. I think he sussed that I had the instinct for selling. He wrote to me the next day, offering me the job and telling me to turn up in three weeks' time, when I would meet all the other recruits.

Problem: I've got to tell my father that I'm leaving Richard Thomas & Baldwins.

Bigger problem: I've got to explain that I'm leaving the job that was going to help me become a professional to become a *salesman.*

I could predict the flak I'd get. 'All those years of studying, all those years of going to school, all that investment in wanting to become something like a scientist, then a statistician, then an accountant, and now you're going to be a bloody salesman? You could have been a salesman two years ago and worked in a shop.'

I was spot on in my assessment of what he would say. However, I pointed out to him that the two jobs I'd had were deadly boring. Also, I reminded him that Mr Harris, my headmaster, had continually told him at school meetings that commerce was in my blood.

'Besides,' I said, 'you should know that I get up to loads of shenanigans with all my schemes. I've already got two other jobs: one on a Saturday, one on a Sunday. And I'm making loads of money. Plus, I'm paying my way at home. So that's it.' And that *was* it.

*

I have to say, my persuasive powers applied exclusively to marketing and selling – I never had the gift of the gab when it came to the girls. This was in stark contrast to my friend Geoff Salt, for whom sweet-talking the girls was his finest attribute.

Steve Pomeroy was the best-looking boy in our group. He was tall and looked like Michael Caine, and the girls would flock around him at the clubs. But he was also a bit like me – not very forward when it came to chatting up the birds. I remember one occasion when my lack of charm lost him an opportunity with some rich bird from north-west London. We were in the Coronet club, near St John's Wood station, when two rather posh young ladies came up to him. I was by his side and they were chit-chatting about where they'd been on their summer holidays. They mentioned that they'd just come back from Cannes. Little did they know that Steve and I had just come back from Margate.

'Do you know Cannes?' one of them said to me.

I took an immediate dislike to this snooty cow and said, 'No, love, the only cans I know have baked beans in,' at which point they turned and walked away in disgust.

Steve gave me a bollocking. 'What are you doing, you schmock?!'

'Never mind, Steve, you don't need those people. They're not for you, son, they're not for you.'

A few weeks later, Geoff used his charm to persuade an old school-friend called Maureen to invite us all to her birthday party at her house in Highgate. The usual suspects were there, and that evening Steve met a beautiful young lady called Sandra. After many twists and turns over several years, she became his wife, but that's another story.

Sandra worked in a hairdresser's in Liverpool Street with a bunch of other girls, one of whom was a young lady called Ann Simons. Sandra told Ann that her boyfriend Steve had a mate called Alan who was . . . 'Yeah, quite a nice bloke. He's all right.' And she talked about the possibility of us going out as a foursome.

Unbeknown to me, Sandra arranged for Ann to have a pre-inspection of me at the Whisky A Go Go club in Wardour Street one night when I was there with Steve. We must have mingled – certainly Sandra wouldn't have ignored Steve, so there must have been some small talk amongst the four of us – but I have no real memory of it.

A couple of days later, Steve told me I was going out in a foursome with this girl Ann whom I'd bumped into at the Whisky the week before. Though I didn't know it, I'd been inspected and approved. I had no idea what to expect, but we met up at St Anne's Club off Shaftesbury Avenue and, as you do as a young man, I kind of gave her the once-over and decided pretty quickly she was really nice. We didn't have too much to say to each other that night – I don't know who was more shy, her or me. Funnily enough, the foursome wasn't with Steve and Sandra, but with Malcolm and Maureen, who had become boyfriend and girlfriend since meeting at her birthday party in Highgate. This was the first time I officially met my wife. Amazingly, the destiny of *three* couples was determined at that birthday party. Had it not been for the party, Malcolm wouldn't have met Maureen, Steve wouldn't have met Sandra, and Sandra wouldn't have put me forward for inspection by Ann. We still jokingly call it 'that fatal day' and blame Geoff Salt for this travesty.

Forty-odd years on, we still meet up as a group. And each and every time some funny stories from the past come out. On one occasion not so long ago, Maureen, like a bolt out of the blue, exclaimed, 'Here, Alan, do you know that Rod Stewart fellow?'

'No, not really. I might have bumped into him a few times at football, but I've never spoken to him. Why?'

'Well, you tell him, he owes me sixpence.'

'What are you banging on about, Maureen?'

'Well, Rod Stewart used to hang out at my house forty-odd years ago with my brother Steve,' she said. 'He was always in and out. My mum used to make him tea sometimes.'

'Okay, but what's that got to do with anything?' said I.

She continued: 'One night I was at the Marquee Club in Wardour Street and he asked me for sixpence so he could get a bus home.'

'Right, so?'

'Well, he still owes it to me!'

'Shut up, will you? You sound like an old groupie who claims to know someone famous. So what you're asking is that if I ever bump into Rod Stewart, I should tell him that a certain young lady named Maureen Gavril lent him sixpence forty years ago for his bus fare, and that she wants it back with interest? Okay, I'll make it a priority . . . If I ever did meet him and said that to him, he'd think I was nuts.'

'It's true. I'm not making it up. I swear it's the truth.'

Malcolm was shrugging his shoulders with a wry smile, as if to say, 'You're right, she's nuts.'

At this point, Tony Kaye jumped into life with his handheld equivalent of an IBM System 400 and calculated that, with interest compounded at say 10 per cent per annum for the past forty years, the grand sum owing would be £18.50.

'No chance, love,' I said. 'Even if it *is* true, he is Scottish after all.'

*

After our date at St Anne's Club, Ann and I started going out regularly. Because of who I am today, people often ask her what she saw in me. All I've ever heard her reply is, 'He was different.' Maybe it's her polite way of saying that I wasn't a schmoozer, meaning that other boys would come and pick her up from home with a box of chocolates and a bunch of flowers, whereas I would say, 'I'll see you at St Anne's Club,' or 'I'll meet you at Bethnal Green tube station – you can get a Central Line train there from Gants Hill.'

To be perfectly honest, I don't know what she *did* see in me. As a journalist once put it, 'Sugar seems to have had a charisma bypass.' A bit harsh perhaps – maybe a charm bypass.

I am what I am. Unfortunately, the niceties weren't instilled in me by my mother and father. They were very direct and didn't engage in small talk. I was never taught any social graces, not even simple things like saying, 'Hello, how are you?' to people or showing interest in their lives or situations. We never used to exchange birthday cards or Christmas cards or anything like that at home. Consequently, the idea of sending someone flowers, chocolates or a card was alien to me. This was to come back and bite me on the nose later in my relationship with Ann, particularly when it came to her family.

I guess if you're not trained as a kid to do the decent things in life, you simply don't think to do them. However, I can assure you that whatever I lack in that direction, my wife makes up for a hundred times over.

I guess this lack of charm has followed me throughout the course of my business life. Whenever I enter a meeting and a bunch of fellows are sitting there talking about yesterday's cricket, or about Chelsea beating Arsenal, or the weather, or some other topic, I think, 'What a waste of bloody time.'

I'm straight in – bang! 'Hello, right we're here to talk about this, that and the other . . .'

I've shocked a few people in my time with my blunt entrances and lack of small talk. I have no patience at all. I know it's wrong, but I feel like it's cheating to be talking a load of rubbish, particularly when you're going into a meeting where everybody knows what has to be resolved and what you're there for.

*

I was now going for my third job in less than two years since leaving school. I duly turned up for my first sales training session, part of a week-long course at the Holloway head office of Robuck Electrical. S. J. Robinson started by telling everybody about the products and what was so special about their tape recorders. We then moved on to a series of fake presentations, to learn how to present and sell the product to a retailer. We were asked to pitch to our colleagues, all of whom were much older than me. There I was, a seventeen-year-old who had to make his first trade presentation, albeit fake, to Robinson – with all the others looking on too. It reminded me of being back in that party when I was fifteen and having to make up a joke about Surf.

I was very nervous. Suddenly the chirpy chappy had drained out of me. I was useless, absolutely useless. Robinson had a stony look on his face, as if to say, 'What the hell have I done here?'

'That's no good,' he said. 'Sugar, you'd better go away and think about that again. You haven't told me about this feature and that feature. You're stumbling on your words, you're looking down at the floor, you're not looking me in the eye. What's the matter with you? You're not the same man who came here for the interview three weeks ago.'

'Sorry about that, Mr Robinson,' I said. 'Give me a few moments, let someone else have a go, and I'll definitely do better.'

Another four guys did their pitches. Watching them, I picked up a few tips. Later in the day, I pitched again, and this time, I put a smile on his face.

'Well done,' he said. 'Very good, young man. If you do it like that, you're going to do well.'

The next Monday was D-Day, so on Friday I picked up my sample tape recorder and record-player and put them in the van. That weekend, it was no longer a case of getting the bus to Bethnal Green to pick up Ann. I proudly rolled up to meet her in my new minivan, with 'Robuck' printed on the side. After exchanging a few niceties, Ann said to me, 'Why are you talking funny?'

'What do you mean?'

She said, 'You're talking with an accent. You sound like a northerner.'

I'd spent the whole of the previous week with guys from Birmingham and up north, and it made my accent change. This strange phenomenon stuck with me later in life. When in the Far East, I developed a new way of speaking based on the way my Asian suppliers talked to me. I branded it 'Export English' – a very slow way of pronouncing every word clearly and leaving gaps between them, and it was much appreciated. The Japanese would say, 'Sugar-san speaks the best English.' If they but knew! I'm sure that would make the elitist journalists chuckle a bit.

I picked up my first order from a shop in Wood Green. Nervously, I walked into the shop and presented the products to the owner. After a short demonstration, he gave me an order for one record-player. That was my first trade sale, on the first day I was out on the road. But as far as tape recorders were concerned, I don't think I sold a single one all week.

In those days, although there were some multi-retailers, the radio and TV industry was fragmented into hundreds of individual retailers who owned one or two shops. One thing I quickly discovered on visiting these retailers was that Robuck was not a new company. It had once reached dizzy heights as a leading supplier of tape recorders, but had then lost the market. This latest recruitment was a new initiative to relaunch the company.

The retailers told me, 'Yeah, we know about Robuck all right. They ended up flogging off loads of these machines in Gamages at low prices and screwed us all.'

Gamages was a large department store in Holborn that was known for bargains and often flogged off discontinued lines. This was before the abolition of retail price maintenance (RPM), so in those days retail prices were adhered to very strictly – there were no such things as discount warehouses. Therefore, one can understand the response I was getting, which was 'Bugger off, why should we buy from Robuck again?'

Later, when I questioned Robinson about this, he told me that the tape recorder *was* actually a new product, but in reality they'd only changed the colour of the plastic material used to cover the wooden cabinet. The tape deck mechanism was exactly the same and was instantly recognisable as the old model – not an easy sale.

When I think of it now, the territory I had – Greater London – was massive. It was the biggest commercially intensive area in the country, and it had been given to this seventeen-year-old.

Anyway, I got stuck in and as the weeks went by, I started to pick up orders. I called a few of the boys up north to find out how they were doing. Some of them were experienced salespeople who'd previously worked for companies like Philips or Ferguson, and they were just picking up a few orders here and there – so I was doing quite well.

I visited one particular customer in Hounslow, a very large, busy and prosperous shop, and managed to see the boss, a lady. She told me they would never deal with Robuck again, as they'd been let down badly by the Gamages fiasco. In my weekly report, I deliberately wrote this down in a way that would, I hoped, spur Robinson into action. He took the bait, got on the phone to this woman as he knew she had buying power, and smoothed matters over with explanations and apologies. He managed to sell them six machines on my behalf.

This technique of getting Robinson on the case worked for me several times. I'd come into the office with a tale of woe and persuade him to get people on the phone. He was a super salesman in his own right.

It was around this time that one of the most important realisations in my business life dawned on me, and it led to a big breakthrough. Here I was, spending all my time visiting individual retailers who

owned one or two shops. The decision-making process of the individual in charge was an important one – I had to put in a lot of effort to
sell to them, and in the end they might buy one or two tape recorders.
On the other hand, it occurred to me that Currys had about 150 shops
in the London area alone. It would require the same amount of effort
to persuade the boss there to buy from me, and if I *did* persuade them,
the order would be huge. So I decided to make contact with the head
office of Currys and, eventually, managed to get through to Michael
Curry, one of the bosses.

I reported this back to Robinson who gave me a real bollocking,
telling me that I shouldn't have contacted such a big retailer. He told
me it was out of my league, and that things like that were *his* domain.
Then he said, 'You actually got through to Michael Curry?'

'Yes.'

'How did you manage that?'

'Persistence. I phoned about ten times and kept leaving him messages. Maybe he was intrigued to hear from someone with the name
Sugar, I don't know, but I got him on the phone. He said that he
wouldn't buy bulk lots.'

But he had also mentioned to me that some of his individual managers at store-level did have a certain autonomy to buy goods locally if
they wanted to. I managed to get a verbal okay from Michael Curry
that I could offer them hardware like tape recorders. My eyes lit up as
if I'd won the jackpot. There's nothing better than investing buying
power in the bloke who normally has to rely on head office to send him
stock. Most shop managers relish the chance of picking products to
sell other than those foisted upon them by some buyer sitting in his
ivory tower at head office.

Once given permission by Michael Curry, my boat had come in.
The easiest sell in the world was to go and see a Currys manager and
tell him that *he* now had the power to buy. I gave up dealing with the
other retailers for a while and concentrated solely on Currys branches.
I must have sold at least fifty or sixty machines to the various branch
managers and I was looking forward to receiving my pay slip showing
my commission at the end of the month.

*

By now I'd decided to give up my Saturday job at Mr Allen's chemist's, mainly for financial reasons. As nice a guy as he was, what he could afford to pay wasn't worth my while any more. On top of that, the photographic side of his business was going down the pan, migrating to Dixons, who were expanding rapidly. He had taught me a lot and I remained in contact with him for many years.

My brother-in-law, Harold Mazin, who was a salesman in Silver's menswear shop in Tottenham Court Road, told me that Silver's had a big demand for Saturday salespeople, particularly in their two Islington branches, and that they would pay £5 plus commission for a Saturday. He got me an interview with Mr Silver and I took a job in the smaller of the two Islington shops.

There I met a man by the name of Mr Shuster – not shyster, Shuster. He was the greatest salesman I've ever seen, and he could talk the hind legs off a donkey. He would stand outside the front door of the shop with his arms folded and accost anyone who looked at the window.

'Can I help you, sir?'

'No, I'm just looking.'

'Well, come inside. Let me see if I can help you out.'

'No, really, I'm just looking.'

'No, no, come on, sir. There's no obligation, please come in. Let me see if I can help you out with something.' The amount of times Shuster did this and persuaded some poor, innocent punter to buy something was incredible.

Sometimes we worked in the larger shop. There, Shuster really came into his own. It was like watching an artist at work. Having sold someone a suit, he would then move on to their need for a shirt.

'No, I'm okay for a shirt, mate, thank you very much.'

'No, no, no, let me show you a couple of shirts to match the suit.'

And before the customer could refuse, Shuster would have two or three shirts tucked into the jacket. Then, without even mentioning it, he would bring out six or seven different ties. 'Look at that – a wonderful match.'

Normally the customer would be with his wife or girlfriend. 'Yes, it is nice, it's beautiful,' she would say.

'Absolutely. Which one would you like, sir? The pink shirt? The white shirt? Or both?'

He didn't stop there. 'Good, now how about some socks? Socks we sell at one pound ten shillings for half a dozen pairs.'

Instead of saying the socks were 5s a pair, and selling only one pair, he would present six pairs. He would also do this with handkerchiefs, which he'd offer at £2 a dozen. By the time the poor sod had walked out the door, laden with bags, he'd spent a fortune. And many times the fellow had just been casually looking at the window.

When I was back in the smaller shop with another manager, I couldn't resist emulating Mr Shuster and started to adopt his techniques. It was obviously successful, as a week or two later, Mr Silver asked me to work for him full-time, but I wasn't interested in a long-term job as a menswear salesman.

One day, my antics had my colleagues rolling up. I had a customer who wanted a suit to go to a wedding party that night. As ever, the suit needed alteration and it was a case of getting it altered quickly or losing the sale. To the amazement of the other salesmen, I said to the guy, 'No problem, it'll be ready by six o'clock tonight. Leave it to me.'

The customer duly paid and left the shop. One of the salesmen turned to me and said, 'How are you going to do that? There are no alteration hands working here at weekends – normally we quote three days for alterations.'

I told them I'd do it myself. The fellow had tried on the suit in the shop and I had pinned up the jacket sleeves and trouser bottoms.

Taking up the trousers was a walk in the park. No problem at all – my dad had taught me how to do that. However, the sleeves were a different matter. There were four buttons on each cuff and a lining inside, all of which had to be disassembled, shortened then put back together again.

I was in deep, deep trouble. I'd undone the lining, but I couldn't work out how to cut the sleeves shorter, put the buttons back on and reattach the lining. And the customer was coming back in a few hours. I was panicking, while the others were cracking up at the fix I'd got myself into. In the end, I took two of the buttons off and sewed them on further up the sleeve. Then I folded the end of each sleeve over and cross-stitched it underneath. Needless to say, it was quite a thick sleeve ending – a real mess.

When the chap came in, I slung the jacket on him and told him he looked great. Luckily, the trousers fitted perfectly, and he was happy as Larry. I told him that because he needed the suit quickly for the wedding, I'd just done a temporary job on the sleeves, and that if he brought the suit back on Monday, the seamstress would be in and she'd do it properly. I thought about saying, 'Don't do too much dancing or bend your arms at the wedding,' but resisted. Next week, one of the boys told me that the seamstress was killing herself laughing at this disaster I'd perpetrated, but she managed to recover the sleeves.

At Silver's on Leytonstone High Road, I met a new manager who was a friend of Harold's. Harold referred to him warmly as 'Boxer', as he had a boxer's muscular frame and a squashed nose from too many punches landing home. Boxer was a bit of a character, particularly with the women – he could charm the birds off the trees. But he had one big problem: gambling.

I had a lucky escape in this direction because Boxer started to show me how to gamble on horses. He was always popping into the book-maker's next door and placing a bet. Sometimes he'd come back laughing; other times he'd tell me he'd lost his money. On one occasion, he told me he had this great tip and that I should put ten shillings on this horse, which I did – and unfortunately it won! I think I got about £5. With the money, I went to the jeweller's shop and bought a ring for Ann. It wasn't an engagement ring, more what I think you'd call a friendship ring – a small opal.

I'm delighted to say that over the course of the next three weeks or so, I gave back that £5 to the bookies, plus at least £5 more – I didn't win another penny. A great lesson learned!

I presented the ring to Ann that Saturday night. I said, 'I saw this ring and I thought it was nice, so I bought it for you.'

She was kind of embarrassed. Delighted to receive it, but embar-rassed in the sense that normally someone would give you a ring if they were suggesting there was something more formal in the offing. I suppose, in the back of my mind, that *was* what I was thinking, but I didn't have the courage to say it.

It was that Saturday night that I dropped Ann back home and met her family for the first time. Strangely enough, I wasn't nervous at all. I walked into their lounge, bold as brass. 'Good evening,' I said to her mum, dad and grandfather (who lived with them). Ann went off to the kitchen and I started talking freely, as if I'd known the family for years. They asked the usual questions: 'Where are you from? Where do you work? What do you do?'

That was my first introduction to Johnnie and Rita Simons, as well as Izzy Schneider, Ann's grandfather. There's a funny story to tell about him later.

*

While working for Robuck, I got one of the first smacks in the face that would toughen me up for my later business life. I walked into an electrical retailer's shop in Stamford Hill, near where I lived, and told him that I was Alan Sugar from Robuck.

'Robuck? Who are they?' he said.

'The tape recorder company.'

'Oh yes,' he said. 'I'm so pleased to see you. I've heard about you and I've been wanting to see you. Tell me what you've got to offer.'

I showed him a tape recorder and he said, 'Excellent.'

He bought six. This was the easiest sale I'd had so far. I was very naïve.

I called on him a week or so later to see how he was getting on. 'Great,' he said. 'I've sold a few of them already. In fact, I'd like to order another four.'

A month later, I was asked by Robuck's credit controller to go down to the shop and chase payment. When I got there it was closed. Empty. I went to the shop next door and asked, 'What's happened to them?'

The chap told me, 'They've done an LF, son.'

'LF? What's an LF?'

'Long firm, mate, long firm.'

'What's a long firm?'

A long firm turned out to be an organisation that buys loads of stuff on credit then sells it very quickly and cheaply with no intention at all of paying the supplier. At Robuck's expense, I'd learned a tremendous lesson in life.

When I looked at my payslip that month, I was shocked to see my commission was not what I was expecting. Fair enough, the long firm sales were deducted, but on the upside I'd sold fifty-odd units to Currys.

I called up Robinson and said, 'What's going on?'

He told me he'd cut the commission on Currys as their head office had cottoned on to the fact that I was selling to them. They wanted a lower price, which Robinson had to give them. And because of that, he decided he would reduce my commission to a quarter of what I was getting when I sold to small retailers.

I told him it was bang out of order, since I'd spent the whole of the month plundering these Currys stores. Had I known there was no money in it for me, I wouldn't have bothered spending my time talking to all these branch managers. I had effectively opened the door to Currys for Robuck, especially bearing in mind the problems caused by selling stuff to Gamages.

I was quite angry. 'I'm not working for you any more,' I said as I walked out of the office. 'You've cheated me.'

Mum told me that Robinson had called a few hours after I'd stormed off, wanting to speak to me urgently. I got hold of him and he asked me to meet with Mr Korobuck the following morning. We went to the factory just around the corner from the office. This was the first time I'd met Mr Korobuck, a quiet-spoken gentleman, about fifty years old, with a slight stoop. After greeting me, he told me that he was very pleased to have heard how well I'd done in such a short time and he let me know that I'd become their top salesman, something that Robinson hadn't told me.

Mr Korobuck had heard I was quitting and, in an effort to change my mind, he shared his plans with me and showed me some new models.

I told him that I would think about it, but I reiterated my disappointment at not being paid the full commission on the Currys deal.

He sympathised with me, but told me this was a matter to take up with Robinson, who stood resolute on the issue.

A week or so passed. I happened to notice an advert in the *Evening Standard* placed by the electrical wholesalers R. Henson & Co. in Finchley. They were looking for salesmen to sell electrical goods, and the job came with a car. I contacted them and went up to north Finchley for an interview with Mr Henson Senior and his two sons, John and Peter, who were also in the business. Henson's product range was vast, with items such as miniature tape recorders, transistor radios, record-players, electric lamps and loads of other things – all under brands I'd never heard of. If I got the job, I wouldn't have to concentrate on selling just one product.

I told Mr Henson I wasn't interested in working for peanuts. I wanted a minimum of £20 a week, clear of tax, as a basic, plus some commission structure. Twenty quid a week clear was a lot of money in those days. The trio stepped out of the meeting for a few minutes. When they returned, Mr Henson said he was prepared to give me a trial.

My next question was, 'What car have you got for me?'

He told me he had a Wolseley.

Wow, a Wolseley! That was a great car, real quality. I couldn't believe what I was hearing. I had visions of pulling up at my flats and parking the Wolseley out the front in Upper Clapton Road. It would look out of place amidst the Ford Populars and Ford Anglias. I grabbed the job. It turned out that the Wolseley was a Baby Wolseley, an oddball of a car – it looked a bit like a Beetle with an elongated bonnet – *and* it was second hand. Still, it was better than a minivan.

I duly resigned from Robuck, much to the disappointment of Mr Korobuck. Time to explain to my dad that I was about to change my job yet again. I had a good patter by now – it was all about career advancement and being paid a fair amount for the job I was doing. I told him that I'd been diddled by Robuck and that this new firm was paying me much more money. Thus the transition to my fourth job in two years came without the usual recriminations.

I spent the first couple of weeks out on the road with John Henson, learning the ropes. Then, on the Friday of the second week, I collected a bunch of samples to put in the boot of the Wolseley so I could be off and running the following Monday morning.

The storeman there told me, on the quiet, that the Hensons were the most suspicious people you could ever come across. They assumed that everyone was going to nick stuff off them. Indeed, Peter Henson was rather hesitant in giving me the samples and told me I should bring them back at the end of each day. I said, 'If you don't trust me, then I don't think I should take the job.' It was a bit of a gamble, but I stood my ground. I also suggested: 'If you list down every sample I've got, then once a week, when I come in, you can do a spot check to see that they are still there.' To me it was a no-brainer, and he finally conceded.

Working for Henson was a great eye-opener. Naïvely, I had believed that their products were stock items which I could continue to sell. I soon found out that this was not the case when I successfully sold some Remington razors to Gamages – I ended up getting a rucking from Henson Senior! He called me into his office and told me that I shouldn't have made promises of being able to supply 200.

That's when I learned that Henson did not manufacture anything. They simply bought parcels of items from various places; there was no consistency in the product range. This was not a problem for me, but, as I said to old man Henson, it would have been nice to have been told about the business model when I joined.

In a way it was interesting because there were always different products coming along. Some weeks we had electric fans, transistor radios, mini tape recorders and loudspeakers; other weeks we'd get a parcel of Hoover toasters or Remington razors.

As time went by, I could easily identify which customers would be interested in the new items. One day I was told there was a parcel of 250 Hoover toasters coming in.

I called one of our customers and told him that I had 250 Hoover toasters.

'What price are they? What's the model number?' he asked.

I told him to hold on, asked Henson Senior and relayed the details down the phone. I sold the toasters on the spot, in front of the boss, hung up the phone and said, 'There you are, they're sold.'

Do you think I got any thanks? No. Not even a 'well done'. Instead it was just 'Okay,' followed by, 'You didn't offer him any settlement discount, did you?'

I said, 'That's a matter you'll have to sort out with him when you deliver the goods.'

Henson and sons were not very complimentary. As with S. J. Robinson, you never got a pat on the back for selling, and sometimes you'd receive bollockings when you'd done well!

Who knows? Maybe I picked up *my* traits from them. Perhaps that's what you do as a boss. It's certainly miles away from the schmooze culture which exists nowadays, with bosses or managers spending half their time dishing out insincere compliments. I certainly missed out on that. Information on this *is* available, for those interested, in the Harvard Business School manual.

Working for Henson, sometimes I would literally do the deal, deliver the goods and collect the money. On one occasion, they'd bought thousands of seven-inch vinyl records under the Blue Beat label. Blue Beat was a kind of Jamaican music popular during the sixties, but the producers had overcooked it a bit and we had boxes and boxes of these records lying around waiting to be sold.

Fortunately, I'd had dealings with customers in Brixton's Coldharbour Lane. One of them, Clint Atkins, a big, burly black guy from Jamaica, was a real character. Clint couldn't consume the volume we had, but he liked the product. He gave me some tips on other places in Brixton and Streatham where I could sell them, and I did quite well.

Months later, I visited a customer and couldn't help noticing some Blue Beat boxes piled up in the corner of his shop. I'd had nightmares about those bloody boxes, so spotting them was easy. I asked the man, 'What are you doing with those records there?'

'Don't ask!' he said. 'I got lumbered with these things. I thought they were a good idea, but basically it's Caribbean music and my clientele are not into it. Plus, I don't have the facilities to put them on display or play them, so they're the most useless commodity you can think of. I'd just like to get rid of the blooming things.'

'How many have you got?' I asked.

'About ten thousand.'

'How much do you want for them?'

'You can have them for a hundred quid.'

I asked him if I could use the phone in his office to call my boss. In fact, I called Clint, who was always asking me if I could get any more, and did a deal with him. The difference in price between what I bought them and sold them for was £80. Now, considering I was earning £20 a week plus commission and this transaction had been done in a quarter of an hour or so, I thought this was a fantastic bit of business.

The next day, I got Henson's storeman to come out with me in the van to pick up the records and deliver them to Clint. I told the bloke we purchased them from that my firm would send them a cheque tomorrow. We drove to Clint's, delivered the records and he duly paid up, which was unusual for him as he liked a bit of credit.

Back at Finchley, I proudly walked into the boss's office and said, 'Here's a cheque for a hundred and eighty pounds. You've got to write a cheque out to Mr So-and-so for a hundred.'

'Why's that?' he said.

I told him I'd found some records, bought them and sold them, and that £80 was the profit. To my shock and amazement, he said, 'You should have sold them for much more.'

I was devastated. 'Mr Henson, I make twenty quid a week plus commission and I've just made you eighty pounds in the course of a day – is that all you've got to say?'

'But you knew the price of these records was much more, so why did you sell them so cheaply?'

I could not believe I was getting a bollocking. I walked out terribly upset at this situation.

My travels around retailers while working for Henson coincided with a boom in TV sales. Retailers would take the customer's old TV in part-exchange, which meant that many small retailers were stockpiling old TVs.

On visiting a retailer in Holloway, I noticed he had all these TVs stacked up.

I asked him, 'What's all this stuff piled up everywhere?'

'I know,' he said. 'We can't swing a cat in here. We'd like to get rid of it all.'

I thought of my mate Malcolm, who was a TV engineer. He could fix the sets and I could flog them. I said, 'I'll take them.'

'Great,' he said. 'You can *have* them. Free of charge. Get rid of them.'

To be honest, I was doing a bit of moonlighting here because I was on Henson's time. I gave Malcolm a call that night and asked him whether he'd be able to borrow his firm's Dormobile van.

'What for?' he asked.

'I'll tell you later.'

We bowled down to this shop the next day and loaded up the Dormobile to the brim with these tellies. Unfortunately, we had nowhere to store them, so we ended up humping them up the stairs to my flat and putting them all in my brother's old bedroom/my ex-darkroom. My mum watched this procedure. 'What's all this rubbish?' she moaned.

'Don't worry, Mum, I'll tell you about it later. Malcolm and I are going into a little business sideline here.'

We also cleared out a Rumbelows shop in Walthamstow, taking more TVs. Malcolm started repairing them, while I advertised them in the *Exchange & Mart* as an 'unwanted item' supposedly belonging to someone getting married and moving out (well, I would one day). When a punter showed up, I'd take a reconditioned TV into my bedroom, put a small V-aerial on the top and switch it on.

My mother was going nuts. Strange people were coming into the flat and humping TV sets down the stairs, with the neighbours watching inquisitively, wondering what was going on.

We were doing so well that Malcolm's repair rate couldn't keep up with my sales rate. Malcolm is a very nice man and we're still great friends to this day, but, to put it politely, I must say he lacked the killer instinct, the passion to want to make money. He'd jog along, while I'd be badgering him. 'Malcolm, I need some more stock. Can you come round on Friday and fix a few more because I've got a lot of appointments on Saturday.'

He told me he couldn't. He spent every Friday night with Maureen and he didn't have time to do the TVs.

I was disappointed. I was sharing the proceeds with him fifty-fifty, so I wasn't legging him over. We were making quite a few quid out of this venture, but he wouldn't budge on his Friday nights, despite me pestering him and telling him we'd already spent money on advertising. The *Exchange & Mart* came out on Thursdays and I'd have to turn away all the customers the advert had drummed up. It was frustrating telling punters the TV had been sold.

My brother Derek once told me he was walking along Kingsland High Road and saw an advert in a newsagent's window for a second-hand TV. He thought to himself, 'I recognise that number – Upper Clapton 7875.' He phoned home to ask about it and my mum and dad told him what was going on. Derek thought it was a tremendous coincidence; all it told me was that it pays to advertise.

On the subject of Kingsland High Road, Malcolm and I sometimes used to buy our valves and spare parts from an electrical shop there. One Saturday, there was a man looking at a television in the window. I said to him, 'What are you looking at?'

He said, 'That second-hand TV there.'

I said, 'I've got a much better one than that.' This was a touch of Mr Shuster. 'It's made by Ultra and it's much more modern. Plus, that thing there is twenty quid – the one I've got is fifteen quid.'

I convinced the guy to jump in the car with me and I took him up to the flat. My mother opened the door and saw my new friend, a rather tall Nigerian, an unusual addition to a Jewish home on a Sabbath, when the ritual lunch was about to be served.

'Who's this?' she said. 'Shabbos lunch is ready.'

'Yeah, don't worry, Mum. He's not here for lunch; he's just come to buy my telly.'

Mum shrugged, and I demo'd the telly to the punter, who was delighted with it. The only problem was that he didn't have a vehicle, so I asked him to give me another quid and I'd take him home, somewhere up Lea Bridge Road.

Thanks to Mr Shuster, that deal paid off very nicely, though Mum was not a happy bunny. In fact, the whole TV venture came to a sudden end due to Malcolm's lack of ambition and me getting a flea in my ear from Mum.

*

In my travels around London working for Henson, I always allocated Thursday as my day to do the City. On Thursday lunchtimes, I would pull up at Liverpool Street, where Ann worked, to meet up with her for half an hour or so. This became a regular routine. Ann worked in a first-floor hairdressing salon and when she came out to the car, the other girls would chuck hairclips out the window and we would hear them bouncing off the roof.

One Thursday, unusually, one of Ann's colleagues came downstairs from the salon and knocked on my car door. I opened the window and she gave me an envelope. It contained a Dear John letter. It was from Ann, telling me that she wanted to break off our relationship. My heart sank. I wondered what I'd done wrong.

A few moments later, Ann came down and sat in the car with me. She looked embarrassed and nervous – there was no real eye contact. She said she was sorry about the letter, but that's exactly what the position was. She said something like: 'We're getting too serious – we're too young to be tied down.'

I drove off gutted. I don't remember where I went, but I know I didn't do any work that afternoon. The whole thing had come as a bolt out of the blue. I tracked down one of my friends, either Geoff or Steve, to tell them what had happened. I wondered if maybe Steve could find out from Sandra whether there was a deeper reason behind this.

There *was* – but it's amazing how oblivious I was at the time.

4

'Who Is Going to Pay You on Friday?'

The A M S Trading Company

1966–8

Throughout our early courtship, I spent a bit of time at Ann's house, getting to know her family. Johnnie Simons, Ann's father, was a very tall man with an air of authority – you wouldn't want to get into an argument with him. He was very domineering and over-powering. This was in stark contrast to Ann's mother, Rita, who had a really soft nature. She was a wonderful, supportive wife and went along with whatever her husband said. My early conversations with Ann's father usually revolved around religion. Johnnie would lecture me on how religious the family was in general; how they observed all the Jewish traditions of running a kosher home; how he attended shul (synagogue) regularly on Saturdays and observed every Jewish holiday.

In fact, whereas most people chat about their football team or their hobbies when making small talk, Johnnie would talk about religion – I think it's fair to say that *was* his hobby. The problem was that if you didn't comply with his religious standards, then you were effectively a pleb. There's no other way to describe it. I obviously fell into that category because he would ask questions like, 'Does your mother keep a kosher home? Do you go to shul? Do you go regularly?'

Being Honest Al, I would reply, 'Well, not really. My mum buys kosher food, but to be honest we don't go to all the trouble of separate knives and forks and all that stuff. And no, the last time I was in shul it was for someone's wedding. I don't go. I find it boring. In fact, sorry to say, I don't believe in God.'

I believe we're right to be proud of our religion and traditions, but people should be able to choose the level to which they comply. In hindsight, my responses to Johnnie's inquisition were quite mature, especially bearing in mind that there are plenty of even stricter Jews who would think that Johnnie was a heathen. However, my answers went down like lead balloons.

There were occasions when I felt I was being frowned upon due to my inability to debate kashrus. It's not as if the Simons family was anything special. They were people who came from the same place as my family did – from the East End of London – but they were part of the circle of Jews who wanted to try to elevate themselves and, as such, maybe felt they were somewhat superior.

Sometimes, when I visited Ann's house, other family members would be there. Johnnie had many brothers and sisters. Uncle Sammy and Uncle Alf were really nice fellows. They used to play the game of being ultra-religious, but still managed to be down to earth. You could have a laugh with these guys – they didn't project themselves as something they weren't. It was quite funny when the family got together. It was like watching a pub quiz, seeing them argue over which Sedrah (portion of the Jewish law) was going to be read this Saturday.

On the other hand, three of Johnnie's sisters felt they were a cut above. When you spoke to them, you could be forgiven for thinking you were talking to royalty. I'm afraid that Johnnie also sailed close to the royalty bracket. He'd broken free of his old East End values and, as I said, Rita would faithfully go along with him. In some of my conversations with Ann's wider family, I would have them laughing at my carry-ons, and get them arguing over my views on religion. I remember on one occasion, I apologised for being hoarse and explained that I had a sore throat. Rita heard me and chimed in. 'Froat?' she asked. 'Is that how you say throat – froat?'

So to sum myself up in the eyes of Johnnie and Rita:

a) I couldn't doven (recite Jewish prayers) from scratch, nor did I read Hebrew or observe the Jewish religion.

b) I was not a university graduate destined to become 'my son, the lawyer', 'the doctor' or 'the accountant'.

c) I spoke with a very broad East End accent.

Unfortunately, what I didn't understand at the time was that poor Ann had been put under extreme pressure to ditch me by her domineering father. So much so, it drove her to write me the Dear John letter.

Twenty years later, a *Financial Times* journalist wrote a book on me and made reference to a certain Gulu Lalvani (I'll tell you about him later) who said, 'Ann's father never wanted Alan – he wasn't good enough for them.' This infuriated Johnnie. At first he denied the accusation, but when I reminded him about Ann's letter, he blustered, 'Well, you just wait till *your* daughter is grown up – see what you're like.' I think the point he was making was that he just wanted the best for his daughter. Fair comment, I guess.

That Thursday night, after receiving the letter, I met up with my pals and discussed the situation. To be honest, they weren't interested. Some of them felt that it was just a girlfriend. So what? It's over. I don't think any of them really understood how upset I was. So I just shut up about it.

On Friday, I found it very hard to concentrate. Despite trying to sleep it off and think positive, move on, all those clichés, I didn't have a good day. As it was the end of the week, I went back to the office and had my samples counted by Peter Henson to check that they tallied with the previous week's count. I was very short on words. Mr Henson Senior was doing his usual uncomplimentary summary of my week's work. I just wanted to get out and go home. I called to Peter, 'Right, would you check this lot of stuff here.'

On counting my samples, Peter said there was a set of walkie-talkies missing – I had no idea why. In fact, the walkie-talkie sets were now totally out of stock, so there was no reason why I should have a sample. Nevertheless, in theory, the set should have been there. Peter asked, 'Well? Where has it gone?'

And at that point I exploded and started effing and blinding, swearing at him, telling him what a prick he was. 'I've no idea where it is,' I yelled. 'And I *don't* like being treated as if I'm a thief.' And then, unbelievably, I burst into tears of frustration.

The guy must have thought, 'Bloody hell, I only asked where the walkie-talkies are!' He started to get a bit worried.

'What's the matter with you, Alan? What are you crying for?'

Obviously this pent-up depression over breaking up with Ann had been buried inside me. I'd hardly spoken a word to my mum and dad on the Thursday or the Friday; in fact, I'd hardly spoken to anybody, since my mates weren't interested. Come Friday afternoon, Peter Henson must have pushed the wrong button.

'Calm down,' he said, 'calm down. What's the matter with you? Is there something else wrong?'

I was on my way out, so I turned to him and said, 'Look, I just want to go home. Is that okay?'

He followed me, saying, 'Don't drive in this state. There must be something wrong. Come inside and sit down.'

Henson Senior rallied round as well. 'What's going on?'

'Nothing, nothing,' I said. 'Just a bit of aggravation, that's all.'

'Where? Here?'

'No, no, at home. Don't worry, it's all right, I'm okay.'

The storeman joined in, thinking my outburst was about the missing walkie-talkies, and said, 'Here, Alan, I've worked it out. After you brought your box in last Friday, Peter was looking for a set of walkie-talkies, so he actually took the set himself and flogged it. I told Peter and he remembers this now, so he knows you didn't nick it.'

I finally went home. That night I met the lads and we all agreed that tomorrow we'd go out to the Whisky A Go Go club.

Although Steve and Sandra had met a while ago, they weren't an official couple yet. Steve still felt he was a free agent, although I'm not sure Sandra did. So when we turned up at the Whisky A Go Go on Saturday, it wasn't surprising to see Sandra there, loitering with intent. What *was* surprising was to see Ann. Head down, I weaved my way to the other side of the room with the lads and just let the evening take its course.

At some point, Sandra came up to me and said, 'Ann's very upset and she's sorry for what she did on Thursday. She'd really like to get back together with you.'

I told Sandra, 'Well, that's heart-warming, but it would be better if the message came from her.' Ten minutes later, another of Ann's friends came up to me with the same message and I sent her off with the same reply.

Knowing Ann's nature as I do now, I can understand how tough the next move was for her. Eventually, she came over, apologised, slung her arms around me and said, 'I'll *never* do that again. That's it. If we ever break up, it'll be you that does it.'

I was in a bit of a daze, to be quite honest. What had I done to deserve that treatment on Thursday? And now what had I done to deserve this treatment on Saturday?

I wasn't bargain of the century, so when I think back, considering the amount of pressure she was under from her parents and considering she was a lovely-looking girl, sought after by many other fellows, I can't see what the bloody hell made her so determined to stick with me. She could have had a prospective doctor, lawyer or accountant, and she'd have made her father happy. To this day, I still wonder at her determination and courage in sticking with me.

Even braver was her next move. At the end of the evening, she asked me to take her home. At this point, I didn't know that Johnnie had been putting pressure on Ann to ditch me, so I walked into the lion's den, cocky as you like. You can imagine the looks I got.

'Hello, Alan, I'm surprised to see you here,' said Rita, as she glared meaningfully at Ann.

'Really? Why are you surprised to see me?'

'Just surprised to see you *here*,' she said, continuing to glare.

Ann's grandfather, Izzy, was sitting with Johnnie watching football on TV. 'Who's playing?' I asked.

'Who knows?' came from Johnnie, as if to say, 'Why are you asking *me* about football?'

*

The following Monday, with my personal life sorted, with all the troubles of the world off my shoulders and with new fire in my belly, I was out selling again.

Peter Henson was still apologetic, not understanding what had gone on the previous Friday. 'Are you all right, Alan? Everything okay?'

'Everything's fine, Peter. Sorry about Friday. Right, anything new in this week? Anything I should know about?'

'Yes, actually, we've got some high-intensity lamps coming in. Take one of these samples.'

I couldn't resist rubbing it in. 'Can you write that down, Peter, only I think when you took the walkie-talkie out of my samples box a couple of Fridays ago, you might have forgotten about it.'

'Yes, I realise that,' he said, knowing exactly what I was playing at.

Earlier I mentioned Henson Senior's Scrooge-like manner. As I continued to work for him, my thoughts increasingly ran along the lines of: 'Here I am riding around selling this stuff, which basically is purchased from third parties. On some occasions I do *all* the donkey work – picking up the boxes from the importer, delivering them to the customer, collecting the money. And I don't even get thanked for it. I get my wages of twenty quid a week clear and a bit of commission here and there, but that's it.'

Once again, let me underline the fact that £20 per week plus, say, £5 commission and another £10–15 from my sidelines, such as selling TVs, meant that I was earning £35–40 a week clear. That was a hell of a lot of money in 1966–7, without a question of a doubt. Nowadays, forty years later, it is, perhaps, the equivalent of someone earning £2,000 a week. Consider that a packet of twenty cigarettes was half a crown (12½p), as was a gallon of petrol (3p per litre in today's money).

Some weeks my TV sideline brought in as much as £30–40, but one couldn't guarantee the consistency of these windfalls, as some weeks I'd hardly sell any. Nevertheless, selling something for myself that brought in £30–40 made the £20 I got for working five days a week, on the road, reporting to a boss, look stupid. And then, when I remembered the £80 I'd made for Henson in a single day . . . well, that tipped the scales.

One Friday night, I came home and I said to the family, 'I'm going to start working for myself. I told Henson today that I'm leaving.'

Henson wasn't actually upset. He said, 'Fair enough, if you want to go, it's up to you. What are you going to do?'

I said, 'I might work for myself.'

'Fine,' he said. 'But let me tell you, you haven't got very good contacts.' Always full of encouragement.

My father looked at me as if I were mad. 'What do you mean, *you're going to work for yourself*? Who is going to pay you on Friday?'

That was an expression I'll never forget, and it really sums up his whole outlook on work and life: 'Who is going to pay you on Friday?'

I told him that I was going to pay myself on Friday.

Fortunately, Daphne, Shirley and the two Harolds were there at the time. Being of a different generation from my mum and dad, they were smiling enthusiastically, really encouraging me. I tried to reassure my dad that the profitability of my sidelines *proved* I had nothing to lose by going it alone – and I think it sunk in.

'So what are you going to do?'

'Well, I'm going to get down to the Post Office and take out a hundred pounds. I've seen a second-hand minivan in the garage over the road for fifty quid. I've already made enquiries and found out that it's eight pounds for third party, fire and theft insurance. And with the rest of the money, I'm going to buy a bit of gear to sell and get on my way.'

Shirley's Harold pointed out to me that I needed to get a National Insurance card and buy a National Insurance stamp once a week. That was another item on my list of chores.

The following day, I sprang into action. I withdrew £100 from my Post Office account, bought the van and took out the insurance.

And then, a really nice thought from Shirley. I received a telegram on Monday which said, 'GOOD LUCK ALAN IN YOUR NEW BUSINESS.' It's a pity I didn't keep it.

I set off in the minivan to Percy Street, just off Tottenham Court Road, and walked into the premises of the first supplier to A M S Trading Company, my new company. Many of the big importers in the marketplace used to name their companies after themselves, but I thought Sugar Trading wouldn't have gone down too well, so I decided upon A M S Trading, which stood for Alan Michael Sugar.

I didn't form a limited company. Effectively, it was Alan Sugar trading as A M S Trading Company. I never had any printed letterheadings or order books, simply a blue carbon-paper book with 'INVOICE' printed at the top of each page.

At the supplier's, I was greeted by a Mr Ronnie Marks, who didn't know me from Adam. He was standing behind his trade counter. 'Hello, how are you?' he said, as if he'd known me for years. This was part of Ronnie's charm – he made you feel comfortable.

To cut a long story short, I bought about forty quid's worth of car aerials off him, which ate up the balance of my £100. Car aerials, I'd learned from my Henson days, were quite an easy sale.

No one, including myself, ever imagined I would succeed in the electrical business in the manner I have. When industry people started talking about me, suddenly everyone claimed to be the one that started me off. One such person was Gulu Lalvani (more about him shortly). So let me officially go on record and say this: *no one* actually started me off as such because no one gave me any merchandise on credit. But it is true to say that my very first supplier greeted me cheerfully, treated me decently and sold me some car aerials – and that gentleman was Mr Ronnie Marks. There you go. That's the start-off story, like the beetroot story, all officially logged.

My first customer was P. W. Thaxton of East India Dock Road, who bought six car aerials. I had known this customer from my days with Robuck and Henson.

I turned up and said, 'Good morning, Peter, I'm now working for myself – it's A M S Trading Company – and I've got some aerials to show you. I know you've sold them in the past.'

I wonder to this day whether he gave me an order because of my sales patter or out of the kindness of his heart. If it was the latter, I'm forever grateful.

By Thursday of that week, I'd sold my first batch of aerials and had been back to buy some more. I had made £60 profit. Now £60 profit was inconceivable at the time, but it then became my weekly target to earn that by at least Wednesday. I must be sounding like a bit of a nutter now. After all, a) what's Wednesday got to do with the price of cocoa? And b) where did the figure of £60 come from? Well, it was a target, and as the weeks went on, nine times out of ten I did achieve this £60 target by Wednesday. The discipline was to carry on through Thursday and Friday and make some more because at some point a rainy day would come.

And rainy days did come because my showroom, my warehouse and my business were all, in fact, the minivan. And this fifty-quid heap of junk kept breaking down. It was always at the garage, and without wheels I was wiped out.

*

Now let me officially introduce you to Gulu Lalvani, a character who has crossed paths with me time and time again, as you'll find out later. He was an importer with premises in Paul Street in the City area. When I first met Gulu and his brother Partap, they both wore turbans. However, not long afterwards, Gulu decided to remove his and take on more of a Western style with a closely trimmed beard. He was rather tall and well-built, and had a sort of charm that women found attractive. Many years later, I would see him doing his familiar party-piece to impress the ladies by telling them he was some kind of psychic. He would hold their hands and bullshit his way through reading the lines on their palms – of course, he made it up as he went along. When I ridiculed him about this, he told me he was blessed with this power and he knew what he was talking about. I was amazed to see the ladies fall for this crap.

The name of Gulu and Partap's company was J. Parker & Co. Ltd, an unexpected name for a company run by a couple of Asian brothers. It's rumoured that one of the first products Gulu sold was a replica Parker pen and he tried to overcome copyright infringement by printing the name 'J PARKER' on it, with the 'J' being quite faint. I have no idea if it is true or not but it's a great story. On reflection, my take on their choice of business name is that it was their way of trying to anglicise the company. Racial discrimination was rife in those days. It was bad enough against Jews in business, but it was even worse against Asians. Gulu employed a stand-up British sales manager, attired in a pin-striped suit and blue spotted tie. This gentleman headed up sales to the outside world – the interface when dealing with traditional British companies.

I first met Gulu and Partap when I was working for Henson. Apparently, Gulu was a bit of a lad and they used to say that he and John Henson would share some rather interesting evenings, boozing and birding. Now that I was in business for myself, Gulu would sell me goods for cash only. I had expanded my range beyond car aerials to transistor radios, but would only be able to afford one carton at a time, which might contain twenty radios. Initially, Gulu would ask me to pay him in banknotes; he wouldn't even take a cheque.

I was coming back every couple of days to pick up more radios and eventually he accepted my cheques, although, if I remember rightly, he cleared them specially. But to be fair to the man, after a while we got to the stage where if I gave him a post-dated cheque, he would allow me to take more than one carton of radios. When I came back to pick up some more stock, then, and only then, would he present my cheque.

For any youngsters looking in, there's a business lesson to be learned here. What I've just described to you is building a relationship with your supplier. I don't blame Gulu one tiny bit for demanding cash up front because he was dealing not just with me, but with loads of market traders, as well as a bunch of flyboys. I would come across these crooks in the months and years ahead; people who would think nothing of writing out cheques that bounced.

So what happened over the course of maybe a couple of months was that I established myself with Gulu to the extent that, although he perhaps didn't quite trust me 100 per cent yet, he made the calculated decision to give me a bit of credit – and that was because I hadn't let him down. And I've never let anyone down since. It illustrates an important point: it's what you do in practice that gains you business credibility, not hype or empty promises. I guess it comes down to the old adage: actions speak louder than words.

The whole area around the City of London, from Middlesex Street to City Road, had importers of 'fancy goods'. Things like transistor radios and high-intensity lamps fell into this category. However, most of the importers were effectively selling the same stuff, just branded differently. Some importers, such as East West – again run by an Asian family, the Shahwanis – sold rather more up-market technical goods. Fronting for them was a gaunt-looking gentleman called Peter Jones, their sales manager.

Around this time, I became aware that all these importers had brand names. Gulu had Binatone (Bina being the name of his sister); others I bought from had names like Vantone and Fantavox. It was a prestige thing – it gave you a kind of credibility with the retailers. If nothing else, it was a statement that you must definitely be the importer.

Most of the time, traders like me wanted to make sure we weren't buying off a middleman. You knew you were buying from a middleman if the diamond-shaped panel had been cut out of the shipping carton. Every importer had its name printed in that panel, so that the dockers could recognise the batches of cargo. If you saw 'J PARKER' printed in the diamond, then you knew the stuff had come from Gulu. So if you didn't want the next guy to know where the goods had come from, you cut out the diamond.

I decided that I would use my own brand name on some products, even though I bought them from an importer. I came up with the name 'Amstrad', from A M S Trading. My first Amstrad-branded product was 1,000 gas cigarette lighters, bought from an importer by the name of Ezra Elias, who was just round the corner from Gulu's gaff. His brand was Vantone. And from East West I ordered 1,000 intercom sets, again branded Amstrad.

The goods took six weeks to arrive. When they came, I was so pleased I proudly showed them around. Most people didn't give a toss and said, 'Yeah, that's the same as the Vantone or the East West product,' or 'Who cares – what's the price?' But the smaller punters, outside London, maybe were impressed.

*

Meanwhile, Johnnie hadn't given up. He was still doing his best to try to get rid of me. One Sunday, I got a phone call from Ann. 'Alan,' she said, 'you've got to get round here quick.'

It turned out that Johnnie had arranged for a boy to come to their house to meet her. This boy was recommended by Auntie Hettie, a real sergeant major. He was a professional, could recite from the Torah from scratch, came from a lovely family and spoke with a rather posh accent – the absolute epitome of Johnnie's target son-in-law. Johnnie had only gone and set this up without Ann's knowledge! And she was supposed to sit there, all prim and proper, with this fellow.

Ann was quite smart. She immediately phoned her friend Susan

Frunt and asked her to come round at the same time and she hauled me in too. It was a most ridiculous situation. The poor fellow turned up on this arranged date to find Susan Frunt, myself and Ann. Ann's idea was maybe this geeky SuperJew would be right up Susan's alley. And I would be there with Ann, so the message being sent to this fellow was '*Hello?* This is my *boyfriend!*'

It's unbelievable to think of the lengths Johnnie went to. He must have been fuming. I cannot for the life of me understand, knowing Ann's character over all the years we've been married, where she found the strength to overcome this pressure. Bearing in mind that she was not the type of person to do something out of sheer belligerence – just to upset or offend her parents – she really must have felt I was worth the hassle.

Johnnie must have got the hint eventually because a few months later, when Johnnie and Rita had disappeared into the kitchen, Izzy whispered to me, 'Here, Alan, why don't you introduce Ann to *your* parents? Why don't you get engaged?'

'What?' I said.

'Yeah, introduce Ann to your parents. And why don't you get engaged? You know, do something about it? *Are* you going to get engaged?'

This was in my mind, but I guess I didn't have the courage to bring it up.

Later, I told Ann what Izzy had said. She was a little embarrassed and just laughed, but I pushed her further on it and asked, 'Where is all this coming from?'

She told me that Izzy had been in the room when Johnnie and Rita were having a conversation about me. They'd mentioned how unusual it was that I hadn't yet introduced Ann to my parents and wondered whether this relationship was really serious.

Ann's family was right. It suddenly dawned on me that in all the time I'd known Ann, she hadn't met my mum and dad. I then realised that a lot of my friends also hadn't met my mum and dad. In fact, most of them hadn't even been to my flat. My honest belief is this: my flat was in a completely different league to the houses of Steve, Tony and, to a certain extent, Geoff. I guess I was embarrassed. How ridiculous.

It's quite sad, when you think about it, to be ashamed of your family home, although I certainly wasn't ashamed of my parents. Anyway, this was a wrong I had to put right immediately. All at once, I realised my selfishness; my complete lack of thought.

I hauled Ann up there as soon as I possibly could. Of course, she was well received by Mum and Dad, as well as by Daphne and Harold, who happened to be there that day. Daphne said to me afterwards, 'Ooh, Alan, I didn't realise she was such a tall girl, your girlfriend. Funny, I had visions of my baby brother having a little girlfriend.' I never quite understood what she meant by that.

A few days later, all the boys came up to my flat. I must have been as thick as a plank because Steve had been dropping hints for the past couple of years. When I eventually said, 'Come up,' he couldn't stop himself from saying, 'At last!'

Of course there was no problem when they came into the flat. They're nice blokes, no airs and graces. They just sat themselves down and started chatting with my mum and dad. No trouble at all. What an idiot I'd been. And, on reflection, how selfish I must have seemed, going to their homes and accepting their hospitality for years without reciprocating. It wasn't that I was stingy, but I *was* embarrassed. Quite unjustifiably so.

Ann and I went out to the West End one night and on the way home we started to chat about past events and how funny Izzy was with his interventions. And then, as you do, I went a bit quiet.

Finally, I popped the question. It wasn't really a blunt 'Will you marry me?' It was more of a discussion between us along the lines of 'I suppose we should get married then.' Both of us were completely committed to each other and I guess getting married and spending the rest of our lives together was something we both felt was inevitable.

We were both quite shy at the time and there was a kind of embarrassment and difficulty between us in getting it out in the open. There was certainly no going down on one knee, with a rose, in a restaurant. In fact we were going over the Stratford flyover in the minivan at the time – can you imagine? Now you must *really* be asking what the hell she saw in me.

I don't recall Ann's response being one of great enthusiasm. I think she said, 'Well, I suppose so.' Maybe my character was already starting to rub off on her!

The next step was to discuss this with Ann's parents. I would have to build up to that. One day during the following week, when Ann's parents were in the kitchen, I said to Izzy, 'We're thinking of getting engaged.'

'Well, tell *him* then,' he said, nodding his head in Johnnie's direction. There was mutual respect between Izzy and Johnnie, but you wouldn't think so if you saw them together. Izzy was Rita's father and she, being the kind person she was, insisted that he come and live with them and the two children. To give credit to Johnnie, he was a gentleman in accepting this situation – not many people would. It did lead to friction sometimes, though. If you can imagine a scene from *The Royle Family* – with Jim constantly resenting his mother-in-law – well, it was a bit like that. Nowhere near as brutal, of course, but there was definitely some banter going on. Sometimes they wouldn't speak to each other for a while; other times they seemed okay. It was hard to keep up with them.

Looking back, Izzy loved Johnnie and thought he was a great fellow, but I never noticed any warmth from Johnnie towards his father-in-law, though he would always sing Izzy's praises as a master carpenter, and a master carpenter he was.

Anyway, Izzy said to me, 'Tell him.'

Of course, I had to wait for the right moment. In came Johnnie, who sat himself down on the armchair to watch TV, and Rita joined him. Ann sat next to me on the sofa and good old Izzy looked at me, nodded, then got up and shuffled out of the room with his walking stick.

'You all right, Dad?' Rita said.

'Yes, I'm fine, I'm fine.'

And that was the moment. Johnnie's back was turned to me when I started to speak to him. 'Ann and I have thought about it and we want to get engaged.'

He certainly didn't spin round and say, 'Congratulations.' He said, 'Fine, okay. Well, have you thought about what you're going to do, where you're going to live, how you're going to make a living?'

I said, 'Yes, I'm working for myself and I'm doing all right. Ann's working too, and everything will be fine.'

They reluctantly accepted the situation. And, to be fair to Rita, she sprang out of the chair and said to me, 'Welcome to the family.'

Johnnie, to use one of his terms, must have been silently plutzing. One day I'm going to write an English–Yiddish dictionary. It's difficult to explain just what plutzing means to a non-Jew, but I'll have a stab at it. It's a word that encapsulates how you feel when you have to grin and bear something you don't really agree with and you don't want to happen. It can be used in different ways – 'He's plutzing,' 'He plutzed,' 'He will plutz.' But you can't say, 'He's a plutzer' – that doesn't work.

My half-Jewish hairdresser, Robert Bell, sometimes uses Yiddish expressions completely out of context and makes us all laugh. It's like watching a white man trying to rap.

Anyway, that was it. Officially engaged. Now I had to go home and tell my mum and dad. I got in about half past ten and they were already in bed, so I stood outside their door and whispered, 'Are you still awake?'

They said, 'Yes. Why, what's up?'

Through the door, I said, 'Ann and I got engaged tonight.'

Silence.

Would the door be flung open any moment? Would there be jumping for joy? No.

'Oh! Okay, good, very nice. Very, very nice,' from my mum. And a barely audible grunt from my dad.

That's the type of people they were, I'm afraid. To be fair, when you look at the horrible upbringings they had, particularly my mother, who had nasty, uncaring parents, it's no surprise. Mum was a hard-nut, no question about it, but with a kind heart.

Ann also agrees that my mum was very tough, but quiet and obser-vant with it, intelligently picking up things and really understanding what was going on, but keeping things bottled up inside her. In Ann's opinion, my father came across as a more caring person.

Ann's family set great store by saying and doing the right thing, and I had a lot to learn in this area. On several occasions during our courtship, I was invited to Ann's house for a traditional Friday night dinner. After four or five such occasions when I'd turned up without bringing anything with me – not so much as a bunch of flowers or a box of chocolates – Johnnie got annoyed. Sadly, I had put Ann under a load of family pressure again.

Looking back, it makes me cringe to think of turning up without showing some gratitude, but it gives you an indication of how unaware I was of these social graces. Eventually, Ann plucked up the courage to tell me, 'If you come round to our house for dinner, please bring something along for my mum because my dad's getting a bit annoyed.'

I was embarrassed and I swung the other way to such an extent that Rita turned to me one day and said, 'Please stop this – you don't need to do this each and every time you come round.'

I also spread the news of our engagement to all my friends. If I remember rightly, Maureen and Malcolm had beaten us to it and were already engaged. Steve was being silent, while Sandra, to use the new word you've just learned, was plutzing. Geoff and Tony didn't want to listen. They were not interested in this settling-down stuff.

Ann and I agreed on a savings strategy. She was doing very well as a hairdresser, and had been since the time I was at Richard Thomas & Baldwins. She still reminds me to this day that she was earning more than I was then. She was a great hairdresser and although her basic pay was peanuts, she was sought after by the clients and earned nearly all her money from tips. We decided to start saving for a house of our own, an unbelievable objective in that day and age. For example, when Daphne and Harold got married, they moved into a rented flat above a shop in Clapton. When Derek got married to Brenda, they did the same. Shirley was the only one who had her own house, her Harold being rather well-to-do. But most people tended to start off by renting a flat somewhere.

Johnnie would remind me from time to time how important it was that I worked hard. Not that I needed reminding; I knew what responsibilities I was taking on.

'How's this business of yours going?' he asked one day.

'Well,' I explained, 'to be honest with you, it's hard work, but I've set myself a target to make sixty quid by Wednesday.'

'What?'

'Sixty quid by Wednesday – that's my target.'

'What do you mean?'

'Sixty quid by Wednesday,' I repeated. 'That's what I've got to earn.'

'Oh, you mean that's what you've got to *take*?'

'No, that's what I've got to *earn*. But I normally make much more than that – maybe eighty by the end of the week. Unless my van breaks down, then I'm stuck.'

Now, Johnnie was not one of those people who deals with things in a polite way. 'What are you talking about – sixty pounds, eighty pounds a week? Who are you bloody kidding? There is a difference between *taking* sixty pounds and *making* sixty pounds, you know.'

'Excuse me? What do you mean?'

'Are you telling me that you're *making* sixty or eighty pounds a week in this business?'

'Yeah, that's exactly what I'm telling you. I know the difference between what I take and what I make.'

'Nah. Rita, what's he talking about? You don't know what you're talking about. I don't believe you.'

'Well, it's true.' I shrugged my shoulders and thought, 'Why am I arguing? Who have I got to convince? Why do I have to justify myself?'

Johnnie looked at Rita and said, 'I'm knocking myself out working with your brother in that bloody factory and we can't make a profit there.' This was the first time I'd heard about the state of Johnnie's business – a furniture factory.

Beerite Furniture in Hackney Road was a typical cabinet-making business in the East End, but what was coming through loud and clear to me was that this business was in the pits. They had about ten employees and were trapped in an endless cycle of trying to achieve orders and compete. So when I told Johnnie I was making £60–80 a week, he thought it was some fantasy of mine.

Slowly, the truth of the matter dawned on him. No way was he jealous – he most certainly wasn't – but to his generation it was unprecedented that a nineteen-year-old kid would be taking home £60–80 a week while he, as he put it, was knocking himself out in a factory, five days a week, out on the lorry, business going down the pan, and only being able to draw a minimal salary. Picture that scenario and you can understand his frustration.

Johnnie pressed me further. 'Show me how you do this then. What are you talking about – sixty, eighty pounds a week – are you nuts?'

So one day, I brought him my books. I had no idea about book-keeping, but I had this big red ledger-type thing in which I entered the day's takings, how much the items had cost me, how much I'd sold them for and, subtracting one from the other, the running profit. Totally the wrong method of accounting, but it was the way I kept control of things. I knew I had to be disciplined about this because I was told that one day I was going to have to give all my bills to an accountant and pay some tax.

'Show me the book,' said Johnnie incredulously. 'Let me see what you're on about.' I talked him through it. Not that it was any of his business, but bear in mind that I was his future son-in-law, not yet fully approved and passed for quality control. The cold shoulder was warming up slightly, so I guess I was kind of schmoozing a bit, to get into his good books.

He started examining the ledger sceptically. Within about ten minutes of studying the book, his expression had changed to one of utter disbelief. He looked up and said, 'Here, Rita, look at this – he *is* making the money!'

He turned to me. 'Are you really doing this?'

'Yeah,' I said.

'What do you sell then?'

'Well, car aerials, transistor radios – that type of stuff.'

'This is ridiculous. If you can do it, I can do it,' said Johnnie.

Rita picked up on this. 'Well, Johnnie, you've been moaning about the business for months, if not years. You say it's bankrupt – well, shut it down.'

'I think I will. I think I will shut it down. I'll go out and sell,' he said. 'If he can do it, then so can I.'

Johnnie put his company into liquidation, took some of his savings and went out in his Ford Zephyr to some of my suppliers and bought some car aerials and transistor radios to sell. He must have been about forty-five at the time, so it was a massive step he was taking. After all, he was now going into a completely different world to try to make a living. He set himself up under the title of J & M Wholesale – the M stood for Mark, Ann's brother's name. Mark wasn't old enough to drive at the time, so he would travel around with Johnnie. Sometimes he'd take samples with him on foot, and remarkably pulled off a few sales himself.

Word about my success must have spread throughout the Simons family because on subsequent occasions, when I was round their house in Redbridge for a gathering of the clans, I could see, slowly and surely, an increasing level of respect shown towards me. This, I was to find out later, was down to Johnnie and Rita singing my praises to the family.

I mention this point because I think that was the first time I'd ever experienced earning respect. I guess it boils down to this simple fact: it's not what you say, it's what you do. Time is your greatest friend if you really want to show who you are.

Mind you, I'd have to say that Izzy always loved me, right from the day he clapped eyes on me.

*

While running around London in my minivan, I decided to pop in and see my old boss Sam Korobuck to say I was now working for myself and, as a long shot, to see if there was any stuff I could buy from him. I discovered that his business was going down the pan and Robinson had gone. Sam was one of these people who are devoted to the *science* of their business – a 'teckkie' rather than a marketing man. The only thing he had for me to buy was equipment which had come back from retailers. As we walked round his warehouse and I spotted piles of record-players and tape recorders, my thoughts turned to Malcolm. Repairing tape recorders was beyond his scope – they were complex mechanical items – but record-players were certainly within his capabilities. Sam was desperate for money and the business was really suffering. I offered him a ridiculous price for the record-players because not only did they need repairing, but also the exterior cabinets needed cleaning up and the whole lot needed repacking. To my surprise, he accepted my offer.

The only problem was that I didn't have the money or the space to store them. Mum wanted all my 'junk' (the TVs) out of the second bedroom. And I was definitely banned from having strangers coming to the flat. So I found a small storeroom in one of the big houses in Rushmore Road, Clapton. This house accommodated a few cottage industries. I moved all my junk in, including the record-players – after I'd worked out where to get the money from.

I went back to see Sam and told him that I'd take the whole lot, but I was a bit short of cash. However, if he'd give me a week, I'd be able to give him all the money. I convinced him there was no point in me going backwards and forwards taking a few at a time and he should trust me to take the whole lot at once. I think I gave him about £300 there and then as a deposit, but I needed to find well over £1,000 in total.

With my minivan and Malcolm's firm's van, we did about four trips back and forth between Holloway Road and Rushmore Road. We whipped all the stuff away before Sam changed his mind!

The major fault with these record-players was that the valves in the amplifiers had died. All we had to do was replace them. The other problem was that some of the record-players were quite dirty. So, with a scrubbing brush and some Ajax, Malcolm not only applied his electronic skills, but also cleaned up the plastic 'leatherette' cabinets. Within a week or so, I'd sold the lot and paid Sam in full.

It was a real eye-opener because the margin I'd made was amazing, something like 125 per cent. I even gave some of the machines to Johnnie to sell. He shifted them easily and was soon pestering me to give him a few more.

The Robuck record-player venture stuck in my mind, and the thought of making a 125 per cent margin drove me on to try to find a product that nobody else had. Of course, it sounds a bit naïve – *everyone* wants a product that nobody else has. Usually, I was buying things for £5 and selling them for £6 – margins were slim and you had to sell a lot of stuff to make real money.

I was on a treadmill, buying and selling stuff for low margins. I was able to make a bit more money by selling further afield in places like Birmingham, Cambridge, Portsmouth and Norwich. Unlike the hard-nosed London dealers, these retailers were willing to pay my prices. But it was a very hard slog and the minivan was conking out every week. When it was in the repair shop, my alternative was to try to do business over the phone, but then I'd have to parcel my orders up at Rushmore Road and wait for British Road Services to turn up and take the parcels away – all time consuming.

Johnnie advised me, 'If you have an old banger, it's going to break down all the time. You need a *new* car – it's as simple as that.'

Regrettably, I didn't take his advice. I bought a second-hand Vauxhall Viva from some dodgy bloke who insisted it had been driven by a little old lady once a week on her way to church. He said I might even find a Bible on the back seat. He took my minivan in part-exchange. I should have known there was something wrong when he offered me sixty quid for it – I'd only paid fifty in the first place.

My cash flow was a problem at that point, so I asked my mum and dad whether they'd lend me a few quid for a couple of months to buy this car. I told them this one would be more reliable and had a big boot. They agreed, and one Sunday morning we went to their Benevolent Society office in the East End. They withdrew £250 and gave it to me as a loan to buy the car.

Young, thoughtless and in a hurry, I grabbed the dosh and was just about to shoot off and pick up the Vauxhall when my mum turned to me and said, 'Aren't you going to say thank you?'

'Oh yeah, sorry – thank you.'

Typical of young people.

The Vauxhall Viva turned out to be a total disaster. The boot capacity was much smaller than the minivan's and the car was breaking down all the time – worse than the minivan – and I was racking up more and more bills trying to fix it. But this was my first real car – I guess my choice was swayed by wanting to impress my mates.

Finally, I went to Wood & Lambert in Stamford Hill and looked at a brand-new automatic Ford Cortina Estate. This would kill two birds with one stone. As an estate, it would double up as a van and as a car, it would be a beautiful set of wheels.

I couldn't afford the £1,050 price tag, so I decided to pay for it on hire-purchase. The salesman pointed out that I was under twenty-one and therefore ineligible to sign an HP agreement. On Friday night, during dinner, I explained what had happened and asked my father whether he would come with me tomorrow and sign the agreement on my behalf. 'I'm *not* signing a thousand-pound bill,' was his reaction.

I can now understand his feelings. He was sixty years old at the time and must have been thinking back to the days when a thousand pounds was like a million pounds now. Back then, I couldn't understand his problem – I was *sure* I'd be able to make the payments. I explained how the Vauxhall Viva fiasco had taught me that I needed a vehicle that wouldn't conk out – a new one with a guarantee – so I could be out on the road five days a week. Despite this, my dad wouldn't budge.

Then, remarkably, Shirley's Harold said, 'Don't worry, Alan, I'll come down and sign for you.'

There was a stunned silence. My dad turned to him and said, '*You'll* sign?'

Harold said, 'Yes. Alan's explained everything clearly – there's no problem. He'll pay off the monthly payments. He's earning good money.'

This embarrassed my dad into turning up on Saturday and signing the HP agreement for the car. I fully understand his mentality and I can appreciate his hesitation. That said, at the end of the day, he *did* back me.

*

Ann and I had two engagement parties. The first, organised by Ann's parents at their house, was for close family only. The second, I organised myself in a small community hall in the flats, so we could invite our friends. An engagement party was traditional, but in my eyes it was a bit of a waste of time, not to mention money. A low-key event was best, as far as I was concerned. I've long since realised that parties are not for me, particularly if they're in my honour – I find them a bit embarrassing and intimidating.

Ann and I were married on 28 April 1968 in Great Portland Street Synagogue. Johnnie pulled out all the stops and laid on a wonderful wedding reception in the Tavistock Rooms, catered by a gentleman named Bert Barnett.

Again, while I'd have to say it was a memorable and wonderful occasion, I couldn't wait till it was all over. Ann didn't share that view. As a bride, she was very excited. In fact, on the morning of our wedding, she woke up with a howler of a sore throat and couldn't speak. It must have been nerves, as she didn't do too badly later in the day.

At the end of the evening, I shook Johnnie's hand and thanked him very much for laying on a great wedding. Then Ann and I shot off to the Hilton where I'd booked a room for the night.

The next day, just before going on honeymoon to Cala Mayor, Majorca, we popped in to see my mum (Dad was at work). Mum seemed a bit depressed, and I couldn't quite work out why. Looking back now, I think it was the reality hitting home that her last baby had left the nest.

We spent two weeks in Majorca and were treated very nicely by the other hotel guests, who realised we were honeymooners. However, by the end of the first week, I was running out of money fast, having underestimated just how much I'd need. There were no credit cards in those days and certainly the Spanish weren't going to take a cheque.

I phoned Daphne, who was concerned at my predicament. She took a risk and stuck £20 in an envelope, sending it by airmail to our hotel. It turned up about three days before we left and got me right out of jail.

Just before we got married, we'd seen a house we liked in Marlands Road, Clayhall, and bought it for £4,700. We got a mortgage with the Hearts of Oak Building Society with repayments of £32 per month, or £8 a week as I was still thinking in those days. The house needed some renovation, including a brand-new kitchen.

Izzy, who had loads of grandchildren, had made it his policy to pay for their bedroom suites whenever one of them got married. He did the same for us as his wedding present. What's more, he made sure he was there to scrutinise the work of the poor sod who fitted it.

While all the refurbishing was going on, we stayed at Daphne and Harold's, not far away. They made us very welcome, but Ann was keen to settle down in our own place. Eventually, we moved in. Ann was delighted to be there and I was quite proud of the fact that we had our own house, considering this was not the norm for young married couples at the time. The house was semi-detached with a small front garden and a large garden at the rear.

Ann often jokes with me about my attempts to put into practice some of the bricklaying and building skills I'd picked up at Brooke House School. In a mad moment, I decided one day that I would make a concrete path running down the centre of the garden leading to the end, where I planned to build a garage. Ann named this path 'the M1' because I'd made it about 5ft wide! Considering the width of the whole garden was only 25ft, the path stood out like a sore thumb.

Nevertheless, the neighbours were quite impressed by my handiwork. They were even more impressed when I decided to build, from a kit, a garage with an up-and-over door. I saw the kit advertised in a national newspaper. The advert stated that a man and his wife could easily assemble it in a day – they forgot to mention that the wife had to be a twenty-stone Russian weightlifter.

The reason for building the garage was that I had now acquired a Dormobile van. With Harold's help, I racked out the van internally, so that I could carry my stock onboard and deliver the goods – effectively a mobile warehouse. It would have been risky leaving the van parked outside the house with all the stuff in it, so a garage was essential. It was also a requirement of the insurance company.

Before getting the Dormobile, I used to store my stuff in a lean-to behind the kitchen – until one day the whole lot got nicked. The insurance company was not interested – I wasn't insured for running a business from home. When I listed all the stuff stolen, they told me to forget it – they weren't paying. I lost about £2,000 worth of stock, virtually the net asset value of the company at the time, a real knockback. That's what prompted me to get the Dormobile, alarm it up and get insurance cover. But it also put me into debt. Luckily, by then I had suppliers who would extend me credit and I was able to replenish my stocks and get going again, simply by using the cash flow of sales to Peter to pay Paul.

The Dormobile turned out to be a temporary measure, as it was becoming increasingly clear that I needed an office. Having expanded my customer base all over the country, I was spending more and more time sending parcels off. This was something that I couldn't really do from home. Plus, I was starting to get repeat orders without having to chase. Customers would ring me at home, but I'd be out and Ann would be at work, so I was losing business – there were no mobiles in those days.

Luckily, I was dealing with a gentleman by the name of Freddie Ezekiel, a small-time importer who sold me radios now and again. He'd taken a lease on premises at 388 St John's Street, Clerkenwell, but had soon realised he didn't actually need the whole building. I negotiated a deal with him that allowed me to rent the ground floor and the first floor. The front room of the ground floor I made into a showroom, the back room I made into a strong-room, fully alarmed, and I used the first floor as an office. Freddie kept the second floor.

And who was to be my first employee, to man the station? I told my dad I'd like him to come and work for me for £20 a week clear. This was a good wage, considering he was earning £15 a week clear at the time.

Although he could see I had a nice little business and I'd already bought my own house, Dad's cautious nature kicked in. He was hesitant to accept, worried that my success might not last. Eventually, I convinced him and he took the unprecedented step of announcing to his colleagues at the garment factory that he was *leaving* – something no one ever did.

'Why are you leaving, Nat?' they asked.

'Well, I've got a better opportunity that's come my way,' he explained.

At the age of sixty-two, having worked for more than forty-five years in a sweat-shop environment, struggling for money, worrying whether he'd have any work the following week, it must have been a moment of glory for him to be able to tell them, effectively, 'Stick your job where the sun doesn't shine.'

Dad manned the premises at St John's Street, answered the phone and wrapped the parcels. I wouldn't say we were tearing busy, but I was easily able to pay him. And it was useful for me to have him go and open up in the morning while I went out selling with my samples.

Occasionally, we would have customers visit the premises. He would proudly come downstairs and walk into the meeting, as if to say, 'Right, okay, what's going on here?'

The visitors would look up and I would say, 'Yeah, that's my father – he's looking after the place for me.'

There was another great task my father performed at St John's Street. Freddie Ezekiel's wife, who worked with him, was pregnant. She worked right up to the last moment – and I literally mean the last moment: her waters broke while she was on the premises! Freddie was out at the time, so she screamed down the stairs. The only person in the building was my father, who sprung into action and organised an ambulance for her.

Freddie didn't know what had been going on until he got back a couple of hours later. When he heard the news, he rushed to the hospital. Apparently, there were some complications with the birth, but due to Dad's prompt actions, the baby was safely delivered. Freddie and his wife didn't stop thanking my dad for at least a year afterwards. They even bought him a present.

As well as being a supplier of mine, Freddie also became a supplier to Johnnie. It was interesting to watch the two of them whenever Johnnie came down to negotiate for stuff. Freddie Ezekiel was an orthodox Jew, so when the pair of them got together they were both in heaven, pub-quizzing on which days they could work and which days they couldn't.

It was at the St John's Street premises that the turning point for A M S Trading Company came.

5

The Truck Driver and His Wife

*Learning What People Want
and Developing a Bullshit Radar*

1969–72

One of my suppliers at the time was K & K Electronics who specialised in more up-market items, one of which was something known as a 'plinth and cover'.

Around 1969, the hi-fi stereo market was starting to grow. Instead of buying old-fashioned mono record-players, people were starting to play their records on a stereo system, which comprised a record deck, an amplifier and a pair of speakers. The record deck would be mounted on a small wooden plinth with a tinted plastic cover on top and looked very smart and sophisticated.

The plinth and cover was essentially a lump of wood and a lump of plastic. K & K imported them from Denmark and sold them to me for about £3 10s wholesale. I was able to sell a few to the smaller retailers who didn't know K & K, but most were buying directly. The margin was really slim and the item was quite bulky – just fifty of them would fill up the whole van – but they were selling well. This annoyed me because I instinctively felt that they didn't cost much to make. I was sure there was something for me in this market.

I was getting pissed off selling stuff and just making a few pennies as a wholesaler. I needed to find a breakthrough where I could make some *real* margin. I decided to investigate making plinths and covers myself. The wood side of things was no problem. I explained to Johnnie and Izzy what I wanted made and showed them a sample. Having spent all their lives in the cabinet-making industry, they said,

'It's easy – it's a piece of nothing. We know twenty people in the East End who can make them for you.'

'How much do you think they'd cost?' I asked.

'That? The plinth section? No more than a pound.'

'You're kidding me. They're charging me three pounds for it.' A total rip-off.

Johnnie took me to see some fellow in the East End. I gave him a sample plinth and sketched on a piece of paper how I wanted it modified – I had an idea how to enhance the Danish design and make it look a bit bigger. Within a couple of days, the guy had made me some samples. I negotiated him down to 17s 6d and ordered 1,000 pieces.

I'd located someone in Highgate who could make plastic lids for me using the vacuum-forming process. This entailed taking sheets of tinted Perspex (which they bought from ICI), cutting them to size, sticking them in a hot rig and, by using suction, shaping them. The cost was 18s each.

So, with a 17s 6d plinth and an 18s cover, I was in business for less than two quid. I started selling loads of them. It made hustling around buying transistor radios from Gulu and others look a bit silly, but I carried on running the two different businesses at the same time.

One of the customers I picked up from Henson was Rex Radio in Kilburn. Rex, the owner of the shop, was a nice old bloke who had two sons, one of whom ran a second shop a few doors away which sold high-quality Bang & Olufsen equipment. I sold his son some plinths and covers. I can clearly remember being in Rex Radio on 20 July 1969, watching the Apollo 11 moon-landing on one of the black-and-white TVs in the shop.

During my travels in the Edgware Road and Tottenham Court Road areas, I bumped into S. J. Robinson, my ex-boss at Robuck, who had taken a new job working for a Russian company which imported Rega radios from Russia and sold them exclusively to Headquarters & General, a large mail-order and retail organisation, famously run by a Major Collins. I think he called himself Major simply because the name Headquarters & General implied they sold goods of military standard at bargain prices. They sold things like tents, lanterns, army-style boots, anoraks and the like.

Major Collins had never been anywhere near the army, but not only did he give himself the fake title, he also grew himself an RAF-style moustache, so he couldn't even get *that* right (bearing in mind that major is not a rank in the RAF).

I went to Robinson's office to see whether there was any business we could do. Of course, we talked about Sam Korobuck and how Robuck had gone into liquidation. I told Robinson I'd bought a load of old record-players off Sam and had made a few quid. I then said that if *he* had any similar junk that came back from Headquarters & General, then I was his man.

Indeed he did – he had hundreds of Rega radios. These Russian radios were built like tanks and were quite advanced in that they used rechargeable batteries. But they also broke down a lot – a bit like Aeroflot used to.

Robinson was no soft touch. He was trying to get near-cost price for these items, even though they were rejects. I wasn't going to pay that sort of price for rejects, so after a bit of negotiation he conceded to a 35 per cent reduction which, on the face of it, was not a steal. But if I could repair these radios and sell them to retailers for slightly less than Headquarters & General paid, not only could I make a profit, but the retailers would then be able to sell the radios for less than Headquarters & General did.

The reason for telling this story is that I'd found myself a repair man to fix these radios, which contained transistors. I would have asked Malcolm, but, as an old-fashioned TV engineer, he had no expertise in solid-state electronics – he was a valve-changer.

My new repairer was called George Chenchen, a peculiar name which you might have thought was of Chinese origin. He was no more Chinese than I am. In fact, he came from the West Country and had quite a broad accent. He was about twenty years older than me, a squat, balding chap with a scruffy appearance, but he seemed to know what he was talking about. He worked with various importers, restoring transistor radios to pristine condition.

I got my dad to check all the radios first. It's common knowledge that there's nothing wrong with half the items that get returned; end

customers often send them back if they don't like them or don't understand how to make them work.

George was not a happy chappy when he realised he'd been given
100 per cent rejects and that he'd have to fix *all* of them. He normally
enjoyed the lucrative windfall of coming across radios with nothing
wrong with them. He charged me 3s 6d for each repair and wanted to
jack up the price. Poor old George – he had to actually do some work!

Around this time, Gulu had imported a load of miniature radios –
about 3,000 of them. Unfortunately, the whole lot were off-tuned. He
asked if I knew anyone who had a mini production line to retune
them.

'How much do you want to pay to put them right?' I asked.

'No more than two shillings each.'

I laughed at him and said, 'You must be kidding. No engineer is
going to do these for two bob each.' Gulu knew as much about electronics as I do about playing the cello, but he was the biggest
bullshitter in the world. He started talking about frequencies, IF-coils,
ferrite rods and so forth.

I said, 'Shut up, Gulu. You're not talking to some Bar Mitzvah boy
here or some buyer from Gamages. Just give me a box and I'll let you
know if I can get them done.'

I showed George Chenchen some of these radios and said, 'What
do you think is wrong with them?'

'Ah, very simple,' he said, pointing out that all they needed was
two of the coils to be adjusted by a quarter of a turn using a small
screwdriver. Little did he know that I had 3,000 to do.

Having fixed the box of radios myself, I called Gulu and struck a
deal to do them all for 2s 6d a piece. I asked him to give me all 3,000,
so I could get on with them. Gulu, still not trusting me, agreed to
release only 500 at a time. Despite my protestations, he went off into
another load of bullshit about insurance and stuff like that. I'm surprised he didn't send a private detective after me to camp outside my
house.

I took the radios home and showed Ann and Daphne how to do it
– it was dead easy. In the evenings, they set up little production lines
in their respective kitchens and knocked out the whole 3,000 in no

time. They got half the money. Ann had become an electronics engineer – something we joke about occasionally. On the other hand, when I mention it to Daphne, she can't remember it at all and swears I'm making it up. But I recall it as clear as day.

*

The plinth and cover market was booming, but my orders were falling now that other people had cottoned on to the fact that you could get these plinths made in the East End. Plus, there were lots of vacuum-formers around. It was great for the East End chippy, who'd previously scraped a living making bedside cabinets – he was having it off big time now. His factory was awash with plinths, not just for me, but for everyone.

I complained and asked if he felt he owed me anything. He thanked me for showing him a new area to exploit, but that was about it – business is business. I think he might have bought me a bottle of whisky at Christmas. Fair enough! I don't have exclusivity on entrepreneurial ideas, even if they are mine. The competition always catches up, and after they hit the market there's a window of opportunity to exploit them. The secret is to move on.

I had always felt that the plastic cover was expensive, so I decided I needed to find another way to make them, to look at the problem in a fresh way, as I'd done before.

On Sunday that week, Ann and I visited my mum and dad's for tea and I noticed they had a plastic butter dish – a red-tinted one. As I lifted the lid up, I saw a moulding mark, known to me now as a sprue mark – the place where the plastic is injected – and in that moment, something clicked in my brain. Here we had a coloured, see-through plastic butter lid, and all I needed to do was to make a similar item but much bigger, also see-through, with a nice grey tint to it.

The following Monday, I got straight on the phone to the plastic manufacturers' association of the time and described the product I was trying to buy. A helpful gentleman explained to me a process known as injection moulding. Simply put, powdered plastic was squirted into a giant press which had a 'tool' – a custom-made chunk of metal that moulded the plastic into the shape of the product you wanted. In go the powdered plastic pellets – with extreme heat they turn into molten plastic – and out pops the finished part.

I was on to something here. That week, I ignored the rest of the business and went round visiting toolmakers with a sample of a vacuum-formed cover, to show them what I wanted made. The prices for the tooling ranged from £3,500–5,000, a fortune for me, but one company down in Surrey, called Arrowcraft, quoted me £2,800.

I engaged these people to make the tool. In those days, the process was slow. The tool had to be drawn up by specialist draughtsmen and then hand-made by skilled craftsmen. The tooling time was going to be twenty-two weeks. Nowadays, the automated tooling process – from drawing to finished product – can sometimes be done in four weeks.

Big lesson coming up here, folks. Unfortunately, I had picked the Del Boy of the tool-making industry. I'd never heard so many excuses for delays in all my life. The twenty-two weeks went by and they were still drilling the steel.

I was kicking up merry hell. To fund this £2,800, I'd committed the cardinal sin of buying goods from one of my suppliers and flipping them for a very small margin in order to generate cash flow to pay the toolmaker. With vendors of other stuff funding my cash flow, I was obviously incurring liabilities. My accountant told me that the way I was operating, as Alan Sugar trading as A M S Trading Company, had many personal risks attached to it. He suggested it was time I formed a limited company. After all, the investment in the tool was a big gamble; if it all went wrong, the vendors I owed money to might look to me *personally* to pay them back.

On 8 December 1968, I formed A M S Trading Company (General Importers) Ltd, company registration number 942631.

*

I virtually *lived* at that tool-maker's until finally they got the thing made. The tool was then taken to Morning Plastics in Chertsey, a very well-organised company, not like the bunch of monkeys at Arrowcraft. Here was the coup: the dust cover would pop off the moulding machine at 3s 6d each! Remember, up till then the lowest price anyone could buy vacuum-formed covers was 18s each.

Knowing my competitors were paying vacuum-formers 18s per cover, my masterstroke was not to treat these things as one of my normal products and just apply a reasonable margin. I decided that even if they did cost 3s 6d, I would sell them for 16s. The vacuum-formers scratched their heads because 16s was the cost price of the raw material they were buying from ICI.

That was it – the start of the big time for me. Within weeks of starting production, I was making £6,000 per month, at a profit margin of over 400 per cent per cover! No more of the hustling around with Gulu and the others. I was selling thousands of plinths and covers to big companies such as G. W. Smith and Laskys.

Laskys was one of the big retailers at the time, with four or five shops dotted up and down the Edgware Road and Tottenham Court Road. In my days at Robuck, I used to call on Eddie Lasky to try to sell him tape recorders. They were a bunch of hard-nosed businesspeople. Their wholesale division, H. R. Factors in Harrow Road, was run by a fellow named Ted. When I used to walk up and down the aisles of H. R. Factors' warehouse, Ted would follow me around like a shadow. Another trusting character. There must be something about me, what with Peter Henson thinking I was going to nick his walkie-talkies and Ted sticking to me like shit to a blanket.

Laskys, who begrudged anyone making a profit, reluctantly bought the covers off me. They wouldn't believe this small-time-Charlie, who had hustled them over the past couple of years, was making the covers himself. They wanted to find my supplier. They managed to do so, but hit a brick wall – Morning Plastics could not supply anyone other than me with lids because the tool belonged to me.

Laskys were plutzing. They were in a dilemma – should they buy plinths and covers from me at a lower price, or not buy from me out of sheer belligerence and pay more to someone else? Even *they* weren't that stupid.

Ronnie Marks, my first supplier, became one of my customers. So did Colin Lewin, who had a retail shop on Gray's Inn Road. He was a great character. Originally he was a GPO engineer (today's British Telecom) and on his travels he started to pick up bits and pieces to trade – he had a real instinct for business. He opened a trade counter and importers would descend upon him, offering all their job-lots. His customer base was market traders and the likes of me, when I was running around in my minivan. He had the guts to go and buy stuff that other people wouldn't touch with a bargepole. It's interesting to note that the tables had turned and I had now become a supplier instead of a customer.

Gulu was having withdrawal symptoms. He hadn't heard from me for months. Unusually, he called me up to ask, 'Where are you? I haven't seen you for a long time. What are you doing?'

I told him I no longer sold his crap and that I was making plinths and covers. 'Oh yes,' he said, as if he knew what I was talking about. He didn't have a clue what plinths and covers were. That is, he didn't until a few weeks later.

Colin Lewin and a few others told me that Gulu had realised I was on to a winner and tried to poke his nose in. Like Laskys, he also ended up in a cul-de-sac upon finding Morning Plastics. He discovered that to compete with me, he needed to invest £4,000 in a tool.

Then came the bullshit. 'Look here, Alan, I know what you're doing. It's no problem for me – I'm going to get a tool made. I've got to wait twenty weeks and then I'll have the stuff at the same price as you. So rather than me doing that, why don't you just sell them to me? Make a fifty per cent margin by selling them to me for six shillings.'

I told him to piss off. Nice try, Gulu. Forget it. He wouldn't have known what to do with them anyway. One of the problems Gulu had going forward in the electronics business was that he never changed from being a trader to being a manufacturer.

St John's Street became a hive of activity. One particular customer required plinths and covers ready-fitted with record decks. The customer free-issued us with Garrard SP25 decks and we assembled them on to plinths, wired them up and fitted covers. This was an additional service we were able to charge for. My dad became a dab hand with the soldering iron, and I took on my next-door neighbour's son part-time to help out with the work.

Gulu, thinking he was missing out on something, bought a couple of hundred of these record decks from me. I still can't understand why because his clientele were market boys and fancy goods shops. I guess he's just one of those guys that need to be seen to be *in there*, as a player.

*

It was around Christmas of 1968, after a visit to the doctor, that Ann announced she was pregnant. We were both happy at the news that we were going to have a baby. Ann was only twenty then and I was twenty-one, so we were very young to start a family, but that's how it was in those days.

When the news was announced to Ann's family, it was greeted with delight – immediately followed by questions about our preparations. 'What are you going to do? Where's the baby's room going to be? How are you going to manage?'

I told my mum and dad the news and got the usual responses. My mum's was, 'Oh, very nice – you *are* young.' And from Dad: 'Oh good,' a sort of congratulatory grunt. I got a bit more enthusiasm from Daphne, Derek and Shirley.

Ann carried on working right up to when she was seven months pregnant. Not because I asked her to; it was what she wanted. In those later months, Ann spent most of her time round at Rita's with a couple of relatives, Edna and Fanny. Fanny was one of Ann's aunts and Edna was her daughter-in-law. They lived next door to Rita and Johnnie.

The cackle that went on between Rita, Edna and Fanny – fussing about all the things Ann had to do to prepare for the baby – was a typical Jewish outing. How this must have confused (or bored) Ann!

Rita would often ask me, 'Aren't you excited, Alan? You don't seem to show your excitement. How do your mum and dad feel?'

'Well, my family are, of course, very happy. And as for me, it's not a case of *not* being excited; I'm just a bit apprehensive about the birth, you know, too many cooks spoiling the broth. It'd be nice if we were just able to sit down and think about this ourselves.'

Believe me, Ann was under heavy pressure, albeit well meaning, with everyone telling her what she should and shouldn't do. It was winding me up. My reply didn't go down too well and I got the 'We're only trying to do our best' type of response. And, of course, they *were* only trying to do their best, but it was hard going.

On 7 June, a Saturday morning, when I was about to leave for work, Ann told me she was feeling a bit peculiar. She thought it might be the start of some contractions. Obviously, this being our first child, she had no idea what to expect. She phoned Daphne who advised her to call an ambulance.

When the ambulance arrived, the friendly neighbours gathered outside to wave her goodbye and wish us good luck, and off she went in the ambulance. By now, Daphne had turned up and she came with me as we followed the ambulance in my car.

Rita and Johnnie were unaware of the goings-on. They were at a synagogue in north London, attending a blessing of a friend. Had they known what was happening, they'd have been down there like a shot.

At Wanstead Hospital, Ann checked in and settled into her bed, by which time the contractions had died down. She looked at me as if to say, 'I don't know what I'm doing here – nothing's happening.' But when I popped back later that night, she was definitely in labour. There was a possibility that the baby was in the breech position and they might have to perform a Caesarean section. I was asked to sign a consent form, as Ann was only twenty years old – in those days you weren't considered an adult until you were twenty-one.

Now here's the bizarre thing – something you wouldn't see these days – instead of staying with Ann until the baby was born, helping her through the trauma and pain, I went home again. Hospitals wouldn't let fathers hang around or be present for the birth of their children, so I didn't have any choice (not that I'd have relished the thought). Anyway, instead of sitting by the phone, the following morning I went to play tennis with my mates! Some of them were jibing, 'You're going to be a father soon.' Meanwhile, unbeknown to me, the real action had started. And while I was playing tennis – on Sunday, 8 June 1969 – baby Simon was born. As they'd suspected, Simon had been in the breech position, but thankfully the doctors were able to manoeuvre him and Ann had a natural birth after all.

I went straight round to the hospital. The nurse brought in a trolley with a plastic cot in it, and there I saw young Simon for the very first time. I wheeled him into the ward and Ann and I were together with our son. I have to say, he didn't look like either of us at the time.

Apart from the delight that we had a son, the reality really hit home that we were now responsible for another human being.

Hospitals were very strict in those days and would only allow visiting at certain times, so when Rita and Johnnie turned up that afternoon – in evening wear because they were on their way to a wedding – they wouldn't let them in initially, but after a bit of argy-bargy, they managed to see their first grandson.

Simon was named after my father's father, Simon Sugar. Unfortunately, he was never given a middle name – something he took slight exception to when he was growing up. This was down to the Johnnie influence again – he insisted that Jewish people *do not* have middle names. Frankly, when I look back now, I cannot believe I accepted such bloody nonsense. I have a middle name, my brother has a middle name and my sisters have middle names. But this very domineering man imposed his wishes on me and, because of that, Simon never had a middle name.

Just before Simon was born, my mum and dad went on holiday to Jesolo in Italy. It was the first time they'd ever been abroad. They could afford it now my father was working for me, but, if I remember rightly, I treated them to their trip. However, the timing of their holiday would give rise to another row between Johnnie and me.

In the days after we brought Simon home from the hospital, Rita was by Ann's side quite a lot, as one would expect when a newborn baby comes home with a very young mother. I went to work as usual and called in from time to time to find out how things were. Ann spent a lot of time at her mother's, with everyone flapping around the baby. I joined them all one day after work and sat on the couch next to Ann. The family was banging on: 'You should do this, you should do that, you should make sure the baby's warm. Has he been fed? Has he been winded?' And so on and so on.

At that moment, Ann burst out crying from all this pressure being put on her, not to mention the customary post-natal depression. I put my arms around her and said, 'Right, we're out of here right now. Get up, we're going.'

'No, no, no,' they protested. 'Don't go yet. The baby hasn't had his milk, he hasn't had this, he hasn't had that . . .'

I said, 'We're going. We're going home. Please, leave us alone for a little while. I know you mean well, but look what you're doing. We have to go.'

For the first time, Johnnie saw the anger in my eyes. Even he slid back in his chair, knowing that this would turn into a flaming row. 'Let them go, let them go then,' he said.

When we got home there was a look of relief on Ann's face. She was more than capable of dealing with the baby – it was just a case of letting her get on with it. Looking back, one can't be angry with the care and attention shown by Ann's family – they just didn't understand how heavy it was. In fact, there were numerous occasions when I had to rescue the situation, when the overpowering Simons family tried to control Ann's or the baby's life.

One such occasion was when the trio on Eastern Avenue – Rita, Edna and Fanny – thought they'd detected that Simon had something wrong with his neck, that his head always tended to lean to one side. This latest fuss eventually led to us taking him to the doctor.

Of course, there was nothing wrong with his neck at all. They were driving Ann bloody mad. Again, all well meaning, but as before, I explained to Ann that we had to keep away and get on with our lives – an idea to which, I think, she was warming. The difficulty was that she'd spent nineteen years living in that household and just over a year with me. She was very conscious of not hurting her family's feelings.

A couple of weeks after we brought Simon home, I realised something was burning up inside Johnnie – he was plutzing again. This time it was about my parents. Eventually, he couldn't keep it in any more. Johnnie and Rita invited themselves to our house for tea, or rather, to come and have a word with me.

Johnnie sat down in front of Ann and me and then, presiding like a judge, he said to me, 'Do you think the treatment your mother and father gave Ann by going on holiday was the right thing to do, when they knew she was just about to have a baby?'

I couldn't see what was wrong with it, but I carried on listening to Johnnie, who was explaining how wrong and heartless it was, how they should have been there in case something went wrong. He ended up saying, 'How could they do that? What kind of people are they?'

I was being pressurised by Johnnie to agree with him. He wouldn't let it go. He kept banging on and on, saying, 'You *must* agree with me. Your mother and father are heartless. They've done wrong.'

Eventually, I said to him, 'If my mother and father have done anything wrong, you'd be the *last* person I'd admit that to, okay? So you are wasting your time.'

Again, he must have seen the look in my eyes – up until then I had always spoken respectfully to him, but now he could see I was about to explode, so he backed down, saying, 'Well, I suppose you're showing loyalty to your mum and dad, and I guess that can't be bad.'

When my parents arrived back from Italy I spoke to them about this incident and I think they felt a bit awkward about it and recognised that they *had* done the wrong thing.

*

When it comes to being a young father, I have to say that compared to those of today, I was rotten. When I saw how my two sons and son-in-law carried on when *their* babies arrived, it was quite an eye-opener. There they were changing nappies, taking their turn to bath the baby, being at the birth, taking time off to assist.

Me? I can honestly tell you that I never changed a nappy. Well, maybe I changed one or two, but I certainly never bathed a baby, although I might have watched a couple of times and taken some pictures. In fact, as Ann often reminds me, I never saw the kids when they were growing up, apart from at the weekends. I was out to work first thing in the morning and by the time I got back, they were already in bed. And even at the weekends, I have to admit that I was never one of those smarty-arty, happy-clappy fathers. Of course, we went on family holidays many times and played tennis and all that stuff, but I wasn't one of those fathers who's at the centre of their child's activities. I'm not sure how they feel about it now. My absence during their early years is most often brought up when my children see me messing around with my grandchildren. They make wry remarks such as, 'You were never like that with us.'

*

Back to business. With lessons learned from the plinth and cover exercise, when my suppliers ended up supplying everyone and his brother, I knew that this injection-moulded plinth and cover stuff wasn't going to last for ever. It wasn't going to take long for people to work out that by investing £3,000–4,000 in their own tools, they'd be able to do the same.

It seems I'd put K & K Electronics out of business. They moved on to open a small factory in Hackney Road, where they assembled amplifier modules. They supplied us with these amplifiers which we fitted in our plinth to make a kind of hi-fi record-player that would be sold with a pair of speakers. It seemed to be a good idea at the time and was a transition from the cheap Dansette record-player with its auto-changer to the more sophisticated hi-fi market.

One day, George Chenchen was at St John's Street dropping off a batch of radios he had fixed for me and he spotted all this amplifier stuff going on. George was a cocky kind of fellow and used to talk in a way which implied that everyone else, from a technical point of view, was an idiot compared to him. He looked at the amplifier I was fitting and told me it was rubbish and that he could design a much better one. He asked how much I was paying for it. When I told him, he laughed and said it was a rip-off. To be perfectly honest, I had no idea of component costs and, as it turned out, neither did he. He just said it for the sake of saying it.

The market for this makeshift stereo record-player with a pair of speakers was not really deemed to be the next growth area in the hi-fi industry. Instead, people were warming to the idea of a separate record deck, separate amplifier and a pair of speakers. Crazy as it may sound, people wanted four lumps of equipment instead of three!

The separate stereo amplifier market was starting to boom. It was monopolised by companies such as Armstrong and Leak and Japanese imports were also starting to make inroads. Leak's and Armstrong's amplifiers were very expensive. Teleton, a Japanese model, was cheaper, but still relatively expensive. I reckoned that if I could make an amplifier much lower in price than the Teleton, I'd be able to take a share of the market.

I challenged Chenchen to come up with a circuit design for an amplifier. I said I would invest some of my money and set up a production line to make it. He told me he was okay on the electronics side of things, but had no idea about the mechanical stuff. This was not an issue for me – my Brooke House schooldays kicked in. I drew up a metal U-shaped chassis and designed a wooden cabinet for the chassis to slide into.

I could spend hours talking about every single amplifier and product we ever made, and it would be dead boring to everyone other than the old saddo hacks who used to work for me or buy from me. For the broader audience, I'm going to skip quite a few things and just cover the interesting points.

George Chenchen was fed up scratching around, making the odd few shillings per radio repair, so he asked whether he could come and work for me. I agreed and put him on the payroll. Between Chenchen and myself, we designed this amplifier.

It was impossible to start production at St John's Street, so I acquired a factory floor in Great Sutton Street, just down the road from St John's Street. The building was occupied by a garment manufacturer, but the first floor was vacant. It was approximately 1,000 sq ft, which looked massive when I saw it for the first time.

We moved everything out of St John's Street into Great Sutton Street. George bought a load of wood and made some assembly line benches, I recruited about twenty employees and we geared up for the production of this amplifier – the Amstrad 8000. I called it the 8000 as it was supposed to be eight watts per channel.

Dad was starting to panic again. Until recently there had been just me and him plus a van driver, Harry Knight. Suddenly I had about twenty employees.

'How are you going to pay for all this, Alan? What are you doing?' said my dad.

'Never mind, don't you worry about it. Look over the road . . . You see there's a bank?'

'Yeah.'

'Well, we're going to rob it.'

These jokes went down like lead balloons with my father. He had no sense of humour and couldn't grasp what I was up to.

I took the first production sample of the Amstrad 8000 to Premier

Radio in Tottenham Court Road. The shop was owned by Ronnie Marks, my first supplier. He told me there was no point showing it to him, as he wasn't technical and wouldn't be able to evaluate it, but his manager, Nick, knew about these things.

I can't recall the number of times I drove back and forth between Great Sutton Street and Tottenham Court Road with various samples of this amplifier, only for it to be repeatedly rejected by Nick because of its poor sound. Each time I told Chenchen why it was rejected, he would change a few components in the circuitry, and back I'd go again. This trial-and-error method of product design proved that Chenchen had as much knowledge about electronic theory as I do about butterfly collecting.

Later, I would learn that producing the right sound from an amplifier is relatively easy if you follow basic electronic principles. The irony of it was that any amateur reading *Practical Wireless* could have worked out the problem.

Eventually, we got the amplifier to a state that Nick felt was reasonable, and at that point we started the production line. I think that Premier Radio bought the first six amplifiers off me.

With my plinth and cover business still subsidising the cash flow, I started to sell these amplifiers to all the electrical shops in Tottenham Court Road. At £17, the Amstrad 8000 was much cheaper than anything else on the market. And simply because of the price tag, they started to sell quite well.

A lot of snobbery existed in the hi-fi industry at the time. The way you drummed up business was to advertise in the hi-fi magazines and try to obtain some editorial endorsement by way of technical reviews by the magazines' experts. I placed my first slice of advertising in one of these magazines. Unfortunately, their review of the amplifier wasn't great, and I spoke to the reviewers to find out why. In the end, I suggested the review should not be printed, but that I would still continue to pay for advertising.

Talking to the reviewers was a learning curve. Never mind what the retailers said; it was the *reviewers* I needed to listen to. These guys dictated what was needed. I found out just what they did in their test procedures and what results they expected to see.

I told Chenchen, 'Basically our amplifier is crap. The long and short of it is that the circuitry's rubbish – it doesn't have enough guts in it to produce the sound quality required.'

It was too late to do anything about it. I'd bought over 2,000 kits of components for this unit and we needed to make them. It wasn't that they didn't work – they did – but let's just say that if one were using it to listen to the Royal Philharmonic Orchestra, the gentlemen playing the triangle and the double bass might as well have packed up and gone home, because the higher and lower frequencies were mostly absent.

Around this time, I changed the name of the company to A M S Trading (Amstrad) Ltd, and a couple of interesting stories emerged.

As production started to increase, I saw we had no expertise as far as assembly was concerned. Neither did we have any stock control system in place to ensure we didn't run out of components. I don't know what made me do this, but I called my old boss Sam Korobuck and asked him whether he would come and work for me, as he was a bit of a technical man. Sam accepted the job and started to profession-alise our production process – the sort of thing he'd been doing all his life.

Chenchen, who by now had persuaded me to employ his wife to do the bookkeeping, did not like Sam's intervention. Sam used to talk a lot of sense. He would point out, diplomatically, that parts of the circuitry were not very good and that the assembly process was poor and inef-ficient. The internal construction of the amplifier was a joke, and Sam took it upon himself to design a small PCB (printed circuit board) which would do away with a lot of the wiring.

Chenchen couldn't really argue against it, though he wanted to. He had started to realise he couldn't blind me with science any more – I was learning the ropes fast. He knew he'd have to cut back on the Richter scale of bullshit.

As the years went on, I became very proficient in sussing out bull-shit. The technical people I employed soon realised this and learned to tell the truth and own up to mistakes, or simply admit it when they didn't know the answer.

In spite of the problem with the Amstrad 8000, I was getting loads of orders, but the customer I *really* wanted to land was Comet, who had changed the face of retailing – they started discount warehousing. Most of their business was mail-order, though they did have a few warehouses in the north of England, so customers could turn up and buy in person. They took out full-page adverts in the hi-fi magazines and national newspapers, listing the names and prices of all the products they stocked. Customers would decide on which product they wanted, then simply look up Comet's price and purchase it. This form of retailing signalled the demise of the small electrical shop on the street corner, which simply couldn't compete.

The hi-fi boom was aided by this method of retailing. Manufacturers would advertise in hi-fi magazines and reviewers would give their expert opinions. Based on these reviews, various products would be commended as good value. The manufacturers' adverts would show the retail price – for example, a Leak amplifier at £40 – and Comet would list it at a discount, say £35.

Their chief buyer, Gerry Mason, was nearly impossible to get hold of; he was being chased by every single supplier. I finally got Mason on the phone and tried to convince him that as our amplifier was so much cheaper than the others he was advertising, it would sell well and he should include it in his listings. After a lot of ducking and diving and about five phone calls, he agreed to a compromise: he wouldn't place an order, but agreed to list it in his advertising to see if there was any demand.

I pulled a bit of a stunt which, from a moral point of view, is not something one should be proud of, but business is business and it didn't harm Comet in the end. I got Chenchen, Johnnie and a few others to send orders with cheques to Comet for Amstrad 8000 amplifiers. Consider, Comet had none of these in stock. When they received orders so quickly after the first advert, I banked on it sparking off a large order from them.

I received a phone call from Gerry Mason's assistant who wanted to order six amplifiers to fulfil her mail-order requirements. Now came the big gamble.

'Six?' I said to the lady. 'Are you joking or what? We are a manufacturer – we don't mess about with six. You're supposed to be Comet

– the big discount warehouse company. We cannot ship you anything less than a hundred pieces.'

'I'll get back to you,' she said.

Half an hour later, she did get back to me. 'Right,' she said, 'we'll take a hundred pieces.'

This was another milestone in the Amstrad story – once we had got into Comet, things *really* started to happen.

Comet was originally the only choice for people who wanted equipment at discount prices, though mostly they'd have to buy it mail-order. However, when companies like G. W. Smith and Laskys jumped on the bandwagon, customers had the option (which they preferred) of visiting the shops to see and touch the product before buying. Comet had to spread from their northern roots and open branches all over the country to compete. All these new-style electronic retailers were buying from me. I had the cheapest amplifier in the marketplace, it looked great value for money and it was British-made to boot.

Having witnessed this success, Chenchen and his wife were starting to think that they were my partners, though there were never any such discussions. He had never put a penny into this business and both of them were being paid very well. Nevertheless, they felt that Amstrad's success was down to George. They could not see that it was me, the chief cook and bottle-washer, who made it all happen.

Trust me when I tell you that I am very loyal to my staff. People whom I work with and those that have helped to bring me fortune have nothing to complain about – I look after them all. *This* bloke deserved nothing.

Chenchen was the only electronics engineer we had, so after the products were assembled, they would come to him for final testing before they moved on for boxing and shipping out. There was no one else who could do it, and as a result, he was constantly holding me to ransom over the hours he worked, thus restricting the output of tested amplifiers, and his wife would be harping on at me: 'Without George, you would be nowhere.'

I could see their attitude changing week by week, as the prosperity of the company and sales of the product grew. At the same time, the arrival of Sam Korobuck made Chenchen more and more frustrated. Sam had incorporated some new production methods and, in doing so, had recruited some new people. In turn, Chenchen took on some allies in the factory – a couple of girls from Sunderland who were his favourites. In his eyes, they could do no wrong, and he sat them on the production line close to him.

I'm about to tell you a story that has haunted me all my life, and still haunts me to this day.

Sam had recruited the services of a young black kid, around fifteen years old. In those days, racial discrimination was rife. Chenchen was always dropping hints about black people – 'those people', as he would call them. I won't go into detail, as it makes me sick to think of it.

Sam sat the kid down and showed him how to assemble a PCB by inserting the components then turning the board over and soldering them into place. Sam had explained to him that we needed approximately fifty of these a day, but that he didn't expect him to produce all fifty – he should just do his best, as we had other operators doing the same.

I can visualise that kid now. He was happy as Larry, beavering away assembling these boards. Sam would come up to me and whisper, 'Look at that kid go – he's fantastic, he's really doing well.'

However, Chenchen would get up from his testing seat and go up to the kid and say to him, 'Look here, son, this is what's called a dry joint. *I'm* sat over there, working my arse off trying to fix these amplifiers, and *you* are making more faults with these dry joints, so watch out.'

A 'dry joint' meant that a component on the PCB wasn't making good contact due to poor soldering. In truth, there may have been the odd dry joint – even the Sunderland dollies made them – but certainly there were no more than you would expect from any good operator. Chenchen was just angry that Sam had pulled off a great coup with this kid, who was the star of the factory. Chenchen couldn't stand it that a young black boy was making his favourites look stupid.

On one particular day, at about four in the afternoon, Chenchen cracked. He went up behind this child and screamed in his ear, 'I'm not going to accept any more of this rubbish work you're doing.'

He screamed at him for maximum effect, to impress the two girls, shocking everyone else. The kid must have responded in some way because Chenchen cranked up the volume and started ranting, 'Don't you tell me about this and that – I'm fed up with it, I'm not accepting these faults any more. Get up and get out!'

The poor kid got up. With his head down and his shoulders slumped, he walked off the factory floor past the onlookers. Chenchen sat himself down muttering, 'I'm not going to put up with this. I'm sat here testing these things and he's making more faults than I'm testing.' Trust me when I tell you that the dry joints tale was a total, absolute pack of lies. In his small-minded way, Chenchen hated Sam because he was doing well and could not stand to see the kid progress. Chenchen's outburst demonstrated what a racist idiot he was. The horror of that moment still haunts me and is one of the main reasons why, from then on, I was determined to give the utmost attention and respect to black people.

Over the years, as I became more recognisable to the general public, my wife has noticed something about me. I can be quite dismissive towards people who approach me in public places – sometimes rudely interrupting me – but she tells me that if it's a black person, I seem to have the time and patience for them. Only a wife could spot that.

I've never explained to her why because I never knew myself. It has taken these reflections, while writing this book, to make me understand. By the way, let me make it clear that Ann is the last person on this planet to be a racist or anything like that.

I wish I could find that 'kid', who of course would be well into his fifties by now. Can you imagine his thoughts? How I wish I could be beamed back in time to that moment. I just stood there and let it happen and I hate myself for that. Given my time over again, I would have grabbed George by what little hair he had left and kicked his arse down the stairs – with his wife tumbling after.

When it happened, Sam looked at me, shrugged his shoulders and shook his head. Sam, of course, was much older than me, far more experienced in life, and was diplomatically tight-lipped over the affair. My dad also observed the incident and asked me, 'What was wrong with the kid? He was a hard worker.' My dad had respect for George, the so-called 'technical man', and ranked him as important. I didn't want to discuss this with my dad, as he wouldn't have understood the real motives.

A week or so went by. Chenchen knew he had me by the balls. He told me he wasn't happy with the way the factory was run and that I had to choose between him and Sam. 'It's either me, who's at the end of the production line testing the items, enabling you to ship the stuff out, or Sam, who just makes them.'

Even now, while I'm telling this story, I feel like punching a brick wall in frustration. That lunchtime, I took Sam down to the café and spelled it out to him honestly. Sam understood the situation and took it very well. I can't remember the financial severance I offered him, but certainly I gave him at least a month's pay to tide him over until he sorted himself out.

I was burning up inside. Chenchen had shown his true colours.

My dad asked what was going on with Sam – he couldn't understand what Sam had done wrong – and this time I gave him the full story. I told him Chenchen had me over a barrel, but I would sort it out.

This was not the right thing to say to a born worrier like my dad. He immediately went into, 'Who's going to test the amplifiers if you get rid of George Chenchen?'

I told him I didn't care and that my mind was made up – Chenchen was on his way out as soon as it suited me. My father started giving me his input as to the pros and cons. At this point my patience ran out and, I guess disrespectfully, I raised my voice to him.

'Stop worrying,' I said. 'I will sort it out. No one is going to hold me to ransom. It's not worth any amount of money in the world to be a wimp, so just leave it and get on with your work.'

I made my mind up about two things that day. One, never again would I allow anybody to make any racist or discriminatory comments to any of my staff. And two, never again would I put myself in a position where one person controls my destiny.

*

As our orders were getting bigger, we needed to assemble more and more PCBs. The capacity of the Great Sutton Street factory was limited, so we sub-contracted out to a small assembly plant up in Norfolk, run by Chenchen's friend Stan Randall and his partner Roger. They would take kits of components from us and bring us back finished PCBs. Stan was a fast-and-loose talker and he mentioned one day that Chenchen and his wife had the hump with me. He confirmed my feeling that they imagined they were partners of mine. But what I *didn't* know was that Chenchen had secretly designed his own amplifier and was going to set up production himself. Stan felt that he needed to let me know this.

This was both funny and outrageous. The funny bit was that Chenchen felt he could do what I had done – in truth, he couldn't sell a box of matches to a chain smoker who'd lost his lighter. The outrageous bit was that he'd been busy designing his own product behind my back.

Instead of blowing my top and chucking him out there and then, I decided to turn the situation to my advantage. I took Chenchen to one side and calmly said, 'What's going on, George? I hear you've made your own amplifier.'

To show off in front of his wife and the two northern girls, he raised his voice and started speaking in a very loud, authoritative manner, to such an extent that he could be heard across the whole floor.

I said, 'George, why are you deliberately raising your voice? Who are you trying to impress? Your two girlfriends? Because it's not working. Just calm down a little.'

That put him in his place. I asked him again about his new amplifier. He explained, 'Well, I'm working my nuts off here and all I'm getting is a salary. I feel you owe all this success to me, so now I want to do it for myself.'

Instead of arguing with him and telling him he was deluded, I surprised him by asking him what circuit he'd adopted for the design of his amplifier, and what was its specification.

I think he was taken aback, as he was expecting me to do my nut, but instead here was I enquiring about his new product. He was such an idiot that he rattled off some technical details, the last thing you'd do with a future competitor. I responded, 'That's better than the 8000. Why didn't you do that for me?'

'Well,' he blustered, 'things move on. It's a matter of opinion whether it's better than the 8000.' Complete nonsense. He knew he'd designed a pup in the 8000 and his 'new model' was much improved. I was biting my tongue and I told him I wouldn't stand in his way – he was free to do as he wished. However, he would need to understand that I'd have to replace him.

So I didn't fire him on the spot, and we agreed that he would stay on until I got a replacement. He returned to his position and carried on testing. He must have felt like he'd got away with murder.

I asked Stan Randall for advice on where to advertise for a new engineer. A couple of weeks later, enter Mr Mike Forsey, a slight, feeble-looking fellow with a strange walk and a Hitler moustache. Forsey seemed to know his stuff, though you didn't need to know much to surpass Chenchen. Stan also found another chap, George Shrubsole, who worked for an amplifier company in Wimbledon, and we offered him a job. Stan was proving very helpful. I think he liked the fact I'd come from nowhere and was growing a business with a brand name that was taking on the likes of Armstrong and Leak.

With Forsey in place and Chenchen expecting to stay on for a few more weeks, I waited for my moment. One day, Chenchen was sitting at the end of the production line as usual, with his chest stuck out, like a peacock. He had a renewed sense of pride, having let everyone in the factory know he was leaving to start on his own.

I walked up behind him in a calm manner and told him to get up, get his wife and clear off. He was dumbstruck. He'd expected to stay for a bit longer. 'Right, George, time for you to go, mate. I've bitten my tongue and put up with you and your blackmail for far too long. Get your things and your wife, and go now.' Rather cheekily, I said all this in a loud tone, so the rest of the workers could hear. He was kind of sacked in front of all them and they heard why. He stormed off without saying a word.

I still remember his wife saying to me, 'I don't know why I should be telling you this, but the petty cash box key is under the filing cabinet door.'

I felt good about getting rid of the pair of them, but there I was without a clue how to do the payroll for the week! In desperation, I called my accountant and said, 'I have no one to do the PAYE – what am I supposed to do?' It's quite amazing how, at the time, I felt this was such a massive problem. My accountant simply sent one of his clerks along, who knocked off the PAYE for us in half a morning and told me how much money to take out of the bank to put in the pay-packets.

Now George Shrubsole, under the supervision of Mike Forsey, sat at the end of the production line testing amplifiers. He even managed to train a couple of the line workers to do the tests, so over the course of two to three weeks, Chenchen – this person who I'd thought had me by the balls, this animal who'd screamed at that kid and made me get rid of Sam Korobuck – was nothing to me any more.

It was big lesson learned – no one is indispensable.

*

So there I was, twenty-four years old, running my own factory, employing about thirty people. I'd built a company selling a product bearing the brand name Amstrad and was competing with the rest of the industry. Naturally, news of this success precipitated through my family and they were all very pleased for me. Similarly, Ann's family saw me in a new light, as you might expect.

I remember arranging a fortieth wedding anniversary party for my mum and dad at a venue in Walthamstow. It was quite a nice do and I invited all the family, as well as some of Ann's family. My Uncle Dave, who worked in one of the garment factories in Great Sutton Street, came up to me, full of compliments. The party went well, and it was something my mum and dad would not have expected.

Ann had coped with motherhood very well and Simon was now a toddler, amusing us and our friends, who used to come round to see the baby. We decided to have another child, and on 29 July 1971 my son Daniel was born at Wanstead Hospital. This time there was no traumatic story to tell about the birth. Ann, in common with most women, found the second one much easier.

I phoned my mum to tell her that the baby had arrived and that it was another boy, and she gave me the usual mild congratulations and asked how Ann was doing and if everything was okay. I then phoned my dad at Great Sutton Street to give him the good news. The conversation went like this:

'Hello, Dad, just to let you know, Ann's had another boy.'

'Oh, good, good, very good, congratulations. Look, Morning Plastics are outside with a big van – they want to know where to offload it.'

Even *I*, by then, could see the error of his ways. I said to him, 'Who cares about Morning Plastics? Did you hear what I just said to you? You're a grandfather again. Ann has just had another boy – we're going to call him Daniel. And everybody's fine, in case you're interested.'

He was obviously embarrassed and said, 'Yes, of course. I'm sorry, I'm sorry – it's just that I was flustered. Yes, it's wonderful news, mazel tov, congratulations. Ann's okay? Good, good, good.'

I took Simon along with me when we went to pick up Ann and Daniel from the hospital and I'll never forget the expression on his face when he saw me bring out the carrycot containing his baby brother and put it on the back seat of the car. He looked into the carrycot, as if to say, 'What's that? Who is this? How's it going to affect me?'

With the new addition to the family, Marlands Road had become a bit crowded. Simon had his own bedroom, but Daniel needed to be fed throughout the course of the night and would be keeping everyone up. We could afford to buy somewhere bigger, so we decided to move.

By 1971, the house I'd bought for £4,700 in 1968 had tripled in value. In fact, it was Ann who sold it. She actually gazumped someone, which is not in her nature at all. It was originally sold for £15,300 to somebody, then the agent brought round some people whom Ann described as 'a really nice family' – the Robinses (Mr Ivan Robins was the local photographer). And as Ann put it, 'They were such nice, lovely people, I said they could have it for fifteen thousand, seven hundred.' She was right, they *were* nice people, and we went on to deal with Ivan and his son for many years to come.

After her gazumping exploits, Ann found us a new house in Chigwell – 10 Chigwell Rise. I bought the house outright for £27,000 cash, with no mortgage – an unprecedented thing at the time.

Chigwell was quite a posh area in those days, full of rather typical

English-style country folk. The migration of people like me, an East End boy, into the area was, to say the least, not popular. My migration – from Hackney to Clayhall in Redbridge, and then to Chigwell in Essex – was kind of the way it worked.

After buying our new home, we really smashed the place to pieces and spent a load of money on it. If I say so myself, we made it into a really top-class house. We even built a swimming-pool in the back garden. Chigwell Rise was a great house and it was to become our home for the next ten years.

I don't quite remember how it happened, but me and my old friends Steve, Geoff and Tony kind of drifted apart at this stage of our lives. However, Malcolm and I were still in touch for business reasons. Human nature being what it is, you tend to make new friends as you get older, usually from the local community.

*

The 8000 had done me proud. We made it for about eighteen months, but its specification wasn't good and I needed to bring a new model into the marketplace. There was also a big demand for higher-powered amplifiers, and this time I wanted to make sure the triangle player in the Royal Philharmonic didn't get a complex. The quality of this amplifier and its frequency response really had to be the bee's knees.

Forsey had explained that the 8000 had been designed without a pre-amplifier. It had no guts in it to drive the bass and treble controls, the things that make the sound richer and sharper. This time, we were going to ensure that any new product we embarked upon was designed properly. It was time for Mike to show me what he could do. Stan Randall (who was now on the payroll as an Amstrad employee) and Mike Forsey came up with some research on the company Toshiba, who were selling Power ICs (integrated circuits). I won't bore you with the technical stuff, but take it from me, ICs were *the* thing in those days, and I figured that if I could incorporate them into one of my new products and use the phrase 'Pioneers of Integrated Circuits' in my advertising, it would work well. The IC2000 amplifier was duly conceived.

Because our orders were now too big to produce at Great Sutton

Street, I acquired new premises at 89 Ridley Road in Dalston. Ridley Road was famous for its market, where my mother regularly shopped and would take me as a kid. It was where I'd worked on Mr Phillips' stall as a young lad.

At Ridley Road, I took 4,000 sq ft of refurbished factory space – four times the size of Great Sutton Street. It felt like I had taken on an aeroplane hangar.

Stan Randall arranged the construction of the production line at Ridley Road and Mike Forsey got on with the design of the IC2000. I did the mechanical drawing for the cabinet and chassis. This time, we moulded some very fancy silver knobs and slider controls. The front panel layout design of the product was down to me. I designed some flash aluminium toggle switches and the whole thing looked a real mug's eyeful. Moreover, it was a bloody good amplifier and it ticked all the boxes as far as the specification was concerned.

There was a demand for a tuner to go with the amplifier, so Stan asked his ex-partner Roger to come up with a design for a tuner chassis, as by now my capacity on the mechanical engineering side was running out; it was getting beyond my comprehension.

Because the *look* of a product – the cosmetic design – was starting to assume great importance, we employed our first draughtsman. Enter Bob Watkins, a bearded, heavily built chap in his early twenties who had previously worked for the Ford Motor Company. We set him up a drawing office next to Mike Forsey's design laboratory.

The production line was being run by a no-nonsense fellow by the name of Dave Smith, the accounting was done by Derek Burford and we had a secretary, Joyce, who answered the phone and did the typing. As with all electronic products, we did get returns, so we set up a service department which was run by Simon Angel, a young hippy lookalike who joined the company from the London Electricity Board. Simon took on a young man by the name of Ivor Spital, someone who's still employed by me today. I recall that he came in for his interview carrying an umbrella, but he swears he's never owned an umbrella, and this argument has gone on for around thirty-seven years now.

We also employed a couple of black guys who were brothers – Richard and Michael Davis. Richard worked on the production line while Michael became an unofficial assistant to my dad, doing odd jobs around the place, packing parcels, opening the incoming mail, sending the outgoing mail, running up to the bank and that sort of stuff.

In all, we must have had fifty or so employees in that building. The one who gave me the most trouble was my dad! There were times I could have throttled him, as he embarrassed me in so many ways with his penny-pinching behaviour. Because he'd struggled all his life to scrape together a living, he simply couldn't get it that I was at the races by now. Although I was only twenty-four, I was a mini-mogul – making loads of money and owning a nice house – yet he would carry on as if we were still living in the dark ages.

The staff had to bite their tongues when they spotted him getting up to his shenanigans. If it wasn't for the fact that he was the boss's dad, they'd have given him a real hard time.

He would intercept the incoming mail before the secretary opened it, to see if any of the stamps had been left unfranked by the Post Office. If so, he would steam off the stamp (probably using more energy than the stamp was worth) and reuse it. You would often see outgoing mail with LePages glue oozing out from around the stamp on a clean white envelope.

Another of his disgusting habits arose because he couldn't come to grips with the idea of the plastic cups from the vending machine being discarded after use. Many's the time Dave Smith would come to me and show me a cup of coffee he'd just got from the machine – the cup would have blackcurrant stains on the outside from previous use! I went berserk with him, but it seemed that the more I screamed, the more he couldn't resist doing these things. He said, 'I'm saving you money! I wash the cups before I put them back in.'

There was a corner of the floor where a heap of used brown paper and odd rolls of string were piling up. In a rage one day, I told him to chuck the whole lot out. He refused, so I asked Harry Knight, the van driver, to take it all downstairs and chuck it in the bin.

You would have thought I'd sent my father's prized Bentley to the crushers. It was like a farce – he was grabbing bits of paper and lumps of string from Harry, saying, 'Don't throw that away, I'll take it home.'

'Take it home?' I said. 'Where are you going to store it all, and what the bloody hell are you going to do with it?'

One day, I lost my rag completely. I had a small office where I made my calls and met customers from time to time. The main floor heating didn't reach the office, as it was sectioned off, so I used a fan heater in the winter. My day-to-day routine was to walk the factory floor, talk with people and generally help out in all areas. One very cold day, I noticed that every time I came back into the office, it was freezing. The first time, I just thought that I'd forgotten to turn the heater on, but after the second and third time, I realised my dad was switching it off whenever I walked out of the office.

I called him over and asked a few others to come and witness what I was about to do. I opened the window, switched on the fan heater and placed it on the windowsill, so the hot air was blowing outside. I then locked the office door and told him that the heater would be staying there all day, as I was sick and tired of his stupid antics.

It was agony for him! He kept coming to me, saying, 'Okay, okay, you've made your point. Don't be silly – switch it off now and close the window.'

I punished him for at least an hour.

*

Around this time we started taking exhibition stands at the various hi-fi shows around the country. There I was, suited and booted, on my own stand at Olympia, exhibiting my own brand of hi-fi equipment.

There were some funny and embarrassing moments at the exhibitions. Some of the old customers I used to visit in my minivan would walk past the stand. They'd see me and do a double-take, as if to say, 'I know that face.' Sometimes they'd come up to me, as was the case with Clint Atkins from Brixton.

'Hello there,' said the big Jamaican. 'I haven't seen you for a while. So, are you working for Amstrad now?'

'No, Clint, I *am* Amstrad!'

'Ha ha, what do you mean, man, you *are* Amstrad?'

When I explained to him that this was my company, there was a look of shock, followed by the 'I suppose you don't care about your old mates now you're in the big time' look.

Similarly, the two brothers from Rex Radio would stop by to have a chat. They remembered who I was and had been following my career. It was ironic that these former customers of mine were now too small for me to deal with – they only had the potential to buy one or two items. Mind you, the Rex Radio boys with their Bang & Olufsen shop wouldn't have touched my stuff with a bargepole. Amstrad was frowned upon as the Ford Motor Company of the hi-fi world. The so-called 'Rolls-Royce' end of the market was dominated by the likes of Leak, Wharfedale, Kef and a host of other posh brands.

I didn't mind Amstrad's image. My interest revolved around designing, manufacturing and selling. To manufacture, you have to be conscious of your costs. As for selling, it's always helpful if you have a good retail price that undercuts the competition. This was to be my philosophy going forwards. I wasn't cut out to be at the top end of the market. My formula was to observe what the higher-price market leaders were up to, then do the same (if not better), undercutting them on price to generate a mass market for products that normally would have been bought only by well-to-do people. There was no question about it – when I got going in the electronics industry, I was *always* going to be at the 'pile 'em high, sell 'em cheap' end of the market, targeting the truck driver and his wife.

Despite being viewed as the Ford of the industry, it didn't matter to me what the retailers or competitors thought – it was the buying public I was concerned about. I would bring perceived value to the average guy who could not afford the expensive kit, but wanted something that looked the part. And, let's face it, half of the people who bought the expensive stuff did so out of snobbery, simply because they were told it was the best. In reality, the sound from the Amstrad kit was perfectly adequate for 99 per cent of the public, in the same way that today a seven-quid Swatch does the same job as a twenty-grand Rolex, if you get my drift.

I could have gone in the other direction – the Bang & Olufsen way – trying to sell high-price, superior-quality items, but my *character* most certainly is mass volume/low price. I couldn't pull off this high-quality Rolex-type image or indeed have the patience to schmooze and convince people to part with £100 for an amplifier – mine was £19.50! More by default, I was right, because as technology moved on and the microchip world became more advanced, it would be fair to say that most manufacturers used the same circuit, so there was no difference in the end, quality-wise.

6

A Taste of Japanese Culture

From the East End to the Far East

1973–6

In the early seventies, when the consumer electronics industry was in its infancy, Japan was the undoubted leader in technology. Some of the Japanese hi-fi equipment had wonderful-looking silver knobs, toggle switches and the like on the front panel. When trying to procure these items in the UK, I soon realised I was dealing with middlemen who imported these components from Japan and stuck on a profit for themselves.

I decided to go straight to the source. We were too small a company at the time to buy switches directly from giant manufacturers such as Matsushita; instead, we would need to use an agent in Japan. Looking through the *JEA*, a Japanese trade magazine, I spotted a small quarter-page advertisement for Shomei Trading Company which looked promising. Within it there were pictures of electronic components such as switches, resistors and capacitors – all very exciting for me. The advert gave a telex number and a telegram address: SHOMEI TOKYO. The contact name was Mr A. Imai.

I applied to the Post Office for our own telegram address and we were allocated AMSELEC LONDON. Initially, I sent Mr Imai a letter by airmail, inviting him to send me a telegram if he was able to help. About a week later, I received a telegram asking for more details. There followed a back-and-forth exchange of telegrams. Although telegrams were expensive, time was of the essence. For me, this was a new culture, dealing with Japan – product designs and specifications were changing rapidly and you had to be fast or get left behind.

Mr Imai airmailed me the Japanese Components Industry catalogue – a massive book, about four to five inches thick. This was the *Glass's Guide* of components; in it you'd find every type of component you could possibly require. I identified several manufacturers for parts I wanted to buy, and Mr Imai sourced them and sold them to me.

I was sending many telegrams and costs were running high, so I decided to invest in a telex machine. Those of you old enough will know what a telex was, but for the younger reader, the telex system was effectively electronic typewriters connected via the phone line. The Post Office allocated us a separate line for the machine. Naturally, I chose the callback ID AMSELEC LONDON.

We had created a brand name for products such as amplifiers, tuners and speakers, but I could see that there was a great market for peripheral items such as headphones and microphones. I was encouraged to move into this area by Nick Lightowler at Comet, a high-level buyer in the hi-fi division. Nick and I were roughly the same age and he liked my cavalier approach. He also admired the way I'd screwed his Japanese suppliers by taking a chunk of the low-cost amplifier and tuner markets away from them. Our heavy advertising in the hi-fi magazines fed straight into the Comet business model. Customers would see our adverts, see that Comet was the cheapest seller and buy what they wanted from them. We became a big supplier to Comet in the hi-fi sector.

Nick would call me and say, 'You know, if only we could get hold of headphones that had two knobs and three bells and five whistles, that sold for nine pounds ninety-five – they'd be a massive hit.'

I owe a lot of my success to the interactive relationship with Nick. He saw merit in advising me of what he wanted, because I could pull it off quickly. This type of feedback was manna from heaven to me. I would get in touch with Imai and ask him to send me details of headphones. In a short space of time, not only could I come up with the exact specification Nick wanted for £9.95 retail, but a whole range of headphones starting from £5.95 up to £15.95.

The speed at which Imai and I worked was incredible. Bear in mind that there was no email, no DHL, no FedEx or UPS in those days. We are talking 1973–4 – samples had to be sent by airfreight, letters had to go by express airmail. There was no fax machine, so you couldn't send pictures instantly. And even if you did take a picture, you'd have to wait for it to be developed before you could airmail it.

I made up a range of headphones with our brand, allowing Mr Imai to work on the artwork for the boxes. They were an absolute smash hit when they got to the UK. They sold really well at Comet, as well as at G. W. Smith, Laskys, Henry's Radio and all the other companies offering discount hi-fi equipment. This peripheral business – where I imported goods fully assembled and ready for sale – was looking quite good.

I added a range of magnetic cartridges to our product line, a cartridge being the small device fitted at the end of the arm of a record-player which contained the stylus that picked up the music from the grooves in a vinyl record. Shure and Goldring were the big brand names for cartridges in those days. These small lumps of plastic with diamond styli sold for a load of money and looked overpriced to me. It was all one-upmanship, snobbery and hype. Using Shomei, I found a maker in Japan, and we put together a range of three cartridges that I think, to be honest, were all the same but were different colours. They had different model numbers and different types of stylus, such as elliptical. According to the gurus in the hi-fi magazines, elliptical styli were the best, so I simply asked Shomei for elliptical and got them.

The telex became my business tool and I'd bang out messages to Shomei all day long, going home at seven or eight at night and getting into work early in the morning to see the replies back from Japan. Because they were eight hours ahead of us, there was only a short period of overlap during which one could get direct answers from them. By about ten thirty in the morning (UK time), you'd lost them; they'd gone.

You may recall that earlier I mentioned a gangly looking fellow called Peter Jones who used to work for the company East West. He suggested he should come and work for me, as he was so well connected in the industry. What a turn of events – Peter Jones, someone who used to take the piss out of me as I was humping cartons from the loading bay of East West, now asking me for a job. I naïvely believed that he *was* well connected and engaged him as a salesman.

One day, he told me that he'd got himself a free two-week trip to Japan, courtesy of his old employer at East West. By now, I couldn't have cared less if he was going to spend two weeks or two years in Japan. The guy had turned out to be totally useless. I remember discussing him with Gulu when I bumped into him at a trade exhibition. Gulu had followed my career and was already starting to develop his 'I started Alan Sugar off' myth. He was singing my praises to everybody walking past. 'Do you know him? Do you see this man, Alan Sugar? He started with me. I used to give him stuff to sell, and now look – he's making all this hi-fi now and it's very good,' and so on.

Gulu asked me how I was getting on with Peter Jones. I remember joking that Peter, whom I referred to as Rigor Mortis, had taken his kid to Madame Tussauds and was told by the security man to keep moving, as he was being mistaken for one of the dummies. Gulu loves a good joke. He laughed, but in truth I think that summed up the pale, gaunt Peter Jones.

Before going off on his jolly to Japan, Peter asked me if it would be okay for him to pop in and see Mr Imai, as a representative of Amstrad, while he was there. I thought there was nothing to lose with this exercise and agreed. When he finally got back, he told me he'd placed an order for 20,000 toggle switches!

'Why?' I asked in disbelief.

He said that he'd been treated so nicely by Mr Imai that he just *had to* place an order. I went crazy, telling him I couldn't understand what he thought he was doing, slinging his weight around without any consultation, without any phone call or telex message. The man was a liability and was bringing nothing at all to the party. I think he got the message and left the company.

*

Although business was booming, like the rest of Britain, we were to be dogged by the three-day week between January and March 1974, a consequence of the miners' strike. To nutshell it, all companies could use electricity only three days a week. Of course, we couldn't operate without electricity. The authorities didn't actually cut off the supply, but if your factory or shop was seen to have the lights on on the prohibited days, there were significant fines and possible jail sentences. It was taken seriously and companies had to abide by the rules. It was a nightmare – I was unable to fulfil orders.

We came up with the idea of buying twelve-volt soldering irons – powered by car batteries – for the girls on the production line, so they could still assemble PCBs. However, as the end-of-line testing could only be done using mains power, we were stumped. That was until an enterprising person in Holland advertised generators in the *Evening Standard*. With a bit of swift action at the bank, I sent the money to the Dutch company, and a few days later this monster turned up on a flatbed lorry.

With some difficulty, it was manoeuvred into the goods lift and offloaded on to the factory floor. When we fired it up, the bloody thing made such a racket, it nearly deafened everyone. It was not practical – the staff couldn't work in such an environment.

The next day I got hold of my builder. We punched a hole in the wall for the exhaust pipe, fitted a muffler and built a complete wall around the generator, using two layers of plasterboard spaced four inches apart, with fibreglass wadding in the gap for soundproofing. This worked to a certain extent, but as the floor was concrete, the generator vibrated like mad and the noise was still unacceptable. Finally, we found some rubber mounts that took away the vibration, and we ended up with an acceptable electricity supply with the minimum of noise.

One of our employees was not a happy camper. He thought this three-day week meant he could look forward to two days off per week for the duration, so this idiot secretly went to the trouble of filling up a gallon bottle with water and poured it into the fuel tank. When it came to starting the generator up, the diesel, being lighter than water, rose to the top of the tank and the machine wouldn't start.

We had no idea what was wrong, but after a bit of troubleshooting by George Shrubsole and myself, we did the obvious to see if the fuel was getting through. On draining the tank a little, we were shocked to see that water was coming out – we couldn't understand it. We drained the water from the tank and finally the generator kicked into life, but we'd lost a whole morning of production.

Angry at this obvious sabotage, I went on to the production floor and started ranting, demanding to know who had done such a stupid thing. No one owned up there and then, but, typical of the workplace, the message got back that it was this particular idiot. The guy was a manual worker of quite low intelligence and it was clear that he hadn't thought up this prank himself, but was goaded into it by others. In the end, you kind of felt sorry for him. I made it clear that the people who'd put him up to this had been noted. There were a few red faces.

*

There was another machine that fascinated me around that time. It was situated next to Ann's hospital bed in Barking Hospital. She was pregnant with our third child and at the first sign of an ache or twinge, Rita suggested we ring for an ambulance. As an experienced mother by now, Ann was well up for the delivery and just wanted to get it all over with as quickly as possible and move on.

Alas, this was not to be. The baby would not pop out. There was no medical problem at all; it was just a false alarm. However, the hospital would not let her check out, so she spent the next three days doing her nut in this place.

The family and I came to see her at visiting times. Not being the greatest conversationalist on earth and having said the usual 'How are you?' and gone over how fed up Ann was, the remainder of visiting time saw me poring over the machine they had linked to her, trying to see how it worked. Apparently, it was pumping some stuff into her to induce the new baby. Ann was very frustrated. She just wanted it over with and vented her anger on me. 'You're more interested in that bloody machine than in me!'

We often laugh about that moment, and it reminds me to put the record straight about something. Ann is perceived by the rest of the world to be this quiet, dignified, kind and shy lady. That is 100 per cent correct – except when it comes to me! Trust me, she ain't that shy and quiet. As I tell people, she knows how to open her mouth to me all right!

One of the days I visited Ann, her grandfather Izzy wanted to come along. I picked him up and on the drive to the hospital, he said to me, 'I've changed my name, Al.' He used to call me Al.

'What are you talking about?' I said.

'Yeah, my name is now Ian Taylor.'

'Ian Taylor? What are you on about?'

'Well,' Izzy said, 'all the others have changed their name to Taylor, so I thought I should.'

'What others?'

'You know, Jack and Harry.' He was referring to his sons.

I'll stop here for a while and explain the rationale behind name-changing. When Jews came to England with names like Schneider, they felt it would be a good idea to change them to something a bit more anglicised. They didn't want their names to stick out like a sore thumb when applying for a job or a council flat, as there was a lot of anti-Semitism in the days of Jewish immigration. Moreover, in the workplace, they felt more comfortable with their anglicised surnames.

In the case of Izzy Schneider, his sons changed their surname to Taylor. Schneider in Yiddish, I was told, means 'tailor', but there are conflicting stories, as I'm also told it means 'cabinet maker' or 'woodworker'. Anyway, who cares? They changed their name to Taylor.

Now you have the background, I can explain why this was so funny. You see, Izzy's sons had changed their names *forty years earlier*, when they were about eighteen and Izzy was about forty-two. And here he was – forty years on, at the grand old age of eighty-two – announcing that he was now Ian Taylor. It was hilarious. I could not stop laughing. Actually, I think he got a bit angry at me.

I'm convinced to this day that it wasn't the machine that induced Ann into labour – it was me telling her this story at her bedside, with Ian beside me. She was biting her lip trying to hold back the laughter, not wishing to upset her granddad.

I went home that night after visiting and, for some reason, Ian stayed at my house – I think Rita and Johnnie had taken the boys to theirs. At four in the morning, on 10 March 1974, Ann rang me from the hospital to say that we'd had a girl. Great news.

In those days there were no ultrasound scans to let you know the sex of the unborn child, so predictions were all down to old wives' tales, with everyone putting in their two-penn'orth. 'It's laying in the front – it's a boy. It's laying high – it's a girl. Your bum is much bigger

than when you had the first two – it's a girl,' and so on. During the
pregnancy, Daphne, who I called a ringer, would say with absolute
authority, 'Ann is having a boy.' Then, four weeks later, she'd forget
she said that and come out with, 'It's going to be a girl.' Finally, when
the baby arrived, she exclaimed, 'There you are – I told you I was
right.' That's what a ringer is.

I'd just fallen back to sleep when the phone rang again, about thirty
minutes later. It was Ann, who exclaimed, 'We've had a girl!'

'I know,' I said. 'You told me that half an hour ago.'

'Did I?' she said. 'I don't remember.'

She must have been pumped up with some drug. When I got to the
hospital in the morning, she said to me, 'We have a girl.'

'I know! You've told me three times now.'

We named our daughter Louise Jane; Louise after Ann's cousin
Louie who, with his wife Edna, had lived next door to Rita and
Johnnie. Sadly, Louie had recently died from a rare heart condition.

Ann and I were delighted to have a baby girl, as was Rita. To Edna,
Louise was her special niece in the years to come, for obvious reasons.
And Daphne was so happy, as she loved baby girls. So, all in all, Miss
Louise Jane Sugar had a lot of love coming her way from all directions.

*

It's all very well selling items from £5.99 to £19.99 retail, but at the end
of the day you need to sell loads to make real money. It's very simple.
Say I made 25 per cent on those products – after the dealer's margin
and VAT, I'd be lucky if the net amount in my bin was £1 for an item
retailing at £5. Sell a product for £50 and you get £12 in your bin. This
realisation was to become another of my philosophies that would lead
me to fortune in the future. I needed to concentrate on high-ticket,
high-margin items.

A booming product at the time was the hi-fi cassette deck, a piece
of equipment which enabled people to play cassettes through their
hi-fi system and make recordings. The Japanese had cornered the
market on these. I noticed an advert in the *JEA* magazine for a cassette
deck by the company Orion and contacted them, only to be told they
were already selling the item to an importer in England. I tracked

down the importer and found that he was a real small-time Charlie – a nice chap of foreign origin. I explained my interest in buying these cassette decks, but also made clear that it wouldn't be practical to buy from him – there was no room for two margins.

Amazingly, he agreed to put me in touch with his equivalent of Shomei Trading – Waco Trading in Japan. He made arrangements for me to buy these cassette decks from the manufacturer, Orion, via Waco. In return for this, a commission would be paid to him on all my purchases.

Waco Trading Company was run by Walter Colson, a man of German-Jewish origin who had escaped Nazi Germany in the war and set up a trading company in Japan. We started to import these cassette decks from Waco Trading with our brand on them and they were a phenomenal success; once again I managed to undercut the market and the units really complemented my range of amplifiers.

Because I was importing more and more products and components, I felt it was about time for me to go and visit the Far East. But prior to me telling you about my first trip to Japan, I need to share with you an amazing story which made me a load of money.

One day, sitting in my office in Ridley Road, I got a call from a gentleman from the United Africa Company who'd seen our advertisements in all the hi-fi magazines. In a rather posh City accent, he told me that he had been contacted by his principals in Nigeria – Kingsway Stores – who wanted to buy some of our equipment.

I knew the word Nigeria meant *beware*. There were lots of scams going on there, so I was very frosty to this man on the phone. Nevertheless, he insisted on coming to visit me at Ridley Road. During his visit, I told him I would be concerned about shipping any goods to Nigeria, as Nigerian companies were notorious for not paying. I didn't want to waste his time, so I told him there was no chance of me dealing with him, even if he were going to propose issuing me a letter of credit drawn on a Nigerian bank, which was about as useless as a second-hand Kleenex.

He responded that the United Africa Company actually *owned* Kingsway Stores in Nigeria, and if they decided to do any business with us, he would pay us for the goods in England. My ears pricked up at that, and I took him through our range of products and gave him prices. He said he would go away and consider it.

A day later, he called and informed me that he was going to give me an 'indent'.

'What's an indent?' said I, wondering if he was going to whack me with a hammer.

'An order, Mr Sugar,' he said.

I was poised with pen in hand, ready to take down this massive order. He announced that he wanted two pairs of each of the speakers we produced, two of each of the amplifiers we produced and two tuners. On top of this, they would need to be packed in wooden crates, no straw (in case of fire), with special markings, etc., etc.

I put down my pen. Rather than be rude to him, I just said, 'Yeah, okay,' but in the back of my mind I thought, 'What a waste of time that was,' and just ignored the whole thing.

A week or so went by and I got a call from the chap asking me what was happening about his indent. I told him, quite frankly, that it was too small, that we didn't deal in ones and twos.

He explained that these were merely *samples* he needed to send to Nigeria by air for them to give their final okay on a bigger order. He convinced me to send the samples to my forwarding agent, assuring me that the United Africa Company would pay for all the special crating of the goods. He said that payment would come shortly, as indeed it did, the next day.

A couple of weeks went by and I was contacted by this fellow again.

'Right, we're ready to give you a big order.'

If I remember rightly, it was for 500 amplifiers and 500 pairs of speakers – and here's the bit that's incredible. He wanted them delivered in the next three weeks to Gatwick, where the whole lot would be sent by highly expensive airfreight to Nigeria. Can you believe that?!

To put it into perspective, in those days to airfreight a box the size of a suitcase would have cost about £100 and this order would have filled at least one forty-foot lorry. They had chartered a big freight jet!

My streetwise upbringing kicked into play. Where was the sting? Was it: 'Be nice and polite, send the money for the samples on time and then, when you get the five hundred units, don't pay'? I pleaded poverty and told him that to produce such an order, we would need the finance for it.

He replied, 'No problem at all – we will send you the money tomorrow.'

In those days, there was no telegraphic transfer system. There *were* ways of transferring money from bank to bank, but it never happened instantaneously – sometimes it took a few days. This all seemed too good to be true. I wasn't going to ship one thing for this fellow until I had the cash.

Sure enough, in the next morning's post came a massive cheque from the United Africa Company. I called my bank manager at Lloyds in Islington and asked him whether he'd ever heard of this company. It shows you how cocooned I was in my narrow-minded way – it turned out that this was a massive organisation which had been trading in Africa for many years and had many African assets. The bank manager said that he'd look at the cheque and if it was authentic, he'd give me an assurance to go ahead. I sent my dad straight up there with the cheque. The manager phoned me back saying it was okay.

Bloody hell! I'd hit the jackpot!

It was time to get back on the phone to this fellow and do a bit of schmoozing. It transpired that the Nigerian government, for reasons best known to themselves, had declared a bonus of the equivalent of £200 to all civil servants. These civil servants were taking their windfalls along to Kingsway Stores to buy up anything that was considered luxury goods, including hi-fis. It was clear that this fellow was no expert in electrical goods; he had merely been given the job of filling Kingsway Stores with hi-fis, fast. What also occurred to me was that everybody else he'd contacted in the UK must have given him the cold shoulder. His other ports of call would have been people like Philips, Sony and the Rank Organisation, companies where he could never have got an audience with the boss. He would have had to go through layers of management, by which time he would have been too late, whereas I was on to it like a flash. But let's not forget that Amstrad was a known brand in hi-fi and the Nigerians did read the UK hi-fi magazines.

I saw the potential straightaway and asked this fellow if there was anything else that he might require, as I was off to Japan shortly. He asked me if we could get a supply of portable radio cassettes with shortwave radio. I mentioned that even though portable radio cassettes, tape recorders, etc. were not part of Amstrad's line-up, I was sure I could source some and fulfil his needs, though I didn't really expect anything to come of it.

Back to my Japanese trip. I hadn't travelled overseas much before; the furthest I'd flown was to Majorca and Italy. So going to Japan was to be an adventure. I decided to take Ann along and her mum and dad offered to look after the kids.

As I was making real money by now, I bought first-class tickets. So there I was, twenty-eight years old, sitting in first class with my twenty-seven-year-old wife, getting some rather strange looks from other more mature and worldly passengers. I think people thought we were from some pop band – how else could people who looked like us afford to travel this way?

It was an exciting adventure. In those days, the plane had to stop to refuel in Anchorage, Alaska – there were no non-stop flights from London to Tokyo. The duty-free area in Anchorage was like a little town, full of shops selling everything from cosmetics to cameras. One thing that sticks in my mind was a giant polar bear in a glass display cabinet in the departure lounge. It was a real, stuffed polar bear, and all the Japanese people surrounded the display, taking photos.

A strange thing happened to me when we got to Tokyo. As the plane touched down in what was unknown territory, a wave of insecurity came over me. Here I was, thousands of miles away from home, in a strange place with a strange culture.

I'd told Waco Trading that I was coming and they had booked us into the Okura Hotel in Tokyo, opposite the American embassy. Mr Imai met us at the airport. As we came through customs, I saw him, a thin little grey-haired man with glasses. If ever there was a stereotypical image of a Japanese man, he was it. He was standing there, diligently holding a sign with my name on it. As I approached him, I said, 'It's me – Mr Sugar.'

His immediate reply was, 'Where is your father? Are you Alan Sugar?'

I said, 'Yes, I am Alan Sugar.'

He was stunned that the person he'd been communicating with all this time was this young fellow with long hair and a leather coat. I introduced him to Ann, but he was still in a state of shock. In Japan in those days it was virtually unknown for young people to be in business. My visit there was to be full of surprises for the people I'd meet.

Mr Imai drove us from the airport to the Okura Hotel. For the first time in our lives, we experienced jet-lag. We were shattered and went to bed soon after we arrived, at about nine o'clock at night, only to wake up three hours later thinking we'd slept through the night. I stuck the telly on and tried to watch an Elvis Presley film with his voice dubbed in Japanese. Really funny.

The next morning, Mr Imai took us to his office – just one room on the third floor of a small office block. I was astonished to see this company working out of one room – I guess I'd had visions of Shomei Trading being some massive organisation. In a way, it was comforting – here was a very small company with a hunger to do business and a boss in control of his costs.

Mr Imai introduced me to his three members of staff. He went on to explain that everyone there thought that the man who'd previously come to see them – Peter Jones – was the boss. He'd told them *he* was in charge. I explained that Jones had left and he was never the boss. They didn't understand and, to be honest, I didn't have the will to explain it, other than to reiterate that *I* was the boss.

It transpired that Jones had slung his weight about and was taken to the finest restaurants in Tokyo. Obviously he'd gotten himself into a situation where he felt he *had* to place an order. I wouldn't have minded, but he didn't even know what a bloody toggle switch was.

Ann was sitting beside me wondering what she was doing there. She was aware, of course, that I was in the business of hi-fi and electrical stuff, but never knew any of the details. I have to say, in my defence, that I never prevented her from getting involved – she simply wasn't interested. In fact, she hadn't even been to any of my business premises.

She must have been bored out of her mind listening to all this nonsense. At least in the afternoon Mr Imai took us to the centre of Tokyo, to see some of the big department stores and a place called Akihabara. Akihabara was my Disney World – a street of giant shops, seven or eight storeys high, with elevators taking you to different departments, as well as a bazaar-style market where you walked through passageways lined with stalls selling every electrical gadget you could think of. I was in heaven collecting brochures and taking pictures. Akihabara provided loads of food for thought and was to be my hunting ground for years to come.

Mr Imai's first name was something like Akira. I found it hard to remember, let alone pronounce, so as we warmed to each other, I asked him if he minded me calling him Harry. He was delighted, as if it were some kind of compliment. In fact, I was to go on to discover that a lot of Oriental people I dealt with in later years had given themselves Western-style first names to make their customers feel at home, particularly American customers. Harry told me that that he would call me Sugar-san, a term of endearment and respect in Japanese culture.

I was scheduled to meet Waco Trading the next day, so I sent a telex from the hotel to the fellow from the United Africa Company giving him my contact details and saying I'd get in touch if I could help him with the purchase of some radio cassettes.

Seeing Waco Trading was an interesting experience. In stark contrast to Shomei, Waco's headquarters were quite plush. Walter Colson, an elderly man in his seventies, sat behind his giant desk in a grand, wood-panelled office. Outside sat what looked like some quite serious executives, including one European-looking gentleman who turned out to be Walter's son, Ronnie. I discovered later that Ronnie was fluent in both Japanese and English, which he spoke with an American accent, and was a bit of a playboy, mixing with Tokyo's mostly foreign elite.

Walter expressed the usual surprise at my age, then introduced me to his general manager, Mr Sakai, a round-faced man in his forties with slicked-back silver hair. He was Japanese, but dressed like a Westerner, in fashionable clothing. He was a real smoothie and must have spent some time in the USA, as he also spoke with a slight American accent. He was totally untypical of what you'd expect a Japanese man to be like. Walter also introduced me to a trendy young man called Joe Oki, allocated to me by Waco as my contact man.

After the niceties and introductions, Walter sussed that Ann would be bored out of her brains and offered to send her around Tokyo with his wife, so as to free me up for his band of vultures. Walter's wife was Japanese – tall, attractive and thirty years his junior. She spoke perfect English and I was happy that Ann would be in good hands.

Most of that first meeting with Waco was spent exploring what else they could sell me. Joe and Sakai gave me a grand introduction to all their staff and so-called specialists.

Sakai had heard that I was Jewish (as was Walter, of course) and thought it quite cool to include in his spiel a few Jewish words here and there. There is nothing worse than a non-Jew using Jewish quips and expressions in the hope of impressing a group of Jews. It's bad enough when English gentiles attempt it, but when someone Japanese tries it, it's like watching white police officers trying to dance at the Notting Hill Carnival. Embarrassing.

I've witnessed lots of attempts by non-Jews to speak in this way and, looking back, I guess Sakai would have got 4/10 for effort. Colin Lewin would get a creditable 8/10 and Gulu, bless him, 9.9/10 – he had great pronunciation with his 'huchs' and 'nuchs'.

Anyway, despite the plush offices and trendy staff, it was clear that Waco Trading were agents sitting between manufacturers and overseas importers. I placed some more orders for cassette decks, but stipulated that they had to have the new Dolby noise reduction system; without it, orders would dry up. As middlemen, they fed this back to the manufacturer, Orion.

I also gave them some information about the United Africa Company's requirements and they told me that Orion also made radio cassettes and could accommodate some orders for a version with shortwave radio, as required for the Nigerian market. They quoted me some prices later that day. I added a big margin and telexed the United Africa Company chap in London. I wanted to honour my promise that I would look for radio cassettes for him, but having thought about the logistics of him paying me, me paying Waco and then arranging all the shipping from Japan to London to Lagos, I thought, 'This isn't going to work – it's just a dream.' So I gave him a 'go away' price, a price so high he would say, 'No thanks,' and go away. And that would be it.

When I woke up next morning, a light was flashing on the panel beside my bed – it was a message from the hotel's Business Centre. I rang them and, with impeccable service, a telex was immediately brought up to my room.

I couldn't believe my eyes! The fellow told me to order as many shortwave radio cassettes as I could get hold of in the next two weeks, taking into account the limitations of component supply and factory output.

I told Ann about this. She didn't understand how crazy this situation was – she must have thought that this was how business *is* – but she could see I was excited. All she said was, 'Oh good, that's good.'

I was on a roll with this nutter. It seemed that he was going to buy bucket-loads of every product I offered him. Clearly the guy did not know what he was doing and, quite honestly, I knew deep down that this couldn't go on.

Here comes another business lesson, one that I used for many years afterwards. I've got an order with a big margin – so that's in the bag. I've got the prices from the supplier, but they don't know I've got an order. The stupid thing to do at this point would be to rush back to Waco Trading and say, 'Okay, we'll take so many of these and so many of those.'

As soon as it was office hours, I called them from the hotel and said, 'Okay, I could use 3,000 of these and 2,000 of those and 1,000 of those, but I think you must have made a mistake. The specification is correct, but the prices you have quoted are surely the retail prices I've seen in Akihabara.'

What must have seemed strange to the Waco Trading people was that they'd offered me some products that were alien to my range and within twelve hours I was interested in buying some – this was not normal practice. Anyway, Waco went into some bullshit about how domestic prices were really low because Akihabara sold at low prices to attract customers, blah, blah, blah. I told Sakai that, as he liked to try to speak like a Jew, he really should understand that I was twenty-eight years old and my Bar Mitzvah had been fifteen years ago – so cut the crap.

Truth was, I never saw any of this stuff in Akihabara. I made Waco a counter-offer, which I just plucked out of mid-air, about 30 per cent lower than their price, while still banging on about what retailers' margins would be.

Time was of the essence, of course. In truth, there was just a small window of opportunity to juggle with and get this thing done, but it's never a good thing to be seen to be rushing to conclude a deal. I took a risk and told them to forget it, that their prices were a joke. They must have thought *I* was the joker because no one makes their mind up that quickly. One minute I'm saying I can take thousands, the next I'm saying forget it. Anyway, it paid off because they left some frantic messages for me at the hotel to call them.

To cut a long story short, after a few twists and turns, we made a deal. Then there was a bit of dancing around, with them trying not to be rude. What they were trying to ask (but didn't have the balls to) was: could I come up with a letter of credit or guaranteed payment, because they didn't really believe in me that much. To be fair, it must have seemed odd that someone of my age could just swan in one day, ask for a quotation on products I hadn't even seen or tested, then give them an order a day or so later.

I'm quite perceptive at recognising this type of thing, so I came out and told them to their face, 'I can see you are worried about getting paid. I can understand this and it's no problem.'

I explained the unusual set of circumstances and was able to confirm with my office that I had been paid upfront by the United Africa Company, which meant that I, in turn, could get the money to Waco within a few days.

When I confirmed with the chap at the United Africa Company that everything was going ahead, I also supplied him with some specifications for clock radios made by Orion. Sure enough, the next morning the light was flashing beside my bed.

Ann must have thought, 'This seems easy, this *work* that you do. You send a message and quote a price, they send a message back and say they want to buy it, and you just organise it – quite easy.'

I told her, 'What you are seeing here is an absolute, one-off phenomenon.'

Very rarely in life do you come across opportunities like this, and you have to grab them. Realistically, this was not long-term business – it was opportunistic; strike while the iron's hot, make some money and get out.

Two factors combined to bring about this windfall. Firstly, as I've mentioned, it was quite clear that this man was not an experienced electrical buyer, as he never negotiated on the prices; and secondly, there was the one-in-a-million situation in Nigeria, whereby all civil servants had been given loads of money to spend on themselves. Obviously it all dried up in time, but I reckon I must have earned around £50,000 from that episode, a phenomenal amount of money for a twenty-eight-year-old in 1975.

One evening, we arranged to meet Walter Colson at the American Club, where they were screening a Western film for American and British ex-pats living in Japan. It was close by, so Ann and I decided to walk there from the hotel. On the way, we were stopped by a policeman who demanded, 'Identification! Identification! Identification!'

No one had told me that we needed to walk around with identification. My passport and business cards were at the hotel. There were no such things as credit cards in those days and we certainly didn't have identity cards. In fact I had nothing at all on me to show who I was.

The policeman only seemed to know one word of English. Fortunately, we were just about outside the American Club and Walter's wife was waiting for us. She saw the policeman talking to us and came over. I asked her to tell the policeman that we were willing to get in his car and go with him back to our hotel room to show him our passports.

He wasn't interested in hearing that. I asked Walter's wife to reason with him that if he took Ann and me back to the police station, what would he then do other than go to our hotel and get our passports, which is what I was offering?

He finally agreed and got on his walkie-talkie to call a police car. Then something must have happened because he just waved us on, as if to say, 'Okay, go away.' Walter's wife explained that there were student uprisings going on at the time, and some American students were involved. I guess to this cop, Ann and I looked like a pair of Western hippies. From that day onwards, I kept my passport with me whenever I was in the Far East.

This first visit to Japan was a great eye-opener for me in all sorts of ways, not least in helping me start to get an understanding of Japanese culture. First of all, they are very nervous and are always seeking assurances that the people they're dealing with are honourable. Honour ranks very highly in Japan. An early message came through from both Harry and Waco that it is better to bite your tongue than make idle promises. Respect within the Japanese business community is gained by actions rather than words. This was to influence my future ethos – I adopted a Japanese mentality from then on. Regrettably, I would find that this mentality was not shared by many of the people I did business with outside Japan. One's word had to be one's bond – simple as that. One's promises had to be honoured. I think it is fair to say that if you speak to any supplier of Amstrad over the past forty years, they'll tell you that a handshake from me is better than any letter of credit or hundred-page contract. This would be my hallmark going forward, a decision that paid dividends in the end. I built up a trust with my suppliers – I would not lead them up the garden path or intentionally cause them any financial embarrassment.

We were entertained very well by Harry and Waco. Harry kindly invited us to his house, where we met his wife and two children. Talk about a culture shock! The first thing that was alien to Ann and me was that we had to take our shoes off. Okay, no problem. What *was* very difficult to live through, however, was the slap-up meal Harry's wife had arranged and had no doubt spent the whole day preparing. In the middle of the table was this metal object boiling away and in it were lumps of meat and odd-looking vegetables. Also on the table were strange looking shellfish, creatures I'd never seen before in my life. Having been brought up in a Jewish household, one didn't really know about shellfish. Up till now we'd mostly eaten Western-style food in the coffee shop at the Okura Hotel, but here we were in the embarrassing situation of being confronted with what looked like items you'd be forced to eat if you were a contestant on one of those reality shows in the Australian jungle.

I tried to explain politely to Harry that we were suffering from jet-lag and that in England we prefer very plain and simple food. I apologised for not eating some of the stuff. In hindsight, this must have been a tremendous insult to his wife, but both Ann and I simply couldn't consume what was put in front of us. We struggled through that meal.

The evening was topped off with a traditional green tea ceremony performed by Harry's daughter. It reminded me of doing art in infants' school, when we used to prepare the paints out of powder, because what was served up in my cup was a lurid liquid that looked like bright-green paint. The evening was becoming more and more embarrassing. As part of this ceremony, the guest of honour, namely me, had to drink the first cup of this stuff, which I reluctantly did. It was *atrocious* – worse than Milk of Magnesia or Pepto-Bismol. How I didn't throw up, I don't know. To be honest, we couldn't get out of there quick enough. And when Harry dropped us off at the hotel, we rushed to the coffee shop to get something to eat.

Regrettably, the hospitality continued, and inevitably Walter's wife invited us to dinner. They had a far more Westernised apartment, as Walter's origins were German, but alas, once again the food was Japanese. We were served stuff which turned my stomach so badly, I had no alternative but to ask to go back to the hotel. Again, very embarrassing.

I don't know whether it was the fact that we'd travelled thousands of miles to the other side of the planet, but something had thrown my metabolism into a complete tailspin. So much so that on returning to England, I visited a number of doctors to try to find out what was wrong with me. Their best diagnosis was that my trip had kick-started a duodenal ulcer. Can you imagine – an ulcer at the age of twenty-eight? I thought that ulcers were associated with stress in people who are much older. As life moved on, I would find that one of my weaknesses on the health front was my stomach, but that's another story.

Ann occasionally called home from Japan to find out how the children were and to check that everything was okay. Johnnie and Rita had moved into our house, which seemed the sensible thing to do, as the kids could carry on with their usual routine. I would listen in on the handset in the bathroom when Ann spoke to her mum.

On one occasion, Ann noticed a distinct despondency in Rita's voice. When she got off the phone, she said to me, 'There's something wrong at home. I can tell from my mum's voice.' To be honest, I hadn't picked it up, but Ann is very perceptive. We discussed whether we should call again, but decided to leave it, as we'd be home in a few days.

We flew back to very bad news. While we were away, Rita had been diagnosed with bowel cancer. The whole family was very shocked and rallied round with whatever comfort they could give. She was only forty-six years old. Everyone's hopes lay with Mr Noone, a specialist in this area. There was a real sense of closeness in the Simons family, a strong bond between Ann, her brother Mark and their parents. As the months passed, the only topic on the agenda was the welfare of Rita, with constant meetings and discussions about her progress each time she visited Mr Noone.

Rita embarked on what was a very primitive form of chemotherapy, but eventually it was decided that she would undergo surgery to have her bowel removed. This would mean she'd have to use a colostomy bag for the rest of her life. Nasty as it sounded, this was a ray of hope for the family – if it meant she *survived*, then that was how it would have to be. We'd just be thankful she was alive.

When people go through this terrible ordeal, there are ups and downs. For a while there was light at the end of the tunnel and it seemed that perhaps the combination of the chemotherapy and the operation had got rid of the cancer. But then things got worse in the Simons household. Izzy, now known as Ian, was complaining of problems with his waterworks, a common ailment in men of his age. It was troubling him to such an extent that this brave old chap decided he would have surgery. The doctors told him that the operation was pretty routine, but added the caveat that anaesthesia in someone of his age was not without its risks.

Nevertheless, as Izzy's surgery wasn't life-threatening, the family's primary concern was of course Rita. Even Izzy himself was only concerned for his daughter. He was recalling how his own wife, Annie, had also died early and I guess he wondered whether perhaps Rita's condition was hereditary.

We all wished him well as he went off to hospital. As he left, he said, 'I know I'm eighty-two years old, but it's the *quality* of life that matters.'

He underwent surgery and woke up after the anaesthetic to be greeted by Rita. His first words were, 'Not bad for an old boy of eighty-two, eh?' But that night, sadly, he died of a heart attack. It was a real blow for everyone. It seems the anaesthetic took its toll and his heart conked out.

As is customary in the Jewish religion, the family mourned the passing of Izzy with an event known as a shiva. This takes place at the house of one of the bereaved close relatives. The close relatives sit on low chairs while other family members and well-wishers visit the home and offer their condolences. On these occasions, one will often hear people reminiscing over stories and fond memories of the deceased. The process of sitting shiva continues for several days. Obviously, because of Rita's condition, it wasn't appropriate to have the shiva at her house, so it was held at the home of Izzy's son, Harry.

Izzy's family was happy that he'd had a long life, but agreed, in view of Rita's condition, that his departure was perhaps a blessing in one way, because Rita would no longer have to worry about the welfare of her father.

There had often been minor altercations between Johnnie and Rita's brothers, Harry and Jack, over why the onus of looking after Izzy should fall upon Rita. Considering that they had homes too, they could have taken Izzy from time to time to give Rita a rest. A week's respite here and there would have been most welcome, particularly when Rita became ill. But there were always excuses and reasons why they couldn't do it.

You have to take your hat off to Johnnie. To offer your father-in-law a home and treat him the way he did over the years was no mean feat. I guess it goes to show how much family life meant to Johnnie. All in all, he gave Izzy a great home and made him part of the family, something that perhaps wasn't fully appreciated by Izzy's sons.

*

Everyone makes stupid mistakes from time to time, and I'm about to tell you about one of mine. My friend Malcolm had taken a shop a few doors away from my factory in Ridley Road. By now he was working for himself, carrying out TV repairs, and he'd teamed up with another chap, Dennis Hart, whom he had met when they both worked in a TV shop in Walthamstow. He had told Dennis about the TV business he used to have with me, and they tried to resurrect it together.

Dennis was a rather strange-looking fellow with a very odd nature. When I heard his dopey way of talking and listened to his ideas and methods, I could tell he wasn't the brightest star in the sky. It also made me doubt his honesty and integrity, which is possibly unfair, as I didn't really know him.

Dennis wore a white coat to make out he knew what he was talking about. In fact, he knew nothing as far as electronics were concerned. One of his scams was to go to people's homes with a device that looked like a pen with a light on it. At one end of the pen was a metal spike and at the other, a wire leading to a crocodile clip. If you touched the spike and the crocodile clip together, the light would come on. He used this device to mesmerise customers. Under the guise of diagnosing what was wrong with their TV sets, he'd prod around with his pen and on would come the light. He'd tell them that their TV was in fatal trouble and needed to be taken away for major repairs, which he'd charge over the odds for. I have to emphasise that Malcolm never had this dishonest streak in him – he had far more integrity.

Dennis was very curious about my business. I let him see my factory and he looked enviously at the production lines, wondering how someone of my age could have built such a business. I knew he was thinking that he and Malcolm could do something similar.

I told them that the products I sold – plinths and covers, amplifiers and tuners – were all advertised in hi-fi magazines, so the simple formula was this: advertise a list of products at slightly lower prices than everyone else's and – bingo – you'll receive orders through the post.

Dennis didn't need telling twice. I suggested that if they wanted to start a business, they should call it something like Audio Supplies, a name that just rolled off my tongue in a moment of inspiration. Sure enough, that's exactly what they did. Dennis and Malcolm took full-page adverts in the hi-fi magazines, listing an array of products, none of which they stocked. Within days of their advert appearing, loads of envelopes were arriving through the door of their tiny little shop in Dalston Lane. Suddenly, thousands of pounds was coming through their letterbox. Dennis was elated, completely blinded by this massive turnover, but he hadn't applied any thought as to where he was going to obtain the items he was advertising. All he'd done was unilaterally list products such as Leak amplifiers and Wharfedale speakers at a few quid lower than everybody else in the magazine. And sure enough, the bargain-hunters sent in their orders. I explained to him that he needed to establish a method of supply and told him about a company called Dallas, in central London, who wholesaled most of the big hi-fi brands.

So much money was coming in that they moved to a much larger shop with storage capabilities in Stamford Hill. It was relatively simple to obtain supplies by buying goods from Dallas or contacting the manufacturers directly. Dennis and Malcolm started to build up relationships with suppliers, as they were able to pay cash and take advantage of the 2.5 per cent cash-settlement discount. These relationships flourished to such an extent that the suppliers were pleased to extend them credit terms.

The cash flow was about £15,000 per week – an amazing figure in 1976 – and Malcolm and Dennis started to take large salaries from the company. I'd never seen a person transform as quickly as Dennis did. The money had gone straight to his head. He became a real bigshot. But he was falling for the oldest trick in the book – massive cash flow. He'd paid no attention whatsoever to profit or costs.

The more orders poured in, the bigger their adverts became and the more outrageous their offers were. I have to say that even I was dazzled by this success at the time, especially since I'd given them the idea in the first place. Bigshot Dennis started attending the hi-fi exhibitions – I'd see him suited and booted in immaculate clothing, striding down the centre aisle, stopping at all the stands and slinging his weight around.

My mistake, based on the other man's grass, was to suggest to Ashley Morris, the husband of Ann's friend Brenda, that perhaps he and I should start up one of these discount warehouses ourselves.

Ashley worked in the fashion industry. He was a tall, slim fellow with a beard and long, lank hair who spoke with a sarcastic air of superiority, belittling those who challenged his so-called wisdom. He would often take the piss out of people's mannerisms, but one felt, on the face of it, that he was quite clever. He was always alluding to starting his own business.

I explained the business plan to him and told him how I'd helped Malcolm and Dennis Hart set up Audio Supplies. We visited their shop in Stamford Hill on a Saturday. Seeing the hustle and bustle was certainly an eye-opener. Such was the clamour, you'd have thought they were giving away ten-pound notes for a fiver. There were people turning up from all over the country to pick up their goods in person.

Ashley tried to exhibit the air of a shrewd entrepreneur. With a kind of reluctant acceptance, he said that he'd give it a go and put a few thousand pounds into the venture if I matched him fifty-fifty. This was really the first sign that perhaps he wasn't quite what he tried to portray. However, as I had some stupid death wish to do this, I agreed to the partnership and came up with a name for the business – Global Audio.

We found some premises in Pentonville Road, and within weeks Global was operating and there was a large cash flow coming in. The shop was terrifically busy on a Saturday.

This upset Ann, who was doing a great job looking after the children Monday to Friday in my absence. She was very annoyed that I would now be out on Saturdays too, helping to grow this discount warehouse business.

Ashley made Dennis Hart's bigshot attitude pale into insignificance. The massive cash flow went to his head big time. As I was busy running Amstrad five days a week, the deal was that he would totally run and control Global Audio. Naïvely, I believed that I would be sharing in the profits. Every so often, Ashley would declare a dividend and give me a cheque for £2,000, what he called 'personal money'.

After Global had been operating for about nine months, Ashley decided to take an exotic holiday somewhere. I took the helm at the shop on the Saturday. Out of interest, I started to look through some of the invoices coming in from suppliers. I became a lot more interested when I looked at the cost price of the equipment compared to what we were selling it for. It didn't take me long to see that items such as giant Celestion speakers, for which we paid about £91 plus VAT, were being sold for £88 plus VAT. So for every pair we sold, we were losing money! That wasn't all; when I delved deeper through the invoices, I saw that we were selling many other products below cost.

This was a bombshell to me. I had trusted Ashley and assumed that common sense would prevail, that he would be applying the simplest principle of business – buying something at a certain price and selling it at a profit. My earlier suspicions that he wasn't as clever as he made out were really coming home to me.

I spent most of that Saturday ploughing through the paperwork. When Ashley arrived back from his holiday, I called a meeting with him and told him what I'd discovered. He was very abrupt, angry and dismissive. He told me he had special arrangements with the suppliers for quantity discounts. He said that he got retrospective kick-backs every three months if he reached a certain level of business and that, eventually, everything we sold would be making a profit. While this practice might have been possible in the motor car trade – where targets were set by the manufacturers – I'd never come across it in the electrical game, and I didn't believe it.

Although there was no intention to do anything deliberately fraudulent, some might argue the business was effectively a type of mini electrical 'Ponzi scheme'. The term isn't really used with reference to electronic retailing, but the principle is the same. To simplify, imagine you have a turnover of £30,000 a week and growing. You obtain up to six weeks' credit from your suppliers, such that, at any time, you can owe them £150,000. So with losses of £2,000–3,000 a week, it would take a very long time to get to the point where you didn't have enough cash flow to pay your bills, particularly when the market was expanding.

To make matters worse for me, the industry had become aware that I was something to do with Global Audio. I had a rather heated exchange with Derek Smith of G. W. Smith & Co., one of the largest retailers in Edgware Road and Tottenham Court Road. He told me point-blank that he was not going to buy any more Amstrad equipment from me while I was effectively a competitor. Clearly Audio Supplies and Global Audio were disturbing the market by undercutting the likes of G. W. Smith and Laskys, effectively costing them money.

I told Ashley that I was under a lot of pressure from the industry and mentioned G. W. Smith's threats. What's more, my friend Nick Lightowler told me that if rumours about my Global connection got through to Gerry Mason, Amstrad could be finished at Comet. Gerry was a very impulsive character and would cut us off just for the sake of it. I explained to Ashley that it was time for me to get out of retailing.

To be honest, this was only part of the reason I wanted to get out of Global Audio. My main concern was the fact that this company was going nowhere and was losing money. I knew that the bubble would burst eventually and I didn't want to be associated with it.

Ashley's response was one of shock. He couldn't understand why I would want to withdraw from a company which was taking £25,000 a week. His attitude was, 'What's the catch? Do you know something I don't?'

I reiterated that there wasn't any other agenda. I guess I misled him a bit by saying this, but I just didn't want to debate with him that the business was going to go down the tubes. I emphasised that the problem was that my main business was going to suffer because of my association with Global, and therefore, if he paid me £25,000 there and then, I would resign as a director and give him my 50 per cent share of the company.

He was amazed – he thought he'd done the biggest deal of his life. The following week, he wrote me a cheque for £25,000 which, let's face it, was a week or so's takings for him. I duly signed the resignation forms and quickly informed Derek Smith at G. W. Smith that I was no longer associated with Global Audio. I also sent a copy of my resignation in the mail to both him and Nick Lightowler. Ashley still couldn't believe I'd given up this pot of gold. He thought I was an idiot, and it suited me to let him think that.

Dennis and Malcolm had seen Ashley and I build a business in direct competition with theirs, but there were no hard feelings. Let's face it, there couldn't be, as I was the one that put them in the business, so our relationship was quite amicable. In fact, Dennis used to arrange social gatherings for all eight of us – Dennis and his Finnish wife Daria, Malcolm and Maureen, Ashley and Brenda, and myself and Ann. He would find the most exotic restaurants in the West End and we would dine like kings. From my point of view, they were real 'on top' gaffs – the food was rubbish, but it was served up in beautifully decorated establishments with lots of pomp. There were waiters wearing silver goblets round their necks and other nonsense.

Like me, Dennis also grew up in a council flat. He saw his new status as a massive elevation. Ashley viewed it as something he was *always* owed and was *always* going to achieve one day. Malcolm went along with the flow, while I sceptically looked on at these deluded moguls.

I haven't bothered to mention the usual trappings of wealth, such as cars, but by that time I was driving a Jensen, Dennis was running around in an Aston Martin, Ashley also had a Jensen and I think Malcolm had something a little more modest, like a Jaguar. To be honest, I was the only one who really warranted such a prestigious car – the others were simply living off the cash flow generated by their schemes.

If there's one thing I learned from this exercise, it was this: if you decide to work with a partner, make sure you know their abilities. Also, do a bit of due diligence to see if all that glitters really *is* gold. It just so happens that I had the foresight to get out, but I should never have got into that business in the first place.

*

As I've said before, in comparison with modern fathers who get involved in the upbringing of their children, I have to admit that I fell a long way short. I missed out on a lot of my kids' childhoods. Most days I would leave the house before the kids were up and I'd get home after they were in bed. At weekends I was quite selfish – I was tired and really needed to recharge my batteries. Weekends normally consisted of taking the kids round to see my mum and dad or Rita and Johnnie. Occasionally, there would be the odd treat, like taking them to the zoo, but apart from that, the only time I really spent with the kids was when we went on holiday.

One thing I did do regularly was take the two boys for a Saturday morning ride in the car. Our journey took us by the local airfield at

Stapleford, where we would stop and have some refreshments and watch the small planes taking off. During my visits there, I started to ask what was involved in flying aeroplanes. It looked very exciting and after talking to some of the people in the flying club, I decided that I would embark upon a course and get my flying licence. This didn't go down too well with Ann. She felt it was a dangerous hobby that I shouldn't take up, considering all my obligations. More to the point, it would consume some of the little time I had to spend with the kids at the weekends.

I guess I *was* a bit selfish, but it was something that interested me and allowed me to relax a bit away from work. I accumulated fifty-five hours and passed my aviation exams and flying test. I became a qualified pilot in 1976 and went on to buy my first aeroplane, a single-engine Grumman AA-5, G-AZVG.

I used to take the kids flying sometimes, although they were a little nervous, particularly Simon. Daniel was more up for it, but Louise was too young. She wasn't big enough to sit in the passenger's seat.

My flying exploits took me across the Channel to places like Le Touquet, Toussus-le-Noble and Paris. But mostly I went to other airports in England, such as Biggin Hill, Shoreham or Elstree – just for the sake of landing.

I won't waste too much time talking about flying because it's something the majority of people wouldn't understand. To most people, flying is all about the need to get from A to B, but most of the time we flying saddos just go up, fly around in circles and then come back to base. To have control of a brilliant piece of engineering, defying gravity, is a great feeling, one that's hard to convey.

*

In early 1976 Johnnie and Ann recognised that Rita's health was deteriorating. Mr Noone told Johnnie there was not much more he could do. For many months, Ann would bring Rita round to our house during the day, so that Johnnie was able to concentrate on his work. Everyone was trying to keep Rita's spirits up. It was a terrible time. Sadly, in December 1976, less than two years after that phone call in Tokyo, Rita passed away.

As young people, both Ann and I were devastated. While we had witnessed Izzy's death, it was the first time that we had experienced the death of a parent. We'd also never seen anyone deteriorate the way Rita had. Towards the end, Johnnie arranged her bed down in the lounge, as she couldn't even make it upstairs.

The plans for the funeral were hampered by the fact that Rita died on a Friday and it was too late to arrange her burial that day, due to the Sabbath. In the Jewish religion it is customary that one has to bury the deceased as quickly as possible. Regrettably, Rita's body remained at their home in Eastern Avenue for two days. Meanwhile, the house was swamped with relatives bringing condolences to Johnnie, Ann and Mark. My mum and dad came to visit. I remember my mum catching a terrible fright when she came across Rita's body on the floor of the lounge, wrapped in blankets.

As many of us know, the death of a parent or someone close to you is a very traumatic event. The week that followed – with the funeral and the shiva – was a terrible time in Ann's life, and it must have been the same for Mark.

Johnnie was absolutely devastated. It was difficult for him – this upstanding, confident man – to try to hold back his emotions. But the whole family gathered round and stayed throughout the whole shiva. Then came that hollow moment when, on the last day, the family left and Johnnie was on his own. He put on a brave face. Nearly two years of a nightmare was over. Rita died at forty-eight, an incredibly young age.

Rita's death also changed our home situation. Effectively, Ann had another person to care for, as Johnnie spent lots of time round our house during the day while I was at work. Ann would make him meals and generally look after his welfare.

One highlight for Johnnie after Rita's death was the arrival of Mark's second child, a girl, and she was named Rita. This Rita was to go on to become famous as an actress in *EastEnders*.

Mark was working in his father's electrical business, but after a while it became clear that there wasn't enough work and income for two people. Johnnie was operating from home, selling stuff over the phone, and it was a nice little niche, but it only brought in just enough money for himself.

I introduced Mark to Ashley, who had decided to open a second branch of Global Audio in Redbridge. Mark was installed as the manager of that shop. It was a job he needed, despite the fact that I suspected it might not last.

*

Sticking to my principle of concentrating on high-ticket items, my sales success, in particular with cassette decks, must have made an impact with our ultimate supplier, Orion. This was no longer small-volume business by anyone's standards and one day I received a phone call from Mr Yonezawa from the London office of Orion Electric Company summoning me to meet the Orion boss, Mr Otake, at the Churchill Hotel. Initially I refused, thinking this would be unethical. I'd never had any direct dialogue with Orion – all my transactions had been through Waco. I'd learned that one had to respect the supply chain – it's very bad business practice to go behind one's supplier's back. However, I was assured by Yonezawa that if any new business did result from the meeting, it would be transacted via Waco. In fact, an hour or so later, I received a telex from Ronnie Colson saying I would be contacted by Orion and, as far as he was concerned, it would be fine for me to meet the boss. He warned me that Mr Otake was a very strange man and that I should take care in how I spoke to him, as he was very proud and pompous in the traditional Japanese mould, where bosses were like emperors. I didn't pay much attention to Ronnie, but I was to find out at the meeting, and over the next few years, what a raving nutter Otake was.

I was met in the lobby of the Churchill Hotel by Mr Yonezawa. With typical Japanese efficiency, he had a photo of me (taken by Ronnie) so he could recognise me. He took me to Mr Otake's suite and invited me to take a seat while we waited for the boss.

And then, the Emperor made his appearance. He was a short, plump man in his mid-fifties with dyed, jet-black hair. He shuffled as he walked across the room and placed himself in the larger armchair. I had remained seated and realised later that Otake had already taken exception to me, as I hadn't sprung to attention and stood up. Speaking in broken English, Otake expressed his surprise at how young I

was. Yonezawa spoke good English and translated the finer details of
our conversation.

Clearly Otake was no fool. He'd recognised that sales of our cassette decks were larger than he'd seen in any other market, and he was
eager to find out what made my business tick.

I went on to explain to him the necessity of producing a Dolby version of the cassette deck. Dolby was a noise-reduction system designed
to eliminate the hiss commonly experienced on tape-recordings. It
was my initial thought to run two models: the existing one and one
with Dolby, for which I could charge a premium.

I advised him that if his company needed any technical assistance
in incorporating Dolby, we would be able to help. Suddenly, in a
Tommy Cooper-like move, he produced a box from beside his chair
and showed me a sample of a new design of cassette deck – with
Dolby! The sample was a mock-up, a non-working plastic model
with no guts. The mock-up had the Dolby logo printed on it, although
at this point Orion did not have a licence to produce Dolby products.

The mock-up was very impressive, much better than the cassette
deck we were buying, but I didn't show that much enthusiasm.
Instead, I abruptly asked the price.

Otake got the hump and exclaimed, 'I don't like this way. You do
not say, "It is good." I don't like aggressive asking price. This not way
I do business.'

I was taken aback – all I'd asked was how much!

He got up and walked out into his adjacent bedroom. 'I don't like
this meeting. You go, Sugar.'

I would learn later that this was one of the games he would play.
Yonezawa explained that Mr Otake was a very important and
respected man in Japan and he did not take to people being as blunt as
I was. I was being warned to watch my ways when talking to him.

I shrugged my shoulders. 'I don't understand what I've done
wrong, but in any case, if I have insulted Mr Otake, please apologise.'

I wasn't so stupid as to let my feelings rule my head. Instead, I put
business first and humoured Mr Otake. After some ridiculous farce
with Yonezawa going to and fro between Otake's bedroom and the
living room, the Emperor re-emerged.

He announced, 'We don't need your business. We have big business in England with Mr Michael Raymond. We are making twenty thousand per month music centre for Mr Raymond. Your cassette deck business is peanut business for me. I am here to help you.' Uncharacteristically for me, I just sat quietly and let him rant. Then, after about ten minutes, it got to the point where it was acceptable for me to enquire as to the price.

When I first started trading with Shomei and Waco, the Japanese yen was 685 to the pound, but the rate had deteriorated to around 530. The proposed price Otake quoted me for this new model, albeit a superior product with Dolby circuitry, would have meant a 50 per cent increase in the retail price over the current model. I explained to Otake that the Japanese yen was causing me problems and that even the model I was buying was becoming unprofitable. I told him I'd been hoping to explain why we needed a price reduction on the existing model, let alone discuss a new model.

And then came a glimmer of light, a clue as to what rang this guy's bells. As all manufacturers will understand, he liked continuity of supply. The comfort of having orders not just for one month, but for *six* was manna from heaven for him.

I explained that the current product was selling well and had found its niche in the market. I told him I'd be prepared to place an order for 10,000 units at the rate of 2,000 pieces per month. He raised his eyebrows and I could see his interest had been sparked.

He said, 'What price you need now because of Japanese yen crisis?'

Yonezawa handed me his calculator. I made some quick calculations and gave my reply.

Otake exclaimed, 'Impossible! Not possible. Stupid request.'

I shrugged my shoulders and told him, 'I may not know a lot about business, but one thing I *have* learned is there's no point buying stuff just for the sake of turnover. If you cannot meet my price, then regretfully it will mean that I have to give up buying this model.' Otake was not going to be seen to compromise in front of a member of his staff. He ended the meeting abruptly, with a quick goodbye, and I left him thinking we were not going to buy any more of his product.

Two days later, I received a telex from Ronnie Colson saying he'd heard I was ready to order 10,000 units. He gave me some bullshit that the component supply chain was tight and if I wanted 10,000, I'd need to book them now. When he phoned me to discuss things further, I took the same position I'd taken with Otake, that I was losing too much margin at the current price to continue with the product.

'What price do you want then, Alan?' he asked.

I told him that I wasn't going to place an order for 10,000 unless he met a certain price, but that I might increase the order to 15,000 and take them at the rate of 3,000 a month.

After a bit of argy-bargy over the next day or so, he accepted my price. The quantity and comfort of five months' worth of orders had rung Otake's bells. I would use this technique for many years to come.

Very often people would promise the same thing to me in order to get lower prices, then come up with some rubbish about why they couldn't take the second or third month's orders. Retailers, for example – I soon learned that their forecasts were not worth the paper they were printed on. I found that the way to impress my suppliers was to lay down long orders and, more importantly, *take the stuff*. This built a bond of trust between us.

I also learned from this episode that Otake was one big bluff. As the Japanese say, he didn't want to lose face, he didn't want to be seen to capitulate. What's more, he didn't want to let on that he wasn't acquainted with the details of the costing.

To finesse this bluff, a day later, Ronnie called me again. He said Otake would prefer me to take the new model instead of the old one. This came as a surprise to me, as I'd seen the new model as some dream that might take shape in the future, with maybe the two models running side by side, the Dolby version being at a price premium.

I told him this was out of the question, expecting to hear that he only wanted me to buy the higher-priced item. For some mad reason, I tried it on and told him I wasn't going to pay one yen more and that in the long term, the addition of Dolby was a *must*. Ronnie argued his corner for about twenty minutes, but I rejected his bullshit.

I had them on the hook and, remarkably, I ended up with the *new* model at *my* price! And at that price there was no point running the two models. This turned out to be a good lesson for me. I would discover that in the ever-advancing electronics industry, the newer models might have more bells and whistles, but they are cheaper to produce. Orion had engineered the cassette deck down to cost less, yet at the same time had made it look great. We helped Orion get a Dolby licence and the machine was a great success when it hit the market.

That wasn't my only encounter with the Emperor. The second time I met him – in Japan – was even more painful. By now, I had taken on a designer by the name of John LeCount – his name alone will give you an idea of this artistic genius. Smartly dressed, long hair, posh accent, you get the drift. He redesigned the 8000 amplifier in keeping with the new Orion cassette deck.

At the time, Goodmans, a Southampton-based company, were having great success with their tuner-amplifier. We produced the Amstrad 5050, a brilliant competitor to it which cost about half the price and became a very big hit.

These products all looked great, but the market was moving on again. Companies such as Pioneer, Trio and JVC were gaining momentum with a new style of equipment. Their amplifiers, tuners and cassette decks had shiny, brushed-aluminium fronts and recessed black metal cases. They were wonderful pieces of engineering with smooth-action knobs, coloured flashing lights and front panel meters. The products looked like they were straight out of a laboratory rack and commanded high prices. Alarm bells were ringing for me and I knew we needed to get into this business. It would take us into a whole different world of engineering.

I decided it was time for a second trip to Japan to research the latest trends. Once again, I met Harry, who was still supplying us with lots of stuff. He'd heard we were buying cassette decks through Waco Trading and asked why I wasn't putting the business his way. He suggested he could find me other manufacturers.

The fact of the matter was that I had a better payment arrangement with Waco. It's important to understand the concept of a letter of credit (LC), effectively a bond issued by a bank that guarantees payment to a supplier. My bank was relatively supportive, but my LC facility was always peaking out and holding me back from doing bigger business. Waco knew this and agreed to ship me goods on 'open account', without an LC. Harry was a small-time operator and could not finance a large volume of business.

Due to this open account financing, I dealt through Waco to buy goods from Orion. Ronnie Colson advised me that once again it was time to pay the Emperor his dues. He and I would have to get a train to Fukuoka, out in the Japanese countryside, to meet Mr Otake. I asked why, but on reflection it was a stupid question – I should have known the Emperor would never come to see me.

We were to meet at a spa resort where the speciality was the hot springs bath. My Western clothes were whisked away by the staff and I was issued with a kimono. Meanwhile, Otake waddled around, dishing out instructions on the day's agenda. At one point, we had to strip off and jump into a giant, boiling spa.

This crazy culture was getting on my nerves. I would have been quite happy sitting in the coffee shop at the Okura Hotel discussing business over a hamburger. Instead, here I was in a hot tub with this little chubby chap and Ronnie. We weren't allowed to discuss business in the hot tub – Otake's rule.

I now know what a lobster must feel like – the water was red-hot. The next torture was to go into a freezing-cold shower, then a couple of sumo-type wrestlers started whacking me with a loofah-type implement. I looked at Ronnie who was trying to get into the spirit of things, but clearly didn't want to be doing this either. He was under Otake's spell – he knew that to do business with this nutter, you had to go along with his mad ways.

Finally, we ended up in a dining room. The table was laid out with all this Japanese tutt. Otake looked at me. 'What is wrong? Food no good? This is best Japanese food.' I told him that I was allergic to shell-fish.

He rattled away in Japanese. Ronnie turned to me. 'Would you like a sandwich or something like that?'

'Absolutely,' I replied. And then, speaking very quickly so Otake couldn't understand what I was saying, added, 'As long as this nutcase here doesn't get the hump.'

After dinner, Otake showed me a range of car radio-cassettes, an area I wasn't active in but which was an up-and-coming market. Cars in those days were not fitted with radios as standard and certainly not with radio-cassettes. Otake told me he'd opened a factory in Korea and it was possible for car radio-cassettes to be imported into Europe duty-free because of some special arrangement between European governments and Korea, which was considered to be a developing nation. That's a joke in itself – little did we all know back then that they would become giants in all industries.

I ordered 10,000 of these car radio-cassettes. I don't know what possessed me – it was just a gut feeling. I also placed another 15,000 order for cassette decks. Otake was quite intimidating and in a way I was trying to impress him with these large orders.

To round the whole episode off, my bedroom had no bed and I had to sleep on a bloody mat on the floor. If anything, I needed another hot tub experience the next day, as it was the worst night's sleep you could possibly imagine. I was full of aches and pains.

Back in Tokyo, I asked Harry to host me around Akihabara. We spent the whole day there and I examined every single product on display, taking as many brochures as I could, as well as photographs. The shopkeepers must have thought I was nuts, taking close-ups of knobs and switches.

I was due to fly home on the Saturday. The British Airways 747 flight to London always left at ten o'clock at night, to arrive at a sensible hour. Before that, Ronnie Colson invited me for lunch to tidy up some of the business we'd done that week. I knew Ronnie felt I was a business commitment he was obliged to see – he was always saying he had better places to be and more interesting things to do. Throughout lunch, he was name-dropping. 'Then so and so said this and that to me when I was in blah, blah, blah . . .' It was really getting on my wick. He'd done this to me before, boasting, for instance, that at the opening ceremony of the Tokyo Olympics, he had the honour of riding with the Emperor's son, with whom he was educated. On that occasion, it got to the stage where I was starting to take the piss out of him, asking him whether he'd met the Queen of England and things like that.

After lunch, we met a friend of his at the Okura Hotel, an American fellow who was trying to sell a new type of Instamatic camera. Kodak had just brought out their rather novel Flip Flash camera, where you popped a small film cartridge into the back. The guy told me that Kodak was selling millions of them in America and that he had tooled up a replica. He asked if I wanted to sell them in Britain and gave me a sample to keep.

There are times in life when you should keep your nose out of things you don't understand, and this was one of them. I wasn't interested. This was not my business – I had no contacts in the photographic industry and it was a low-priced item which meant low margins. Why would anyone buy an Amstrad replica when you could buy the Kodak for a couple of quid more? The Kodak business model was based upon selling a low-priced camera with a view to making the *real* money on the film and processing – it was the classic Gillette blade syndrome.

After the meeting, Ronnie couldn't get rid of me quick enough. He obviously had better places to be, probably meeting up with his beautiful Argentinian girlfriend. He got me a taxi to take me to the hotel – that was it, goodbye.

I had a few hours to kill and sat in the lobby of the hotel, worrying that perhaps I'd bitten off more than I could chew with the big order I'd placed. I did some long-hand calculations on cash flow and realised I'd created a bit of a problem for myself. I wondered how I was going to finance this stuff, in particular the car radio-cassettes.

Then I went to the hotel's shopping arcade and bought Ann a row of pearls. The Japanese are known for the best pearls in the world. I also popped into the photographic shop to see if I could buy a film for the little camera I'd received as a gift. Outside the shop was a big, black minder-type guy, quite a strange sight in Japan, and three Japanese security men. I couldn't understand why until I went inside and there, standing at the counter talking to the salesman, was Sammy Davis Junior. I couldn't believe my eyes. He looked at me and said, 'Hello.' I froze, and then returned his hello.

He was discussing a high-tech Nikon camera with the shop staff and very politely told me, 'You go ahead. I'm going to be a while here, so just ask the man for what you want.' Then he noticed my little camera. 'What have you got there?' he asked.

I said this was a newfangled gadget which took a special film, and we engaged in conversation. He was very interested in the camera. The photographic shop sold me one of the cartridges and I popped it in. I couldn't resist asking Sammy if he'd mind having a picture taken with me. Otherwise, who'd have believed that I'd bumped into Sammy Davis Junior? He was really polite. He stuck his arm round my shoulder and the guy behind the counter took the picture. As I always kept my passport with me (after the last experience), I whipped it out and asked Sammy to sign his name in it.

I was laughing up my sleeve. Ronnie Colson, poseur extraordinaire, had missed Sammy Davis Junior. Unbelievable! He would be plutzing no end. He would have milked every minute of it, but he'd dumped me at the hotel and missed the opportunity to meet one of the world's greatest celebrities.

When I got back to England, I rushed the film to a processor and asked them to print ten copies of the picture of me and Sammy Davis Junior. I express airmailed one to Ronnie with a letter saying that it was very nice of him to host me and that I happened to have bumped into Sammy Davis Junior and we'd had a great afternoon. I wrote, 'Sammy was intrigued by the camera your friend gave me, so much so, he invited me up to his suite and I spent a couple of hours there, which really helped kill the time before I had to go to the airport. Shame you missed it, Ron. Never mind.'

I knew this porky would wind him up no end, and I was right. He called me a week later and put on an American accent, making out he was Sammy Davis, just to check if it was true. I wound him up so much – it was great. 'Such a shame you had to leave, Ronnie. You'd have loved it up there in Sammy's suite – you know, the Imperial Suite on the top floor.'

7

'Young Man, You Have a Good Business'

Should I Take the Money and Run?

1978–9

As the company grew, so did the number of staff. The new people I took on experienced the rapid growth and success of Amstrad, and they shared in the excitement. This applied to all the staff, from those who sat on the production line to those in managerial positions. I wasn't one of those bosses who appointed a manager and left them to deal with the 'lower level' people. I was heavily involved with everyone. In fact, it's fair to say that I was chief cook and bottle-washer.

Now that I reflect on it, I can remember seeing the confusion on the faces of people like Dave Smith, the production manager, when he saw me talking directly to his workers. He'd give me a look as if to say, 'What are you doing? I'm supposed to do that.' It wasn't always easy for the managers to get to grips with my style as a boss, but in the end they understood it and, more to the point, understood me. I've always believed that I shouldn't ask anyone to do what I can't do myself. Many's the time when we started making a new model that I would sit on the production line and assemble the first units. This exercise helped me when I was envisaging future products; it gave me an idea of the complexity of the production process we were about to embark upon.

In truth, I am not happy unless I know every detail of what goes on – that means assembly, material costs and supply chain, as well as the technical workings. The commercial side of sales and marketing just comes naturally to me. In the future, Rupert Murdoch would say, 'This fellow Sugar knows where every nut and bolt in his company is,' a description I was happy with!

My style of management meant that the staff felt I was speaking to them on their level and in an informed manner. I really believed I'd created a family culture at Amstrad. For this reason, I was hurt to discover that a member of staff had betrayed my trust.

One day, our accountant at Ridley Road was off sick, so Dave Smith went into his office to pick up some uncollected paypackets for the people who hadn't been in the previous Friday. In a drawer, Dave noticed paypackets for people who'd left the company a while ago and had been paid in full. He sussed out that something was wrong and brought it to my attention. I asked my accountancy firm to investigate the PAYE and they discovered that our accountant had been embezzling from the company for several months. I called in the police and he was well and truly nicked. This was the first time I had encountered someone stealing from me.

I recruited a new accountant, a very nice fellow, quiet and unassuming, which is why he was shaken when two Scottish labourers we employed phoned him up and told him that they were leaving that Friday and if they didn't get their money, they were going to 'come down and punch his fucking head in'.

They worked at our overflow factory in Shacklewell Lane, just a few hundred yards from our main premises. I'd acquired this extra factory as we were busting at the seams at Ridley Road and needed more space for bulky items such as loudspeakers.

From my regular visits to Shacklewell Lane, I knew who these two were, but hadn't realised they were trouble. They were causing havoc in the factory – they had no regard for timekeeping and came and went when they fancied. When I told Dave Smith I was going up there to sort them out, he warned me that they were a pair of big bruiser lunatics and that everybody was petrified of them. He advised me to take care. With that in mind, I grabbed a crowbar and stuck it in my car before I went up to Shacklewell Lane.

It was about midday. When I asked the factory manager, Colin Baker, where these two were, he told me they were in the pub.

'In the pub?' I asked. 'Why would they be in there? They're supposed to be working here.'

He shrugged his shoulders, as if to say, 'I can't control them – they're a law unto themselves.'

I walked down to the pub on the corner and, like the Milky Bar Kid, pushed the saloon doors open. I saw these two yobs sitting with a group of people. With crowbar in hand, I pointed at them. 'You two, get out here.'

Like two little lambs, they put down their drinks and came out. I screamed at them to get their stuff from the factory and get the hell out. I threw their paypackets at them. By the time we were back outside the factory, they were over their shock and getting angry. One of them said, 'You've embarrassed us in front of our drinking pals – now put that doon.' He was referring to the crowbar I was nervously tapping against the side of my leg.

I said, 'I'm not stupid enough to put this down. If either of you come anywhere near me, I'll wrap it round your head.'

This stand-off at the OK Shacklewell Lane Corral lasted about five minutes. One of them picked up an empty milk bottle as if he were going to throw it at me – instead, he threw it to the ground and it smashed. As they edged towards me, I lifted the crowbar again, warning them, 'Come one step further and I promise you, this will be landing on your head.' By now, a crowd had gathered. After a few more verbal exchanges, they finally walked off, muttering that they would get me in the end.

That was the last time we saw those two idiots. Why am I telling this story? Well, it does have a funny ending. I was going on holiday with Ann and the kids the next day and when I got out of bed the following morning, my right leg was stiff. I couldn't understand why, but when I looked down at my thigh, it was black and blue from all my nervous tapping of the crowbar. Ann was killing herself laughing when I showed her my bruising and told her the story behind it.

The accountant left shortly afterwards, and I recruited a new fellow, Jim Rice, to replace him. Jim was a qualified accountant, a nice-natured, shortish chap with blond, curly hair. To cope with the company's growth, he expanded the accounts department and introduced some new systems.

Also important in the life of Amstrad was Dickie Mould, who joined around this time. Dickie had watched from afar our meteoric rise from minnow to major player in the hi-fi market. He introduced himself as someone who had his own business manufacturing loud-speakers. In reality, his business was going down the pan, but, in hindsight, knowing Dickie's character, I can see how it would have been impossible for him to admit it.

He explained that he was well connected with all the hi-fi retailers and that while I had made inroads into the larger companies, he would be able to sell to all the smaller retailers, some of whom advertised in the hi-fi magazines and had two or more branches. He talked a good game, so I employed him as sales manager. To be fair, he did have con-nections and he did generate some sales with the smaller retailers.

Trouble was, I was always trying to keep him at a distance. He was continually trying to edge his way into the upper echelons of power. It was starting to feel like shades of Chenchen and wife. The best way to describe Dickie is to liken him to the character Boycie in *Only Fools and Horses*. He had the same sneering air of superiority and even looked a bit like Boycie, with his Brylcreemed, slicked-back hair and small, spivvy moustache. He was taller than me and always wore a three-piece suit with a waistcoat.

I had never come across someone so protective of their status. Dickie would say things such as, 'Of course, Alan, *you and I* fully understand everything that's going on, but the others [referring to the other members of staff] don't.' He saw the other staff as plebs and himself as some superior being. Think about Boycie and you'll get the gist. He continually spoke about his big house in Rochford and how he had his own snooker table. He'd go on about how he too was a private pilot and once owned an Auster plane.

Dickie's mannerisms gave rise to a lot of jibing within the com-pany. He would keep his cigarettes in a specially made pocket inside his jacket and would take out the packet, open it, whip out a cigarette and return the packet to his pocket in one swift movement. Never did he think of offering one to others.

What made people laugh most was the chain that hung inside his jacket which was connected to a wallet containing his credit cards. I asked him once why he had the chain. He said that it was a precaution, in case his wallet fell out of his jacket. In those days, credit cards weren't as widespread as they are now. Nevertheless, Dickie had the lot: Diners Club, American Express, MasterCard, Barclaycard – you name it, he had it. And, of course, he was a 'premier member' of each one – what else would you expect from Boycie? Despite this show of wealth, he was a bit tight as things go, and was always rather shy in coming forward to buy a round of drinks. Once when he did, I recall jibing him, saying, 'Blimey, Halley's Comet must be due this week!'

He also had a funny way of speaking. Instead of agreeing with an 'okay', his favourite expression was 'Righto, ducks.' I never did understand what it meant, but I'm told it's some East End expression. It was something you'd always hear when people were mimicking Dickie. Some called him Tricky Dickie or his full title, Tricky Dickie Righto Ducks.

When we visited our customers, I would exchange pleasantries with most of the bosses on first-name terms. However, in those days, things were still rather formal and you would not expect a member of staff lower down the chain to address Comet's Gerry Mason or Derek Smith of G. W. Smith by their first names. When I took Dickie along to meetings, it would wind me up no end to hear him calling these people by their first names, as if they were his best mates. You could see from the expression on their faces that it wound them up too.

Dickie had to be brought down to earth a few times during his first six months of employment, sometimes by my deliberate put-downs in front of the other staff – *they* were just as valuable to me as he was, if not more so, and they were clearly getting the hump over Dickie walking around as the big I Am. But eventually the penny did drop with Amstrad's own little Boycie and he tweaked up his people skills and calmed the situation down within the first year.

*

By the mid-seventies, we were flat out trying to produce amplifiers. The prospect of expanding our production line was daunting – it was very labour-intensive, very technical and a giant headache in the overall scheme of things.

I took stock of my business model. It was to design products (aesthetically and technically) that were needed for the marketplace – and market them. However, in the middle of all of this was the nightmare of assembly and manufacture, which I viewed as an occupational hazard. If I could subcontract this element of the business out, we'd be left with doing what we were best at – designing, controlling the cost of the bill of material and brilliant marketing. In those days, we were still assembling our PCBs manually. This entailed placing the components into the boards and hand-soldering them. This was only practicable if your production runs were low. Large-volume manufacturing used auto-insertion machines which mechanically picked and placed components onto the PCB and then processed the board through a flow-soldering machine. I was not prepared to move in that direction. To me, expanding the business by investing in mechanisation was a no-win situation.

Stan Randall pointed out to me that the company Fidelity, run by the great industry icon Jack Dickman and his three sons, made large volumes of music centres by totally sub-contracting out their PCB assembly, which just left them with the job of final assembly. This rang my bells. I got Stan to contact Fidelity's sub-contractor, L & N Radio in Chatham, Kent, who specialised in electronic assembly. Using them would result in a win-win situation. They'd be promised orders from me, they'd have no headaches about where their business was coming from and they wouldn't need to procure materials, as we would free-issue them the parts. All they'd need to do was concentrate on what they were best at – assembly and quality control – and deliver us finished modules ready for final assembly and testing. If I could negotiate a good assembly price for every module, I would fix my costs by adding the bill of material to their labour charge.

This was to be the key to Amstrad's future.

We went ahead with this arrangement, which also assisted us with component storage, as bulky items were delivered direct to L & N. Even so, we had run out of space at Ridley Road and by 1977 the subject of expansion was rearing its head again.

When I host seminars and Q&A sessions for businesspeople and students, a question that comes up time and time again is 'When do you take your next step for expansion?' Of course, I can only speak from my own experience. I tell my audience that I was always very cautious – it took wild horses to make us move from one premises to another.

We had been bursting at the seams at St John's Street and again at Great Sutton Street and had moved both times out of sheer necessity. Once again, we were in the same situation – there was literally no more capacity at Ridley Road, even with our overflow factory at Shacklewell Lane.

When it was time to leave these two premises, I learned my next hard lesson: if you've signed a lease, you're responsible for paying the rent, even if you don't need the premises any more. I'm sure I must have been advised of this when I signed, but I guess it's something I brushed aside at the time. Now I found myself in a position where I had to pay the landlords a surrender fee on both premises, something I did not like at all.

With that in mind, I took the bold move of deciding that I would *buy* our next premises outright. I located a massive building with over 40,000 sq ft of factory space in Garman Road, Tottenham, no more than 500 yards from Tottenham Hotspur Football Club. I bought the place for £300,000 and we moved our whole operation there. Reluctantly, I settled with the landlords on Ridley Road and Shacklewell Lane.

When we finally moved, in September 1977, a look of worry came over my father's face again. He still hadn't got the plot that I was making bundles of money. He looked at this giant building in amazement. 'What are you going to do with all this?'

'I'm going to start a ballroom dancing business, Dad. What do you think I'm going to do with it?'

'But how can you pay for it all?'

By now I couldn't be bothered explaining it to him, so I just said that we needed to expand. I added, 'Don't worry, Dad, I'll find you a nice little office here.'

'Office? Me? An office? I don't need an office.'

'Well, you need somewhere to do your post, you need somewhere to keep your balls of string and your brown paper, so I'll find you a little office.'

He walked off mumbling, 'Office? Why would I need an office?'

I called out after him, 'And just to make you happy, there'll be no heating in there,' which made Dave Smith and a few of the others laugh.

Even then, my dad didn't get the joke. 'Heat? I don't need heat. I don't like it too hot. It's hot in here already. How do you heat this place?'

We all shook our heads and turned away.

This new factory enabled us to produce large volumes of loud-speakers – very bulky, but also very lucrative.

One of the things about the electronics industry is that innovation is very much a matter of fashion and not just technical change. Having kept an eye on trends in the UK and Japan, I knew it was time to give my products a facelift and design a new range of brushed-aluminium-fronted products to follow the Japanese trend. I named the range the 'executive series'. I took note of reviewers' comments on the Japanese products and enhanced my models accordingly. We made a new range of amplifiers, tuners and tuner-amplifiers fronted by aluminium extrusions. Orion produced a cassette deck to complement the range – we changed its design from the old horizontal flatbed style to what became known as the front-loading cassette deck.

Imagine a separate amplifier, tuner and cassette deck all stacked on top of each other, all with gleaming, brushed-aluminium fronts, beautiful knobs and switches, lots of lights and meters – the ultimate mug's eyeful. It had a real high-quality technical look about it, and we proudly displayed the British flag on our packaging and marketing (with the exception of the Orion cassette deck, of course). We had beaten the Japanese at their own game because our pricing was far below theirs.

At that time, the effects of free circulation in the European Community had not really kicked in. In France, Germany, Italy and Spain, the importation of tuners from the Far East was restricted. Not only would importers have to pay import duty, but thanks to protectionist measures from French and German giants such as Thomson, Philips, Telefunken and Grundig, there were quota restrictions. This played into my hands. The fashion was a stack of hi-fi equipment and since the Japanese were restricted to importing small quantities of tuners, this in turn restricted their sales of complete stacks. The same import restriction did not apply to tuners made in Britain and with this in mind I looked towards the export market. The likes of Leak and Armstrong were slow to react to the change in fashion. We really were ahead of the game.

At the Sonex exhibition, held annually at a hotel at Heathrow, a good-looking man with a bushy moustache walked into our suite. His name was Pierre Sebaoun. Pierre was the archetypal charming Frenchman, a real schmoozer. He'd seen our adverts in the hi-fi magazines and wanted to import our products to sell to the French retailers.

Pierre was accompanied by a very attractive lady, Marion Vannier, who ran the business for him. Pierre, Marion and I struck up a very good relationship at that first meeting and I agreed to appoint his company, Cogel, as the representative for Amstrad in France. This was later to flourish into a massive business.

My first order from France via Pierre Sebaoun came a few weeks later. It was the first single order of over £100,000 I'd ever received. However, I didn't know the company we were going to supply, so I insisted they open a letter of credit (LC) in our favour.

The boss of this company, Mr Shuarki, wanted to visit our factory, so Pierre and I hosted him around the plant. Pierre also promised Mr Shuarki a big night out in town, something I wasn't accustomed to. Hospitality wasn't my greatest forte – quite frankly, I think it's boring talking a load of nonsense to customers who are just out for a good jolly.

We spent a tedious night at the White Elephant on the River, which was an excellent restaurant and had been a stamping ground for Ann and me and our friends. Pierre spent much of the time talking in French to Shuarki while I sat there bored. The only good thing was that they

Mum as a young woman, with her family. From left to right: Mum, Auntie Libba, my grandfather Aaron, Uncle John (who had a hardware shop) and at the front is Uncle Jack.

My dad in 1927.

Five months old and I've already survived being abandoned in a pram outside Woolworths. This was taken on 2 September 1947.

You can see why Shirley nicknamed me Mopsy. Here I'm about two years old.

Woolmer House, where we had
the top corner flat.

I was a page boy at my sister Shirley's
wedding to Harold Regal in March 1952.
My cousin Denise was a bridesmaid.

With Mum and Dad in
Springfield Park.

And about the same age,
in more formal attire.

With Mum and Dad on the way to
my cousin's wedding, May 1956.

Derek's engagement to Brenda. From left to right: (back) Harold Regal,
Harold Mazin, Dad, Derek, Mr Press; (middle) Shirley, Daphne,
Mum, Brenda, Mrs Press, Brenda's grandma; (front) me and Adrian.

A page boy at Derek's wedding to Brenda. I'm on the left, and Adrian Press, Brenda's brother, is on the right. We were to meet again a few years later.

Already showing fighting spirit. With the Hackney School Boys Boxing Club, 1958. I'm third from right, top row.

Happy at school, 1959.

The stamp I used when I set up as a 'professional' photographer.

In my mid-teens.

On the beach with my best friends. From left to right: Steve, Tony, Geoff and me, with Malcolm sitting.

With Ann, Easter 1967.

I set up Amstrad in 1966 when I was nineteen. This is the very first Amstrad branded product – a cigarette lighter!

Ann with her beloved grandfather Izzy on our wedding day, 28 April 1968.

Ann's parents, Johnnie and Rita, dancing at our reception.

Mum and Dad dancing at our reception.

My wedding day. A memorable and wonderful occasion,
but I couldn't wait for it to be over!

confirmed the order and that they'd be paying by LC. It was my first big order in the export business.

*

I'm sad to say that holidays were something I saw as a necessity for the family rather than something I looked forward to myself. Pitiful as it sounds, that was the truth. Some of the great holidays we had were down to Gerry Eriera, the husband of Ann's cousin Norma. Gerry was a partner in a fashion firm. We became very friendly with Gerry and Norma and would spend many holidays together. Since I could never be bothered working out itineraries and stuff like that, I left it all to Gerry. He would always come up with something special. Gerry and Norma were from the same kind of stock as me – ordinary, down-to-earth people from Stamford Hill and Clapton – and we spoke the same language.

The first trip organised by Gerry was Ann's and my first experience of America. We stayed for two weeks in a resort in the Catskill Mountains in the state of New York. I was dead ill with a virus for the first four days and only saw the inside of my hotel room. When I recovered, it was a real eye-opener to see how these Yanks carried on. Maybe I met a bad sample of Americans, but these people were so insincere and full of shit. They seemed to transmit and not receive. One interesting thing that happened at our hotel was that we saw a young man by the name of John McEnroe practising on one of the tennis courts.

On one of Gerry's trips, I branded him Sierra Eriera, a good name he could use for a travel agency. He had organised a two-stop holiday in Los Angeles and Hawaii around Christmastime. In LA, we stayed at the Beverly Hilton and took the kids to the usual attractions – Hollywood, Disneyland, the Farmers Market and all that stuff. Then we flew on to Hawaii.

During flights, Western Airlines ran little competitions to keep the passengers occupied. One competition was to guess the exact time we would reach the halfway point between LA and Hawaii. As a pilot, this was a cinch for me. I filled out seven forms, one for each of the people in our party. Each form had a minute's difference in the answer.

Before we landed in Honolulu, the hostess read out the names of the competition winners over the intercom. 'In first place, Simon Sugar. In second, Alan Sugar. In third, Louise Sugar. In fourth, Karen Eriera, and finally, in fifth place, Daniel Sugar.' Amusing, but quite embarrassing.

We arrived in Hawaii, a fabulous place with a completely different culture from mainland America. It was just as you'd imagine – grass-skirted girls welcomed you with flowery garlands as you stepped off the plane.

Before leaving England, I'd mentioned to Gulu Lalvani that we were going to Hawaii. He told me that his wife Vimla's family lived there and that he too would be visiting at Christmas.

The hotel we stayed in was the Kahala Hilton, the best in Honolulu. There was a large pool containing dolphins in the hotel grounds! We meandered onto the beach where we came across celebrities such as the Brotherhood of Man, who had recently won the Eurovision Song Contest, and megastars like Diana Ross. Interestingly, no one pestered these famous people. They were able to relax in peace, which they must have found quite refreshing.

Sure enough, during our stay, Gulu phoned me. I asked him and his wife Vimla to lunch at our hotel. Vimla was a tall and beautiful Asian lady who spoke with an American accent, having been brought up in Hawaii.

Sitting with Gulu over lunch was like being on *Mastermind*. He'd fire his questions at you as if he were using an M16 machine gun – probing, impertinent questions that businesspeople don't normally ask each other. 'How many of those did you buy? Who did you buy them from? Who did you sell them to? How much did you pay? Are you finding they're selling well? Are you going to get into this business? Are you going to sell that? How are car stereos doing?' Even before you had a chance to answer, he'd unleash his next question.

In the end, I called him Magnus Magnusson, which went over his head – he obviously didn't watch much TV. I asked the others to get me a black chair and put a spotlight on me because this guy was like a KGB interrogator. They all knew Gulu's ways and couldn't help but laugh. Gulu must have realised what he sounded like. 'So sorry. So sorry to spoil your holiday. I am always talking business, always talking business.'

He was right there, but to be perfectly honest, around that time of my life – at the age of thirty-one – that was all that was on my mind too. On holidays, as long as the hotel had a telex machine, I was happy. I called the office in London every day. I would be visualising the goings-on at the factory, wondering what was happening on orders and outgoing shipments. Communication was absolutely vital to me. It became my major tool in business advancement in the years that followed.

So, let's step back a moment and recap. There I am in Hawaii, sitting by the pool, best hotel in the world, Diana Ross on the beach, and Gulu there for lunch. This was Gulu Lalvani, the man who used to sell me a box of radios which I'd have to hump off his loading bay into my clapped-out minivan, no more than eight or nine years earlier. How times had changed! Those thoughts must have gone through my mind that day – they were certainly going through Gulu's mind because it was at this stage that he started to become my greatest ambassador.

He invited us to Vimla's mother's house for dinner a couple of days later. It was a fabulous place, full of servants, with a beautiful ocean view. Gulu sat there singing my praises to the family. 'You see this man? He used to come to my place, I gave him credit, I gave him some goods, I started him in business. And now he's one of the biggest manufacturers of hi-fi in England. He used to come along with his little van and sometimes Ann would be in the van to help him unload . . .'

'Hold on, hold on!' While I was quite happy to let him babble on, I drew the line there. 'Gulu, thank you for the accolades, but please, now you're getting carried away with yourself. Ann was *never* in the van; she was *never* unloading.'

'You sure? You sure, Alan? I'm sure I saw her in the van.'

'I don't think so. In fact, Gulu, the first time you actually met her was a couple of days ago in the Kahala Hilton!'

'Is that right? Is that right, Alan? I didn't realise that. Maybe I'm getting a bit confused.'

'Yes, you are getting a bit confused. But carry on, carry on, Gulu –

I'm enjoying hearing my life story,' at which the family and friends started to laugh.

I told him, 'If you could speak English properly, or write English properly, I'd let you be my biographer.'

'Oh, you're so funny, Alan, a very funny man. Yes, not only a good businessman, but a very, very funny man.'

So Gulu had become my PR consultant and still to this day tells the same old stories. It's funny how if you convince yourself enough about something, then as far as you're concerned it's a fact. He still swears blind that Ann used to be in the van with me. Total nonsense.

Earlier in the holiday, I had broken away from Ann and the kids and flown from LA to San Francisco to visit the head office of Dolby Laboratories. I needed to obtain a Dolby licence and get our latest cassette deck approved. After making the new range of aluminium-fronted amplifiers, we had decided to design our own front-loading cassette deck and stopped buying from Orion.

I spent a whole day in Dolby Laboratories with a test engineer, checking the unit out. Sadly, it failed. I urgently telexed Mike Forsey with the reasons. We submitted a new sample and finally got approval. We had become a Dolby licensee. This might not sound much now, but in those days it was a big deal. Dolby licences were only granted to large companies, so we had joined the big boys.

The car stereo market was doing very well for us and, as a quick learner, I soon found that Orion were not the be-all and end-all in this area; in fact, there were others who made better stuff. So, as well as moving my cassette business away from Orion, I also looked elsewhere when it came to sourcing car stereos. Otake's main henchman, Itakura, who had been present at our past meetings, was fully familiar with the Amstrad/Orion history. This bloke was always very serious and had the sternest face I have ever seen – in another life he could have been the commandant of a Japanese prisoner-of-war camp. Despite severing our relationship with Orion, he always kept in touch.

My new car stereo supplier was a company called Unisef, an arch-competitor of Orion. I used to love winding up Otake by telling Itakura that his car stereo prices were now off the radar and not only were Unisef cheaper, but they had a far better range. Otake's attitude was one of disdain, as if he didn't care. But his henchmen used to ask me privately afterwards how many we were buying. This, I knew, was under instruction from the Emperor, so I embellished the quantities to wind him up a bit more.

*

Wally for Wireless was a shop in Mile End Road, originally founded by Wally Segal, but now run by his son Harold. I had formed a friendship with Harold, who was a very nice fellow. He was the sort of retailer who was behind the counter every day; he touched and felt the products and knew where the market was going. Feedback from Harold was priceless. The quantities of goods he would order were much smaller than I would normally accept, but I made an exception in his case and supplied him. This turned out to be a good move. Of course, I could have consulted the buyers from the larger companies who *in theory* should have known what was going on, but the real insights came from Harold, who was there on the shop floor. From him, I'd get the inside track on the way the market was moving, much quicker than I ever would from the giant companies. Harold was later to accompany me on a trip to Japan to source new ideas.

Harold's cousins ran a company called Stella Electronics, who expressed an interest in my car stereos, but wanted them under their own brand name. It is interesting to look back on how flexible I was at the time. Although I was intent on promoting the Amstrad brand, my mind was open to supplying these guys with their own branded car stereos to sell through their own channels of distribution. The way I saw it, it was extra volume and margin to a new market I had no connections with.

The problem with being a middleman between Stella and Unisef was not disclosing my supplier to Stella and not disclosing my customer to Unisef. I asked Ronnie Colson to handle the shipping. To do this, Waco formed a trading name – Amstrad Japan. This arrangement gave credibility to the notion that Stella was importing from Amstrad and it kept my supplier and customer isolated from each other.

The exercise also gave me first-hand experience of OEM trading. OEM stands for original equipment manufacturer. These manufacturers have no trading brand and don't sell to retailers but rather to others who *do* have their own brands. It showed me how one could make a margin on products without even touching or seeing the goods and OEM turned into quite a lucrative business.

*

By the late seventies, Japan wasn't the only country on my radar when it came to the latest technology. Hong Kong had just started to make transistor radios and small tape recorders as the technology migrated from Japan – the margins in low-cost stuff were no longer of interest to the Japanese; their culture was always one of moving on to the next technology. But what I was starting to see – and would witness over the course of the next twenty-five years – was the emergence of South Korea and the explosion of the electronics industry in Taiwan, culminating in the world domination of manufacturing in mainland China. I would also witness the more flexible and versatile nature of the Chinese compared to the very cautious and formal nature of the Japanese.

In February 1978, I ventured to South Korea for the first time. Downtown Seoul – what a dead-and-alive hole that place was. When I returned home, I told people that if the world had haemorrhoids, *that's* where they'd stick the suppositories.

I was warned by Waco Trading that a military-imposed curfew existed in South Korea and all Korean subjects had to be off the streets by ten o'clock at night. Foreigners *were* allowed on the streets after ten, but the problem was that there were no taxis, no cars, nothing. So if you were out somewhere at nine o'clock, there was a mad rush for a taxi to take you to the Chosun Hotel, the only Westernised hotel in the city.

While in South Korea, I visited a firm by the name of Lucky Gold-Star, a large electrical company which mainly supplied the domestic market. Lucky GoldStar, known today as LG, grew over the next thirty years into the massive giant it is now. I was there to discuss the possibility of buying twelve-inch black-and-white TVs. The importation of TVs was restricted by European government quotas in order to protect giants such as Philips, Thomson, Telefunken and Ferguson. An import licence was required, and I had obtained one to import 3,000 black-and-white TVs.

I negotiated the deal with Lucky GoldStar on this one-day visit. When I got back to the hotel, I rang Gerry Mason in England. I wasn't an important supplier to Comet back then, but he was intrigued when he heard I was calling long-distance from Korea.

I told him I had 3,000 black-and-white TV sets. His reaction was, 'You need a licence for those, sunshine.'

'I've got that, Gerry.' He went quiet for a while.

'You got a licence? How did you get a licence?'

'Well, Gerry, I have, so just take that as fact. I'm calling to see whether you want to buy them.'

After a bit of negotiating, he took the whole lot. He wanted them exclusively. It was a done deal as far as I was concerned, but the word 'exclusive' lodged in my mind. It's a word I would come to hear many times. Exclusivity was something that every retailer would ask for and it was something I would struggle with in years to come, needing to juggle orders to maximise volume. I mastered the art of juggling as the years went on.

Leaving Korea was like being let out of prison – I felt I was going to be shot any moment. Most people were dressed in uniform-like black jackets done up to the neck and they looked at me and my Western clothes as if I were some kind of alien. They had seen foreigners before, but perhaps not so many of my age.

Outside the Chosun Hotel, I waved down a taxi to take me to the airport. A smartly dressed Korean businessman in his forties was standing next to me and asked if he could share the taxi to the airport. We exchanged business small talk and when we arrived at Seoul Kimpo Airport, he wished me farewell and plonked a copy of *Playboy* magazine in my hand. I couldn't quite understand why. 'Read it on the plane,' he said.

I flew to Osaka in Japan, the nearest airport to Otake's offices. When I arrived in the customs hall, a customs officer grabbed the *Playboy* magazine and asked me, 'What is this?'

I shrugged my shoulders, 'It's a magazine.'

Within minutes, four or five officials had gathered round. 'What's the problem?' I asked.

The officer opened the magazine and showed me the pictures of nude women, telling me, 'This is not allowed in Japan.'

That bastard at Kimpo Airport knew what he was doing. Instead of chucking this forbidden magazine away, he dumped it on me. They took me to some special room where they studied my passport and wrote down my details.

Thankfully, one of them spoke English. I explained what had happened. 'I am in the electrical business and someone gave me this magazine at the airport. I am not an importer of men's magazines.' The officer sort of smiled and told me that they would have to confiscate the magazine. I didn't object – I was just happy to be free from this interrogation.

The UK market was moving towards car hi-fi. In-car graphic equalisers and massive bass speakers were becoming quite popular. You would stick the two speakers on the back shelf of the car, mount the graphic equaliser under the dashboard and connect it to the car radio, and the effect was twenty-five watts or so of music power blasting out. Many Taiwanese factories made this stuff and I was interested in buying it. We spent a couple of days visiting factories and I placed orders for some of this kit to enhance my now large range of in-car entertainment.

Like Harold Segal at Wally for Wireless, Colin Lewin, one of my old mates, had transformed his business to in-car entertainment, concentrating on selling high-ticket items made by Blaupunkt, Grundig, Pioneer, Bosch and Sony. He had his ear to the ground and I used him as my own personal product manager.

Colin wanted to stick to the big leading brands, but as his roots were that of a trader, he couldn't resist dabbling in the low-end market. He stocked Amstrad in-car entertainment as what he called his budget range and he gave me some great advice as to what kinds of specifications were required. I had learned another lesson: never forget your old colleagues from the early days, as they may come in handy later on.

My product range had become quite diverse: hi-fi equipment, cassette decks, black-and-white TVs and in-car entertainment. In fact, it was so diverse that it was becoming difficult to formulate an advertising strategy. Up to that point, individual products had taken the hero positions on full-page adverts.

One day, Gerry Eriera asked me whether I had a job for a young man, Malcolm Miller, who had trained at Birds Eye in the marketing department and was now looking to move to a smaller, more dynamic company.

Marketing – another word for advertising? Some would argue not. I argue that most of our marketing budget went on advertising, with things such as exhibitions included. We were unsophisticated in those days and didn't recognise the power of PR that we'd come to know in later life (though even now I'm not convinced it's *that* powerful).

Malcolm seemed a quite clean-cut fellow with a nice way about him and he put across what he thought he could bring to this dynamic company. I'm not so sure he knew too much about the products technically, but he'd done his homework and certainly understood what we were selling and who we were selling to. Malcolm came at a good time. I needed to employ someone who could deal with the donkey work of the advertising we were doing. I wanted to be involved with the ideas and direction in general and leave it to someone else to handle the photographers and generate the final artwork.

One of the first projects I gave Malcolm was to come up with a packaging design for a new range of car speakers and also work through some advertising ideas. My unpaid marketing expert Colin Lewin told me that the bee's knees in car speakers was Pioneer – their kit was selling like hotcakes and the Taiwanese were effectively copying them. The packaging design for our kit looked identical to Pioneer's – even the typeface was the same, albeit Amstrad's was in our corporate plum colour while Pioneer's was blue.

He'd done a good job in conjunction with our advertising agency, who handled all the artwork, which was swiftly sent to Taiwan. Within weeks, we started to sell these speakers and they were a tremendous success. Colin Lewin lapped them up, as did Comet, Laskys and G. W. Smith.

One day, Colin asked me, in passing, 'Are you sure you're not going to get into trouble with these, as they're virtually identical to the Pioneer ones?'

I didn't quite understand what he meant at the time, but I would certainly find out later!

*

Because the electronics industry was really booming in the mid to late seventies, a merchant bank had suggested to Laskys, G. W. Smith and a wholesaler called Eagle Products that they should combine their powers and form a public company known as Audiotronic. This sounded like a good idea, as the shareholders of all three companies would get a large capital payout when the new company floated on the stock market. They went ahead and offered 40 per cent of the shares to the market. The money received was divided between the original shareholders in the appropriate proportions. The company seemed to run smoothly for a while, but very soon rumours were rife within the industry that all these personalities and egos were having problems, jockeying for power. From what I recall, there were various management reshuffles internally.

After trading for a year or so on the stock market and not seeing any significant increase in share price, some directors became disenchanted and had the customary 'irreconcilable differences' with the board. They left the company and no doubt disposed of whatever shares they had left in Audiotronic. Audiotronic got itself into poor financial order and appointed a so-called company doctor to help them through the rough times.

One day, Kenny Lasky asked if he could come to see me. This was a rather unusual move. Kenny's father and uncle were nice enough fellows – tough but fair – although it was hard doing business with them. I guess they remembered me as the little hustler and I always felt they were reluctant to purchase from this kid, but then again, as true retailers, they had to buy what was selling.

Kenny was also a decent fellow, but he had this air of aloofness about him. When I spoke to him, he would be a bit dismissive. Some might say he was slightly jealous – after all, he must have heard from his father how this young kid from Clapton had grown this big hi-fi business. I don't know whether that was on his mind, but it's certainly the impression he gave.

So there I was, meeting with Kenny Lasky, who, in one of the innumerable reshuffles at Audiotronic, had been promoted to be the man who buys all the stuff. During his visit, he explained that his strategy was to expand Audiotronic's business. He asked whether I would mind meeting privately with the company doctor at his father's flat at Regent's Park.

Intrigued, and with nothing to lose, I agreed to go along. His father, Harry, was hovering in the background in a very nice lounge overlooking the park. Kenny introduced me to the company doctor, a slim, bespectacled Jewish man in his forties, who did all the talking. The long and short of it was that Kenny had recommended to the board of Audiotronic that an acquisition of this new up-and-coming company, Amstrad, would be very interesting. They had done some calculations and suggested to me that they'd like to acquire 75 per cent of my company, leaving me with 25 per cent. And they offered to pay £2 million for this 75 per cent share.

This was around November 1978. Here was I, the boy from Clapton who used to hustle around with empty Tizer bottles, now being offered two million quid. I guess this sum would equate to around fifty million in today's terms.

I'm quite proud of myself when I think back to the response I gave at the time. Instead of jumping at the offer, I coolly asked for clarification. If Audiotronic were going to buy 75 per cent of my company, I wanted to know whether they'd be running it as a separate company or as part of the Audiotronic group.

The company doctor bullshitted that they had expertise in the public company area and saw an opportunity of floating Amstrad separately on the stock market, and that when they did, they would make a lot of money on the 75 per cent they owned, as indeed would I on my 25 per cent.

I went home and told Ann about this. Typical of her, she said something like, 'Very nice, what are you going to do?' To Ann, if it were two million, twenty million or two hundred million, it would make no difference. All she was interested in was good family life and the welfare of those she loved.

The offer, of course, was preying on my mind. I didn't really have anybody to consult with. I had no partners; I certainly wasn't going to tell Tricky Dickie or any of the others about this, as they wouldn't understand. It might have even demoralised them, as they enjoyed the family dynamic of the firm and wouldn't relish the prospect of being part of a large group.

I did mention the deal to Ashley Morris, who said I should take the money and run. And I talked to my accountant, Neville Shaw. He was very excited and told me how proud he and his partner Guy Gordon were of me. I'd been using their small firm in Old Street since I started and they'd both seen me grow from this acorn into an oak. Neville enthused about how unbelievable this was and that I should grab the opportunity – again, take the money and run. But, at thirty-one years old, where was I going to run to?

I was in a quandary. Suddenly it dawned on me that if I were to go ahead with the deal and be acquired by Audiotronic (who owned Laskys and G. W. Smith), my other big customer, Comet, would get the raving hump. There was no way that Comet would buy goods from, in effect, Laskys and G. W. Smith, which is what I would become if I agreed to the deal. Neither would my smaller customers, such as Henry's Radio and a host of others, buy from Audiotronic. It's just one of those things – people don't want to buy from their competitors, even if it means cutting off their nose to spite their face.

It occurred to me to go above Gerry Mason's head and speak to his boss, Michael Hollingbury. I had only met him once or twice very briefly, when I visited their Hull headquarters and popped into his office to shake his hand. I was quite nervous about phoning this guy – he was the big boss of Comet, and Comet was the leading retailer in the country.

Michael Hollingbury was a gentleman. Although his family and background was in Hull, he was obviously educated at a public school. He spoke with a very posh accent and was ideally positioned as the chairman of a large public company.

I explained the situation to Michael. I guess I was testing him for two reasons. One was to see whether, if I did go ahead with the Audiotronic deal, he would threaten to stop buying products from me. The other was to see whether I could elicit a counter-offer from him.

I figured he might think that if Audiotronic were going after this, then perhaps he should step in and do the same.

He listened quietly to what I was telling him and gave no reaction other than to tell me he would get back to me in a couple of days. When he did, he said this to me: 'Young man, you have a good business and these Audiotronic people know that. In fact, I think you have a better business than they do. They're going nowhere, but you *are* going somewhere. However, we at Comet are *retailers* and we need to stick to what we know, so we would not be interested at all in being associated with any manufacturer [that was nice to hear – he classed me as a manufacturer] because of the obvious negative effect it would have with our other suppliers – in other words, your competitors.'

He finished by telling me that he'd made contact with Kleinwort Benson, a merchant bank in the City of London, and had set up an appointment for me to talk the matter through with them, as they would give me good independent advice. I went along to the meeting and was introduced to a gentleman by the name of Tim Holland-Bosworth, a typical City gent, rather tall, very posh-sounding, slicked-back hair, tortoiseshell glasses, pin-striped suit, striped shirt and a bright-red tie. We spoke about the company and Tim agreed he would visit me and investigate what advice, if any, they could give me.

Tim's initial instinct was that Audiotronic was trying to leg me over. He reckoned if they were offering me £2 million for 75 per cent as a starting point, they were trying to steal the company and it must be worth more than that. He suggested I could go back to them and demand more, but at the same time I should seriously consider whether I wanted to work for someone else again. I told him straight-away that I didn't like that idea at all; indeed, the so-called company doctor looked a real slimy git to me.

That's when Tim told me his other idea – that Amstrad could be floated on the stock market. This was an exciting prospect, but he immediately added that a lot of work would have to be done before-hand and the timing would have to be right.

This was around spring 1979. He told me that he would come

back to me, possibly at the start of 1980, to see if anything could be done.

*

Amstrad had grown to such a size that the accounting firm I used was getting out of its depth, so I moved to Mordant Latham & Co. The senior partner was a gentleman called Neville Shearman who also acted as a liquidator specialising in the electrical industry. I knew this because after a few of my customers went bust, I naïvely attended the creditors' meeting, thinking there might be a chance I'd get paid what I was owed, only to find it was a waste of time. Normally, by the time the liquidator gets involved, there's hardly any money left to be paid out. And even if there were, it would be something like ten pence in the pound, which you'd get two years later.

Neville informed me that a supplier of mine – a company by the name of Fircastle Ltd – had gone into liquidation. They were a wood-working factory who supplied us with speaker cabinets of our own design. We'd then fit the speaker units, wire them, test them and finish them off.

It was bad news to hear that Fircastle was going bust, but it occurred to me there was a deal to be done. Perhaps it was time for me to move into the cabinet-making business. Neville told me that tenders were going out to the industry to see whether there would be any par-ties interested in buying the company as a going concern. From my point of view, losing Fircastle meant that I would need to find another cabinet supplier, so I moved very swiftly and made them an offer of £50,000 to buy the plant and all the machinery. However, Neville told me that there was another party interested – guess who?

Gulu Lalvani had heard on the grapevine that my supplier had gone bust and he was poking his nose around, making a bloody nuisance of himself. I called Gulu and asked him what he was doing sodding around, knowing that he had no intention whatsoever of run-ning a woodwork factory.

'No, Alan, we are very serious,' he said. 'We really want to buy this factory. We are going to start making speakers, just like you do. We are going to move into the hi-fi separates market.'

I knew that Gulu's customers were not the type that bought speakers; they bought radios and tape recorders, or fancy goods like watches and lighters. I accused him of simply messing around trying to put a spanner in the works, which he denied. When you put all of Gulu's bullshit about how he admired me and all that to one side, he had this perverse streak in him. I wouldn't say it was jealousy, but he had this tendency to try to scupper his competitors. He obviously thought I was one of them. In the end, I agreed to give him five grand to go away.

This was typical Gulu. Of course he didn't need £5,000 – he had a good business. The money was insignificant, but the fact that he'd managed to pull the wool over my eyes delighted him.

I acquired the assets of Fircastle Ltd and had the option to keep the factory in Stock Road, Southend-on-Sea. It was a move away from my ethos of not getting involved in manufacturing, but this was a different situation – speaker cabinets were the lifeblood of the company and the margin on speakers was fantastic.

I shot down to Stock Road and met the factory manager, Harold Livesey, who was anxious to find out what my intentions were. At the meeting was an engineer by the name of Mick O'Malley, who was responsible for keeping the machinery running, as well as a burly Geordie called Norman Thorne, the production manager.

They must have seen me as some kind of Santa Claus. I assured them there and then that no one was going to lose their job and that Amstrad was going to take over this factory and keep it running. However, we would no longer be selling speaker cabinets to other manufacturers – the factory would be making them for Amstrad only. What's more, I told them I would be transferring the *entire* assembly process to Stock Road. This would mean they'd have to learn how to wire up the speaker units and circuit boards inside the cabinets, and pack them up as finished products ready to ship to customers.

Harold was a bit wary. He was a cautious fellow and worried about whether the layout of the factory could accommodate this additional work. I later found out that this was typical Harold. He was one of those guys who would say, 'No, it can't be done, it's impossible,' and then a day or so later he would tell you that he'd worked out a way of doing it.

By sheer coincidence, Nick Lightowler at Comet informed me that one of their speaker manufacturers in Norway, with whom they had exclusivity on a full range of speakers, had gone bust. It must have been fate! Nick could not have known about the major commitment I'd just made. I told him I had just acquired a cabinet-making works and would like a chance of tendering for that business before he rushed off to other speaker manufacturers.

I'll fast-track this story, as there's a lot to tell. After several weeks of liaising with Comet's technical people, we got the order for a whole range of new speakers branded Solavox – a name owned by Comet.

When I look back, I can see how I managed to beat people like Wharfedale and Kef. These manufacturers had their heads so far up their arses about promoting their own brands, they were reluctant to make speakers on an OEM basis. Comet had cleverly realised the massive margins that could be made on speakers and, to be fair to them, they brokered a great deal with me. When I saw the retail prices they were selling these speakers for, they were doing pretty well for themselves too, earning much more margin than they would have ever got using Kef or Wharfedale. It was a win-win situation.

Often, people who bought hi-fi amplifiers or tuners would fix on the brand they wanted, then leave it up to the retailer to suggest a pair of speakers. Naturally, Comet's salesmen strongly recommended Solavox.

Harold, Mick and Norman must have thought I was a magician. Within weeks, they had to set up another production line to make these new speakers. The staff got into the spirit of Amstrad. Previously, they'd been treated as faceless workers by their paymasters. Now they were dealing directly with the boss in a more exciting way, getting involved with me on product design, costings, sizes and so on.

The process of making speaker cabinets in those days was rather cumbersome. Most were made of high-quality chipboard and had teak veneer glued onto the outside, which would then go through a series of processes such as staining and polishing. It was real craftsmanship. But important changes were afoot in speaker manufacture.

When I was in Taiwan, I came across suppliers of a vinyl material on which was printed a wood-grain effect in teak, walnut or oak. The only process required was to lay the vinyl on the chipboard. Although it was just plastic sheeting, it was very realistic.

The problem with vinyl however was *psychological*. I spoke to Nick Lightowler and showed him some samples of a speaker we'd assembled using vinyl, pointing out to him the consistency of the grain. He was easy-going and agreed with me that the cabinet was much cleaner and that most consumers wouldn't know the difference. Regrettably, both Gerry Mason and his technical manager had a different view. They wanted real teak veneer cabinets, simply because that was the tradition. I had also upset Comet's technical manager, Bill Coupland, by arguing with him on the phone over this matter and he had gone into belligerent mode and was not budging from his position. I needed to move fast before the whole thing went tits up.

I loaded the back of my small plane with some sample cabinets, flew from Stapleford to Beverley Airfield in Hull, got an audience with Gerry and Bill and showed them the various shades I could offer and the beautiful consistency of the graining.

I convinced Bill that, from a technical point of view, the sound quality would not be compromised – a fact he could not deny. He could see I was no mug and knew what I was talking about. It was important to win this point in front of Gerry, as it then became just a cosmetic issue.

Gerry piped up that the process surely must be much cheaper than veneering and he wanted a reduction in price. Here was some light at the end of the tunnel – another business lesson to learn. Let your opponent win *something*. There I was, banging my point home like a sledgehammer, when I realised that it's no good boxing people into a corner; if you really want to succeed, you need to let them win a little and leave them with a nice way out.

I went into reluctant mode and moaned, 'I'll be losing money,' and all that stuff. I grudgingly agreed to reduce the price by £5 a pair for the largest speakers, £3 for the mid-size and £2 for the smallest. They had won something and they agreed to the deal. I was at the races! Vinyl was the way forward and we had made a bold move in being the first to produce hi-fi speakers with vinyl-covered cabinets instead of veneer – something that the rest of the industry rapidly caught on to.

I gave the good news to Harold and told him he needed to sharpen his pencil and get the costs down as I'd given away some of our margin.

The vinyl manufacturer in Taiwan had never sold vinyl in volume before in the UK, so he was hungry to get it off the ground. I said to Harold, 'Let me loose on this Taiwanese mob – I'll have a chat with them.'

With a bit of nifty work, I managed to get the vinyl supplier to provide the special machinery required free of charge to our chipboard supplier, on the basis that it was an investment for them. In return, I convinced our chipboard supplier not to charge us for the additional labour involved in gluing the vinyl onto the chipboard; just to charge for the chipboard and the vinyl. It was another win-win situation – I'd done the chipboard supplier a big favour and in time he was able to expand his business and supply everyone and his brother with vinyl-laminated chipboard.

*

My limited company was formed on 8 December 1968. By June 1979, turnover had risen to £5.6 million, with profits of £908,311.

I didn't realise it at the time, but behind the scenes Tim Holland-Bosworth and his team had been beavering away investigating Amstrad independently. They couldn't just take my word on the company's performance because the owner of a company will obviously sing its praises. I always say that you have to take whatever claim is being made, divide it by two and take away the first number you thought of, and then maybe you'll get to the *real* situation. People are passionate about their businesses and tend to overlook certain issues which others may deem negative. Kleinwort Benson made sure that I had no skeletons in my cupboard, such as a criminal record or problems with the Inland Revenue. Just before Christmas 1979, Tim called me to say that he felt it was time for us to explore the possibilities of a public flotation. It was an exciting way to end the year.

8

'Amstrad to Go Public'

A Towering Success

1980–3

In January 1980 I got my first taste of City life and City people. The boy from Clapton went to the headquarters of Kleinwort Benson and sat in a boardroom with a load of posh-talking bankers to discuss the possibility of floating Amstrad on the stock market.

They were discussing *my* company, but the terminology that was flying across the table was totally alien to me. Terms such as P/E (price/earnings) floated around. The last time I'd heard the term P.E. was at school, where it had stood for physical exercise. Imagine me sitting there and being asked questions like, 'What do you think your P/E should be?' I had no idea.

One of my better traits is that I'm open and honest. I remember saying to these people, 'I'm a simple man from Hackney and, to be perfectly honest, I am in your hands. I haven't got a clue what you're talking about, but I'm a very, very fast learner. So if you wouldn't mind, perhaps you could explain things to me in simple terms. The things you're talking about may be common knowledge to you, but they're completely foreign to me.'

I think they found this refreshing and they certainly seemed to enjoy going into educational mode, debating amongst themselves the best way to explain things such as P/E to me, the thicko. It was quite amusing watching them jockeying for position to see who was best at putting these things into layman's terms.

We decided to go forward and draft a prospectus or 'offer document'. Tim Holland-Bosworth was cautious, telling me that the market was vulnerable, and he made it perfectly clear that the effort which was about to be expended on this exercise may come to nothing, as they might not be able to get the offer away. I didn't really understand what he was banging on about, but agreed to go forward.

Apparently, the first thing I needed to do was clean up the limited company. At the time, the only directors were Ann and I. Tim explained that we needed to have a proper board structure. He suggested we keep it simple, but as a minimum we would have to have a financial director. I duly appointed Jim Rice as financial director and Ann resigned. We also needed to assemble a team of advisers. As I was completely out of my depth in this area, Kleinwort Benson arranged a fashion parade of advisers for me. To cut a long story short, I agreed on accountants Touche Ross (now known as Deloitte), lawyers Herbert Smith and stockbrokers Greenwell.

The adviser from Touche Ross was Mr Michael Middlemas, a very serious professional who acted not only on the flotation committee, but also as an independent financial adviser to Amstrad. Herbert Smith's team was made up of Edward Walker-Arnott, a well-respected corporate lawyer who went on to become the senior partner, and his sidekick, one Mrs Margaret Mountford. Greenwell's representative was Mr Howard Miles.

Margaret Mountford, who was then in her late twenties, came across as a real fiery character, very serious and exact – you could see she knew her stuff. She was short and very smartly dressed, as one would expect a City lawyer to be. Howard Miles was another typical City gent, quite tall and slim and decked out in standard pin-striped attire.

We all got together on a regular basis for what were called 'drafting meetings'. After the fourth or fifth meeting, a draft document appeared which would eventually be sent out to the public if and when the flotation happened.

Hours and hours were spent over many days drafting and redrafting this document. This continued throughout January, February and March. Between meetings, Tim Holland-Bosworth would come out to our premises to investigate the new products we were making. Kleinwort Benson was putting their name and reputation behind the offer for sale, so they had to make sure they had a great understanding of the company. In those days, reputation was of prime importance. The institutional shareholders' trust was based upon recommendations from bankers such as Kleinwort Benson.

On one occasion, Jim Rice and I were given a tutorial by Edward Walker-Arnott and Tim Holland-Bosworth about 'the yellow book' – the stock market rules. We were warned about things such as insider trading and how the financial figures and results of the company must always be kept secret, and how directors had to ensure complete openness and independence. They made their point very well. It really registered with me that confidentiality and adherence to the yellow book was a matter that had to be treated very seriously.

It suddenly occurred to me one day, while sitting in the luxurious offices of Kleinwort Benson, enjoying the wonderful sandwich lunch that was always served at these meetings, that somewhere along the line there must be some costs ticking up. There must be something in it for all these people. Was I going to get a whacking great big bill? How stupid of me only to realise this after a couple of months! I had the audacity to raise the subject, which caused a few red faces around the table. Michael Middlemas told me that the fees for the advice given by Herbert Smith, Touche Ross, Greenwell and Kleinwort Benson would have to be paid for by Amstrad, and they would be in the order of a quarter of a million pounds – at least!

I went mad at him, quite unfairly. He couldn't understand why I was so angry. Obviously these people wanted paying, but I had stupidly overlooked this. I ranted on, 'There is no way I'm going to pay a quarter of a million pounds with no guarantee that the company will be floated.'

Moreover, no one had discussed with me how much money I was going to get, or how many shares I would have to sell, or even the value of the company in the market. Talk about quick learner! Once the penny had dropped, I was on the case and made it quite clear that these drafting meetings should be cut down to a minimum, so that costs would not escalate.

In March 1980, I was informed that we needed to pad out the board a little, with what were known as non-executive directors. These were independent directors who would sit on the board and represent external shareholders, making sure the company was run correctly. I appointed Neville Shearman, my former accountant and auditor, and Ronald East, who was put forward by Kleinwort Benson. Our accounts were audited by Touche Ross.

I recall a meeting around early April 1980 with Tim Holland-Bosworth, Michael Middlemas and Edward Walker-Arnott that turned out to be the most important meeting of this whole saga.

For a new flotation, one would normally look at the industry sector and find another company in the same business, then take their P/E and apply it to the profits one was going to declare at flotation. In simple terms, post-tax profits multiplied by the P/E number will equal the market value of the company. Once you have that figure, you simply divide it by the amount of shares the company has issued and you get the share price we all see listed in the financial papers. So if your post-tax profits were, say, £625,000 and the P/E ratio for the sector was 12.7, the stock market valuation of your company would be around £8 million. And if the company had ten million shares in issue, the share price would be 80p. So the higher the P/E ratio established for Amstrad, the higher the value of the company would be and, when we finally got down to discussing how many shares I was going to sell, the more money I would receive.

Initially, the discussions revolved around what the profits of the company were going to be at the year-end, post-flotation. In 1979 we had £908,000 profit on the clock, verified by Touche Ross. The profits forecast for the year in which we were going to float were around £1.3 million.

Bearing in mind the 52 per cent corporation tax at the time, this would result in a £624,000 post-tax profit and the P/E ratio, established at 10 by Tim, put a value of £6.24m on the company. He made a point of saying that as Amstrad was rather unique, there was no sector to compare us with and as such he had to 'stick his finger in the air' and break new ground and *invent* a P/E. In a mad moment, I told him that this was totally unacceptable. After all that hard work, he was trying to tell me my company was worth only £6.24m. To cut a long story, we established a new P/E ratio of 12.7.

With a 12.7 P/E ratio, the company was valued at around £8m, and Holland-Bosworth suggested I offer 25 per cent of my shares to the public, which would earn me about £2m.

He added, 'See what we have done for you, Alan – do you see? Audiotronic offered you two million pounds for seventy-five per cent of Amstrad – we're bringing you almost two million for twenty-five per cent.'

To this day, I don't know whether his P/E suggestion of 10 was a tactic or not, but I couldn't argue with his logic over the £2m for 25 per cent as opposed to Audiotronic's £2m for 75 per cent. It goes to show one thing about these City people – when you cut all the bullshit and highly technical nonsense, at the end of the day, the value of the company was simply fixed at what Tim fancied, as indeed there *was* no direct comparison to Amstrad. The good news was that after months of meetings and deliberations – and some impatient chants from me along the lines of, 'Are you going to put up or shut up?' – Tim finally announced, 'Okay, we are going ahead – we are going to float your company.'

It was a great deal for me. Up until then, I had no personal wealth – everything was in the company. It was time for me to cash in, in part, on all my efforts from back when I'd started trading in my own name fourteen years earlier.

On 23 April an announcement was made to the public, by way of a press release, that Amstrad was going to be floated. The *Evening Standard* newspaper stands had posters splashed across the front of them: 'AMSTRAD HI-FI TO GO PUBLIC'. It was an exciting time.

All this public company stuff had been kept secret. Even my family and friends didn't know anything about it, so it came as a big surprise to all of them. There were also constant phone calls from some of my customers and suppliers, congratulating me on this unbelievable event. Small-time guys I'd dealt with in the past sent me telegrams.

While I had established myself as a good brand within the hi-fi industry, now, from a public perception point of view, I was the rags-to-riches success story. The boy who was born into a poor tailor's family and brought up on a council estate in Hackney now had a company valued at £8m and was collecting a cheque for nearly £2m. It really captured the imagination of the media.

We had just come out of a recession and Amstrad was the first flotation to occur after those depressing days. The Thatcher administration had been voted in the previous year and the meteoric rise of Amstrad was seen as a welcome sign of better financial times ahead. The rags-to-riches story was right in line with the culture that Thatcher was to trying to nurture – the ethos that 'anyone can do it'.

The offer-for-sale document was sent out. Adverts were placed in the *Financial Times*, the *Daily Telegraph* and the *Evening Standard* inviting members of the public to subscribe to the shares. One thing that was always emphasised in the drafting meetings was the need for the flotation to be over-subscribed – this would show confidence in the company. As it turned out, the shares were *ten times* over-subscribed, which was quite phenomenal.

What this also meant was that over £20m had been sent to Kleinwort Benson awaiting fair distribution of the shares. Prospective shareholders would each get approximately 10 per cent of the shares they requested.

Michael Middlemas asked me whether I'd made any arrangements with Kleinwort Benson regarding the interest that would accrue on the £20m during the month or so that the money sat in escrow. I didn't quite understand what he was driving at. He elaborated, telling me that if I wasn't careful, Kleinwort Benson would keep all this interest for themselves and that I should insist upon it being paid to Amstrad.

I didn't need further prompting and called Tim Holland-Bosworth. He told me it was traditional that the interest accrued on over-subscriptions was always taken by the sponsoring bank and that he felt disappointed I was laying claim to it, particularly since I'd been so stingy when agreeing the fee for flotation.

He went on to explain that I had broken another record – that Amstrad had managed to float with costs of no more than £225,000. He added that I should be satisfied with this result and that any interest accruing in the escrow account would be a little icing on the cake for all the hard work that Kleinwort Benson had done over the previous few months.

I might have known sod all about the workings of the stock market, but I showed Tim he wasn't dealing with some wet-behind-the-ears schmock. Although I'm not suggesting for one moment there was a deliberate attempt to deceive me – the situation regarding the interest was simply an anomaly we'd never discussed – I had carefully consulted with Edward Walker-Arnott and Michael Middlemas as to whether Kleinwort Benson had entitlement to the money from a legal point of view. It turned out they had no claim on it whatsoever and, in fact, the money was Amstrad's, not theirs.

Armed with this information, I said to Tim, 'Naïve I may be, slow I am not,' and I reminded him of that first meeting three months ago when I'd warned him I was a quick learner. I started to rattle off some legal terminology I'd written down in consultation with Edward Walker-Arnott. Frankly, I didn't have a clue what I was saying, but Tim must have sussed out that I'd taken advice and he was stuffed.

With Tim's back to the wall, I started to feel a little uneasy. Perhaps I was being ungrateful. After all, here was the man whom *I* had consulted and who had brought me around £2m of personal wealth, an amazing sum for a thirty-three-year-old. This guy wasn't against me; he'd been helping me. I didn't want to leave a sour taste with Tim. He genuinely felt hurt – he had taken this young bloke from Hackney and made him into a legitimate player. I remembered some of the lessons I'd learned: always give the people you're dealing with an elegant way out and share some of the prosperity with those that help you make money.

I suggested to him a fifty-fifty compromise, which he graciously accepted, and we shared the accrued interest. The bank base rate in 1980 was 16 per cent. If you had money on deposit, you could get 14 per cent easily. Think about twenty million quid on deposit at 14 per cent for a couple of weeks or so – you're talking over fifty grand's worth of interest per week.

Going public had some benefits for my staff, as they each received a 'pink form' which gave them preference in the share allocation process. I explained that if they sent the form off with a cheque for however many shares they wanted, they would get them all. To be fair to the staff, not many of them had much money, so they subscribed to modest amounts.

My brother Derek dabbled in these new offers; not just in

Amstrad, but on other flotations. The game was to get an allocation of shares which, when trading started in the market, would be at a premium. If the punter then sold them, he or she would make a profit. Derek had successfully done this a few times and now he explained to my father that the pink form was like gold dust – he could not lose. My father subscribed, almost begrudgingly, still not understanding the process, wondering whether his son Alan was up to some scam. Amazingly, he still had this air of mistrust about him when it came to this public company stuff – very sceptical, very suspicious. He simply didn't understand what was going on.

The shares launched at 83.3p and as soon as trading started, they rose to 95p. All the flyboys got out quickly, selling their allocations, which were taken up by institutions. The shares settled back to about 87p after the first couple of days' trading, but quickly rose to 95p again.

Then my dad finally got the plot. 'I like this game,' he said. 'I laid out eighty-five pence and now they're worth ninety-five! Can I have more?'

'No, Dad, it's too late now – just stick with them and leave them.'

These were euphoric times. I had become a mini-celebrity in financial circles. My face was appearing in countless newspaper articles, as the rags-to-riches story ran and ran. It had not occurred to me that my fame would have an effect on my children.

Simon, now eleven years old, came home from school and told me his teacher had seen me in the papers. Daniel said the same. The kids at school were asking them what this all meant. 'Your dad's a millionaire – lend us a few quid,' the kids would say. Children can be spiteful and sometimes it would be a bit upsetting for Simon and Daniel.

My mother cracked me up. Typical Fay, she'd be in Ridley Road market buying her groceries and people who knew her would stop her in the street. 'Ooh, Fay, I read about your son. Isn't it wonderful? Isn't it marvellous?'

She would get the raving hump. 'Yes, wonderful, marvellous. What's it got to do with you?' would be her reply.

My sister Daphne would kill herself laughing when she went shopping with my mum in those days. 'Mum, this is a great thing. Why are you telling people off? Why are you telling them to keep their nose out of your business?'

'It's not my business – it's Alan's business. Who needs people coming up to me saying all these things?'

'Mum, they're being nice; they're being polite. They're just saying how wonderful it is.'

'Yeah, well, they should mind their own business. What's it got to do with them?'

She couldn't stand the publicity. I think it stems from the fact that Jews had a bad name for money-hoarding, so it was best to be understated rather than ostentatious about one's wealth. It was bad enough that I had been riding around in a Jensen, but the newspaper articles about me having lots of money was a nightmare for my mum and, I guess, for my dad too. This instinctive self-protection mechanism from the aftermath of the Holocaust was deep in the psyche of many Jewish people of that generation.

*

I duly received my cheque from Kleinwort Benson for £1,941,931.25. It was an unbelievable feeling to have this in my hands. I took it home and showed it to Ann. Typically, she shrugged. 'Wonderful, very, very nice.' She had no real enthusiasm.

I photocopied the cheque and immediately rushed it to the bank. I showed the photocopy to my brother and sisters, who did share my excitement. I had two million quid in the bank – unbelievable!

Unfortunately, the Chigwell Mafia was alerted.

Alan Sugar, the chap they'd previously passed on the shopping parade with their noses held high, had suddenly become a local celebrity. People were now saying to me, 'Hello, how are you? How are things?' and trying to engage in conversation.

A bit of my mum came out in me. Not over the wealth issue, but more that these people wouldn't have given me the time of day before and now suddenly they wanted to talk to me. It wound me up a lot and I'm sure I must have come across as rude and dismissive.

The same thing happened with Ann. Suddenly people who had previously ignored her wanted to talk to her. In fairness, it wasn't a case of them expecting any financial favours; it was more that they wanted to be associated with Alan Sugar of Chigwell.

In the Jewish circle of the Chigwell Mafia, the Don at the time was Mr Clive Bourne. The whole community looked up to him. He was a wealthy individual who had inherited part of his fortune from his family business. He resided in Roding Lane, in a house previously owned by the boss of electronics giants Plessey. Clive would hold court with his admirers and was perceived to be *the* man. I think I had dethroned him somewhat, though I still lived in what was considered a modest home compared to those in Roding Lane or Manor Road.

Sitting at home one evening, there was a knock on the door. Standing outside were two gentlemen, Mr Paul Balcombe and Mr Stuart Rose, two of the Don's admirers. I was surprised to see them and didn't really know who they were. I invited them in and they sat down in the lounge.

Paul Balcombe explained that he led the fundraising within the local Jewish community and that I now needed to join the club and start contributing. His attitude came across to me as very arrogant, dictatorial even. He spoke with a real insistence in his voice, telling me I *had* to do this and I *had* to do that. Stuart Rose sat there quietly, nodding in agreement. It was clear that the Chigwell Mafia had appointed these two to make an approach to me.

Balcombe had heard that I was a man of few words and rather blunt, so he decided to adopt an aggressive attitude, which perhaps he thought might impress me. He was wrong. I was burning up with fury at what I perceived to be this very presumptuous and supercilious fellow. How dare he dictate to me what I should do as regards charitable donations? In fact, the matter hadn't crossed my mind at the time, but I certainly wasn't going to be dictated to by people who, up till then, had passed me by on the street.

Finally, my temper overcame me and I told Balcombe to mind his own bloody business. I didn't need him to tell me which charity I should or should not support. I swiftly showed them the door and effectively kicked the pair of them out.

Ann told me I was too harsh, but I was furious. She tried to calm me down while I stormed up and down saying, 'I don't like the attitude of these people. Who the hell do they think they are?'

It was a few years before I actually got on speaking terms with Paul Balcombe. Stuart Rose was actually a very nice fellow. He was the local optician and everybody went to him for their glasses. He lived opposite me, next door to Gerry and Norma, and on some occasions when we socialised with them, Stuart and his wife Valerie would pop in. I think Stuart apologised to me for the famous meeting.

My £2m was sitting in a deposit account earning an amazing 14 per cent interest – over £5,000 a week, an incredible figure. Meanwhile, I had met up with a chap called Howard Stanton, a very nice fellow. He was well respected in City circles and chaired fundraising for the local Chigwell & Hainault Synagogue. The synagogue had debts following the recent addition of an extension to the main building. Together with Howard, I worked up a scheme. The synagogue would open an account at Lloyds Bank in Islington and I would deposit the whole £2m for a period of nine months, by which time it would have accrued a lot of interest. At the end of the nine-month period, the £2m would be repaid to me and the £200,000 interest would go to the synagogue.

This was an innovative and tax-efficient way of making a donation to the building fund and it worked like a dream, after some nifty work with the lawyers. In gratitude, they put a plaque in my name at the entrance of the synagogue. This was a proud moment for Johnnie. He came to Chigwell & Hainault Synagogue one Sabbath – instead of his usual Beehive Lane haunt – probably just to look at the plaque and boast to a few of his mates whom he'd dragged along. Well, good luck to him, it was his moment of glory – his son-in-law had done something he was *really* proud of. This donation to the synagogue showed the Chigwell Mafia how I really operate.

*

Ann has never been a demanding person, but she's very funny in some ways. When she gets a bee in her bonnet about wanting to do something, she becomes very determined.

The children were getting older and, while Ann is not materialistic in any sense, she wanted us to move to a larger house with more space. She employed the services of local estate agent Cyril Dennis (after a few minutes' conversation I got the impression that if you shook his hand you'd need to count your fingers afterwards – but I often feel that about estate agents). Loads of property details came through from Cyril, none of which we liked.

Manor Road was deemed the place to be, but I never really liked it. It occurred to me that we should drive around the Chigwell area ourselves and look at houses we wouldn't mind buying. Ann thought this was a nutty idea, but at least she saw I was signed on to her desire to move. We drove around and identified four or five homes that looked good. I wrote a letter to each of the owners. Next day, I went out with Daniel in the car and he shoved the letters through the letter boxes. Interestingly enough, we received replies from most of them, polite responses thanking us for our interest but telling us they had no intention of selling. All apart from a Mr Derek Higgins, the owner of a house known as Bramstons in Roding Lane, the most prestigious road in the area – the Don's house was in Roding Lane. It had actually come onto the market four years earlier and we'd had a look at it, another of Ann's whims. The lady who'd lived there for the past eighty years, Mrs Pratt, had passed away and it was in a completely dilapidated state. I'll never forget the first time I viewed Bramstons. In what's now my study, there was an old Bakelite telephone on the windowsill and in the centre of the dial was written 'CHIGWELL 8'. This was the number that had been allocated to the Pratt family dating back to the earliest days of telephony – they had the only eighth telephone in Chigwell!

We didn't buy the house at the time, as it was derelict and really needed to be bought by a builder – Derek Higgins was just that. He was a well-respected man who ran a very big firm, D. J. Higgins & Co. Now, three or four years on, he had decided to sell it and contacted me. Ann and I were round there like a rocket, having noticed the magnificent refurbishment that had taken place.

While Derek and his wife showed us around the house, Ann was digging me in the back, as if to say, 'This is it. You're buying this whether you like it or not.' Each room we walked into, she'd dig me in the back one more time – I was getting the message loud and clear.

We sold our house in Chigwell Rise to a young couple. It was nice to see these newlyweds wanting to buy the house that Ann and I had enjoyed for so many years. I never really negotiated hard on it and sold it to the fellow for £100,000. Ten years earlier, I had paid £27,000 for it.

Once we moved into Bramstons, we built a swimming-pool and a pool house, as well as a state-of-the-art tennis court on the land adjacent to the house. Tennis is a passion I still have today.

With all this work going on, we needed to landscape the garden and I was introduced to one of the funniest characters I've ever met – Arthur Sewell. His claim to fame was that he was the chief groundsman for Valentines Park in Ilford, and what he didn't know about landscaping and horticulture wasn't worth knowing. The trouble with Arthur was that he did not stop talking. Yap, yap, yap, yap, yap. He had this way of saying, 'Righto, sir. Okay, sir. With respect, sir. Understand that, sir.' Everything was 'sir', or 'madam' when he spoke to Ann.

Arthur would get hold of me as I was about to leave for work and quote the Latin names for shrubs. 'There you are, sir, this is a *Cupressus Wilma*, known for its lemon smell if you rub the leaves in the palm of your hand. Just smell that, sir – lemon, see, sir? That is *Cupressus Wilma*, sir.'

'Righto, Arthur. Well done, son. Nice.'

'Well, I hope you appreciate the work, sir. I'm working very hard, sir. With respect, very hard, sir, making sure you're going to have the best garden in Essex.'

'Fair enough, Arthur. I've got to go now.'

'Righto, sir. See you on the weekend then. By the way, sir, I've noticed around the tennis court they haven't done a very good job in laying the stones. May I respectfully suggest, sir, that you allow me to put in some paving around the area that will allow you and your lovely lady wife to walk up to the tennis court without getting your shoes dirty.'

'Fine, Arthur, fine. Just go ahead and do it.'

'With respect, sir, I wouldn't do it without you giving me the okay, sir. I don't know how much it's going to cost; I'll give you a price later on, sir.'

'Fine, Arthur. Get on with it. Now I've got to go.'

'Righto, sir. Have a good day.'

If you've ever watched the TV programme *Columbo*, you'll know that one of Lieutenant Columbo's traits was to look as if he was leaving and then come back and say, 'There's just one more thing, sir . . .' It was the same with Arthur.

'Sir, just one more thing, with respect, we need to buy some Hayter mowing machines, sir. The rubbish we've got here at the moment is no good, sir, with respect. Is it okay with you, sir, if we go down to the garden centre and buy some mowing machines, sir?'

'Yes, Arthur, go and buy some mowing machines. Go on, off you go.'

'Well, once again, sir, I don't want to spend your money without you knowing.'

'Right, Arthur, I'm going now. Please don't talk to me any more today, thank you.'

'Righto, sir, I know you are busy. Thank you very much, sir.'

You could never escape from him. I used to get the kids to go outside and see if he was around and when the coast was clear, I'd make a quick dash for the car.

I also inherited a gardener called Dennis Croak, who used to do the garden for Derek Higgins. Dennis was a lovely chap and he still works for me today. Arthur took Dennis under his wing, instructing him how to mow the grass, how to deal with the flowerbeds and all that stuff. Dennis, who's a little deaf and wore a hearing aid, would look at me, shake his head and shrug his shoulders, as if to say that Arthur was driving him nuts. Many's the time I would call after Dennis and get no response. When I walked up to him, he would say, 'Sorry, Alan, I switched off my hearing aid because Arthur was driving me mad.'

Arthur had planted an array of trees around the swimming-pool to protect it from the wind. One evening, there was a knock on the door. Arthur had a solemn look on his face.

'Sir, I've come to report a disaster. A disaster of the highest proportions, sir – a death, sir.'

'What?! Who's dead?'

'Sir, young Dennis has *murdered* a Leylandii.'

'What are you banging on about, Arthur?'

'Come with me, sir, I will show you.'

We walked out to the garden, near the swimming-pool. The trees that had been planted no more than a year earlier had a stake adjacent to them to keep them upright. Apparently, Dennis had used some plastic string to tie the tree to the stake. As the tree trunk grew, the string had cut into the side of the trunk and, according to Arthur, this was murder.

'I told him, sir, that there are special things you can use which expand as the tree grows. But did he listen to me, sir? No, he didn't, sir. He's used plastic string and here is the result of it, sir – murder in the first degree!'

'Will you shut up, Arthur, please. It's a bleedin' tree.'

'It's not a bleedin' tree to me, sir – I watched this thing grow. And now I'm going to have to find you a tree of a similar height, so that it will grow to the same level as the others.'

'But, Arthur, the tree doesn't look dead to me.'

'Trust me, sir. With respect, this tree *will* die. The tree will die, sir.'

'Well, I don't think it will. It looks very healthy, so give me a pair of secateurs and I'll cut the string. You put one of your expandable straps on there and let's leave it for a while.'

'Sir, you are questioning my horticultural knowledge.'

'Shut up, Arthur. Just leave it for another six months and see what happens. If you're right, we'll replace it. If not, we'll leave it.'

'Righto, sir. With respect, you're the boss. I'll do as you say, but don't blame me when the lovely lady of the house looks out of the window and sees this thing wilting. With respect, sir, just remember my words.'

On this particular occasion, Arthur was wrong. The tree is still there today. It's scarred, but it has grown to over fifteen feet.

*

While I was working on the details of Amstrad's flotation, our newest product, the tower system, was flying off the shelves. The idea for the tower system had come to me the year before, partly as a result of the success of the executive series. These gleaming-fronted hi-fi separates looked superb when mounted in a complementary wooden rack.

Originally, the Japanese had taken the lead on this concept of providing a wooden rack to stack the hi-fi on. The fashion for wooden racks fell straight into our lap – they were easy to make and we supplied them in a flat-pack format for end-users to assemble themselves. The rack had three shelves on which to place an amplifier, tuner and cassette deck. On top you'd place a record deck, while at the bottom was a storage area for cassette tapes and LPs. The rack was fronted by a smart tinted-glass door and the whole system was complemented by a pair of speakers.

The whole package was quite expensive by Amstrad standards, but still half the price of its Japanese competitors. It sold very well, particularly in France. In the UK, this equipment sold predominantly in hi-fi stores such as Laskys, G. W. Smiths and Henry's Radio. However, it was still too expensive for the mass retailers such as Dixons, Currys and Rumbelows to stock. They tended to concentrate on more consumer-oriented products such as TVs, music centres and portable radio cassettes.

Cogel was exhibiting my stuff at the Festival du Son in Paris in February 1979, so I flew over there to visit the stand. There's a lot of spare time at these exhibitions when you sit around waiting for customers and, while talking with Pierre during one of these spare moments, I had a brainwave.

We were discussing what scope there was for reducing the price of the racked hi-fi system to make it a mass-market item. Through this stimulating debate, it dawned on me that each of the items on the rack – the amplifier, the tuner and the cassette deck – had its own power supply, transformer, power cable and plug. There was also a whole mass of spaghetti behind the rack, where the separate components were connected to one another – a real jungle of cables. These alone were very expensive. On top of that, there were a lot of other duplicated electronics residing in the separate units. If I were able to make an item in a simple wooden cabinet which, from the front, looked as if it had a separate amplifier, separate tuner and separate cassette deck, but was in fact one lump containing all the electronic guts, with one power cord coming out of the back, this would save a tremendous amount of money.

On the back of some scrap paper, I started to sketch the profile of a proposed front panel with deliberate gaps between the amplifier, tuner and cassette deck sections. The gaps would be cleverly designed to give the illusion of separate items.

Pierre was excited and very helpful – it's fair to say that part of the idea was down to him. People in my position often find it hard to give credit to others – I guess it's the male ego. For most famous business-men, it's true to say that *somebody* helped them on their way, but many are a bit frugal in dishing out praise to others. *I* am happy to say that Pierre Sebaoun is one of the people who deserves some of the credit here.

I couldn't get back on that plane quick enough. When I got home that evening, I called Bob Watkins and asked him to come into the office early the next day, as I wanted to tell him about this great idea. We met at 8.30 and sat sketching at his drawing-board. By the end of the day, Bob had drawn up a brilliant-looking front panel and our engineer Mike Forsey had already thought about the elimination of redundant components.

In a couple of days we had a complete construction drawing of what was to be known as the Amstrad 'tower system'. I was already scheduled to go on another trip to the Far East later in the month and this time I took Bob Watkins with me.

We had been purchasing some tuner modules from a company called Morse Electrophonics in Hong Kong, who were owned by Morse USA. Phil Morse was the boss and effectively the king of audio in America. They made large, silver-fronted music centres, but the market in America was down for that type of junk, so their Hong Kong factory was struggling for things to make. Their salesman was Moshe Mor, an Israeli whose job it was to solicit additional business.

We set up a meeting with Morse and showed them our design con-cept. They were very excited and started rambling on how they could sell them in America. I put a stop to that immediately – I told them that if they made this product for me, they'd have no right to sell it anywhere else, as the tooling and design would be 100 per cent owned by Amstrad. In the end we spent four days in Hong Kong negotiat-ing with Morse, going through the bill of material on every single component, item by item, ending up with an agreement to pay them a labour and overhead cost, plus a 5 per cent margin.

One has to admire the industriousness and efficiency of the Chinese. They are unbelievable in their work ethic. The deal was struck at the end of February and my requirement was for them to ship the finished product by August, for it to arrive in September, so we could start supplying the market. It was a tight deadline and they started beavering away. A week later they'd produced a mock-up sample of the front panel. It looked a million dollars, with its shiny silver knobs, switches and meters.

As soon as the mock-up arrived, Harold built a cabinet around it and we photographed it. The target price for this product, fully assembled in a rack, with a record deck mounted on the top and supplied with a pair of speakers was £199 retail. This would undercut the Amstrad separates version by £150, let alone the Japanese competition.

Armed with photographs of the new tower system, we set about calling on all of our dealers and raised a lot of interest in the traditional channels we sold to.

In May there was a trade show held in Kensington. We took a room in the Kensington Palace Hotel and proudly displayed the mock-up of our tower system – model TS40 – in its cabinet. John Drazin, the buyer from Woolworths, popped his head round the door. He was a funny-looking fellow, strange and very abrupt. He didn't know me from Adam, but I happened to be standing next to the TS40, so he asked me, 'How much is that?'

I told him that the trade price was around £120, to which he immediately replied, 'When can I have some?'

I knew he was Woolworths' buyer, so my ears pricked up. I explained that they would be available in September.

'Have you got a sample for us to test?'

'Not yet, but possibly in a month or so,' I replied, not really knowing when we would get the first working sample.

'Right, well, subject to me testing the working sample, we'll take a thousand of them.'

I was taken aback, but tried to remain outwardly calm.

Throughout the course of that exhibition, we must have taken orders for 5,000 of these units, all based on a mock-up sample. Clearly we had a hit on our hands.

In early August, Bob Watkins went off to Hong Kong to start the production line running at Morse's factory. By the end of the month, the first thousand pieces had been produced and loaded onto a container, the fastest vessel we could get, which had a thirty-day transit time from Hong Kong. Bob arranged for ten of these chassis to be air-freighted to the UK, so we could make up working samples and jigs at the factory. Harold did a great job setting up the production line and as soon as the bulk cargo arrived, we flew into mass production and started to honour the Woolworths order.

Malcolm Miller, in conjunction with an advertising agency, took some three-quarter-page advertisements in the national press, which sparked the attention of Comet. I'd mentioned the product to Nick Lightowler, but bearing in mind that his division of Comet specialised in true hi-fi, he'd given a lukewarm response, saying it wasn't suited to Comet.

However, the day after our first advert appeared in Thursday's *Daily Mirror*, Nick phoned me to say that perhaps he *would* like to try some of these things. His branch managers had been calling him, knowing that Comet normally sold Amstrad products, asking whether these tower systems were on the way.

At the bottom of the advert, it said, 'Available at Woolworths,' as well as a few other smaller retailers' names. Nick asked me to add Comet's name on the next bunch of adverts.

We started supplying Comet, but I received a rather irate telephone call from Gerry Mason. He bellowed down the phone, 'If you supply Woolworths then you're not supplying us!'

I tried to reason with him that the tower system was more of a consumer electronics product rather than a specialist hi-fi item. I also reminded him that there were other electrical goods that both Woolworths and Comet sold, but Gerry was furious and wasn't going to give way. There I was, faced with the buying boss of Comet telling me that he was going to halt the purchasing of all Amstrad products unless I agreed to pull out of Woolworths.

I phoned Nick Lightowler after Gerry's call. Nick was rather relaxed and told me to forget it. He said, 'Gerry's just in a rage – this is his rant of the moment. It'll all die down in a week or so.'

I wasn't convinced, but Nick knew Gerry better than anyone else did, so I guessed it was best for me to keep quiet. Comet started to sell hundreds of tower systems per week, which was good news in the sense that they'd already been delivered, so even if Mason meant what he said, it was too late.

Around this time, Ashley Morris joined forces with Dennis Hart and Malcolm, amalgamating Audio Supplies with Global. The combined group continued to trade as Global Audio and they then expanded, opening several branches.

By now, Dennis Hart had changed his surname to Hadleigh, for reasons best known to himself. We all assumed it was to try to replicate the lifestyle of the TV character James Hadleigh, a dashing, handsome country toff. Dennis had illusions of being one of the gentry, with a farm and stables, going horse-riding, clay pigeon shooting and all that stuff.

However, he had one of those 'irreconcilable differences' with the board and decided he didn't like being relegated from kingpin to effectively Ashley's lackey. They agreed to part company and Dennis started again on his own. He opened a shop in Edgware Road, right opposite Paddington Green Police Station, and another shop up north, near Leeds.

As before, the business model was flawed – it was simply selling stuff at low prices to get cash flow. By now, Ashley's Global Audio was offering Green Shield Stamps to try to boost sales. For every pound they took, they were losing ten pence.

One day, I received a phone call at home and heard Dennis's dopey drawl. 'Alan, if I ask you for some invoices for stuff, will you give them to me?'

'What did you say?' I replied. 'Why do you need invoices?'

'I'm going to have a robbery and I need you to give me some invoices to support my insurance claim.'

'What? Are you fucking mad, Dennis? Get lost and don't even talk to me about this.'

'No, really, Alan, if you give me some invoices, I can make a killing.'

'Dennis, I'm going to hang up the phone now. Don't ever talk to me about such things again. Don't be silly – don't do this.'

What happened next, you wouldn't believe. Picture the scenario. His shop is bang opposite Paddington Green Police Station – the biggest and most sophisticated police station in London. As the story goes, he got a young boy who worked for him to smash a hole in the shop ceiling. He then claimed there was a break-in and that all his stock had been stolen. The police took the fact that this robbery had occurred right under their noses as a slap in the face and swung into action. Straightaway they smelt a rat and within a day the young boy had confessed that Dennis had asked him to bash the hole in the ceiling.

The next call I got was to tell me that Dennis was in Brixton Prison, awaiting processing. What a bloody idiot. I felt sorry for him and went to visit him. I remember bringing him some apples, which were confiscated by the guards who said he could only have two, not the whole bag.

I was led through a maze of locked doors before getting to the visiting room, where I saw Dennis dressed in a grey prison jacket. His eyes were bloodshot as he cried to me, 'They locked me up and put me in a cell.' It was pathetic to see this stupid man, who had tried to run with the hares and hounds, now banged up behind bars and one could only feel sorry for him.

I couldn't get out of there quick enough. When I got home, I told Ann what I'd experienced and called Ashley and Malcolm to report this pitiful sight. That was the last time I saw Dennis. He was sentenced to two years in prison and I have no idea what happened to him after that.

The inevitable happened at Global Audio and they called in the liquidators. They went well and truly bust, with debts of £400,000, catching Amstrad for about £20,000 in the process.

One of the side-effects of their demise was that my brother-in-law, Mark Simons, was out of a job and asked if I had a position for him in Amstrad. Mark was a good salesman and at the time we were weak in the sales area. With the addition of our tower system, we needed to expand our customer base to companies such as Currys, Rumbelows and other big chains.

Mark came onboard and was tasked with breaking into the electricity boards, which sold electrical goods in their High Street stores. I concentrated on Currys, which was trusted by the public as the place to go if you wanted a TV, a hi-fi, a fridge or a washing machine. I had tried to contact Michael Curry on several occasions, but he wouldn't take my calls any more, which fascinated me since many years earlier I *had* managed to get him on the phone. I think what happened was that their business had grown so large, he'd become a real bigshot who would no longer talk to suppliers.

I was therefore left to deal with the buyers – a real arrogant lot. I cannot tell you the number of times Dickie Mould, aka Boycie, and I sat in the reception of Currys House in Ealing looking at the fish pond. You'd see the buyers coming down in the elevator, then they'd look at you and simply walk past, saying they were going for lunch. We would have to sit around waiting for them to come back and only then would they graciously grant us a few moments of their time. Now you have to understand that Currys (and later Dixons) had huge buying power and could make or break a business. The buyers knew this and could not help but come across as high-handed and arrogant.

I managed to get an appointment with Ken Sladen, Currys' audio buyer, and took Boycie with me. Ken was a bit of a cool character, trying to make out he wasn't impressed by the numbers I gave him on how many tower systems Comet and Woolworths were buying. Eventually, he agreed to sample a quantity of 200 units in selected branches to see how they went and I told him I'd add Currys' name to our advertising, along with the words 'selected stores' in brackets.

They started to sell like crazy in Currys. The speed at which the first 200 left the stores was incredible, so much so that, unusually (normally you had to *chase* buyers), I received a phone call from Ken. Again holding back, not wishing to show too much excitement, he told me that the units had gone *relatively* well and that perhaps he should roll them out to all the branches and he casually asked whether I'd be able to supply 2,000 units.

They were on the hook and it was time for me to have a bit of fun. I told them it was very nice to hear they wanted to roll them out, but my production was flat out. I couldn't deliver 2,000 units quickly, but I'd try my best. The truth was, they had taken customers' money and were now selling the samples. They already had orders for 450 pieces and they needed them urgently. It was funny to hear Ken suddenly switch from his laid-back tone into desperate mode. Of course, I was fully aware of the importance of a breakthrough into Currys and we managed to accommodate his requirements over the course of the next few weeks.

Before we knew it, we were making and selling approximately 25,000 tower systems per month, and we hadn't even scratched the surface as far as France was concerned, the place where the product was first conceived.

By this time, our business had got so big that we needed to open our first office in the Far East. Stan Randall was at a loose end, having regrettably had some matrimonial problems, so I approached him to see if he would like to start a new life running our Hong Kong office and liaising with all our Asian suppliers. He said yes. The Amstrad Hong Kong office was to become the hub of design. We recruited a couple of young mechanical engineers, Vitus Luk and Isaac Ip, who were to become two of Amstrad's longest-serving employees and, in fact, are still employed by them today.

Stan also appointed a secretary, Callen So. This highly intelligent young lady spoke perfect English and had a brain like a computer. She got to know every detail of the business within a month, and would remember every price, every shipment and every costing. She was so good, I eventually brought her over to England and she became my right-hand 'man'. I have to say, she was the nearest thing to *me* when it came to knowing every aspect of the company. Simply amazing.

Stan had put together a good team who were going to become very important to the future prosperity of Amstrad.

*

Word got around the Far East about Amstrad buying large quantities of chassis from Morse. We had become a big fish in the pond and as a result I was contacted by the Taiwanese company Hawson. I had heard of them and knew that their expertise lay in making loudspeakers. Although our speakers were being made at our own factory, Bob Watkins and I agreed to visit the Hawson factory in Taipei, where we were guided around their speaker production lines.

They quoted some prices for speakers and, after a few calculations in consultation with Bob and Harold by phone, we found they were able to supply fully assembled speakers at a much lower price than ours because the speaker drive units inside the cabinets were made in Taiwan, whereas ours were made in Italy. Also, with lower labour costs and economy of scale at their factory (which was also supplying the American market), they had a greater buying power with the chipboard makers, the drive unit makers and, of course, the Taiwanese vinyl suppliers.

There was one problem – the bulky size of the finished speakers. While they were cheaper than ours, when one added $4 per pair for shipping, it didn't look so great. It occurred to me that if we got Hawson to produce the speakers in such a way that we could pack more into a container, then freight costs would come down.

This next statement is going to make the real hi-fi nutters cringe. The depth and height – in fact, the overall volume of a hi-fi speaker – is something that should be calculated scientifically on the basis of producing the best baffle effect for the sound, but my criteria were different. I asked Hawson to attend another meeting and, after lots of sketching and calculations, we worked out how to get the most speaker shells out of the eight-by-five sheets of wood. We decided the speaker's dimensions should be the most economic size to ship, rather than be designed for perfect sound quality. Under these criteria, we were able to stuff at least 50 per cent more pairs of speakers into a container, thus reducing the freight cost to about $2 per pair.

At the last minute, I also insisted that the price must include the speaker cables to connect to the tower system. This eleventh-hour piece of chutzpah shook them a bit, but when I told them we were talking 25,000 pairs of speakers per month, they agreed.

Hawson was an aggressive and growing company who wanted to go into electronic production and, under their own initiative, they bought some of our tower systems from England and examined the chassis. They suggested that *they* could manufacture them in their newly acquired factory, which was fully equipped with Toyota-style production line belts and lots of auto-insertion machines. It was far more efficiently laid out than Morse's factory, which was a typical Hong Kong workshop, with people humping assemblies around left, right and centre.

Hawson's boss told me that he would tool up, at his expense and with no obligation, a copy of our tower system and make me some samples. I didn't want anyone copying my product, so I insisted that if he *did* tool up the front panel, then we would pay for the tool and have the ownership of it. In fact, I said that I wanted to pay the toolmaker directly, so there could be no misunderstanding, and he agreed.

The decision to go with Hawson turned out to be quite fortunate, as unbeknown to me there were problems ahead with Morse. Stanley Neichin, the managing director of Morse Hong Kong, asked if I would meet up in Hong Kong with his boss Phil Morse, whom he'd told about the success Amstrad was having.

Phil Morse was in his mid-sixties and looked like a cross between Walter Matthau and the Jewish comedian Jackie Mason. His opening gambit was that he was a legend in America – he was Mr Audio. Apparently, this was true at one time, but what he'd forgotten to mention was that he was talking about five years ago. Since then, his company had failed to move with the times and its finances were starting to wane. But what shocked me was that he started to talk about *his* tower systems and how he was going to display them at the forthcoming consumer electronics show in Chicago.

'Hold on a minute,' I said, 'they're not *your* tower systems, they're *my* tower systems. I paid a hundred per cent for the tooling.'

'Nah, you may have paid for the tooling, but we've put in all the effort and all the engineering. We lost a lot of money designing and developing them in the early days. Let's look at it this way – they're not yours, they're ours.'

'No,' I said, 'they're mine. And, with respect, you are not going to show these things in Chicago, as you would be exhibiting a product that belongs to me.'

'Don't worry, don't worry, I'll put them on display as samples. We won't take any orders. If we get any orders, we'll talk about it.' A compromise was reached on that basis.

Phil Morse was from a Polish-Jewish background and would come out with typical Jewish sayings. Surprisingly, he mentioned that Otake had been one of his suppliers in the past and I thought it quite interesting to pump him a little on his opinion of the Emperor. 'An arrogant meshuganah – you have to know how to deal with him.' Those few words summed him up beautifully. Meshuganah is a Yiddish word meaning madman – not mentally ill, but someone who's highly strung with some weird ways and crazy mannerisms.

Later that year, I attended the CES show in Chicago, the biggest electronics show in the world. I realised how big a company Morse was when I saw their stand, which was the largest one there, right by the main entrance. I'd agreed to meet Phil Morse at their stand and when I arrived, I couldn't help but notice my tower systems were on display. Before I announced myself to Phil, I thought I'd ask some of his staff about the product. Typical Americans, so full of shit. They spoke about how they'd developed it themselves and how it was the new direction in hi-fi, following the Japanese trend, and they told me it was red-hot as far as sales were concerned. I took that with a pinch of salt, but nonetheless they *were* taking orders.

To cut a long story, I had a blazing row with Phil Morse and started to get lawyers involved. I told Morse that I was finished with them – completely. What's more, they had to stop selling this product immediately unless they came up with some financial compensation. This fell on deaf ears. Phil Morse didn't believe I would take it any further. He had a big shock coming because I'd already learned a bitter lesson about copyright.

I referred earlier to Malcolm Miller designing a range of car speakers, which basically we copied from Pioneer. This was to bite us on the nose. One day we received a very formal solicitor's letter containing lots of drawings and documents in legalese. I knew this was serious. I consulted a partner at Herbert Smith – Tony Willoughby, a specialist in this area.

He took a look at the letter and at the products and told me, 'You have a seriously big problem. What idiot in your company would have done something as blatant as this? Do you not understand the world of copyright? Didn't the corporate people do due diligence on your company before it went public to ensure there was no chance of litigation?'

I agreed with him. We had made a naïve and stupid mistake and we were most probably about to learn a hard lesson. In fact, Colin Lewin had tipped me the wink that Pioneer were up in arms and were going to take legal action. To cut to the chase, the result was that we had to deliver about 2,000 sets of speakers to Pioneer, who duly destroyed them.

So, armed with this prior experience, it was clear to me that Phil Morse was bang in trouble. One thing he hadn't realised was that I had taken the precaution of getting a signed piece of paper from Stanley Neichin and Moshe Mor saying that the tooling and design were my property, that we had fully paid for it and that they had no right to use it without our permission. I showed this to Phil Morse, but he kept going on about the fact that they had lost lots of money developing the tower system and that he felt we were partners.

Herbert Smith wrote to Morse's lawyers in America, telling them to stop producing immediately. Herbert Smith also had offices in Hong Kong and they teed up the partner there to serve some sort of injunction on Morse Hong Kong. It took a while for the penny to drop with Phil Morse. The guy was such a bigshot, he felt he was untouchable. He didn't expect me to go to these lengths, but he must have been alerted by his attorneys that he was now up against it. It finally brought him to the table and in the end they agreed to pay us $5 for every unit they sold.

Stanley Neichin was a bit of a slippery customer. He had made several mock-up samples of products just different enough from Amstrad's tower system to avoid infringing our copyright. Shortly afterwards, they went into production and shipped them to the USA. More significantly, and nastily, he went on a trip to Europe touting these products around. And guess who he bumped into?

You got it – Gulu Lalvani.

Gulu had no assembly plant at the time; he was just an importer.

Nevertheless, he would bullshit, saying that he wanted into this business. He had no intention of doing so – he didn't know the first thing about assembly – but he took great pleasure in calling me to say that he'd just had Stanley Neichin in his office and was going to place an order with Morse for these units.

I gave Gulu a bit of his own punishment. 'Really? How much has he offered them to you for?'

'How much does he sell them to you for?' he said.

'No, how much has he offered them to you for?'

'Fifty-seven dollars.'

'Oh, very good, very good, Gulu. Good price, you've done well.'

'What do you mean? What do you mean I've done well? Is it a good price or not?'

'Let's just say you've done very well, Gulu. Not like you to pay over the top though.'

'What? Is it too expensive? Too much?'

'Do you expect me to tell you what price to pay? And anyway, what am I wasting my time talking to you for? You've got no intention whatsoever of starting up a production line.'

'Yes, yes I am, at Wembley. We're going to get a big place and we're going to start assembling. And we also have new premises at Milton Keynes and we're going to set up a production line there.'

'Good. Well, good luck to you, but I have to tell you that Stanley Neichin's mock-ups are crap and we've already moved on with another model.'

'Another model? What other model? What features has the other model got? Who's making it for you? Morse?'

'Mind your own business. Wait and see.'

This slippery lot at Morse were *out* as far as I was concerned. It taught me to be very careful about choosing new partners and subcontractors when inventing new items.

Hawson had come at just the right time. Bob and I flew off to Japan and had our usual trip around Akihabara before visiting Hawson in Taiwan. Bob referred to me as Hawk-eyes because he didn't know how I managed to observe every single detail of something I'd spotted in Akihabara. In one of the stores selling up-market equipment used for professional recording, I noticed in the corner an industrial unit made by Sharp with a twin cassette deck for copying tapes.

Bingo! Something sparked off in my mind. On the plane from Tokyo to Taipei, Bob and I sketched up a tower system with a *double* cassette deck mechanism. One of the cassette mechanisms would be play-only, while the other would be the normal play-and-record type, the idea being that consumers could dub their own tapes.

When we arrived at Hawson's factory the next day, they had diligently prepared a mock-up sample of our tower system. They had enhanced the design of our TS40 and, frankly, it looked much better. I found out later that they'd used the services of a proper industrial designer, and it showed. I told them that we would be interested in going ahead on the basis that the bottom cassette section was modified to a twin cassette deck. Bob had drawn up something with a bit more detail overnight, which he handed to their designers, and within two days, they'd modified the mock-up sample. It was a drop-dead killer product.

From my previous experiences with Morse and Pioneer, I was becoming a bit of a copyright lawyer. I called Willoughby from Taiwan to ask what kind of paperwork I'd need to ensure these people couldn't rip me off. The problem was, Taiwanese law was a bit ropey and it would be very hard to enforce any judgement against them.

He telexed me with some details and I got a secretary at the hotel's business centre to type up an agreement. They were so hungry for this business – their first venture into the electronics market – that they signed it immediately. The contract was based on English law, which gave us a little bit more security, but the reality of trying to enforce a judgment in Taiwan in those days was complicated to say the least.

The twin cassette version of the tower system, the TS55, was launched in September 1981 and took off like a rocket. I think it's fair to say that we set the template because in the years that followed, every single audio manufacturer in the world – including the Japanese and European giants – produced twin cassette audio units as staples. Our head start meant that we had a good eighteen-month to two-year run at it.

Our national newspaper advertising was being cranked up. I told

Malcolm Miller to take the precaution of putting an asterisk beside the picture of the new TS55 twin cassette tower system with its 'tape to tape' logo and at the bottom of the advert, in large, bold printing, we stated, '*It is illegal to copy copyrighted material. This machine should only be used to copy material you have generated yourself.' If you picture a full page advert in the *Daily Mirror*, the warning was in bold black letters about a centimetre high.

This was a cheeky tactic. People would read it and think to themselves, 'Hey, that's a good idea! I can use this machine to copy my mate's Abba cassette.' *That* was the effect the warning had, yet there was I, keeping within the law, whiter than white, telling people that the product should *not* be used for that purpose. Is that called reverse psychology?

While on the subject of copyright, the BPI (British Phonographic Industry) – the organisation responsible for collecting royalties on music – started to make noises that our twin cassette product was inducing the public to copy tapes. The first few letters they sent me, I chucked in the bin, but they started to get a bit heavy, so I contacted Tony Willoughby who made a statement I've never forgotten, one that has haunted him throughout his career no doubt. He said that if they kept harassing us, we wouldn't wait for them to take proceedings against us, we'd go to court and get a declaration that we were doing nothing wrong. In other words, attack is the best form of defence. He said that if he lost this case, he would give up being a lawyer and become a pig farmer. That's how sure he was.

Well, nine months later, all I could say was, 'Oink, oink.' The judge ruled for the BPI. I wouldn't have minded, but the BPI hadn't even brought an action against us. It was Willoughby's brainwave to try to get a court declaration. Naturally, he was totally embarrassed by this.

Representing us in court was a top-flight barrister, Tony Grabiner (now Lord Grabiner), and a junior counsel. As the story goes, when the judge read out his judgment, Grabiner turned to Willoughby and said, 'Don't worry about this – the judge has gone mad. We'll win it on appeal.'

We had to take the thing all the way to the House of Lords where eventually we did win. It was an historic victory which set a legal precedent – many subsequent disputes over breach of copyright have cited the Amstrad v BPI case. From my point of view, though, I could have done without this aggravation.

Through our Hong Kong office, we went on to develop the twin cassette concept onto portable radio cassettes – nobody had ever done that before either. It was a massive hit and once again became the industry standard.

It makes me laugh when I reflect on showing new products to someone like Currys' buyer Ken Sladen. Initially, he greeted my twin cassette products with great enthusiasm, but as time went by and everyone jumped on the bandwagon, he would refer to 'the Sanyo twin cassette' or 'the Sony twin cassette' or 'the Philips twin cassette' as if they were commonplace products, as if twin cassette were some sort of natural progression rather than a brainchild of Amstrad.

This was typical of retailers – they have no loyalty whatsoever. Maybe I'm a bit old-fashioned, but they conveniently forgot who put them in the twin cassette business in the first place. Instead, they would throw other manufacturers' versions in my face to try to get me to compete. The twin cassette concept was, of course, not patentable as there was nothing novel in it – industrial duplicating machines already existed.

*

In the meantime, a new market was emerging in 1981 – citizens' band radio (CB). This was effectively a glorified walkie-talkie which up until then was illegal in Britain because there was no allocated frequency for it. In the USA, CB radio had become very popular for people to install in their cars and trucks to communicate with each other while driving. Enthusiasts gave themselves 'handles', colourful names like Rubber Duck.

In Britain, the industry lobbied the government to make CB radio legal and after a lot of pressure, the government agreed. However, they allocated a frequency that was different to the USA's, which meant that instead of importing the products already being made (in the Far East) for America, the electronic circuit had to be completely redesigned. Customers were contacting me, asking whether we were going to be active in this market, and it was clear to me that as soon as there was a product available, they would buy it in volume. The first one to market was going to win.

Many Japanese suppliers were reluctant to invest in what they perceived to be the small UK market, especially bearing in mind they would have to redevelop their existing USA version. I finally found one fellow who would be prepared to make them. He told me that his company had a great relationship with Sanyo, who had embarked upon the fast-track development of a new chip for the British CB market. The first company to have a PCB ready for this chip would be the first company to be in the British market.

Things were moving very fast. In March 1981 I agreed to make a one-day trip to Japan, as crazy as that may sound. At the time, there was a British Airways Boeing 707 which landed in Moscow for refuelling, then went on to Tokyo. I jumped on a plane, landed at around 3 p.m. Japanese time and was met at the airport by Mr Shigano, the boss of the company. We immediately went to the Okura Hotel to discuss the supply of CB radios to Amstrad.

I could see this company was quite small, but to check them out thoroughly would have meant a delay we couldn't afford. The bottom line was that he promised a delivery date which would mean we'd be first to market. I wanted to get an LC to him quickly, so he could see we were serious.

The meeting went on till about 9 p.m. and after negotiating on price and exclusivity, Mr Shigano agreed to supply me. He then dropped a bombshell. In order to meet the delivery dates, he needed to have my front panel design drawing by the following morning! He warned me that if the drawing were to be delayed for a week, then so would the shipment.

My Brooke House education kicked in. I phoned room service and asked for a pencil and ruler to be brought up. Then, on Okura Hotel notepaper, I drew up the front panel design of our new CB radio based on the dimensions Mr Shigano had given me. I had to take into account where all the knobs would poke out and where the LED display would be and design the plastic front panel accordingly. I came up with two different designs: a basic model with fewer features and another up-market model which had more knobs and lights on the front panel. I intended to buy the basic model in small quantities, simply to obtain what was known as a lead-in price.

Consumers are quite funny people. They are attracted by a lead-in price, such as £39.99, but when they arrive at the point of sale and see the up-market model for £49.99, human nature makes them enquire about the better model. The salesman in the store then explains that this is the deluxe version and, nine times out of ten, the customer buys it. This technique would prove successful in the years to come.

It was 11 p.m. and I had just about drawn the outline of the front panel. I was stuck because I had no implement to draw the circles for the knobs. The Okura Hotel sewing kit came in very handy here – the shirt buttons in the kit were proportionally the right size for my drawing (it was drawn to half scale) and so I drew around one to create the four knobs on the front panel. Shigano was very surprised at our breakfast meeting the next morning when I presented him with the drawings and told him I had produced them myself. Can you imagine explaining that?

'How did you arrive at that design?'

'Er, with shirt buttons, mate!'

I had taken the wind out of Shigano's sails and I told him that now he had no excuse and could immediately start tooling the front panel. Being Japanese, he could not lose face. I then set off back to London. In the one-hour layover in Moscow I bought a set of Russian dolls as a present for Ann and the kids. This, I understood, was a typical Russian novelty. Credit to Shigano, he stuck to his word. We airfreighted in the first shipments of CB radios at great expense and hit the market in November 1981, before anyone else. This enabled us to open up some new customers, such as Rumbelows, with whom we'd not previously dealt. These were giant chain stores with hundreds of shops all over the country.

Through Ken Sladen, I'd managed to sell tower systems to Currys, but CB wasn't his department. He told me the buyer who dealt with this was Ian Radley. On this occasion, Currys' rude and arrogant attitude was dispensed with. As soon as I entered their headquarters and spoke to the receptionist, I was told to go up to the ninth floor to see

Radley. He was hot to trot to buy CB radio and wanted to be the first in the market.

He tried it on, saying he would not buy from us unless Currys had exclusivity. Then he started bullshitting about having other suppliers who had products coming, but I knew from Shigano that we had consumed the first quantities of the Sanyo chips and that we were the only company with cargo on the way.

I told Radley that there was no chance I was giving him exclusivity and, to Dickie's surprise, I closed my notepad, as if to say the meeting was over, and made as if I was going to stand up and leave. The guy got my body language, backed down and booked a massive order for quite a few thousand units. In fact, I had underestimated the size of the market, so unbeknown to Currys, their order was so large that they got exclusivity by virtue of the fact that I had nothing else to ship! I didn't let Radley know that.

I asked Shigano to see if he could ramp up production. He did accommodate my wishes, though not immediately; we had to wait a few more weeks for production to increase. There was tremendous demand in the early days of CB radio. My other customers, including Rumbelows, were starting to question me, justifiably I guess, as to why I couldn't supply them with Amstrad CB radios when they'd seen them in Currys' stores.

I explained to them that Currys had bought my first lot and paid extra for airfreight. I was stuck between the devil and the deep blue sea – either I would have to pay an extra £3–4 per unit to airfreight them in or wait an extra five weeks for them to arrive via the sea route. Many of the customers agreed to pay an extra £5 per unit for airfreight and, looking back over the whole CB exercise, we must have airfreighted in 90 per cent of what we sold.

Like all fads, CB radio died very swiftly. We supplied the market with tens of thousands of units and the first wave of nutters scrambled to buy their CB radios. This gave the false impression that there was a gold rush on. It was another lesson learned: when dealing with big retailers like Currys, their large orders fill the pipeline and can cause confusion and create a false market as far as volume is concerned.

Come the downturn in CB radio by the summer of 1982, Currys

demonstrated just how mercenary retailers are. They simply pulled the plug on taking more goods, despite the fact that they had given me firm purchase orders! The options open to me were to sue them for breach of contract or swallow it on the basis that you don't want to alienate a customer for life. This shoddy treatment by Currys taught me that an order from a big chain retailer is not worth the paper it's printed on. You can only consider that you've had an order when you've delivered and been paid.

Currys was a good barometer. Clearly they had seen their sales drop dramatically and the buyer's alarm call to me indicated that we should give up CB radio quickly. I instructed Dickie Mould to start dumping them in the marketplace at just above our cost price, which was the right decision. Some of the other customers didn't have sophisticated enough radar to see that the market was dying, so when we slashed the price of our CB radio, they thought their boat had come in, only to find they were well and truly lumbered.

We all played around with the CB radio sets, installing them in our cars and giving ourselves handles. I also arranged a base station at home for my two boys to play with – they would speak to people driving by. It was fun, but a classic example of a passing fad. The speed to market and realistic acceptance of when the market was dead was a classic case of get in, make a killing, get out, move on. I know I might sound a bit of a bigshot talking about pulling off this coup, but at the time I had no idea it would be a passing craze. It taught me a big lesson.

The shirt-button story floated around Amstrad's engineering department for years to come. They thought it was quite funny that the design of our CB radio and the dimensions of the knobs were based on the shirt buttons in the Okura Hotel's sewing kit. It *was* funny, when you think about it.

*

When we floated the company in 1980, the forecast profit published in the prospectus was £1.25m and, as recommended by Kleinwort Benson and all the advisers, we would need to comfortably beat that figure, which we duly did. That said, the share price didn't change much, remaining pretty stable. It had risen from its initial 83.3p to around £1.20, dipping to about £1.10 from time to time.

I didn't know much about the workings of the stock market, but I'm a quick learner. One of the first things I learned was not to accept everything Kleinwort Benson told me! Quite early on, they explained I would have to get used to playing the public company game and this included attending what they called 'special investors' meetings'.

I was summoned to a meeting with a bunch of people from the Middle East who expressed interest in the hi-tech sector. We were told to set up a display of some of our products in the meeting room at the conference centre and provide a member of staff to demonstrate the equipment. When I got there, the room was full of gentlemen dressed in thobes and ghutras (the traditional Arab white robes and head coverings). Apart from a couple of fellows from Kleinwort, we were the only ones in Western clothing. Tim Holland-Bosworth told me to mingle with the crowd, but I didn't have a clue what to do or say. In fact, one of the Middle Eastern guys must have mistaken me for a waiter, as I was in a black suit, because he asked me for a glass of sparkling water.

I popped over to my bloke demonstrating our stereo equipment to enquire if there had been any interest shown and couldn't resist telling him, 'Watch what you play – three choruses of "Hava Nagila" won't go down too well here.'

I felt the meeting was a total waste of my time, but Holland-Bosworth came over to me and commented on how well the event was going.

'Going well? What are you going on about, Tim? I've had Lawrence of Arabia asking for a Perrier and no one's asked me any questions about the company or the products. I don't know what I'm doing here. Perhaps I should run around with some canapés: "Here, sir, try the sheep's eye and pineapple, they are very good."'

'No, no, Alan, these things take time. Trust me; we've done a good selling job here. I'm sure they will invest.'

'Maybe I'm missing the point here, Tim. I've done my deal; I've got my money for the shares I sold – where am I going wrong?'

I still don't know what that meeting was all about. Needless to say, it was the last one I attended.

*

My next lesson came on 30 June 1981 when I got a strange phone call from some fellow at Greenwell, our stockbrokers, who introduced himself as being on the corporate side of the company. He advised me that within the company there was an impenetrable Chinese wall. People like me – the chairman of a public company – could talk to the corporate side confidentially about the way the company was performing and that this information would be kept secret from the Rottweilers on the other side of the Chinese wall – the actual traders. At the time, I just had my head down and was getting on with business. I was very happy that I'd copped my two million quid and figured that we'd just keep moving on by way of organic growth and that the share price would grow steadily.

Jim Rice had run the accounts and informed me that in actual fact we were looking like making £2.4m to the end of June 1981 – in other words, we had doubled our profits. The stock market was expecting a moderate growth of around 20 per cent, in line with what they were told a year earlier.

When Greenwell's corporate bloke rang me, he said, 'Well, Mr Sugar, it's the end of your first financial year as a public company. Do you have an indication of how well the year has gone? Is there anything I need to hear in preparation for the publication of your accounts in October?'

Without a thought, I said to him, 'Well, actually, we're doing all right. Looks like we've got two point four million on the clock.'

There was silence for a moment, then he said, 'That's fine, it sounds very good. Okay, right, I must go now, I've got a lunch to go to.'

What a bunch of bloody gangsters they were.

That afternoon I was at my desk minding my own business when Jim Rice came and told me that he'd been receiving phone calls from the *Evening Standard* saying our share price had shot up from £1.10 to £2.80 and they wanted to know if there was any reason for this.

Suddenly the penny dropped. This bloody gangster who was supposed to be on *my* side of the Chinese wall had run off to his trading
department, who had obviously started to sell stocks to their mates.
The share price was running away. My second lesson on the stock
market was well and truly branded on my forehead: don't trust anybody in the broking firms – they are full of gangsters and monkeys.

I called Edward Walker-Arnott and explained what had gone on.
He kind of chuckled and told me that I hadn't done anything wrong,
that if I was speaking to the corporate side of my brokers, then it was
quite right for me to give them the heads-up. He said that if there *was*
an inquiry, I would be completely clean. He added, 'That is, as long as
you, your family or any of your employees haven't bought a lot of
shares.' Of course, none of us was minded to do that.

I had been very naïve and didn't understand the possible effects of
our profits doubling. It was only when the results were finally published in our preliminary announcement in late September that it
dawned on me what a great achievement we'd made in catching the
market by surprise. There were great headlines about us doubling our
profits and a lot more interest was directed towards the company. The
share price rose to somewhere in the region of £4 and Howard Miles
at Greenwell (not a gangster or a monkey) told me that there was only
a very small amount of stock in the marketplace.

I remember going to Currys with Boycie to take Ken Sladen to
lunch one day. Long before the days of mobile phones, I had a Storno
phone in my car, made by a Swedish company. You called a central
operator and gave them the number you required, then you were put
through to the person. The phone worked on a push-to-talk basis and
I can't tell you the number of times I had to say to people, 'I'm on a
special phone – let me talk, then I'll stop, then you talk and when you
stop, I'll talk again.' It took people a while to get the hang of it.

While driving to Ken's head office in Ealing, I received a call from
Howard Miles. He told me that if I were prepared to sell another 8 per
cent of my shares – reducing my holding to 67 per cent – he could get
me £4m for them.

Was I becoming a bit blasé or what? 'Righto, Howard, go on then,
do it.'

As we sat down to lunch with Ken Sladen, I told Boycie that I'd just flogged another four million quid of shares. Sladen couldn't believe the relaxed manner in which I made that statement. The way I saw it was that after the excitement of selling 25 per cent of my shares for £2m about eighteen months ago, it didn't seem a big deal to be selling just 8 per cent for £4m.

The next year, we doubled the profits again to £4.8m, and the year after that (to June 1983) we did it yet again – an £8m profit. We were flying in the stock market and I was the City's blue-eyed boy, doubling profits three times over since we'd floated.

I can't recall exactly how many shares I sold on the up, but I adopted this policy of selling a small percentage every time the share price doubled. My original £2m had paled into insignificance and I was now a multi-millionaire.

*

I wasn't the only Sugar selling shares in Amstrad. Dad was loving watching his shares double and triple. One day, quite sheepishly, he asked me if it would be okay if he sold some. When he did, he made what he felt was a fortune.

By now Mum and Dad had moved from Woolmer House to a brand-new council estate in Stamford Hill. Their old neighbour, Ivy Moore, had also moved into one of these flats, but sadly her husband Percy had passed away by then. The location was good for my dad to get to work in Tottenham – he simply caught a bus from Stamford Hill up to the Spurs ground, then walked through the back doubles. He was really only working because he wanted something to do and spent his time running up to the bank for Jim Rice and doing various other bits and pieces.

One day, he came into my office, in a rather formal manner, and said that he wanted to jack it in. He'd worked all his life and now he felt it was time to retire. This was no problem to me. I knew he was now financially secure, with me occasionally backing him and Mum – when they'd let me! I'd sent them on holiday to Israel for the first time and even to Miami – all expenses paid, of course – but Dad still wanted his independence and insisted on paying for their European holidays with his own money.

Long after he'd left Amstrad, I was sitting in my office in Garman Road when Butch Cassidy and the Sundance Kid (aka Dad and his mate Sid) burst in. This was typical of my father – he had no regard as to whether I was in a meeting or on the phone, he would just barge in. He told me that he and his mate had booked a package holiday through a travel agent in Clissold Road, Stoke Newington. Unfortunately, my dad's mate got sick and was advised by his doctor not to fly. They'd paid a deposit up front, but when they spoke to the travel agent that morning, he'd told them it was non-refundable.

Dad was aggravated. I knew my father's mentality – this was going to really wind him up and make him worry like crazy. After he had explained the situation, he said, 'We want to know what you can do about it.'

'What *I* can do about it?' I asked. 'What am I supposed to do?'

'Well, you know what to do with these things. Go on, phone up the man at the travel agent and tell him to give us our money back.'

I knew there was no chance of getting his money back because unless you took out some insurance, there were no refunds when it came to these package deals. In any case, the only refund would be to his mate and not to my dad, as there was nothing wrong with him.

My phone was ringing and I dismissed him quite quickly, saying, 'Okay, leave it to me. I'll get on to it.'

Two days went by and my dad was phoning me up. 'Well? What have you done? Did you get my money back yet?'

'No, Dad, I haven't had time.'

'Well, when are you going to do it?

'I'll do it tomorrow, leave it to me.'

Eventually, after a few more calls from Dad, I worked out what I hoped was the solution. The total amount of the refund was roughly £650 (£325 each). I called the travel agent and asked him which company the trip was booked through and he told me it was Laker. After assuring him I wasn't going to make a fuss, he reluctantly gave me their phone number.

I called Laker and spoke to some lady. 'Madam, you don't know who I am, but could you please listen very carefully. My father and his friend have booked a holiday with your firm and regrettably the friend cannot travel. They are very old, in their seventies, and they're driving me round the bleedin' bend. Now, I know they haven't got a leg to stand on and I'm not going to ask you to give them a refund, but this is what I'd like you to do: I'm going to write out a cheque now to Laker Airways for £650 which I'll post to you immediately. When you receive this cheque, could you please write out two cheques for £325 – one to my father, the other to his friend – and send them to me.'

I had to repeat this at least twice before she got the plot. I told her that my father was driving me mad and that this was the simplest solution, otherwise he'd have a heart attack. In the end, she agreed and about a week later the two cheques turned up at my office. I phoned the old man up and told him to get down to Garman Road, as I had some good news for him – I'd got his money back. The pair of them were there within the hour and I presented them with their cheques.

'There you are,' my dad said to his friend. 'I told you he would do it. I told you my Alan would give 'em what for. Didn't I tell you he'd get the money back – see?'

He turned to me. 'What did you tell them, Alan? What did you say? Did you tell them you were going to get a solicitor on to them?'

'Don't worry, Dad, I sorted it out, just leave it at that. See you later, bye. Hope you get better soon, Sid.'

As they walked out of the room, I could still hear my dad saying, 'See, I knew he'd do it, I told you.'

A week or so later, Sid sent me a little present. They never did find out the true story behind their refund, but Daphne, Shirley, Derek and Ann were impressed with my little scheme and found it quite funny. Dad had been driving *them* mad too.

Meanwhile, there was some good news on the home front when Johnnie met a really kind and caring lady called Minnie, who had the patience of a saint. They married and she would go on to be called Auntie Minnie by my kids. She was warmly welcomed into the family.

Minnie was also a SuperJew and immediately fitted in with Johnnie's ways of kashrus and attending synagogue, so he was in heaven. They moved to Westcliff-on-Sea, near Southend, where there was a large Jewish community. They found a very nice flat with a lovely view of the sea, which we purchased in Ann's name. They lived there for quite a few years and gained a whole new bunch of cronies – serious synagogue-goers, of course; what else would you expect? We spent many a Sunday driving down the Southend Arterial Road with the kids to visit Johnnie and Minnie.

9

Young Businessman of the Year

'And the Award Goes to the Amstrad Blockbuster Computer'

1982–6

In February 1984 I received a letter from the *Guardian* informing me that their committee of experts had selected me as the Young Businessman of the Year and inviting me to attend a big bash at the Mansion House in the City.

Tim Holland-Bosworth told me it was one of the highest accolades a businessperson could achieve and that it was a really big do, attended by all the City dignitaries, including the Lord Mayor. He added that I would be the guest of honour and would most certainly have to make an acceptance speech. Bloody hell, I thought, the last time I made a speech was at my wedding.

My mood at the time was not that great. I was concerned that the Amstrad bubble might be about to burst. Since flotation, we had doubled our profits year on year, but I knew there was no way we'd achieve this in 1984 and I was worried about what my next business move should be.

Ann and Jim Rice were with me in the car on the way to the Mansion House. I was very nervous at the prospect of speaking to all these people, so while Jim was talking to Ann about what a wonderful event this would be, I was being my usual sceptical self. I felt like a bit of a fraud, accepting this great accolade knowing that the overhyped expectations of me were about to evaporate. Both Ann and Jim told me to stop being a killjoy and shut up. They reminded me how far we'd all come since the days of Ridley Road and told me I should stop being silly. It didn't help.

When we arrived and I saw the size of the room and the hundreds of people there, I *really* got cold feet. I sat through the lunch at the top table, nervously trying to exchange pleasantries (ha, ha – *me* exchanging pleasantries!) with the Lord Mayor and other dignitaries, and then it was time to accept the award and make my speech. Heaven knows what I said. I just blurted out some words, including a joke that got a mild grumble of a laugh, but that's all I can remember. Nevertheless, I'd picked up my first gong.

*

By 1984, sales of our tower systems had flattened out. Like all boom products, they were starting to reach saturation point with profits starting to plateau out at £9m on a turnover of £85m. The figures would have been worse if we hadn't moved into the growing market for colour TVs and VCRs and, once again, the Emperor was to play a role in the Amstrad story.

A couple of years earlier, I had received a call from Itakura of Orion. We had not done any business with them for a long time, but they had noticed the phenomenal growth of Amstrad in the UK audio market. Itakura, obviously prompted by Otake, called to say that they were very interested in supplying us with audio chassis and, if we agreed to this, they might supply us with the colour TV they were now making. He also mentioned that they planned to start VCR production and that when they did, we might be able to buy these also. I didn't need to kiss Otake's arse any longer, so I was quite dismissive. I fired some prices at him which were ridiculously lower than those we were paying Hawson, thinking that he'd simply go away.

To my surprise, a couple of days later, he told me that they would be eager to produce at those prices. I sent Bob Watkins to Korea to check it out. Bob called me from Korea and told me that their factory was virtually idle. Orion's audio business with Michael Raymond had gone down the pan – my tower systems had taken over and wiped out the music-centre market completely. It was clear that Otake was desperate for work to fill his Korean factory and, typical of him, he used the carrot of selling colour TVs and the promise of supplying VCRs to tempt me to transfer production of my tower system chassis to him. It was nice to have Otake in a position I was comfortable with for once and I took the decision to switch production of the tower system chassis to Orion in Korea on the proviso that he would sell us fourteen-inch colour TVs immediately and VCRs when they started production.

From an engineering point of view, Orion was a far more professionally run organisation than Hawson or Morse. The speed of reaction into production was brilliant and the quality of the tower system chassis was a cut above what we'd been used to. Our after-sales service department had been suffering due to the poor quality of some batches of Hawson chassis, as had our reputation as a result. This reputation for poor quality had to be nipped in the bud quickly, as it was the only argument our competitors could raise against us, so we took the opportunity of sorting this out while we were changing manufacturers.

You have to take your hat off to Otake – he had a nose for the market. He wanted to move away from the audio business and had spotted that the VCR market – monopolised by JVC with their VHS system – was starting to boom. By the early eighties, JVC had won the video war against Philips, who originally introduced the Video Home Recording system, and Sony, who were next to market with their Betamax system.

Otake duly started a VCR production line, but for some strange reason he was desperate to get his first orders, so desperate that he made an unexpected visit to England, during which he was uncharacteristically pleasant and schmoozy. This wily old fox was up to something and I couldn't quite work out what. Here he was with his new charming persona, begging me to buy VCRs. He didn't need to beg Amstrad to enter the VCR business – it would be a great boost for us – so while I was confused over his strange change of nature, I didn't care about the reasons; I was delighted to get into the VCR business.

Our VCR had a retail price of £399, the highest-priced Amstrad product ever, but one had to consider that JVC's and Ferguson's VCRs were at least £200 more. Knowing that the market was desperate for VCRs, I made an appointment with the buyer at Currys, Ian Radley, the same guy who had bought CB radios from us a couple of years earlier. He placed an order for 10,000 units, exactly the amount I'd bought from Orion.

Stanley Kalms, the chairman of Dixons, had always had a pretty negative mentality towards Amstrad. He didn't want to buy from me if he thought I was buying from someone else – he wanted to buy direct. Dixons' buyer, Terry Fitt, used to buy a few tower systems from us simply to maintain the credibility of their stores, as they couldn't be seen to be without the best-selling kit. I would go so far as to say that *all* my business with Dixons in years to come would be on that basis – I would generate the demand through my ground-breaking products and advertising. There were never any favours coming from Dixons. They bought what they had to buy because the market demanded it.

In this case, Stanley knew who my supplier of VCRs was and went directly to Orion. Otake struck up a relationship with Dixons and cut me out. I complained bitterly to Otake that this was not ethical. Dixons knew that I'd pulled off a coup in getting low-cost VCRs, so they went to Otake who did a deal behind my back. However, we were buying audio chassis from Orion in large volumes and I would be cutting off my nose to spite my face by moving that business elsewhere, so I reluctantly swallowed this dirty double-dealing. I would constantly jibe at Otake, telling him how disappointed I was that he'd gone against what I understood to be the honourable Japanese ethos. This would wind him up no end, which was my only consolation.

Around this time we purchased our first fax machine, which stood as tall as a washing machine. It was a mass of computer-type PCBs, with a huge and complicated paper transport mechanism. You had to pour black toner into it and load it with a massive roll of thermal paper. No longer would we have to airmail drawings or pictures around the world; and instead of sending an urgent message by telex, we'd simply type a letter and fax it. It was a fantastic breakthrough, a real must-have business tool.

*

The family and I would regularly go to Florida around Christmas, staying in the Boca Raton Hotel. At the tail end of the holiday, I'd take them to Las Vegas, to coincide with the Consumer Electronics Show, and we'd fly home from there. During our 1982 Christmas holiday, one of the kids cut their toe in the swimming-pool, so I went off to find a drugstore to get some plasters. On the way, while walking through the hotel lobby, I noticed a sales display for a nearby development of houses in a place called Boca West. I stopped to talk to the lady there and she showed me some pictures of the new houses going up – they looked great. I started to wonder, now I was in the money, whether it would be the right time for us to own a home abroad.

I went on the missing list for about two hours and visited the site to look at one of these homes. The lead salesperson from the developers, Arvida, was so full of shit that inwardly I was killing myself laughing listening to his crap.

It went a bit like this: 'Sir, these are *quality* homes. We at Arvida only produce *quality* homes. The hospital I was born in was built by Arvida. The school I was taught in was built by Arvida. The church I was married in was built by Arvida. And the house that I live in was built by Arvida.' I thought he was going to burst into some Gospel rap at any moment.

I shut him down pretty quickly and asked him to give me the price and show me which lots were available. There was one location where there were two lots together and I asked him whether it was possible for me to buy them both, so that I could build a tennis court as well. This put the guy into a tailspin – I was asking him to deviate from his robotic sales script. He said, 'Sir, we only sell one lot at a time.'

'Okay, if you only sell one lot at a time, what shall I do? Shall I come in the door, buy the first lot, then go out the door and come in again and buy the second lot?'

'Ha, ha, you English, you're so funny – you have a great sense of humour.'

'Will you please cut the crap and tell me how much for two lots? I want a house on one lot and a tennis court on the other.'

This was far too much for him to take in. He told me that I needed to meet with the actual contractor himself, a guy by the name of Sol Slosberg, who gave me a price for the two lots, including a house and a tennis court – $525,000 – and we virtually shook on it there and then. It dawned on me that I'd better get back to the hotel. More to the point,

I'd better tell Ann that as well the plasters I went out for, I'd bought a house! I casually bowled up to the swimming-pool and told her that after lunch she should come with me and see what she thought of something I might buy.

I guess if you speak to Ann, she will tell you that I never fail to surprise her with my crazy ways. In fact, she was delighted, though she did wonder whether this was going to be one of my mad whims. She let me know her concerns, but added, 'Well, as long as we actually *use* it, then it's great.' As far as I was concerned, as long as I could install a fax machine, there was no problem. This wonderful new invention was the lifeblood of communication to me. I could easily work from Florida by phone and fax.

I did a deal with the builder to make sure the place was ready by the following July and we arranged our summer holiday in Florida, inviting Gerry and Norma to stay with us. During this holiday, I had a couple more strange experiences with Americans.

Ann decided we needed a small fridge for the TV room in the new Florida home. I measured the cabinet where the fridge was to go and popped out to Sears Roebuck to buy one. As I walked through to the white goods department I saw a couple of fridges which looked suitable. A salesman, who must have been in his sixties, came up to me. 'Good morning, sir, welcome to Sears Roebuck and Company.'

'Morning,' said I. 'Do you have a ruler?'

'A ruler? What is a ruler, sir?'

'A ruler – you know, you measure things with it. Or a tape measure?'

'A tape measure? What is a tape measure, sir?'

'Something to measure the height of the door on this fridge. I need to know whether it will fit into a cabinet.'

Now consider, this bloke and I were standing no more than two feet away from the fridge. He turned to me and said, 'Sir, Sears Roebuck and Company have a policy – every refrigerator on our display has the dimensions on the door.'

I looked at him and said, 'Would you turn your head and look at the doors of these two refrigerators and show me where the dimensions are.'

'Oh my Gaad, you're right!'

'Yes, I know. That's why I'm asking you for a ruler, so I can measure it.'

'A ruler, sir? What is a ruler?'

'Please, I need you to get me something to measure the door. When you get me something to measure the door, I will know whether it's the right size.'

'Okay, I got it. You wanna measure the door, don't ya?'

'Yes, please.'

'Okay, please wait, I'll be back momentarily.'

I watched him walk off, right to the end of the store. Five minutes later, he turned up with a tape measure.

'Thank you.' I quickly measured the fridge – no problem at all. 'Good,' I said, 'I'll have this white one.'

He said, 'Saarry, we don't have any in stock.'

I asked him, 'Why didn't you tell me that when we were discussing the size of it?'

'Well, I thought maybe you wanted a rain check.'

Now it was my turn. 'A rain check? What's a rain check?'

'It means, pay for it now, then come back and get it when it's in stock.'

'No. I don't want a rain check, I want a fridge. Okay, forget the white one. What about the black one next to it – do you have one of those?'

'Yes, sir.'

'Good. I'll buy it. Thank you.'

'Thank you for your custom at Sears Roebuck and Company.'

'Okay, good, good. Let's get on with it. Here's my credit card.'

'I'm sorry, sir, we don't accept credit cards at Sears Roebuck and Company, unless you have a Sears credit card?' (That was their policy back in the early eighties.)

'No, I'm English. I wouldn't have a Sears credit card because I don't live in America. I'm from England – I'm on holiday.'

'Oh really, sir? That's very nice. Where are you from?'

'London.'

'London! Oh, I know some folk in London.'

'Yeah, yeah, fine. Look, I don't have a Sears credit card; I only have American Express or Visa.'

'We don't take credit cards, sir.'

'Okay. How much is this fridge?'

'One hundred and twenty-eight dollars plus tax.'

'Fine, I'll pay cash.'

'Cash? That's very unusual, sir.'

At this point, he called across to a female assistant standing in the aisle. 'Myrtle, how d'ya do cash?'

She stopped the conversation she was having with someone else and said, 'Whaaat?!'

'Cash! This guy wants to pay cash.'

She walked over and drawled something to him and eventually I was able to pay. Unbelievable. This exercise took at least an hour and there was still more to come. I had to go to the loading bay at the back of the shop, present the paperwork and pick up the fridge, which took another twenty minutes or so.

That was the last time I went out shopping for Ann in Florida. I just cannot take those people behind the counters in department stores – I have no patience whatsoever. Ann totally agrees with me, but it doesn't stop her having a good spend-up.

On that same trip, one of my friends, Dennis Baylin, was visiting and we had a game of tennis. Unfortunately, he made the fatal mistake of not clearing the court and trod on a tennis ball, twisting his ankle badly. I'd never seen an ankle balloon up so quickly. We had no alternative but to take him to hospital, as he was in agony. I drove him to the Boca Raton hospital and was met at the emergency entrance by a burly nurse.

'What can I do for you, sir?'

'I think my friend here may have broken his ankle.'

'Okay, hold on, sir.'

They sat him in a wheelchair and wheeled him into the hospital reception. I stood beside him at the check-in counter while the lady started entering Dennis's details on her computer. After taking his name and date of birth, she asked, 'Social Security number?'

I piped up, 'Er, we're English, he doesn't have a Social Security number.'

'You gotta have a Social Security number otherwise we can't check you in.'

'We are from England, do you understand? This man is a visitor – he's on holiday. He has had an accident and he needs urgent treatment. He's in agony, can you see?'

'I can see that, sir, but we need a Social Security number.'

'Well, he hasn't got a Social Security number.'

'I can't get past the computer program to move on to checking him in.'

'Well, stick any bloody number in then!'

She called across to one of her assistants. 'What do you do when someone don't got a Social Security number?'

'You type in XXX999, then you'll find the program will work.'

She typed it in and turned to Dennis again. 'We need your home address, sir.' He gave her his address in England.

'What is your ZIP code?'

'No, look,' I chimed in again, 'we're from England; we don't have ZIP codes there.'

'You don't got a ZIP code?'

'No, we don't have a ZIP code because we are from England – and *he* is in agony. Do you see this? Can you get him to a doctor?'

'I have to get through this form, sir.'

Once again, she shouted across to her assistant, 'What do you do when they don't got a ZIP code?'

'Put in XXX999 again.'

Her next question was, 'What is your insurance company?'

'We don't have an insurance company – we'll pay by credit card.'

'Fine.' *That* she understood.

Eventually, after fifteen minutes of interrogation, they allowed him to be wheeled off to see a doctor. I told him to call me at home when he was ready to be picked up – which he did, two hours later. Before he could leave, they insisted he sign the discharge forms and, of course, his credit card slip. He was balancing on his crutches, his leg in plaster, having spent two and a half hours in this hospital putting up with all their ridiculous formalities, when the woman at reception finally turned to Dennis and said, 'Thank you, sir. You have a nice day now.'

At this point Dennis, who has a rather volatile nature, turned to her and said, 'Have a nice day? *Have a nice day?* Are you taking the piss? I was sitting here in agony while you were asking me for Social Security numbers and ZIP codes before you would even bleedin' look at me. Then I sat around for another hour and a half waiting for some bloody doctor to come and see me. And now I'm balancing on two crutches, trying to sign the credit card slip and you're telling me to *have a nice day?*' It wasn't funny at the time, but it's one of those things we look back on and laugh at now.

That's America for you. I don't think they'll ever change. Regrettably, all the people I know in Florida don't know about anything outside their great country. Plus, they expect everyone to understand what they're talking about.

*

Amstrad was on the move again in April 1984. We acquired an office block in Brentwood which was to become our headquarters. The premises had great communication links, as it was smack bang opposite the mainline station with direct trains to the heart of the City and just a few minutes' drive from the M25. To put into perspective how far we had come, my first premises (part of the factory space in Great Sutton Street) was 1,000 sq ft; our new offices in Brentwood were 40,000 sq ft!

By this time it was clear that our amazing growth had levelled out. The market had become accustomed to our profits doubling and they obviously felt that we'd run out of steam, and this was reflected in our share price. Typical of the media, there were comments like, 'Has the boy from Clapton run out of steam? Was this all a flash in the pan?' The same people who had bigged me up in the rags-to-riches stories had now turned the other way. I guess this was my first taste of adverse publicity, so understandably I was a bit worried. One of the things that has always fascinated me is how some so-called friends and associates of mine were always quick to report to me when they'd read a negative article in the paper, but never made a point of telling me they had seen the positive stuff. I have to say, that still goes on to this day.

Amstrad obviously needed to diversify. We had done a good job on audio, but I could see we had reached saturation point. Competitors had caught up and prices were dropping and I knew that we needed to move on and find another sector or product to bring us back to profit growth. We had been observing that personal computers made by Sinclair, Commodore and Atari had gained popularity over the last few years, and Bob Watkins and I had discussed getting into this market. Having bought lots of samples, we looked inside the machines and found there were hardly any electronics in there – just a few chips on a PCB. Ignoring all the high-tech bullshit spouted by the nerds who were seen to be the pioneers of the industry, we looked at how much this lump of plastic and silicon would cost to make.

We decided to make our own personal computer. I thought – and later publicly said – that the Sinclair computer looked like a pregnant calculator; it didn't look like good value for money. Also, at the time, people would buy a Sinclair computer and then have to buy a separate cassette player to connect to it. On top of that, they'd have to wire it all to the back of their television sets, which they'd use as monitors.

My concept was simple: Mum and Dad don't want little Johnny taking over the TV set, so our computer should come with its own monitor, have a full-sized keyboard and a built-in cassette mechanism for loading software *and* hit a target price of £199. This way, little Johnny could have it in his bedroom, freeing up the family TV. A great concept.

At the speed of light, we drew all this up and made mock-up samples. There was just one problem – we were clueless when it came to things such as software and didn't know how to make the main PCB. So Bob engaged the services of a couple of long-haired hippies who had helped us out previously by tracking down an epidemic problem with some Orion TVs. They claimed they would easily be able to design a PCB to go inside this beautiful exterior hardware we showed them. We were moving into unknown territory and what happened next, I guess we can only look back on and laugh at.

Again, I don't want to be too technical, but I'll try to explain in simple terms what went wrong. Computers work using an operating system (OS) of some kind and the software for these operating systems takes thousands of hours to write. What one of these hippies claimed he could do in a month would, in reality, have taken a team of fifty software engineers a year, but Bob and I didn't know that at the time.

This new software would be contained in one chip which would be the whole heart of the computer. We designed the PCB, which effectively had a hole in the middle, ready for the chip to go in. At this point, our computer would spark into life.

After about four weeks, Paul Kelly, the lead rocket scientist of this dynamic duo, went on the missing list. Bob received a phone call from his father one day saying that he'd found Paul drunk, lying on the floor. Paul's father accused Bob of being responsible because of the undue pressure we had put him under, hassling him for the software.

What a bloody cheek! We'd not put anyone under any pressure. Naïvely, Bob and I had simply believed what this fellow had told us – that he could provide this software within a month.

The guy *did* eventually provide us with some software, which we believed was the finished item. We sent this software to Toshiba, the chip manufacturer in Japan, only to find that the data we had sent was total garbage. The fellow had just supplied us with some rubbish to keep Bob quiet. It was an absolute disaster. We'd learned very quickly that this computer business wasn't just a case of chucking a bunch of chips into a box and putting a plastic cabinet around it. We were entering a new world and, with our heads in our hands, we wondered what we would do next.

Bob knew another guy, Bill Poel, who was an academic, rather tall, very well spoken and knowledgeable about computers. Bill is one of those people who has great ideas, but has difficulty in executing them. There was no question of a doubt that Bill could spot trends in the computer industry – he still does to this day – but there is something missing, something which I've never been able to put my finger on, which means he's been unable to turn his expertise into pounds, shillings and pence.

Bill introduced us to another brilliant chap called Roland Perry, a shortish fellow with thinning hair. When this Cambridge graduate and Bill discussed things, you could see they knew what they were talking about and, in fact, a week later, they'd come up with a masterplan. They wanted to use a design by the company Locomotive Software, who had already developed approximately 80 per cent of what we required. Bill and Roland also suggested that we engage the services of Mark Jones, a hardware specialist.

The secret to low-cost computers in those days was to condense lots of electronic circuitry into one chip. We had been led down the garden path by the two hippies – Mark Jones explained that for *their* version of the computer to have worked we would have needed two giant PCBs filled with hundreds of chips. However, Mark told us it was possible to condense all these chips into one superchip known as a gate array.

The development of this gate array was going to take at least ten to twelve weeks. The technology was in its infancy, but Mark Jones was one of the foremost experts in the field. Bill and Roland had put together the A-Team and we were pressing ahead.

Our computer project was given the code-name 'Arnold', an anagram of Roland. It was typical in those days to give such projects a name because in the fast-moving, ultra-competitive market, manufacturers wanted to keep their work confidential. So rather than quote a model number, which would give the game away, we would liaise with component suppliers and ask them to quote on materials for Project Arnold.

We designed the hardware based on lessons learned from the success of the tower system. It was clear in my mind that the solution to be sold to the public had to be one of *simplicity*, not only in the operation of the computer, but also in the way it was set up. We decided that the computer system would comprise just two items: the monitor and the main keyboard. We'd also make it look like a *real* computer, like the thing people saw at the airport when they were checking-in. The charcoal-grey keyboard was about two feet long with multi-coloured keys and a built-in cassette data recorder. The monitor also looked great, with the same charcoal-grey, high-tech cabinet, but in reality it contained nothing more than standard black-and-white television circuitry.

The industry was full of snobs who spoke in haughty, intellectual terms, trying to imply that the electronics involved in computers was something way above that used in the general consumer electronics industry. Fortunately, I recognised at a very early stage that this was a load of bollocks. The way I looked at it, chips are chips, PCBs are PCBs and plastic is plastic. Simple as that.

In the case of the monitor, we originally designed it with a standard twelve-inch black-and-white TV tube. However, when one saw the characters displayed on the screen, it didn't look very good. So I decided to get the manufacturer to change the phosphor inside the tube to green, so it looked like a computer screen – when you typed the characters, they appeared light green on a dark green background.

We also decided that the power supply to drive the main computer keyboard should be built into the monitor. This would provide the same simple solution we employed on tower systems. In other words, plug in the monitor at the wall, then plug the keyboard into the monitor. Easy. This was my brief to Bob Watkins and his team.

One of the things about Emperor Otake, when you put to one side his bullshit, arrogance and mad ways, was that he was a fantastic manufacturer. His speciality was getting products straight to market, so he could capitalise on sales in new trends. Like everyone, he had his good points and his bad points. On this occasion I had to put up with his nonsense and massage his ego in order to motivate him to enter into this new computer venture with me. Orion was much like Amstrad and the wise old fox Otake knew that computers were an up-and-coming market.

Despite the fact that he'd screwed me on the VCR deal with Dixons, I put my personal feelings to one side simply because of his ability to act fast. Besides, there was no way he could screw me on computers because we were entering a world where intellectual property meant that we owned the product and nobody could sell it without our permission. What's more, we would supply him with the custom chips, which were the heart of the computer, on a free-issue basis and as these chips were made exclusively for Amstrad, the chip-maker could not sell them to anyone else.

I had a meeting with Otake in London and I explained to him that we would have to do business in a completely different way when it came to these computers. We were the designers of the product; he had the assembly facility in Korea. We pooled our knowledge of component prices and established a labour cost for assembly and, in view of the fact that he had no risk (as our orders would be irrevocable), agreed on a 5 per cent profit margin for his company.

Initially, this was difficult for Otake to accept. He didn't like the idea of being treated as a sub-contractor and often reminded me not to call him that. Nevertheless, once his ego got over it, he agreed to this arrangement. To get him to agree, I played him at his own game and implied that I had other options open to me. I told him there were plenty of Taiwanese manufacturers who would be willing to work in this way. In truth, I didn't have any other maker in mind, as my best experience to date had been with Orion. My bluff worked and he backed down and agreed to my suggestion.

This method of doing business was to be the way forward for Amstrad in the computer industry. We were to learn that the prices of components would tumble, week by week, and it was important that we never placed too many orders for certain components, particularly things like memory chips.

Our biggest struggle was with the British electronics company Ferranti, who allegedly were experts in the gate-array technology we were using. We had a bad experience with them and I'm ashamed that this company, which was supposed to be a glowing example of British technology, caused us such problems. I won't go into detail, but at the eleventh hour we realised we were getting nowhere with these people. The promised production and launch dates were getting close and there we were without the heart of our computer.

One of the things I've learned is how to cut through all the smoke and mirrors to get to the heart of the matter when faced with problems and delays in production. I tended to get involved with the technicalities which, in the early days, upset a few of my people, who saw it as interfering. Under normal circumstances, the boss of a company such as mine would ask his lieutenant, in this case Bob Watkins, to sort out the problem. Unfortunately for people like Bob, despite me doing just that, I still wanted to hear things first hand. To Bob's frustration, before he knew it, I was on the phone to Bill, Roland and Mark Jones, as well as the technical people at Ferranti, wanting to understand why the thing wasn't working and why we wouldn't be receiving our order on time. Having built up a load of enthusiasm about our forthcoming computer, the reality was that we weren't going to be able to ship any because Ferranti was holding us up. Armed with all this information, I asked my people a simple question, 'Isn't there anyone else who can supply this stuff?'

A lesson I learned was that for all the genius of the people working on our project – and trust me when I use the word genius – their technical expertise did not extend to entrepreneurial nous or, dare I say, common sense when it came to solving problems in a clear-thinking way. The answer I got from my line-up of geniuses – Bill, Roland and Mark Jones – was a casual, 'Oh yes, there are others who produce this stuff. Ferranti aren't the only ones – in fact, the Japanese are quite good at it now.'

When I heard this casual, 'Oh yes, there are others,' I felt like smacking them round the head. I asked, 'Why the bloody hell didn't you tell me this six weeks ago when we knew we were in trouble with Ferranti?'

'Well, Alan, I thought we were ... erm ... well, I don't know really.'

They had focused on the fact that we'd engaged Ferranti and paid them a development fee and it didn't occur to them that writing it off and moving on was an option. That development fee paled into insignificance when one considered what was at stake.

After letting off steam, I told them to ditch Ferranti and start again with a reliable Japanese maker. I think Ferranti got there in the end and we did buy a few chips off them, but had we relied solely on them, it's fair to say we would have never succeeded in the computer business the way we did because *time to market* was the essence of our success. That episode served to demonstrate the difference between brilliant academics, bless 'em, and entrepreneurial businesspeople.

By early 1984, rumours were rife throughout the industry that Amstrad was about to launch a microcomputer. We'd built a couple of samples by using two giant PCBs spanning the entire length of the keyboard and containing over a hundred chips. In fact, we could have mass produced computers like this, though they would have been really expensive, but until we had the new superchip, it was the only way of demonstrating a working computer.

We launched the CPC464 in the Great Hall of Westminster School on 11 April 1984. The place was jam-packed with City analysts, as well as a vast array of journalists from the press and computer magazines. The launch had been organised by Malcolm Miller and a certain Mr Nicholas Hewer, a PR consultant from the firm Michael Joyce Consultants, Amstrad having now grown to a size where it needed a PR firm to deal with its affairs with the media.

As I stood there in the packed room, I couldn't resist using my one-liner about the Sinclair computer being just a pregnant calculator, which the press picked up on. I seem to have this knack of coming up with one-liners that the press, I am told, call 'Sugarisms'. That was the first of many.

I went on to tell the audience that we had made a major breakthrough. I showed them the two giant PCBs covered with chips and explained that the sample computers that were being demonstrated here were being driven by these PCBs. However, we were going to make a breakthrough in price and sell the whole computer, including monitor, for £199 because we were going to condense the contents of these two PCBs into one tiny chip. I remember holding up the two PCBs in one hand and a blank Ferranti chip in the other. The audience was amazed. The general media couldn't quite believe it, but some of the technical people there knew exactly what I was talking about and the story grabbed the headlines. Prior to the launch, as I have explained, the market had felt that Amstrad was on the wane, but after this press conference in Westminster, our share price shot up.

We took advantage of this by having a rights issue on 11 May 1984, offering additional shares in the company to existing shareholders, raising £12m to help finance the stocks we required to build up the computer business. On top of this, we were in the process of constructing a 400,000 sq ft custom-built factory in Shoeburyness, which needed funding.

With supplies of the superchip in sight, we could see that computer production would be starting shortly. However, another big issue suddenly reared its head. While we had produced the computer itself, no software existed that would run on it! This was a point which I personally, and naïvely, had overlooked and it became a top priority.

We needed to have a range of software available, otherwise the young-sters wouldn't be driving their mums and dads mad to buy the computer itself.

With computers the hot new item, parents at the time thought it was a great thing to buy for the kids. They had visions of themselves sitting down with little Johnny at the keyboard, accessing educational stuff, helping him with his homework and other worthy things. The truth of the matter was that the kids only wanted to play games, so it was necessary that interesting and attractive games were made avail-able. Roland and Bill were tasked with finding software companies who had already been successful writing games for people such as Sin-clair and Commodore and convincing them to invest their time developing games for the Amstrad platform.

Many of these software companies were run by technically smart people who had started out as engineers and thought that they'd turned into businesspeople – these were the worst kind. The problem was that in many cases they'd stumbled upon a gold mine and these hairy hackers who wrote games in their spare time now found that people wanted to buy them in big volume. They surrounded them-selves with lawyers and accountants and before you knew it, you were confronted with a bunch of people who thought their shit didn't stink. Their policy was, 'We'll write games for the company which has the most computers in the marketplace.' On the face of it, this was a logi-cal way to go, but if you continued with this philosophy, you would never move forwards or allow any other computer to come into the market.

Because of this, I was hauled in from time to time to sit in front of these geeks who'd made a few bob to try to convince them that we were going to put thousands, if not millions, of our computers into the European marketplace and thus it would be worth their while to con-vert some of their games to run on our platform.

I recall one such meeting with an arrogant bunch of tossers from Psion, a leading player in the software market. The boss, Dr David Potter, was having it off big time, selling hundreds of thousands of games based on the Sinclair platform. He didn't come along himself, but instead sent some skinny little posh twit, all suited and booted. He spoke *at* us rather than to us, as if we were some low-level pond life that had no right to be in the world of computers. His attitude was, 'This sector is confined to the fine intellects emanating from Cambridge. How dare you vulgar Amstrad people, who sell those audio things, encroach on our elitist world?'

Bob Watkins, who knew my temperament very well by then, took one look at my face and, just before I whacked this tosser, jumped in and said, 'Alan, I think you have an appointment upstairs. Shall I carry on with this meeting?'

Psion declined to work with us, but with the combined efforts of Roland, Bill and my persuasive, if slightly muscular, charm, we did manage to get some software companies to support us. In the end, there was a respectable amount of software for our machine when it hit the retailers.

With the software in place, the next plan was marketing. The price for the complete system with a green monitor was £199, but I added a colour monitor version of the system for £299. It was the same tactic I'd adopted on CB radio and tower systems and, as before, consumers at the point of sale tended to choose the more expensive version, even though £199 was the lead-in price that hooked their attention. I would say that 90 per cent of the total sales of CPC464 were for the colour version, but had our lead-in price been £299, the computer would not have had the impact it did when it hit the market.

The CPC464 went on sale for the first time in the UK on 21 June 1984. We had only a limited supply to distribute, so we did a deal with Rumbelows whereby they would be the first to launch the computer, in return for them pushing it in their advertising. It was a fad in those days to announce the exact date and location of when a new computer went on sale, so that the first wave of saddo anoraks could get their hands on them. We chose the Edgware Road branch of Rumbelows. As expected, the queue started to form early in the morning, at about 7.30. Within three hours, Rumbelows had sold out.

The all-in-one concept had really captured the imagination of consumers and the CPC464 took off like a rocket in the UK market, outselling all the competition. Sales of this item dwarfed what we had seen before, even with our tower systems, and although they did not impact our 1984 financial results, by June 1985, our profits had jumped to £20m on a turnover of £136m, with computers representing 70 per cent of sales.

The CPC464 was the product that really broke us through into Europe. The German market was the biggest in Europe (the biggest after America for consumer electronics) and we'd started doing business there with a company called Schneider which was very similar to Amstrad, focusing on audio equipment. We had hammered out a deal whereby we would supply them with raw chassis for our tower system under the Schneider brand, and the tower system became as successful there as it was in the UK. During the development of the CPC464, I'd been discussing with boss Bernhard Schneider the possibility of selling it in Germany. Schneider was a very conservative company and the thought of diversifying from their traditional audio and TV business into an area such as computers was completely alien to them.

I sent a sample to Schneider with one piece of software – a chess game. Being a typically efficient German, he sent it to a so-called expert he found in Munich, who reported back to him that our CPC464 was a very good computer compared to some of the other machines in the German market, such as Commodore. Schneider agreed to take some CPC464s, but wanted them under his own brand name. I agreed at the time, simply because we were *all* entering new territory and his brand was well known and well connected in Germany's retail trade, whereas no one had heard of Amstrad.

His first order was for a few thousand units which, when they hit the stores, sold within days. This made Bernhard Schneider panic like crazy. He asked me to supply him with more, as if I had some kind of tree in the garden I could pick them off. I had a big row with him, telling him that as a manufacturer himself, he should see how stupid his ranting was. How could I immediately click my fingers and deliver him 20,000 or 30,000 units? No, he would have to place an order for them in the normal way. It's strange when people panic like this – they suddenly forget the basic principles of manufacturing. I reminded him that *he'd* insisted on having his own brand name on the product, so even if I had more stocks of Amstrad computers in England, he couldn't take them anyway.

The success in France was just as phenomenal and changed the fortunes of Amstrad SARL, my first European subsidiary. The company had been set up in 1981 at the suggestion of Marion Vannier, Pierre Sebaoun's sidekick at Cogel. She'd called me and I'd known from the tone of her voice that something was wrong. The long and short of it was that there had been a falling-out between her and Pierre.

She told me that she no longer worked for Pierre, who had sold the Cogel business and was concentrating on a new venture.

I was due to visit Paris later in the week and she asked me if we could discuss opening a small office there for Amstrad. In hindsight, our business in France *had* slowed down somewhat, but it really hadn't bothered me, as we were so busy in the UK.

I had a meeting at the Méridien Hotel in Paris with both Marion and Pierre, the purpose of which was for me to ask Pierre whether he had any objection to me employing Marion and letting her take over the Amstrad business in France. There was a very tense atmosphere between the two of them, who were clearly not on speaking terms, and I was stuck in the middle. Pierre agreed there was no problem and that we could go our separate ways. Over the course of the next few weeks, Marion's enthusiasm returned. She was not only a fantastic salesperson, but also a great organiser and, under her management, Amstrad SARL established a respectable position within the retail trade.

Like Bernhard Schneider, Marion was sceptical about computers. However, news had travelled fast in the French media about Amstrad launching a computer and she was being contacted by them asking what stance Amstrad would be taking in France. The CPC464 really grabbed the imagination of French consumers due to its all-in-one appeal. In fact, I believe we sold more CPC464s in France than we did in the UK.

It also took us into Spain, where we had no representation and no understanding of the Spanish market, which was very protectionist. As an example, the importation of items containing a radio tuner was banned so as to protect home-produced products. Amstrad had never been successful in Spain – even with audio equipment – but that was about to change.

Just before we moved to Brentwood in 1984, Bob told me that he was being driven mad by a Spanish gentleman called José Luis Dominguez who wanted to do business with us. Dominguez was so keen, he flew over from Spain and turned up unannounced at Garman Road demanding an audience with me.

I don't quite know why I agreed to meet Dominguez – I think Bob persuaded me he was worth listening to. I walked into Bob's office in a rather flippant mood and told Dominguez that I was very busy, but that I'd give him a few minutes. He hardly spoke any English, but managed to explain that he had a company, Indescomp (essentially a two-man band), and wanted to represent Amstrad in Spain for our computer. In exchange, he would give us ten software programs that they had written for the CPC464, free of charge, for us to sell in all markets throughout Europe.

This was an attractive offer because the more software titles there were for the computer, the more successful the product would be in the marketplace. The games Dominguez had were very colourful and gripping, although they needed a little modification. We named the hero character after Roland Perry and the games were called Roland on the Ropes, Roland in the Caves, etc. I didn't realise what an ego boost this was for Roland within the computer industry. People thought it a rather exciting move to name a series of games after one of the senior engineers at Amstrad and it attracted a lot of media attention.

As we didn't know Dominguez from Adam, we insisted that he come up with letters of credit. I remember being very couldn't-care-less with him, an attitude I could afford to take because we were selling so many computers in other markets.

Somehow or other, Dominguez managed to find the finance to open LCs and started to sell the CPC464 in Spain. Once again, it was a massive success. To this day, I still don't know how Dominguez managed to finance the business in Spain, but he was now buying unbelievable quantities of these computers, similar volumes to those going to France.

One day, he invited all of Amstrad's distributors in Britain, France and Germany to a giant press launch and dinner in the Meliá Hotel in Madrid. I didn't quite get the purpose of this, but, according to him, the audience would be full of customers from across the whole of Spain and they would deem it an honour if I were to attend with Marion and other members of Amstrad. He booked me into the biggest suite in the hotel, so big you could have held a football match in it. Marion told me that her room was also massive.

That evening, Marion and I walked into this grand hall and took in the music and the glitz, the big stage with a set and flashing lights and the hundreds of people assembled. We looked at each other as if to say, 'How is this guy *paying* for all this? And what's the purpose of it?'

I remember shrugging my shoulders and saying, 'I don't care – we're getting the letters of credit,' to which she replied, 'You're right, that's all you have to worry about.'

Dominguez was an unbelievable showman. What rung his bells was personal fame and fortune. There were ten photographers standing strategically in the walkway approaching the main table, so that as Marion and I walked through, the cameras flashed away. It was similar to the way you see the paparazzi chasing after celebrities these days.

When we finally sat down to this grand dinner, I asked Dominguez where all these photographers were from and why they were taking pictures. He openly admitted that he'd hired them to impress upon the audience that we were very important people. Again, I remember looking at Marion and shrugging my shoulders as if to say, 'Not only is this guy nuts, I think he's a bit sick.'

*

We certainly were the darlings of the computer media, so much so that we started to get nominated for awards. Nick Hewer pestered me to attend some bash in Birmingham, the Computer Trade Association's annual dinner, which he assured me was a very important industry event.

To be honest, I wasn't interested in these things. I always find they turn out to be a bloody bore, with people pestering you and slipping you their cards, trying to do some business one way or another. By this time, I'd already done my fair share of corporate entertaining – wining and dining customers and talking a load of bullshit. For the punters, it was a big night out and the staff saw it as some kind of treat, but as boss of the company, I didn't see it as anything special – I'd rather have been sitting at home watching TV and relaxing.

So there I was, all dressed up in a dinner jacket and talking to a load of boring people on my table, looking at my watch and wondering when I could get out of this place. The award ceremony started and went on for about half an hour until it got to the final top award of the night. While drifting away with boredom, to my surprise, I heard the Master of Ceremonies declare, 'The Product of the Year Award goes to Alan Sugar of Amstrad for the CPC464.' The whole room stood up and applauded, except me. I was stunned. Nick nudged me, as if to say, 'You'd better get up there and accept the award.' I guess it was a nice thing to have. I am terrible when you think about it – I made no fuss or showed any sign of elation.

*

There comes a time when a business grows to such spectacular heights that, regrettably, some of the staff initially tasked with jobs such as accounting or sales find themselves out of their depth. This was the case at Amstrad with Jim Rice and Dickie Mould.

Jim had been employed back in the days of Ridley Road, taking over an accounts department that was run by one person. He was perfectly qualified to run the small department and transform it into something larger, but by now we were becoming a giant public company and we needed a heavier hitter. I appointed Ken Ashcroft as our new finance director. Ken, who was quite well known in the City, had held the same position at Comet and was recommended to me by Nick Lightowler.

It's a tricky subject to bring up with one of your loyal staff members – to tell them it's time for them to move aside and let someone else step in – but the new job I had in mind for Jim was no small task. Though he was initially upset at the prospect of someone else taking over the accounting reins, he finally accepted that it was the sensible thing to do. Instead, he would move into the newly created position of operations director, controlling our distribution and warehousing logistics for the whole of Europe.

Dickie Mould – Boycie – was good in his day, dealing with the small retailers, but was totally out of his depth handling the Rottweiler-type buyers at companies such as Dixons, Rumbelows, WHSmith, Littlewoods, BMOC and Argos. My philosophy of selling in Britain was to stick to large organisations such as these, who would buy in bulk, and, to be perfectly frank, I largely ignored the individual and smaller dealers, but we had appointed one wholesaler in the Midlands who would supply the smaller retailers on a ones-and-twos basis.

I could never understand where there was any margin for small retailers. Since I wasn't prepared to sell to the wholesaler at a lower price than I was selling to Dixons, and since the wholesaler would have to make a profit when selling it to the retailer, how could the retailer compete with Dixons' price? Nevertheless, we bought this small wholesale company in Stoke-on-Trent because I saw this as a convenient opportunity to help Dickie Mould save face. There was no job for him at our head office and it would have been unfair to get rid of him through no fault of his own – he was simply a victim of the dynamic growth of the company. Instead, I created a new company, Amstrad Distribution, and appointed him as managing director to run the wholesale side. Effectively, he was trading with the Amstrad head office on an arm's length basis by buying from us and selling to small retailers.

All of this coincided with a general expansion of our executive staff. We were still very much in the audio business – I was not prepared to ignore the business upon which Amstrad was founded, despite the temptation to concentrate solely on computers.

Malcolm and I decided that we'd bring in a new tier of management, known as product managers. On the audio, TV and VCR side of the business, Malcolm took on a young man called Anthony Sethill as our consumer electronics product manager, and on the computer side of the business, we employed David Hennell as our computer product manager, along with Keith Collins as a specialist computer salesman.

In entering the computer business we became more and more entangled in legal documentation, especially with software companies, who were paranoid about being ripped-off. We found that we were using a lot of external legal resources, which were costing an arm and a leg, so we decided to recruit our first corporate lawyer, David Hyams, to deal with the increasing number of licence agreements and contracts.

With new markets opening up in Spain and Germany, we also needed to employ someone who was familiar with the logistics of export so we asked Joe Oki, formerly of Waco in Japan, to come to England and be our export sales manager, handling orders to France.

While on the subject of personnel, I had asked Mike Forsey to leave the company a while back, as he just didn't fit in with the Amstrad culture – he dithered and pontificated and was somewhat awkward in his manner – and I promoted Bob Watkins to technical director.

In discussion with our corporate advisers, I decided to initiate a share option scheme for the staff. In simple terms, it was a way of giving my employees the right to purchase Amstrad shares three years after the options were granted. As an example, if when I granted the options the share price was £1 and three years later the share price had risen to £10, the employees would have the right to pay £1 per share, sell at £10 per share and make £9 per share profit. I am sure some technical guru will disagree with my simple explanation, but trust me, that's more or less the nuts and bolts of it in simple Hackney terms.

Share options were granted to all my key staff. Naturally, the directors got a lot more than the general staff. Most employees didn't realise the benefits that were about to be bestowed upon them. They thought it was similar to the various incentives that sometimes crop up in companies – in other words, to be taken with a pinch of salt as some kind of management gimmick to try to make the staff feel wanted. The scheme was put into place at a time when Amstrad's share price had dropped back a bit, due to what the market perceived as disappointing results at the end of June 1984.

*

Roland, Bill, Bob and I had been talking about the next model of our microcomputer. We decided to get rid of the archaic method of downloading games via cassette and replace it with a floppy disk drive, which was clearly the way forward. This would raise the profile of the computer into a different league and would allow more sophisticated programs, such as spreadsheets or word processors, to be run on it.

We brought out the CPC6128 in August 1985, a very slick and slim-looking grey computer with a floppy disk drive in place of the old cassette mechanism. We also doubled the amount of memory to 128k. It became a massive seller in all markets due to its perceived higher technology. People considered it a *real* computer.

The success of our computers was seriously threatened at one time by a lack of components. This was a new phenomenon for me. In the audio, TV and VCR markets, I don't think there was ever a time when our style was cramped by a lack of materials. However, in the computer market, memory chip manufacturers (basically a handful of giant American and Japanese companies) would suddenly decide to give up making certain sizes of memory chip as technology advanced. No one wanted to supply us with the 64k D-RAM chips we used any more and there was a severe shortage of memory chips throughout the world. It got to the stage where production was stopping and we couldn't manufacture computers.

Thankfully, Samsung had just started to enter this market and, like all new boys, they decided to start with the lowest technology, namely 64k chips. We ended up persuading Samsung to continue to run their 64k chip production and we bought millions of chips from them in order to keep the CPC464 and CPC6128 running.

It was a worrying period for me as a manufacturer, but it also reminds me of a funny incident at the time. At home one Saturday, I was preparing to play tennis with a friend of mine, Ivor Spiro. We were sitting in the kitchen chatting about things in general when suddenly the doorbell rang.

Standing at the door were two rather smartly dressed gentlemen. They announced that they were sorry to disturb me, but were here on ministerial business. I automatically assumed that these two blokes had come from the council to discuss some planning consent we'd applied for on the field next to the house. Then it dawned on me that it was Saturday, so it'd be highly unlikely that any officials would come round.

It took another couple of minutes of conversation for me to realise that they were Jehovah's Witnesses, and that the ministering they were doing was on behalf of the Lord. They asked whether there was anything the Lord could do for me. How funny that two Jehovah's Witnesses had turned up to confront me and Ivor Spiro, two Jewish fellows.

I decided to humour these two chaps. 'Perhaps there *is* something you could help me with,' I said, keeping a straight face.

The more senior of the two gentlemen looked interested and pleased that I was about to call upon their assistance. 'How may the Lord help you, sir?'

'Any chance you can get two and a half million 64k D-RAMs?'

He laughed and replied that the Lord has been known to do many things, but that one was rather challenging.

Anyway, these two fellows didn't want to leave, so I cut them short by telling them that, in actual fact, I had a special consultant there who dealt with these matters and if they wouldn't mind, I'd call him over and leave them to explain their work to him and then he would report back to me.

They agreed quite readily, at which point I shouted over to Arthur the gardener, who was hovering in the background wondering what was going on.

'Arthur! I'd like you to help me out here. I have two gentlemen that need your specialised attention.'

'Righto, sir. Leave it to me, sir. With respect, sir, you go and play tennis with your friend, sir, and I shall deal with the two gentlemen and report back to you, sir.'

'Thank you, Arthur. Yes, would you kindly do that. They're here on important matters. Would you please take them away and deal with them.'

This was the first time I'd ever found a good use for Arthur. He would bore the pants off these two to such an extent that they'd never come back. About ten or fifteen minutes later, when Ivor and I had started our match, Arthur stormed up the path to the tennis court.

'Thank you very much, sir, thank you very much. You lumbered me with those two blokes. With respect, sir, I'm a gardener – what do I know about the Lord's work?'

'Never mind, Arthur, you've done a very good job. Have they gone?'

'Not half, sir. I told them to clear off and not to bother you again!'

*

I mentioned earlier about protectionism in Spain. In August 1985, I had a panicked telephone call from Dominguez telling me there was a serious problem, that all computers of 64k and below were now banned from importation into Spain. This was because a Spanish manufacturer was producing a 64k computer and had managed to get the Spanish government to impose a rule blocking all others. This was a disaster for Dominguez and Amstrad – by now we were selling thousands of computers in Spain. This new rule would effectively shut us down.

If anyone knows about dealing with Spain, they will be aware that it would be an insurmountable task to try to argue this point legally with the Spanish customs and government – we had to find another way to overcome the problem. The simplest and most obvious solution was to increase the computer's memory, but that would mean some high-level design changes and re-engineering. Even at the fast pace Amstrad worked, there was no way we could pull it off in time for the forthcoming Christmas market.

The computer boffins out there will cringe when they hear what I did next. I felt the trick I was about to play was morally justified because the Spanish government was trying to impose import regulations simply to protect one of their mates in the local market. I remembered that nearly twenty years earlier there was a fad in the portable transistor radio market, whereby the more transistors in the radio, the better it was claimed to be. The fact was, those radios only needed six transistors to work, but some Hong Kong manufacturers used to stick four extra transistors – which did nothing – on the PCB, simply so they could label their sets 'ten-transistor'.

We needed to do a similar sort of thing on our computer. We

added a chip to increase the memory to 72k. I also asked my technical geniuses to come up with some justification as to what this extra chip was doing. They did – but don't ask me what it was! A bit of poetic licence if you ask me – I'm not exactly sure it did anything.

We rushed the new design to Orion. This was the brilliance of Orion and why it was so worthwhile putting up with Otake's nonsense. Once he got behind something, he moved at a speed I've not experienced in all my manufacturing life, neither before nor since. I don't know how he motivated his staff to do it, but within two weeks we were producing a special CPC464 for Spain with 72k of memory – all with new faceplates, books and packaging.

We had basically stuck two fingers in the air to the Spanish government, who were trying to screw our business, and there wasn't much they could do about it because at the cargo's point of entry into Spain, customs had to allow them through. We never received a technical challenge from anybody in the Spanish market. The bottom line was, we beat their system. Eventually, they scrapped the ruling, at which point we magically changed back to our standard 64k product. As a result of this exercise, we managed to sell at least another 50,000 units in the Spanish market that Christmas season. We'd have been in trouble otherwise, as all the advertising had been booked and the retailers had placed their orders.

*

Marketing was to play a big part in the Amstrad success story. On reflection, I'm a marketing person, effectively an advertising agent in disguise. Maybe that's why so often I didn't feel the need to seek the advice of advertising agencies in coming up with killer catchphrases for our adverts. Most of the headlines and punchlines in our adverts came from me. Rightly or wrongly, they seemed to work.

Originally, I thought that advertising agencies had some secret talent. They would come along and pitch their great ideas to me, the client. It transpired that the great idea was limited to the main punchline of the advert and from then on, the only great idea they had was to send you big bills for doing three parts of sod all. There were unbelievable charges for photography – things like setting the lighting scenes and the ambience, with a whole crew out on location in Lake Ullswater in the north of England, waiting for the right moment to see the moon setting on the lake, with the rippling lights on the water and all that bollocks. I put up with one bout of this crap and then kicked their arses out.

Amstrad's philosophy was simple – pile 'em high, sell 'em cheap. Adverts had to be full-frontal: show the product, show what it does, show the price and tell the punters where they can go and buy it. Simple as that.

Never would one of my adverts win an award at an advertising fraternity bash at Cannes or Montreux. These people consider a good advert to be one that everyone remembers because it's funny or clever. How many times have you said to your friends, 'Have you seen that advert with the car parts all falling over each other – brilliant, isn't it?'

Yes, you're right – it *is* brilliant photography. The problem is, when you ask what company it was for, nobody remembers. Ask what car they were selling and nobody knows. The amount of money pissed up the wall by marketing managers for the sake of boosting their personal egos within the advertising fraternity is incredible. The bigger the firm, the bigger the waste. My idea of a good advert is something that shifts kit off the shelves, something that these creative geniuses seem to forget. And I wasn't having any part of joining this game.

I had rows with Marion in France when she tried to engage one of these creative twits. The guy was not prepared to reveal his advert until he'd talked Malcolm Miller and me through some twenty-minute presentation on the whys and wherefores of what a Frenchman does on a Thursday afternoon when he sticks his left leg out of the window in Toulouse on a rainy day. I told the guy that I wasn't interested in listening to all that demographic crap – just show me the bloody advert or I'm getting up and walking out, which is exactly what I did. I left Malcolm there to sit through all this boring bullshit.

When it finally got to the stage where we saw the adverts, they were crap. His whole concept was a pair of red boxing gloves. I looked at Malcolm and Marion and said, 'What are we sitting here talking to this twit for? What's a pair of boxing gloves got to do with flogging computers?'

Apparently, there was some subtle message, whereby the boxing gloves were there to show that we were going to punch everybody out of the marketplace. Brilliant. To add insult to injury, there was a tiny picture of the computer, about the size of a postage stamp, at the bottom corner of the advert, along with some subtle strapline in French.

It took a while for me to convince Marion this was not the way we were going. She was a lady who had a strong personality; not an easy person. She stood up and argued her corner, but in this particular case she started to realise I was right. It did help somewhat when I told her that I was controlling the advertising budget in France and that she was hereby not authorised to spend one penny on this crap.

In Spain, Dominguez followed the Amstrad pile 'em high, sell 'em cheap model, replicating our adverts and sometimes bettering them. He'd really caught on to my train of thought.

It seems I didn't get it too wrong, as Amstrad went on to win the Marketing Society Award in 1985, 1986 and 1987, as well as the RITA Award 1986, the Management Today Award 1986, the British Micro Awards 1985 and 1986, the Golden Chip Award 1985 and the BEW Toby Award in 1986. It's a wonder I wasn't head-hunted by Saatchi & Saatchi!

*

Exhibitions were an important part of the computer industry, as they were with consumer electronics, and our first exhibition stand at the Olympia computer show was so popular we had a near-disaster. The stand was inundated with young people and trade buyers and at one stage I was becoming concerned that the raised floor would collapse. I'd never seen an exhibition stand so packed, nor have I since. It was as if we were giving away tenners for five quid. It was an unbelievable sight to stand back and watch, but, as I say, quite frightening at the time. In today's climate of health and safety, we would have been shut down.

José Dominguez's exhibition stands, which I visited in Madrid and Barcelona, were the most flamboyant. José would walk down the central aisle of the exhibition hall and people would virtually be bowing to him, as if the Don was arriving. Who knows how he'd got himself this reputation in such a short period of time, but if you imagine this short, dark-haired, heavily bearded man walking through the exhibition wearing a black suit with an overcoat draped over his shoulders, you'll get the picture. It was like a scene from *The Godfather*.

I remember Nick Hewer standing with me and commenting on this while José once again pulled his fake paparazzi trick, with a few photographers flashing cameras at him. Other people were looking on, wondering, 'Who *is* this important man?'

I told Nick, 'Don't worry, we're still being paid by letter of credit.'

By now, José Dominguez was not satisfied just selling Amstrad computers in Spain; he also wanted to sell our audio equipment. The design of our tower systems had changed quite a bit by then – it was more compact, with twin cassettes and the newly invented CD player.

Imports of audio equipment to Spain from the Far East were on very strict quotas, but they couldn't ban the importation of equipment assembled in the UK. And while our tower system chassis were from the Far East, they were assembled into cabinets in England, with British-made BSR record decks and British-made speakers, so due to the high content of British material, the product could be classified as British-made and we were free to ship to Spain.

When José visited our factory in Shoeburyness, he spotted a small micro hi-fi with twin cassettes and a pair of speakers. We had managed to engineer it down so that it sold through UK mail-order companies at £99 – quite amazing. He said if he could sell this item in Spain for 29,999 pesetas, it would be a big hit. I wasn't going to argue with him as long as he could pay.

He gave me an order for 50,000 units and sold them to El Corte Inglés. Unbeknown to me, the 29,999 pesetas price point was an incredible breakthrough in the Spanish market, which had been heavily protected until its entry into the European Community. We were the first to exploit the fact that by assembling the products in England, we could classify them as British, so we were first to market.

José was right – these things sold like hot cakes. There were unbelievable queues outside El Corte Inglés in Madrid, Barcelona, Valencia and Seville. He sent me a video of a TV clip showing people swarming to the stores as if they were giving away gold bars. I believe he bought 150,000 units over the next six months. Of course, as usually happens in business, other people caught on. Nevertheless, we exploited that moment in the market, which is what I love about Amstrad. José came up with a phrase to describe our series of successes – the Amstrad Effect.

By now you must be getting the picture that José Luis Dominguez was no longer a man to take lightly and it's true to say that he had more of an audience with me each time he came up with an idea. However, his next idea was a disaster.

He had been contacted by an old friend of his, Jaime Pero, who was living in Chicago and allegedly was some kind of computer expert. He had seen the success of Amstrad in Spain and, being of Spanish-South American descent, he had read a lot of the Spanish computer magazines talking about Amstrad. Pero wanted to represent Amstrad in America. I told Dominguez that this was a total, absolute joke. The Americans had already forgotten what we'd yet to learn about microcomputers and they were moving on. The CPC464 and CPC6128 would be laughed at in the American market. I told him to forget it.

José was not the type to give up. He threw my philosophy back in my face. 'Why are you arguing, Alan? If we can get a letter of credit from the marketplace, *you* don't have to worry. Pero is very confident he can sell the CPC6128 in America.'

It was difficult to argue against this reasoning. Even though I knew the product would bomb in America, if I was being paid by LC, I couldn't argue. Reluctantly, I agreed to meet Pero on one of my visits to Chicago for the CES exhibition. José had flown in, as indeed had Malcolm Miller, and we set up a meeting.

Jaime Pero was a very convincing South American character, taller than Dominguez and older – in his fifties, I would guess. If you'd been a fly on the wall in that meeting, you'd have seen a bizarre sight – Alan Sugar trying with all his might to talk people *out* of buying his product! I put up every obstacle, explaining that this was a disaster waiting to happen, that the CPC6128 was no great revelation as far as America was concerned. I told them that nobody would buy this thing and I didn't want them to walk into a hornets' nest and get lumbered with all the stock.

Despite my protestations, I reluctantly agreed to move forward and develop the CPC6128 for America on the basis that we would not lift a finger from a technical point of view unless we received £250,000 up front for development which I would refund to them over a period of time if they purchased 100,000 units. (To sell to America, your product needed to comply with very strict regulations.) If ever there was a go-away offer, this was it. But they accepted and, sure enough, £250,000 arrived with us a week later.

Being in Chicago also meant it was time for the quarterly summit meeting with Emperor Otake and his crew. As ever, Otake had booked himself into a very royal penthouse suite at the Conrad Hilton. Itakura and his other slaves were there, including the engineers from Japan who worked on Amstrad projects. The meeting took the usual form. Otake pretended to ignore the fact that I'd even walked into the room (there were about ten to fifteen of his staff in there, plus three or four of mine), then he looked up and said, 'Ah, Sugar-san! I didn't know you were coming! I am surprised!'

Total bullshit. He knew perfectly well I was coming.

He continued with his charade, 'Ohhh, I don't know if I have any time to discuss business with you. I didn't know you were coming. I'm so busy with my VCR business and my TV business. This computer business is really not big business for me – I do it just to help you.'

Now, anybody who knows me would be very proud of the fact that I just sat there and let him ramble on. The fact of the matter was that twenty fax messages had been exchanged setting up this meeting, specifying which of his slaves were coming and what we were going to discuss. Everyone in the room knew what we were there to talk about. Mr Ogami, Orion's chief engineer, was chuckling to himself knowingly.

Then Otake said, 'Okay, let's see . . . Itakura, please telephone Mr Dieter Latha, my German distributor, and tell him we now delay our meeting with him until tomorrow just to accommodate Sugar-san here.' Otake turned to me. 'Sugar-san, in future please make sure you make appointment with me!'

Whenever the discussions started to get technical, Otake would get

up and walk out of the room. He didn't like it when he was out of his
depth or couldn't control the meeting. Business ought to be fun sometimes, and it was fun to listen to Otake's nonsense. It actually used to
relax us, so I managed to keep my mouth shut while this little game
went on. I have to say, I do miss those days. I miss playing games with
this nutcase and massaging his ego. And in the history of Amstrad, he
was one of the greatest manufacturers I've ever used.

This time, I explained to Otake that we wanted to get the CPC6128
adapted for the American market and he gave me the name of a company who specialised in getting things approved.

I realised that apart from the £250,000 Pero had paid, I had not yet
seen an LC for mass production. I put this to Pero and, after cutting
through a load of his bullshit, he informed me the *actual* importer of
the product was going to be the giant Sears Roebuck group.

Sears, who have department stores throughout America, had
apparently set up a separate division known as Sears World Trade. The
purpose of this division was to import goods and sell them to the retail
trade in general.

Again, this sounded a crazy idea to me. It must have been one of
those decisions made by some brain surgeon inside Sears Roebuck
who, not being satisfied with Sears simply buying stuff from suppliers
and selling it in their department stores, now wanted them to become
distributors as well. They believed that they would be able to sell to
other retailers like Target, Best Buys, Bloomingdale's and Burdines.
Absolute blind naïvety. Never would retailers in the marketplace buy
from, effectively, another retailer – you may recall Michael Hollingbury of Comet telling me that years earlier.

However, it seemed that Pero had managed to stumble across
them at just the right time. Sears World Trade had not started business
with anyone yet and Pero's proposition was one of the first.

Sure enough, we received LCs from Sears World Trade and started
to ship CPC6128s to America. Pero took an exhibition stand at CES
in Las Vegas that January 1986 and invited me along as some kind of
guest of honour. He'd also arranged for press and media coverage and
had decided to plaster the Amstrad brand all over the stand. People I

knew from the industry were walking by. It was pathetic – I was feeling a bit of a dickhead. Most of the people who knew me were saying, 'What are you doing, Alan, trying to sell this technology in America?'

As I predicted, the launch of the CPC6128 in America was a total flop.

10

'I Am Changing Your Lives, Gentlemen'

And Burning the Harvard Business School Manual

1985–6

By summer 1985, we were working on another project which was to make the £20m profit we'd just announced look like small change.

I was walking around Akihabara on one of our regular Far East visits in February 1985, when my attention was drawn to a bizarre-looking electronic typewriter in one of the shops. It looked like a computer screen with a printer mechanism on top. We had been asked many times if there was a printer available to complement the CPC464 and CPC6128, but I wasn't interested in the printer market. We would simply recommend a printer produced by Seikosha (known today as Epson).

But now a sense of excitement came over me and I had the spark of an idea. While flying from Tokyo to Hong Kong, Bob Watkins and I started to discuss the possibility of making a custom word processor using the Amstrad all-in-one philosophy – plug in and go. On the back of a Cathay Pacific serviette, I sketched what is known today as the PCW8256 word processor. I envisaged a keyboard connected to a monitor which also contained the floppy disk drive and a separate printer module. The monumental challenge here was to get a printer manufacturer to sell me the printer mechanism only (which they used in their finished printers) – they would obviously think I was out to compete with them in the printer market.

Most of the printer manufacturers were Japanese. I contacted

Seikosha and met a quiet young man and a senior official. I explained that I wanted to buy the mechanism only. I showed them my concept for a complete word processor and assured them that it wouldn't affect their business. I offered to sign any legal agreement they required to say that I would not use the mechanism to produce a stand-alone printer.

I had their attention, but I also had to make another difficult request. Not only was I trying to convince them to sell me their mechanism, I also needed the software codes, which was effectively asking them to give away the whole shop! I kept reminding them that I was never going to be a competitor.

As is typical of Japanese meetings, they said they would come back to me, but when I left I didn't feel very confident. Without a printer mechanism, we'd never get a word processor off the ground, so I virtually ditched the idea.

Then, a few days after my return to London, I received a call to say that two Japanese gentlemen from Seikosha were staying in the Great Eastern Hotel at Liverpool Street and wanted to know if they could come and see me.

'Shouldn't we go and collect them?' Bob asked. 'They're in a huge city in a strange country – how are they going to find their way to us?'

'Listen, Bob,' I said, 'their grandfathers found Pearl Harbor. Trust me, they'll find Brentwood.'

Now I was very excited! At the meeting, the jigsaw puzzle started to fall into place. It turned out that the quiet young man was the son of the boss of Epson (at that time Epson was Seikosha's export brand) and he'd been thrown in at the deep end for training. Being young and enthusiastic, he quite liked the idea I'd come up with. In fact, I think he quite liked me. We struck a deal on the mechanism and I managed to get them to supply the software details. I wrote them an order there and then for 100,000 pieces – it was the only way to convince them to cooperate with me. What a lunatic I was in those days! A hundred thousand pieces, all from the seed of an idea that started with me catching something out of the corner of my eye in a shop in Akihabara. I was now taking a massive gamble before even showing the idea to the market. Was this computer business going to my head? My thinking was that we'd already sold hundreds of thousands of

CPC464s and CPC6128s and I just had this gut feeling that an all-in-one word processor – targeted at £399 – would change the face of office work.

The word processor's code-name during development was 'Joyce'. Bill Poel, with his usual sense of humour, decided to name it after my long-standing secretary at the time – she had been there since the Ridley Road days and still typed the occasional letter for me.

Now the challenge was to come up with a product that could sell for £399 yet offer the dealer a margin of at least 25 per cent. Once again, we commissioned Mark Jones to develop it and this time we chose the giant Japanese company NEC as our partner to produce the superchip, which they did very diligently.

We tasked Locomotive Software with developing the word-processing program and they beavered away to try to meet the very aggressive launch date I'd planned. In conjunction with Roland and Bill, they designed the software with new features such as drop-down menus, a really flash way of displaying things on the screen. It was something which hadn't been seen before, but had been trialled in the USA on some sophisticated word processors used by the company Wang, which was a major supplier of word processors.

Nick Hewer had arranged the launch of the PCW8256 in the centre of London in September 1985. Nobody had any idea of what we were about to unveil – they thought it was just another computer, possibly the next step up from the CPC6128. Perhaps that's why attendance at the launch was quite modest, but the usual suspects turned up from the press. They were amazed when we pulled back the curtains and ran the video for the new Amstrad PCW8256 and they were further shocked when I announced the price.

Let me take you back to Chelmsford market and the man on the stall selling a pair of pillowcases, a couple of sheets, two blankets, five towels and six handtowels. 'Hold your money, ladies! Hold your money, ladies! The whole lot for five quid.' Picture that. Then picture the promotional video. 'Here's the new Amstrad word processor, complete with floppy disk drive, 256k of memory, dot matrix printer, large twelve-inch green display, full QWERTY keyboard, plus the new LocoScript word-processing software.' Imagine seeing the drop-down menus in the video; imagine seeing someone typing on the machine, then pressing a button and seeing the letter come out of the printer. And then – bearing in mind that IBM and Wang were selling word processors for around £5,000 at the time – imagine the reaction when the final shot came up on the video: 'And all this, gentlemen, for £399.'

You can understand why, with our price, the market was about to explode.

The press were totally, utterly gobsmacked. In the Q&A session that followed, they were asking me, 'Why sell it for £399? Why not £3,999? Why so cheap?'

I explained that Wang and IBM were supplying a very niche market of lawyers, accountants, etc. *Our* product was for the mass market. I continued, 'Many of you gentlemen here in the audience are journalists. No longer will you have to hack out your stories on your typewriters; no more will you have to use Tipp-Ex to correct your mistakes. You can copy and paste paragraphs, delete and insert text, search for words, do bold and italic formatting and, finally, save your masterpiece onto a floppy disk. I am changing your lives, gentlemen.'

This statement proved true and there are some journalists out there, like Hunter Davies, who still sing the praises of the PCW8256. What's more, I told the audience, 'It won't just change journalists' lives. Think about every person in every office up and down the country who uses a traditional typewriter – just imagine how the whole face of office automation will change.' We had announced an amazing breakthrough in technology.

After the Q&A, we led everyone into another room where twenty of the machines were lined up. The journalists clambered over them. Some of them had already called their offices and loads more people started to turn up, particularly photographers. We'd done it again – we'd created excitement for a product. But now we had to start delivering.

By September of that year, with only weeks to go before they were meant to be on sale, there were still technical issues and the main processor chip inside the monitor was crashing.

We made twenty or thirty of them work, but when we started to run the production line in Korea, we found the processor chip was crashing again. Harold Livesey, our factory manager, had employed John Beattie as a right-hand man specialising in production engineering and he was seconded to Brentwood to look into why this product was causing trouble. Urgent work had to be done in the laboratory to solve the problem.

I dived in myself, not knowing what I was talking about, but listening to all the engineers' theories as to what was going on. At eleven o'clock at night we still had our heads in our hands, wondering how to solve the problem. I've spent many hours like that, scratching my head over seemingly insoluble technical problems. Eventually you do solve them, but at the time it looks like you are stuffed – up a gum tree with nowhere to go, a terrible feeling.

Everyone had been working on the thing since nine in the morning, so I told them to go home and go to bed, then, in the morning, jump in the shower and think about it from another angle. One thing I've learned is that when you get into these burning-the-midnight-oil sessions, you get tired and lose focus and end up chasing your tail.

The problem was that we didn't know how to replicate the crash – and I'm ashamed to tell you how we finally managed to do it. One of our engineers, young Ivor Spital, who had started in the service department at Ridley Road and been promoted throughout the company's growth, had deduced that the problem was linked to radiation caused by what's known as spikes on the mains supply. It's difficult not to get technical here, but the mains supply to our houses and offices is not always 'clean' – sometimes it contains spikes, which can cause equipment like computers to crash. Typically, these spikes are caused by things like refrigerator compressors (we've all heard our fridge compressor kick in). So, with this in mind, we tried to replicate the factory problem by getting hold of an old fridge compressor and plugging it in next to the computer. By switching the compressor on and off we could prove that this crashed the processor every time.

The reason I'm embarrassed to tell this story is because there are pieces of test equipment that replicate mains spikes, whereas our Heath Robinson method of using a fridge compressor to do it was, in technical terms, a total joke. Obviously, in years to come, we had the full monty of test equipment to simulate these things, but in those days we didn't. So thanks to an old fridge compressor, we replicated the problem and fixed it by adding a few components. Together, John Beattie and Ivor Spital had solved the issue.

The announcement of the PCW8256 had created a lot of demand and the senior buyer from Dixons, Brent Wilkinson, asked me to come in and demonstrate the product to his boss, Mark Souhami.

It's hard to explain, but when you think you've got a hot item on your hands which hasn't yet proved itself in terms of physical sales, you still feel nervous about whether it's going to be a hit or not. Would it capture the imagination of the public? Would it sell? Sometimes you can panic and do silly things. In this case, I nearly did something silly in giving Dixons exclusivity in exchange for a big first order.

I duly arrived at Dixons' headquarters in Edgware and met Mark Souhami and the buyers. When I showed them the product and demonstrated it, their eyes were popping out of their heads. Pathetically, they tried to play it down and act cool, but they knew that, at £399, they had a killer product on their hands. So much so, I was told that Stanley Kalms, the chairman, would be joining the meeting. In walked Stanley, who was about the same height as me, though I'd have to say much heavier (to put it nicely). He took one look at the product and got it straightaway.

Stanley, a man of few words, acknowledged me by looking up and simply grunting, 'Hello.' We had never met before, but obviously he knew of me, as he'd screwed me on VCRs and had been selling my tower systems, albeit reluctantly.

Stanley asked, 'How many of these have you got coming?'

I explained that this was not a job-lot – he wasn't buying a load of Canon cameras that were being discontinued – this was a regular product. What was 'coming' was simply what was on the high seas. We had started to produce at the rate of 5,000 per month, ramping up to 40,000 per month.

He asked, 'How many will be arriving in the next three months or so?'

I estimated, 'About twenty thousand between now and Christmas.'

'Right,' he said, 'we'll take the lot, but we want them exclusively.'

I didn't answer. I knew I would be alienating my other customers if I agreed to this. However, in Stanley's mind I *had* agreed and he walked out of the room thinking he'd struck an exclusive deal. I had mixed feelings. On the one hand, I was delighted – my product was going to be a hit; I'd got the top boss of Dixons to endorse it with a big order. On the other, I was feeling nervous – I could not give away the shop to Dixons. In fact, I'd deliberately under-committed on quantities earlier in the meeting, so I'd have some left for my other customers.

The advertising campaign for this product was another challenge. How do we transmit to the public the death of the typewriter? We came up with two concepts. One was a large lorry filled with old typewriters being taken to a dump. The lorry turns up, tips all the typewriters off and they fall into a big pile, then we cut to someone using the PCW8256, showing how it works.

The other advert, which I favoured (and was also a favourite of Margaret Thatcher), was the one where a secretary picks up a typewriter, opens the office window and throws it out, so that it lands in a rubbish skip in the street. The secretary then replaces her typewriter with the Amstrad word processor. This was one of the most successful adverts we ever ran, as it told the whole story. It was dreamt up by Malcolm Miller and myself and the advertising agency worked to *our* rules. They were given a budget of no more than £25,000 for filming the advert (as opposed to the usual £150,000 one would expect to pay one of the leading agencies). We also dealt with the media ourselves by negotiating with them directly or by using a media-buying organisation that took a small commission.

We were a big advertiser in those days, but we certainly weren't going to waste money on advertising agency fees. My philosophy was: if we're going to piss £1m up the wall on a campaign, I want it all spent on the actual advertising; I don't want a large chunk of the budget wasted on production and creative fees. You can see why I'm not on the Christmas card lists of most of the advertising fraternity.

One of the ways we convinced an agency to work with us this way was to tell them that when the ad was aired and people asked who the agency was we'd keep schtum and let them take the credit (and go on to rip-off other clients who think they are geniuses). We'd also let them go on their jollies to Cannes and accept any awards going. Trust me, this worked!

It seemed our advertising was spot on. Even John Major, the then Chancellor of the Exchequer, bought one of our word processors. He sent me a picture of himself with the PCW8256 in the background.

In Spain, José Dominguez bought some television time and copied our advert. The product was fantastically successful there, as well as in Britain and France. However, I was told that in Germany there were laws whereby you could not slag off market sectors. An advert with typewriters being thrown out of the window into a skip was effectively illegal as it would imply that typewriters are rubbish and be disparaging to German typewriter manufacturers. Because of this restriction, the PCW8256 wasn't such a great success in Germany, though they still must have sold over 100,000 there.

When the product launched in Britain, there was a queue outside Dixons at Brent Cross on the Saturday. This was not some pre-planned PR stunt – people were genuinely falling over themselves to get these word processors as soon as they came into the shop.

Stanley Kalms must have been plutzing. Never mind that he was making 25 per cent on every unit sold, he hated the fact that he was buying from me, knowing he couldn't get them from anyone else. He also hated the fact that there was no negotiation on price, no negotiation on quantities and no real negotiation on exclusivity. Then he got the raving hump when he saw the product on sale in Comet. One of his underlings, Eddie, the acting MD, called me to complain. I told him that no official agreement had been made as far as exclusivity was concerned – it was all in Mr Kalms' mind. It certainly wasn't in *my* mind.

Eddie threatened that they would no longer stock Amstrad products. The conversation ended with this fellow saying something like, 'Well, that's it. We're closing our account with Amstrad.'

I said, 'Fine. That's a decision which you'll have to live with.'

I have to admit that at the time I was worried. I wasn't really so arrogant as to believe that one could exist without Dixons – they were growing in the marketplace. They had acquired Currys in a hostile takeover bid in December 1984 and they had a tremendous distribution network throughout the country. However, it was just one of those stand-off situations. Should I get on the phone and start kissing the arses of Stanley Kalms and Mark Souhami? Or should I just sit back and be quiet? More by luck than good judgement, having been distracted during the next day or so by other problems, I didn't do anything about it.

Then I received a phone call from Souhami, who was a bit of a smoothie. He was a short, well-groomed gentleman with a very posh, City-type accent. 'Now, young Alan,' he said, 'you've upset Stanley. And when you've upset Stanley, you have to understand that people like me have to sort it out. Now, what can we do about this?' I told myself to keep my mouth shut and not fan the flames by arguing over whether I'd offered exclusivity or not. Just be quiet.

After a moment I spoke. 'Well, I don't know what to say, Mark. According to your managing director, Eddie What's-his-face [I never *could* remember his name], we haven't got an account with you any more, so . . . there you are, that's it. What do you want me to say?'

'Well, this can't go on, obviously. We need your products, you need us . . .'

Best to shut your mouth, Alan. Keep quiet. 'Yeah, you're right, Mark, you're quite right.'

'Now, we're right out of these word processors – what are you going to do about it?'

'Er, sorry, Mark, I was told by Eddie that our account is closed – what do you *want* me to do about it?'

'No, no, take no notice of Eddie! We need some units – how many have you got?'

Alan, keep your mouth shut, don't be spiteful, don't rub it in. Don't start bullshitting that you've allocated all the stock to someone else and make it even worse. Just shut up.

'Let me call you back, Mark, and I'll see if I can get some stuff to you quickly.'

I had been a good boy and restrained myself from my mischievous ways. We were obviously back on track with Dixons without the need for further confrontation. But the episode did endorse something that was to become part of my philosophy: never rely on the retailers to help you. Don't listen to any bullshit that they love you and they'll always support you. No, you have to generate a demand for a product which drives consumers to the retailers. You must create a situation where the retailers need you and you *don't* need them because, as I was to find out through painful experience, the minute you're no longer the darling of the market, they'll drop you like a hot potato and forget about all the help and support you've given them in the past. And with the exception of my relationship with Nick Lightowler in the early days, they *all* fall into that category.

We were extremely successful with the PCW8256, selling 350,000 in the first eight months after the launch, and we went on to make a big brother version, the PCW8512, with two floppy disk drives and 256k more memory to justify sticking the price up by another £100. The same old trick worked every time – £399 for the lead-in model, £499 for the twin-drive/larger-memory version. As ever, the margin on the additional £100 per unit was exceptional.

In June 1986 we announced a turnover of £301m and profits of £75m – almost four times the profits of the previous year.

*

In America, as I'd predicted, the CPC6128 was not selling. But despite this, Pero was now driving me crazy about the PCW8256. I said, 'It's bad enough you can't sell the CPC6128s which are arriving in volume – now you're talking about buying something else that isn't suited for the American market! Haven't you learned your lesson yet?' He explained that it was the people at Sears World Trade who'd picked up on the publicity for the PCW8256 – it was *they* who were showing enthusiasm for the product.

These Americans, bless 'em, they're ever the optimists and you have to take them with a pinch of salt. I was very sceptical, but Pero insisted on coming to London with a representative of Sears World Trade, Karl Flummerfelt.

This guy was scary. He'd obviously found out every single detail about me personally. He spoke about virtually everything I'd ever done in business and while he was trying to be complimentary, it made me feel uncomfortable. This was before Google made it easy to find the ins

and outs of everything. To have this level of knowledge meant someone had done a lot of work. Perhaps I hadn't realised how much people
pored over stories that documented Amstrad's meteoric rise in magazines like *Business Weekly*. Flummerfelt was a mine of information,
what you'd call in this day and age 'Wikipedia on Alan Sugar'. The
long and short of my meeting with him was that Sears World Trade
wanted to represent Amstrad on the PCW8256 in America.

I was not enthusiastic about this venture, but Flummerfelt insisted
they wanted to buy the product. His attitude also made it quite clear to
me that this Jaime Pero guy was now becoming an irritation. He had
talked Sears World Trade into financing the CPC6128s and, surprise
surprise, they didn't sell. What's more, the people in California who'd
promised Pero they would take the goods didn't! So they were well
and truly lumbered with the first batches of CPC6128s. They asked
whether it would be possible to cancel some of the new shipments on
the way, as Pero couldn't even sell the first lot.

At the time, demand for the CPC6128 was big in Spain and France
and we were turning customers away because we hadn't ordered
enough. So it suited me to flip the production over and divert the
American ones to the French market. However, there would be some
costs involved in writing off redundant components used solely on the
American versions.

Before I even broached the subject of payment for the redundant
components, Sears World Trade offered to pay a 50 per cent cancellation fee for the next 20,000 units on the way (in fact, it turned out that
no more than 10 per cent of the total sales price would be redundant).

Some people might have bitten their hands off at the 50 per cent
offer – *I* felt it would have been a bit of a cheek, total greed considering I badly needed the units in Spain and France. It does show you
how stupid people from these giant companies can be when they're
dishing out what is effectively shareholders' money. Maybe they had
their reasons, but I couldn't understand them. I told Flummerfelt there
was no need to pay a 50 per cent cancellation fee, though there would
be a small charge, around 10 per cent. I told the truth – I needed the
product in another market and could divert it.

I also took a big stab at Pero, saying how full of shit he was and that

I'd warned him a hundred times that this product would not sell in America, but despite those warnings he kept insisting he had orders. I lost my rag and told him that his orders weren't worth wiping my arse with and that he was a typical bullshitting American.

Part of my anger over the situation in America was because I was growing up in a business sense and was no longer prepared to be as opportunistic as I'd been when dealing with the United Africa Company or importing CB radios. Amstrad was now a public company and we had to be careful and try to build our brand.

While there was a lot of praise from the media over our phenomenal growth, there were also snipers. The *Daily Mail*, for example, never joined the Alan Sugar fan club during my rise to fame. Success stories are not on their agenda, but they are always ready to pounce on a failed venture – and Amstrad failing in the USA would be right up their alley.

It didn't seem a good thing to ship stuff to America, even if payment *was* guaranteed, but despite witnessing the bollocking I'd given Pero, the Sears World Trade people still insisted on going forward with the PCW8256.

I told them they had to be realistic – there was no way they could sell the PCW8256 for $399. In simple terms, if I gave them the same price as I gave Dixons, fine – they might be able to add a 25 per cent margin and sell it in their own retail stores. But if they expected to make a profit *and* sell it on to another retailer, who in turn had to put their own 25 per cent margin on it, the product would end up ridiculously overpriced at $800.

It was clear that Flummerfelt had been given the job of running Sears World Trade and he was treating it as his little empire. It was also becoming clear to me that they didn't have any products other than the CPC6128 – and now they wanted the word processor too! When I asked him what other things they were importing, he was very vague and couldn't tell me. It seemed that this new business unit, Sears World Trade, had to start proving it could do something otherwise it would be shut down.

These deluded people ordered 100,000 PCW8256s and opened the LC for the first 50,000. They told me they were going to push Pero to one side and that this deal had nothing at all to do with him – it was between Amstrad and Sears World Trade.

On the face of it, the story of Amstrad selling to the mighty Sears organisation in the USA sounded good and people in the UK thought we'd pulled off a major coup. But deep down, I knew it wouldn't be successful. Nevertheless, I reluctantly agreed to develop an American version of the PCW8256. The following summer, at the Chicago Consumer Electronics Show, Sears World Trade displayed the PCW8256. They had taken on a team of salespeople to sell these into the trade.

Finally, the penny had started to drop with them that although the product was conceptually excellent, the pricing was too high at $899. They asked me if I would be prepared to contribute to advertising, on the grounds that they were promoting my brand. They wanted to put our advert – the one trashing the typewriters – on TV. I explained that we were not responsible for paying for their marketing – that was part and parcel of their privilege of being the sole distributor for Amstrad in America.

I remember having a row with their sales manager on the stand. He started getting sarcastic, slapping me on the back and saying, 'You're a clever man, Alan, you really are. You take all this money from us, all these letters of credit which we can't cancel, you won't give us any money for advertising and I'm stuck with the job of selling the product. Seems you've stitched us up quite well.' I turned to this loud-mouthed idiot and told him that he was just a simple salesman and that he should keep his mouth shut and his nose out of business that didn't affect him.

Not that I had to justify myself to him, but he wasn't at the original meeting the previous year, when I'd told his bosses not to buy the bloody stuff! I raised my voice so loudly that everybody started to look around. He went bright-red in the face.

Although the stuff wasn't selling, the shipments were still piling in. However, this time there was *no way* I was going to cancel the order because the number of components required in the construction of the PCW8256 for the American market was significant. Plus, this time we weren't short of units for our other markets.

Flummerfelt asked me whether we could slow down the shipments. I wanted to shut those thoughts down immediately and said, 'The CPC6128 was a one-off situation and it ain't happening here. You've *got* to take this whole batch of 100,000 units. And, by the way, you'd better open the LC now for the balance.'

They never did open that LC. To be honest, we only produced 35,000 of the first 50,000 units, so we were not financially exposed for the balance of the order. Instead, David Hyams and I negotiated with the legal department of Sears World Trade a $2m cancellation agreement for the balance of the order. This time I didn't feel morally obliged to let them off the hook. They had been warned very clearly not to try to sell this stuff. Being backed by the mighty Sears, they coughed up. They realised that they had no chance of fighting the compensation because we had done nothing wrong. We were quite within our rights to sue them for loss of profit on the 50,000 units they wanted to cancel.

The story of Sears World Trade doesn't end there. It got a bit messy. Pero believed he was diddled out of a great business opportunity and he went to an ambulance-chaser lawyer in Chicago and started a class action against Sears World Trade and Amstrad.

The ambulance-chaser was obviously working on a contingency fee. He was banking on the fact that if he caused enough aggravation to a giant organisation like Sears World Trade, they would just pay him some money to get rid of him. He made the fatal error of thinking that's also what I'd do.

To cut a long story, we employed lawyers in Chicago to fight the issue on our behalf. Pero had contacted Dominguez and told him that if I were to agree that Sears World Trade had screwed Pero and give a witness statement to that effect, he would drop the action against Amstrad – all he wanted to do was get a lot of money out of the subsidiary of the giant Sears.

Under the American laws of deposition, the lawyers acting for Pero came to England to take a statement from me. In that statement I had to explain everything that went on, as far as transactions were concerned, in the relationship between Amstrad and Sears World Trade and also declare anything else that had gone on which may influence the case.

These smart-arse lawyers were firing questions at me all day long till it got to the stage when they asked me if I'd had any contact with Pero since the last meetings in Chicago.

'Yes,' I replied.

'What did he say to you?'

I told the lawyers, 'I'm sure you don't want to hear what he said to me.'

They thought they'd struck gold. '*We'll* decide whether we want to hear it or not. What did he say to you?'

I replied, 'Are you sure you want to push me on this – on what he said to me?'

'Yes,' they said impatiently. Bear in mind that also in the room was a lawyer from the main Sears legal department.

'Well, you asked for it. What your client said to me was, "Alan, if you write me a witness statement saying that Sears screwed me, I will let you off the hook and I will not sue your company." Okay? Are you happy with that?'

David Hyams couldn't hold back his laughter. He turned to them and said, 'He did warn you! He asked you twice whether you wanted to hear it, you said yes, so he told you. Now it's in the deposition.'

'When did my client ring you and say this? Last week? A couple of weeks ago?'

'Dunno,' said I, 'but he also said it to Mr Dominguez. I'm sure that when Mr Dominguez is called into the courtroom in Chicago, he will also give witness to this fact.'

The ambulance-chaser was not a happy bunny. He was deflating like a balloon.

A couple of weeks later, the Sears corporate lawyers decided to settle with Pero and give him some money to get rid of the irritation. His lawyers must have copped a large share of this, leaving Pero with the dreg ends. *We* told them both to get stuffed – they got nothing out of us. Unfortunately, under American law, there's no way to claim back your legal fees, even if someone brings a failed action against you, so the ambulance-chasers rely on large corporations realising it's going to cost them a fortune to defend their position and deeming it cheaper simply to pay some money for them to go away.

In truth, it would have been cheaper for Amstrad to give Pero $100,000 and tell him to piss off, because the bill we got from our high-class Chicago lawyers, Mayer, Platt & Brown, must have been for well over a quarter of a million dollars. But it was the principle that mattered in this particular case.

People often argue that my principles are wrong if they cost me money. There have been times when I've spent a fortune on lawyers just to get a point over, knowing I had no chance of getting all the money back. I don't know whether I'm right or wrong – commercial people would say I'm wrong. I defy the principles of business which say, 'Pay a few quid and tell the people to clear off.' Somehow I don't think I could ever bring myself to do that.

*

Otake was never one to dish out compliments, but he used to say to me, 'Sugar-san, you are a gambler. I like your fighting spirit.' By this he meant that he'd never come across a person like me who was prepared to place large orders based on unproved concepts. In the Harvard Business School manual, they advise that before anyone embarks upon large-scale production of any item, they should test the market with sophisticated market research techniques. Then, and only then, should they sample the market by making a small production run to see how the products are accepted.

This is all well and good in certain sectors, but in the dynamic electronics industry of the eighties, there was no time for this nonsense and I had to trust my gut instinct when it came to gauging what consumers would go for. This ability took in things like spotting trends and tendencies, observing what competitors were doing, trying to condense and feature-pack a product (Amstrad was the Swiss Army knife of electronics) and at the same time bring it down to a price affordable by my target consumer, whom I warmly referred to as 'the truck driver and his wife'.

I'll now tell you a story which will be hard for so-called business experts to understand. What I was about to embark on, you can't learn from a book. Nor can you go into Boots and buy a bottle of entrepreneur juice to teach you how to do it.

In February 1986, Bob Watkins and I were on one of our regular trips to the Far East. I was staying at the Peninsular Hotel in Hong Kong, on the Kowloon side, a fantastic place that brings back so many great memories for me. While there, I received a message asking me to call Mark Souhami of Dixons at the Mandarin Hotel.

I thought this rather strange and called him back to ask what he, a retailer, was doing in Hong Kong. He explained he was there with Stanley Kalms on a general trip around the Far East and that Stanley thought it would be a nice idea for me to pop over and have tea at the Mandarin.

'Have tea with Stanley?' I said, puzzled. 'What are you going on about? Stanley doesn't have *tea*. What's going on, Mark? What do you really want?'

'Alan, why are you so sceptical? Why are you so suspicious? We're friends! We're all in Hong Kong. Pop over, have tea. What's wrong with that?'

'Nothing wrong with that, Mark, but rather strange, to say the least.'

Intrigued by the invitation, next day I took the ferry from Kowloon across Victoria Harbour, which dropped me right outside the Mandarin Hotel. I went up to Stanley's suite.

'Good afternoon, Stanley, I'm surprised to see you here. What are you trying to do – contact my suppliers, as usual? You're wasting your time, mate. You can't screw me any more, you know.'

Usually, nobody would talk to Stanley in that way, but I had this cheeky knack of getting away with it, as it came across as half-joking. I am like an elephant – I never forget – and this was my little dig at him for the way he'd screwed me on VCRs. While Stanley liked me personally, there would be no favours coming from him in business terms. And the feeling was mutual.

'So, what do you want, Stanley? What have you schlapped me over here for? I'm busy. I've got no time for tea.'

'Calm down, Alan. I just thought it would be nice for us to touch base.'

'Yeah, okay, Stanley, forget all that touching base stuff and tell me what you want.'

'Oh, you are terrible, you really are terrible, Alan. All right, well, look, let me tell you this – this Clive Sinclair fellow is going bust.'

I was shocked, but seconds after digesting the statement I remembered hearing rumours that he was running out of money fast and I'd seen a front-page story in the *Mirror* about how the mogul Robert Maxwell was going to rescue Sinclair.

'Right, okay . . .' I said cautiously.

'Well, we sell hundreds of thousands of his products and we've been approached by Price Waterhouse to see whether we would take over his company to get him out of trouble. Now as you know, Alan, we are retailers. We're not interested in this, so I'm giving you the heads-up. You need to jump in quickly and see if you can sort a deal out.'

Wow! Now that *was* interesting. It actually took the wind out of my sails.

First of all, I couldn't help feeling some satisfaction that my arch-competitor was going down the pan. I know it's not a nice thing to say, but I'm being honest. Secondly, the acquisition of the Sinclair brand would be a massive coup for Amstrad.

After further discussion with Mark and Stanley, the story became clearer. The truth of the matter was that the man at Price Waterhouse had *not* suggested that Dixons buy the company, but had actually asked for an introduction to me, knowing that I was also a supplier to Dixons.

Dixons quite selfishly realised that if Sinclair went bust, they would be stuffed in two ways. One, they would lose a lot of business because they were selling hundreds of thousands of Sinclair Spectrums; and two, they would have no after-sales service path for the millions of Sinclair units they'd put into the marketplace.

From Stanley's suite in the Mandarin Hotel, we called London to speak to the guy at Price Waterhouse. From what I could gather, Sinclair was in dire financial straits. Barclays Bank had a debenture over the company and by 31 March 1986 either Sinclair had to cough up the money they owed them or they were going to force them into administration.

Clive Sinclair at that time was a national treasure, and the guy at

Price Waterhouse explained to me that there were deep political con-notations here. They could not allow Sinclair to go into bankruptcy – it would be deemed a disaster for the flag-bearer of the British com-puter industry to go under. So many songs had been sung about his enterprises and Barclays Bank would be seen to be the people that shot Bambi's mum. It's true to say that if Clive Sinclair, who by then had been knighted, wasn't as famous or popular as he was, the company would have simply been slung into liquidation and no one would have heard any more about it.

I agreed to call the guy from Price Waterhouse back in a couple of hours as I didn't want to discuss my business affairs in front of Stanley and Mark. On my second call with the chap, it became clear to me there was a deal to be done. I discussed this with Bob Watkins, who was very excited at the prospect and understood what a blockbusting event this would be.

Now, here is where I defied all business logic. With no deal done, I decided there and then – before meeting Clive Sinclair or discussing numbers with banks – that I was going to buy the Sinclair business one way or another.

We rushed over to our Hong Kong office and instructed the designer to look up pictures of the Sinclair computer in some trade magazines. My concept was to redesign the Sinclair Spectrum to incorporate a built-in cassette data-recorder in line with the Amstrad philosophy. By noon next day, with a bit of tweaking from Bob and myself, we had a full colour picture on the drawing-board of our ver-sion of the Sinclair computer. Remember, still no deal discussed.

Bob called Colin Heald, the production director of Avnet, a Tai-wanese manufacturer we used, and asked him to jump on a plane and get over to our Hong Kong office. The night before, Bob had tele-phoned Ivor Spital back at Amstrad and instructed him to go and buy a Sinclair computer at Dixons, open it up and report back to Bob in the morning with a list of components on the PCB – this was to be our preliminary bill of materials for us to cost in Hong Kong.

With the usual Amstrad efficiency, this information was waiting for us first thing in the morning. In our meeting with Colin Heald, we realised we could produce a fantastic new version of the Sinclair

Spectrum with a built-in data-recorder and sell it at a retail price of
£139.

By that afternoon, Isaac Ip, one of our draughtsmen in Hong
Kong, had drawn up the external cabinet dimensions of this new
Amstrad Sinclair. His drawing included details of the internal construction and showed the size of the PCB and cassette mechanism
module. We faxed the whole lot through to Avnet and asked them to
give us an estimate of the tooling cost. Again, still no deal with anyone.

If we were to get stocks into the market for the Christmas season
of 1986, we would have to press the button on tooling there and then
and if we wanted to bring 100,000 computers into the market quickly,
we would need at least three sets of tools.

Now, here's another reality check: I'd done no deal to buy the company (I'd never even met Clive Sinclair) and I hadn't discussed
anything with his bank. Despite this, I pushed the green button and
told Avnet to go ahead with the tooling, an expenditure of approximately $100,000 for three tools. The way I saw it, if everything went
tits up in my negotiations when I got back to England, it was just a bad
outing that didn't come off.

While Mark Souhami and Stanley Kalms were still on their Far
East trip, Souhami met up with his senior buyer, Brent Wilkinson. I
invited them over to Amstrad's Hong Kong office and we showed
them the drawing of the new Amstrad Sinclair. Not only that, one of
the Amstrad Hong Kong engineers had carved out of polystyrene the
profile of what the thing would look like in real life. They had stuck the
drawing on top of it and generally painted it up, so that one could get
an idea of the size.

Souhami and Wilkinson couldn't believe their eyes. Souhami said,
'I only met you a couple of days ago, Alan. My God! What are you
doing? You haven't bought Sinclair yet – you haven't done a deal.
What are you playing at?'

I explained to Souhami that I'd spoken a bit more with Price
Waterhouse and my gut feeling was that this deal would happen. I
said, 'All *you* need to focus on is whether you want to be the first to buy
these. The retail price is £139.99 and I've already pushed the button on
making the first production of a hundred thousand units. So, do you

want to buy them – yes or no? You've got nothing to lose really – if it doesn't happen, you've lost nothing.'

Incredible as it may sound, they placed an order there and then for 100,000 units on the basis that we would start shipping them to Dixons in mid-September.

It was time for me to get back to England and meet the Price Waterhouse chap for the first time, as well as Clive Sinclair. The following week, Clive Sinclair came to our Brentwood headquarters late in the evening, slipping in through the rear fire escape. If anyone from the industry or the media had seen him creeping into my offices, it would have been front-page news.

As I had recalled, a few weeks earlier the *Daily Mirror* and their infamous owner Robert Maxwell had declared, 'We are going to rescue Sir Clive.' The guy from Price Waterhouse told me that Maxwell was full of shit. When it came to putting some cash on the table, he was all talk.

The purpose of the meeting was to try to come up with a mutual win-win situation. It was a momentous event meeting Clive for the first time – after all, he was a national hero, the so-called father of the computer industry in Britain. He was quite polite, even humble, with no hint of arrogance, and admitted that his passion for research had caused him to take his eye off the ball and overspend. He was no fool and could see there was no way out for him. With his reputation about to go down the pan, he was clearly looking for an elegant way to preserve his image.

I was very polite in return and showed him the respect he deserved. Having said that, I did need to keep the meeting on track and every so often, in a diplomatic way, reiterate that he was bust and I was there to find a mutually acceptable way out. Clive was angling for me simply to rescue the company and allow him to run it, but there was absolutely no chance of this. All I was interested in was acquiring the intellectual property rights and the brand name Sinclair – and that's it. I had no intentions of inheriting any of the problems his company had got itself into.

Clive left the meeting very despondent. He'd thought I was a white knight who was going to rescue his company, leaving him in charge to continue developing his new ideas.

I was also disappointed – it seemed the arrangements I'd made in Hong Kong the week before were premature. Perhaps I'd jumped the gun.

Next day, the Price Waterhouse man called me and told me that Clive wanted to see me again. Clive had digested the very blunt stance I had taken and was starting to realise that there weren't any other options. I jumped in a car with Bob Watkins, who was very excited at the prospect of meeting Clive, and drove to Cambridge. We met Clive at his house rather than his famous research centre, as that would have caused a furore in the marketplace and the media. This time, the Price Waterhouse people were not present, as Clive wanted to see whether he could come out of this deal with some money for himself.

Once again, I had to be blunt. I told him that I was a simple-thinking man with a very narrow focus on my objectives and that I didn't like over-complicated situations. *All* I would be interested in was acquiring the Sinclair rights so that Amstrad could make stuff under the Sinclair brand, with no other strings attached. (I had not mentioned the model we'd designed to Clive or Price Waterhouse.) This second meeting with Clive was his last throw of the dice to try to rescue his personal integrity and secure a few quid for himself for this massive albatross he had built.

Things went quiet for a few days. I was not prepared to move from my stance.

On 20 March 1986 I was due to fly to Florida with the family. I was contacted by Price Waterhouse who asked me whether I would be prepared to attend a meeting on 24 March (which happened to be my birthday) at Barclays' headquarters in the City. I agreed and suggested that Ann and the kids travelled to Florida ahead of me. Family holidays were important to Ann, so she was not a happy bunny, but I promised her that I would be there on the 24th, one way or another. I worked out that if I left the City at about 3.30 p.m., I could catch the 5 p.m. Concorde to New York and from there fly down to Fort Lauderdale, which would get me into Boca Raton by about 10 p.m.

I arrived at Barclays' headquarters and was greeted by the guy from Price Waterhouse who asked if I'd mind waiting outside for a while. I agreed but said, 'Whatever happens, I'm leaving here at half three, so you can forget about these City meetings that go on till midnight – I'll be gone, like it or not.'

He'd obviously relayed this to the people in the meeting and I was rapidly called in. It was a massive boardroom packed with people from Barclays. Sitting at the other end of the boardroom table was Clive and a few of his blokes. More importantly, his suppliers and subcontractors were there. One of these was the company AB Electronics, who were based in Wales. They were his main sub-contractor and were very badly exposed by events. If Sinclair went bust, then AB would lose millions, as would their other sub-contractor, Timex in Scotland, who were in the same boat.

They wanted to hear my proposition and I spelled out very clearly that I would throw £5m on the table today in exchange for all Sinclair's intellectual property rights, including its brand name and any software applicable to the operating system. I made it plain that I was not interested in anything else. I did not wish to take on any of their staff, I did not wish to acquire any of their premises and neither would I be responsible for any of the work in progress at AB or Timex or any other sub-contractor.

I could see this was a massive smack in the face for all the people at the table. I don't know what the guy from Price Waterhouse had told them about me, but they must have had visions that I would come in as a white knight and rescue the situation. Not only had the bank presumed that I was going to step into Sinclair's shoes as far as its debts were concerned, AB and Timex had presumed I was going to simply take over the reins and it would be business as usual.

They asked if I would step outside again while they discussed my proposition. The guy from Price Waterhouse escorted me into another room and I asked him, 'What the hell have you told these people? It seems to me that they were all shocked at my offer. Have you been bullshitting and telling them that I was going to rescue the company?'

'No, not at all, Mr Sugar, not at all. Look at me as a kind of *catalyst*; look at me as someone who's just trying to come up with a win-win situation for everyone. Barclays is very embarrassed here, as is Her Majesty's Government. Grants have been given to Sinclair up in Scotland to help employment in the Timex factory and AB employs

With Ann in Tokyo on my first trip, in 1975, looking like a hippy.

I bumped into Sammy Davis Junior at the Okura Hotel, Tokyo, May 1976.
I knew no one would believe me unless I had photographic evidence.

The tower system that changed our fortunes.

SOFT EJECT DOOR

The flotation of Amstrad made the front page of the *Evening Standard*. I kept one of their advertising banners.

CITY TODAY

AMSTRAD HI-FI TO GO PUBLIC

Evening STANDARD

Mr Otake, the boss of Orion. I put up with his mad ways as no one could beat Orion for quality and speed of production.

Lord Carrington handing me the *Guardian* Young Businessman of the Year Award in 1984. Inside, I was worried the Amstrad bubble was going to burst.

The CPC464, which took off like a rocket, outselling the competition.

'And all this, gentlemen, for £399.' The PCW8256 word processor.

With Marion Vannier in 1986 at one of the Amstrad exhibition stands.

With Sir Clive Sinclair at the press conference to announce that
Amstrad had bought his company, 1986.

The Amstrad Team, around 1988. Seated from left to right: me, José Luis Dominguez, Marion Vannier, Malcolm Miller. Standing from left to right: Jim Rice, Colin Heald, Bob Watkins, Ken Ashcroft.

Dickie Mould, aka Boycie.

With Mr Funai outside the Funai-Amstrad factory in 1987. The venture turned out to be a bit of a disaster.

Showing Prince Charles a new PC at an event in Birmingham in 1988.

With Ann and Gulu Lalvani.

Ann with the kids on holiday.

Simon's Bar Mitzvah, with his proud
grandfathers and dad.

Daniel's Bar Mitzvah, in the
garden at Bramstons.

With Mum at Simon's
engagement party, 1991.

At the launch of Sky with Rupert Murdoch, June 1988. I'd just promised in front of the media to make satellite dishes for £199 – and I didn't have a clue how I was going to do it!

Receiving my honorary doctorate from London's City University, December 1988.

hundreds of people in Wales. The whole Sinclair image is now about to go down the pan. You *are* the white knight.'

He was trying to big me up, to play to my ego, and I have to say that in some cases that might have worked – sometimes people do silly things that cost them a lot of money if they don't think rationally. In this case, my ego wasn't going to get in the way. While this was going to be a great coup for Amstrad, I knew enough about Sinclair's business to see it was double-barrelled bust and I wasn't going to get involved with taking over its debt. What's more, their way of manufacturing was wrong – they should never have made their low-cost computers in the UK, but rather in the Far East, as we did.

I reminded the guy from Price Waterhouse that 'In one and a half hours' time, I'm walking out of here and frankly I don't care what they say; I'm catching my plane.' Just at that moment, the door opened and Clive appeared and asked me whether there was any possibility of me increasing my offer. I knew then that I had them on the hook. I rejoined the meeting.

It occurred to me that one of the ways to win over this deal was to see if I could find a way out for Timex and AB. This would also be good politically – the last thing I wanted was to be branded as the person who put a load of people out of work in Scotland and Wales.

I came up with my final offer: £5m on the table there and then, plus I would take responsibility for all of the work in progress that Timex and AB had for the current model. In other words, if they had 50,000 computers in various stages of assembly, they should finish assembling them and I would pay a fair price for them and take responsibility for selling them. I had Dixons in the back of my mind to dump this lot of cargo on, even if I had to sell them at the price I negotiated with AB and Timex.

Once again, they asked me to leave the room and now AB and Timex joined me in a small sub-office. They wanted to know how much I would pay them per unit. I told them that I was going to get them out of jail and they should be happy if they recovered all their costs and not start looking for any profit.

I asked them to tell me there and then what their costs were. After a few phone calls backwards and forwards, they presented me with some figures which I didn't believe. When I compared their costs to the retail price of the Sinclair Spectrum, there was a big discrepancy. They were trying it on. I made them an offer of £40 per unit – take it or leave it. A few more phone calls, a bit more negotiation, and they agreed at £48. We went back into the meeting. Now that Timex and AB were onside, this just left Barclays Bank.

'In half an hour's time,' I warned them again, 'I'm going. I'm sorry, gentlemen, but I have to leave to catch my flight.'

Having been coached by the man from Price Waterhouse, I made a little speech to Barclays that must have rung their bells. 'I understand that on 31 March 1986 you have no alternative but to foreclose on Sinclair, as the debenture expires. It is now 24 March and you have exactly seven days to find another solution. I have bent over backwards trying to help AB and Timex with their employment problems in Wales and Scotland. What happens now is entirely up to you.'

They still hadn't made a decision, so I stuck to my guns. I wished them farewell and departed for the airport.

As you can imagine, my head was spinning on the journey to Florida. I was wondering whether I was going to get this deal or not. I was also wondering whether I should throttle-back and cut my losses with Avnet in Taiwan.

The next day, in Florida, I got a call from the Price Waterhouse man. He told me that he *thought* everybody had agreed, though Barclays would make the final decision. They wanted to know whether I could come to a meeting with lawyers to draft up an agreement.

I replied, 'You know my number – you've just called it.'

'Yes . . .' he said in a puzzled voice.

'Well, then you'll know you dialled America. I am not coming to any bloody meeting in London. I'm over here with my family. Now cut the crap and tell me what the next move is. Have I got a deal or not? If I have, then I'll get a team of my people to meet with you – they are more than capable of thrashing out a contract. I don't need to be there.'

'Fair enough, Mr Sugar, we'll do that then. I'll let you know where and when the meeting will be.'

The meeting was scheduled for 30 March, which was a bank holiday weekend. I insisted that someone from my lawyers, Herbert Smith, together with David Hyams, Ken Ashcroft and Bob Watkins attended this meeting. My people were happy to do this, but Herbert Smith sent a junior intellectual-property lawyer who was unfamiliar with the computer industry, but was the only one prepared to work over the bank holiday. He wasn't the brightest star in the sky, but it turned out that we didn't really need him in the end. Bob was at the meeting, even though his wife was on the verge of having a baby.

The meeting started at 9 a.m. UK time. When I woke up in Florida at 7 a.m. (noon UK time), I got in touch with Bob and Ken and they told me we'd got virtually nowhere. Barclays, Sinclair and everyone else had been trying to throw in all sorts of other obligations, such as after-sales service. I'd already told them that I had no interest in inheriting their past problems, but they still tried it on.

Throughout the course of the day, the phone was red-hot. My team was going backwards and forwards, speaking to me then arguing with the Barclays mob. Finally, they got to the stage of having a draft contract, which Ken insisted I see.

At my house in Florida, I had installed a giant Panasonic fax machine which would make a real racket. It was in the dressing room adjacent to my bedroom and if faxes came in at night, all the clanging, clattering and beeping would wake Ann up and she would give me a load of stick. I had to train my staff in Hong Kong and England not to send faxes until 7 a.m. Florida time. On this occasion, however, the fax machine was running right through the night. I stayed up the whole of that night and, by 8 a.m. the following morning, 31 March, we had finally agreed a contract.

There's a bizarre ending to this amazing story. Part of the deal was that Sinclair had to deliver us proof that they owned the source code in the main heart of the chip, which, incidentally, was made by Ferranti. We needed an irrevocable letter from Ferranti saying that they would continue to supply us the chip and would accept that we were now the owner of the intellectual property rights.

It then turned out that Sinclair *didn't* actually own the intellectual property rights to the software in the heart of the chip! At the eleventh hour, on 31 March, just before the debenture was due to expire, they discovered that some bloody hippy had written the software code for them and they would need *his* signature to assign the whole deal over to Amstrad.

And where was this hippy? He was fishing by a river in Cambridgeshire. And would he come to London to sign an agreement? Absolutely not – not on bank holiday weekend. But if someone would come to this river in Cambridgeshire with a cheque for £20,000, he would sign. I know you must be thinking that I'm making it all up, but I swear it's the absolute truth. A taxi was sent from the City of London to somewhere near Ely to locate this long-haired chap sitting on the banks of the Great Ouse river. A banker's draft from Barclays was handed over to him and he duly signed over the rights. The lawyers must have missed this and if it wasn't for me and Bob pushing this point, we could have been bang in trouble with a claim after we'd started making the stuff.

Finally, the deal was done. Everyone agreed that the matter would remain confidential until I returned from my holiday and that it would be announced officially at a press conference.

Ann didn't often take much notice of my business life, but on this occasion she realised what a massive coup this was. Even *she* knew that Sinclair was a big-time brand. When I told her the news that morning, she congratulated me and gave me a kiss and a hug and said, 'Well done.'

Bloody hell, it must have been a big coup if she was interested!

I spent the next week or so in Florida speaking to Bob and giving Avnet the go-ahead for production. As well as tooling, we would now have to commit to ordering large volumes of components in order to meet the very tough delivery schedule. There was no way we could afford to airfreight these products over – they would have to be produced by August and put on a fast vessel to arrive in England by mid-September to catch the Christmas trade.

On 7 April, a press conference was called in London and the media was invited to receive an announcement from Alan Sugar and Clive Sinclair. The media wasn't as clued-up in those days as they are now. There was no Sky television, no internet and there had been no leaks, so nobody had any information. People must have thought we were going to join forces or something. The market perception of Clive Sinclair was that he was still kingpin in computers.

One of the things I recall about the press conference was that it was televised and to avoid the lights reflecting off Clive's bald head, he had to be brushed with some anti-glare powder. Funny what sticks in your mind.

Then came the moment when I experienced my first real paparazzi event. Both of us stepped out of a room and walked down a corridor towards the main meeting hall. There were at least twenty-five photographers flashing their cameras at us. Even *I* hadn't realised what a sensational story this was going to be.

I was very careful in choosing my words at that press conference, to make sure that everybody knew what the deal was about. I was at pains to point out that we were *not* inheriting the past business of Sinclair or its after-sales obligations, but at the same time I had to be careful not to kill off the existing Spectrum, as I had to get rid of the ones I'd agreed to take from AB and Timex. I didn't mention the new model we were developing and managed to deflect questions about the destiny of the existing Spectrum and what we would be doing in the future.

I had agreed some words with Clive. There was no merit in me gloating and I wanted to big him up and leave him with some dignity. He announced that I had allowed him to use the Sinclair brand name in a very limited fashion on some of the new and exciting projects that he was going off to develop in the future.

It did end up a win-win situation because Clive kept his dignity and, I think, deservedly so. Throughout the course of our many meetings and conversations, his assistants told me that he really *is* just a boffin. He admires the fact that I'm a businessman and accepts that he is not.

Dominguez could not believe we'd got the Sinclair brand. He was absolutely delighted and got busy advertising it heavily in the Spanish market. In fact, now that Amstrad had acquired the Sinclair brand name and taken out one of its main competitors, it was about to dominate the European market in microcomputers.

We sold the AB and Timex stock to Dixons at cost price, which made Dixons very happy. I think they took delivery of over 80,000 of the old computers. I had honoured my deal with AB and Timex and, as far as I was concerned, I'd done my bit.

Colin Heald and his team at Avnet also did a great job. The cargo duly turned up in the middle of September. We increased our order to over 350,000 units to be shipped to Europe before Christmas, but more to the point, we actually *sold* 300,000 in that period.

Following that first meeting at the Mandarin with Mark and Stanley in late February, we had done the deal, tooled up and made and sold 300,000 units by early December. You won't find a story like that in the Harvard Business School manual.

*

During my Q&As on businesses and enterprise with young people, one of the most frequent questions I'm asked is, 'Who do you aspire to?' Of course, I've aspired to different people at different stages of my life. Initially, the only person I *knew* in business was my Uncle John, who had his shop, but, as the story tells, I rapidly overtook him. Then there were the suppliers – the likes of Gulu and Colin Lewin – whom I also overtook and indeed became a supplier to. Then, later on, I had, and still have, a great admiration for Rupert Murdoch and the late Lord Weinstock, as well as Bill Gates and Sir Richard Branson.

One event sticks in my mind regarding business aspirations. It seems that around 1985–6 a couple of young entrepreneurs by the names of Richard Schlagman and Mark Futter aspired to *me*, which I guess is rather complimentary. They had tracked my success and, to a certain extent, had successfully emulated it.

Richard Schlagman was the grandson of Alfie Goldstone, one of the old warhorses from the early days of electrical wholesaling and fancy goods. Alfie was deemed to be the kingpin in the marketplace, though he wasn't an importer. He told his grandson to try to follow my example and Schlagman and Futter set up a non-manufacturing electronics company which imported goods from the Far East. They made a clever move in acquiring the brand name Bush from the then defunct Rank Organisation – it was a rather popular brand in the seventies and the two lads bought it while it still had some life in it.

We kept in contact and on my way back from the annual Berlin Electronics Fair in September 1986, Richard Schlagman sat next to me on the plane. As part of his usual questioning of me – about what he and his partner's next move should be – he mentioned that he'd sold his company to Alba. The duo was now looking to see what else they could do.

My advice to him off the cuff was, 'You should step back a moment and enjoy the money you've made.' He asked me if he should invest in Amstrad, but I told him, as he knew, that I couldn't give him any inside information. And even if I could, I didn't want the responsibility of worrying whether their money would go down the pan due to stock market fluctuations. Nevertheless, he said that the future for Amstrad looked bright, so he and his partner might well consider buying shares. I did what I normally do in these situations: I didn't answer. It transpired that they did invest a substantial amount of money in Amstrad and made a packet when the shares went up over the course of the next year. They decided they would buy me a present – a portrait of me, done in oils.

To be perfectly honest, I wasn't interested but they were rather insistent. They told me they'd commissioned the artist Bryan Organ to paint me. I didn't know who he was and, quite frankly, I couldn't have cared less. It had never occurred to me to have my portrait painted and I guess my initial reaction was ungrateful – even hostile. After saying, 'Thank you very much, it really wasn't necessary,' I added, 'Look, I have to tell you – I'm not going to sit in front of some bloody artist for hours on end posing for a bleedin' picture. Please get that idea out of your heads because I don't want to upset this artistic genius you've booked.'

Schlagman called me a few days later to say that the artist just wanted an hour of my time so he could take some photographs of me and I reluctantly agreed. He wanted me in a pose which represented me at work and painted a portrait which today hangs in my house. As I've said, I had no idea who this bloke Organ was, but later found out that he was a very famous artist who'd painted portraits of Prince Philip, Princess Diana, Prince Charles and Harold Macmillan. Some of his work hangs in the National Portrait Gallery. However, as far as I was aware, he could have been one of those blokes you see at the seaside.

I found out later that his commission for painting this picture was somewhere in the region of £60,000. Considering how much money that was back in 1987 – a small fortune – the boys certainly *were* very grateful for the money they'd made on their Amstrad shares. I was less than gracious, moaning about wasting my time with the artist.

Schlagman and Futter never got back into the electronics industry. They flirted with the idea of representing Amstrad in America and opening up a branch there, but the discussions became rather complicated and we gave up the idea.

On the subject of share dealing, as Amstrad shares at the time were growing year on year, personal friends and relatives came to realise the gains they could have made had they bought Amstrad shares. You can imagine the number of times I was pestered by people to give them the proverbial tip-off as to whether to buy or sell. My stock answer to everyone, including close relatives, was, 'If I give you a tip and you make a lot of money and people find out I'd been tipping you, you will have to come and visit me in prison because it's illegal. I can't do it – it's as simple as that.'

This really upset a few people, who felt it was their divine right, being a close associate of mine, to have some insider knowledge. The problem was that even if I *were* so inclined, you can imagine how any tips I gave them would precipitate down to their contacts and beyond. So, because of this, I became very tight-lipped.

I was just as careful not to leak information on shares going up or down. Yet, despite this, people outside my circle of friends and family – particularly those in the City who purport to be honourable people working within the Chinese wall in their organisations – would still try to prise the information out of me before anyone else had it. My stock answer to them was, 'I don't care whether you represent some massive pension fund; I have to be mindful of the poor old retired colonel sitting in his deckchair in Devon. He has as much right to know about the fortunes or misfortunes of the company as you do. And so we will publish our results every six months and that's about all I'm prepared to say to you.'

*

While all the Sinclair stuff was going on, I was also looking into the possibility of producing an IBM-compatible computer, something my people in Brentwood, France and Spain had been urging me to do. The real personal computer market was about to explode and we could see from the USA that it was the IBM format that was gaining momentum as the ultimate business tool. I asked Bill Poel and Roland Perry to get some IBM computers so we could take a look at what was inside these things. I wanted to see how they justified a sales price of over £2,000 for the main system unit alone – not including the monitor!

It didn't come as too much of a surprise to Bob Watkins and myself that when we opened the cabinet, we just saw some PCBs with a load of chips. Even Bill and Roland, hovering over our shoulders, found it hard to justify that the computer should cost more to produce than a standard piece of hi-fi or audio equipment.

I think that the Amstrad way was a tremendous learning curve for them. When someone is cocooned in a particular industry, such as computers, with no other point of reference, such as to low-priced consumer electronics, it is understandable how they can believe the hype that there's some mystique in computer technology. External snipers talked about Amstrad buying cheap components to make computers, but this was rubbish. There's no such thing as cheap plastic, a cheap D-RAM or a cheap floppy disk drive – they cost what they cost.

After a little discussion with Bob Watkins and a quick back-of-a-fag-packet calculation, I said that we had to target our first IBM-compatible computer – with monitor – at £399 plus VAT. The 'plus VAT' was a good way of achieving my magic price point while under-lining the fact that it was going to be a business computer (as retail prices for consumer electronics products already included VAT). Had there been any aggro from the advertising standards people, my argu-ment would have been that the £399 plus VAT pricing was justifiable, as I was claiming this was a business computer. The important thing was that I made the 'plus VAT' clear in the advert.

It's strange how I was already starting to think about the target price and VAT issues when all we'd really done was take an IBM PC to pieces in the lab. But to my mind, and Bob's, it was a done deal – this was what we were going to do. The question now was: how were we going to make them?

We called a meeting with Roland Perry, Bill Poel and Mark Jones to discuss the way forward and discovered that in order to get to the target price, we would have to make three custom gate-array chips. On top of this, Bill insisted that we needed something called a 'mouse'. Bob and I didn't know what this was at the time – that's how early-days it was. The specification was defined and I pressed the button to go ahead.

The plan was to again offer an all-in-one unit with one power cord to fire the whole lot up. We could incorporate the power supply for the whole system into the monitor. We decided to have two types of monitor: a monochrome 'paper-white' version and a colour version offering a palette of sixteen colours. This was highly unusual at the time, as all IBM computers offered just four shades of grey mono-chrome. Toshiba developed our three custom chips and we were able to assemble some samples of the Amstrad PC1512 – code-named 'AERO'.

Now, there's an argument about where we got this code-name from. I always spelled it AERO and have suggested that it came from a discussion where I said, 'If we make this computer and get it out there for £399, it'll fly off the shelves, so we should call it AERO.' Others spelled it AIRO standing for Amstrad's IBM Rip-Off. The debate still goes on amongst some of my old colleagues as to which one was right.

Now that we had a clear road map of the hardware, we needed to supply the computer with some software for the DOS (disk operating system). Up till then we had been dealing with the company Digital Research whose version of DOS (called DR-DOS), Bill and Roland explained to me, was exactly the same as Microsoft's MSDOS. At the time, all I knew about Microsoft was that they had dabbled in a games computer and had some kind of operating system which they hadn't been successful with.

I wasn't interested in Microsoft at all and certainly had no intention whatsoever of paying them a high royalty per box for every piece of MSDOS software I shifted. Up till then we'd been paying tiny royalties to people like Digital Research for packaging some of their software, while in other cases we were buying the licence outright. Companies like Locomotive Software, who wrote LocoScript, were paid a moderate royalty on every item we sold. Therefore, we took the decision to ship DR-DOS with our computer.

One of the things I regret, on reflection, was not adhering to certain industry standards. As an example, the only mouse that was available on the market at the time was manufactured by the company Alps in Japan for Microsoft. The cost of this mouse was approximately $25, a ridiculous amount of money and certainly not acceptable as far as Amstrad was concerned.

I commissioned Vitus Luk in our Hong Kong office to develop the Amstrad mouse from scratch and, to his credit, he did a superb job. Where we made our mistake was the plug we chose at the end of the cable to connect it to the computer – it was non-industry standard and therefore made the mouse an odd-ball item. Similarly, the physical format of our PC was different from the IBM. In hindsight, it would have been better to have followed the same format. I was to find this out later, when the corporate market became interested in our products. They would always want the industry standard format for everything.

The motivation for us to do it *our* way was, of course, true Amstrad cost-saving. The plug and socket used on the Microsoft mouse cost $2, whereas that used on the Amstrad mouse cost 20 cents, though they did exactly the same thing. The expression 'penny-wise, pound-foolish' comes to mind, and I'm the first to admit that this was a classic example.

As soon as we had working samples of the computer, we called a meeting with Schneider's people, Marion's people in France and Dominguez's people in Spain and disclosed what we were doing. There was an atmosphere of excitement that I can't put into words. We were in a dynamic, growing market and I'd just come up with another world-beating product. Credit to Schneider, Marion and Dominguez, the feeling was one of camaraderie. There was no arguing over price or jockeying for the first orders or anything like that – it was just a celebratory feeling.

At that meeting, we decided on a launch date for the PC1512: 2 September 1986. Nick Hewer arranged the PR for the launch at the Queen Elizabeth Conference Centre, Westminster, and about 1,200 people turned up – it was absolute mayhem. You can't really keep things a secret in business and rumours had been flying around the marketplace that Amstrad was going to launch a PC compatible, but nobody knew what the price was going to be.

With the usual fanfare and video screens and presenters, the launch took place, with the French, Spanish and German visitors wearing headphones connected to a translator. Having shown that the average PC cost £2,000 at the time, we eventually announced our price of £399 and there was a gasp of amazement from the audience. The Q&A session afterwards went on for about an hour, with journalists firing one question after another.

One of the funny things I recall was that Nick Hewer had invited the whole world and his brother to the launch. I'm convinced to this day that there were people in the audience from *Knitting Weekly* and every other magazine in the country. One woman asked a question which had nothing at all to do with the new PC1512 – she wanted to complain about the printer ribbon supplied with her PCW8256 running out too quickly! I was stuck for words for a second, but then responded, 'Ah, now we know where that one went,' and there was another wave of laughter from the audience. That shut her up.

It was getting to the stage where people were wearing me down with their questions. It felt as if every one of the journalists there wanted a piece of me. I had to go into a side room for a while to keep away from them, as my head was pulsating to near bursting-point. They didn't want to talk to Malcolm or Bill or Roland – they just wanted to talk to me. In actual fact, they'd have got far more information from the other guys.

There was an annexe area where we had about fifty of these computers on display, and the only way I can describe the scene is to say that it was like the Saturday before Christmas in Oxford Street. You could not move. All the staff we had there to advise people about the computers were completely drained by the end of the day.

There were massive headlines in the business pages of the next day's newspapers, followed by write-ups in all the trade magazines. The Amstrad share price shot up to a level whereby the company had a market capitalisation of £1.2bn.

This is possibly a time to step back and reflect. I'll say that again – one point two billion pounds – £1,200,000,000. Remember, I started from selling tar blocks as a kid. These kinds of numbers meant nothing to my mum and dad. It was mumbo jumbo; it was a figure they simply could not comprehend. I was holding 45 per cent of the shares at the time, so theoretically, on paper, I was worth £540m.

*

Schneider immediately pestered us to buy the PC1512 for the German market, but with MSDOS. I explained that DR-DOS was exactly the same; I could honestly put my hand on my heart and say that our computer, with DR-DOS, could do everything that an IBM PC could do. There really was no need for me to pay out money to Microsoft. They could either take it as it was or leave it. I also decided at this stage that I would no longer supply Schneider under their own brand name. By now, the German retail industry knew that *we* were their suppliers and while it suited me at the time to supply previous models under Schneider's brand, there was no way I was going to do this on the PC1512. I agreed a compromise with Bernhard Schneider: the front panel of the unit would say 'Amstrad PC1512 by Schneider' – a joint brand name. Again, this was a take it or leave it offer.

A week or so after the launch of the PC1512, Roland came into my office and told me that some smoothies from Microsoft had flown over on spec and wanted to speak to me about the benefits of putting Microsoft software in every computer box we sold. Bill was also hovering, telling me (off the record) that from a credibility point of view, while it was true that DR-DOS *was* the same, psychologically people wanted Microsoft's MSDOS. It was one of those marketing things. I suppose in this day and age you could equate it to having an Apple iPod or some other branded MP3 player. Both do the same, but you go for the name.

In those days, people were very snobbish about the software they ran on their computers. There were always claims that other programs would not run correctly unless you used Microsoft. None of this was true, but when you were trying to sell to a corporate market, to some jobsworth who worked on the principle 'you never get fired for buying IBM', you had to appreciate that there was no point trying to convert people; you just had to give them what they wanted.

Reluctantly, I agreed to a meeting with these guys. They tried to convince me to pay $4 per unit for this MSDOS. I told them I had absolutely no intention of doing that and effectively I couldn't care less about MSDOS. As far as I was concerned, I had produced an IBM-compatible PC at £399 that worked perfectly. I sent them away with a flea in their ear.

I think these guys must have stayed overnight in Brentwood because the next morning, they asked to see me again. This time the Microsoft arrogance had evaporated and they were desperate. They must have been given instructions by Bill Gates to 'get in the box'. There was no way that he could afford to have hundreds of thousands of IBM-compatible computers thrust into the market without Microsoft in the box.

I am not going to disclose what I paid (it's been one of the best-kept secrets in the computer industry) save to say that I agreed to take one million licences with Microsoft, at a price that suited me. I'm not sure whether the non-disclosure agreement has run out by now, but for safety's sake, I'll let it remain a secret. No matter what you may read in the industry archives and what other tittle-tattle you might hear in the computer industry, this was the true story of how Microsoft got itself into Amstrad products.

After the launch, Dixons were champing at the bit, as usual demanding all the stock that was coming in, but there were lots of other customers in the marketplace for this type of product. Large computer distributors who were already selling IBM were chasing to stock our product to sell on to the dealer networks throughout the country. It's true to say that we were now dealing with a completely different customer base. The PCW8256 word processor was deemed a consumer product; the PC1512 had moved us into another category.

Then came the sniping. IBM salesmen were running around telling customers that our product was rubbish. Mind you, what would *you* do if you were an IBM salesman trying to flog computers for £2,000 when ours were £399? The computer magazines had endorsed our computer from a compatibility point of view, explaining clearly to the trade and the public that everything the IBM did, the Amstrad did. So what was the best argument these IBM salesmen could come up with? 'There's no fan in the Amstrad – it will overheat and if it over-heats, it will conk out. Therefore it's unreliable.' It was a complete load of cobblers, but it does go to show how the whole market can change its opinion about a product based on a rumour spread by a competi-tor.

As I explained earlier, the power supply for the whole system was actually in the monitor. The reason IBM computers had a fan inside them was that *their* power supply was in the base unit and therefore needed a fan to cool it down so that the sensitive microprocessor circuits wouldn't get hot. In our computer, there was nothing inside the base unit that got hot, so it didn't need a fan.

Despite this, the BBC put out a statement saying that they wouldn't buy these Amstrads because they had no fan. Understand-ably, I went berserk. I got hold of our corporate lawyer, David Hyams, and asked him to deal with the BBC and a few others. Within a week, the BBC were forced to make a public apology. The managing director of IBM UK, Tony Cleaver, called me to say that this rumour was not a corporate position they were taking; it had been put around unoffi-cially by some of their sales staff. He started rattling off the IBM employees' manual guidelines stating what measures were going to be taken against these individuals, but I wasn't interested at all. The damage had been done. People were still saying, 'Don't buy the Amstrad because it hasn't got a fan.'

Believe it or not, I immediately asked the factory to fit a fan in the base unit of the PC1512. The fan did absolutely naff all – it was cool-ing a cool area – but we could now say that the Amstrad PC1512 had a fan.

I am a marketing man – I give people what they want. It seemed an obvious solution to me. As I said to the *Financial Times*, 'If they want a fan, I'll give them a bloody fan. If they want a computer with pink spots on, I'll give them a computer with pink spots on. I'm not here to argue.' That statement made a lot of people at Amstrad laugh and as I walked around the engineering floor, I could see everybody had stuck pink spots all over their computers. Stanley Kalms called, laughing (unusual for him, the miserable sod) and saying, 'Now, now, young Alan, we're very proud of you here at Dixons, but you know you really shouldn't talk to the *Financial Times* in that way.'

Adding the fan stuffed IBM and the BBC.

*

The original Amstrad PC1512 was sold at £399 with a paper-white monitor and a floppy disk drive. The twin floppy disk drive with paper-white monitor was an extra £100 and the twin floppy model with colour monitor was £649. To our amazement, the biggest seller was the dearest machine. Clearly we had moved into a marketplace where businesses were buying this product. It was the dawn of office automation, when the computer rapidly became a must-have, one-per-desk item.

Then there was the advertising campaign. I came up with the strapline 'Compatible with You Know Who. Priced as only We Know How.' The advertising agency we used at the time tried to change a couple of words, so they could claim that the brilliant strapline was theirs. I said to Malcolm Miller, 'Tell them to forget it and use my strapline without changing it. Tell them they'll still get their fee and can still tell the world it was their idea.'

Imagine my surprise a month or so later when I visited the Comdex Computer Show in Atlanta, Georgia, and saw that some American monkey manufacturer had copied our strapline and plastered it all over their stand. Malcolm and I contacted the exhibition organisers to explain to them that this guy was using our strapline on his stand without our permission. He'd nicked it from us. This is typical of Americans – they feel it's their divine right to take something they see in the colonies and use it without any repercussions. Well, they hadn't yet come across me.

Amstrad was becoming the biggest personal computer supplier in

Europe, but these Yanks claimed they'd never heard of us. My complaint to the organiser was met with derision, as if to say, 'Who are you?' Nevertheless, we kicked up a fuss and told them we'd get an injunction not only to shut down the stand, but also to close their show. This got their attention and in the end the manufacturer was forced to take down its signs.

The strapline was used by Dominguez in Spain and Marion in France. Of course, Schneider was unable to use it, due to the goody-goody law in Germany that made sure that IBM's feelings weren't hurt.

So great was the impact we'd made in the market, I was contacted again by Tony Cleaver, the managing director of IBM UK, who told me that we needed to enter into a licence agreement with them over certain patents they held. Most certainly, some of the techniques used in our design did infringe IBM patents, so we needed to sort this out to avoid any legal problems. The royalties offered were very fair and we duly entered into an agreement for worldwide sales.

My mind went back to 1963. There I was at sixteen, failing IBM's aptitude test and here I was twenty-three years later, signing a licence agreement with them. Within three months, I'd taken 27 per cent of the total European market away from them. Mr Gates was right to want to be in our box.

11

Everything Was Going Wrong at Once

Losing the Midas Touch

1987–9

By now, Amstrad was such a big player that I was constantly being invited to attend government functions. I recall getting invitations from Prime Minister Mrs Thatcher, the Chancellor and various other ministers, as well as Prince Charles. Naïvely thinking these might be interesting events and that maybe I'd get to meet the person who invited me, for a one-to-one chat, I schlapped along to a few of these bashes, but soon realised that most of the time they were packed with hundreds of people and if you stood on a chair you might see the Prime Minister somewhere in the middle, mingling with the crowd.

Margaret Thatcher in particular used to haul me out from time to time as a glowing example of the new breed of chirpy-chappy entrepreneur, a kind of role model to help endorse her policy of widening the opportunities for anyone from any background to become successful in business.

I soon put paid to these bashes, as they were a waste of my time, plus there was the risk that you'd get lumbered with a load of boring people. I told my secretary, Frances, 'Ditch all these invites and reply that I'm busy. If they come back enquiring why, try to suss out if it's one of these bum-rushes with hundreds of people or whether it's more intimate. If it's the latter, I might go.'

One day, Frances came to me all excited. 'You've received an invitation from Her Majesty the Queen and Prince Philip to attend Buckingham Palace.'

'Calm down, Frances,' I said. 'This is bound to be another of those bashes with five hundred people. Tell them I'm busy.'

A few minutes later she came into my office and said, 'Sorry, Alan, but you *are* going. I've been told by the Palace that you *will* attend.'

'What do you mean, I *will* attend?'

'Alan, this is a private lunch, just you and no more than five others with the Queen and Prince Philip, and I've been told to tell you that you *will* attend.'

Bloody hell – of course I'd attend! Can you believe it? Alan from Clapton was going up to London to see the Queen.

An official invitation duly arrived along with security instructions telling me to turn up at 12.30 p.m. on 25 February 1987. I took it home to show Ann, who couldn't believe it either, and she in turn called all our family and friends.

On arriving at the main courtyard of the Palace in my chauffeur-driven Rolls, I was met by some fellow who escorted me up the stairs into the very grand dining room. It was a beautiful room with a high ceiling decked out with gold leaf and a wonderful large dining table with ornate chairs to match. One of the equerries hovering about said, 'Hello, Mr Sugar, please come this way. May we offer you a drink before lunch?'

I don't drink at lunchtime, as it gives me a heavy head, so I replied, 'Yes, a tomato juice, please.'

I can't recall who the other five guests were, apart from the actress Wendy Craig, famous at the time for being in the TV series *Butterflies*. At lunch, I sat opposite the Queen and next to Prince Philip. He spoke to me of his interest in computers and we exchanged some chit-chat, including a disagreement about whether IBM printers were made in England – he thought they were; I told him they weren't.

We also chatted about his dietary tendencies – how he had to watch his weight what with so many of these lunches and how he would eat just a little of every course. Scintillating stuff. I would rather have watched paint dry, but, to be fair, I'm sure he was bored with me also. He must have been totally fed up with making polite small talk.

After lunch, we were all invited to go into the anteroom, which was as opulent as the dining room. The Queen and Prince Philip stood at the end of the room and the guests were invited to go and chat some more. The other five were like bees round a honeypot. 'Hello, Queen, I'm so and so. Yes, Queen, no, Queen. I've done this, Queen. I've got that, Queen . . .' all that stuff. I decided to stand back and let them get on with it, mainly because I hadn't got a clue what to talk to the Queen about.

One of the equerries spotted me lurking at the back of the room and told me to go ahead and speak to the Queen. He put his hand behind my back and gently nudged me forward. During that walk across the large room, I was so nervous. What the bloody hell was I going to say? What could we talk about? I have no idea what BS came out of my mouth, but I'm pretty sure the Queen didn't care. Nonetheless, it was a great event for me, and a great honour.

I had arranged to meet Ann that evening in town for dinner with a bunch of friends. As soon as we sat down, they wanted chapter and verse on the day's events. 'Well, Alan, what did the Queen say to you? What was it like? How was the lunch?'

You can imagine their excitement, but there was nothing much to tell, so I went into mischievous mode. Putting on a serious face, I recounted the bit where I had to walk across the room to speak to the Queen on a one-to-one basis. I told them I didn't know what to talk about so I had to think up something quickly.

'So what did you say?'

'Well, as I got to the Queen, I just burst out with, "Your Majesty, I feel like a fraud. I arrived here today by car when instead, Your Majesty, I should have mounted a white horse at the Tower of London, put on a cape and ridden along the embankment, with the mane of the horse and my cape flowing in the wind, before galloping along The Mall and finally entering the great courtyard of your palace. I should then have dismounted from the horse, run up the stairs and thrown my cape to the floor in front of you."'

They were glued to my every word. 'You're kidding! What did she say?'

I paused for a few seconds. 'Well, she turned to Prince Philip and said, "Hey, Phil, who is this fucking nutter?"'

Ann gave me a whack on the shoulder for winding them all up. Of course I was joking – the Queen would never use a word like 'nutter'.

*

By now I had moved my mother and father out of their council flat in Stamford Hill and bought them a nice flat in Barkingside, Essex, near where Daphne lives. This effectively brought them much closer to the family. On the odd occasion, my dad would still pop up to the Brentwood office to chat with some of his old colleagues. When he did come up, he'd be walking around the place, rudely poking his nose into people's meeting rooms. The visitors and the newer staff would look up from their meeting and wonder who on earth this old man was. Of course, the old hardcore Amstrad staff knew him and he was obviously quite welcome around the place.

On one occasion, he came to the office using his free bus pass, explaining to me that he'd caught a bus from Barkingside to Gants Hill, then another bus from Gants Hill to Romford, then yet another bus from Romford to Shenfield and finally a train to Brentwood! He quite enjoyed getting out of the house and doing a little bit of travelling and it must have been a godsend to my mother to get him out of the way for a while.

On this particular day, the heavens opened up and it was belting down with rain. I told him that there was no way he was going home on this epic journey by train and bus and that my driver would take him.

No. He insisted he wanted to go by public transport rather than be chauffeur-driven in a Rolls-Royce. Unbelievable, but there comes a point when you just give up arguing. I'm convinced that it was because he was getting the travel free of charge. I asked him to let me see his train ticket, but he was reluctant to show it to me – he must have thought I'd pounce on it and tear it up so that he'd *have* to go home by car. We ended up doing a deal whereby he'd allow my driver to walk him across to Brentwood station with an umbrella.

On another occasion, when he *did* accept a lift home, my driver told me that my dad had complained a bit about back pains. Over the years, my dad had been in hospital a couple of times – once to have a pacemaker fitted and later for a serious operation in the men's water-works area. He was odd in that he would never tell anyone about it beforehand – he'd simply announce that he was going into hospital. This time we would soon learn just how serious the situation was.

Initially, when he started complaining of these pains, I got my private doctor to go and see him. He suggested that it might be a fault with Dad's pacemaker and he felt he should go to back to the Middlesex Hospital, who had fitted his pacemaker and had his records. It wasn't until my second visit to see him there that a nurse took me aside to say that the doctor wanted to see me. He told me that my dad had cancer. It transpired that the operation he'd had two years earlier was for the removal of cancer which, in hindsight, I think was in the prostate gland. He'd never told anyone what his operation was about.

Even if we had known what was wrong, what could we have done? It was hard enough getting him to accept a lift in my Rolls. I had murders getting him to see my private doctor, who would attend at an hour's notice, as Dad protested strongly that he would rather go and see his NHS doctor. Can you imagine trying to take charge of his medical care and sending him to a top doctor in Harley Street? I know how that argument would have gone. 'Why should I?' he would have asked. 'I've paid for the National Health all my life.' Could we have preserved his life a little longer? I don't know and, of course, none of us will ever know now.

The doctor at the Middlesex told us the cancer was so advanced that, while they could give him a bout of radiotherapy to slow it down a bit, there was nothing more they could do for him. I moved him to a local private hospital in Redbridge, where he had his own room, and he hated every minute of it. He wanted to be back at the Middlesex Hospital on an open ward. On reflection, I can quite understand how he must have felt. I wouldn't like being confined to a room on my own, knowing I'd got only a few weeks to live.

I remember visiting him there one day. He'd got himself out of bed and was staring out of the window with a glazed, worried look on his face. In the end, he pleaded with us to let him go home, which we did. I arranged for a couple of nurses to look after him in his own bedroom, in the comfort of his own flat. He was certainly much happier with that arrangement.

It's at times like this that business takes second place. From the time I first learned about my dad's back pains, I spent a nasty ten weeks watching him fade away until eventually he died on 7 May 1987. As with everyone, there comes the first time you lose a close member of your family. It's not until then that the harsh reality of such a loss hits home. Obviously it was a very sad occasion for my brother and sisters too.

Our attention turned towards the welfare of Mum and what she would be like afterwards. Although she was eighty, she was still a very capable lady and, bearing in mind that she lived close to Derek and Daphne and relatively close to me, she was never too far away from help. The funeral, obviously, was a terrible day and we decided that my mother should not attend. The traditional shiva was held at my house and went on for a few days. Hundreds of people passed through, expressing their condolences.

*

In spite of the success we were enjoying with our computers, I was determined not to ignore the old core business of Amstrad – consumer electronics. We had turned to a new manufacturer, Funai, to supply us with VCRs and the boss, Mr Funai, was a completely different character from Emperor Otake. He was just as you would expect a Japanese person to be – very polite and humble, and anxious to do business with Amstrad. But he was no pushover, for sure. He tended to step back and allow his staff to conduct the discussions and instantly report back to him. At one of our meetings, he sat in an office a few doors away while they ran backwards and forwards telling him what was going on. That way he didn't lose face in matters of negotiation.

Funai's main interest was to try to convince me to take the computer business away from Otake – they were obviously business enemies. One of the side benefits of dealing with Funai was that I could wind up Otake by telling him what nice people they were, how cooperative and keen to learn about new technology. In truth, I wasn't about to take computer production away from Otake, but I did do a deal with Funai to produce dual-speed VCRs.

I'd noticed the American VCR market was tending towards these dual-speed VCRs. Effectively, this meant that an E120 videotape (which normally had a maximum recording time of two hours) could accommodate four hours of recording in long-play mode. I knew this would be a big selling feature if we could introduce it to the UK market. The only drawback was that when one used fast-forward or rewind to skip through things like adverts, the picture would have fuzzy stripes across the middle. I was sure this would not be a problem for consumers, as they could easily see when the adverts were over and the programme had restarted and then they'd simply press the play button and the normal, good-quality picture would be restored.

I instructed Funai to make me some samples and I showed them to Nick Lightowler at Comet. His technical people weren't happy, believing that the fast-forward/rewind issue could create a lot of problems with consumers thinking it was a fault. My solution was to state in the instruction book that the stripes were a normal part of the technical operation of the product. In this way, the consumer would accept it. On top of this, I suggested that if we printed the same warning on a big red label and stuck it over the face of the product, we would pre-empt any consumer enquiries. In his usual way, Nick signed on to this. He was still quite cautious, but he agreed to take some stock and try it out. In our advertising, we displayed our low price with a large bomb-blast flagging the main feature: 'Now you can record and playback up to four hours on one tape.'

We hit it off again. It was a great success and we started to take a big share of the VCR market in the UK.

Inevitably, this dual-speed feature became the industry standard after about a year or so and people like Orion followed suit, but we'd already taken a grip on the market. Due to our advertising, Dixons *had* to buy these products – reluctantly, of course – because the Amstrad brand name was now much stronger than their own Matsui brand.

You might remember the days of VCR and just how difficult they were to set up and programme. One of the things that Amstrad was famous for was keeping things simple. We came up with a new idea for the remote control, which we sub-branded 'User-Friendly VCR'. On these machines, by following a few simple steps, it was easy to set the timer to record. At the time, this was a godsend, certainly for the older generation.

We also became a big player in the French VCR market. But another problem was looming. European manufacturers were up in arms about the dumping of Japanese VCRs. Our French cousins, bless 'em, came up with a very innovative solution. They could not break any trade agreements with Japan for the free flow of merchandise, so they decided that all non-European VCRs had to be imported through one small town – Poitiers.

Imagine one customs bloke with his dog in a hut. I'm perhaps exaggerating, but that was the idea. Hundreds of containers of VCRs had to be cleared at Poitiers and, of course, the customs officials were on a work-to-rule, so just one or two containers got through every day. This was the French way of imposing import restrictions. Meanwhile, European-made VCRs were able to flow freely. There was pressure mounting in Brussels to impose anti-dumping duties on all VCRs coming into Europe from Japan in order to protect the so-called European manufacturers.

The only way to overcome this would be to set up production in the UK or another European country. Orion, for example, had set up its own factory in Wales. I never visited it, but from what I understood it was a 'screwdriver plant'. Basically, they imported the modules that made up a VCR, then screwed them together and finished off the unit. They could then say, 'Made in Wales' and ship them around Europe.

I suggested to Mr Funai that we should start assembling VCRs at our Shoeburyness plant. To fast-track the story, in May 1987 we formed a company – Funai-Amstrad. Because of the impending anti-dumping duties, a lot of the British retailers immediately turned to Amstrad, desperately seeking supplies. Granada gave us a very large order, the first to be produced in the Funai-Amstrad factory. This turned out to be a bit of a disaster. It seems that Mr Funai's idea was that he would sell the individual modules to Funai-Amstrad *at a profit*, and that Funai-Amstrad, which was financed by us, would assemble them and sell them to Amstrad for Amstrad to sell on to its customers.

I have to say that I took my eye off the ball in this negotiation. My understanding was that Funai-Amstrad would get these modules at cost price and make their profit by selling to Amstrad. This would result in the same cost to Amstrad as if we'd imported them from Japan.

Mr Funai was no schmock – he was laughing all the way to the bank. Amstrad financed the purchase of the materials; meanwhile, he'd effectively made his profit on the modules he shipped to Funai-Amstrad from Japan. The fact that the factory in England had to assemble them and ship them was a mere technicality in his mind. The whole venture turned out to be a fiasco.

After a year or so, the penny finally dropped with me. I told Mr Funai we were shutting this business down. What's more, the arguments coming from the European Community manufacturers were waning – they realised they were losing the battle and many of them gave up their own production in Germany and France and started to import fully assembled VCRs from the Far East. All mention of anti-dumping had magically gone away. Even Poitiers was shut down. That was the final nail in the coffin which led to my decision to end the Funai-Amstrad fiasco. Nevertheless, to give you some idea of how we plundered the market at the time, we sold 450,000 VCRs in 1987.

We reverted to importing fully assembled VCRs. Having made a mistake with Funai-Amstrad, we walked away and wiped our faces! This Funai-Amstrad outing had cost us a lot of money and Mr Funai got off very lightly.

So, was I losing my touch? You have to remember that up to this point, pretty much every business decision I'd made had worked out. When you've experienced this, you start to think you can walk on water and it's difficult to imagine that your next move will go wrong. In some ways, Funai-Amstrad was my first warning that in the not-too-distant future, many things would start to go very wrong. But in June 1987, as we announced we'd doubled our profits yet again to £135m (on a turnover of £511m), I had no idea that these normally reliable instincts of mine were going to start blowing up in my face. It seemed like business as usual as, once again, we proved we could successfully and quickly adapt to the ever-advancing technology of the PC market by producing computers which now included a hard disk drive. These were massively expensive at the time, costing in the region of $300 for a 20MB hard disk drive. Consider, most cheap computers you can buy these days have a 500GB hard disk drive – that's 25,000 times the capacity of the machines back then!

This hard disk drive market was very vulnerable. American manufacturers were the leaders and the technology was advancing all the time. Every three months they would suddenly announce a doubling of capacity from, say, 20MB to 40MB and if you got lumbered with any 20MB drives, you might as well chuck them in the river because no one wanted them. It was all specmanship, particularly in the corporate market.

*

I've not yet touched upon my philosophy on profit margins. Working on slim margins like 5 per cent or 10 per cent was not for me. However, the only way to achieve larger margins – say in the region of 30–33 per cent – is to think of a product that is sought after and that no one else has, and then ensure that you beat down the cost price to achieve a great retail price. A no-brainer, right?

As I have explained, I learned early on in my business life that selling £5 items is a waste of time. I was now fully focused on raising the ticket value of the products we sold. Say I wanted the retail price of a new product to be £399 including VAT (which was 15 per cent at the time). To work out the *cost price* I established a simple formula:

£399 ÷ 1.15 to take off VAT (15 per cent) = £346.95
£346.95 ÷ 1.35 to allow for the dealer margin (approx 25 per cent)
 = £257
£257 ÷ 1.54 for Amstrad's gross margin (approx 35 per cent) = £166
 which is the target cost price (including labour cost).

Once we had established the target cost price, we worked diligently with our suppliers to reach it. The way we achieved low material costs was to bang down large firm orders on the table to the vendors – nothing got their attention better. This was a science in which we became expert. Bob Watkins and I trained up a couple of other buyers and together we formed a crack team. We constantly monitored the prices of major components and had our own database of prices on all the materials we were buying. Each and every time we were notified of reductions, the database would be updated and from this database, we were able to assemble a bill of material for any new item we dreamt up. My rule was never to compromise on my 1.54 ratio and I have to say that this contributed to the phenomenal success of Amstrad.

Of course, it's not unusual for manufacturers to have such large gross margins as 35 per cent. But what *was* unusual was for those gross margins to flow through and result in a tremendous 25 per cent net margin. The difference between Amstrad and other manufacturers was that our formula was based on *sub-contracting* the manufacturing – we included the labour cost charged by our sub-contractor as part of the target cost price. Our costs after that were simply those of admin-istration, marketing and engineering. I had a winning formula and became stuck trying to do things the same way I had in the past, blindly thinking the success would continue endlessly. However, as my story moves on, cracks start to appear at the seams. Sometimes running a tight ship without the correct financial control and deeper engineering and research facilities takes its toll.

Part of my philosophy of maintaining margins meant that dealing with people like Schneider and Dominguez would inevitably end in tears. The European market was becoming more and more competi-tive and to maintain the retail prices in those markets and generate volume sales, there would be no room for two margins. By 1987 I was starting to think that opening more overseas subsidiaries was the best move.

At the same time, more advanced computers were coming on to the scene which used a new generation of processors – the 20286 and 20386 from Intel – and both Schneider and Dominguez were starting to think that they'd procure their computers from other sup-pliers. As Amstrad was developing new 20286 and 20386 machines, it was inevitable that the PC1512 and PC1640, both based on the 8086 processor, would cease production. Allowing Schneider and Dominguez to buy their next-generation PCs from others would mean that our grip on the Spanish and German computer markets would eventually die.

I called a meeting with Dominguez and discussed the possibility of us buying his company. In exchange, he would take some shares in Amstrad plus a wedge of cash. As he was a great marketing man, I really liked the idea of him joining the board of Amstrad to assist in overseas marketing, along with Marion Vannier.

We acquired Indescomp in September 1987 at a value of approximately £25m in shares and cash. At the same time, we opened subsidiaries in Holland, Belgium, Italy and Australia.

I also believed that the potential for the PC1512 in America was great, but there was no way of selling it through Sears World Trade. For one thing, the senior bosses there had put the kybosh on any more irresponsible dealings, due to the cock-ups on the CPC6128 and PCW8256, although the latter did become a runaway success once the price was right. Flummerfelt had come to see me at the Las Vegas show in January to discuss whether I had any ideas on how to dispose of their stocks of PCW8256 word processors. I told him that the first loss is the best loss and suggested that Sears should put them in their own stores at a retail price of $399. If they did this, I was sure they'd fly off the shelves.

And that's exactly what they did. Amazingly, they sold all 30,000-odd units they had in stock in one week, across the whole of their distribution in America. I repeat – one week. This may sound incredible, but it shows the appetite the American market has if something is the right price.

The funny thing was, Flummerfelt called me a few weeks later, asking me if it was possible to buy some more to sell at $399, as he reckoned they could sell hundreds of thousands. He had not signed on to the fact that if he were to sell at $399 on an ongoing basis and tried to make at least 20 per cent margin, he would need to buy them for $300. There was no way, even with our aggressive buying, that we could produce them and make a profit at that price. It makes me wonder sometimes how such senior positions in giant organisations can be given to people who seem as thick as a plank when it comes to simple business principles. Maybe I was missing something.

So Sears were out and instead we opened our own subsidiary in America too.

The following year, I parted company with Schneider and opened a subsidiary in Germany. We recruited a heavy-hitter, Helmut Jost, who was previously the managing director of Commodore Germany and was very well connected in the marketplace. We did an interesting bit of business with the PC1512 out of our German office after the reunification of East and West Germany. One customer in Berlin told us he had been visited by lots of Russian and East German students who were somehow managing to ship our computers into Russia. Export to Russia was virtually impossible from a commercial point of view, due to import bans and because they lacked foreign exchange to pay, but these enterprising people had found a way into the Russian market. In recognition of this, I sent Mark Simons to Russia to suss out the situation and see if he could find a technical guy there who'd be able to translate our instruction manual and MSDOS into Russian.

Microsoft did not have a Russian version of MSDOS at the time, as there were restrictions imposed by the American government under CoCom's rules (this was the committee set up after World War Two by Western Bloc countries to prevent the export of weaponry to the Eastern Bloc). I guess that Amstrad's commissioning of the translation of MSDOS by some Russian hack was sailing a bit close to the wind. You never know, I could have caused World War Three or been banged up in some American jail.

Effectively, we had created the first Russian IBM PC-compatible with Russian MSDOS and a Russian Cyrillic keyboard. As you can imagine, sales of this computer shot up dramatically through the Berlin connection. I guess it's another example of entrepreneurial spirit, though still sailing a bit close to the wind as far as CoCom was concerned. My justification was that we, Amstrad UK, were selling the goods in Berlin, which was now a Western economy and what the Berliners did with them was not our problem. I don't think that would have gone down too well in a Washington courtroom, but that was my stance.

*

My sons Simon and Daniel were educated at Chigwell School, which, coincidentally, was adjacent to our house, Bramstons. Growing up with a father who was a well-known and established businessman was quite difficult for them at times.

I tried to keep their feet on the ground when it came to pocket money. If Simon and Daniel wanted some extra cash, they had to go and get a Saturday job, just like I did when I was their age. Simon worked on Saturdays and school holidays serving up hamburgers at McDonald's in Ilford. He left school at the age of sixteen with a few GCSEs and went to Loughton College to study art and design.

He did express a desire to work for his dad's firm, but I told him that he wasn't coming to work for Amstrad until he'd spent at least a year as a shop-floor salesman in a retail outlet, to give him some training at the school of hard knocks. He needed to see what consumers wanted and what was involved in dealing with them on a day-to-day basis.

I asked Stanley Kalms if he could arrange a job at Dixons for Simon and insisted that he should not be given any special treatment in respect to pay or seniority; after all, he was just a kid. Stanley took this onboard and sent the message through to the shop floor. However, everybody knew that he was Alan Sugar's son and it was assumed by some of the staff that he had special privileges. As a result, he found it tough trying to be one of the boys.

After spending over a year working at Dixons, Brent Cross (a good hour and a half's journey every morning from Chigwell), he moved to Oxford Street to get the feeling of an up-market branch. Finally, he went to the other end of the spectrum, working at the Ilford branch. It was great experience of what's involved on the retail side of things.

He then joined Amstrad to work in the audio, TV and VCR department as a junior sales and marketing person, under the guidance of Malcolm. Once again, I insisted there should be no special treatment; he would come in on the same salary level as everyone else. As far as I was concerned, this was part of his training in life, to get some values.

Both Ann and I wanted to ensure that our children became nice, level-headed people when they grew up. We've seen so many cases where the children of wealthy individuals go off the rails and we were intent on ensuring that our three children's feet were firmly on the ground.

At Amstrad, because Simon and I worked in the same building, people could see there was no special treatment when I walked the floors. He was either going to be good at what he did or not. Most people inside Amstrad observed this and respected the situation. Of course, there were the odd few who couldn't see the wood for the trees, still thinking that Simon had privileges. New employees in particular assumed that he must have been given some form of seniority.

Daniel, who is two years younger than Simon, joined the company as a junior clerk in the sales department. We'd found a great niche for him – while he wasn't suited to design and development, he definitely had a trader's instinct. Part of his job was the disposal of B-grade merchandise, an important side of the business. During the dynamic rise of Amstrad, our sales people were focused purely on new sales and we hadn't highlighted the issue of disposing of B-grade merchandise. This was merchandise returned from mail-order companies for various reasons – either it was faulty or a customer simply sent it back because they didn't want it. With lots of stock building up in the warehouse, I realised we needed to pay attention to this and find an outlet to dispose of it – otherwise it was just cash sitting around. It had to be disposed of quickly, while the product was still in fashion, to avoid it becoming 'obsolete technology'.

The customers who would buy this stuff were job buyers. They would test and repair the merchandise and sell it to wholesalers, who would sell it on to market traders or ship it abroad to Eastern Bloc countries. It was important that the B-grade merchandise never came into the normal distribution channels in the UK, as this would ruin our reputation. All consumer electronics companies have these problems and it is a special art to ensure that the disposal of the product is conducted in an orderly fashion.

The buyers for this stuff were a real bunch of characters; some of them were a little bit sharp to say the least. Talk about shake their hand and count your fingers afterwards – that's putting it mildly. Daniel got a good grounding in dealing with these tricky people and it showed him a side of business that sharpened his wits. Be under no illusion, the sales volume here was not peanuts. It was important to convert this returned merchandise back into cash. Naturally, there were laws one had to comply with – refurbished products could not be sold as brand-new goods.

*

As I've mentioned, I had been selling shares in Amstrad while the price was on the way up and had accumulated very large sums of cash. My thinking was, 'Amstrad is my business gamble,' and it's true to say that I did embark on some very risky strategies. I needed a kind of personal piggy bank that was secure in case of disaster at Amstrad and by now this piggy bank was substantial. It would be enough money for the family to live on for the rest of our lives in the style we'd become accustomed to.

I often tell people that a lot of my success is down to knowing what *not* to do, a statement based on the lessons I've learned through my failures. People say that the best thing about casinos is that they show you how quickly you can lose your money. Similarly, one failure of mine turned out to be one of the best things that ever happened to me.

A lot of people in my position, who have made loads of money out of business, find themselves faced with a so-called 'high-class dilemma' – what should they do with the cash they've amassed? Sticking it in a bank to earn interest is deemed boring. Many people I know have entrusted money to so-called stock market experts to put into various funds.

Shortly after I floated the company in 1980, and just after I got the money I lent the synagogue back, I was approached by the Japanese bank Nomura. A little Japanese fellow came to see me and told me that Nomura had opened a stockbroking arm in London. He said they were experts on trading in the Japanese market and explained that I should invest my money with them and they would make it grow at a far greater rate than I could achieve with it lying stagnant in my bank. Like a mug, I gave this bloke a quarter of a million quid to play with.

A couple of days later, my people were telling me that the telex machine was totally blocked by this lunatic sending through telexes, sometimes three yards long. Completely uninterested, I would glance at these telexes, which turned out to be transactions this fellow was making. I was just annoyed that he was blocking the telex line, as it was my only way of communicating with my suppliers, and called him up to give him a bollocking. I told him that I didn't need to see these telexes. If he wanted to send me the stuff for the record, he should put it in the post. That's how ludicrous the situation was.

I only realised what was going on when, at the end of that financial year, my personal accountant pointed out to me that this fellow was losing me money as if it were going out of fashion. It transpired that he was buying and selling hundreds and hundreds of different companies' stocks every day, taking a commission for buying, taking a commission for selling and using his discretion as to whether to get in or out.

He had lost me a small fortune. I went berserk at this little man, but it seems I had signed some piece of paper that exonerated Nomura from any cock-ups. This was a lesson learned. I got out and cut my losses.

From that day onwards, I've taken no notice whatsoever of any of these so-called experts in the stock market or fund managers who want to look after my money. If these bloody people know so much, why haven't they got yachts and private planes themselves? Why do they need to do it for other people?

I'm so happy that Nomura taught me a lesson. Putting it in perspective, it was cheap at the price because there are some *real* disaster stories to be told about the losses made by brokers and bankers on their clients' behalf. It's amazing how these companies can bamboozle you into signing forms that totally insulate them from any of the risk. Clearly what they do is not unlawful – the devil is in the detail of what you sign.

Instead, I decided to invest my cash in property, based on the following simple criteria. Buy a building that is occupied by a well-known and respected tenant, in a good location. Look at the length of the lease the tenant has signed and if it's longer than ten years, it would appear that this is a safe place to invest my money, as long as the return is at least equivalent to what I could receive by placing the money in a bank on deposit. The upside is that the values of the properties will increase as the years go by. Pretty damn boring, but it suited me down to the ground. It's not that I am a distrustful person – certainly not – but I have absolutely no respect at all for the brokers, fund managers and all those other tossers in the City.

*

What to do with your money is a good problem to have and in the summer of 1988, my staff were to share this dilemma. The share options I'd granted them three years earlier were about to mature and kick in. My directors became millionaires overnight while other employees each made in the region of £150,000–250,000. These were ordinary people and this was a load of money in those days, so you can imagine the elation.

I was delighted for everybody. It was real payback for a loyal group of people who had helped this dynamic company grow. I guess if you spoke to all of them today, they would say that never in their lifetime would they have imagined that just by being a simple employee they'd hit the jackpot like this.

Bob, Malcolm and Mark decided to buy themselves new luxurious homes with their windfall. People like Jim and Ken, being typical accountants, were more streetwise and cautious and would never go down the path of getting themselves into potential financial problems. But there were some sad stories, similar to those you read nowadays about people who win the lottery and blow the lot. One member of the junior engineering team, a Scouser, was quite blunt when the big payday came. So much for loyalty – he copped his £250,000 and immediately resigned, saying that he was retiring to Spain with his wife to open a bar there. He was around thirty years old. When I heard this news, I shook my head, as if to say, 'You poor, poor fellow. You'll be back in a couple of years – a quarter of a million pounds is going to get you nowhere because there's something called inflation.' I don't know what happened to him, but I suspect, like so many other people in those days who thought £250,000 was going to last them a lifetime, he must have got a wake-up call somewhere down the line.

One sad story that emerged before the share options kicked in concerned Dickie Mould – Boycie – who was up in Stoke-on-Trent running Amstrad Distribution. It turned out he'd got himself into a lot of trouble. The first I knew about it was when Jim Rice told me that Dickie was banged up in Pentonville Prison. We were both shocked. Jim had found out that this had happened after the fourth or fifth time the police had been called to his house because of matrimonial disturbances. Unfortunately, this news was reported in one of the national papers, which must have been a further hammer-blow to him. I received a hand-written letter from Dickie, apologising to me for the shame that he'd brought on the company and asking me to accept his resignation.

What also came to light was something that surprised us all – he had successfully disguised the fact that he was an alcoholic. As usual, after the event, you start hearing stories. The staff up in Stoke-on-Trent were saying that he was always pissed in the evening; sometimes he didn't turn up; other times he'd make irrational decisions. I guess it's easy to spot the signs in hindsight.

I recalled a day when Dickie and I had visited Argos in Edgware. The fellow we went to see had an empty bottle of whisky in his dustbin. As we left his office, Dickie said to me, 'Did you see that? There was an empty bottle of whisky in his bin – he must be on the sauce.' I didn't think anything of it at the time, but I guess it goes to show that it takes one to know one.

Poor Dickie. Obviously things had got out of hand. I don't know whether this was because he had to spend most of his time up in the Midlands or whether he was struggling with his own ego, in that he'd had a sideways promotion and was no longer a kingpin at Amstrad's head office. Apparently, he was always telling the staff at Stoke-on-Trent that he was 'talking to Alan every day' when in fact he wasn't. I guess I kind of left him on his own up there to get on with things and he must have craved my attention. To this day, I don't know what sparked off his alcoholism, but what had I been thinking? How come I hadn't known that this man was so troubled? One of the saddest parts about this was that, due to his resignation six months earlier, he was not eligible for his share option windfall.

Jim kept in close contact with Dickie afterwards, so we knew that he'd decided to move to Spain to try to start a new life. It hurts me to say this, but the man we had so much fun with – taking the mickey out of him for his mad ways – one day, in a deep depression, committed suicide.

There was a terrible feeling around the company. I felt guilty and vented my anger on people like Jim Rice, Bob Watkins and Malcolm Miller, unfairly saying that it was our fault. *We* had taken the piss out of him, *we* had ostracised him, *we* had sidelined him.

Malcolm and Bob told me that we shouldn't feel guilty. We never knew of his secret alcoholism, we never knew anything about his private life. In fact, we'd never met his wife, not even at Amstrad Christmas parties. It was a really sad time and I think all of us felt bad seeing a colleague who had grown up with this monster company not being able to live with himself for reasons known only to his inner demons.

*

By the autumn of 1988, we were ready to enter the new Intel 20286 and 20386 PC market. We were already seen to be late entrants into the 286/386 market, considering we were supposed to be the bigshots of the PC world, having taken over 30 per cent of the total European sales. What's more, rumours that companies like Olivetti were also about to bring out low-cost 286/386 machines added to our panic. We rushed and made a bad product – the PC2000 series.

I won't get too technical, but to understand the disaster that was about to unfold, I need to explain something about hard disk drives and how they work. In those days, the hard disk drive had to be connected to the computer using a hard disk controller card which would plug into one of the slots available on a standard IBM PC. The card itself was a very expensive item.

Amstrad's philosophy had always been to condense everything onto one PCB and not have separate items, so I commissioned our team to design our own hard disk controller chip and lay it down on the main PCB instead of buying a separate hard disk controller card, which I believe in those days cost around £60. The chip that we laid down on the PCB would cost some money, but we saved approximately £45 this way.

We bought the hard disk drives from two different companies –
Seagate and Western Digital, the world's leading manufacturers of
hard disk drives. We obviously assumed their products would be of
good quality – one didn't even think of questioning it, just as you
wouldn't think of questioning Sony or Philips if you bought their
screens to use in monitors.

Soon after launch we hit a snag. We had problems starting production on some of the models because, like a couple of years before, the
supply of D-RAMs completely dried up. Due to a general downturn in
the market the previous year, the price of D-RAMs had bottomed out,
so much so that many manufacturers gave up making them, as they'd
ended up selling them at a loss. The only way to encourage manufacturers to produce them again was to start paying high prices.

My next disastrous move was down to a knee-jerk reaction. I
decided to take some money off the cash pile we'd amassed and buy
a 9 per cent shareholding in the American D-RAM manufacturers
Micron in exchange for them loosening up some of the supply to us.
However, we then discovered it would take them several months to
ramp up additional production to accommodate us, so by the time
they were in a position to supply D-RAMs to us ad infinitum, we
didn't need them any more, as all chip-makers were now supplying
freely again. This episode added insult to injury.

Then, shortly after the PC2000 series hit the market, we started
receiving complaints about hard disk drive errors on the 286 and 386
machines. Generally, when you hear the first one or two complaints,
you think maybe the customer got something wrong, but the complaints started to increase, not only in the UK, but throughout Europe.

It pains me to talk about this situation, so I want to be as brief as
possible. We had to admit there was some unknown fault with our
PC2000 series and we recalled the whole lot from the market. Imagine
the disaster of such a move and the negative publicity it attracted, not
to mention the effect it had on our share price. 'At last,' some of the
sniping commentators said, 'Amstrad stumbles!' They were right.

Further cracks were starting to appear. To be honest, the level of
engineering we had back then was not capable of recognising the root
cause of the problem. I made an assumption that it was all our fault –

we'd been far too adventurous in trying to design our own hard disk controller chip. We were warned by the suppliers of hard disk controller cards that we'd be stirring up a hornets' nest, that it was no simple thing to design. They said they had spent many man-years developing this technology and that Amstrad couldn't do it on its own. So with these 'I told you so's ringing in our ears, Bob and I made the reasonable assumption that the culprit was our own hard disk controller.

We sent samples of our products to Seagate and Western Digital and asked them to give an opinion as to why things were conking out. They told us, 'It's not our hard disk drives; it's definitely this non-standard hard disk controller you've designed.'

So the first phase of our attempted recovery of the PC2000 series was to disable our own hard disk controller and buy hundreds of thousands of hard disk controllers from the supplier who'd warned us not to go it alone. That supplier was Western Digital.

We set up a production line at Shoeburyness and converted all the computers drawn back from the market, as well as all those on the way to us. On top of this, we sent thousands of hard disk controller cards to Orion in Korea, so that they could restart production.

We relaunched the computer into the marketplace the following spring, apologising to our customers and telling them how we'd now fitted new hard disk controller cards and that everything was hunky-dory and back on track.

Wrong.

After the relaunch of the PC2000 series containing Western Digital's hard disk controller cards, we were *still* getting complaints of hard disk failures. We turned to Seagate and Western Digital again. 'What's your excuse now?' They told us that our box was too hot and the hard disk drive was overheating. The sad thing about this whole situation was that we did not have the engineering capability within Amstrad to look at this situation independently. We'd made the assumption that Seagate and Western Digital knew what they were talking about – they were the industry leaders in hard disk drive technology, after all. Surely there was no way the fault could lie with them, could it? It *had* to be something Amstrad was doing wrong.

Eventually, one of our engineers, Bill Weidenauer, working closely with John Beattie and a few others, learned enough about hard disk technology to realise that a gigantic coincidence had occurred – both Seagate *and* Western Digital had shipped us faulty hard disk drives! Who could have dreamt of that scenario? No wonder we thought that *we* were doing something wrong. We had poured good money after bad changing all the hard disk controllers and relaunching the product, only to find that it was their drives to blame. It was our misfortune that both suppliers had shipped us rubbish. If at least one of them had shipped us good stuff, we'd have known far earlier that the problem didn't lie with Amstrad.

I make no excuse for the fact that I was too focused on launching new products at the time. I didn't give enough care or attention, or allocate enough funds, to building up an engineering department with more analytical resources in high-level technology. I wrongly thought that this would lead to having non-productive people hanging around. This was a big error. We were entering the 16-bit computer business. The philosophy of viewing a computer like a piece of audio equipment might have been fine in the early days, but now we were moving into territory where the technology was beyond the scope of the guys that had made us successful so far.

*

In the midst of these dark times, one positive event occurred. On 5 December 1988, London's City University awarded me an honorary Doctor of Science degree in recognition of my so-called contribution to the information technology industry. It was a rather formal ceremony in a grand hall and all the students being awarded their gongs were present. They dressed me up in a long robe and I had to wear a large flat cap. I climbed the stage and said a few words about how honoured I was to receive this great accolade. I felt a bit out of my depth and was quite nervous, as I didn't want to make a fool of myself by saying or doing the wrong thing during the ceremony.

From now on, I was to be known as Alan Sugar DSc. I was very honoured to have my first title, so to speak, though as most people will tell you, these honorary things are not really respected by true academics. Nevertheless, I milked it amongst some of my family, friends and close colleagues, jokingly telling them they had to call me 'Doctor' from now on.

In fact, I had been invited to make a speech at the university previously, at the time when I was flying high and Amstrad was ruling the world in the PC business. It attracted a full house, so much so that the managing director of IBM UK, Tony Cleaver, was locked out of the room and missed it!

It started off with a bang when I addressed the question I'm most frequently asked – 'How did you make all your money?' Bear in mind that the audience had already read many stories about me selling car aerials from my £50 minivan, so with a deadpan face, I explained, 'It's very simple. I started at the age of nineteen selling car aerials and bought a few for forty quid. I sold them all the same day and bought a load more with the profit. Then I realised there was a *new* style of car aerial which came in a coloured blister-pack, so I only bought and sold those. Then I decided to cut out the middleman and buy the aerials raw and get my own blister-packing machine.' I paused for a few seconds, with the audience hanging there, waiting for my next pearl of wisdom, and then said, 'Then my uncle died and left me fifty million quid.'

The audience laughed. They were loosened up. As for the rest of the speech, it rambled on a bit and was quite boring. However, there was one Sugarism within it which was to be quoted many a time afterwards by the media. I was trying to explain Amstrad's philosophy compared to those of other large companies. I said, 'Pan Am takes good care of you, Marks & Spencer loves you, IBM says the customer is king. At Amstrad, we want your money!'

Maybe not the cleverest thing to say, but the most honest. All that crap spouted by those companies is nonsense – they're in business to make money from their customers. Anyway, I was young, honest and inexperienced in public speaking and, more to the point, in gauging media reaction.

Any negative coverage I got then was mild compared to what was heading my way now. The PC2000 series ruined Amstrad's credibility in the market and this was the first time that I started getting real stick from the media. The praise I got from the media on the way up never went to my head, but when they started slagging me off, I'd be lying if I said it didn't affect me. It was quite a depressing time.

Companies such as Olivetti and Dell started to get a grip in the marketplace with low-cost 286 and 386 machines. We made an attempt to re-establish ourselves with the PC3000 series, which was well engineered and worked perfectly, but the damage had been done. What's more, by the time we came to market with this model, prices had dropped tremendously and we were no longer miles cheaper than the competition. Everybody had jumped on the low-cost PC band-wagon. And because the PC2000 series completely bombed, we lost the whole computer market.

An inevitable fall in profits resulted. In June 1989 they dropped from the previous year's £160m to £76m, but, strangely, based on our last published set of financial results, people in the outside world who didn't follow the UK media so much still thought we were high-fliers!

During this disastrous time, I was visited by Andy Grove, the founder of Intel, who'd come to see this 'genius' who'd taken 30 per cent of the European PC market. Little did he know what was around the corner. When he arrived, I was very depressed, and the meeting lacked anything of significance. I couldn't be bothered; I had nothing to brag about. He was banging on about some new processor they were working on and I just drifted through the meeting, preoccupied with our troubles.

It never rains but it pours. My secretary took a call from Bill Gates's office. He was over in Europe and he too wanted to meet face-to-face for the first time. He planned to fly into London on a Saturday, come and see me at my home, then fly back to the USA. I agreed to meet him, but again, in a deep depression, I was at a loss to think about what we would discuss.

Bill arrived at Bramstons in a chauffeur-driven car. Like most Americans, he had thought London was about the size of his home town. He wasn't expecting a two-hour slog around the M25 to get from Heathrow to Chigwell and when he arrived he was flustered to say the least. Ann popped into the lounge to offer him some refreshments and he asked for a Coke. We don't do Coke at my home, but we did have some Diet Coke, which he reluctantly accepted.

We spoke for an hour or so. Again, I had no real enthusiasm. He must have gone away thinking that this Sugar guy was no big deal, no spark of inspiration at all, and that this meeting had been a bloody waste of his time.

Everything was going wrong at once. Inventories of our PC2000 series, as well as a lot of our other consumer electronics products, had reached an all-time high. We had £335m of unsold stock and I owed the bank £114m. Lloyds Bank was starting to get sweaty and they came in for many meetings to try to understand where we were going.

I recall one meeting with Lloyds' senior management when I told them quite openly that things had got out of control. The subsidiaries had been ordering stuff based on their sales forecasts; we had made the goods, but they weren't selling. On top of this, the PC2000 series inventory was massive, but we couldn't ship any until we'd fixed them. These were the reasons we had such high levels of inventory and borrowings. To be fair, there was never a suggestion from Lloyds Bank that they would bring in the administrators, but clearly they were worried. In any case, I didn't need them to warn me – I knew that if I couldn't resolve the situation in the next six months the inevitable would happen.

After that meeting with Lloyds, I called a meeting with all of Amstrad's senior sales staff and told them that we were going to have an organised fire sale. I put the situation to them bluntly. 'If the bank were to call in a receiver or a liquidator, the outside world would know they could nick the stock from us. I've told the bank, "I will deal with it." And now I'm telling you, "*You* will deal with it."'

We spent the whole of September through to December 1989 doing deals. I remember calling Stanley Kalms and telling him I had 40,000 camcorders in stock. Stanley explained that Amstrad wasn't the only company in trouble; Dixons was experiencing a terrible downturn in business at the time, due to the recession that was about to kick in. He said there was no way he was going to buy stock from us and take the risk.

I told him, 'The stock is sitting in my warehouse doing nothing.

You might as well stick it in your shops and sell these camcorders at £399 [which was an amazing price]. They will fly off the shelves over Christmas.' He had nothing to lose and he agreed, but of course he wanted his 25 per cent margin.

We reduced the price of our audio equipment and cleared the stocks through giant chains like Rumbelows, Currys and the Dixons group. Marion did the same in France, reducing stocks of VCR and audio.

By 30 June 1990 we had managed to change the situation. We'd slashed our inventory to £188m and we had £24m in the bank. I remember Lloyds inviting me to lunch and telling me they'd never experienced anything like this before when they'd seen a company in trouble. They were highly complimentary of what we'd done. I recall joking with them and asking to look at their accounts – I wanted to see if they were worthy of holding our £24m.

The majority of the £188m inventory on hand was the PC2000 series, which was still being reworked. The market prices had dropped so badly that we had to make a decision about this product. Do we spend a load of money buying hard disk drives from reliable Japanese sources such as Sony and Hitachi, then rework the whole series again and relaunch it? Or do we just cut and run and sell the stuff at any price to a jobber? Even if we spent good money on new hard disk drives and the labour involved in reassembling the machines, the market had moved on, plus there was now a stigma attached to the Amstrad PC2000 series. So Daniel was tasked with getting rid of the inventory, and someone bought them off us at a steal.

I had rescued Amstrad from inevitable liquidation when our business was in the pits, with the computer side of things gone. The near demise of Amstrad was as horrible a period as anyone could imagine and our annual profit plummeted from its peak of £160m in 1988 to £44m by June 1990. And worse was yet to come.

However, while all this was going on, another market-changing event was about to take place.

12

'Who on Earth Is Rupert Murdoch?'

When You See a Satellite Dish, Think of Sugar

1988–90

'Alan, I've got Rupert Murdoch on the phone,' my secretary Frances said. 'Can I put him through?'

'Nah, not really. Tell him I'm not in – do the usual,' I said.

About five minutes later, she walked into my office and asked, 'Do you know who Rupert Murdoch is?'

'No, who is he?'

'He's the man who owns the *Sun* and *The Times*. He's the man who had that trouble down in Wapping with the strikes and all that.'

It suddenly dawned on me that I hadn't bothered to pick up the phone to speak to one of the world's biggest media moguls. I was totally cocooned in my own little world – I knew everybody's names in the electronics business, but I couldn't tell you the names of any government ministers, pop stars or other celebrities.

'Okay, Frances, get him on the phone straightaway.'

Rupert told me that my company had been recommended to him and he wanted to come and talk to me about the possibility of launching a satellite TV service in England. He'd heard that at one stage Amstrad had joined Granada and Virgin in a consortium to bid for the right to put up a satellite TV service known as BSB. He was right – we *had* done that. However, when I got the measure of some of the people in this consortium, and their lack of ideas, I decided I was no longer going to play. Richard Branson followed shortly afterwards.

Murdoch's idea was to broadcast sixteen additional TV channels in the UK via a satellite launched by the company Astra. In those days, only four television channels existed: BBC1, BBC2, ITV and Channel 4. When I heard his idea, I knew immediately it would be a great consumer product – the punters would go bananas for an extra sixteen channels if it could be done cheaply.

We agreed to meet and Rupert was driven from Wapping all the way to my headquarters in Brentwood. To be fair, he told me straight-away that he had done the rounds – he'd gone to the likes of Sony, Philips and even GEC, but no one was prepared to make any decisions unless he was willing to lay out a lot of money for development.

Lord Weinstock, the chairman of GEC, told him, 'Go and see Sugar, he's the man who can bring a consumer electronics product to the market faster than anyone else. In fact, while Sony and Philips are still thinking about it, he will have them in the market for you.' Those are the very words Rupert told me he'd heard from Lord Weinstock.

The proposition I put to him was this: 'If you, Mr Murdoch, pro-vide sixteen channels of additional television, including movie channels, news and sports, I will find a way of making satellite receiv-ing equipment so that it can be sold in places like Dixons for a hundred and ninety-nine quid.' It was my opinion that if we could achieve this, the whole thing would work. In fact, I told Rupert I was so confident about this that he didn't need to underwrite any orders. If he would agree to press the button on renting the space on the satellite and putting up the sixteen channels, I would be prepared to start develop-ment and production at my own risk. There was no official agreement, just a handshake. His transmission date was February 1989 – *my* job was to make sure that we had equipment in the marketplace by then.

It was now June 1988, so we had eight months to do it. Rupert called a press conference and asked me to attend. It was a massive bash held in the BAFTA auditorium in Piccadilly. After promising to launch Sky Television by February 1989, he turned to the audience and said, 'And this man here is going to make the equipment to receive the broadcasts – and it's going to be available for a hundred and ninety-nine quid! The proposition is, ladies and gentlemen, sixteen more channels of television for a hundred and ninety-nine quid.'

I started to feel a bit nervous, sitting there in front of the world's media, smiling as if to say, 'Yes, that's right.' Little did Rupert know that we didn't have a bleedin' clue how to make them yet – it was just my gut instinct that we could do it. I didn't realise what I'd let myself in for.

A few days before the press conference, I spoke to Mark Souhami and told him what was about to happen. As ever, Dixons wanted in on this new and exciting market and agreed to buy 500,000 units.

One thing you'd have to say about Stanley Kalms is that he understood his products and he understood his consumers. While his company had layers of product managers, marketing managers and buyers who used industry statistics to gauge product sales, all these systems could do was track and assess *existing* product categories. When something new came along, like satellite, this threw a spanner in the works. That's when old-fashioned gut feeling kicks in. Stanley had that feeling and he backed this new satellite business. So, to give myself more to worry about, I proudly announced in June that these units would be available in Dixons next February.

The press conference created a load of attention, but after the euphoria wore off, while walking down Piccadilly to my car, I was thinking to myself, 'What have you done, you bloody lunatic?!'

I got back to the office and told Bob Watkins, 'I've only gone and committed to supply this stuff! Now we need to work out how we're going to do it.' Bob and I had done a quick bit of research after the first meeting with Rupert as to what was available in the market as far as satellite receivers and dishes were concerned. We'd seen some very expensive pieces of equipment capable of receiving satellite transmissions from the Middle East – these were normally purchased by rich Arab customers. Looking inside the box, as usual, we could see there wasn't really much in there.

Bob and his team got weaving and we got on stream for developing the receiver. The bigger question was: how would we be able to make the receiver plus dish for £90, so that we could sell it to Dixons for around £120, so they could sell it to the customers for £199? Remember, satellite receivers and dishes in the market at the time were around £5,000!

I learned that there's a device which is mounted at the front of the satellite dish called an LNB (low noise block), which picks up the signal from the satellite after it bounces off the dish. People like Marconi were the experts in this field and, as Marconi was owned by GEC, it was time to call Arnold Weinstock. First, I thanked him for his intro-duction to Rupert Murdoch, then I asked him whether he could put me in touch with his mob who made these LNB things. I told him, 'I want to pay a couple of quid for them, not two million pounds each.'

Arnold quite liked my sense of humour. His background was also in consumer electronics – he'd taken over his father-in-law's business fifty years earlier and built it into the giant GEC. After a series of dis-cussions with his technical people, we managed to get GEC-Marconi to talk sensible consumer electronics prices.

At the time, Arnold's company was dealing in high-level stuff – they were getting contracts from electricity providers for huge gener-ators, council contracts for traffic lights and military contracts for radar-guided missiles. Yet here he was on the phone to me, negotiat-ing like a market trader back in the days when he used to make televisions and radios under the Sobell brand. I could detect he was enjoying every minute of it. In fact, people told me afterwards that Arnold didn't usually get involved in price discussions. We had some good banter over the phone and after a lot of backwards and forwards bartering, I agreed to place an order for a million units at £28.50 each. This was a major breakthrough.

The gamble I had taken telling Rupert Murdoch I'd have his prod-uct in the market was massive, given we had no idea about the technology, but we were learning fast. We had one final nut to crack. Where on earth were we going to get a satellite dish made, not forget-ting all the brackets required to mount it on the wall? Bob's mechanical engineering people drew up the bracketry – that was easy, we were conversant with steel prices and we knew how much it should cost – but there was *science* behind the dish.

As one would expect in the early days of satellite, a number of so-called 'specialist satellite dish manufacturers' sprang up. We spoke to some of these people, who really tried to blind us with science about the angle of curvature of the parabola and all that stuff. When we sent a drawing to one of these fellows and asked him to quote for this bowl-shaped disc, he came back with some ridiculous price of around £30. We thought he'd made a mistake and it was supposed to be something like £3, but no, he was serious – thirty quid for just the dish. On questioning him, he continued with his bullshit about the tooling accuracy required, the close tolerances involved and other such nonsense.

Bob and I sat down and looked at it in the good old-fashioned Amstrad way.

'Just what *is* this we're looking at, Bob?' I said. 'Look at the dish from a different perspective – it's a bit like a dustbin lid, and a steel dustbin doesn't cost much, does it? Why don't we find the people who bash out dustbin lids and start from there?'

We needed to get some special material that wouldn't rust, bearing in mind the dish would be exposed to the elements. We thought of plastic-covered steel, as used on the top cover of one of our cassette decks. Logically, it *had* to be as simple as that – there was nothing special about this dish, it was just a lump of steel.

Bob got on to the British Steel Corporation and asked them to quote us for blank sheets of a steel known as Stelvetite that was laminated on both sides with a rugged plastic covering. A couple of days later, he told me, 'You're not going to believe this. British Steel's raw material cost for a piece of steel large enough to punch out one of these dishes is . . . guess what?'

'No idea, Bob. Go on, tell me.'

'Seventy pence.'

We couldn't believe it.

'Seventy pence? And that tosser was asking for thirty quid? Can't be right, Bob.'

'I'm telling you, it's seventy pence. If we buy the amount of steel needed to make a million of these dishes, they've quoted me a raw material price which equates to seventy pence a pop. All we need to do now is find some metal-basher who's prepared to take the steel in, make a tool, bash them out and we'll give him a few bob for his labour and overheads. Up in the Midlands, there are great big car plants and car part suppliers who make wings and boots and bonnets – these guys have got the size of press needed and can do these dishes with their eyes closed.'

Brilliant stuff! Brilliant Amstrad stuff, sitting there brainstorming. Can you believe being quoted 70p and someone had asked £30 for it? Now we were really at the races on this satellite thing. There was light at the end of the tunnel. We'd cracked the LNB and now the dish. We were on target to meet our costs and I was able to relax a bit – I had made a promise to one of the world's biggest media moguls and at one point it had looked like we weren't going to be able to pull it off.

Bob and one of the buyers found a Midlands company, Concentric, who were delighted to take on this work. We made a three-way arrangement between Amstrad, Concentric and British Steel whereby Concentric bought the raw material directly from British Steel, bashed out the dishes and then supplied us with the finished product. At the same time, we slung in all the bracketry for them to make and we offered them the opportunity to pack the whole thing up in a card-board box. In other words, the satellite dish was delivered boxed and ready to go – we didn't have to touch it. Concentric agreed to make the dish for £1, plus another couple of quid for the bracketry and packaging, so for around £3 we had a fully packed satellite dish ready to ship.

The schedule was very tight, so who was the best man to make these satellite receivers quickly for us? Emperor Otake. As usual, he got his team working diligently and they managed to produce the receivers on time. Of course, we owned the intellectual property rights, so Otake couldn't go flogging them to other people. Also, as the chip in the tuner belonged to Amstrad, the manufacturer would not supply it to anyone without our permission.

We met the £199 retail price target, but it was very tight, so we pulled our old trick – we made another receiver which included a remote control and priced it at £249. Of course, everyone went for the £249 model and we were well in the money.

Credit to Rupert Murdoch, he started broadcasting in January. We got to market by February and were the only supplier at the time. Dixons advertised the hell out of the product and, sure enough, started to sell them in great volume. It was the first time the British consumer had a choice of television beyond the four terrestrial channels.

Meanwhile the BSB consortium had finally got their act together and raised some money. They were peddling a new technology using a small square dish which they called a 'squaerial'.

There was a lot of snobbery about the BSB service. They tried to project themselves as being superior, both technically and in terms of the programmes they'd broadcast.

Sky got to market first in February 1989, with a great advertising campaign that showed a Sky dish and the competitor's BSB dish. The strapline on the advert said, 'Sky: on air – BSB: hot air.' BSB didn't start transmitting until March 1990.

As with all new technology, you get what are known as 'early adopters'. My gut instinct had told me that if consumers were offered a package of sixteen television channels for £199, the product would fly off the shelves. However, it turned out that only a certain number of early adopters were interested. Dixons sold around 150,000 units very quickly and then sales started to slow down.

This was obviously a learning curve for Rupert Murdoch. It was clear that if his objective were to be achieved – if Sky Television were to become profitable – he would need *millions* of viewers so he could make money from advertising or subscriptions or whatever – 150,000 was absolutely useless.

As Sky Television began to take off, out came the snipers with their adverse comments about the 'ugly' dishes which were changing the face of the country's masonry. Some people vowed they would never have such a hideous thing stuck on the walls of their homes and, on reflection, it *was* a cultural change. These days there are over ten million around the country, so I guess if I am remembered for anything, it might be as the man who changed the face of the suburban landscape – when you see a dish, think of Sugar. Of course, if I had my choice, I'd prefer to be remembered more like Sir Christopher Wren, the man who built St Paul's Cathedral.

In rushing to the market, no thought had been given to a method of encrypting signals so that Sky could charge consumers on a pay-per-view basis for viewing movies or sports events.

I suggested the smartcard system to Rupert and we used the

company NDS in Israel, who specialised in making smartcards for banking and security purposes. We also needed signal encryption, the thing that scrambled the signal so that viewers couldn't watch the programme if they hadn't paid their subscription.

Rupert Murdoch's technical people chose the French company Thomson, who owned the scrambling system VideoCrypt. Thomson insisted that if he signed up to a licence for VideoCrypt technology, then they themselves must make the satellite receivers exclusively.

I told Rupert that this was totally unfair on Amstrad – after all, *I* was the one who'd had the balls to make a load of units on spec to help him launch Sky. Now he was trying to soft-land me into a situation where Thomson would be the only ones allowed to make the units for him. This was typical of the bloody French, who always want to keep things for themselves.

To be fair, Rupert took my point. He told Thomson that they weren't getting any deals unless they granted Amstrad a licence to make units with VideoCrypt technology. He argued that there was no way any broadcaster would ever place all their eggs in one basket, relying upon hardware supplied by one company.

Thomson reluctantly agreed to give us a licence, but insisted we send our staff to Paris to negotiate the agreement. I sent our corporate lawyer David Hyams over and asked Marion to get involved because I knew what these French bastards were like. Just like their VCR protectionism in Poitiers, we had to make sure there were no banana skins we could slip up on.

Sure enough, Marion called me from Thomson's offices and said, in her very dramatic French way, 'Alan, I'm telling you, they will never give you a licence. They are messing around and neither David Hyams nor I can convince them. They are being typical Thomson. They hate you. They don't want you to have a licence.' It was true. David Hyams confirmed that these people were being totally unreasonable and were throwing demands on the table that no one in their right mind would accept.

I got on the phone to Rupert and explained what was going on. I can only imagine that Rupert must have gone in to bat for me and beaten them up some way or another, because the following day they did sign an agreement with us. All their bullshit had gone away. Well, at least I *thought* it had gone away.

Part and parcel of being a Thomson licensee was to ensure that the product we shipped complied with their specifications. Or maybe they were being tricky and this condition only applied to us!

Rupert wanted me to stop production of the simple satellite receiver, so that *all* production would incorporate the VideoCrypt system and smartcard. Sky's requirement was for a combined receiver-decoder.

One of the other exciting aspects of entering this satellite business was that there were far more than the sixteen English-speaking channels on this service. In fact, there were over fifty channels, many of them being German. Germany was worse than England in that they had only two official terrestrial channels. German companies had decided they would start broadcasting stuff via satellite and our German subsidiary was being pestered for Amstrad receivers.

Meanwhile, Stanley had honoured his obligation and taken into stock about 350,000 of these receivers. As I've mentioned, he'd sold the first 150,000 or so, but the balance was sticking. Dixons was well and truly lumbered with the old stock.

What I'm about to tell you now doesn't bother my conscience at all, because Stanley Kalms and Dixons were a real hard-nosed bunch of people, which of course they were perfectly entitled to be. During the demise of Amstrad's computer business, when I organised a fire sale to reduce our inventory, Dixons commercially raped us and exploited our predicament. There was no sentiment, no camaraderie, no loyalty due to the fact that we'd put them in the serious IBM-compatible computer business in the first place. They'd never sold a bloody PC in their lives before we came along and yet now, when you walked around their stores, they were decked out with IBM, Apple, Dell and all the others. The fact was, *I* had put Dixons in that business and it now represented over 40 per cent of their total business. There were no thanks whatsoever. As a realistic person, I didn't really expect any, but I just want to create a clear picture here, to justify what I was about to do in my next move.

One of Dixons' senior managers, Danny Churchill, called me up and said, in the typically arrogant Dixons manner, that they had stocks of the Amstrad satellite receiver that weren't shifting and what was I prepared to do about it?

I told him, in a very straightforward way, that he could forget about bullying me like he did all his other suppliers. He could forget about asking me to take them back because, in short, Dixons weren't buying anything else off us. They weren't buying computers, they weren't buying audio – all they were buying was satellite.

'In fact, Danny Boy,' I said, 'all you *ever* buy off me is what's shit-hot and what the market wants. The minute we get ourselves into trouble or our products stop selling, you drop us like a hot brick. You don't do *me* any favours and frankly I'm not going to do *you* any favours.'

That was the general gist of the conversation. However, in the back of my mind, I knew I could sell all 200,000 receivers to Germany and make a huge profit. There was massive demand and we had no stock. It would take sixty days at least to get fresh stuff from the Far East, but I certainly wasn't going to take them back from Dixons at the price I'd sold them for, only to go and sell them again at the same price in Germany. Why should I bother?

After a few backwards and forwards phone calls with Churchill, I told him, 'In business, you have to know when to cut your losses. I'm quite prepared to take these things back off you for half of what you paid for them. Remember, I never held a gun to your head; it was Souhami who wanted to buy half a million pieces. In fact, you're lucky I didn't ship you the other 150,000 you were supposed to take – you only took 350,000. Anyway, that's my offer.'

Sharp as a needle, Danny said, 'Well, what are *you* going to do with them then?'

I told him it was really none of his business. I mentioned that I might try to sell them in the European market through one of my subsidiaries, but that's about all I was prepared to say. I struck a deal with Dixons and we sent a load of trucks to their Stevenage warehouse to pick up the stuff. We shipped the whole lot to Germany and sold them again for a handsome profit.

Should I feel guilty? Absolutely not. There was no love lost between Dixons and Amstrad – we both knew where we stood. To be fair, Stanley took his loss in the same way that I took mine when I had that fire sale a year or so earlier. I should add at this point that *outside* business, Stanley and I got on very well.

*

Rupert Murdoch appointed a series of people to run Sky initially. The first one I came across was Andrew Neil. He was the editor of the *Sunday Times* and had been promoted to try to run this Sky business but didn't last too long there.

Rupert had put a hold on everything until the market could be supplied with receiver-decoders so he could start charging subscriptions. The lesson learned from Dixons was that the number of people who were willing to fork out £199 for the product was limited to around 150,000. If Rupert's Sky was going to grow to the millions of subscribers he wanted, there was only one way of doing it, and that was to give away the boxes and dishes for *free*. This was something I'd been discussing with him as an alternative.

I have to say, you very rarely come across a bloke like Rupert Murdoch. He has got balls of steel because the risk he took in this business was unbelievable – his decision to *give away* the equipment was remarkable. Now Sky would have to buy the stuff from me, as well as finance a team of salespeople and installers to go out and fit them in people's homes.

I remember being called to a meeting in Wapping where the topic on the agenda was this gigantic decision – whether or not to change their business model and buy a load of satellite receivers to give away in order to build up a subscriber base.

Rupert invited me in to talk and I threw my tuppence ha'penny worth in, saying that it seemed to me to be a reasonable bet – if you gave the equipment free to customers, they would pay a monthly fee to receive additional television channels as long as the content was good. For example, there had to be movies that customers couldn't rent from Blockbuster. I also mentioned other programme content, such as sport. There had to be a mixture of some free telly and some subscription channels. Finally, it would be down to how much they expected punters to pay per month.

I remember one guy in the meeting hinting that *I* should join in the initiative and supply my boxes free of charge in exchange for a share in Sky Television. I remember half joking with him, saying, 'Well, why don't you, News Corporation, buy my company Amstrad? Then you'd be getting the products at cost price.'

It was quite amusing banter, but I'm not sure he had thrown his suggestion across the table as a joke. Certainly, I wasn't laughing, as that was the last thing on my mind, although, using that wonderful thing called hindsight, if I *had* said yes, it might have been the biggest and best decision I'd ever made in my business life, given the subsequent success of Sky (or BSkyB as we know it today). But I was a manufacturer and I'd always been a manufacturer – I wanted to stick to selling stuff and getting paid for it.

I was asked to leave the room while they discussed the matter. Eventually Rupert walked in and told me that they'd agreed to give me an order for half a million boxes. We dealt with it there and then. After a bit of to-ing and fro-ing, with News Corporation's lawyer running in and out of Rupert's boardroom, we did a deal on two sheets of paper. Both Rupert and I instructed the lawyers that we didn't want a fifty-page document; it had to be very simple.

I walked out of that building with a £78m order. At this time, late 1989, I knew it would be such a shot in the arm to all the boys back in Brentwood, considering the tough times we were going through on the PC2000 series.

After the meeting in Wapping, the focus was now on getting these new receiver-decoders to market quickly. Thomson had also been given an order and promised to get their units to the market on time. My parting comment to Rupert was, 'I bet you ten dollars that even though I'm using *Thomson's* technology, I'll have our unit to market quicker than they do, even if they *are* the inventors of VideoCrypt.' He shook my hand in front of his board of directors as I left.

To show you how horrible these Thomson people were, I'll share another story. Our chief engineer, Ian Saward, was a specialist in satellite receivers. He was tasked with developing the new receiver-decoder and obtaining technical approval from Thomson. We had already engineered the product and got it working and were ready to push the button on production. However, we couldn't do so until we'd received approval from Thomson. Ian told me that we'd sent them a sample over three weeks before, but they hadn't tested it yet.

I went nuts. I called some person in France and asked them what the hell they were playing at. This was their answer: 'Yes, you have sent us a sample, but the sample is currently in customs. It is not our job to clear your sample with customs – it is your job to deliver your sample to the doors of our laboratory.' Bastards. They were deliberately slowing us down.

I suggested that Ian get another sample, jump on a plane, go to their offices and stand there while they tested it. Ian went, but they would not allow him into their laboratory or give him a time when they would start testing it. They said, 'We are very busy and we do not know what time slot we can give you. We will let you know.'

Two weeks passed. Nothing.

We screamed down the phone at them, asking what was going on. They told us, 'We have tested your unit and it has failed.'

'How did it fail?'

'It is not for us to tell you how it failed; it is for you to look at our specification and make sure it passes.'

'Well, just tell us which *part* of the specification it failed.'

'No, we have told you – it is not for us to tell you which part of the specification it failed; it is for you to make sure you present an item that passes.'

This was getting out of hand now. We knew there was nothing wrong with the product. I spoke to David Hyams who advised me that what they were doing was tantamount to being illegal.

I got on to News Corporation's lawyers and, together with Herbert Smith's lawyers, we sent a stinging letter to Thomson threatening that we would report this matter to the European Community's Restrictive Practices organisation. These letters went by fax the next day (getting lawyers to work that fast was a miracle).

We must have touched a nerve because the engineering people at Thomson were instructed to inform Ian Saward exactly which part of our satellite receiver had failed. When we got the unit back and looked for the problem they'd outlined, we found that, in fact, nothing had failed. We tested the unit thoroughly in our laboratory and it sailed through. One of our engineers was sent on a plane to Thomson, who retested the unit and finally gave us technical approval.

Sky Television was steaming ahead, taking premises in Isleworth, west London, where they built studios to transmit Sky News. Rupert had employed a Scottish fellow, Liam, to be in charge of the logistics of taking the satellite receivers from us and installing them for customers, including setting up a network of salespeople and installers.

At the time, apart from the opportunity of buying movies on a pay-per-view basis, Sky did not own any other major rights such as football or cricket. I think it fair to say that in the early days of Sky, the sales team were a bit like double-glazing salesmen – they were incentivised to get subscribers. Who knows what bullshit they were giving people, but they were certainly getting a lot of product installed around the country. The viewer base was growing.

However, what Liam had organised was *chaos* – although to be fair he had an almost impossible job when you compare his small team with the infrastructure that exists at Sky today. We started to hear rumours that installers were stealing boxes and dishes, that there was no control on inventory or the quality of the subscribers they were signing up. The running joke was that a salesman would turn up at a house, see a kid and say, 'Do you want to watch cartoons?'

'Yes.'

'Sign here.'

Bingo. That was an installation. It was a real shambles. Nothing compared to today's brilliantly slick Sky operation.

The boss of Sky at the time was another one of Murdoch's editors, Kelvin MacKenzie, who had successfully edited the *Sun*. It was clear that changes were needed and Rupert took action, appointing a heavy-hitter from Australia, Sam Chisholm. He was the first guy to come onboard who had some actual knowledge of the Pay TV industry. Sam had successfully worked for Kerry Packer in Australia and he was brought in to take over as top man at Sky.

I'll never forget my first meeting with Sam Chisholm, a short, round-faced fellow, in his mid-fifties I guess, with a broad Australian accent. You could see this bloke had fire in his belly and he talked with an air of authority – you got the feeling he was a tough street-fighter. He came to my offices in Brentwood with Liam and when we offered him coffee or tea, he abruptly said, 'No, thank you, no. I've got to get down to business. These orders you're shipping us have got to stop. We've got stock coming out of our ears – you simply have to stop.'

That was his opening gambit. We had shipped all the goods ordered at the meeting in Wapping and Liam had placed more and more orders, as he was putting more and more units into the market. Now people were sending them back or telling Sky they didn't want them and a lot of people weren't paying the subscriptions. Chisholm had been thrown in at the deep end to try to stop this fiasco and get the business on the right track. His first port of call was me.

Sam sat in my office, opposite me, with Liam behind him. You could see from his body language that Liam resented Sam Chisholm's presence and was revelling in seeing Chisholm try to cancel the massive orders. Liam had obviously briefed Chisholm that I was not someone to mess with because, despite Sam's bravado (I can remember it as if it were today), his hands were actually shaking. Liam, meanwhile, was smiling at me.

I am a realistic person. This wasn't the Nigerian United Africa Company, this was not a case of taking the money and running; this was a serious business and it was clear that it had got totally out of hand. There would be no future for Amstrad in this business if it were to carry on this way. I knew this had to stop. In fact, I was surprised it had taken so long for someone to come along and pull the plug.

I decided to help out. I assured Sam that I would do everything in my power to slow production down until he got himself sorted out, but this might mean the cancellation of a lot of components which were particular to his model. I was honest with him – I told him I'd be able to re-use 65 per cent of the components in a model which I could sell in Germany. He was very relieved at my reaction, as he'd thought his first meeting with me would end up with us having a big legal battle.

I told Sam not to worry, that I was standing alongside him as part of the family. I had seen Sky Television announced back in June 1988, launched in 1989 and had kept my promise to have equipment in the

shops by February 1989. I'd even won my $10 bet with Rupert by get-
ting our receiver-decoders to the market first. I said to Sam, 'As far as
I'm concerned, apart from making money selling these things to you,
I'm actually enjoying watching this new television network being
born, so I'm onside with you. I'll come back to you in a week or so,
when my people have done the calculations, and I'll advise you of the
financial exposure on the components we can't use.'

The specialised components for the outstanding orders came to a
few million quid and we were able to convert the rest of the stock for
the German market. It must have come as a great relief to Sam when I
told him that the orders currently outstanding – which were worth in
the region of £40–50m and which he was contractually *obliged* to take
– could all be cancelled for a few million. We struck a deal and they
paid up.

*

Once BSB had launched, they and Sky were beating each other up. This
wasn't a healthy situation for Murdoch. It was like his newspaper business, where the *Sun* was forever competing with the *Daily Mirror*. There
was also some inevitable confusion in the marketplace amongst retailers. BSB had commissioned Philips and Tatung to make the receivers
(which worked on a different system to Sky's) and retailers stocked both
BSB and Sky (Amstrad) equipment. BSB was burning money like there
was no tomorrow. They were a totally useless, uncommercial mob compared to the great marketeers at News Corporation and Sky.

In late October 1990, I took a call from Sam advising me of a big
summit meeting being held with BSB and Sky. Rupert had flown in
and was currently in a hotel room, locked in negotiations. I learned it
was likely that an agreement would be reached whereby Sky Television
would combine with BSB as a single entity. This sounded the sensible
thing to do.

Later that evening, Rupert called me to say the deal was done, but
that it wouldn't be announced for about a week while some technicalities and contracts were being sorted out. Until then, everything was
confidential. He finished the call in a strange way, saying he was going
to send me a letter the next day. What was that all about?

A couple of days later, Frances gave me a single sheet of paper. It was from Rupert Murdoch and read, 'Dear Alan, it has taken me three hours to write this letter. You should be aware that it is the first letter I have ever written on a computer. Thank you very much for the laptop you gave me – it's great.' I'd forgotten that I'd sent Rupert a real leading-edge portable computer which we'd recently launched – the ALT1000.

Now, just to show you that I'm not a nasty guy to my friend Stanley Kalms, Dixons was, of course, selling Philips and Tatung BSB receivers and squaerials, having disposed of all the Sky ones. Effectively, they had placed their bets with BSB. Little did Stanley know that in a week or so's time there was to be an announcement which would render his BSB inventory at Dixons redundant.

I called Stanley and suggested he take me out to lunch at Harry's Bar, around the corner from his office, as I had something that was important for him to know. He was intrigued. During lunch, I said, 'I'm about to do you a favour. Now don't forget this because I know you wouldn't do the same for me. I swear you to secrecy.'

I quickly explained the situation and told him, 'You're going to be well and truly lumbered with all that Philips and Tatung stuff you've got in stock. I suggest you get back to the ranch quickly and get Danny Churchill to come up with some cock-and-bull story – because he's very good at those, as you know – and tell Tatung and Philips that you're sending all the stuff back. And might I suggest,' I added, 'that because Tatung and Philips need you more than you need them – in that you sell their TVs, VCRs and everything else – you have far more bargaining power in getting *them* to take the stuff back than you had with me when I made you cut your losses.'

I warned Stanley, 'This time, even if you agree to take *half* of what you paid for those satellite receivers, they're totally useless – there will be no more broadcasts to watch on them! So you need to go and do what you're best at doing, and screw Philips and Tatung.'

Stanley was dead shrewd and he got the plot straightaway. I think he grunted a thank you to me and he might even have paid for lunch!

About a week later, Sam Chisholm called and asked me whether I would show up at a television studio to be interviewed in front of ITV and BBC cameras about Sky taking over BSB. They wanted some comments from me, as the leading supplier of equipment in the marketplace.

The deal was announced late on a Friday night, 2 November, and on Saturday I went to a studio somewhere in the West End. Rupert had given the BSB mob a little bit of dignity in that the name of the company going forward would not simply be Sky Television – it would be BSkyB, standing for British Sky Broadcasting. I heard a rumour that the company name was one of the things that clinched the deal. If so, it shows you how pathetic some people can be in business – little things please little minds.

*

Looking back on Amstrad's spectacular growth, one of the things I regret was the lack of financial control for a company of our size. We certainly allowed the entrepreneurial spirit to flourish through Marion, Dominguez, Jost and myself, of course, but we were all marketing people who paid little attention to detail when it came to general housekeeping. That was fine when everything was going well and we had hot products that everyone wanted, but caused problems when things started going wrong, as with the PC2000 series. Despite the excitement of the satellite business, realistically, it was only part of the whole. The computer side was slugging us down, people were not paying, and stocks were building up in the subsidiaries.

When you get to that stage, desperate for sales, you start making arrangements you wouldn't normally make with customers – things like offering goods on sale-or-return, or agreeing extra-special discounts if they bought a certain volume.

Alarm bells started to ring in early 1989. Ken Ashcroft and I decided to appoint one of our accountants as an internal auditor and send him regularly to the overseas subsidiaries to see what was going on. It must sound crazy to think about doing this after the horse had bolted, so to speak, and it goes to show how lax we were in those days of spectacular growth. We posted a senior accountant, Tony Dean, to Germany on a permanent basis. Jost was turning out to be a bit of a Jack the Lad – he was running the company as if it were his own, with no regard for authority or policy.

As a result of these internal audits, a horror story emerged – terrible financial control and customers owing us lots of money with no clear road map as to when we would get paid. Spain was particularly bad, with the debtors' list getting bigger and bigger and payment running out further and further. I discovered that some customers had been allowed over 180 days' payment and in many cases payment terms weren't even specified. The exclusive distributor in Barcelona owed Amstrad Spain a fortune.

When we delved into the financial arrangements, it was as clear as mud. Dominguez had let the thing run wild. He had lost his enthusiasm when he realised that Amstrad had run out of ideas and that customers were no longer begging for stuff. He was confronted with having to deal with mundane housekeeping and problems with customers and he didn't like this at all. He wanted to focus on new blockbuster products and create advertising campaigns and sell hundreds of thousands of units, but those days were gone. He'd cashed in a load of money when we bought his company and I was hearing rumours that he was dabbling in real estate and property and not focusing at all on the shit we were in.

I liked Dominguez as a person and it was a sad day that September when I flew to Madrid with Malcolm Miller and told him that he and his senior staff were fired. We needed to put in some sensible people with a good accounting background to try to sort the mess out. Similarly, in Germany, Jost was a loose cannon. We removed him and promoted the sales manager, Franz Simias, to take over the company.

We were in fire-fighting mode. Every single week there was another problem. My focus turned to shrinking the company and stopping the bleeding. In Spain, France and Germany, we shed our luxurious office premises and incorporated them into the warehouses we rented. This cost-cutting exercise also entailed the removal of a lot of staff. I had turned from an entrepreneur – thinking up products and ideas – into a liquidator.

We had chased our tails on the PC2000 series for over eighteen months – including the fiasco of exchanging the hard disk controllers – till eventually, in 1990, we threw in the towel and flogged the stuff off. The full ramifications of this meant write-downs which affected our accounts. It was clear we'd been legged-over by the hard disk drive manufacturers. This rankled with me and I instructed David Hyams to engage Herbert Smith to investigate whether we had any legal claims against Seagate and Western Digital. Both denied any liability for effectively ruining Amstrad's computer business.

We decided to issue legal proceedings against Seagate through the English courts and, for some reason better known to the lawyers, we issued proceedings against Western Digital in the United States. The preparation for these highly complicated court cases was such that it would be years before we ever got to court to fight the cases. There was no quick solution.

It was an awful time and very demoralising. Ken Ashcroft came to me one day with some story about wanting to retire. He explained that he'd spent his whole life working and now he'd made some money on the share options, he wanted to move on. He wasn't at retirement age; I think he was one of those people who liked to be associated with success. Clearly the Amstrad bubble had well and truly burst and there was no single product or idea that was suddenly going to elevate us to our former glory. All Ken could see was aggravation ahead and he wanted out. Eventually, we promoted Tony Dean, one of our existing senior accountants, to the role.

Marion was very frustrated. She had seen her shares-wealth dwindle and she kind of blamed me for the fact that she'd held on to half of her shares. I reminded her (and some of the others) that I'd *gifted* them their share options and that the million-pound windfalls they'd enjoyed a couple of years ago were just that – *a gift*.

Also, her reputation had waned in the French marketplace as our fortunes declined. She had become a legend there. She'd been bigged-up by the press and had won lots of awards, such as Businesswoman of the Year. She was now suffering a bit of a downer, like a fallen star.

*

In between bouts of fire-fighting, I used to cheer myself up with new ideas. I was always on the lookout for new innovations. One of those ideas came from thinking back to how we went from the single cassette tower system to the twin cassette version. I wondered if the same philosophy could be applied to VCR. I was conscious of copyright issues, however. I had to think carefully about how we could justify a twin-deck VCR without getting ourselves into lots of trouble, because in those days people rented pre-recorded tapes from Blockbuster and a twin-deck VCR might be thought of as a means to copy them.

However, after a bit of fancy work in the software and electronics, we designed a product that would allow a customer to load the double-deck VCR with two tapes and set the thing to record for eight hours. Bingo – that was it – the true justification of why we would make a twin-deck VCR.

It was not easy to convince Funai to produce this product. They started to worry that the product incited copyright infringement, but eventually we managed to convince Funai that the product was viable. I knew if we could reach the magic £399 price point, it would be a big hit.

Of course, our advertising displayed a bold warning of how it was illegal for people to copy copyrighted material and we also put large red labels on the front of the unit and outer packaging. There was uproar within the media industry about this product, but despite their protestations, there was nothing they could do. Amstrad had cleverly warned consumers – using the same reverse psychology trick as we used on our audio units – that the Double Decker must *not* be used for illegal purposes. The product was born and became a tremendous hit in 1990.

It was something positive, as was our business with Sky, but overall it was still a pretty horrible time.

13

'Terry Will Look After the Eleven on the Pitch . . .'

'I'll Look After the Eleven Million in the Bank'
– Buying a Nightmare

1991–2

As a kid, my dad and Uncle Jack used to take me to see Spurs play. We always stood in the East Stand, on the right-hand side, and my dad would lift me up and put me on top of one of the crush barriers so I could see. Sometimes he'd lift me up over the turnstile to avoid paying for me, winking at the man in the cubicle at the same time. He also used to take me to reserve games quite a lot, which in those days were played at White Hart Lane. I don't want to portray myself as a fanatical Tottenham supporter, but most people tend to follow one football club – and Spurs was my club. It's one of those things you do for life – every Saturday you watch out for your team's results and follow their progress. My brother Derek *was* a real Spurs fanatic. He had a season ticket and he'd go to every game with his mates.

I was so busy during Amstrad's early days that I never had time to go along to Spurs. Ann's brother, Mark, was a big fan and would take Simon and Daniel to White Hart Lane sometimes and one of our neighbours up the road in Chigwell was also a massive Spurs fan and would take the boys there occasionally. I went along a few times with Mark and Ann's cousin, Melvin, another fanatic. So that gives you an honest background to me as a Spurs fan.

Around 1991, I couldn't help but read in the newspapers about a load of aggravation going on with Spurs' finances and how it was on the verge of bankruptcy. My friends and my kids were telling me that the club was in danger of being shut down. It was one of those things you tended to hear in the background but not pay too much attention to.

On Saturday 18 May 1991, I was at home watching the FA Cup Final. Spurs were playing Nottingham Forest. A deal had been done by Spurs to sell Paul Gascoigne to the Italian club Lazio for £5.5m at the end of the season, which would pay off part of Spurs' debts. The fans were not happy, but accepted it as part and parcel of the survival of this famous club. We beat Forest 2–1 that afternoon, but regrettably Gascoigne suffered a serious knee injury, which meant that his transfer to Lazio was off and the £5.5m obviously wouldn't be coming. Nevertheless, Spurs had won the Cup and were in Europe the following season.

To this day I don't know what possessed me, but on the following Monday, I put out a call to Spurs' manager, Terry Venables. I'd met him previously, as he once took part in an advertising campaign for our hi-fi tower systems – we'd used the strapline 'Great Players'. I'd received a call a few years earlier from the Inland Revenue, asking us to provide details of the fee we paid him, and I'd called him out of courtesy, marking his card that we had to supply the Inland Revenue with these details.

The newspapers had reported that various consortiums were going to buy the club from the existing owner, Irving Scholar. All failed because none of them had any money! There was also talk that Terry Venables, who'd been managing the club for over three years, was going to try to get his own consortium together to buy the club off Scholar. From what I could gather from the newspapers, Venables was at loggerheads with Scholar who, as chairman, had been cast as the bad guy, responsible for the demise of the club. Reading the papers, you got the impression that everything wrong with Spurs, both on the pitch and in financial terms, was down to Scholar. Scholar was the devil and Venables was the white knight – only without any money.

I made the fateful phone call on Monday 20 May and got through to Venables immediately. I agreed to meet him and his adviser, Eddie Ashby, at the Hilton Hotel in Park Lane later that week. It was the same night I was due to attend an industry dinner.

I couldn't quite understand why people were hovering around as we sat openly in the Hilton lobby. Naïvely, I didn't grasp that the mixture of Alan Sugar, the multi-millionaire, and Terry Venables, manager of financially struggling Tottenham Hotspur, was bound to get tongues wagging. To be honest, I didn't realise how high-profile football was.

The first indication I had that our informal meeting at the Hilton had attracted some attention came on Saturday night. I was out for dinner at Langan's Brasserie when suddenly a journalist from the *Sunday Times* appeared at my side and asked, 'Did I hear that you're buying Spurs?' I was shocked.

'No, it's not true – I haven't bought Spurs. I haven't done anything like that at all. I was just discussing it. I've really got no comment to make.'

Ann turned to me and said, 'What's all this? Spurs?' as did the friends we were having dinner with. When I explained to her that I was thinking of taking over Spurs with Terry Venables, she looked at me as if I were nuts. 'Since when have you been interested in football? Bad enough you used to be out flying every Saturday – now I suppose you're going to be at football every Saturday!'

'Calm down,' I said to her. 'It's only a discussion at the moment. It could be a good financial deal because it's a public company and I believe there's potential in football.'

Sure enough, the headlines in the business section of the *Sunday Times* the next day read, 'Sugar to take over Tottenham Hotspur'. It was at that point that I realised what a high-profile thing this was. My phone didn't stop ringing that Sunday. Everywhere I went, people were asking me, 'Are you going to do it? Is it true? Will it happen? Are we going to buy any players?'

Daniel and Simon were very excited at the prospect. Daniel in particular wanted to know every detail. He'd followed the Spurs situation closely and, like all fans, understood that the devil was, allegedly, Irving Scholar. Daniel asked me on a daily basis throughout the course of the next week what was happening. Were we going to end up buying it or not? What was Scholar doing? What was Scholar saying? He called him 'Swerving Irving'.

At the Hilton meeting, Ashby had explained that Venables had £3m available and if someone else would match that £3m, then between them they would have enough of a fighting fund to buy Scholar's shares and take control of the company.

I'll say it again – I have no idea what prompted me to get involved, but I agreed to meet Ashby at my offices in Brentwood, so we could sit with my accountants and go through the financial situation at the club.

According to Ashby, unless this great institution, Tottenham Hotspur Football Club, was rescued, the next move would be the Midland Bank calling in the liquidators to shut it down. I told Ashby I was prepared to go ahead on the basis that Terry put up his £3m. I would then match it with my £3m and we'd each own the same number of shares acquired from Scholar and another shareholder, Paul Bobroff. (It was necessary to acquire both Scholar's and Bobroff's shares to take control of the company.)

My vision of Venables at the time was of a chirpy chappy, a shrewd lad. He was rumoured to own lots of clubs and pubs and he was a so-called football genius. He'd played for Spurs in the past and had a couple of England caps.

It never dawned on me to challenge whether Venables actually *had* £3m of his own money. You must be thinking now, 'Is this Sugar *really* a clever bloke?' After years of wheeling and dealing, making millions, I was now about to enter a transaction without bothering to check whether my new partner had any money or not.

Venables and I enlisted the services of a merchant bank, Ansbacher, to act on our behalf in buying Scholar's and Bobroff's shares. To fast-track this part of the story, a bunch of lawyers and accountants drafted up an offer document, I had discussions with Scholar at his home in Monaco about acquiring his shares and we near enough agreed on a price of 75p.

There was a lot of publicity surrounding this possible acquisition and media mogul Robert Maxwell, owner of the *Daily Mirror*, was making noises on the front page of his paper that *he* was going to rescue Spurs. I was really hyped up to ensure that Maxwell would not scupper the deal. Andrew Neil, now back as editor of the *Sunday Times*, called me trying to be helpful by bringing me up to date on what his market intelligence was telling him about Maxwell's inter-vention. As I was so hyped up, I rudely said, 'That's not news, Andrew, I know that already.'

Andrew saw this as a massive insult. He was trying to help and I was so dismissive. He got very angry on the phone and basically told me to get stuffed. It was a case of my mouth working faster than my brain – instead of thanking him, I came across as a real bigshot and deserved the bollocking. A few minutes later, I called him back to apologise, but he was still fuming and from that day on he's been quite hostile to me. Obviously a man who doesn't forgive and forget.

The whole thing reached a climax at Ansbacher's offices on Friday 21 June. Venables, Ashby and I were present when Bobroff turned up to sign some documents and sell his shares. Scholar had sent his lawyer along, but had still not agreed to sell to me. Something fishy was going on. Then the officials at Ansbacher told me they'd received an eleventh-hour approach from Robert Maxwell, who was sending a team of people there to scupper the Venables/Sugar deal, stating that he'd agreed to buy the shares off Scholar and Bobroff.

I was still digesting this information when one of the officials from Ansbacher told me that Robert Maxwell was on the line and wanted to speak to me. Maxwell told me to back off from this transaction, that Venables was not a man to be in partnership with. He suggested that the better partnership would be him and me.

Maxwell said he could assure me that he would be a passive investor. I'd seen enough of this outlandish man to know there was *no way* he could ever be passive about anything! He was already the owner of Derby County FC and I remembered watching this fat oaf running across the pitch on TV after his team had won an important match. I also remembered the days of the Sinclair deal and how Maxwell had plastered himself across the front page of his paper, claiming he was going to rescue Sir Clive.

After listening to his rant, I told him, 'I deal in simple facts. We have bankers' drafts here on the table, ready to do the deal. With respect, Mr Maxwell, you do a lot of talking – as you did on the Sin-clair deal – but when it comes to putting your money where your mouth is, you seem to back off. I've been told you don't have any money. Does this mob you've sent down here have a banker's draft with them?'

Maxwell went nuts, spouting off a load of rubbish. I cut him short and said, 'Okay, that's all well and good, but do you have the money – yes or no?'

He started waffling again and again I cut him short. 'You *don't* have the money, right? So in that case you'd best tell your team of lackeys to piss off and let me get on with this deal.'

He hung up.

I'd sussed out that Maxwell had no intention of buying the club; he was just looking for another front-page story on how he was going to rescue Spurs. Nevertheless, he'd sent a team of lawyers and bankers down to Ansbacher's offices. I instructed Ansbacher's people to lock them in another room and keep them away from Bobroff.

Bobroff, meanwhile, had received a call from Scholar telling him that Maxwell was about to make a counter-offer and that Maxwell's people were actually there in Ansbacher's offices. He told Bobroff to insist on seeing them. We couldn't stop him, so he went off for about a quarter of an hour, then came back and said, 'They've offered me eighty-five pence per share and you're only prepared to pay seventy-five.'

Everybody was panicking. I pointed out to Bobroff that this was his one-time opportunity of walking away with a banker's draft for his shareholding. My bank manager was there in the building with the banker's draft ready. I said to Bobroff, 'Maxwell can offer you eighty-five *pounds* a share, as far as I'm concerned, but you're not getting one penny more from me. The difference is, we have the money and they don't.'

I explained to him that Maxwell was full of shit. He always talked about buying things, but did not perform. He tried to impress people as 'Robert Maxwell, the billionaire'. No one other than me would have had the audacity to ask him whether he actually *had* the money. The bottom line was, he *didn't* have the money – simple as that.

I said to Bobroff, 'I'll come with you, if you want. I'll talk to Maxwell's financial advisers. Just ask them if they have the cash to give you today.' Bobroff went off on his own and came back ten minutes later, talking some bullshit that Maxwell wouldn't pay him the money until Scholar had also agreed to sell to him.

I reiterated to Bobroff that, surely, as a clever businessman, well respected in the property business, he could read between the lines and see that Maxwell was full of crap. I finally convinced him to sign a share transfer to me and we gave him a banker's draft in payment for the shares he owned, at 75p per share. I asked Bobroff to call Scholar in Monaco and tell him that he'd sold to me, but he was frightened to do so, as I think he'd made some kind of gentleman's agreement to sell to Maxwell.

I ended up calling Scholar in Monaco. I told him about the fiasco which had just taken place and that he could check it out with his lawyer, who was standing next to me. An hour or so later, Scholar called back to say he'd accept the deal. He congratulated me and told me to make sure that we won the European Cup-Winners' Cup now that we'd won the FA Cup.

The deal was done. We had bought Scholar's and Bobroff's shares and we now had control of the company in sight. There was just one problem. Where was Terry Venables' three million quid? It was at this point that Ashby casually said, 'Oh, by the way, Alan, there's a bit of a delay with Terry's three million.'

'A delay? What do you mean by delay? You knew this was the completion meeting. You knew that we had to turn up and pay out the money! What do you mean delay? You sat there watching me beat up Bobroff, negotiate with Scholar and fight off Maxwell – you saw it all – and now you tell me your money's not here?!'

'No, no, it's a technical issue. It'll be here Monday for sure. It was just a problem with the bank transfer. I promise you, it will be here on Monday – no trouble at all. I guarantee you, you'll have the money on Monday.'

I was faced with a dilemma in Ansbacher's offices. I'd signed and agreed a deal with Bobroff and Scholar. I had given Bobroff an £822,000 draft for his shares; meanwhile, Scholar's lawyers were waiting for me to hand over a £3.2m draft for Scholar's shares and repay a loan he had made to the club. I had no alternative but to shell out over £4m for the full acquisition that night.

As you can imagine, I was thinking, 'What the bloody hell have I let myself in for with this Venables and Ashby pair?' Venables couldn't see anything wrong with the whole thing; he didn't understand the procedures, as he'd left everything to Ashby and, in his mind, my having to wait till Monday was no problem. He never spoke to me about this, but hid in another room and let Ashby do the talking.

By now, there was another person hovering around, a barrister called Jonathan Crystal who had popped in during the evening session. He said he was a good friend of Terry and I assumed that, as a barrister, he was part of his advisory team.

When I was having a row with Ashby about the funds not being there, Crystal stepped in and said, 'I can vouch that Terry's money will be coming through next week. You can take my word for it as a barrister.' I suppose this gave me some comfort at the time.

The following Saturday, there was a press conference at White Hart Lane and it was announced that Terry and I had taken over Spurs. It's easy to speak in hindsight, but if I thought I'd had aggravation with the PC2000 series and winding down Amstrad, that was a walk in the park compared to the hornets' nest I had now entered.

In the end it took ten days for Venables' £3m to turn up and even then I never thought of asking whether it was from Venables' own pocket or whether it had come by way of some form of funding or loan. I was just grateful to receive it.

The essence of this deal, as I saw it, was that Terry Venables would look after the football side of things, while I would oversee the business side and finances. That was supposed to be the dream ticket.

Back at Amstrad, Bob Watkins turned to me and said, 'You aren't gonna last ten minutes with that Terry Venables bloke.' I couldn't understand why he would form that opinion – it was quite uncharacteristic of him. I think what he was referring to was a clash of egos. Little did he know how spot on he was.

I got a load of phone calls from people congratulating me or expressing surprise over this deal. One such call was from Edward Walker-Arnott, now senior partner at Herbert Smith, who told me that I needed to take care on entering this football business. He said, 'It's not meant for your culture, Alan.'

Naïvely, I agreed to Venables' suggestions about reshuffling Tottenham's board of directors. It would now comprise myself, Tony Berry, Terry Venables, Jonathan Crystal, and a man by the name of Igal Yawetz who was an architect and a friend of Venables.

I also appointed a finance director, Colin Sandy. He was not associated with Amstrad, but was someone who had handled my personal finances and those of my property business. Tony Berry was declared the chairman of the football club, while I was declared the chairman of the PLC holding company. I didn't really understand what that meant; I just went along with it.

In August, we were due to play Arsenal in the Charity Shield, the traditional pre-season match between the winners of the league and the winners of the FA Cup. We were due to go on holiday that day, so you can imagine how pleased Ann was when I told her that first we were going to Wembley to see a football match. It was the first time I would be able to see the team I'd bought.

Before the match itself, it's traditional for the chairmen and dignitaries of both clubs to gather and have a grand luncheon. However, I was informed that the seats had all been taken – apparently this had all been worked out long before the acquisition. I didn't think anything about this at the time and, quite honestly, I didn't really care.

All became clear when I got to Wembley, however. I was waiting outside the grand dining hall when eventually the diners started to exit and make their way to the stands. Out came Terry and all his mates, including Jonathan Crystal. Having enjoyed their slap-up lunch, they were pouring out of this place, while I, the so-called owner and chairman of the club, was standing there like a schmock. I didn't know how to feel at the time.

The game ended in a draw and the Charity Shield was shared. After the match I made a quick getaway to Heathrow to catch my private plane down to Sardinia. We landed two and a half hours later, unloaded the luggage and asked the taxi drivers to take us to the Cala di Volpe Hotel. They looked at us as if we were mad, shrugging their shoulders and shaking their heads. We said it again, 'Cala di Volpe Hotel. We want to go to the Cala di Volpe Hotel.'

One of them got out a map of Sardinia and showed us that the Cala di Volpe Hotel was located in the northern part of the island – we had landed in the south. It turned out that if we wanted to get there by car, we'd have to make a journey the equivalent of Hyde Park Corner to Penzance. We had landed at the wrong airport!

I'd spoken to the pilots earlier in the week and they'd asked me, 'Which airport are we going to?'

I thought Sardinia would only have one airport, so I looked at the map and flippantly said, 'Okay, we'll go to that one.' Apparently there were two airports.

It sounds funny now, but consider six people stranded with loads of luggage, 250-odd miles away from where we should have been. Fortunately, the flight crew were still there, so we lugged all our stuff back onto the plane and flew to the other airport. Eventually, we turned up at our hotel.

Apparently, this hotel was owned by the Aga Khan, for whom Nick Hewer was a PR consultant. It was one of those hotels that were very sought after and difficult to get into. The elite all stayed there, and even they had to book years in advance. So as you can imagine, we were eager to see what was so good about this hotel.

As we were led to our room, I thought that someone, perhaps Nick, was having a joke – it was the biggest dump I'd ever been to in my life. I said to my friends, 'Have we made a mistake? Did we not only go to the wrong airport but also the wrong hotel?'

But no – this *was* the famous Cala di Volpe Hotel.

When we walked through the reception, the men and women were dressed in very smart and exotic outfits, so I wondered if they'd dumped us at the staff's quarters by mistake. What's more, Nick had booked me into what was called 'the Grand Suite'. The air-conditioning grille on the wall was black with soot and looked as if it hadn't been cleaned for twenty-five years. The bed was a simple metal-framed affair, the so-called patio windows were stuck slightly open and there was just one little wardrobe to hang a few clothes in. One of my friends told me to come and look at his room. It was a total joke – he didn't even *have* a wardrobe.

We went down to complain at the reception. The man behind the counter shrugged his shoulders, as if to say, 'Yes, I know it's a problem, but that's how it is here.' Unbelievable. One of the most expensive hotels in the world and it was a bloody rip-off. And to add insult to injury, when we came to check out and tried to pay by credit card they said, 'No, we only take cash or cheques here.'

During my stay that week, Eddie Ashby phoned me from Tottenham and told me that Terry had identified a Scottish player, Gordon Durie, who was playing for Chelsea, and he wanted to buy him. Eddie was looking to me for authorisation to go ahead with this transfer.

'Are you joking, Eddie?' I said. 'We've just used our money to buy Bobroff's and Scholar's shares, plus the others – there's no money left. We've got Midland Bank currently working out an arrangement for us to repay the eleven million quid we owe them, plus the Gascoigne deal's not going through. So, Eddie, please explain to me where the money for this new player is coming from? Why are you even bothering to ask such a stupid question?'

'Look, Alan, Terry is confident he is going to sell some players. With the money, we'll easily be able to pay for Durie. Actually, Alan, I'm just letting you know as a courtesy that the transaction *is* going ahead.'

By now, I was starting to get a bit concerned. 'Hold on a minute, Eddie, have you actually got a contract for the sale of the outgoing players? Who are these outgoing players anyway?'

'Terry doesn't like to publicise that certain players are up for sale, otherwise we won't get much money for them, so he needs to keep it to himself.'

'Never mind keeping it to himself – he can surely share it with me. Can you tell me who these players are and at what stage of negotiations are we? How far down the line are we in concluding these deals?'

'Well, Terry won't be happy to tell you all that and he needs an answer today on this Chelsea deal.'

'I don't give a fuck whether Terry's happy or not and I'm getting a bit pissed off being treated as if I'm some kind of idiot. I am hereby telling you, in plain and simple terms, that you are *not* allowed – repeat, *not* allowed – to buy this player until you show me a road map of where the money's coming from. I'm not sticking one more penny in until we've got to grips with what's going on.'

I slammed the phone down on Ashby.

By the time I got back from holiday, Venables had gone ahead with the Durie transfer without my permission. He'd called me while I was in Sardinia to assure me the deal would be financed by the sale of other players. Bearing in mind I hadn't been in business with him long, I accepted this on face value. I reminded him that I'd given my personal assurance to Midland Bank on the eve of the acquisition of the club that there would be *no* spending on players – the priority would be to reduce the £11m debt.

Venables seemed to be oblivious to this. He buried his head in the sand like an ostrich, always referring me to Eddie. Needless to say, he *didn't* sell any players, so we had to finance the deal from the cash flow on season ticket sales. The bank was very angry and demanded a meeting with me and Colin Sandy to discuss the matter.

*

As the new season started and I began attending games, I was told that I'd been allocated a few seats in the directors' box, in about the fifth or sixth row back. Tottenham directors and guests were in the right-hand side of the directors' box; the left-hand side was for the visiting team's directors. The front rows, right and left, were for the chairmen and directors of Tottenham and their opponents. I, the owner, was stuck five rows back! A number of people, including Ann, asked me why I was stuck in the back rows. Tony Berry was tucked up in the second seat on the front row, leaving a space for Terry Venables. The remainder of the front row was occupied by Venables' family. People were starting to wind me up and I began to feel as if I'd been taken for an idiot.

I got hold of Venables after the second game and told him that this seemed all wrong. Perhaps he could explain to me what all this 'chairman of the football club' and 'chairman of the PLC' meant.

Once again, he shied off, saying that he didn't understand all this technical stuff and I should discuss it with Eddie, at which point I told him, 'Never mind "all this technical stuff", it's as simple as this, Terry – you're taking me for an idiot. You must think I'm some wally with a load of money who's come in here to rescue the club and let you do as you wish. Well, I'm telling you right now, you've picked the wrong bloke because that ain't gonna happen. And while we're on the subject, as chairman and owner of this football club, *I* will be sitting in the front row and so will my family. On top of that, I'll be asking Peter Barnes to explain to me this seating allocation and who gets what because I want to know why all these hangers-on seem to be walking around as if they own the place.'

For the first time, I realised that Venables had no bottle. He was only in his comfort zone when surrounded by his lieutenants. He said he did *not* take me for a fool and that he hadn't been behind anything that had gone on. He told me that Tony Berry was the one who organised everything, placing the blame with him. I never asked Berry if this was right or not. But I did tell Berry that the game was up. I was a fast learner and while it was a nice try to see if he and Venables could put me in the back room, it had failed. I told him to resign as chairman of the club and simply remain on as a director. I took on the chairmanship of the club in addition to that of the PLC.

After a series of meetings with Midland Bank, we had to have a rights issue, which I ended up underwriting. This resulted in me injecting another load of cash into the club, making my total investment £8m. I would have more shares than Venables, as he had no money to underwrite his portion of the rights issue.

Ashby was Venables' right-hand man, though he never had a formal title or position – he just seemed to be the main mouthpiece. Terry placed all the financial decisions in his hands and I think it fair to say that Ashby was running the place. I had agreed that Venables, as chief executive, would have total responsibility for not only the football side of things but also for all commercial aspects. However, when it came to financing everything, there were no ideas forthcoming at all. Ashby was talking about getting mortgages, which never materialised, and the sale of Gascoigne, which would have brought in around £5.5m from Lazio, had stagnated due to his injury. To make matters worse, during his rehabilitation, Gascoigne got involved in some incident that resulted in him damaging his knee again, putting the whole healing process back several weeks.

Even telling you this story in hindsight, I'm still shocked as I recall the unbelievable events that were about to unfold.

Venables explained to me that a very well-connected Italian called Gino Santini was going to broker the deal between Lazio and Tottenham to see whether we could get them to pay us the money even though Gascoigne still hadn't fully recovered. This sounded fine to me and all I kept hearing over the next few weeks was 'Gino this' and 'Gino that'. Gino turned out to be a restaurateur in Kensington who spoke Italian and had helped in Mark Hateley's move to AC Milan – that was his claim to fame.

He was absolutely useless in the negotiation of this matter. I thought it was handled in the most unprofessional manner, with stupid suggestions such as, 'Insurance policies will cover Gascoigne's recovery and provide a warranty to Lazio.' Why would anyone in their right mind pay us £5.5m when the player was still injured, without any medical evidence that he was fit to play?

Despite this, Ashby convinced Venables that he would find an insurance company who would cover the risk. Ashby came up with a Mickey Mouse insurance policy and ran up a bill with a broker. The offer put forward by the insurance company was so ridiculous in respect to the premium payable (as well as the limited liability of the policy) that it was a total joke – Lazio would just laugh at it. I shut it down before we started running away with extra costs.

In the end, the sensible thing happened. Lazio sent over a medical team to England to examine Gascoigne at the end of his rehabilitation and finally approved him fit to play. At that point they transferred the money.

In the meantime, Gino Santini had slung in a bill for £200,000 which we paid into a Swiss bank account. It seems Venables and Ashby had entered into an agreement with him that a fee would be payable as soon as the transaction went through. There was nothing much I could do about it other than demand that he send us a proper invoice.

With the further injection of cash from me and the money from the Gascoigne transfer (plus revenues from gate receipts), we were able to get the Midland Bank overdraft down to manageable proportions and at least I had honoured the promises I'd made to the bank.

In his capacity as chief executive, Venables was totally out of his depth. He knew nothing about merchandising and nothing about the commercial side of business, but he was paranoid about maintaining his status. As he saw it, he'd spent all his life as a player and a manager – this was his big opportunity to become an owner and a boss. The only problem was, he didn't have a clue about things like Stock Exchange requirements, accounting, cash flow or marketing – he left it all to Ashby.

I was getting very concerned. On many occasions, at board meetings, Venables would make some totally stupid comment, but Crystal, who turned out to be a real arse-licker, would insist that Terry was on the right lines. Berry would take a schtum powder and keep quiet. I looked to him and Ashby for some support when I explained the logical and professional way things should be done, but they were all shit-scared of offending Terry. It was very frustrating and an uncomfortable atmosphere was growing.

I started to notice that Venables was very distrustful of me. He was always looking to see if I was lining my own pockets in some way or another. Every time I said something, you could see him weighing up how this might disadvantage him. Venables had employed his daughter to work in the merchandising department, which, I was informed by Colin Sandy, was burning money as if it were going out of fashion. There was no stock control – players and other playing staff members were simply coming in and *taking* stuff. 'That's how it's always been' was the famous expression. I insisted we needed to put in a computer system to create some form of control.

Bearing in mind that I was in the computer business, it made sense for the equipment to be supplied by us at wholesale prices. Venables thought that my company selling the club £4,000 worth of computers was going to make me a fortune. It was totally ridiculous. We needed a computer system and I was in the computer business. Venables was sick in the head with his paranoia about anything to do with money I might get out of the club. He, on the other hand, felt that as joint owner, he was entitled to have as much as he wanted and employ who he wanted. It was a case of dual standards.

He had his nightclub, Scribes West in Kensington, where Tottenham Hotspur bashes were regularly held to celebrate various things.

Not that we had much to celebrate, but any excuse: start of season party, FA Cup draw party, winning a game party, Christmas party, New Year's party, any pitiful excuse. Everyone was invited. The irony was that he made his mates pay for their drinks, but for so-called official Spurs parties, Tottenham Hotspur footed the bill. Spurs was paying a fortune to Venables' Scribes West club.

I was told, 'Oh, this is quite normal – football clubs have to entertain all the time and it's better we do it at Terry's club than hold the event in a hotel.' Yet buying £4,000 worth of computers from Amstrad (whose turnover was £350m at the time) was, in Venables' eyes, lining my pocket.

Another of Venables' hangers on was Eric Hall, the resident agent at Spurs, who handled the sales of players, negotiated their contracts with the club and then sent in large bills. Eric Hall would spend seven days a week at Scribes West. He was so far up Terry Venables' arse it was untrue. I gave him the nickname Anusol.

I had never in my life experienced two people like Crystal and Hall, who were so besotted by this messiah Venables that they would literally do anything for him to get his attention.

As the months passed, I could see things were not going as well as had been anticipated with this so-called dream team. The way Nick Hewer had spun it to the press was, 'Terry will look after the eleven on the field; Alan will look after the eleven [million] at the bank.'

Certainly, on the pitch, we weren't setting the world alight. Venables had appointed Peter Shreeves as manager of the team and he wasn't doing well at all. On my side, however, after a lot of twists and turns with Midland Bank and the Stock Exchange, we finally got the shares listed back on the stock market again – they had been suspended at the tail end of the Scholar era.

*

The acquisition of Tottenham by myself and Venables took place in June 1991. In February 1992, the first division football clubs (including Tottenham) resigned from the Football League to form the Premier League. From this point on, there were regular Premier League chairmen's meetings, which I did not attend, as I was told they were just discussing fixtures and the rules of the game, and there was nothing financial to bother me with. Venables, as chief executive, would go, along with Crystal, and the club secretary, Peter Barnes, would also attend and sit at the back.

On one particular occasion, they informed me that a very important vote on television rights was going to take place. Up until then, television rights for English top-flight football were split between *Match of the Day* on BBC and ITV, who were paying around £4m per season to the league for the rights to show a few games live. However, there was a feeling among most of the Premier League that a small nucleus of clubs comprising Arsenal, Manchester United and Liverpool seemed to attract most of the television coverage. They were closely involved with ITV and wanted to keep the next round of negotiations with them.

Rupert Murdoch's BSkyB was making noises that *they* wanted to bid for the Premier League rights. The whole thing had grown to a crescendo and at this particular Premier League meeting, on Monday 18 May, a decision was going to be made by the chairmen as to which company would win the rights.

Rick Parry, the Premier League's chief executive, quite rightly insisted that a proper tender process should be followed. Broadcasters would have to deliver their best and final bids by a certain time. This was no longer going to be a closed shop or a foregone conclusion. For the first time, ITV looked like they might not win and they'd have to come up with a darn sight more than the peanuts they'd paid in the past. More importantly, the Premier League clubs now wanted to share the prosperity from any TV windfall – many of them bitterly complained that in the past, the only winners seemed to be an elite few.

On the day of the meeting, I turned up at the Royal Lancaster Hotel. As we entered the room where the meeting was to be held, Trevor East, an ITV executive, was handing out pieces of paper to the chairmen. This was a last-minute dirty trick and it broke the rules of the tender.

I, of course, wanted BSkyB to succeed, so I went to the public phone cubicles opposite the meeting room and called Sam Chisholm.

Little did I know this call would go down in the annals of football history – some in the media have described it as 'the phone call that irrevocably altered the history of sport and media in Britain'. I told Sam that ITV was trying to pull a fast one at the eleventh hour and he needed to get hold of Parry quickly and find out what was going on.

About half an hour later, I got hold of Sam again. He told me that he had put in his strongest bid in compliance with the tender process, but ITV had somehow found out the details of BSkyB's bid and wanted to top it.

I can't recall the exact numbers, but faced with this type of auction (where, for example, £45m per season was on the table and your opponent could top it and win by offering £46m), I told Sam, 'There's only one way to clinch the deal – you'll have to blow them out of the water!'

'What do you mean by that, Alan?'

'Look, Sam, they won't expect a *giant* increase in your bid – they'll be thinking you'll go up in one million pound increments – so make your final bid £60m per season and blow them out of the water.'

I'm not exactly sure what happened after that – how Sam contacted Parry to get his message through or indeed the actual figure he offered, but the meeting of the Premier League chairmen had started and the TV deal was about to come up.

At this point, I interjected, through the secretary, stating that I wanted to declare a conflict of interests. I explained that Amstrad manufactured satellite dishes and that I was a big supplier of BSkyB, who were one of the bidders for the TV rights. I suggested that due to this fact, Tottenham Hotspur Football Club should abstain from the vote, to avoid any accusations that I was acting in my own interest.

Most of the other clubs, including Chelsea, Leeds, Wimbledon, Manchester City and Nottingham Forest, objected to this suggestion, saying that Tottenham not being able to vote might alter the decision. A motion was put forward balloting all the clubs as to whether Tottenham should vote, in view of my declared conflict of interests.

After a lot of protestations from Arsenal's David Dein and Manchester United's Martin Edwards, the meeting agreed that Tottenham should indeed be allowed to vote. David Dein was dead against BSkyB and was singing songs of praise about ITV. He was throwing all kinds of curve-balls into the discussion, like suggesting the Murdoch empire might not have the money.

Fortunately, I was there and was able to counter all this rubbish. To be honest, my back was up. I was disappointed by all the sniping going on when discussing whether Spurs should be allowed to vote or not and I could see agendas forming. The big clubs were trying to bully the rest – it was undemocratic. It seemed clear that they wanted to line their own pockets by favouring ITV. I was annoyed, so I went in to bat big time for BSkyB.

After a couple of hours' discussion, the motion was put to the room as to whether we should accept BSkyB's or ITV's offer. BSkyB got the deal. Ironically, they won it by one vote – clearly Spurs being allowed to vote *was* important. The ITV people were furious.

The next day, I went off to France for a few days' holiday. My son Daniel called me to tell me the newspapers were full of stories about me telling Chisholm to 'blow them out of the water'. The stories went on to say that ITV were going to take BSkyB to court and get an injunction to stop this deal going through. Daniel told me that, in football terms, I had started World War Three. There were pages and pages on the whole thing in every national newspaper and it was suggested that it was all down to me.

The thing about football people is that they don't like change. They tend to get stuck in their ways and this move to BSkyB, a satellite company who were going to charge a subscription, was alien to most of the football fraternity, as well as some of the old sports hacks in the media. They were happy with the way football had been broadcast in the past and were worried that the face of football would change now that Murdoch had got his hands on it. It was quite negative stuff and the non-Murdoch media was giving me a load of stick, suggesting that, as I was a supplier to BSkyB, I was lining my own pockets. However, I had openly declared my conflict of interests, so there was no foundation to this.

A few days later, in the High Court, ITV were again blown out of the water by BSkyB's lawyers, who argued that the tender for the television rights was conducted in a correct and legal manner. It was a great victory for Sam Chisholm who, coincidentally, was at my offices in Brentwood at the time his lawyers called with the news that ITV had lost again. Sam asked if he could call Rupert and give him the good news.

Was I pleased that BSkyB won the deal? Absolutely. Yes, it was going to be good for the satellite business, and yes, it was going to be good for Amstrad, but I had acted in good faith and declared my conflict of interests. In any case, it was also a good business proposition for the clubs because BSkyB stumped up a fortune compared to the peanuts previously paid. It was good for Spurs too, as we'd get a healthy share of the money.

14

Bungs and Barristers

A Backseat at Amstrad and Shooting Bambi's Mum

1992–4

The affairs of Tottenham Hotspur were not distracting me too much from the core business of Amstrad – at least, not yet. Bob Watkins and I were discussing other markets for Amstrad. The telephone manufacturer Betacom was going down the drain and Bob and I saw our opportunity. In May 1992 Amstrad PLC made a most unprecedented move in acquiring 66 per cent of the shares of Betacom, also a public company.

No one could understand why I didn't buy the whole company outright, but in the back of my mind I had the vision of one day, having squeezed Amstrad down through rationalisation and possibly having found a buyer for it, being able to retain this other small public company on its own and effectively start again. Let's face it, leading a public company had been very good for me. I was able to cash in on large chunks of shares as Amstrad's share price rose. I made far more money than I could ever have done if the company had remained private, as the only way of getting money out of a private company was by dividends from profits. In the crazy Amstrad days, our stock market rating valued our shares far beyond the equivalent of any dividends I could have taken. So I would never complain about being involved in public company life. How could I?

I had this in mind because it was clear that Amstrad was still struggling. We'd lost the PC market due to the failed PC2000 series, the buzz of blockbuster products had gone and I'd spent so much of my time fire-fighting that I was out of ideas. The share price had plummeted from the dizzy heights of £2.35 and was now hovering at around 26p.

Marion's frustration with the retailers as well as the demise of her share options resulted in her resigning in February 1992. I too was frustrated by the situation. I guess the market was losing confidence in us, seeing us shrinking our subsidiaries, shutting things down in Hong Kong, selling off computers at low cost and with profits dropping year on year. Then, in June 1992, we reported a huge loss of nearly £71m – we had taken a realistic view on the value of the massive PC2000 series inventory and had written it down.

Confidence from the market had now totally drained away. From my perspective, this was outrageous. I could see why the market was nervous, but I didn't understand why the share price had dropped to as low as around 22–23p, meaning that the market value of the company was below its asset values – lower than the cash balance in the company! I commented on this several times in the media, explaining that this was crazy. No matter how bad business had been in the last year or so, we still had good assets and potential in the marketplace.

After my summer holiday, I decided to see if it would be possible to privatise the company, so that it would be 100 per cent under my control again. *I* believed in Amstrad, even if no one else did. I'd amassed a lot of cash from previous share sales and the company had cash in itself. Margaret Mountford from Herbert Smith explained the mechanics of how to make an offer and we also discussed it with Tim Holland-Bosworth from Kleinwort Benson. I'd calculated that as the share price was hovering around the 23p mark, then from a logical point of view, if I offered 30p per share, people would bite my hand off.

Margaret also explained that although the company I was trying to privatise had lots of cash in it, it would be illegal under stock market rules for me to try to acquire Amstrad using its own cash. Instead, I needed to find a bank to lend me the money for a few weeks while the transaction was going through, then pay them back quickly once the deal was done.

Tim Holland-Bosworth was not particularly happy with the 30p price. Traditionally, your merchant banker would recommend what they felt was a 'good offer' to shareholders. I argued with him on the basis of simple logic, saying, 'Right now the share price is twenty-two pence and it's been like that for the last six months. Why would anybody in their right mind turn down thirty pence? Why should I offer any more?'

He explained that my offer of 30p was below the total asset value of the company, to which I replied, 'Exactly, that's why I'm so annoyed! If the share price was fifty or sixty pence now, I'd be quite happy and get on with my work. But I'm pissing in the wind at the moment – no matter what we try to do, it is not reflected in the sentiment of the market.' Reluctantly, he agreed to the 30p price and an offer was sent out to shareholders in September 1992.

Margaret Mountford warned me to keep schtum during the privatisation transactions. She added, 'There will be a lot of shareholders – particularly institutional ones who paid a lot of money for these shares in Amstrad's heyday – who won't be happy bunnies to find that *you're* the one buying them back.'

Did I take any notice of Margaret? No.

As soon as the privatisation announcement was made, Nick Hewer was pestering me every minute of the day. Every national newspaper in the country suddenly woke up to Amstrad again, having been quiet for the past eighteen months while we struggled. Like a bloody idiot, I fell for it hook, line and sinker and I got sucked into discussing my reasoning behind privatising the company. Of course, the real reason was that I wanted to get it back on the cheap and effectively pay for it with the cash that was sitting inside it, but I didn't feel I was doing anything wrong. After all, if the shareholders felt the company was worth more, why wasn't the share price 50–60p?

Pages and pages of articles were written, slagging me off. Outraged shareholders were commenting to the press. It was a great story for the financial newspapers and the adverse publicity created a groundswell of anti-Sugar feeling. One chap, Gideon Fiegel, who owned a few shares as a private individual, decided to go on a one-man crusade and was championed by the newspapers as 'this poor fellow being done down by the multi-millionaire'. As you can imagine, he became a star overnight. They practically had to operate on him to prise the microphone out of his hands. He was like Posh Spice, having his photograph taken at every opportunity.

Margaret's advice was 100 per cent right and I will never know whether the deal would have gone through had I taken it. As it was, the shareholders voted it down and my attempt to privatise the company failed. Gideon Fiegel was hailed a hero. I guess he'll dine out on that story till his dying day.

When the dust settled on the failed privatisation, there were complaints from heavy-hitting institutions with large shareholdings that I was too much of an autocrat, that Amstrad was not being run in accordance with public company standards. There were no non-executive directors; I had the role of chairman *and* chief executive officer. They were demanding that I restructure the company in a different way.

It was not a nice feeling, having the investors turn on me while the media was damning me as someone who'd reached his peak and was on the way down. I think it was one of the lowest times in my life. Most people in my position would have taken the view, 'Well, I've made loads of money and I'm a multi-millionaire. These days I'm just left running a load of aggravation, and to top it all I'm getting a load of stick from the outside. Why bother?' The easiest thing to do would have been to hand over the keys to someone else and I even recall Ann saying something to me along those lines. But I had built this baby from scratch and I just couldn't bring myself to walk away.

I don't know what came over me at the time, but I heeded the City's call to adopt public company structures and appointed two non-executive directors and a chief executive to run the company while I remained in the position of chairman.

I wasn't the only one hit hard by these events. Bob Watkins was starting to feel a little despondent about the direction in which Amstrad was moving – in fact, he wanted out. He'd noticed a similar air of despondency in me since I'd failed in my attempt at privatisation.

Bob told me one day that he'd been approached by Gulu Lalvani, who'd clearly assumed that a lot of our past success was down to Bob. In one way, he was right, as Bob got stuff into production in a timely fashion, which was vital to the success of Amstrad in its heyday. Gulu perhaps didn't understand that the product ideas didn't actually come from Bob, though he was great at transforming the rough ideas I'd conceived into production. Nevertheless, Gulu had made him an offer to run his Hong Kong organisation, with a remit to develop products and try to take his company, Binatone, to a different level.

To be fair to Bob, he struggled with his conscience over this – he didn't want to do anything behind my back. He told me quite openly that this opportunity had come his way and he was seriously considering it, but he didn't want to offend me in any way, as we'd kind of grown up together through the good times of Amstrad's meteoric rise. But now we'd lost the computer market and were struggling to come up with new ideas, he saw Gulu's offer as a much-needed fresh challenge.

Although I felt upset that one of my long-term colleagues wanted to leave me and should have expressed my feelings, I just said that if he wanted to go, he should, and there'd be no hard feelings as far as I was concerned. I was very grateful to him for the effort he'd put in over the years, which had helped me make hundreds of millions of pounds. He felt he had an opportunity to better himself and any objection or attempt to stand in his way seemed unfair.

Bob left Amstrad and joined Binatone in January 1993. I'm sure Gulu felt he had pulled off a great coup, although we never spoke about the situation – he was under the impression that his negotiations with Bob were entirely confidential and that he was doing a bit of a dirty on me. I guess, when you analyse Gulu's tracking of my career, it must have been motivated partly by admiration, but also partly by resentment. While Amstrad had been growing into a massive organisation, his company was still messing around trading in low-cost, low-technology products such as radios and telephones.

*

As part and parcel of our rationalisation and cost-cutting, we decided to shut our French, Spanish, Belgian, Italian and Dutch subsidiaries. They really had no more potential, as we'd lost the PC market. For the same reason, we also shut down our subsidiary in Australia run by Bordan Tkachuk. Bordan was a very good salesman and I decided to bring him over to head up the UK sales department.

None of this was helping my mood, but there *were* times when, with the rationalisation behind me, it seemed I'd got my old spark back. For instance, Ian Saward came to me one day in early September 1993, having heard that a Danish company called Dancall was about to go into bankruptcy. They had some great technology in mobile phones and were developing what was known in those early days as a GSM phone, a phone that could be used anywhere in Europe. This was the type of stuff that gave me some enthusiasm again. The mobile phone market was starting to explode and every businessman had an analogue mobile phone, but GSM was going to be the future.

The company Orange, run by Hans Snook, had started to take massive adverts in the national newspapers to say that Orange was coming. They had been talked into this mad scheme by some Hooray Henry advertising agent. On these full-page adverts, 95 per cent of the page was black and in the bottom left corner was an orange square with the word 'Orange'. The idea of this campaign was to get everyone asking, 'What is Orange?' Sure enough, it worked – but who bloody cared? It must have cost a fortune.

Hans Snook sent me a free Orange phone to try out and invited me to the official launch of the Orange mobile network. On the day, when all the guests were seated, the lights went down, the curtain went up and a plump advertising executive came to the centre of the stage dressed in a bright-orange suit to unveil their next brainwave, the new TV advertising campaign. It was a newborn baby swimming underwater, with the strapline 'The future is bright – the future is Orange.'

I was thinking to myself that Hutchinson, the massive Hong Kong investment company who had recruited Snook to launch Orange in the UK, really must have money to burn. The adverts said nothing about the phone, nothing about the service, nothing about how these new phones would work in other countries. It was a total joke.

At the cocktail party after the presentation, Hans was strutting about like a peacock. He grabbed hold of me and steered me over to his Chinese bosses. 'Well, Alan, as a great marketing man, what do you think of that then?'

'All I can say, Hans, is that it's about time you started shipping some of these phones, getting some subscribers and getting the show on the road.'

There was no point expressing my real opinion in front of his pay-masters.

Anyway, a few days after Ian Saward told me about Dancall, I hired a private jet and went there. Scandinavian companies were far more advanced in radio telephony than those elsewhere in the world; indeed, the industry was promoted by the Scandinavian governments. Dancall had received certain government grants to develop mobile telephones, but had got itself into deep financial trouble.

At the factory, I was met by a couple of the employees, who wanted to give me some long-winded storyboard presentation of their history, where they were going and what they were planning to do. I could see this was going to take at least an hour, so I cut them short and asked them to walk me round the factory premises and the engineering department and show me what was going on.

Having spent so long in the industry, I could sniff out a good factory and a good engineering department simply by walking round, seeing how things are made and talking to the engineering people to get an understanding of what they're up to. What I saw in this organisation was a little pot of gold. They'd spent many years developing products and were just at the stage of being able to start production of the only thing that was likely to sell, but they'd run out of money at the wrong time. The employees were about to be made redundant that week. I was starting to feel a buzz again, just like the day Rupert Murdoch talked to me about his satellite plans.

I asked them to call a meeting of all the staff. They assembled in the canteen and I spoke to them openly and honestly. I asked them to do me one favour: even though they wouldn't be paid beyond this week, I asked them to be patient and remain for at least one more week, as I intended to buy the company and take it forward.

The firm of accountants administrating the liquidation quickly sent a representative to England to see me. I struck a deal with the guy to buy the whole lot – lock, stock and barrel – for £6m and agreed to incur the liability of the employment of all the staff.

I decided to send Claude Littner to look into the immediate situation and report back. I'd recruited Claude initially to look after the French subsidiary after Marion's departure. He was introduced to me by my brother-in-law Mark as a kind of company doctor and spoke very good French. He was talented at getting to the bottom line, cutting through the crap and spelling out to me in simple terms the strengths and weaknesses of a company.

Luckily, Bob Watkins had kept in touch with me. His new job in Hong Kong, as I'd anticipated, wasn't as wonderful as Gulu had painted it. Bob said, 'People know where they stand with you, Alan. Gulu's not as straight-talking as you, and you don't know what the direction is.'

I told Bob I'd acquired this company in Denmark and it was right up his alley. All he had to do was to make sure the newly designed products got into production and, more importantly, apply the Amstrad philosophy in cost-cutting and negotiation on component parts. Bob promptly resigned from Binatone and came back to take over Dancall.

I made a second acquisition in June 1994. The computer market had been changing from traditional selling (via retail channels) to direct marketing and I spotted one company, Viglen, which operated in this way and looked attractive. It was run by four of its founders and, having appraised the business, I suggested to the board that we purchase it, but take extreme care that we didn't allow the vendors simply to run off after we'd paid them the money. My suggestion was that we pay £60m for this company by way of an up-front payment of 50 per cent, then structure an arrangement based upon three years' profits, over which the other 50 per cent would be paid. In this way, we could at least get our own management's feet under the table before the lucky vendors were able to come up with the inevitable 'irreconcilable differences with the board' and clear off with their money.

Meanwhile, we tried to find a chief executive for the Amstrad group – someone who'd be able to take this tiger by the tail and professionalise it. Most of the applicants were certainly not experienced in consumer electronics, others were quite hesitant to take on the role because they feared they would be suppressed by me. Eventually, we found David Rogers, an ex-Philips executive based in Eindhoven. I wasn't that impressed, but we weren't having any luck getting anyone

else to join, so I reluctantly agreed he could be employed. To be perfectly honest, I had lost my fighting spirit.

Rogers' arrival was welcomed by people like David Hyams and
Ian Saward, who became good allies of his, signing on to his new large
corporate systems. Hyams was the type of person who tends to get
deflected away from what they're good at and wants to be more
involved in the business side of things. I've seen this many times, with
engineers, lawyers, accountants, even football managers who don't
want to play to their strengths, but feel they have some entrepreneurial spirit and are better at other things. I could clearly see this was a
disaster waiting to happen.

Malcolm Miller, another long-term employee from the early days
of Amstrad, left just before Rogers arrived. He was head-hunted by the
games company Sega in Japan and, like Bob Watkins before him,
couldn't see any prospects at Amstrad – there seemed to be no direction and, more to the point, no further opportunity for large windfalls
by way of share options. However, his departure was not conducted in
the same manner as Bob's.

Out of the blue, Malcolm told me one Monday morning that he'd
flown to Japan the Friday before, met Sega in Tokyo over the weekend
and had flown back on Sunday. He told me flatly that he was taking the
job. There wasn't much I could say – I had to let him go.

Miller, like Watkins, was head-hunted in the belief that he might
be able to help replicate Amstrad's successes. I could have expressed
my disappointment about the lack of loyalty in the manner Miller
went about his departure, but instead I bottled it up inside me.

*

After a few months, Rogers presented the board with his going-
forward plan. His idea was that every product category we were active
in should be called a 'line of business' (or LoB – he liked abbreviations
and buzzwords). His master plan was to have LoB managers for computers, satellite, fax machines and audio/TV. He named the UK sales
office and the subsidiaries Betacom, Dancall and Viglen 'business
units' or BUs.

I could see problems on the horizon. Why on earth would you set up a line of business for fax machines when, in fact, the market was already dwindling? Not only that, every Tom, Dick and Harry in Hong Kong and China was now making a cheap fax machine. If anything, he should have decided to get *out* of that business, not try to expand it. Similarly, in the satellite market, he employed some product manager who decided to expand the range beyond that of the products we were shipping to BSkyB. They came up with a new series of specialised satellite receivers – complex and up-market models, none of which had a hope in hell of succeeding.

Through all this, I had to button my lip. If I'd started to impose any pressure and suppress any of these ideas, it would have been seen as me trying to take back control of the company and undermine Rogers. If ever the expression 'watching your mother-in-law drive your brand-new Ferrari off a cliff' was appropriate, it was now. During this time, I noted that people such as Hyams and Saward were disregarding me and my comments. They were simply in awe of all this LoB and BU jargon floating around the company.

Meanwhile, at newly acquired Viglen, Rogers would attend board meetings with Hyams, who was enjoying it tremendously. No longer was he going to be bored dealing with contracts, licensing and other minor litigation matters – he now saw himself as a senior executive, making decisions. Be under no illusions, David Hyams was very intelligent and a good lawyer. The problem was, he didn't want to do lawyering any more.

Rogers was also regularly attending Betacom board meetings. The management there, especially the accountant, were able to wind Rogers around their little fingers. The managing director, Norman Becker, and his finance director had this bee in their bonnet that even though Amstrad owned 66 per cent of Betacom, Betacom was still a separate public company and they had to ensure it was not influenced by the 'big, bad wolf' Alan Sugar. I could imagine this being Becker's big boast down the pub – how *he* was running this business and how Alan Sugar couldn't do anything about it.

My son Simon had moved to Betacom, as it was the only company in the group that was still involved in consumer electronics. Simon had some very good contacts in supermarkets and mail-order companies to whom he'd sold loads of TVs in the past. He tried to implement the sale of TVs through Betacom, to increase their turnover. It was a no-brainer – a 15–20 per cent margin could be made and selling TVs at £80–90 trade price would dwarf the turnover of their stupidly priced £3–4 telephones. However, this was a 'not invented here' idea as far as Becker was concerned so Simon's idea was buried.

*

During this period, I was still interested in new technology and ideas. Apple were making noises about a new product they named 'Newton' – a small, flat device with an LCD screen. Using a stylus, you could write on the screen and operate all the functions, which included a simple word processor and an electronic address book. We got wind of this and in 1993 quickly initiated our own version, known as the PenPad. It was a great device which incorporated handwriting recognition and had a full contact and diary section. It was real leading-edge technology and I was rather excited about it, having lived through the recent disasters.

The problem was, I was used to making 100,000 per month of everything new we came out with – that was *my* idea of a hot item. I'd experienced this sort of success in the mid-to-late eighties with other products I'd launched, but things had changed. Sales of the PenPad were disappointing – the market wasn't ready for it. We'd made 100,000 and had to start flogging them off. Unbeknown to me, we *had* hit upon the right direction; it was just a case of it being too early. However, with the acquisition of Dancall and their knowledge of paging technology, I decided to commission a mark-2 version of the PenPad to incorporate some kind of mobile phone paging system, so that people would not only have an organiser, but also a mobile radio device to send and receive messages.

In the meantime, Rogers and I visited Hans Snook and presented the idea to him for Orange to buy and market. Hans really had the hots for it and told me there and then that they would buy loads. He said they had many services they could transmit to the unit, such as weather and traffic updates. I told him this was just the start of a range of products that would ultimately lead to the incorporation of a full-blown mobile phone. However, Rogers and Saward decided to can the project due to technical development problems.

Why am I telling you all this? Simple. What happened later was that the US company PalmPilot sold tens of millions of the product I've just described. We should never have given up. To add insult to injury, this technology would have been the road map to what is today known as the BlackBerry or iPhone. How sick is that?

I don't want to give the impression here that it was someone else's fault we missed out on a massive market. The fact was, I was really in despondent mode at the time, so it was a case of, 'Okay, if that's what *you*, the CEO and the chief engineer, have decided, then fine.' Had I been *really* fired up, I'd have got to the bottom of why the mark-2 didn't work, as I used to do in the high-flying days. But what with Spurs to run and all the fire-fighting *that* involved, my mind was elsewhere. This was one of my big business errors and it cost me dearly.

In the end, the senior staff didn't need to be told by me that David Rogers was not working out. They could see with their own eyes that none of his plans had come to fruition. He was making bad calls and they'd seen me step back and allow it to happen. Eventually, in December 1995, Rogers resigned and took up a job in some giant organisation. He was more suited to the large corporate environment.

Bordan had been very despondent under the David Rogers regime. In the end, he'd resigned and planned to go back to Australia. Now I told him to hang on, as I needed him to run the Viglen business and he agreed to stay. We also took on another accountant to help sort out some of the problems in places like Dancall and Betacom, a guy by the name of Guppy Dhariwal, an unusually tall and strapping Indian fellow.

Guppy was very much like Claude Littner in the sense that he had no time for bullshit or small talk. When we sent him to Dancall or Betacom, he would come back and tell it like it was, without any embellishments or enhancements. I was in a board meeting just after Rogers had left, listening to all his leftover jargon being thrown across the table – '. . . the LoB this and the BU that . . .' – and I said to everyone, 'I've bleeding had it up to the neck with all that LoB/BU crap.'

With an angry and serious face I added, 'Since you love it so much, here's a new buzzword for you – I'm going to send the FBI into Beta-com to sort them out once and for all.'

'The FBI, Alan? What does it have to do with the Federal Bureau of Investigation?'

'No,' I said, 'I'm talking about Guppy Dhariwal – the Fucking Big Indian.'

*

While juggling Amstrad and Tottenham hadn't seemed a problem to start with, I had no idea what I'd taken on. Sadly, I still had a lot to learn about how the world of football operated at the time.

One match day, Venables uncharacteristically came into the boardroom and asked to speak to me. He told me he was interested in a player at Nottingham Forest by the name of Teddy Sheringham, but there was a problem because, as Venables put it, 'Cloughie wants a bung.'

I told him I wasn't interested in listening to anything involving corruption and bungs. I'd heard it went on in football, as there had been some scandals in the past, but I told him it was absolutely and totally out of the question. Spurs would have no part in anything like that.

He immediately said, 'Sure, yeah, that's what I thought you'd say, but I was just checking it out with you, just letting you know. I mean, Teddy's a great player, but that's how it is – Cloughie wants a bung.'

I repeated, 'Just try to pursue getting the player in the conventional manner.' And, as far as I was concerned, the matter was closed.

This was around September 1992. Over the next couple of weeks, there was constant discussion about the acquisition of Teddy Shering-ham and how the transfer was being delayed. Tony Berry asked me whether I knew about the situation and Brian Clough's demands for a bribe. I asked how *he* knew about this and it transpired that Venables had told him over lunch at Langan's Brasserie.

I'm not sure whether Berry was sounding me out to see whether I would change my attitude, but I certainly reinforced that I would never be involved in anything corrupt. I told him it was a criminal offence and that we were a public company – we must *never* be associated with it.

Berry agreed. 'Of course, Alan, of course. No, I'm just mentioning it, you know, just mentioning it.'

The next thing I heard on the Sheringham transfer was that an agent, ex-player Frank McLintock, had handled the deal, which Ashby claimed was now done. Venables had agreed to pay McLintock a £50,000 fee for arranging the transfer of the player to us. With the transaction about to take place, I received a phone call from Colin Sandy who told me that he'd been instructed by Ashby to go down to the bank and withdraw £50,000 in cash to pay McLintock.

I told him this was absolutely ridiculous. If McLintock was an agent, he should simply send his bill to us and we'd pay it in the normal way, by cheque. Colin said he'd already explained this to Ashby, but that Venables had *insisted* he went down to the bank now to get the money. I told Colin he was absolutely *not* allowed to do it and that he should go back and tell Ashby to tell Venables that if we had to pay McLintock a fee, we wanted an invoice showing VAT.

A few hours later, Colin called to say that McLintock had agreed to issue an invoice to the club for his services for the transfer of Sheringham, but was paid in cash.

From a technical point of view, Colin had done everything he possibly could. I found out afterwards that Ashby had instructed one of the club's accountants to go down to the bank and withdraw £58,750 in cash and the money was given to McLintock to settle his bill.

When I asked Venables what was going on, he stuck his head in the sand as usual, saying that Eddie knew all about it and I should discuss it with him.

Peter Shreeves had been the manager in the first season after we had acquired the club, but he hadn't done a good job and was asked to leave. Venables took over the managerial position, jointly appointing Doug Livermore and Ray Clemence to assist him. In the 1992–3 season, one could see Venables was actually getting a little more involved on match days, going down to the pitch when things weren't going well.

One match day, Venables came to me saying he'd just had a great shock. He'd been told by Ashby that he was a bankrupt and Venables just wanted to let me know. I was a bit surprised at this sudden declaration of Ashby's personal status, but things started to make sense as I recalled numerous occasions when Berry had suggested that Ashby should be one of the directors, since he seemed to be operating in a chief executive position. The reason Ashby didn't put himself forward to be a director now became clear – bankrupts may not become directors of public companies.

My reaction was to say to Venables that he must have known about this way back at the acquisition stage or he would have suggested Ashby as a director. Venables denied any prior knowledge and said he'd only learned about it that day.

The truth behind this revelation was that one of the national newspapers had got hold of this information and had called Venables for his comments. It was inevitable that the story of Tottenham's virtual chief executive being a bankrupt would soon be splashed across the papers and this was the reason Venables was telling me now.

In fact, Ashby seemed a reasonably intelligent and fair-enough fellow. Nothing he had said or done so far seemed illegal or unprofessional. I said to Venables, 'I don't need to know the reasons for Eddie's bankruptcy. On the face of it, he seems a reasonable chap and there's no reason why he shouldn't remain employed as your assistant.'

The person who actually gave me the most grief was Jonathan Crystal. As I previously mentioned, Venables had this mental block whereby anything I said or did was in order to line my own pocket or disadvantage him in one way or another. Crystal would, out of blind devotion to Terry, raise these issues at board meetings, acting as Venables' mouthpiece, aggravating situations, deliberately winding me up and engaging me in arguments. Crystal was so far up Terry's arse it was sickening to see. In fact, on one of the occasions I met Terry's wife, Toots, she made me laugh by telling Ann and me how Crystal would appear everywhere and drive her nuts sucking up to Terry. She said she had nightmares that Crystal would appear at the end of their bed.

It was clear, from some of the discussions we'd had, that Crystal didn't know much about public company life from a corporate law stance, yet he would always say, 'I'm a lawyer, I know these things.'

Actually, he knew sweet FA and I wouldn't have used him to get me off a parking fine. Some of his tactics and ideas were outrageous.

On one occasion, Venables had agreed to enter Spurs into a tournament with a few foreign clubs, to be played at White Hart Lane. We would receive a fee for taking part in the tournament on one condition: the tournament had to be televised. Crystal told me the deal had been struck, but the problem he faced was finding a broadcaster. The opponents we were going to be playing weren't top-notch teams such as Real Madrid or Barcelona, so there wasn't much interest from ITV or the BBC. Crystal asked me to enquire whether Sky would like to transmit this tournament. I called the director of sport at Sky, but once he heard who the opponents were, he politely turned it down.

Crystal reiterated that unless we got this tournament broadcast by *somebody*, the whole deal would be off. He pointed out that it didn't actually say in the contract that there had to be a *fee* from the broadcaster, merely that it had to be broadcast.

On that basis, we agreed that I would go back to Sky and ask them to do me a favour and broadcast the event for no fee. Even *that* turned out to be a difficult job. Sky explained that the amount of viewers they'd get wouldn't warrant the cost of sending out cameras and crew and putting the event on the air. I pleaded with the director of sport and told him he'd be doing me a great favour if he did it for me, as a friend of the company, and finally they agreed.

The tournament went ahead and Sky broadcast the games, but then a week or so later, Venables called me up, shouting and screaming down the phone. 'Why is it that Sky got the deal and didn't pay a penny for it? Why are you helping out your friends?'

I was dumbfounded. 'What are you talking about, Terry? Talk to Crystal – he'll tell you everything that happened. No one wanted to take the bloody tournament and because of Crystal's genius in drafting the contract, we were lumbered with having to get it shown on TV. The only people prepared to do it were Sky and at one point they were actually asking *us* for payment for sending out the camera crew.' Venables was so thick, he couldn't grasp what was going on. He had it in his head that, some way or another, me arranging this deal with Sky was lining my own pocket.

I was really frustrated and angry. I got hold of Crystal and asked him, 'What the hell is going on? How dare Venables call me up and make such accusations?' I reminded Crystal that he was completely responsible for this mess and told him to go and sort it out immediately.

A couple of days later, I got the pair of them in a room to have this out. To my utter amazement, Crystal said he'd never discussed broadcasting for no fee with me. I couldn't believe what I was hearing. It showed me what an absolute liar and cheat Crystal was and how he'd say anything to remain in Venables' good books.

From that moment on, I decided this arrangement with Venables was not going to work. It seemed the man loved to have an enemy. In the past, Venables had constantly harped on to me about how bad Irving Scholar was, how he'd messed up this and ruined that. It seemed that Venables was not happy unless he had a fight of some kind on his hands – a 'them and us' situation. His allies were people like Crystal, Hall and Brian Fugler, all boosting his ego, and it seemed, now that Scholar had gone, that *I* was the enemy he had to fend off.

To be fair to Ashby, he was always silent when these altercations were playing out. In hindsight, I believe that his silence was because he could see I was right, but as Venables' right-hand man, he obviously found it embarrassing to contradict him. From time to time, Ashby would tell me, 'Just ignore Crystal – he's an idiot.'

I wasn't prepared to take any more of this nonsense. I'd previously spoken to Margaret Mountford at Herbert Smith about the goings-on at the club and the things I wasn't happy with and now I decided to call her and ask her to explain exactly what the legal position was if I wanted to dismiss Venables as chief executive.

At the time, I held 44 per cent of the shares in the club while Venables held about 27 per cent. The rest were held by people like Berry (who had about 8 per cent) and the fan base. There were hardly any institutional investors, as they had no interest whatsoever in football clubs at the time.

I explained to Margaret that I wanted to try to be fair and give Venables a clean way out of the situation – I'd offer to give him his £3m back and pay off the remainder of his outstanding contract.

Together, we drafted a letter to Venables spelling out my reasons for asking him to resign and outlining my offer to pay him back all his money. There was a board meeting coming up in a few days and I was planning to give it to Venables after the meeting. But during the meeting, Crystal started to wind me up over some issue where, once again, he didn't know what he was talking about. I ended up losing my temper with Crystal, almost to the stage of actually getting up and whacking him! He was such an annoying fart. Venables was smirking at my ranting and, I guess, was quite enjoying seeing Crystal wind me up. I was so fired up, I knew I had to get out, otherwise I would have definitely hit Crystal and maybe put him in hospital. So I stood up, opened my briefcase, drew out the letter and threw it at Venables, telling him he'd better read it and call me back later that day.

The letter obviously came as a shock to everybody. I'd been told by Margaret that technically the board of directors was capable of firing Venables and that if certain members of the board voted for it, it would be a straightforward transaction. During the course of the next week, many phone calls were made to try to resolve the situation. Venables knew I was serious, but arrogantly believed he would be able to outride this challenge of mine.

Sometimes I used Venables' office at the club to discuss commercial or legal matters with visitors. On more than one occasion, he asked his secretary what I was doing in his office. He would then hide behind her as she popped in to say that Terry needed his office back for some important matters he had to deal with and would I please relocate my meeting somewhere else. There *was* nowhere else at the time – there weren't any other offices, as everything was open plan. I recall once having to stand in the hospitality room with a senior barrister to finish a meeting. This was Terry's pathetic attempt to exert his seniority.

I was told by Herbert Smith to call a board meeting where the item on the agenda would be the removal of Terry Venables as chief executive of the company. The date was set for Friday 14 May 1993. On the evening before, an event was taking place at one of the big hotels in London – the annual Football Writers' Dinner. Venables and his associates leaked his imminent dismissal at the dinner and the next day the newspapers were full of 'Venables about to be sacked' stories.

As we arrived for the board meeting, the forecourt of the club was packed with press, cameramen and fans, all screaming for my head. I was forewarned about this by Peter Barnes, the club secretary, who told me to get my driver to drop me at the back entrance of the stadium in the East Stand rather than attempt to come in by the main entrance.

In the week leading up to the meeting, Berry had made it plain to me that his vote would be in my favour. With Colin Sandy and Berry voting with me (and Venables having to abstain), I believed the result would be a formality. To my surprise, Berry turned up at the meeting with Peter Leaver, a senior barrister, one-time club director and mad Tottenham fan. Berry told me Leaver was there as his legal adviser.

When the agenda to remove Venables from the company was read out, the board was asked to vote. Crystal and Igal Yawetz voted *against* removing Venables, while Colin Sandy and I voted *for*. Berry abstained. He said I didn't need his vote, that in my capacity as chairman, I would have the casting vote, which was correct. But it showed me for the first time a new side of Berry. It seemed to me that, not knowing how this would pan out, he simply sat on the fence in order to keep his options open. Venables was officially fired there and then, but still maintained his director status. As soon as the decision was made, Venables got up and walked out.

After the meeting, Nick Hewer drove out through the baying mob at the main entrance relatively easily (as no one recognised him) and came round to the East Stand to pick me up and take me home. To the disappointment of the fans and thugs at the main gate, my driver, who had positioned my car inside the ground, drove out of the main gate alone – the mob could see there was no one in the car other than him, so he escaped relatively unscathed.

At 5 p.m. that Friday, I received a call on my mobile phone from David Gold, chief of Herbert Smith's litigation department. Gold told me that Venables had gone to his lawyers and they had served an *ex parte* application to the court to have the decision overturned. This came as a big shock to Herbert Smith, and particularly Margaret Mountford, not to mention myself. A hearing was called for around 6 p.m. that night, giving us hardly any time to prepare our counter-arguments and engage a barrister.

The hearing took place in front of a judge who was completely out of her depth with regard to football matters. Venables' lawyers put forward the argument that the club would be badly disadvantaged, that players would leave the club on the announcement of Venables' dismissal. On top of that, they claimed there was a tournament the club had agreed to play in South Africa where Venables' presence was a contractual requirement. All of this was a pack of lies. What made it worse was that these lies had been given credibility by being included in a statement by Brian Fugler, a solicitor, who had presumably sworn this on the basis of what he had been told. Venables employed the lawyers Kanter Jules, a small firm known to be difficult. Bombarded with all this nonsense, the judge reinstated Venables!

As we had a disaster on our hands, David Gold agreed that he and another litigator would come and visit me at my home on Sunday to start compiling evidence to put forward to appeal and overturn this judge's decision. Meanwhile, Eric Hall got together a bunch of people, including a load of thugs and some players' wives, to form a protest group outside my house. My driver slowly edged the car past them. I told him to just drive – they would get out of the way. When I got in that Friday night, Daniel told me that this time I really *had* caused World War Three. Never mind Bambi's mum – I was the man who'd shot Bambi! The Adonis of football, God's gift to the game, the chirpy chappy Venables was culled by the money-man Sugar.

Daniel told me, 'Give it all up, Dad. Let Venables give you your money back and get out.' Apart from the fact that Venables had no way of paying the £8m I'd injected into the club so far, I was adamant I was not going to be pushed out of this situation and was determined to fight the matter.

That Sunday, David Gold introduced me to Alan Watts, one of the younger litigators in the firm. Gold had chosen him as his credentials in this matter, apart from being a good litigator, were that he liked football and was a Liverpool supporter! At least it wasn't Arsenal.

I explained to Gold and Watts that the judge had been lied to. It was obvious that players *wouldn't* leave the club, as they were contracted to us – they couldn't simply walk out. Anyone who knew anything about football would have known this.

Gold agreed that the judge didn't understand this point and most probably thought the players were like any other group of workers, who could simply leave. Of course, if players *did* decide to walk out, they wouldn't be able to play for another club unless they had Tottenham's permission.

I also told Gold and Watts that this so-called South African tournament had been cancelled over a week earlier. I even showed them a memo from Peter Barnes to that effect, *proving* they'd lied to the court. And not only had they lied, but Fugler's statement had misled the court.

Gold asked me if I knew how to contact Fugler. I found his phone number, called him and asked why he had done such an outrageous thing. Fugler started to waffle about how he'd been assured that Spurs *were* going to South Africa. The following Monday, Fugler sent a notification to the court to cover his arse, excusing himself and saying he'd made a mistake. Gold had coached me to tell Fugler a few home truths on how he was compromising his position as a lawyer and how I could report him to the Law Society. However, despite Fugler's letter to the judge, the judgment was cast in concrete.

It took two weeks to get a new hearing in front of another judge. Throughout the course of that fortnight, I put together a witness statement, as did Colin Sandy. Included in this witness statement was every single thing that had happened to date concerning my involvement with Tottenham. I also disclosed to Herbert Smith the 'Cloughie wants a bung' incident and the McLintock arrangement. Herbert Smith wanted a copy of the McLintock invoice to add to the witness statement, but when Colin asked Tottenham's accounts department for a copy of it, they said they had lost it. We kicked up merry hell until someone, who must have had a conscience, anonymously dropped it into Colin's in-tray a day later.

Herbert Smith had employed the services of a brilliant barrister by the name of Philip Hislop. We met with him prior to the hearing and he told me that while I'd gone into great detail in my witness statement, most of it was irrelevant, as he would be arguing this matter purely on company law. All the issues about bungs and Venables' other wrongdoings were actually a sideshow and he had no intention of presenting these to the judge. He was going to stick to the letter of the law as far as the Companies Act was concerned and he told me we had a 99 per cent chance of winning. As for the judge who had been hijacked a few Fridays ago, she was totally and absolutely wrong.

On arrival at the High Court in the Strand for the first day of the hearing, there were huge crowds standing outside, screaming my name, snarling abuse at me and calling me 'Judas'. As we walked up the staircase inside the court building, crowds of fans were standing above, spitting on me and Ann, who'd decided to be there to support me, as the whole world had ganged up on me. As we entered the courtroom, we needed security to clear a pathway, as the fans' abuse was increasing.

As soon as proceedings started, Venables' lawyers, Kanter Jules, a firm made up of Jewish partners, stood up and declared they hadn't had enough time to prepare for the case due to the Jewish holiday of Rosh Hashanah. They requested more time and, frustratingly, the judge granted it to them. Unbelievable! If they were so observant of Jewish law, they wouldn't have been in court on Friday night two weeks earlier.

It would take another three weeks to get a hearing. Kanter Jules's people were constantly making excuses and delaying matters, saying it wasn't convenient for one particular partner or another. Eventually, however, we pinned them down and got to court. Once again, the street outside was packed with fans. Venables had employed a public relations company, who had probably printed the banners saying, 'SUGAR OUT!' that appeared everywhere.

Crystal had delayed putting his witness statement in and, one day at White Hart Lane, I bumped into him and suggested that he was purposely holding up the court hearing. I also reminded him, half-jokingly, to make sure he didn't put a pack of lies in the statement, bearing in mind he was a barrister. I mentioned this to David Gold in a casual conversation, at which point Gold explained to me that what I had done was tantamount to tampering with a witness. I couldn't understand what he was talking about. He said that I wasn't allowed to intimidate or interfere with witnesses and now he felt that he needed to write to Crystal and tell him that his client, namely me, had meant no wrong.

I protested to Gold that this was nonsense – such a letter would pour more oil on the fire. I told him it was just a throwaway remark on the stairs at Tottenham, but he insisted on writing this letter. As I expected, this opened up a whole new can of worms. It was manna from heaven for Crystal. He knew I'd meant nothing by what I'd said, but because Herbert Smith had gone to the trouble of writing to him, he sensed they were worried. Lawyers have no bloody common sense sometimes – they can't see their actions will *cause* trouble, they can't adapt and use a bit of shrewdness. They are trained robots who do things according to procedure! In hindsight, I was lucky I hadn't whacked Crystal in the boardroom a few weeks earlier, as he'd have done me for GBH.

Crystal employed the services of a solicitor in Manchester to issue contempt of court proceedings against me on the basis of my trying to intimidate and tamper with a witness, namely him. Margaret told me that this was a very serious matter which, if proven true, could mean imprisonment. She said I would need to be represented by a separate set of barristers at this contempt of court hearing, which would have to take place before the main case could continue. This was the first time Margaret really worked with Nick Hewer and she told me, in a way only Margaret could, 'Now look here, Alan, you keep that Nick fellow right out of this; he's done nothing but cause you trouble, what with the privatisation media circus, and now he could land you right in it.' Funny how things work out – they are the best of pals now.

All this aggravation was caused by Gold, who could not see further than his law books. I'd warned him that Crystal was slippery. We employed the services of a very senior barrister, Derry Irvine (who later became Lord Chancellor). He sent his junior counsel to Herbert Smith to draft a witness statement for me in defence of this contempt of court allegation. One of the things I needed to show the court was what a twisting liar Jonathan Crystal was. Nick Hewer told me about an occasion when, by pure accident, he had seen Crystal's antics in court. He and Margaret Mountford were attending a hearing, when proceedings were interrupted by Jonathan Crystal, who walked into court and asked the judge for a couple of minutes' recess. Crystal requested that the judge postpone a hearing that was to take place later in the day because he wouldn't be available to represent his client. He said that he had an *emergency* hearing in another court scheduled at the same time. The judge granted Crystal his wish.

The plot thickened when Nick met me that afternoon for a meeting at Tottenham. When the meeting started, he saw that Crystal was also there. Nick thought this was strange, as he'd seen Crystal that very morning in court and heard him tell the judge that he couldn't attend a scheduled hearing this afternoon because of some other emergency hearing – yet here he was at Tottenham for a board meeting!

I included this incident in my witness statement in my defence of the contempt of court matter. Alan Watts obtained the transcript of that day's court proceedings, which showed that Crystal had lied to the judge. Armed with this information and copies of the minutes of that day's Tottenham board meeting, we had conclusive proof that Crystal had lied to the judge and wasn't to be trusted. We worked through the night preparing this witness statement, as the court hearing was the next day.

Crystal and Venables were standing outside the courtroom smirking, thinking I was in deep trouble on this contempt of court issue. Their barristers insisted it should be the first thing to be heard. The smile was wiped off their faces within fifteen minutes, when Herbert Smith handed them copies of the witness statements and the brief being put forward by Derry Irvine.

Crystal went white. There was a lot of shuffling around with his lawyers and then they asked the judge, Vice-Chancellor Sir Donald Nicholls (the most senior judge in the Chancery Division), to delay the contempt of court hearing. The judge had also been served a copy of my witness statement – he knew very well what all the fuss and delay was about, and he kind of smiled knowingly.

Philip Hislop, acting for me, stood up immediately and stated that this case had been delayed several times already and that the contempt of court issue was a sideshow, created to cause further delay. The judge accepted this and the contempt of court issue was put to one side, clearing us to continue with the main case. Alan Watts turned to me, smiled and said, 'One–nil to you.'

I never forgave Crystal for the aggravation he caused me. He was a wicked man. I had the bit between my teeth and I was going to teach him that messing with me was the wrong thing to do. I instructed Herbert Smith to draft a complaint about Crystal to the Bar Council – I wanted him reported as the cheating liar he was. The process took about a year, after which the Bar Council suspended him for a month.

When we resumed with the main case, Philip Hislop stuck to his guns and ran the case on technical Companies Act matters, steering clear of all the other issues. Unfortunately, Philip had a speech impediment and that repulsive animal Eric Hall, who was in the public gallery, kept taking the mickey out of him by mimicking his stutter, to try to upset his flow of words. There were lots of fans in the gallery shouting throughout the hearing and every so often, the judge warned them they'd be thrown out if they didn't keep quiet. Eric Hall continued his heckling of Philip Hislop, who nevertheless put his case clearly.

Then a rather stupid and unprecedented thing occurred. Venables' barrister stood up and, for reasons best known to himself, started to read out the section of my witness statement about Cloughie taking a bung, along with other issues I'd raised about Gary Lineker's transfer to the Japanese club Grampus Eight.

Alan Watts and I were shocked – we had resigned ourselves to the fact that all this stuff wouldn't be disclosed. However, in their wisdom, Venables and his advisers decided to get in first, as it were, rather than allow my barrister to read out all this damning stuff. Little did they know that my barrister had no intention of doing this as he considered it irrelevant to the case.

This revelation must have affected the rainforests – there'd be barely enough trees to make the paper for the newspaper industry over the coming days. The media went bananas. In the national newspapers the next day, there were front-page headlines, back-page headlines and double-page spreads – all about the Clough bung allegations. Venables had shot himself in the foot trying to be clever and getting the information out first.

The case went on for two days. At one point, Edward Walker-Arnott, the senior partner of Herbert Smith, turned up to show his face. I wondered what he was doing there, but Alan told me it was a psychological tactic Edward employed sometimes. He was very well known and respected in court circles and his presence was a way of showing the judge that his client, namely me, must really have a serious case.

The judge called a halt to proceedings halfway through the second day and said he would be reading out his judgement in the next half-hour. This looked positive for us. Alan Watts explained, 'Normally, judges can take a couple of *weeks* to formulate a judgement. This must mean he's made up his mind.'

Shortly after the court adjourned, Alan received a message from the judge telling me that immediately after the reading of the judgement, I should exit the courtroom through his chambers and out the back entrance. He advised me to have my vehicle standing by. Meanwhile, there were hundreds and hundreds of raging fans outside the front of the courts.

When the court reconvened, the judge read out his decision and upheld the firing of Venables, overturning the renegade judgement on that fateful Friday night. He also ruled that, technically, there may have been a contempt of court; however, taking into consideration all the pressure I was under and the threats from the fans, he decided to waive the issue and call an end to all the proceedings.

Looking back on this incident, you can see that the judge had made his mind up before calling a halt to proceedings, but allowed the half-hour gap so I could make preparations for my escape. My brother Derek and Ann were also in court and we all scurried through the judge's chambers and were guided to the back entrance, where Nick had arranged a taxi to stand by. We jumped straight in and the cabbie, as instructed by Nick, whisked us away quickly to a nearby square, where my driver was waiting in my Range Rover. We switched vehicles and shot off. When we turned on the car radio, it was already on the news that Venables had lost the case and had finally been sacked.

The newspapers were driving Nick mad to get interviews from me. They wanted more detail on the Clough bung situation. This time, I took Margaret's advice and completely clammed up. I hoped that if I didn't wind him up in the press, Venables would now do the sensible thing, accept my offer and graciously move away from the situation.

Unfortunately, this was not to be the case. Egged on by Crystal and

Eric Hall, Venables started to give interviews to newspapers giving *his* side of the story, making me look like a monster. A few days later, Venables called a press conference at his club, Scribes West, where he told the media he was going to continue his fight against me.

Throughout the course of preparing the defence for these court actions, Colin Sandy, using the services of Deloitte, had done a lot of background work on Venables and Ashby. It appeared that Ashby had been involved in no fewer than forty-three bankrupt companies! It also transpired that Venables had borrowed a large proportion of his £3m to buy Spurs from a company called Landhurst Leasing in exchange for leases they had granted him on pubs that turned out not to be under Venables' ownership!

Deeper investigation revealed that Landhurst Leasing was given a free executive box and free tickets at Spurs. We also uncovered loads of invoices which the club had paid to Scribes West for so-called 'entertainment'. Even club property, such as Tottenham's dance floor, had been taken up and put into Scribes West! Venables had been on trips to New York and had used the club's credit card to pay for things like carpets and other gifts for himself. There were loads of bills from Eric Hall for services rendered on transfers and the negotiation of players' contracts and outrageously large bills from Fugler – far in excess of what a large firm like Herbert Smith would charge. It was a total financial mess.

Eric Hall decided to take legal action against Tottenham after our refusal to pay some of his monstrously inflated bills. Alan Watts pointed out that Hall had acted illegally in the case of representing the player Justin Edinburgh. Not only had Hall charged Spurs for negotiating the player's contract, he'd also charged Edinburgh himself. This, I was informed by Alan, was a breach of the Prevention of Corruption Act, whereby an agent may not take fees from both sides. Nevertheless, Hall pursued the case until, on the steps of the courtroom, he backed down when his own lawyer warned him that he'd be walking into a hornets' nest. I instructed Alan to go after Hall to recover our costs, which he did.

The case brought against Tottenham by Venables' company Edennote went on for about a year. Rumour had it that the company had no money and he was not paying many of his suppliers or advisers.

David Gold suggested we applied to the court for security of costs, which meant Venables would have to prove to the court that should he lose the case he was bringing against us, he would be able to pay our legal fees. After a lot of twists and turns, Venables finally threw in the towel. He was unable to prove to the court that his company had any money.

While I was fighting this case, Gulu Lalvani thought it would be a good idea to employ the services of a PR consultant. He chose Nick Hewer! Shortly afterwards, Nick called me and told me that Gulu was banged up in a suite at the Dorchester Hotel – with Venables! He even gave me the room number, but told me not to let Gulu know he'd told me.

I decided to surprise Gulu by phoning him. 'Hello, Gulu, it's Alan Sugar here. How are you?'

It's a shame videophones weren't available in those days. All I got was a stunned silence. Eventually, he said, 'Oh, hello, Alan, how are you? What can I do for you?'

'It's not what you can do for me – it's what I can do for you, my friend. It seems you're getting busy poking your nose into my business.'

'No, no, not all, Alan. I am just having a business meeting here.'

'I know who you're meeting with and my suggestion is that you chuck him out.' I slammed the phone down.

An hour or so later, Gulu called me to say he had met with Venables at Venables' own request. I told Gulu that he was a bloody busybody who always got involved in things that didn't concern him.

He denied it, saying he was trying to *help* me by finding out what Venables wanted. He told me that Venables had his back to the wall and needed someone to finance his court case against me. Venables was offering Gulu a chance to get a share of Tottenham Hotspur if he would stump up the money for security of costs.

'Alan, you are my friend. I would never go against you, you know that. I was trying to help. I was going to call you to let you know what had happened. By the way, who told you I was in a meeting? How did you know?' What a load of bullshit. Gulu had this pathological obsession with me and wanted to try to scupper whatever I was involved in.

A few days later, to my shock, on the back page of the *Sun* there was a big headline and an exclusive interview with Gulu Lalvani. The headline read: 'Sugar is a ruthless, hard man.' It was a terrible story – all lies, of course. Maybe they twisted Gulu's words, but I was gutted. How could someone whom I'd socialised with and considered a friend – albeit a bit of a rogue – do such a low thing? Ann was also very upset, as she too had spent a lot of time socialising with Gulu and his wife.

He tried to call me the next day, but I refused his calls. In desperation, he eventually got me on my mobile and started to blurt out that they had twisted his words and he'd never said this and he'd never said that – all that bullshit. I said I didn't want to hear his excuses – he should never have spoken to them at all – and I told him that he and I were finished. I never wanted to speak to him or see him again.

From that day on, I never had anything more to do with Gulu.

*

Long after the initial court case, around the time Venables finally threw in the towel, businessman Philip Green called me to let me know that Venables was prepared to sell his shares to me for £3m – what he'd paid for them. I was a bit surprised to receive the call, as I didn't really know Philip Green, other than having seen him in the boardroom at Tottenham a couple of times as a guest of Venables.

I told Philip I wasn't interested in dealing with Venables at all. After all the aggravation he had caused me, he could stick his shares where the sun doesn't shine. I reminded Philip that Tottenham was a public company and that Venables could sell his shares in the market-place – *I* certainly wouldn't be buying them from him.

It appears that Philip Green and Tony Berry knew each other and, allegedly, had both used the services of Landhurst Leasing on occasions. Maybe it was Philip or Tony who had put Venables in touch with Landhurst and Philip was now trying to broker a deal to get me to buy Venables' shares (I've since learned that Philip likes to broker deals).

One of life's lessons is never to form an opinion of a person based on information given to you by others. I have to confess at this stage that I was rather short with Philip Green on the phone. A couple of people whose names I won't mention had warned me to steer clear of him. They never gave me any specific reason *why* – they just tipped me the wink as if to say, 'You don't want to get involved with that bloke.' I guess this was in the back of my mind at the time and it made me a little dismissive.

The reason I mention this is because Philip Green is now known as one of Britain's most successful entrepreneurs and wealthiest businessmen. And while we do speak to each other occasionally these days, I can detect an air of coolness from his side, probably because he remembers the time I was offish with him. Now that he is who he is, it must look suspicious that I'm suddenly prepared to talk to him. To be fair, I know exactly how he feels and if the boot were on the other foot, I wouldn't have anything to do with me either! So, to his credit, the relatively polite relationship that exists between us now is perhaps more than I deserve.

In truth, I should have learned this lesson a long time earlier. How many times in the old Amstrad days would Stan Randall mouth off about someone, resulting in me disliking that person without even meeting them! Look at Venables and his opinion of Scholar. When I finally met Irving Scholar, he seemed an ordinary, honest type of guy. I fell for this so many times. Nowadays, I've adopted a policy of not forming an opinion on someone until I've experienced them first hand.

Venables went on to publish an autobiography in which he told a pack of lies about me, and I sued him. His publisher's insurers took the rap for his lies and paid out £100,000 to me, which I donated to Great Ormond Street Hospital. Venables would not apologise, so the best I could get was an announcement read out in open court. I arranged for a giant cheque to be printed – sarcastically from the Porky Pie Bank – made out for £100,000 and signed by Terry Venables. I had my photo taken outside the court with a Great Ormond Street nurse and gave the picture to the media – quite fun.

*

All this was very time-consuming. I'd become obsessed with it, devoting seven days a week to fighting this legal battle. I'd completely taken my eye off the ball at Amstrad. What's more, I realised things could potentially get worse, as without Venables I was faced with having to run the *whole* football club.

The players were very unhappy with the situation. Some of them had been negotiating with Venables for new contracts and were demanding an audience with me to resolve outstanding issues. I had no experience whatsoever in discussing contracts with players' agents and was about to embark on a whole new world of ducking and diving!

The most important thing to put in place was a new manager. Tony Berry, who was now onside (he *had to be* once Venables was booted out), became very friendly, offering me assistance in choosing the new man. Two names were put forward: Ossie Ardiles, who was manager at West Brom, and Glenn Hoddle, who was rumoured to be signing a contract to become manager at Chelsea.

Berry told me he knew Hoddle quite well and would discuss the issue with him. Hoddle explained that he had virtually agreed on a deal with Chelsea's Ken Bates and was ready to sign. Had he been approached a week earlier, he may have been able to take the Spurs job. He said he was very frustrated, but what came across was that he didn't want to take the job of Spurs manager only to be forced out one day by Venables.

I told Berry that this was a load of rubbish; Venables was *not* coming back, however much the newspapers insisted he'd be suing me. The papers had quoted Venables as saying that *when* he won the court case (not *if* he won) he would retake control of Spurs. Still, Hoddle felt this was a risk he didn't want to take, so he took the job at Chelsea.

We were left with Ossie. Tony Berry had made contact with him and he agreed to meet me at my house to discuss the job. Ossie was very excited. To use his words, I think he said he would crawl on his hands and knees to get the job.

Louise, Daniel and Simon happened to be round when Ossie arrived and were quite excited to meet him, as he was a Tottenham legend. Ann was there too, but she didn't really know much about football and footballers. Ann has a kind of olive complexion and on that particular day she had her hair tied back – when she did this, people often thought she looked Spanish or South American. In her normal, quiet way, she brought some drinks into the room where I was meeting with Ossie. I introduced her to him and she shyly said hello. Ossie started to speak to her in Spanish and she looked nonplussed. I asked him why he was speaking in Spanish and he told me, 'Your wife looks like a Spanish or South American lady.'

Ossie agreed to sign for the club that night and was announced as the new manager on 19 June 1993. He employed Steve Perryman, another ex-player, as his assistant and took control of the club for the start of the next season. This was a big relief to me. I had employed an ex-Tottenham hero, hoping the fans would be receptive towards him, which they indeed were. They gave him a great welcome on his first day.

However, the players were still angry at the dismissal of Venables and a lot of stuff was still going on behind the scenes. There seemed to be a clique of players that I suppose you could describe as Venables' allies and they were torn between playing for their club and supporting Venables. Some of them would visit Venables' nightclub, tittle-tattling about what was going on at Tottenham. In my opinion, that little mini-mafia gave Ossie a lot of headaches at the time. I think he found it hard to win them over, but the way you win players and fans over is to win games on the pitch. Of course, you're only ever as good as your last game.

The season started off brightly, but soon we were struck down with a few injuries, including one to our main striker, Teddy Sheringham. In the end, we struggled through the season, romancing the relegation zone. In the last week, we had two games to play – the first was at Oldham and the final game was against QPR. If we'd lost both matches, we would have been relegated.

I remember travelling up to Manchester by plane for the Oldham match. It was touch and go whether the game would be on, as it was pouring with rain and the pitch was a mud-heap. Happily for us, the game went ahead and, thanks to some great passing by Vinny Samways, we won 2–0. On the following Saturday, now safe from relegation, we lost our final game to QPR at home.

In order to sort out the mess at White Hart Lane, I decided to transfer my son Daniel from Amstrad to Tottenham to assist in the

administration and running of the club. Claude Littner was also seconded and put in place as chief executive to sort out the financial
issues. Claude's appointment turned out to be very unpopular, as he
tightened the purse-strings within the organisation, which was very
much needed. Allegations were flying around that he was cutting off
the benefits that players had enjoyed in the past. It's terrible how
snipey people can be, leaking malicious stories to newspapers. One of
the lies printed in the papers to try to make our management regime
look bad was that Claude had refused to allow Gary Mabbutt, our loyal
captain of the club and a diabetic, to have Diet Coke on the club coach.
This was absolute garbage, but the sort of below-the-belt stuff that can
turn fans against you.

Claude got rid of all the accounting people, put in place a senior
finance director – releasing Colin Sandy back to his duties at Amshold
– and took on some other management, including a new physiothera-
pist and club doctor. In addition, the merchandising department was
professionalised, with proper credit control and inventory control, as
well as new warehousing for the mail-order department.

We also had to comply with new laws applying to football
stadiums following the Taylor Report, commissioned after the
Hillsborough disaster. All Premier League stadiums now had to be
all-seater, and reconstructing the whole stadium required a tremendous amount of capital expenditure. Claude handled all these matters.

Within a year or so, we looked like a professional organisation. It's
a shame that the efficient way in which we streamlined the affairs of
the club was not reflected on the pitch. The external sniping did not let
up, as the newspapers continued to write bad stories about Tottenham
and, in particular, me.

Throughout the course of this fiasco, a couple of television channels decided to make programmes about Venables. BBC's *Panorama*
did a big exposé of his company Edennote and the fact that he'd raised
money against assets that didn't exist. It also looked into Gino Santini,
the Swiss bank account his money was paid into, and made claims he
was being pursued by the Inland Revenue for tax evasion. Channel
Four also ran a similar exposé.

Venables by now had been appointed England coach. FA chief

executive Graham Kelly was getting a bit concerned that all these revelations were making Venables' appointment look a bit ill-judged and he was desperate to protect Venables in any way to try to maintain his credibility. The Department of Trade and Industry had started an inquiry into Venables' affairs (which eventually resulted in him being banned from acting as a director of limited companies for seven years). News of the inquiry did not send out a good message to the FA either and the newspapers made a lot of play of it at the time.

At the end of the 1993–4 season, we were approached by Granada television, who told us they had been given loads of documentation to do with illegal loans Tottenham had made to its players during the previous regime under Scholar. Not wishing to get too complicated, FA rules stated that everything you paid to a player had to be expressed in the player's contract. If you incentivised a player *outside* his contract, this would be deemed a serious breach of the rules. Past examples of this had resulted in some clubs being punished by relegation.

The information leaked to Granada resulted in them making a rather stupid programme. However, what happened next was quite remarkable. An impromptu press conference was called by Graham Kelly at 5 p.m. on Friday 12 May 1994. It took place on the doorstep of the FA headquarters at Lancaster Gate.

Kelly read out to the gathered media that Tottenham Hotspur were about to be charged with illegal loans dating back over ten years, including some initiated when Terry Venables was manager under the Scholar regime. If the charges were upheld, it could mean relegation for Spurs, possibly by two divisions. After all, there was a precedent – just a few years earlier, Swindon Town had been relegated by two divisions for similar misdemeanours. It was a very serious matter.

This sudden action by Kelly made no sense. He had been advised of the loans at a meeting I'd previously held with him and Rick Parry, the Premier League CEO. As far as I was concerned, the matter had been disclosed and I was shocked that the FA was now bringing charges. Indeed, the issue of illegal loans was brought up at a board meeting back in the so-called 'friendly days' just after Venables and I took over the club. In fact, on discovering this information at the time, it was my suggestion that Venables and I go to the FA and inform them that, as the new owners, we had just uncovered this and wanted to clear the decks. This suggestion was turned down by the brain surgeon Crystal, who advised that even if we were up front with the FA, we would still get into trouble.

Instead, they consulted Peter Leaver, the ex-director and barrister, for advice. He was at a board meeting one day and gave his opinion, saying that, *technically*, these were breaches that occurred under the Football League administration and we were now in the Premier League, a completely separate entity which had no jurisdiction over past events. Moreover, he suggested that the Football Association had no jurisdiction over these events either. The only organisation which could have jurisdiction would be the Football League, which now governed the old second, third and fourth divisions. His legal advice was that we had no case to answer. Had we been relegated that season, then we *would* have been under the jurisdiction of the Football League and if we'd then been found guilty of past misdemeanours, we could have been relegated a further two divisions – to the old fourth division!

Though I had no proof, I was pretty sure Venables or his hangers-on had had something to do with this and were rattling Kelly's chain. I guess Kelly's idea was cooked up in the midst of the poor season we were having. However, he had overlooked the fact that as we didn't get relegated, any action would be limited to a Premier League inquiry rather than a Football League inquiry.

Once again, our contribution to global warming kicked in. The newspapers were full of this story, which seemed like a deliberate attempt by Kelly to pay me back for giving him so much aggravation over his England coach.

At the meeting held with Kelly and Parry, apart from discussing the loans, we also talked about the Clough affair. This resulted in a separate FA inquiry being called to look into the Clough bung situation. Rick Parry also recalled this meeting in which I showed them all the documentation and invited them to take it away as part of their inquiry. Included in it was our disclosure to them of the illegal loans we had uncovered, as well as board minutes documenting the discussion. Despite seeing all this, Kelly called upon the Premier League to disclose to the FA *just* the findings relating to the illegal loans, *not* the Clough bung allegations. And on the basis of that report, Kelly called his kangaroo court press conference that Friday night.

Rick Parry was furious with Kelly – he could see straight through this whole charade. Rick saw that this was a *political* matter and was totally on our side. He knew these illegal loans had been openly disclosed to both of them – there were no secrets – and he was fuming that Kelly had pulled this stroke.

A hearing about the illegal loans was set for two weeks later. It was held at a conference suite at Wembley, allowing the press to have their fun with comments like, 'This is the only way Spurs will ever get to Wembley.' The FA assembled their panel of so-called experts to adjudicate on this issue. We employed the services of Tony Grabiner (now Lord Grabiner), another Tottenham fan and leading QC, to put forward our case in front of the tribunal.

Just to show what a sham this was, Alan Watts, who was there representing Herbert Smith, was taken aside by someone from the FA who suggested that if we were to plead guilty, the matter would be over quickly. We struggled with this offer, as we had no indication from them what sort of punishment they had in mind. We spent an hour discussing this amongst ourselves and concluded that we couldn't risk it, as they might be thinking of relegating us.

The hearing went ahead and the result was that we were going to be deducted twelve points next season, banned from the FA Cup and fined £600,000.

Starting the season twelve points down was tantamount to relegation, but we were told afterwards that we should be thankful! In fact, one person, a director from Southampton FC, who sat on the tribunal, had argued that we be deducted twenty-four points.

I immediately lodged an appeal against the FA, which was heard two weeks later. Having experienced this kangaroo court, I refused any form of legal help and ran the appeal myself. I was warned that failing at the appeal tribunal could mean not only the punishment being upheld, but there was a risk it could be increased. I decided I'd take my chances.

The appeal was heard by the chairman of the Football Association,

Bert Millichip, along with a couple of other old hacks from the football industry. I pleaded that this was a most ridiculous and punitive decision made against us. I told them that all this stuff had been openly disclosed to Kelly and Parry ages ago and I also alluded to the vendetta against me by Graham Kelly.

My protestations seemed to succeed in part. The twelve points' deduction was lowered to six, but the fine was increased to £1.5m. And we were still banned from the FA Cup.

15

The Prune Juice Effect

And Carlos Kickaball, Tottenham

1993–5

It's hard to describe the gut-wrenching anguish you feel when, day after day, you read twisted lies about yourself in the press. Worse still was to observe the effect on those close to me – my family, friends and people like Nick Hewer and Margaret Mountford, who kind of shared the suffering. They were all very supportive as my involvement in football found me engulfed in a battle being played out in the media.

What I *hadn't* realised before I sacked Venables was that he was the Messiah of football. He had managed, through his PR machine and support from his mates in the media, to portray himself as some sort of genius, as though his life in football was touched by the gods. It was brilliant marketing when you think about it. Compared to people like Sir Alex Ferguson and Arsène Wenger, Venables had achieved virtually nothing of significance.

The words of Edward Walker-Arnott warning me to be wary of football people rang in my ears, as did those of my son Daniel, who early on had told me to walk away, wipe my face and let Venables have it all. Some could argue that this aggravation was self-inflicted, as I had walked into a hornets' nest after being warned off. And just to inflame matters, I was still ignoring Margaret's advice to keep schtum.

Via a friendly journalist, Harry Harris at the *Daily Mirror*, I was giving the snipers back as much as they were giving me. So much so, Piers Morgan, when he was editor, joked that *I* was running the back pages of the *Mirror*! I gave Harry some great stories, which he followed up in style, winning Sports Journalist of the Year in 1994.

Almost as bad as the press were the two-faced people who feigned support – those who enjoyed the privileges of boardroom hospitality and the associated match-day tickets. On match days, they would grovel around me and say things like, 'Oh, it's terrible, Alan, what they're saying about you – it really angers me.' Then, on occasions when Venables visited Tottenham in his capacity as England manager (to check on the form of Spurs' England players), I'd see the same people hovering around Venables like bees round a jam pot.

*

One thing keeping me sane during this period of my life was my family. One of the memorable milestones in Ann's and my life was Simon's marriage in 1992, which took place at Bramstons. In fact, our wonderful house has hosted many parties over the years, including Daniel's Bar Mitzvah in 1984 and Simon's engagement party in 1991.

For Simon's wedding, a very grand marquee was built on the field adjacent to the house, decked out with wonderful chandeliers. On the morning of the wedding there were some high winds and the chandeliers were swinging wildly as the roof was blown from side to side. Luckily, the wind died down and the wedding ceremony went off exceptionally well, as did the party afterwards.

Then, in August 1993, our first grandchild, Nathan, was born. He was named after my father. It felt a bit strange for us to be grandparents, as we considered ourselves quite young – I was forty-six and Ann was forty-five. Needless to say, little Nathan was spoilt terribly by the whole family, being the first arrival.

The marriage of my son and the birth of my first grandchild are all part and parcel of life. But these events *do* tend to have an impact on your way of thinking as you get older. I found myself thinking more about my childhood and my parents. I remember them as very quiet and undemanding. My mum would never poke her nose into the affairs of my married life, nor would she tittle-tattle to me about the affairs of Daphne, Derek or Shirley. That said, I think she did confide in Daphne a little more than anyone else.

My mum did make me laugh sometimes when she tried to digest

my rise in fortune. She often told me that she'd read something about me in the paper.

'Alan, I see you're going to make car phones now!'

'No, Mum, that's rubbish. It's not true.'

'It *is* true – it says it in the papers.'

'Mum, I'm your son and I'm telling you it's *not* true. Don't believe what you read in the papers.'

She would turn and waddle off, mumbling, 'Well, it's in the papers . . .'

One of the things I used to like doing with my mum was getting out all the old photos and going through them with her, listening to her stories about this person and that person. One day, when I visited her and asked her to get the photos out, she told me she'd thrown them all away! She said they were old and there was no point holding on to them any more and thinking about the past. I couldn't believe what she was saying, but in hindsight I think this act was the result of one of the fits of depression she was prone to at the time. This was such a shame, as we now have very few family photos to look back on – indeed, in this book, there's a lack of photos of me as a young lad for that very reason.

As Mum was becoming less able to look after herself, I spoke with Daphne about placing her in some kind of warden-assisted home. Daphne found her a place in Ilford, where she had a small room, a bathroom and the use of a communal lounge. On reflection, it was a horrible place. Mum was not very happy about it, though she never came out and said so. I have struggled with my conscience about this ever since. I suppose there's no other way to put this: I was being very selfish. Although I provided all the finance and ensured that she got the best treatment, what she probably craved most was my personal attention. Despite visiting her every week and bringing her home on Sundays for lunch, I still feel there was a hell of a lot more I could have done.

I discussed this with Ann on numerous occasions. She would tell me not to look for consolation from *her* to try to allay my guilt: 'If you feel that bad about it, then *do* something. Spend more time with your mum. Let's have her round here for longer.' To be brutally honest, I was too involved in football and business and I never gave her the time she must have craved.

Then Daphne told me that Mum had gone into a strange sort of mental state after meeting someone at the home whom she'd known many years earlier. Apparently, this woman had driven Mum mad by reminiscing about the old days. As Daphne put it, 'It's done Mum's head in.' Regrettably, that unprofessional diagnosis was wrong. Mum had suffered a stroke. Through my family doctor, I arranged for her to have the top people look at her, but sadly there was nothing they could do. She was in such a bad state that the people at the warden-assisted home were no longer able to look after her.

I had previously made a donation to Jewish Care which enabled them to build an intensive-care home for elderly people incapable of looking after themselves. I contacted them now and said I needed them to take my mother in. The people at this home were excellent, but it was a depressing place to visit because the condition of most of the residents was dire. I recall visiting Mum, who was completely out of it, and seeing her being spoon-fed by one of the attendants – it was an awful sight. Daphne told me that many a time she'd gone there only to find the food the attendant had fed my mum was still in her mouth, undigested – she wasn't even capable of chewing.

The last occasion I saw my mum, she was lying in the bed at the care home, very depressed and silent. 'Mum, it's Alan, I'm here,' I said, trying to get through to her. 'Do you know who I am? Mum, can you hear me? Do you know who I am? It's Alan, I'm here.'

There was silence and I repeated this about four or five times, 'Mum, it's Alan. Do you know who I am?'

Finally, she blurted out, 'Of course I know who you are! Who do you think you are – Lord Beaverbrook?'

I was taken aback. She always did have a sarcastic sense of humour, but I suspect this comment contained some anger too. It may have been her way of telling me I'd not given her enough attention. Maybe it was a final swipe, in her depressed state, and she was expressing how poorly she felt she'd been looked after by her own children. She *knew* I was there, she just couldn't be bothered to talk to me. She was preparing herself to leave this world.

As one can imagine, this last visit panged my conscience. I had left it too late to try to make the tail end of her life a happy period. On 4 June 1994 she passed away peacefully at the age of eighty-seven.

It was a terribly sad occasion for the family and once again the shiva was held at my home and was attended by hundreds of people. My mum was buried beside my dad at the burial grounds in Cheshunt, run by the Jewish Burial Society. My parents had joined the society back in 1920 and had continued to pay the burial service fees over many years. Knowing my dad, I imagine he'd finally be thankful he got value for money.

Watching my own children growing up now, I kind of wonder what will happen to Ann and me when *we* get older, whether their own lives will be so busy that we might be treated the same way. I somehow know that that won't be the case. I think about how caring and considerate they were towards Ann's father, constantly visiting him and keeping him in the loop as far as their own children (his great-grandchildren) were concerned, so I don't think we have any concerns there.

But it does make me wonder whether my coldness as an individual has something to do with my upbringing. I never experienced any warm feelings of closeness and caring from my parents – a complete contrast to my own family now. I don't know whether it stems back to how my mother and father were treated by *their* parents. Certainly, some of my mother's ways have rubbed off on me. Ann and I are not at all intrusive when it comes to our own children and the way they run their lives – we tend to keep our mouths shut and not interfere. Neither are we the kind of parents who bowl up at their kids' homes expecting an immediate audience – not that we wouldn't be welcome. Of course, this may be interpreted by my children as a lack of interest on my behalf, which it is not.

My mother was much cleverer than people thought. She bottled a lot of stuff up inside and never expressed an opinion, but she knew everything that was going on in the family. I have to say that in that respect, I'm the same. And because Ann has lived with me for so many years now (she was sixteen when we met) perhaps my ways have rubbed off on her too. She also seems to bottle up her true feelings about things – although, as two great minds think alike, we *do* share our inner thoughts from time to time.

I don't know whether it was my tough upbringing in the business world, but I find it very difficult to express emotion when people do things that are hurtful to me. Not wishing to show that I am angry or upset about something, I remain silent. I'm not sure this is a good trait – perhaps I *ought* to express myself and tell the offending party I'm not happy. I'm not confining this to just my family life, but also to business, when colleagues let me down or do things which are hurtful or disrespectful.

Fortunately, this is not a problem between Ann and me. As I often tell people, while Ann may come across as a very quiet, prim and proper lady who never seems to open her mouth about anything, she's never silent when it comes to letting me know when I've done something wrong and there have been many occasions when she's put me back in line and pointed out the error of my ways. Ann's input has often served as a great wake-up call. Having said that, I can't think of many occasions when I've had to reciprocate and tell her that *she's* done something wrong. In fact, I don't know anyone who has a bad word to say about Ann, nor indeed anybody who'd have the *right* to say a bad word about her.

*

It was July 1994 and we were about to start a new season. How would we be able to attract new players when the club was already down six points and out of the FA Cup? All credit to Ossie, he was optimistic. He told me that I'd done a good job in reducing the twelve points to six and said I should just look at it as losing two games over the season.

I was still furious with Kelly and decided I was going to take on the FA again. At the press conference after the appeal hearing, I told the journalists I wasn't going to leave it there. I spelled it out very clearly – Mr Kelly had overstepped the mark in protecting God's gift to football, his England coach, and this was clearly a vendetta against me for the aggravation I'd caused by embarrassing the FA over Venables' financial affairs.

I was determined to kick Kelly's arse and asked Alan Watts at Herbert Smith what options were open to me. He told me it would be hard, if not impossible, to challenge the FA's decision in the courts. Normally, you could challenge such a decision by way of judicial review, but since the FA wasn't a governmental or quasi-governmental authority, this wasn't possible.

There was, however, another path. I could threaten to take them to court on a breach of contract claim. FIFA, world football's governing body, had strict rules stating that no football association from any nation must engage or allow one of its members to engage in legal action. This FIFA directive meant that all national football associations had to make sure any disputes were settled out of court. If Tottenham were to take the FA to court, there was a chance the English FA could be punished by FIFA, even to the extent of banning England from a future World Cup! One country had recently been banned from all FIFA events because it had allowed such a dispute go to court.

So we came up with what I suppose could be deemed a risky and divisive plot – directly attacking Kelly and threatening to take the FA to court. Since Herbert Smith would never threaten legal action if there was no real intention of carrying it out, we agreed that all communication on this matter would be written by me personally, on Tottenham letter heading.

Before moving on to this story, I'd like to tell you about a little present I bought myself to cheer me up during the Venables litigation nightmare. Ann and I had got into the habit of chartering a boat for our summer holidays. On a visit to the South of France around June time – shortly after winning the Venables court case – the broker we'd previously chartered boats from, Nick Edmiston, took us to pick one for that year's holiday. Only one was any good – *The Margo Rose*. He explained that it was actually locked up by a bank, who had repossessed it from its previous extravagant owner, a Swedish millionaire.

Nick suggested I ask the bank whether they'd be prepared to let me charter the boat for a couple of weeks. The bank, being a bank, rejected the proposition, but they *did* say they'd be ready to take a write-down on this asset and flog it to me for $7m.

In the same way that Ann had poked me in the back when we first set eyes on Bramstons, she was doing it again as we were walking around this luxury boat. It was much better than the one we'd previously chartered. I told her she was nuts. 'What am I going to do with a bloody boat? We only want it for a couple of weeks.'

She suggested we could spend more time on it in summer, taking a few days off here and there. I must admit, it sounded a great idea at the time. Ann was very excited, as the boat was done up really well, with a cinema, great bedrooms, dining rooms and all that stuff. On top of this, it was full of immaculate art and furniture.

I told Nick there was no way I was interested in buying a boat, but my wife was quite insistent that I pursue the matter. Then I laid it on about the recessionary times we were in and how the bank would have to wait a long time before they found another Hooray Henry to buy it. I put in a 'go away' offer. 'Tell them I'll give them five million dollars and I'll do the deal within a couple of days.'

'Don't be silly, Alan! That's ridiculous! There's no way they'll sell this boat for five million – it's worth at least eight. It cost *fourteen* million to build four years ago.'

I reminded him, 'If it's worth eight million and you're such a bleedin' good agent, why is it still sitting here in Golfe-Juan clocking up lots of costs?'

'Well, it's the economy at the moment.'

'Exactly! Now, you go and tell the bank that I'll give them five million dollars and if they're interested, get back to me.'

Like all good agents, he was like a dog with a bone and of course he *did* get back to me. He told me he'd spoken to the bank and, as anticipated, they'd totally rejected my offer.

'Great,' I replied. 'Now I can go and tell Ann they didn't want to sell it.'

'No, no, no, come on, Alan, you can do a bit better than that. How about six and a half million?'

'Nick, you're not hearing me, are you? I do not want a bloody boat, do you understand? I just thought that, as an impulse buy, it wasn't a bad bargain for five million.'

'But you're not going to get it for five million.'

'Yes I know, Nick. You've already said that. And I'm telling you the same thing again – just find me a boat to charter and I'll be a happy bunny. Forget *this* boat and tell the bank to clear off.'

A couple of days later, he phoned me to say he'd got the bank talking sensibly and they were prepared to take $5.8m. By now I knew I had them on the hook. This type of asset was not the kind of thing people normally bought on the spur of the moment – you either wanted a boat or you didn't – and in the strained economy at the time, there were no buyers.

'Look, Nick, there's this bloke Venables and I offered him three million pounds to buy his shares in a football club. He refused and took me to court and I've had a very, very hard time. The reason I'm offering you five million dollars is because, at today's exchange rate, that's exactly the same as the three million quid I was going to give him. Now, either you get me the bloody boat for five million dollars or stop driving me bleedin' mad!'

They agreed on $5m in the end. In boating terms, I nicked it, not only because of the structure of the boat, but because the internal decoration this Champagne Charlie had spent his money on (or more likely the bank's money on) must have been worth $3–4m alone.

According to maritime law, the boat had to be taken twelve miles out to sea, to no-man's land, before the sale could take place and as I was buying it from a bank, they wanted everything conducted in the correct manner. We couldn't have picked a worse day. The sea was choppy and I was turning greener as we were going along. Ann is a great sailor, she never seems to suffer from seasickness, but as a kid I suffered badly from motion sickness in cars. My daughter Louise is the same. I was feeling so ill, I told Nick Edmiston that he should get the bloody boat into port as quickly as possible and I joked that I might even pay him $5.2m – that's how bad I felt.

The captain of the boat was a handsome young Italian by the name of Mario and the rest of the crew were also young fellows. I found out that the previous owner was a bit of a playboy and this boat had a reputation of being a party boat in the South of France. You could see that Captain Mario and his crew had enjoyed all this partying, but if they thought this type of lifestyle was going to carry on, they'd made a big mistake. They picked the wrong bloody owner with me, I can tell you that!

Mario told Nick to point out to me that all the art and other extras like camcorders and computers on the boat were *not* actually part of the assets the bank owned – they were the personal property of the owner. I took this at face value and told Nick that the deal was off. I'd agreed to buy the boat lock, stock and barrel and there was no way I was paying $5m if these items weren't included. This put a real spanner in the works. To cut a long story short, after a load of calls on the satellite phone while we were bobbing up and down out at sea, the bank invited me to make a counter-offer.

When it comes to paintings, I can't tell a Damien Hirst from a Geoff Hurst – I just like what I like, and Ann is the same. How much would twenty paintings and a few statues be worth? Not a clue! I threw a figure on the table of $150,000. The bank was obviously desperate, as they agreed to this reduction immediately, and I signed the sale agreement with the bank representative who was onboard.

Here's the funny part of the story. It turned out that Mario was telling porkies. I knew there was something fishy going on when he suddenly came up with this story out at sea. I suspected that the owner did *not* own the artwork himself and that Mario was trying to nick it. I decided to blag him with a porky of my own. I phoned him a few days later, telling him that I'd made enquiries with the bank and they'd shown me the full inventory of what they'd financed, *including* the various artworks. I wanted to know why he was giving me this load of old bullshit. He came up with some waffle and then I knew for sure he was lying. I told him that I was due at the boat in a few days and warned him, 'I will expect to see all the stuff still onboard – if it isn't, then I won't expect to see you onboard either.'

The cheeky bastard said to me, 'But, Mr Sugar, you just got a hundred and fifty thousand dollars from the bank – why are you worried?'

I told him to mind his own bloody business and warned him that if any of the stuff was missing from the boat I would involve the police. Needless to say, I took the $150,000 reduction from the bank and by blagging Mario about checking the inventory with the bank, I didn't need to buy any additional artwork!

We planned our first trip on the boat for a couple of weeks later. During that week I decided I wanted to make some engineering changes to the boat, to make it a little more streamlined. We called in a German firm to look into some modifications and Mario was poking his nose in while I was discussing the design alterations, telling me I couldn't do this and I couldn't do that, and that I was going to change the *character* of the boat – bloody cheek! I took no notice of him and the design we came up with was magnificent – it really transformed the boat into much more of a family-oriented vessel.

This guy Mario really acted as if the boat belonged to him. He would always speak down his nose to me about what he wanted, how much money he needed to spend. When we first fully explored the boat, we opened every cupboard and saw stores of luxury goods – soaps, shampoos, perfumes, towels, etc. Mario was getting the raving hump as we were finding this stuff because he was planning to nick it all. Having sussed him out as a bloody crook, there was no way I was going to leave him in charge of the finances, so I employed the services of an agent to manage the boat for me.

We planned our last boating trip of the season for the whole month of August and invited some of our friends and family onboard. When we turned up, Mario explained that he'd like his wife to join him in the captain's cabin throughout the voyage. As far as I was concerned, there was no problem with this and, in any case, she would be acting as one of the stewardesses during the day. Then, as we set sail, a beautiful little blond boy came running down the walkway of the boat! Where the hell did he come from? It turned out he was Mario's wife's child from a previous marriage. Mario had forgotten to tell me we were going to have a baby onboard as well. While this was a rather large and luxurious boat, there was no way that a baby could be confined to barracks in a small room for a month.

Ann and I were furious, but we were already at sea and there wasn't much we could do about it. We did discuss with our friends and family whether we should go back to port and send Mario's wife off the boat with the kid, but in the end we decided to leave it as it was. To be fair, the boy never got in our way; in fact, he was a gorgeous little child and we ended up playing with him a few times.

But it showed that this geezer Mario was a right liberty-taker. When we got to Capri, I took him to one side and started to read him the riot act. I told him that any ideas he'd got from the past about this freewheeling party boat should be purged from his brain, because we were not like that. What's more, splashing out money on ridiculous things, as the previous guy did, was *not* going to happen here, because basically the last owner had been spending the bank's money, not his own. I made it clear that Mario was going to have to toe the line, otherwise I'd kick his arse off the boat there and then. I don't think anyone had spoken to him that way before and from that moment till the end of the voyage, he certainly had the hump.

At the end of the summer, Mario and the crew delivered the boat to Hamburg, where it was taken out of the water and the work started. I'd agreed a $2m contract for the alterations. Mario was then summarily fired and the ship's agent employed a new English captain, whose first duty would be to oversee the work being carried out, which would take at least six months at the shipyard. I instructed the captain that on his way back to the South of France, he should take the boat into London and park it by Tower Bridge. We left it there for about a week and invited some guests aboard to see the newly named *Louisianna* – named after my daughter and my wife.

*

It was on the boat the following summer that I embarked on the task of beating up Kelly at the FA. The boat had a satellite phone connection and fax machine, so it became a floating office. Alan Watts and I drafted up the letters to Kelly, threatening that Spurs were going to take him and the FA to court. In each letter, I gave him a deadline to reply by, implying that if I didn't hear from him by this deadline, legal action would be taken without further notice.

He was rattled. He'd realised by now I wasn't one of those typical wimpish football club chairmen who sit around allowing the fans, the manager and everybody else to walk all over them. Day in, day out, for the next five days, I wrote him letters, each one concluding with the same deadline message. It was all a complete and utter bluff. If Kelly had had half a brain and consulted with some external lawyers – or had thrown down the gauntlet and challenged me to go ahead and take him to court – he would have known (as I did, based on Alan Watts' advice) that there was nothing much we could do, and I'd *have to* back down.

It seemed the letters had worn Kelly down a bit and he was softening, so Alan suggested we offer Kelly a fast-track solution to this issue: instead of going to court, we'd be willing to attend an arbitration hearing which was binding to both parties. Kelly took the bait hook, line and sinker. We had pulled off an amazing coup – we'd got the FA back to the table. At an arbitration hearing, I could have another crack at appealing against the six points, the £1.5m fine and the FA Cup ban.

Apart from the shenanigans with Kelly and the FA, that year's boat trip was particularly eventful, as we were also trying to purchase more players. I agreed to help Ossie overcome the disadvantage of the six-point deficit by allocating up to £9m for new players to strengthen the team. The 1994 World Cup had just finished and during Romania's victory over Argentina, Ossie had noticed two Romanian players: Ilie Dumitrescu, an attacking midfielder, and the defender Gheorghe Popescu. Ossie was interested in buying them and told me he'd mentioned it to the agent Dennis Roach.

Dennis Roach purported to be one of the best football agents in England, but from what I'd heard on the grapevine, if you shook his hand, you *definitely* had to count your fingers afterwards. His company, PRO International, was allegedly run out of a shed at the end of his garden at his house in Bournemouth. It used to make me laugh when I phoned him and a woman would answer the phone, 'PRO International, how can I help you?' You'd have thought you'd just phoned some high-rise office in the City.

Roach called me to say he was very well connected with Steaua Bucharest, the club Dumitrescu played for, and would easily be able to pull off a deal for me. This was the first time I'd got involved in any player transfers. Previously, Venables and his cronies had dealt with everything and we went through the first season under Ossie without much transfer stuff going on. So I took Roach's claims at face value, that he actually *did* have some connection with the Romanian club. He was calling me all the time over the course of the next few days, telling me he was getting close to striking a deal for Dumitrescu.

His first lecture to me was, 'These foreign clubs, they like to deal in dollars, Alan. Do you know what dollars are? American dollars? Now, most club chairmen only know about pounds sterling, but these foreign clubs like to talk dollars . . .'

'Dennis, who do you think you are talking to here? I'm not one of these farmer chairmen out in the sticks somewhere. I'm an international businessman, so I think I know what dollars are. I have no problem paying in dollars, sterling or any other currency.'

'Oh, right, okay, Alan. I just wanted to let you know, because not a lot of people in football understand dollars.'

'Okay, well, get on with it.'

'I think I can do a deal for you at four million dollars. It's been very, very hard, but if you agree to pay at that kind of level, then I can sort this matter out. In fact, I'm in Bucharest right now and I have to tell you, while you're sitting out there in the sun on your boat, I'm banged up in some horrible hotel and the food is lousy. Anyway, can you call me back?' He gave me a telephone number and the international prefix was for Monaco! Roach must have been used to dealing with complete and utter brain-deads.

'Dennis,' I said, when I'd got him back on the phone, 'the dialling code 377 is Monaco, not bloody Romania, so what's this bullshit about you being in Romania, in a horrible hotel with terrible food?'

'Oh, no, no, no, sorry, I meant *yesterday* I was in the horrible hotel with the terrible food.'

'Dennis, you told me not more than five minutes ago that you're in Bucharest *right now*. You said you'd just met the guy who's in charge of the club and you're banged up in this crap hotel overnight, waiting to do a deal tomorrow. Now make your bloody mind up, where are you – Monaco or Bucharest?'

'No, I'm in Monaco, Alan. Yeah, you're right, I am in Monaco. I was in Bucharest yesterday.'

'Okay, fine. So how are you going to get to Bucharest tomorrow?'

'Er, I'll catch the first flight out of Monaco.'

'Dennis, there's no airport in Monaco. There's an airport at Nice.'

'Yeah, yeah, Nice, I meant Nice.'

'Now, Dennis, there are no direct flights from Nice to Bucharest – you'll have to fly somewhere else.'

'Yeah, yeah, I know, I know.'

'Dennis, you're absolutely full of shit aren't you?'

'Now, now, Mr Chairman, that is *not* a nice way to speak to me. I'll have you know I am the chairman of the Football Agents' Association – I am a very well-respected dealer. Many of your contemporaries in the Premier League will tell you what an honest trader I am.'

'Shut up, Dennis, will you? Let's just see if we can do this deal or not. Because let me tell you something, sunshine, what I've *forgotten* about bullshit, you haven't even *learned* yet. So just bear in mind you're not talking to some idiot now, okay? I've got your card marked – you're a bit of a ducker and diver. Now stop talking to me like I'm a bloody fool and just get on with it.'

'Fair enough, fair enough. I'll move on.'

A couple of days later, Roach called me back. 'Right, I've got the deal all lined up. There's only one problem – the club is run by the military and the colonel who's in charge . . .'

'Dennis, are you bullshitting again?'

'No, I swear to God, the club's run by the military. The colonel, who's the equivalent of the chairman, insists that he wants an additional donation to the local authority gymnasium.'

'What *is* this load of bollocks, Dennis? What are you going on about?'

'He wants another two hundred thousand.'

'Well, Dennis, tell him to forget it. In fact, do you know what? I'd like to forget this whole deal because it's starting to sound a bit fishy to me.'

'No, no, no, everything's all done, it's all straight. Let me get back to you.'

He phoned ten minutes later. The $200,000 was clearly a try-on. Then he started to explain the rather complex way he wanted us to pay. He said the $4m should be sent to a Swiss bank account, after which it would be split up, with a certain amount going to the club, another sum going to the community and a whole load of flannel like that.

'Dennis, pin your ears back and listen to this,' I said. 'I am buying this football player from the football club – that's the only organisation I am paying any money to. If you can't arrange *that* then the deal is off. I'm not sending any money to anyone other than Steaua Bucharest. So, Dennis, what you need to do is send me a document on Steaua letter heading showing me the contracted sale price of the player, as well as transfer details for any bank they want me to pay the money to.'

'Well, that's going to be complicated, Alan. To be honest, it ain't gonna happen and Ossie is gonna be very, very upset that he ain't gonna get his player.'

'I don't care if Ossie's going to be upset. I can assure you we have enough aggravation at the moment with the FA – there is no way I am getting involved in any dodgy deals. Do you hear me loud and clear? Now, wherever you are, Monaco, Bucharest or Timbuktu, I suggest you get your arse back on a plane and go home, because this deal is *not* going to happen.' I slammed the phone down on him.

Half an hour later, he called me again. 'All right, Alan, all right, it's all sorted, it's all sorted. You'll be getting a fax soon – on Steaua Bucharest letter heading – with their bank details. If you sign that and send it back, then we have a deal.'

'Okay, that sounds fine to me. Just a couple of other things, Dennis. The deal has got to be subject to us agreeing terms with the player and also subject to the player passing a medical test.'

'Oh, yeah, yeah, sure, no problem, he's fit as a fiddle. The player's as fit as a fiddle. And as for terms, I've already told the player he's getting eight grand a week and that's it – no more. Four hundred grand a year, which is what you indicated to me.'

'Are you sure, Dennis? Are you sure the player has understood that's *all* we're paying?'

'Definitely.'

'Dennis, I'm telling you again, don't schlap this bloke over to England with his agent unless you're telling the truth. We don't want to find out when he arrives that he's never heard about these terms. Because I promise you, Dennis, if they disagree with this they can get back on a plane and go home. So, Dennis, don't piss about – you'd better be honest with them.'

'Alan, I swear to you on my grandmother's life . . .'

'Dennis, please leave your grandmother out of it – from what I've heard, she's died twelve times already. Forget your grandmother and just tell me whether the player has agreed to eight grand a week, because that's the maximum we're paying.'

'It's all agreed, Alan.'

'Good. Well then, when you fax me this Steaua Bucharest thing, you might as well also send me some signed piece of paper from the player, showing he has agreed a four-year contract at eight grand a week.'

An hour or so later, documents started coming through on the boat's fax machine. There was a letter from Steaua Bucharest outlining the sale of Ilie Dumitrescu for a fee of $4m, signed by a Colonel Some-thing-or-other, with a space on the document inviting me to sign in agreement. An addendum to this was a letter from the player himself, stating he agreed to sign a contract for four years at the rate of £8,000 a week.

I told Colin Sandy at the club to send the money once Dumitrescu had safely arrived, passed a fitness test and signed his contract with Tottenham. We also had to obtain a work permit for him because he wasn't from the European Community. This was a mere formality – he was a World Cup international.

Ossie called and thanked me for landing this player and asked how I was doing with regard to Popescu, who was playing for PSV Eind-hoven in Holland.

I got in touch with Frank Arnesen, PSV's director of football. When I spoke to Frank, he immediately rejected any suggestion that Popescu leave the club. I reported this to Ossie and felt the matter was dead. However, within a couple of days, Dennis Roach was back on the phone, telling me that he was an expert on PSV Eindhoven and knew Frank Arnesen very well. He said I should leave matters with him and he'd sort out a deal.

'Dennis,' I said impatiently, 'am I not getting through to you? I do not believe a bleedin' word that comes out of your mouth. You're about as expert on PSV as I am at opera singing. You're just poking your nose in again, trying to stimulate a deal. I've already spoken to PSV and they've told me they're not going to sell him.'

'Well, Alan, if that's the case then you've got nothing to lose if I pop over there and see if I can sort a deal out.'

'You're quite right, Dennis, I've got nothing to lose. Go and knock yourself out.'

My family and a few friends were on the boat with me that summer. The family had been pretty well shielded from my shenanigans with the FA, apart from Daniel, who was obviously quite interested as it was to do with football. The next event, however, was going to interest everybody.

We parked the boat up in Monaco to allow the ladies off to go shopping. I remained on the boat and received a call on my mobile from a foreign chap who introduced himself as Andy Gross, the agent for Jürgen Klinsmann. He told me that Jürgen was interested in playing in the English Premier League, having had a very successful World Cup with Germany. I was no expert on football at the time, but even *I* knew who Jürgen Klinsmann was.

I told Gross, 'There's no way Jürgen Klinsmann would play for Tottenham. For a start, we could never agree terms on salary – our maximum pay is eight thousand pounds a week. Secondly, our football club has a bit of a problem at the moment – we start the season six points down because of some so-called misdemeanours. So, to be honest, if Jürgen Klinsmann wanted to come to England, I should imagine we'd be the *last* club he'd want to play for.'

'No, Alan, Jürgen is very interested in playing for your club – the six points are irrelevant. Jürgen is currently playing for FC Monaco and he's not happy with Arsène Wenger. You can get him for a reasonable fee from Monaco, as we have special terms in his contract allowing him to leave.'

I suggested to Gross that this all sounded too much of a pipe dream. I figured if Klinsmann wanted to play in England, there would have been a number of other clubs, offering loads more money, that would have been a far more attractive proposition than Spurs. But despite my frankness with Gross, he insisted there was a serious possibility that Klinsmann could come to the club. To be honest, I didn't take it too seriously. Having had a bellyful of Dennis Roach, my opinion of agents wasn't running high at the time. I thought this might even be a wind-up or someone fishing around.

The next day, Andy Gross called me again and said that Jürgen Klinsmann would like to meet me.

'Andy, I'm on holiday on my boat in Monaco,' I replied.

'Yeah, I know that and I know where your boat is. If you walk to the back of your boat and look up, you'll see an apartment building. I am there, in Jürgen's flat.'

With nothing to lose, I told him that if they wanted to come aboard they could do so. About fifteen minutes later, Andy turned up with Jürgen Klinsmann. Andy was a Swiss national, a skinny bloke with long hair, dressed like an American hippy. If it wasn't for the fact that Klinsmann was standing beside him, I would have still believed it was a wind-up.

Klinsmann turned out to be a very sharp character; not only a great footballer, but also quite clever. He'd played in Germany, Italy and now in Monaco, but recognised that the English Premier League was becoming the most powerful league in the world. And as part of his career, he wanted to play in England. Why he chose Tottenham was a bit unclear. With the benefit of hindsight, I'm convinced it was simply because it was the nearest club to what he considered a fashionable location to live – Highgate. I know that may sound ridiculous and if you asked Klinsmann he would probably deny it, but I'm convinced he had mapped out in his mind that he wanted to play in England, he wanted to be in London and he wanted to live in Highgate – and the nearest club to it was Tottenham.

It suddenly occurred to me that in having these discussions with a player, I was breaking a cardinal rule in football – the chairman should not interfere or decide which players to buy. I hadn't consulted Ossie simply because I thought this was either a wind-up or a pipe dream, but now it was starting to look serious. I called Ossie and told him that sitting on my boat right now were Jürgen Klinsmann and his agent. I explained what had happened over the past day or so and asked whether he would want Jürgen Klinsmann.

Ossie's reply was, 'Are you joking with me? Is this one of your funny English jokes?' Actually, he added a few Spanish expletives which I won't repeat!

'Ossie, I'm serious. He's sitting here on my boat.'

Ossie continued, '*Of course* we will have Klinsmann! Yes, yes, move ahead! You don't realise what you have there. Keep me in the picture.'

I told Gross and Klinsmann it would be a great boost for our fans if he joined, as we had these punishments laid down by the FA. But I made it perfectly clear I was not going to break the bank to secure Jürgen's services. Our limit was £8,000 per week – that's it. Strangely enough, they didn't argue with this. They told me they'd agreed a departure deal with Monaco which meant we would have to pay a transfer fee of £2m.

I started to discuss the personal terms of a two-year contract for Klinsmann. Because of the problems Tottenham was having with the FA and the possibility that we might get relegated, Gross said that any contract Klinsmann signed would have to have a get-out clause so at the end of his first season he could leave – on the basis that someone would pay the same transfer fee I was paying Monaco. This sounded a no-brainer to me at the time. What did I have to lose? With Klinsmann in the team and the new acquisition of Dumitrescu, the chances were we *wouldn't* get relegated and Klinsmann would play out his full two years. Who knows, at the end of those two years we might be able to sell him to someone else or he might stay.

I hastily agreed to this arrangement. It was now sounding too good to be true and I wanted the deal sealed irrevocably. Gross arranged for me to go to AS Monaco and meet the president and Arsène Wenger to discuss the transfer.

Next day, 29 July, we pulled the boat out of Monaco harbour and hung offshore, very close to the coastline, where we could see Monaco's stadium. The small tender took me to the quayside, right next to the stadium entrance. During the meeting, Wenger talked to me about the Spurs player Nick Barmby, saying he was very good. He didn't hint that he wanted to buy him, he just commented that he was a good player. I was surprised Wenger had knowledge of our team, considering we weren't playing in Europe; he must have been following the English Premier League.

I had now done a deal with Monaco and with Klinsmann, who had signed an unofficial note to seal the deal. However, this wasn't legally binding; Klinsmann would have to come to England and pass a medical before he could sign a proper Premier League contract.

Nothing in football is secret and I was aware that this news could leak out through the media and someone else could scupper the deal. So before meeting the people at Monaco, I'd called Vic Wakeling, head of Sky Sports, whom I'd met many times before. He knew I was very friendly with Sam Chisholm and Rupert Murdoch and he always took my calls. I told Vic to listen carefully as I had a scoop for him. If he could arrange for a mobile film crew to come down to the dock outside Monaco's stadium in about two hours' time, I would be walking out of the main entrance and shaking Jürgen Klinsmann's hand to announce he had signed for Tottenham.

Vic was very excited about this and asked me if I was serious. I told him I wasn't messing around and that, to be perfectly frank, I needed his help. Once I got Klinsmann shaking my hand at the dockside live on TV, it would put paid to any snipers trying to hijack the deal. Ten minutes later, Vic called me back and told me he'd arranged a satellite van through Reuters. He said he'd told the crew what I looked like – they obviously knew what Klinsmann looked like! The story would be aired on Sky News as soon as we came out of the stadium.

After Klinsmann and I had shaken hands in the office and completed the paperwork, we walked down the stairs and out of the main entrance. Sure enough, there was a fellow hovering there. 'Mr Sugar, Mr Klinsmann.'

'Yes?'

'Could you come over here, please?'

Klinsmann was taken aback. 'Who's he?'

I said, 'He's a friend of mine from Sky TV in England. They're going to announce that you've signed for Tottenham.'

'Well, hold on, I haven't signed yet – I haven't passed the medical. Maybe it's too early to do this.'

'That's okay, you're a man of your word – let's do it.'

We stood at the edge of the jetty and I put my hand out. Klinsmann had no alternative but to grasp it and shake it, although he was in shock. He knew the media got their stories quickly, but this must have been a record! He was now well and truly committed to

Tottenham and there would be no way he could pull out. All that could go wrong would be that he failed the medical.

I bid farewell to Jürgen and told him I'd meet him tomorrow at Nice airport and we'd fly to England. I wanted to take him back personally, to ensure there were no last-minute hiccups – I wanted to see his signature on the Premier League contract with my own eyes.

I got into the tender and chugged back to the boat. Just as I got aboard, Daniel pulled Sky News up from our onboard satellite dish – and there I was shaking Klinsmann's hand. An unbelievable coup.

My mobile started ringing like crazy. I had a call from Chelsea's Ken Bates, asking me how I'd pulled that one off. 'Is it serious? Are you really getting Klinsmann?'

Ossie called me, tremendously excited, saying, 'You did it, you did it! How did you manage to do it? How much did we pay?' I told him the details and he said it was a fantastic deal and thanked me very much for supporting him.

The next morning, I met Jürgen – and a load of luggage – at Nice airport. A lot must have been going on behind the scenes that I didn't know about. Here was a man who up till the day before was living in Monaco; now he was laden with four or five suitcases, ready to move himself to England, no doubt to an apartment he'd already sorted out – in Highgate.

My head was spinning with excitement on the flight to London. As we got off the plane at Heathrow and walked up the gangway, it was packed with photographers and they followed us all the way through immigration and customs. Peter Barnes, our club secretary, had arranged for a car to meet us and we drove straight to White Hart Lane. Sky News had carried the story again and this generated a load of fans gathering outside the main gate.

We whisked Klinsmann straight up to the medical department and within twenty minutes the doctor had signed him off. I took him up to Peter Barnes's office and, with a few twists and turns, we replicated the agreement we'd made on my boat in Monaco and Klinsmann put pen to paper and signed for Tottenham.

He then met Ossie and asked if it was possible to do a bit of training. I didn't know what he was going on about – it was the close season and training had finished for that day, but Jürgen insisted. We took him to the indoor pitch and Ossie found some kids from the youth team to kick a few balls around with him. They couldn't believe their eyes!

Having secured Klinsmann and Dumitrescu, the focus of Ossie's attention was now on Popescu. I'd really given up on this, but Dennis Roach was still on the case, pestering me, saying he'd spoken to Frank Arnesen and was sure he'd be able to pull off a deal. By sheer coincidence, I was flying to Eindhoven on Amstrad business, so I told Roach that if could set up a meeting on the same day with Arnesen, we could see if there was a deal to be done. I met Roach at PSV's stadium, along with Popescu and his agent. Finally, it seemed they were open to discussions. Clearly the fact that Klinsmann and Dumitrescu (Popescu's Romanian teammate) had joined Tottenham had got the player's attention.

I'd previously told Roach we were not paying any more than £2.5m for the player and Roach promised me he'd done a deal, but – typical of him – when I got there no one knew what he was talking about. They looked at me as if I were nuts when I started talking numbers. To cut a long story, the player and his agent, together with the PSV management, went into a separate meeting to discuss Popescu's severance. The net result was that I agreed to pay PSV £2.7m for the transfer.

We then moved on to the player's personal terms. Roach swore on his grandmother's life – again – that he'd promised Popescu only £8,000 a week plus club bonuses, the terms I'd told him to offer. The problem was, Roach had implied that the bonuses would equate to another £2,000–3,000 a week.

'Dennis, where did you get that crap from?' I asked.

He said, 'Well, it can happen sometimes. You have a good run and your bonus might equate to that.'

'Dennis, there is no chance. Players may get a bonus of two hundred quid a week, five hundred max if things have gone well. You're lying again, Dennis. You've lied to the player and his agent. You've put this vision in their minds that he's going to get ten grand a week total.'

I called Peter Barnes to clarify what the bonus could amount to. I was right – never mind £2,000 a week, they were lucky if they got £2,000 a year!

Dennis said, 'Oh, I'm sorry, I made a mistake.'

I had to spend the next half-hour explaining to Popescu and his agent that Mr Roach's sole objective was to try to broker a deal and whatever he'd told them, they should forget and start from scratch. Eventually Popescu agreed to our terms.

To show again how quickly things happen in football, the player told me he'd pop home right now, get some clothes and come back with me on the plane to England to have a medical and sign the contract. I was amazed at the speed at which these people operated, but it was fine by me! We arrived back at Stapleford airport and I took Popescu home and called Ossie to come to pick him up and take him away for all the necessary formalities.

Ossie now had his Romanian duo, plus Jürgen Klinsmann, Teddy Sheringham, Darren Anderton and Nick Barmby. The newspapers were full of it and they named the Spurs front line 'the Famous Five'. There was a lot of excitement in the media and for once they were being positive towards Tottenham. They were even being kind to me, as I'd laid out over £9m, which was a lot of money in those days. I recall an article on the arrival of the two Romanians in one of the national tabloids with the headline, 'They're used to mad dictators, so they'll do well at Spurs – Sorry, Mr Sugar.' They *can* be funny sometimes.

With the season about to start, I had fulfilled my promise to Ossie that we would invest in players to overcome the punishment laid down by the FA. It looked like the investment was going to pay off as we went into the first game of the season at Sheffield Wednesday. It was an eventful match! A lot of the attention was on Klinsmann, who was making his debut. After the World Cup some of the media snipers had labelled him a diver. With Spurs leading 3–2, Anderton crossed to Klinsmann, who headed in a magnificent goal. He then ran back down the pitch and dived extravagantly onto the turf, sliding to the touchline, followed by a load more of our players, who dived after him. This goal celebration was a dig at the media for their 'diver' accusations. Later in the game, Klinsmann, who clearly wanted to impress, enthusiastically went up for a header and smashed his head against one of the other players, knocking himself out cold. We couldn't believe it – stretchered off the pitch in his first game!

Uncharacteristically, I ran down to the dressing room to see what was going on. Thankfully, he had come round and the doctor was already stitching up his badly cut lip. By the time the game was over, he was up, walking around and ready to talk to the media. Spurs won the match 4–3.

The next game of the season was home to Everton. Klinsmann was fit to play and scored an amazing goal with an overhead scissor-kick. The crowd was going bananas – this internationally famous player was scoring goals for Spurs. Not only were the fans buying shirts with Klinsmann's name on them but, believe it or not, I noticed a couple of fans with 'Sugar' on their shirts! Before we all get carried away, I may have seen the only two fans that ever bought 'Sugar' Tottenham shirts, but it was nonetheless true. Ann happened to spot them on the way into the ground. However, despite the fact that we had the Famous Five, the early signs weren't great as the season progressed. Although we looked good going forward, we were leaking goals at the back, as we were tactically bad defensively. League results were poor, criticism was starting to come from the media and the fans were getting frustrated. Pressure was being put on me to replace Ardiles. With my naïvety about football management and the football industry as a whole, I just couldn't understand what was going wrong. Clearly something was, inasmuch as the team was poorly organised from a defensive point of view and this was making the players lose spirit.

Although we had the six-point penalty and were out of the FA Cup, we were still allowed to play in the League Cup and in October we were drawn against Notts County, a second-division club. Normally, a Premiership club would simply sail through his type of fixture, especially with the star players we had. However, they slaughtered us 3–0 and made us look stupid. This was the final straw. I remember sitting in the directors' lounge at Notts County afterwards with Berry, concluding that Ardiles would have to go.

A couple of days later, I summoned Ossie to my house and told him that, sadly, he'd have to leave the club. To be fair to him, he didn't protest. He requested one thing: that he could call a press conference the next day and get it over and done with in a dignified manner, after which he would not discuss the matter with the press.

The search was on for a new manager. Gerry Francis was an obvious target for Spurs at the time, having been very successful with Queens Park Rangers. His main claim to fame was that he was able to motivate his players and keep QPR in a relatively high position in the Premier League. Gerry's art was buying wisely (as he hardly had any budget to spend). For some reason or other, QPR's owners had decided to employ the services of ex-player Rodney Marsh and bring him in as director of football. Gerry Francis, from what I understood, took exception to this, as the appointment was made without consulting him, and he resigned from QPR.

I met with Gerry and we had a long discussion. He was a very serious chap and was concerned about whether he could do a good job for Tottenham – he felt more comfortable as manager of a club where he had some history. He'd been a player at QPR and would talk in terms of, 'We did this, we played well, we were fifth in the league,' whereas when he referred to Tottenham and me, it was a case of, 'I'll try and do a good job for you.' Gerry was a deep-thinker, quite heavily influenced by his family. He told me he'd go off and think about it and have a chat with his dad. At the time, his only impression of me was all the stuff he'd read in the press, the rubbish that Venables and his cronies had been putting about.

I suggested he talked to someone like Steve Perryman, who'd been Ossie's assistant and actually worked with me at the club. I even offered to walk Gerry through all the Venables crap and let him know where the land lay. He said he didn't want to hear any of the past stuff and made it clear that he would take no stance on the Terry Venables issue. It was a rather strange statement and he seemed a bit angry when he made it. I told him it was merely a suggestion, but if he didn't want to hear it, it was fine by me.

He finally agreed to join the club in November 1994 and his first game was at home against Aston Villa. We were losing 3–0 in the first half, so you can imagine what the fans were thinking, but Sheringham scored just before half–time, so we went in 3–1 down. When we came out in the second half, we were a different team. Klinsmann converted a penalty, then went on to score another to equalise. Unfortunately, Dean Saunders scored for Villa in the last minute and we lost 4–3.

When I spoke to Gerry later in the evening, he told me, 'At half-time I went into the dressing room and told the players, "Right, this is my first game and you don't know me and I don't know you. But what I saw out there in the first half was a bloody joke. If you've got any guts and if this famous football club means anything to you, then you need to get out there and show me what you can do."' He was quite proud of that achievement and indeed they did stage a tremendous recovery.

*

My efforts when it came to beating up Kelly resulted in a two-day arbitration hearing being set up for 24 and 25 November. In my communications with Kelly, I always demanded quick responses from him because the early rounds of the FA Cup were approaching and I wanted the courts to have enough time to rule on whether the FA's punishment was to be upheld or not.

At the hearing there would be a panel of three arbitrators. The chairman was a former appeal court judge and the two parties were allowed to nominate their own (independent) panel member. I asked Rick Parry, who was still furious with Kelly over this fiasco, whether he would act as our nominee, but regrettably, and quite rightly, he said there would be a conflict of interests, as he was chief executive of the Premier League. However, he came up with a great idea to appoint a Scottish barrister called Donald Findlay, who was a director of Glasgow Rangers. He suggested I call David Murray, Rangers' chairman, to see whether this was possible.

David Murray and I had previously done business on some player transfers. I think he quite liked my straightforward approach and the way I'd decided to take on Venables and the rest of the football mafia without backing down. He was sympathetic to the mishandling of our affairs by the FA and said, 'No problem at all. I'll get Donald to do it for you.'

I asked Herbert Smith to find me a barrister who was experienced in this type of thing to put our case at the hearing, someone who had a bit of a sports background. We were represented by Michael Beloff and the FA's barrister was Peter Goldsmith, the fellow who was to go on to become Attorney General under Tony Blair. He was deemed to be the bee's knees of barristers, one of the most respected in the country.

Donald Findlay was brilliant at the hearing, guiding the judge and explaining the technicalities of football to him. Goldsmith, meanwhile, was getting frustrated; he was certainly no expert in football. Edward Walker-Arnott from Herbert Smith was very interested in the case and he spent almost the entire two days there. Once again, he added weight to our side by looking at the panel intensely and nodding sagely whenever our barrister made a good point.

The panel retired on the afternoon of the second day, going into a huddle for about an hour before coming back. As Donald sat down, I looked at him and he winked at me as if to say, 'You're okay, mate.'

The chairman said they had decided in favour of Tottenham Hotspur and that the details would be published later. We suspected that meant we'd got our six points back and were back in the FA Cup but we had no idea about the fine; whether we'd get the money back or if it was to be reduced. Kelly was plutzing; you could see he was gutted – no one had ever taken on the FA and beaten them up in this fashion.

The decision was finally made public: we had our six points restored and were back in the FA Cup. The only thing the arbitration panel didn't overrule was the £1.5m fine, even though they considered that it was bordering on irrational. Instead, they referred the matter back to an FA panel to review in the light of their comments.

I jumped in the car and went down to the training ground, where Gerry was still working with the players. I told him I had some good news and that he should assemble the players together. I walked into the dressing room and told them that we were back in the FA Cup and we'd got our six points back. Teddy Sheringham, who'd never shown any enthusiasm towards me in the past, was beaming – you could see his heart really *was* with the club. Many of the other players sat there silently when I announced the good news, but some of the older ones seemed pleased with the result. Gary Mabbutt, our captain, spoke to me outside, saying he wanted to apologise on behalf of the players that hadn't shown any great emotion when I'd made this announcement. He told me that some of these guys felt intimidated in front of chairmen and tended to shrivel up into their shells. But on behalf of the players, he wanted to let me know this was a fantastic thing which had been achieved and they were all delighted. Nice bloke, Gary.

Back to the ever-dwindling rainforest and our contribution to global warming – the newspapers had a field day and Kelly was made to look a real prat. For once, it seemed I had achieved something positive in the football world.

At the next Premier League meeting, I was invited to debrief the chairmen on the events that had occurred. Sam Hammam, the chairman and owner of Wimbledon, said to me, 'Alan, you're a frightening man – not in the physical sense, but frightening in the impact you've had on football in the short period you've been involved. Look at the TV deals you've helped structure – and now *this*. Perhaps you don't realise it, but you have broken the mould. No one has ever gone against the Football Association in the way you have and won.'

Although Kelly was present, I didn't hold back and told the meeting that the whole fiasco was down to him. I showed him very little respect. He knew his action was a sham and should never have been brought in the first place. He didn't have much to say in return, other than a weak 'Congratulations' to Tottenham for battling their way through this situation, as if we'd been battling with someone else and not him!

The FA were still dragging their heels on the Tottenham Clough bung inquiry, but the media was not going to let it go and the story ran and ran. It finally resulted in an in-depth investigation where a barrister was employed by the FA to look into the matter, assisted by ex-football manager Steve Coppell. Inevitably, this would involve Tottenham having to give evidence.

In delving deeper at Tottenham, we had uncovered a ludicrous situation which supported the fact that the £58,750 paid to McLintock in cash *was* indeed a bung. In tracking down the history of the affair, John Ireland, the club's lawyer, had questioned Peter Barnes, the club secretary, and it was clear Peter knew a bit more about this arrangement than he'd let on originally. At the time, Peter had been in an awkward situation – torn between Venables and me – and, like Tony Berry, he'd sat on the fence. With Venables gone, I'd started to put pressure on Peter to recount the events. He admitted he was given a brown paper bag by Terry, who told him to put it in the fridge.

'The fridge?' I asked. 'What do you mean by that?'

'The safe.'

'And where *is* this brown paper bag, Peter?'

'Er . . . it's still in the safe.'

'Well, go and get it and show it to me.'

Inside this brown paper bag was £8,750 in cash. I went bananas, asking Peter why the hell, over one year later, it was still sitting there. He gave me a gormless look and told me he'd forgotten about it! It transpired that Venables had asked McLintock to return the VAT element of the £58,750, as this was not part of the arrangement they'd made, and the money had been in the club safe ever since.

We suspected that Customs & Excise had launched an inquiry into Frank McLintock's company. At the time of the revelations, McLintock had not filed a VAT return showing the transaction, but once it broke in court at the Venables dismissal hearing (after his barrister blurted out all of the Clough bung stuff), we believe he did so retrospectively. It was clear that when the shit hit the fan, McLintock tried to cover his tracks. I never found out what happened to McLintock – whether he got fined or reprimanded by the authorities – but one of the things that came out of all this was that the Inland Revenue now started to take an interest in football clubs in general; indeed, a task force was set up to hold an inquiry into football clubs' affairs.

The results of this inquiry were, of course, confidential. Nevertheless, the media managed to get hold of a lot of facts. Over the course of the following year, several clubs were clobbered with heavy fines and penalties. Indeed, Tottenham had to repay some taxes. Colin Sandy, who was a tax expert, did a good deal with the Inland Revenue on the basis that since it was Tottenham, and in particular Alan Sugar, who had decided to legitimise the football club, the new regime should not be punished for past misdemeanours. While technically the Inland Revenue could not accept this as an argument, I believe their settlement with us was reasonable.

The Clough investigation dragged on. Eventually, the FA decided, in their wisdom, that due to Brian Clough's ill-health at the time, it was

The Dream Team of myself and Venables on the pitch at White Hart Lane, 22 June 1991. The dream quickly became a nightmare.

I'd dismissed Venables, God's gift to football, and you'd have thought I'd shot Bambi. This *Sun* cartoon amused me, but the fallout, in reality, was hard to handle.

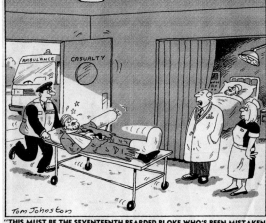

"THIS MUST BE THE SEVENTEENTH BEARDED BLOKE WHO'S BEEN MISTAKEN FOR ALAN SUGAR, TODAY!"

After my libel victory against Venables, I had this giant cheque printed up. The money went to Great Ormond Street Hospital.

With Ossie Ardiles, a Tottenham legend and the first manager I appointed.

The handshake that sealed Jürgen Klinsmann's transfer to Spurs. I'd arranged for Sky Sports to capture the moment.

David Ginola turned out to be one of the greatest players ever to perform at White Hart Lane.

Daniel came to Spurs to help with the running of the club.

My yacht, the *Louisianna*.

With Stanley Kalms on his boat. We got on well socially, but there were never any favours coming from Dixons.

Reunited with my old mates. From left to right: Malcolm, Geoff, me, Steve and Tony, at my fiftieth birthday party in March 1997.

With Gordon Brown, then Chancellor of the Exchequer, in April 1998.

With George Graham, God's *other* gift to football and my last-ditch attempt to find success on the pitch.

I was honoured to accept a knighthood from Her Majesty the Queen in June 2000.

'Arise, Sir Alan'. This photograph was taken after the ceremony. From left to right: Harold Regal, Shirley, Ann, me, Derek, Brenda, Daphne, Harold Mazin.

We had a fantastic party at Bramstons to celebrate our fortieth wedding anniversary. From left to right: (standing) Jake, Alex, Matthew, Daniel, Emma, Simon, Mark, Nathan, Joe; (seated) Michaela, Rachel, Ann, Fay, me, Louise.

I thought it was great being part of a popular show like *The Apprentice*.
Here is a selection of the winners over the years, clockwise from top left:
series 1 winner Tim Campbell; series 3 winner Simon Ambrose;
series 5 winner Yasmina Siadatan; and series 4 winner Lee McQueen.

Nick Hewer and Margaret Mountford
had worked with me for many years
before the show. It was *The Apprentice*
that made them friends, though.

And here I'm with the candidates of *The Junior Apprentice*.

With mates Piers Morgan and Nick Hewer.

It was a great honour to be made Lord Sugar of Clapton. Ann, of course, was already a lady.

On the day of the ennoblement ceremony, 20 July 2009, I got emotional seeing my family and thinking about my mum and dad. From left to right: Brenda, Minnie, Harold Regal, Johnnie, Ann, me, Daphne, Shirley, Harold Mazin and Derek.

not appropriate for him to be called to give evidence at any tribunal. But in August 1998 the FA did bring misconduct charges against Ronnie Fenton, his former assistant at Nottingham Forest, who seemed to take the rap over the bung. Really, the whole industry knew that Brian Clough was involved in the affair, but no one wanted to see a sick man punished. As a result of all this, I got a load of stick from fans, players, managers and ex-footballers, some of whom had taken on roles as media pundits. The attitude at the time was, 'Even if Cloughie *did* take a bung – so what? He's a great football manager, he's been great for football – who cares?'

Yes, he did achieve some great things, but still I found this attitude quite unbelievable. In this whole football litigation issue, one could say that I won the battle but lost the war. To anyone lower down than the chairmen and executives of football clubs, my name was mud. I had come along and upset the status quo. I had disrupted what was deemed *standard procedure* in football.

*

While the Tottenham litigation was going on, I was totally occupied with defending myself, spending much of my time dealing with lawyers. Even on holiday on my boat or in Florida, I'd constantly be reviewing faxes and talking to lawyers. Ann commented that I was becoming obsessed with this football thing in more ways than one and it was affecting me personally. I was losing my sense of humour and becoming very protective. Whenever anyone spoke to me about football matters, I would clam up.

I started to become cynical, imagining that everyone who questioned me was looking for an angle. It was a horrible situation which came about from the constant harassment by the media. I even adopted this attitude with family, friends and Amstrad employees. It was better not to talk; it was better not to explain anything. I entered a bit of a miserable period – some might argue I'm still in it!

Even when I wasn't caught up in constant fire-fighting over legal issues, I had other affairs at the club to consume my time, including attending Premier League meetings. At one such meeting, the topic of discussion was once again the TV rights, which had come up for renewal. The first contract had one year left to run and by now the number of subscribers was rising rapidly. The gamble Rupert Murdoch had taken was really paying off. BSkyB had been floated on the London Stock Exchange and the share price was running away because its operating profits were really substantial.

At the meeting, I found myself in the situation where I had to wear *three* hats, owing to my support for BSkyB, the Premier League and Tottenham Hotspur FC. As usual, I declared a conflict of interests and told the meeting I would like to put my relationship with BSkyB to one side for a moment and focus on the interests of the Premier League and Spurs. I raised the point that the original deal was now looking too cheap. In my opinion, the meteoric success of BSkyB was mainly down to them acquiring the football rights – people were taking up the subscriptions mainly to watch sport. On that basis, the hundreds of millions of pounds' operating profit they were making was something we had to recognise. Like all good deals, *all* partners should share in a win-win situation. So my suggestion to the meeting was that we should not accept anything less than £150m per season.

Everyone in the room started to laugh, telling me I was mad, I was crazy, I didn't know what I was talking about. Consider that many of these chairmen had lived through the era of ITV paying £4m per season and had then seen the first deal with BSkyB, which represented a quantum leap. To them, hearing a figure like £150m per season being bandied around was a joke.

I told them that they weren't looking at things logically. If, for example, BSkyB were making £350m a year in operating profit, that profit was mainly from subscriptions to Sky Sports. I added, 'At the end of the day, if they pay us £150m, they'll *still* be making a fortune. The fact is, without the Premier League rights, they don't have a business.'

While they were still laughing, I decided to tell them another joke. I pointed out that *none* of the clubs had held on to any of the money they'd got from the first BSkyB deal to strengthen their balance sheets. A lot of them were still borrowing heavily and had just jumped on the bandwagon of buying players and overpaying them – based on the prune-juice effect.

'The prune-juice effect, Alan? What do you mean by that?'

'Well, you know what happens if you drink too much prune juice – it runs straight through your body. That's exactly what's going on here. The more money the TV company is going to give you, the more money you're going to spend on players. You are not repaying your debts or modernising your stadiums, you're just paying more for transfers and salaries.'

'So what's your suggestion, then?'

'My suggestion is that if, hypothetically, we got a hundred and fifty million a year, the Premier League should retain, say, fifty million each year and put it into a special trust that's governed by experienced people from the football industry, a trust that can be drawn upon to pay for things such as ground improvements, academy development, training grounds and so on. The trust would ensure there'd be no dodgy dealing – clubs would be prevented from drawing on their share of the trust under the guise of "ground improvements" when really it was to be spent on players.'

You'd have thought I was a cabaret act, some sort of stand-up comedian. This suggestion brought another roar of laughter. I told them all, 'You simply don't grasp the fact that if even we *did* get a hundred and fifty million a year, I'd have a bet with every single one of you that by the end the year, none of your clubs would have anything left in their pockets. We are hiking up the prices of players *ourselves* by competing with each other using the large sums available to us.'

The acquisition of Klinsmann, Dumitrescu and Popescu seemed to have kick-started a new revolution of foreign players joining the Premier League. In the past, players came from the local community, trained in the youth academies and had a real allegiance to the club. I reminded the meeting about this and how we were now being flooded by foreigners coming here for the money, simply because we were the richest league around. We were now attracting these Carlos Kickaballs who had no history with our clubs and would go anywhere for money. The Carlos Kickaball remark got more laughter. To this day it is quoted and remains in the football dictionary.

The trouble with me is, I get too excited when I'm explaining something. I come across as too overpowering and this kind of winds people up and puts them in defensive mode. To me, it was clear the industry was heading for disaster. Piles of money would be given to the clubs, some of which were run irresponsibly by people who were no more than glorified fans, the last people on earth you should put in charge of finances.

I also failed to get my point across when arguing that no other broadcaster could compete with BSkyB. Their model was based upon Pay TV, whereas broadcasters such as the BBC and ITV were funded – in the BBC's case by the licence fee, in ITV's by advertising. I told the meeting that the BBC and ITV would never come up with a massive amount of money. If, hypothetically, ITV were to bid for the forty live games, each game would have a maximum of twelve minutes of advertising time (advertising time slots were regulated in those days and the pre-programme sponsor we now see on ITV was not allowed). The likes of Coca-Cola, Gillette or Nike would pay no more than £15,000–20,000 for a thirty-second slot. It was simple maths: 40 games x 12 minutes per game = 480 minutes (or 960 thirty-second slots). At £20,000 per slot – assuming we were only proposing to allow forty games to be broadcast per year – the total advertising revenue for the channel would only come to £19.2m.

Unfortunately, this logic fell on deaf ears and I got some dumb looks from certain chairmen. A couple of the shrewder ones caught on to what I was saying, in particular Ken Bates and Sam Hammam. But the others just dug their heels in and argued because they didn't understand what I was talking about. David Dein and Arsenal were still banging on about allowing ITV and others to pitch. My maths lesson had been a waste of time and we agreed that the next TV deal would be decided at the annual summer meeting, to be held in Coventry, with an array of broadcasters invited to pitch their propositions to the chairmen.

At the Coventry meeting, a fashion parade of broadcasters arrived. Michael Green, the head of Carlton Communications, came along with a bunch of people, saying that he'd put a consortium together and was prepared to put up a bid. As an eloquent speaker, he got the attention of some of the chairmen. Then I opened *my* mouth and started asking a few questions. 'Mr Green, do you have a proposal as to how viewers will be able to *watch* the programmes broadcast by your consortium?'

'No, no, no, don't worry about that – we'll be putting up a service on a satellite. That's really a minor issue.'

'Excuse me, Mr Green, that is *not* a minor issue. BSkyB have invested hundreds of millions of pounds putting equipment in people's homes to enable them to watch football. Is it fair to say, Mr Green, that your consortium has no way of broadcasting at the moment?'

'My technical people say there is a way that we can use the existing dishes in the market – they can be turned and tuned in to another satellite.'

'No, no, Mr Green, please hold on. With all due respect, my fellow chairmen are not technically up on these issues. I have to say, on behalf of the chairmen here and the Premier League, that I *am*. And there is no way you can simply turn a dish in another direction, nor will you be able to use existing BSkyB equipment to collect your money. Also, Mr Green, if, for example, you were going to offer over a hundred and fifty million pounds to us, we would need to know where the money is or how you're going to get it.'

At this point Green lost his temper, telling me that I was only there to line BSkyB's pockets and that I wasn't being fair. I told him, 'I've asked you some simple and reasonable questions – how are you going to broadcast the stuff? You have given *us*, the chairmen, no answer. You have passed the question over to your so-called technical expert who, with the greatest respect, is talking a load of rubbish. You haven't told this meeting whether you can guarantee the money and, by the way, even if you *could* guarantee the money, we would be a bunch of fools to accept money from an organisation that is not actually providing a service to the public. We all agree that one of the effects of BSkyB's coverage of football is that it has popularised the sport – all our stadiums are now full and there is an excitement about football. *That* has all been brought about by the tremendous job done by BSkyB. With respect, Mr Green, what *you're* proposing sounds like walking two steps forward and ten steps back.'

Green shut up at that point and the meeting was brought to a close.

I wasn't lining the pockets of BSkyB; I was genuinely talking with my Premier League hat on. A further meeting of the chairmen only was convened an hour or so afterwards and we finally decided to go for BSkyB's new offer – equivalent to £150m per season. How did that come about? Well, one of the few people who took notice of me was Rick Parry. He had nothing to lose by hinting to all the broadcasters that they needed to be in the £150m ballpark.

I tried to reiterate my idea of putting some of the money away into a trust, but this was shouted down by Chelsea's Ken Bates and Terry Brown of West Ham. They claimed it was *their* money and they should be allowed to do with it what they wished.

Sam Chisholm was delighted when I called to tell him that the meeting was over and he could pop the champagne, as they'd won the deal again. While I was talking to him, his other phone was ringing – Rick Parry was on the line, about to tell him the same thing.

BSkyB never knew about my intervention with Michael Green. They don't realise to this day what a pivotal moment it was. I spoke to Green afterwards and he told me that all he wanted was to get a consortium together to buy the *rights*, then he would sell them on to someone like BSkyB and make a profit on them. Quite a clever move, if he'd got away with it.

16

A Magnificent Deal

New Inspiration with New Amstrad

1996–8

'Mr Sugar, what is a lie?' Peter Goldsmith demanded.

'I'm sorry – a lie?' I said weakly.

It's a funny thing. When you're confronted by a barrister, all dressed up in his wig and gown, with the judge next to you as well, you tend to get nervous.

It was July 1996, nearly six years since Amstrad had issued legal proceedings against Seagate for the duff hard disk drives they'd shipped us. The case had finally got to court and the hearing was in front of a specialist judge, experienced in technical matters. My staff had given their evidence and now it was time for me to take the stand. I'd spent the weekend reading up on all the documentation as best I could, bringing myself up to date with events that had occurred nearly eight years earlier. There were about ten thick files and it was torturous work. All I could do was scan through the stuff.

This was the first time I'd given evidence in a court case. As you can imagine, I was anxious and this was not helped by the fact that Seagate had employed the services of Peter Goldsmith, the same guy the FA had used in the arbitration with Spurs. He was backed up by two other barristers and a pile of solicitors. David Gold had warned me that Goldsmith was a bit of a Rottweiler – tough, tricky and hard to deal with. His opening gambit had thrown me, but I pulled myself together and decided I wasn't going to be cowed or bullied by *anyone* – I would simply tell the truth.

'Yes, what is a lie?' Goldsmith persisted.

'Well, a lie is when someone doesn't tell the truth.'

'Okay, Mr Sugar, do you lie?'

'Well, not generally.'

'*Well, not generally,*' he mimicked. 'Mr Sugar, do you lie? Yes or no? Do you lie?'

This dramatic opening question obviously caught me a bit off guard. I collected my thoughts and replied, 'Well, there are different types of lies, aren't there? There are serious lies and little white lies.'

'Little white lies, Mr Sugar, are lies, are they not?'

'Yes, they are lies.'

'So you *do* lie then?'

'Well, Mr Goldsmith, I most probably lie as much as you do, or His Honour here.'

'I beg your pardon, Mr Sugar? It is very discourteous of you to suggest His Honour doesn't tell the truth.'

'I didn't say he doesn't tell the truth *in general*. Because you asked me to give you a black and white answer as to whether I lie – "yes or no" to use your words – I used the example of a little white lie compared to a serious lie, but it seems you're not satisfied with that answer. Mr Goldsmith, do you have any children?'

'Er, I beg your pardon, Mr Sugar? What does my having any children have to do with the matter we're discussing here today? And by the way, *I* am the one asking the questions, not you.'

'Well, I would like you to answer me, Mr Goldsmith – do you have any children, yes or no?'

'Well, it so happens I do.'

'Good. Well, when one of your children loses a tooth and you tell them that in the morning they'll wake up and find a fifty pence piece under the pillow because the tooth fairy put it there – that's a lie, Mr Goldsmith, isn't it?'

The courtroom started to laugh. Goldsmith had lost his point and I had put a stake in the ground that he wasn't going to make a monkey out of me.

He then moved on, trying to describe the technicalities of a hard disk drive and how it stores data. I could see he was bullshitting – he knew as much about the intricacies of hard disks as I did about knitting. I chose a moment to raise my eyebrows and glare at him, looking straight into his eyes as he was talking. At the same time, I smiled as if to say, 'You are talking a load of rubbish – you don't know *what* you're talking about.' He started to go red when he realised he was digging himself a bigger and bigger hole.

I kept on glaring at him and he must have thought that at the end of his ramble I was going to tell him he was talking a load of rubbish. Instead, I said, 'I assume, Mr Goldsmith, that someone has coached you on this and, to be perfectly honest, I don't know whether what you've said is right or wrong because I'm not a technical person.' I could see the judge smile. He realised both Goldsmith and I knew sweet Fanny Adams about hard disk drives.

I was on the stand for two days. At one point, Goldsmith led me to one of the files and asked me to turn to a letter from one of our customers, P&P Micro. The letter was packed with complaints – it stated they'd received the first lot of computers and they'd failed, then they'd received the second lot of computers (after we'd fitted hard disk controllers) and they'd still failed. Finally, they'd received the third lot of computers and they were still failing.

The point Goldsmith was trying to make was that we had *alienated* our customer base and had lost the market. In other words, even if we'd been making perfect computers now, we no longer had customers to sell them to. He needed to run with this argument to alleviate the claims we had on Seagate for damage to our business. He was implying that if Amstrad *had* been damaged by Seagate, we would need to refer to Seagate's terms and conditions in their contract, which stated that if they shipped bad merchandise, the maximum we could claim would be the value of the merchandise. If Goldsmith were to get this point home, then even if the judge agreed that Seagate *did* ship us rubbish, the judgement would only be for a small amount of money – the value of the hard disk drives. We, of course, were claiming not only reimbursement for the rubbish they'd shipped, but payment for damages caused to our company and its shareholders.

Goldsmith hadn't realised that I'd read the documents. I remembered that P&P Micro's letter was actually two pages long and Goldsmith had referred only to the first page. Just as he was about to move on and make his next point, I asked him to stop and look at the second page. He reminded me again that *he* was running the cross-examination and it was not my place to interject.

'Mr Goldsmith, you have made the point that you think we had lost all our customers, is that right?'

'That is exactly the point, Mr Sugar. You no longer had any customers due to the way you had alienated them.'

'I see. Well, therefore I think it only fair, Your Honour, that we look at the second page of this letter and read the penultimate paragraph.'

The judge looked at Goldsmith, then turned to me and said, 'Please read it out, Mr Sugar.'

It read, 'Despite all these problems, we are still very interested in supporting Amstrad computers. As soon as you've solved these technical issues, would you please ensure that we are the *first* customer to receive them.'

Goldsmith was very embarrassed. He'd lost his point totally, but blustered on, 'Ah, well, Mr Sugar, everybody wants to be the first, don't they?'

'Mr Goldsmith, you just painted a picture that no one wanted to deal with us any more. Remember the recent crisis at McDonald's because of mad cow disease? Well, Mr Goldsmith, would you want your children to be the *first* to eat the newly launched hamburgers?'

Once again, the court burst into laughter. I was starting to enjoy myself on the stand and I was getting a real feel for how these things went. Goldsmith, meanwhile, had a face like thunder.

The case went on for about ten days, at the end of which the judge announced he would deliberate before arriving at his judgement, which would be made in several months' time. I couldn't quite understand why he needed so long, but David Gold explained that this was a complex case and it was quite normal for judgements to take up to nine months. The judge was a busy person, hearing many cases, and had to find the time to study his notes, the history and the documentation.

*

I'd taken one eye off the ball as far as Amstrad was concerned. It is one of the things I look back on and deeply regret. I have gone on record many times saying I wasted ten years of my business life in football. Not only did football disadvantage me financially (and who knows what Amstrad could have achieved if I'd concentrated on it totally?), but it also took its toll on me *personally*. It made me a miserable sod, constantly involved in arguing and fire-fighting.

Regrettably, I also hadn't concentrated on Dancall under Bob Watkins' management, but had left him on his own to get on with it. When I bought the company, I envisaged it focusing totally on the new booming GSM mobile market – they had the technology and were ready to go. I wanted Bob to do what he was best at: making sure the new GSM stuff was fully developed and getting it produced on time and at the right price. Instead, he allowed the people there to run riot developing other technologies such as pagers and DECT (portable fixed-line home phones). I made a big error in not being there on day one to assert my authority and make them focus on GSM only.

Here is the bloody point. Bob spent years working side-by-side with me and *knew* my philosophy – forget low-price items and concentrate on high-ticket items. Simple. We don't want to be selling audio units at £20 ex-factory and only make £5 profit; we want to sell colour PCs at £1,000 ex-factory and make £200. The writing was on the wall for pagers – they were on the way out. The billing price ex-factory was about £35, so the absolute margin per unit was slim. More to the point, it occupied a lot of our rocket-scientist engineers who were more than capable of turning their hands to GSM. The same could be said for DECT – while it *was* leading-edge technology in those days, it was only usable for home phones and, again, the ex-factory billing was small. A GSM phone, on the other hand, was fetching around £180 ex-factory in those days. Apart from pagers and DECT phones, Dancall *did* develop a couple of new GSM phones and got orders from Mercury in England and E-Plus in Germany. There was no lack of demand in those days, as the market was booming.

When I finally got round to reviewing what had gone on, I looked into the financial arrangements Bob had agreed to and discovered that some of them were outrageous. On top of this, he had awarded the

American company Audiovox exclusivity on selling our phones in Spain. But the biggest issue was that, in trying to act as CEO and businessman, Bob had taken his eye off engineering and production – the bit he was best at. The first GSM phone designed under his regime had a serious mechanical fault whereby the battery would lose contact while clipped on the back. The frustrating thing was that the electronics and software that went into this phone (including all the GSM technology) made up 99.9 per cent of the rocket science involved; the stupid plastic cabinet was just the other incidental 0.1 per cent. We fell down on the simple stuff – on mechanical design. With our wealth of knowledge, we should have been able to deal with this with our eyes shut, but it completely screwed us.

You see, a customer doesn't *care* why a phone doesn't work. They are not interested in hearing that 99.9 per cent of what you sold them is technically brilliant – it's the bloody 0.1 per cent they remember.

It was a sad day when I went to Denmark to relieve Bob of his duties as chief executive there but I still wanted him to remain with the company, to be my consultant as far as technical matters were concerned.

However, Bob had his pride and dignity and in January 1997 he left once again to join Gulu Lalvani, who had been following the Amstrad/Dancall deal. I don't know exactly what Bob was expected to do – I suspect it was to try to put Gulu in the mobile phone business.

I knew I'd done a good deal acquiring Dancall; I was just angry I'd let it run riot. I can't emphasise enough how advanced this little company was compared to some of the big boys. I knew we could never compete *long-term* in the mobile phone market – we could never afford the marketing budgets or have the economy of scale to make millions of phones per month – thus I always had it in mind to sell Dancall to a big player.

However, this latest setback got me thinking that maybe the disposal of Amstrad as a whole would be the best thing for me, to finally sever my relationship with electronics, as nothing seemed to be going right at the time and we'd lost the computer market. Psion, who were enjoying exceptional success with their Organiser, seemed like a good match. I got in touch with Dr David Potter, the chairman and boss, to discuss the possibility of Psion, also a public company, acquiring Amstrad. I explained that in addition to our technology, there was a large cash pile inside Amstrad, as well as a possible windfall pending the result of the litigation with Seagate.

Potter was very interested and we had several meetings to discuss it. Regrettably, somebody leaked these secret discussions to the media and the *Daily Mail* blew the story. Potter was furious, originally blaming me for the leak. It had nothing at all to do with me – I was fully aware of the necessity to keep things quiet and was insulted that he was making accusations like this. As a result, the Stock Exchange asked Psion and Amstrad what was going on and Psion had to put out a statement saying that they were in preliminary discussions with Amstrad, but as due diligence had not taken place, they were in no position to make an offer.

I found Potter to be a very cautious and distrusting person. Even after carrying out due diligence, I think this distrust led him to conclude that I was trying to palm him off with some white elephant. He was so wrong. I was simply trying to relinquish the reins of Amstrad and put it into another company. I just wanted to sit back and let someone else run it, so the responsibility wasn't on my shoulders alone. But at the eleventh hour, Psion got cold feet and announced they were pulling out of the deal.

The bad news came on a Friday, leaving me quite depressed and demoralised. One of the negative effects of Ann having no interest in or knowledge of my business was that at times like this, she never understood how gutted I felt. We were out for dinner with friends the following night and I was in a deep sulk and very poor company. If ever there was a time for her to leave me alone, it was then. Instead, she gave me a bollocking at the table for not being the life and soul of the party.

However, I pulled myself together and started to focus again on Dancall, where we were seeing a new wave of enthusiasm within the management. After Bob's departure, I read the staff the riot act. I told them we were shutting down any projects on pagers and DECT, explaining the commercial rationale. There were some disappointed engineers who saw this as abandoning their first love, but I reminded them, 'I am the boss and that's *it*. We're going to redeploy you where we can make some money. This is not a learning institution or a charity; this is a business. Let me remind you how you got into trouble in the past – by not focusing on where the revenue's coming from.'

We had recruited the services of a super-salesman who specialised in Eastern Bloc countries such as Romania, Poland and Czechoslovakia, which had been left behind as far as the big boys like Nokia, Ericsson and Motorola were concerned. These countries' national telecom organisations all wanted to be in the mobile phone business. We got lots of orders from this market; we pretty much had it to ourselves. So while Western Europe was not really interested in Dancall, Eastern Europe was buying as many phones as it could lay its hands on.

I spent a lot of time with the engineering people, discussing the changing trends in the mobile market. Phones in those days transmitted on one of two bands: GSM or PCN. I decided we should develop what I called a 'World Phone'. The product would be dual-band – a phone you could use in America or Europe, a phone that could roam automatically between the PCN and GSM networks. Obviously it wasn't a new idea – everyone was thinking this way – but no one had yet produced it in an elegant and commercial package. I was keen to demonstrate this dual-band phone at the Hanover Fair in March 1997, because if I *were* to sell Dancall, now would be the time. I wanted to prove that Dancall had advanced technology in order to make it attractive to any serious big buyer.

With some of my enthusiasm rekindled, I contacted Robert Leitao of Rothschild and suggested we look for companies to buy Dancall. It seemed to me there was a one-time opportunity to offer the company to some giant organisation who wanted to catapult themselves into advanced mobile technology, rather than greenfield it themselves. The German giant Siemens was one such organisation and I had already contacted them and pulled off a deal for Dancall to make a Siemens-branded dual-band phone. It was quite amazing to see that Siemens, this giant organisation, was so far behind Dancall technologically that its own factories couldn't produce this.

Rothschild put together a document to target potential buyers, inviting them to make further enquiries with a view to an offer. To our surprise, a lot of companies responded, including Sony, Bosch and a few others. Meanwhile, the boss of Siemens called me to ask if I could give him an indication of how much money we wanted for Dancall. Before answering, I consulted with Robert Leitao.

If you think investment bankers know what they're talking about, here's an interesting example which proves they have no idea whatsoever. Robert, a very nice fellow, had tried to assist me in the Psion takeover and got to know certain things about Dancall. But when it came to putting a valuation on it, he just kind of looked at me, as if to invite *me* to come up with a figure. For no reason other than complete and utter bravado, I blurted out, 'This company will not be sold by Amstrad unless we are offered at least a hundred and fifty million US dollars.'

I just plucked the figure out of mid-air. And here's the bit that'll make you laugh – Robert said to me, 'One hundred and fifty million is reasonable, very reasonable. That's the figure we should go forward with.'

So much for all the investment banking advice! We'd only paid £6m for Dancall and had injected a further £10m, so our outlay over the two years we'd owned it was £16m. Between you and me, if someone had offered me £35m there and then, I'd have bitten their hand off. In fact, if Robert had burst out laughing and said, 'You must be joking, Alan, it's not worth more than thirty million,' I'd have said, 'Okay.' But having seen Robert's reaction, I thought, 'What the hell, there's nothing to lose, go for $150m.'

I told the guy from Siemens that if he thought he was going to *steal* the company, he'd better think again, as other parties were interested. Without mentioning their names, I told him they were substantial international companies and I was thinking in terms of $150m. Siemens pulled out at that price level, but Bosch and Sony really had the hots for this transaction.

There are certain events I will never forget from my electronics days. One of them was the time we announced the dual-band phone at the Hanover Fair. Companies like Ericsson, Nokia and Motorola had massive exhibition stands – they'd spent a fortune at the fair, with their staff all dressed up in matching coloured uniforms, but the crowd was flocking to the Dancall stand. It was inundated with people, even from Ericsson and Nokia, all gathered around our dual-band phone display. Not only had we announced it, we had *proved* it worked – we were demonstrating it there and then, showing how the phone automatically flipped between PCN and GSM without any physical switching. It was a revelation.

So often at exhibitions, companies make big announcements about new items which just turn out to be their *intentions* – we call it 'vapourware'. This was not one of those occasions – word got round the show very quickly that we'd actually *done* it.

The fair's daily magazine placed a big article on the front page, highlighting our dual-band phone as one of the major revelations of the show. This encouraged Sony and Bosch even more. The chief executive of Bosch called for a meeting with me on our stand at Hanover. I told him we were going to send out a final tender document and by 24 March 1997, they would have their last opportunity to put their offer in. He asked me to 'cut to the chase', as the Americans (not the Germans) would say, and give him a definitive price, so I told him that, whatever happened, I wasn't selling this company for less than $150m and that was all I was prepared to say.

With both Sony and Bosch on the hook, it was time to play one off against the other. Sony and Bosch were both informed they were in a race, so to speak, and that their tenders had to be in by 24 March, which just happened to be my birthday.

In 1997 it was a special birthday – my fiftieth – and Ann and Nick Hewer had arranged a real slap-up party for me, which would take place on 23 March. Ann tried to keep the party secret from me, but unfortunately it wasn't a surprise because Nick had written to Margaret Thatcher to see if she'd be prepared to come along and her staff had mistakenly replied to my home address. On opening the mail one morning, I stumbled across a letter from Margaret Thatcher wishing me a happy fiftieth birthday and apologising for being unable to attend.

I had a dilemma as to whether or not I should tell Ann that I knew. In the end, I quickly passed her the letter and said, 'I think this is for you – I accidentally opened it. I haven't read it, but I think it's for you.'

Nothing more was said, but she knew the surprise was blown. However, she did manage to keep a couple of other major secrets from me.

The party was held at Nick's gentlemen's club, the Reform Club in Pall Mall, and as it got underway, I could see the extent of all the trouble that Ann and Nick had gone to. There were some surprise guests, including Tony Blair, the leader of the New Labour Party, our friends Jeremy Beadle, Maureen Lipman and Tommy Steele, and even Nick Lightowler from Comet. But the biggest surprise of all was yet to come.

Cooped up in a side room was a bunch of people I had lost touch with. Ann and my daughter Louise had got together all my old friends – Geoff Salt, Steve Pomeroy, Tony Kaye and Malcolm Cross, together with their respective wives. I hadn't seen Geoff, Tony or Steve for nearly thirty years and Malcolm for twenty years. I was dumbstruck. It was an amazing surprise, but still not the biggest of the evening.

At the end of dinner, Michael Aspel turned up, presented me with a big red book and said 'Alan Sugar, this is your life!' Nick had arranged for Michael Aspel to put on a pseudo *This is Your Life* show. Unbeknown to me, a stage was being set downstairs and the guests were invited to leave the dining room and assemble there. People came on the stage to do the famous *This is Your Life* bit and video messages were played from Rupert Murdoch, Jürgen Klinsmann and Bill Gates. Then out on the stage came Gerry Francis, Tommy Steele, Bill Kenwright the impresario and chairman of Everton, and David Dein from the arch-enemy Arsenal. It was an unbelievable surprise. I was feeling a bit embarrassed sitting through all of this. Loads of people were there, including Stanley Kalms and people from work like Bob Watkins. It was a great night.

The next day, my birthday, we flew off to Marbella, where I'd arranged for my boat to be parked at Puerto Banus. We were going to spend a week there over the forthcoming bank holiday. Early in the afternoon, I received a call from Robert Leitao telling me the tenders had arrived at midday. Bosch had offered $150m. Sony had also put in an offer of $150m, but it was a Mickey Mouse offer – they had done some jiggery-pokery, messing with parts of the balance sheet to make the headline figure look good, but effectively it equated to $50m. The massive gap between the two bids made this a dangerous situation.

Obviously I wanted to accept the Bosch offer, but there was still lots more work to do before we got to the contract stage. By now, Sony and Bosch both knew they were fighting against each other. If it leaked out to Bosch that their opponent (and the only other serious player) was offering $100m less than they were, they'd certainly revise their offer.

Shortly after the phone call from Robert, I received a call from Mr Morita. First of all, he congratulated me on my fiftieth birthday – he'd read about it in *The Times* that day – then he asked me whether I'd received his offer. I told him I *had*, but that it only valued the company at $50m. He started to waffle that his offer was for $150m, but when I cut him short, he asked me to give consideration to his offer rather than reject it outright. I simply told him it wasn't good enough and that he'd have to get closer to the $150m, with no caveats. I needed to keep Sony in the loop in case we ended up with a Dutch auction around the $50m mark.

Morita told me he'd flown a team of executives over to England, ready to do the deal and sign contracts. I thanked him, but told him this was academic, as he was way off on price. Nevertheless, he said his team would remain in England until such time as we formally rejected or accepted his offer. I told him again that his people should go back to Japan now, as they were *miles* out and simply wasting my time and his time. Despite that, they stayed.

About an hour later, I received a call from some high-flyer at Bosch, asking me whether their offer was acceptable. I told the guy that there were other people interested in the company and it was now a case of 'first come, first served'. In other words, all the due diligence was over and that anyone ready to sign a contract in the next two days would get the deal. He called me back ten minutes later and said he was prepared to send a team to my lawyers' office to hammer out a contract. I asked Robert Leitao to get Margaret from Herbert Smith and Tony Dean, our finance director, ready for this meeting. I would fly in the next day on a chartered plane to oversee the discussions. I wasn't going to let this thing go wrong.

In the meantime, I was being pestered by one of the Sony chaps, asking me whether we were prepared to go ahead with their offer. Having arranged the meeting with Bosch, I still wanted to keep the balls in the air in case anything went wrong, but I reiterated to Sony that there was no way we would be selling to them.

I took the plane to London the next morning, arriving at Herbert Smith's office around 11 a.m. Bosch had sent a whole team of senior people over and Margaret Mountford had drafted up a comprehensive contract. I'd been up the whole of the previous night on the boat, talking about the terms on the phone with Robert Leitao.

When you get down to the last contractual stage of any deal, there are always a few show-stoppers. These are normally knocked out of the way by further debate amongst the parties. As the hours passed, the Bosch contingent kept looking at their watches, obviously conscious that the Easter bank holiday was coming up and they wanted to shoot off. It was getting dangerous again. There were four or five show-stoppers still unresolved and they were starting to say, 'Well, perhaps we'll go home and we'll resume this next week, after the bank holiday.'

I reminded them that when I'd spoken to their boss a couple of days earlier, I'd told him the contract had to be signed today, otherwise all bets would be off and we would start pursuing negotiations with another party from Japan. Bosch had the hots to buy this company – I could see they had been told to do this deal by the powers above – so when I mentioned the other party, they must have panicked a bit.

This was a bit of a bluff and a gamble, but it softened them up and they agreed to my next idea. I could see this mob of jobsworths were desperate to get home for the holidays, so I suggested they leave behind their trusted lawyer and we would print out the signature page of the contract, which everybody would sign now with the exception of their lawyer. *He* would hold on to this signature page and would not exchange it with us until the four remaining points were resolved to his satisfaction. In this way, they could all piss off home (I didn't say piss off) and we could carry on working with their lawyer.

They couldn't sign the piece of paper quick enough.

We now had one man left from Bosch. Tony Dean, Margaret and I slowly wore him down with a kind of three-way pincer movement. The poor sod had been up twenty-four hours, but to be fair, he was a tough nut and he was doing a good job for his firm – he was adamant on some points and would not back down. Tony Dean locked horns with him and one could see there was not going to be a winner.

I stepped in and had a look at the points at issue. I worked out with Margaret which of them was of the least concern to us, then told her I would come back into the room in a few minutes and kind of play-act, asking why we were still arguing over this point. I would big the guy up and concede the point, letting him think I was overriding my people. I'd learned previously that if you box someone too far into a corner, they go into belligerent mode. In the end, the guy accepted and the deal was done. I had sold Dancall for $150m. The announcement of the sale was to be embargoed until the first business day after the bank holiday, so although I flew back to the boat, I had to keep the matter secret from my guests.

What an amazing coup! In two years we had laid out £16m for Dancall and now (based on the exchange rate at the time) I'd just sold it for £95m!

At 7 a.m. the following Tuesday, 1 April 1997, the deal was announced. Mr Morita of Sony called me to say I had done a magnificent deal – and of course he could now see I hadn't been blagging him when I'd told him he needed to match the $150m. He was surprised I'd been so honest!

After the deal, I hosted a meeting with the Bosch people in Denmark, who unveiled their plans to the Dancall staff. This included the construction of a massive factory in Aalborg which would increase capacity at least five-fold. The staff at Dancall were delighted. I had secured their future. Many of them wished me all the best and thanked me for rescuing the company two years earlier and now securing this wonderful deal for them. They asked me to have some photographs taken with the engineering team to celebrate not only the transaction, but also the breakthrough on the dual-band mobile phone.

*

After the sale of Dancall and the failed acquisition of Amstrad by Psion, I started considering ways of reorganising the company. There were no blockbuster products on the horizon to replicate the successes of the mid-eighties, plus I was preoccupied with fire-fighting at Tottenham. I guess I'd stupidly lost interest in Amstrad and in the back of my mind, I wanted a graceful way out. Employing Rogers had failed, even though I'd genuinely attempted to cooperate, in the hope that perhaps *someone* could run the company professionally and properly. On reflection, it goes to show I really *am* what I am – a bit of a one-trick pony. I'm as good as the product or venture I'm involved with at the time.

Realistically, I must be a bit of a control freak. I was intimately involved with every single item Amstrad sold over the years. I knew where every single nut and bolt was within my company. I often admire others who run giant organisations – the likes of the great Arnold Weinstock and indeed Rupert Murdoch – who have managed to master the art of delegation, allowing other people to run sections of their business. Clearly the Alan Sugar way had its limitations, but in its defence, we must have broken all-time records in reaching the dizzy heights we did in the mid-eighties. Nevertheless, I was effectively a one-man band, albeit with a lot of good workers around me.

I still quite liked the idea of selling off Amstrad and perhaps restarting again in a small way, with a slimmed-down organisation, so I put the process in motion. Having sold Dancall, Amstrad had amassed a cash pile of nearly £200m. With this £200m in the kitty doing nothing, rather than spend it irresponsibly on some harebrained idea and possibly lose it, it might be an idea to distribute it to the shareholders, one of whom was me.

Margaret came up with an idea called a scheme of arrangement. This would result in the shareholders receiving a share in every asset we owned, by way of a reorganisation.

The scheme was very complex, but also very clever. It got me what I wanted. When the company was split up, I would receive a considerable amount of cash plus a shareholding in Betacom. It was my intention to rename Betacom 'Amstrad PLC' and effectively make it the consumer electronics division. Once the whole transaction had gone through, Betacom (now Amstrad PLC) would be my new vehicle going forward.

Mike Ray, one of Amstrad's accountants, was appointed finance director to the board of Viglen, which became a separate public company in its own right. Based on the pro rata scheme, I held a 36 per cent shareholding in it. From my point of view, I was quite happy to allow Bordan Tkachuk and Mike Ray to run Viglen. It was a specialised business supplying schools, education authorities and corporations, which was not the consumer-oriented market I had grown up in.

I pressed the button on this scheme in August 1997. It received no objections whatsoever from the shareholders, as it was a very fair way of divvying up the giant Amstrad organisation.

It kind of gave me a little injection of enthusiasm, to have a much smaller but publicly listed company again, the newly named Amstrad PLC. There was a start-from-scratch feel about it and all the baggage of the larger Amstrad was now behind me. Internally, going forward, we would call the company New Amstrad. My son Simon became sales director and we appointed a financial director, Martin Bland, who turned out to be a bit of a gem, a really serious and good professional.

Bob Watkins had kept in contact, even though he was at Binatone, and once again he told me there wasn't much going on in Hong Kong – Gulu didn't want to invest in the development and production of mobile phones. I offered Bob another opportunity to come back on the basis that he'd give up any idea of being a business guru and stick to what he was best at – getting stuff made at the right price. I said it was a chance for us to start over again, as New Amstrad. He didn't need much convincing and he swiftly resigned. Even though I'd brought him back to deal with engineering and costs, he was awarded the title of managing director of New Amstrad.

We had a small team of around sixty employees left, including quite a few who had been with Old Amstrad for many years. Now, like me, they felt a buzz of enthusiasm at our remit to try to replicate what we'd achieved in the past. It was a new birth.

Old Amstrad was no more. It was now a shell company, left with just a fighting fund to pay the costs of the litigations against Seagate and Western Digital, as well as some other claims we had from the Spanish market. The Old Amstrad shell *did* need to remain in exis-tence in case we received some windfalls from the pending Seagate or Western Digital actions.

It turned out we were right to leave the old shell running. The judge in the Seagate case, having taken over a year to deliberate, awarded Amstrad the equivalent of $150m! This was made up of a refund for every single hard disk drive we'd ever purchased from Seagate, plus damages, plus the interest which had accrued over the past nine years. Seagate immediately announced they were going to appeal, which was a pain in the arse. After all this hard work, we were going to have to face another three or four years of arguing in court to see whether the judgment would be upheld. We'd won, but we hadn't got the money.

Throughout the course of the Seagate action, it was clear, in evidence shown to the court, that Seagate knew they were shipping us crap. As an example, one of their internal memos clearly showed that the stock they were about to ship us had already been rejected by another customer.

Under American law, there are actions which can be brought to claim for punitive damages if you can prove the company in question had damaged you intentionally and not accidentally. It occurred to me that while we'd brought the action against Seagate *in the UK*, one way of encouraging them to release the money was to start making noises about bringing an action against them for punitive damages in the United States. This was a bit of a long shot, as punitive damages had never been awarded to a company. Typically, they would be paid out to members of the public who had suffered illness or injury – for instance, if a pharmaceutical giant sold duff drugs or a car manufacturer knowingly shipped faulty vehicles. These companies would get punished, sometimes by having to pay sums that are ten or twenty times more than the actual damage caused.

I was advised by Herbert Smith and the US lawyers acting on our behalf in the Western Digital case that bringing a punitive damages case against Seagate would be unlikely to succeed. While we could prove they had deliberately sold us faulty stuff, a company can't be hurt in the same way as a person, so while the principle was the same in theory, in practice their opinion at the time was that *companies* would not be awarded punitive damages.

Despite this advice, I decided to instruct a separate set of lawyers in America to make waves, knowing I wasn't going to take it all the way. This was designed to aggravate Seagate and, more importantly, allow us to ensure that the media and the electronics industry in America knew that Amstrad had won their action in the UK and were now going to bring a punitive damages action against Seagate in the USA. We boasted loudly that our claim could result in Seagate having to stump up ten times the amount we'd been awarded by the UK court.

The basis of my claim was that it wasn't me personally – as a 36 per cent shareholder – claiming, but the other 64 per cent of the shareholders who had been disadvantaged. They had invested in Amstrad in good faith and due to no fault of Amstrad's management, but rather by the fraudulent action of Seagate, individuals had lost out in their pension schemes. I cited the old colonel from Devon, who had retired and was relying on his dividends and growth in his shares to see him through his remaining days. David Gold was impressed by my creative idea, saying I'd become a bit of a legal strategist, having picked up lots of tips from him. Bloody cheek! Yeah, brilliant strategies like writing letters to Jonathan Crystal.

This tactic certainly rattled Seagate's cage. By now they understood I wasn't someone to mess with. And we had a $150m judgement against them, a fact they had to declare in their accounts as a public company. I waited to see what they'd do next.

*

In December 1997 we went to our house in Florida, as usual, for Christmas. I'd made it a tradition at Christmas time, with the help of Vic Wakeling of Sky TV, to have some live Spurs games beamed up to an obscure satellite. I arranged for a giant dish at my Florida house, so I could tune into the games, and would invite some of our friends who were also staying in Florida to join us and watch games such as Spurs v Arsenal or Manchester United.

One day, while I was outside de-rigging the satellite dish, a man came up to me and asked whether the house was for sale. You'll recall that my house was somewhat special in the sense that it had two plots, one of which was used for the tennis court. The fellow told me he wanted to be in this location and that if I was interested in selling, he would buy both plots, as he wanted to redevelop the site. The real estate market in Florida had started to rise since I'd bought the house.

By now my kids had grown up and had decided that going on holiday with Mum and Dad was *not* the thing to do any more. Understandably, they wanted to do their own thing. It occurred to me that maybe Ann and I had come to the end of an era, owning a house in Florida. With that in mind, I considered the offer. I said I wasn't really interested in selling the house, but if I *were* to sell it, he'd need to be thinking in terms of $900,000 (I had paid $525,000 for it in 1983). To my amazement, he stuck out his hand and said to me, 'You have a deal.'

I was shocked. There I was, on the brink of selling the house without consulting Ann, who had gone off shopping. I refused to shake the guy's hand there and then and told him that while his offer was interesting, I would need to consult with my wife.

That night at dinner I confessed to Ann that the house I had casually bought several years earlier when I went out to get some plasters from the drug store had almost been sold, this time while *she* was out shopping. She was surprised and a bit angry. 'What? You sold my house?'

But after a bit of a discussion, she agreed that perhaps we *had* got ourselves into a rut, constantly coming to Florida. Perhaps we should spread our wings a bit and choose different holiday destinations, especially bearing in mind that we now owned a boat. So I sold the house to this fellow and during the remainder of our stay in Florida we arranged for a removals company to pack up some of our things and ship them back to England.

However, over the course of the next few months, Ann and I reflected on the many happy years we'd spent in Florida and realised we'd made a mistake. A friend of mine, Harvey Gilbert, was intent on acquiring a home in Florida in a very up-market community known as Royal Palm, in Boca Raton, right next to the famous Boca Raton Hotel and Club. In September 1998, I told Ann to go with Harvey's wife to investigate the possibility of buying a new house at Royal Palm for us too. Then I flew out to see the house she had found, which was halfway through construction and in a great location on the inter-coastal waterways.

The salesperson was a real Rottweiler. She was working on behalf of a developer and put together a proposition for us. Having looked at the house in its part-constructed state, I agreed a deal. However, there were a few twists and turns to come, resulting in her having to bring the boss of the developing firm along to try to close the deal.

I'm not sure whether it's peculiar to Florida, but the people developing houses there are somewhat slippery. I could tell this Rottweiler-style real estate agent had done some research on me – she was mentioning things like Amstrad and Tottenham Hotspur – and had found out that I had plenty of money. She decided to jack up the price by making outrageous suggestions, saying Ann had requested finishes above and beyond the standard finishes offered – all bollocks.

I'd never seen Ann get very angry with anybody, but even *she* realised, having been part of the discussions on speccing out the house, that this woman was lying through her teeth. It was interesting to see Ann getting excited and telling this woman off. Normally she would never get involved in arguing over matters of finance. That might give you a measure of how tricky this woman was.

At the closing meeting in the lawyer's office, the agent produced a list of what she claimed were *extras*, costs we'd never agreed to pay, and I had a flaming row with her. She pathetically attempted to call the deal off by slamming her file closed and standing up, at which point I told her she could stick the house where the sun doesn't shine, an expression Americans don't seem to understand.

'I beg your pardon?'

'Okay, let me put it in simple terms – stick the house up your arse!'

Finally, her lawyer calmed the situation down and we exchanged contracts at the agreed price.

A friend of mine there, Zvi Levine, told me, 'Alan, you have to expect this in Florida. Once people know who you are, they simply put the price up.'

I've had many debates with Zvi over this. He can't understand why I'm so puzzled. I told him, 'In England, if you call a builder or a contractor to paint your house, it doesn't matter whether the house is located in the finest road in London or out in the sticks – the cost of the paint and the hourly rate is pretty much the same.'

'No, it doesn't work that way in Florida. First of all, they look at your house, see where it's positioned, then they pluck a figure from the air to see whether you'll pay it.'

'Well, she certainly picked on the wrong person here.'

There was one more hurdle before the deal was final. I hadn't realised the Royal Palm and Country Club, where this house was situated, was a private organisation. The Royal Palm Association needed to 'approve' me to be an owner on their estate and a rather strange procedure ensued. Ann and I had to be interviewed to see whether we were *acceptable people* to live within the Royal Palm community.

I was given a bunch of forms to fill out prior to the interview. Typical of Americans, who don't recognise that anything outside America exists, I was asked to put forward various references from US citizens who could give a good testimony about me. These references were required to guarantee that I was capable of paying the association's $800 a year charge for communal landscaping! Having just spent $4m on buying the house and paying in cash, this ridiculous request wound me up.

As I have explained before, when trying to buy something or apply for something in America, you run up against their programmed ways of doing things. Despite telling people I'm not American, they still insist on asking for things like social security numbers. Eventually, you learn there's no way of bucking the system – you have to play their game. So on the basis of 'if you can't beat them, join them', Ann and I both took a driving test in Florida, just to get a Florida driving licence and make our lives easier at times like this.

I was stuck as to who to put forward as my referees for the Royal Palm interview, as I didn't feel I knew any Americans well enough. Then I remembered the two famous Americans I *did* know and got into mischievous mode. I would ask Rupert Murdoch and Bill Gates to write me letters for these local hobos. I called Rupert's office and explained this ridiculous situation to his secretary and asked her to tell Rupert this was more of a wind-up than anything else; I did a similar thing with Bill Gates's people. Sure enough, two letters were faxed to me and, together with a reference from Lloyds Bank, I attached them to the application form.

Ann and I turned up at the interview and presented all these documents. One fellow took a look at the letters from Bill Gates and Rupert Murdoch and passed them to the other three committee members, who coolly tried to play it down. They got my point after I explained to them that I was English and their form wasn't applicable to foreign nationals wishing to live at Royal Palm. I suggested that perhaps they should learn to recognise that there is another place outside the United States, called England, and while they may consider it one of their colonies, people *do* live there and many of them are capable of paying $800 a year. It was quite a funny episode, but we obtained our approval.

*

The Western Digital case was now approaching. Once again, I needed to appear as a witness because of my heavy involvement in the running of Amstrad. The hearing was in Orange County, California, so of course I had to fly to Los Angeles. On the first day, we went into the judge's chambers to have a meeting. The courtroom (an overflow from the main courtroom in Orange County) was an old converted furniture store and the judge's chambers looked like something out of Steptoe and Son's living room – full of old junk. The six or so people attending this meeting included executives from Western Digital and the judge had to shuffle around to find us chairs to sit on. It was so casual, you'd never have believed we were there to discuss a multi-million-dollar lawsuit.

The judge opened his drawer and took out a penknife, then out of a polythene bag he produced an apple. He started peeling the apple with his penknife while telling us all about his personal history, how he'd started as a young lad working in a building yard where they made bricks. As he didn't know any better, he was picking up the bricks with his bare hands and by the end of his first day, his hands were cut to pieces. His boss told him, 'That's the first lesson you learn, young man – you need to wear gloves in future.' I couldn't believe what I was listening to. This lunatic was telling us his life story and we had to sit there quietly and diligently because, after all, he *was* the judge.

When he finally got round to talking about the case, he spent a few minutes asking whether we could settle this matter before it went to trial. It was only then that I realised that no trial was going take place that week – this was merely an unofficial settlement meeting. I went berserk with my lawyers, asking why they'd schlapped me all the way from London – on a ten-hour flight – to sit here listening to this idiot. They could have quite simply told the judge, on my behalf, that any settlement discussions attempted in the past had been negative and we wanted to go to trial. I was very angry with them. I had to return to London and await the new date for the trial.

The Seagate trial in the UK was heard in front of a technical judge. In America, however, we had to plead our case in front of a jury of laymen. I suddenly realised how difficult it was going to be to get our story over and rely on twelve ordinary people to get their heads around the very detailed technical matters. I flew over to LA and spent two days giving evidence in this court case.

Just to give you a perspective of some of the evidence we put forward, there was a particularly damning document which was disclosed by Western Digital, the gist of which was along the lines of, 'The Amstrad engineers have been on the phone again. They have changed all the controllers over to our ones and *obviously* the drives still don't work. The shit is going to hit the fan soon, once they find out we've sent them the rejected drives returned from Tandy Corporation, the ones with the formatting fault on them. I've avoided answering them for the past two weeks and have used the earthquake as an excuse. Please advise what our next move should be.'

Now, anyone with half a brain would say that disclosing *that* document was game, set and match to us. It categorically proved that Western Digital *knew* the drives they'd sold us were crap. Common sense should tell you that at that point, our lawyers should have stood up and said, 'Right, that's it, case over. Can the jury now please focus on the damage Western Digital has caused Amstrad?'

But no. The case continued for another two weeks. Then the lawyer acting for Western Digital stood up and made his final speech, which was basically this: 'You have heard from this guy, Alan Sugar. He is a multi-millionaire from England, worth in the region of a billion dollars. Western Digital is a local company from Orange County, on hard times, employing fifteen hundred of your fellow townsfolk. Do you think it is right that Alan Sugar should get any money from this company?'

This final summation was outrageous. It wasn't *Alan Sugar* bringing an action, it was Amstrad the corporation bringing an action on behalf of its shareholders. It was no different than, for example, if Microsoft were to take someone to court for copying their software and the defence argued that the offender should be let off because Bill Gates is a multi-billionaire. However, that was the summation this guy made.

I wasn't at the trial when it finished and the jury was sent away. If I had been, I would have gone bananas. When I read the transcript of what went on, I asked my lawyers why they didn't stand up and object to this rubbish and focus the jury on the memo and remind them what the case was about. They were bloody useless. The guy defending Western Digital was in a different class – he avoided all the technical stuff and brushed it under the carpet.

Initially, the jury came back hung, which was bad news. They were sent away again by the judge to make a final decision, which was: Western Digital had no case to answer.

All the weeks of pleading with the jury and showing them details of how Western Digital had shipped us junk, and all the technical explanations from the engineers we'd flown over from England were a total waste of time. At the end of the day the record book will show that Western Digital won the case. So maybe they would argue this means there was nothing wrong with their drives. However, the record and transcripts of the case will also show we disclosed papers that any reasonable person would interpret as showing that some Western employees believed we were sold duff drives. Anyway, it seems this is what's called a home victory decided by a jury of local townsfolk whose decision was based not on technical facts, but on good old-fashioned loyalty. The twelve jurors were sympathetic towards the then ailing Western Digital company and were worried about the employees being out of work. That's the American judicial system for you. You can understand why someone like O. J. Simpson got off scot-free.

The whole thing was unbelievable! I complained to David Gold in

England about the decision to go down the American route in the first place, but it was too late now – it was over and done with. Our only consolation was that in America we were not liable to pay Western Digital's legal costs. In the UK, had we lost the Seagate case, we *would* have been responsible for paying all their costs.

On the brighter side, at least my tactic of worrying Seagate with a punitive damages action was working. Seagate's internal senior legal counsel finally contacted my office and asked me to call him. When we spoke, he started to jockey for position with a load of legal crap. He was telling me our claim for punitive damages was ridiculous and not applicable, and that they would strenuously defend it. All the usual fighting talk you'd expect.

I just listened and waited until he finished, then calmly told him we certainly *were* going to pursue it. Here's a little tip I've learned when it comes to negotiation: the art of silence. Imagine the exchange of words I've just described. After I said we were going to pursue it, I just went silent. A silence like this can feel like ages when, in fact, it's just a few seconds and it forces the other person to continue the conversation. This always works.

Normally, the other person will say, 'Hello, hello, are you still there?'

All you need to do is say, 'Yes, I'm still here.'

In the end, he stopped waffling and asked if there was any way we could settle this matter rather than get involved in more court action.

All *I* wanted was the money released. I told him I'd noticed in Seagate's annual accounts – made public in keeping with American Stock Exchange rules – that they had declared a provision of $160m for the Amstrad litigation issue. I pointed out that this was $10m more than the amount in escrow and I put it to him that the $10m was to deal with further legal costs coming from arguing the appeal and the punitive damages case. He didn't comment.

I then told him I had a great idea – if he would agree to pay the $150m and drop the appeal, and we dropped our punitive damages action, then he would be able to release the $10m they had set aside back into their accounts, thus boosting their next financial year's profits. He went silent and told me he'd get back to me. Seagate was suffering a downturn in their business and I had clearly touched a nerve. The guy called me back a few hours later, agreeing to my idea.

We had won and the cash was released.

*

Despite the fact that Claude Littner and Daniel were doing a very good job on the day-to-day running of Tottenham Hotspur, the club still rested on my shoulders with regard to providing finances for the manager to put together a team.

After beating up the FA and getting Spurs back into the FA Cup, we went on a great run. In fact, we did so well that we got to the semi-finals, against Everton, which was to be played at Leeds United's Elland Road ground. I flew up to Leeds in a private plane with Simon and some of the directors. Funnily enough, the minibus taking us from the airport to Elland Road had 'Kelly's Minibus Hire' painted on the side! Considering that Graham Kelly was the person who'd given us so much aggravation, I thought that if we ended up winning today, a photo of us being taken to the ground in this minibus would go down a treat with the media. Someone there had a camera and took a picture of us standing with Kelly's minibus.

Gerry Francis had not been able to train with the players all week, as his son was in hospital and Gerry had spent a lot of time with him, but he managed to come to the semi-final, as his son had started to recover.

At Elland Road, they'd built a new section to their stadium, a massive East stand which held about the same amount of people as the other three sides. The FA had allocated this stand to Tottenham fans. From an acoustics point of view, since the other three sides were full of Everton fans, it sounded as if Everton were at home and we were plonked in an away stand. It all seemed a bit unfair.

Darren Anderton, labelled 'Sicknote' by the fans because he was hardly ever available to play for us, was still complaining that there was something wrong with him. He was finally persuaded to go out and play – with a big bandage around his knee!

We lost the game, but the 4–1 score didn't tell the true story. We were 2–1 down with ten minutes to go, but in trying to press for an equaliser, we left ourselves open at the back and Everton scored twice.

The private plane flew us back to Heathrow, where Simon and I caught the Concorde to New York to connect down to Florida to join Ann. As Simon reminds me, I never spoke a word to him for the entire flight. Our dream of winning the trophy that year was over and I was gutted with the result. We'd gone through so much to get back in the Cup, only to be scuppered by a series of disasters, such as Gerry not being available to train the team all week, the unfair stand allocation at Elland Road and a few stupid mistakes on the pitch.

Despite finishing seventh in the league that year – clearly nowhere near the relegation zone – Popescu decided he no longer wanted to play for Tottenham. At the last game of the season, he told all the players he was leaving and simply walked out!

Popescu had turned into a great player. A lot of people were writing about him in the media and Gerry really admired his defensive skills. Behind the scenes, however, his agent had set up a deal for him to join Barcelona. What Popescu had forgotten when he arrogantly walked out was that he would not be able to play for *anybody*, as he was contracted to Tottenham. Eventually, I was contacted by the chief executive officer of Barcelona, asking me to negotiate a transfer for Popescu. It was clear the player was not going to stay with us, so I accepted a fee of £4m, which was some kind of consolation, as we'd only paid £2.7m for him at the start of the season.

Klinsmann was also making noises about wanting to leave, invoking the clause in his contract that stated he could leave at the end of the first season. I reminded him and his agent, Andy Gross, that the clause was meant as a get-out if we got relegated. Regrettably, in the euphoria of signing him and having taken Klinsmann and Gross at their word, I didn't articulate the point about relegation in the contract. Nevertheless, I was angry with Klinsmann and Gross and said they were reneging on a gentlemen's agreement. Gross kept referring to the strict letter of the contract; he said they were *not* reneging and that Klinsmann was entitled to go. His year at Tottenham had been a great advertisement for him, as he'd played brilliantly and was loved by all the fans. Now he had re-established himself as a top-class striker, he was head-hunted by Bayern Munich's Franz Beckenbauer.

Reluctantly, I had to let him go and Bayern paid us the agreed contractual compensation.

There are some stupid things I did in my football days – maybe it was something to do with my short temper. When Klinsmann left, I made lots of complaints to the FA about the approaches made by Bayern Munich and what the clause in his contract *implied*, but it all fell on deaf ears.

Klinsmann told the media he had enjoyed his year at Tottenham and that he wanted to personally thank the chairman, Alan Sugar, for letting him go to Bayern Munich and that he would give me a signed shirt. The BBC wanted to interview me about this incident because they knew I was very angry. The interviewer came to my office in Brentwood and brought up the Klinsmann departure, telling me he thought it was a nice touch that Klinsmann had given me a signed shirt. I don't know to this day whether he was deliberately winding me up but, on camera, I got up, grabbed the shirt (which was in my office), screwed it up and threw it at him, saying he could go and clean his car with it as far as I was concerned. Not one of the moments I'm proud of.

That incident, of course, was manna from heaven for the media. Next day, the *Sun* ran a double-page spread and a little competition offering the Klinsmann shirt I'd chucked at the BBC reporter as the prize. I guess my over-reaction was a result of real frustration, as Klinsmann was not only a good player, but was expert at manipulating the media. Daniel and I experienced how he would turn on the charm when a camera was there, but off-camera he could be more difficult. I felt that the charm he could turn on at the flick of a switch made him seem a little sly, and in fact on one of our trips on the boat, Daniel and I jokingly made up some new lyrics to the famous *Dad's Army* song.

> *Who do you think you are kidding, Mr Klinsmann,*
> *When you smile upon our screens?*
> *Fans think you're great and you're such a lovely guy,*
> *But, off the camera, you're really a bit sly.*
> *So who do you think you are kidding, Mr Klinsmann,*
> *When you smile upon our screens?*

We now needed to recruit some more players and, to add insult to injury, Nick Barmby, who had signed a new contract with us earlier in the season, also declared he wanted to go to Middlesbrough. Things were crumbling around Gerry – he'd lost Klinsmann and Popescu, Sicknote was never available to play and now Barmby wanted to leave. Gerry didn't want to let him go, but the player wanted away. I put a £6m price tag on him, which in those days was a record fee. Bryan Robson, Middlesbrough's manager, protested that this was outrageous and I was standing in the player's way, stopping him from progressing in his career.

I told him I didn't give a shit about the player's career because Barmby didn't give a shit about us. The player had signed a deal with us no more than a year earlier and now wanted to leave. I told Robson that if he wanted the player, then that was the price.

After a lot of argy-bargy, I ended up doing the deal for £6m with Steve Gibson, the chairman of Middlesbrough and a very nice fellow. Barmby's transfer made the headlines in the next day's newspapers because of the record fee. It was particularly noteworthy because Tottenham had only paid something like £100,000 to Hull when we bought him as a youth player, a fact that got a lot of admiration from my fellow Premier League chairmen, but obviously didn't go down well with the fans.

Gerry had identified a young striker at Crystal Palace he liked the look of – Chris Armstrong. David Hyams, the corporate lawyer at Amstrad, was a mad Palace fan and we were always ribbing each other over our respective clubs. It so happened that Chris Armstrong and his agent came to negotiate a contract with me at Amstrad's Brentwood headquarters. Having signed him for Tottenham, I called David Hyams in his second-floor office and asked him to come up to the tenth floor, as I had some serious news for him that would affect him personally.

He must have wondered what I was going on about. You can imagine his face when he came into my office and saw his hero, Chris Armstrong, sitting there. I said to David, 'This chap has just signed for Spurs and I thought you'd be delighted to be the first to hear it.'

He was as sick as a parrot. 'Thank you very much, Alan, very funny. Very, very funny.' He turned around and walked out of the room.

My actions the previous season to shore up the team with the acquisitions of Klinsmann, Popescu and Dumitrescu had been rather a bold move for a British club. While there were *some* foreign players in the UK before this point, the arrival of this trio started an influx. So much so that when Klinsmann and Popescu left, I was contacted by loads of foreign agents to see if we were interested in replacements. I didn't know half of the players being offered to me. I'd just tell Gerry that so-and-so had been on the phone and offered me a Carlos Kickaball mark-2.

I got a call from a fellow who said he represented Dennis Bergkamp, who apparently was a Tottenham fan and had all the old Spurs players plastered on his bedroom wall when he was a kid. I've lost count of the number times an agent has spun this line to me!

Gerry hadn't really caught on that I wasn't your typical club chairman. They say every football fan is a manager – well, some *chairmen* are glorified fans with power who want to be involved in player selection. Old-fashioned managers like Gerry saw this as the most heinous of crimes, and I agree. However, Gerry misinterpreted my frequent reports about the calls I was getting as me interfering and *insisting* we buy this player or that player. So when I told him someone had called me about Dennis Bergkamp, he exploded. 'Look, I am the fucking manager, right? And I pick the fucking players, *not* you.'

'What are you going on about, Gerry?'

'I pick the players, right? I'm not interested in all these players you keep coming up with. It's *my* job to decide on players.'

'Yes, I know that. I'm not saying we should buy them, I just tell you when people have been on the phone. I am just passing information on to you to see if you are interested or not – that's normal, right? What's wrong with that? Do you want me to ignore these calls? I haven't got a fucking clue who Dennis Bergkamp is – he could be Denis Thatcher as far as I'm concerned.' I don't think Gerry had been spoken to this way by past chairmen. He could see I was angry.

'Oh, okay then, when you put it that way, I suppose you're right. Anyway, Bergkamp is not a striker; he's more of a midfield player.'

'Fine, well, we'll leave it at that then. I'm just passing on the information – you do what you want with it. If you want to pursue any of the leads I give you, it's completely up to you.'

When it comes to managers, *no one*, let alone the chairman, should suggest players to them. It's what I call the 'not invented here' syndrome. I've seen this many a time in business, when the person in charge belligerently rejects ideas they see as an encroachment on their seniority. If I told a manager I could get hold of Zidane, Kaka and Ronaldo for a hundred grand each, I'd see the suggestion rejected with a weak excuse. I learned quickly, both in football and in business, that the art of overcoming this is to put things in such a way that it looks like the idea has come from the person who's supposed to be in charge. On the rare occasions I was contacted by an agent about a player who I felt was a good buy, I adopted this tactic, telling the agent, 'Call the manager directly and don't mention that you've spoken to me.' If it *did* go somewhere, then when the manager informed me, I would feign surprise and say, 'That's a good idea.'

*

In the 1995–6 season, Chris Armstrong had a moderate impact, but regrettably he suffered a bad ankle injury which kept him out for quite a long time. Gerry's team performed reasonably and we finished mid-table, as we did the following season.

At the end of the 1996–7 season, we lost the last game to Coventry at home. Gerry Francis told me after the match that Teddy Sheringham wanted to have a discussion with us both. We all met in Claude Littner's office after the game. Sheringham, who still had two years to run on his old contract, demanded I tell him which players we were going to bring in next season, so he could decide whether or not he wished to remain at the club – this despite the fact that he was in contract and *couldn't* walk out! His attitude wound me up. I told him it was none of his business, save to say there was a budget for players and the manager would decide which ones *he* wanted to buy. *I* was certainly not prepared to discuss target players with him.

Sheringham said, 'That's not good enough.'

I lost my temper with him and told him, 'If that's not good enough, you can go. Clear off – get yourself a contract somewhere else.' I walked out.

When I got home that evening, Gerry called me and said, 'Teddy doesn't really want to go; it's just his immature manner. He thought that was the way he needed to talk to you. He just put himself over badly. He's a good lad really – he doesn't even use an agent.'

I told him that Sheringham had been hostile to me since I'd sacked Venables and, unlike the other players, I'd never had any dialogue with him. He had distanced himself from me. I continued, 'Gerry, the manner in which he has spoken to me, the chairman and owner, is disgraceful. If he wants to stay at this club, he should call first to apologise, then to see if we can discuss a contract. I certainly won't be calling him.'

Gerry should never have allowed this situation to arise – he should have dealt with the player via the club secretary, not put me in a position where a player was arrogantly demanding things from me. It would be a dangerous situation indeed if I were ever to be dictated to by a player.

Sheringham called me at my office. He didn't apologise, he just announced himself. I said, 'I don't want to mess about. Let's cut straight to the point and get this contract over and done with quickly.'

In short, Sheringham wanted £1m a year and a five-year contract. Gerry told me to sign him for three years only because of his age (he was thirty-one at the time). Statistically, based on other players of his age, it was unlikely he'd be good enough in three years' time to perform at the highest level, so Gerry's decision was a reasonable one to make at the time.

Sheringham, however, was adamant he was not signing unless he had a five-year deal. Again, he stated this in a very arrogant manner. Looking back, I think he was trying to be some sort of tough guy, imagining that's the way you deal in business. I think he'd picked up his negotiating skills watching Del Boy on TV. It went down like a lead balloon.

I told him it was impossible for us to sign him for five years and suggested that he take my word for it that if after three years he was still playing well, we would certainly extend his contract.

He refused, but I told him to go away and think about it and call me back later. His attitude was disgusting in that he was dogmatic in his insistence on five years, and made it clear it was non-negotiable. He eventually called me back to say he'd decided he wasn't going to sign for us because we wouldn't give him the contract he wanted. I told him maybe we could agree to four years, but he insisted on five years and told me to take it or leave it. I had to say I'd leave it. I finished by telling him that if he sent me a letter requesting a transfer, I would let him go.

Sheringham went off to join the England squad under the management of Glenn Hoddle and during the close season I sold him to Manchester United for the same amount of money we'd paid Nottingham Forest several years earlier.

The irony was that Sheringham went on to play for a good few years afterwards, both for Manchester United and England. He kept himself very fit and had we given him the five-year contract, he could have played for Tottenham right through. But, as I've said, I was guided by Gerry Francis, who quite rightly assumed that three years was prudent at the time, given Sheringham's age.

I had never met Glenn Hoddle or spoken to him personally, but as a so-called 'loyal Tottenham man through and through', his comments to the media about Sheringham's departure were not helpful. He gave an interview saying that this was a bad time to disrupt poor Teddy with uncertainty over his club future. He said he needed him fully focused, with a clear head, to do a good job for England. On top of this, Hoddle was waffling on about his concerns over Darren Anderton being fit to play for England.

It got to the stage where I made contact with Hoddle at the FA to ask why he was poking his nose into our club's affairs. We had struggled to get Anderton fit after his numerous injuries, as of course it was in our interest to do, and I was wound up by Hoddle's public comments. Effectively, he was suggesting that we didn't know what we were doing.

When I spoke to him, it was clear that he had a dialogue going with Anderton. Hoddle told me that Spurs' training and physio regime was treating Anderton incorrectly. He'd heard that at our traditional pre-season training session, Gerry had taken the players for a run through

Epping Forest to get them psyched up. Hoddle commented, 'This is all *wrong*, Alan – you made Darren run up hills over rough ground.' I couldn't believe what I was hearing.

'What?! What did you say? Oh dear, the poor diddums professional footballer was being asked to run! Are you bleedin' joking, Glenn, or what? Are you taking the piss?'

'No, Alan, I'm not. I've spoken to Darren and he wants to see Eileen Drewery. She's done wonders for other players and I hope you don't object.'

I didn't have a clue who Eileen Drewery was. My immediate assumption was that she was some doctor or expert in sports injuries. I also didn't know that Anderton was seeing her already, in his own time.

I met with Gerry and our club physio Tony and told them about my conversation with Hoddle. I asked Tony about this woman and expected to hear about the special medical techniques she employed. Imagine my shock to hear she was simply a *faith healer* who asked the player to lie on a bed while she hovered her hands over the offending injury.

'So that's it?' I exclaimed. 'Anderton lies on a bed while Eileen waves her hands over him, telling him to have "positive thoughts"? I don't believe it – he's lying there thinking of England while schmock-me is paying him twenty grand a week! Are you fucking joking or what?'

It was amazing how Anderton always seemed to manage to turn up and play for England, but when he returned to Tottenham he claimed his injury had come back again. I could not understand how Gerry was able to stand by and let this go on, but it seems you can't argue with someone who says they have pain.

It seemed to me that some players just did what they wanted, when it suited them.

*

During the close season, I bought Les Ferdinand, a player Gerry wanted, having known him from his QPR days. I also bought David Ginola, who turned out to be one of the greatest players ever to perform at White Hart Lane. Once again, I was on my boat when we did the deal. Ginola called me and asked where I was located in the South of France. In his typical, flamboyant style, he got a friend of his to hire a very fast speed boat – a Cigarette – and came all the way from St Tropez to Monaco to meet me at the harbour at Villefrance. His agent met up with us on the boat and we discussed the terms of the contract and agreed to sign him there and then. Ginola was a revelation for Spurs – I would say he had more impact on the team than Klinsmann did. He really gave the fans a great lift.

One funny incident that occurred during Gerry's reign was an attempt to buy the player Emmanuel Petit to shore up our midfield. Gerry had been following the progress of Petit when he played for Monaco and decided he was a target for the club, so Claude and Daniel agreed to meet with Petit and Gerry at White Hart Lane to discuss the virtues of him joining Tottenham. Gerry and Daniel spoke about the usual sort of things: what players we had, where Petit would fit in and where we were going as a club. Claude, however, wanted to assure him that home life in England would be great and asked what Petit's girl-friend's interests were. Petit said she was 'a dancer'. What sticks in my mind was the report back from Daniel who told me that Claude, who was bending over backwards to try to make Petit feel comfortable, said we could arrange dancing lessons for his girlfriend. Apparently, Gerry gave Claude a strange look – I wonder why!

There was a twist to this story. Petit thanked us very much indeed for our discussions and said he would make a decision within the next day. He asked if we'd kindly call a taxi for him. We imagined that he was going back to his hotel, but it turned out that the taxi we'd arranged and paid for took him straight to the home of Arsenal chairman David Dein. There he met Arsène Wenger, and the rest is history. Emmanuel Petit signed for Arsenal and turned out to be a great player.

Piers Morgan, one-time editor of the *Daily Mirror* and mad Arsenal fan, thought this was hilarious. He must have told the story at least 10,000 times and has the habit, after becoming inebriated, of repeating it six or seven times on the trot. So much so that even Arsenal fans tell him to shut up.

The 1996–7 season didn't go very well for Gerry. At one stage, around late September 1997, he came to me saying he'd reached the end of the road and couldn't do much more for the team. He felt he'd lost the support of the dressing room. He said that despite the investments I'd made and the support I'd given him to try to build a squad, it was clear it just wasn't happening on the pitch. He wanted to throw in the towel and resign.

I asked him to stay and go back to doing what he was good at – motivating the players and getting them back on track. I still had confidence in him. Also, it would be hard for me to find a replacement mid-season. Gerry agreed to stay on, but a month later one could see we were going nowhere. He came to me again, asking me to accept his resignation.

I have to say that, as far as managers go, Gerry was a gentleman. Normally, managers are signed up on big contracts and despite the fact that poor performances on the pitch are usually down to them, they sit it out until they're sacked, in order to claim substantial compensation. In Gerry's case, there was never a suggestion that he wanted any money for leaving. In fact, I remember him telling me he was grateful for the support I'd tried to give him – in particular for purchasing players such as Ferdinand, Ginola and others. He said he couldn't have asked for any more support from his chairman. Regretfully, I had to let him go.

I asked David Pleat to consider the position of director of football and he agreed and joined the board. He also held the fort with the team while we tried to recruit a new manager.

Unfortunately David wasn't very forceful when it came to getting his point over at the right time. Unlike me, he had a tremendous wealth of knowledge about football and I wish that in his position as director of football at Tottenham – with this idiot Alan Sugar not knowing what to do about managers – he'd been more assertive in telling me what to do, as well as talking me out of other people's ideas, usually agents trying to line their pockets.

During our search for a manager, a lot of names were thrown at me. Even David Dein, who was quite friendly with me socially, told me at one Premier League meeting that he knew he shouldn't be helping

Tottenham out, but was aware we were in a dire situation. He was sympathetic about all this stick I was getting when a lot of Tottenham's problems had nothing to do with me and he told me that Bobby Robson was free to leave his job in Spain. Andy Gross, Klinsmann's agent, suggested Leo Beenhakker and another guy by the name of Christian Gross, who was doing a fantastic job in the Swiss league at the club Grasshoppers.

The media was having fun rubbing it in. They implied that the team was going nowhere and that the culture of the club came from its chairman, Alan Sugar, who had no ambition whatsoever and was only interested in money.

Daniel and I flew to Zurich to meet Christian Gross and we ended up agreeing to sign him, along with fitness coach Fritz Schmidt, who was an integral part of Gross's training plans. We explained to Christian Gross and Andy Gross, who was also Christian's agent, that we would hold a press conference at White Hart Lane and we gave Christian specific instructions to turn up at a certain time at this hotel in Waltham Abbey, whereupon Daniel would escort him to the ground in an orderly fashion.

Unfortunately, the press had already made up their minds about Christian Gross, as the appointment had been leaked to the media beforehand. The tone had been set by ex-Tottenham player turned football pundit Alan Mullery, who at the time was dragged out by the media whenever a comment was needed about the affairs of Tottenham Hotspur. They had obviously caught him very early in the morning when they asked if he had any comment on Spurs' new managerial appointment, Christian Gross.

'Christian who?' was Mullery's answer. Cannon-fodder for the media.

'CHRISTIAN WHO?' was the headline the next day. The great Spurs expert Alan Mullery had spoken.

Regrettably, this 'Christian who?' thing seemed to permeate down to the players, some of whom were not blessed with too many brain cells and tended to follow the lead of the sports journalists in the tabloids. In simple terms, players have admiration for a manager if they know what he's achieved. However, if a manager comes in whom they have no knowledge of, irrespective of what his achievements might be, then as far as they're concerned, he's no good. The day Gross turned up at White Hart Lane, some of the Tottenham players simply disregarded him, thinking he was a waste of space. To be fair to the sensible and intelligent players, they *did* give him an opportunity.

The press conference was a total farce. We were all assembled and I was waiting for Daniel to tell me where Christian Gross and Andy Gross were. Daniel phoned to say he was still waiting for them at the hotel in Waltham Abbey, but there was no sign of them. A minute later, the receptionist at White Hart Lane called me to tell me that a Mr Christian Gross and another chap had arrived. I was very confused. We rushed him up to an anteroom next door to where the press were gathered and I asked what the hell he was doing. Why hadn't he gone to the hotel as we'd agreed? I couldn't quite grasp the answer he babbled to me. The person he'd brought with him – some sort of PR guru – said there had been a misunderstanding.

Finally, we entered the press conference and Gross took his seat next to me. I introduced him and advised the room that Schmidt would be his number two and that David Pleat would be director of football. The floor was then open for questions.

The first question to Gross came from a journalist, along the lines of, 'What do you think of the current squad at Tottenham? Will you be adding any more players and if so, who will be your targets?'

Gross totally ignored the question and from his top pocket pulled out a tube ticket and declared, 'This is my Underground ticket. I came like the normal people come to the football club. I travelled like the normal people on the Underground. *That* is how I came to Tottenham.'

We were flabbergasted at his opening statement. This little speech was the brainchild of his PR guru and it had taken us all by surprise. The press managed to get pictures of me looking at Gross with a stunned face. What with Mullery's 'Christian who?' comment and this pathetic PR attempt, I knew from that moment that Gross was dead meat.

Christian was a very nice fellow. He tried to implement professional ways at the club, but basically some of the players were taking the piss out of him. They didn't perform on the pitch and his first home game ended in a horrific defeat to Chelsea. If I didn't know better, I'd say it was as if some of the players wanted him to fail.

He lasted about nine months. It really was an untenable situation and eventually I had to let him go. David Pleat again took over the managerial reins temporarily and did quite a good job while we searched for a permanent manager.

During my time at Spurs, I had started off with Terry Venables, then employed Ossie Ardiles, Gerry Francis and now Christian Gross. We had spent an enormous amount of the club's money trying to accommodate all these managers' requests and still we were getting nowhere. *And* I was getting a load of stick from the fans, mostly fuelled by the media.

George Graham, God's *other* gift to football, who'd successfully managed Arsenal for many years and won a lot of trophies, was a name that kept coming up for the position. I realised that appointing him might be seen as a smack in the face for Spurs fans, but I really *must* have been losing my marbles by then, because I considered it!

17

'Sugar Out!'

Arise, Sir Alan – The Nightmare Is Over

1998–2001

It was a sign of how desperate I was to bring success to Tottenham that I signed George Graham at the end of September 1998. Why did I do it? Well, Tony Berry and Martin Peters, an ex-Spurs player and board member, had insisted he was the *only one* with the credentials to do the job. David Pleat had kind of whispered the idea of Martin O'Neill, but he hadn't put his point across strongly enough. In hindsight, O'Neill was someone we should have pursued most vigorously.

Graham was manager of Leeds United at the time, though he still had a house in north London. From what I'd heard, he was interested in working down here, as travelling up to Leeds each day for training was not really his cup of tea.

David Pleat and Berry warned me that if I *did* appoint George Graham, it would open a can of worms. Not only would I get a load of stick from the media, simply because Graham was considered the arch-enemy, but also he'd been involved in an alleged bribe scandal when he was Arsenal manager – in cahoots with the agent Rune Hauge – and was eventually dismissed by Arsenal and fined by the FA. I took that onboard, but at the same time, everybody was singing his praises as being in the same league as Sir Alex Ferguson and Arsène Wenger.

My line was, if he's a true professional, given the players and the backing we have at this club, theoretically he should be able to bring us success and trophies. I also cited the fact that in business the CEO of an arch-competitor is often head-hunted. Giving the job to George Graham was no different to me head-hunting a bloke from IBM to run my computer business. And while the fans *were* divided initially and some saw him as the arch-enemy, the rest respected him as a good coach and accepted him on the basis that he would do for Spurs what he did for Arsenal.

During his stint at the club, under my chairmanship, Graham spent a hell of a lot of money on players, but didn't actually do much on the pitch, though we did win the Worthington Cup, thanks to an Allan Nielsen header against Leicester at Wembley.

Graham's contract was geared towards personal achievement – he would get bonuses if, for example, we ended up fifth in the league or did well in one of the cups. A big bonus would be payable if he won the Premier League but, according to Graham, that was a pipe dream with the team he had.

The day after we won the Worthington Cup, he phoned the finance director of the club, demanding his bonus payment. The finance director then called me, nervously asking what he should do. Under normal circumstances, bonuses like this would be paid out at the end of the season, in a couple of months' time.

Everyone was kind of frightened to talk to Graham. He was an unapproachable person who had a certain air of authority about him. No one was prepared to question him or say anything that might go against his principles.

I called Graham and asked what he thought he was doing phoning up the finance director and intimidating him the day after we'd won the cup. I told him he was being ridiculous and that it was an insult to me and the club to be asking for his money straightaway. I said it was clear in his contract that all payments would be made at the end of the season. It was then that I realised Graham actually had no bottle. This must have been the first time someone had raised their voice and stood up to him.

'No, no, Mr Chairman,' he said hastily. 'You've got it wrong, you've got it all wrong. I was just phoning John to ask him what the bonus figure will be. Of course I know it's not payable till the end of the season. You've misunderstood what's gone on – I don't think John explained it to you properly. I'm sorry if you feel this way, but I was just *enquiring* about the amount. I only wanted to check what was coming.'

For the first time, I saw that if you questioned Graham and put pressure on him, he wasn't the tough guy he made himself out to be. I tried my best to maintain a professional relationship with Graham and bit my tongue for a long while. Certainly, he wasn't the type of person I would socialise with. He was there to do a job and that was it. He, like Venables, had a load of arse-lickers in the media. As far as they were concerned, Graham could do no wrong. So much so that the media had had the audacity to make Arsenal vice-chairman David Dein the villain when the board had no choice but to dismiss Graham for taking dodgy payments which effectively came out of the Arsenal bank account! *How dare David Dein dismiss him for turning Arsenal over?* This is the type of problem you have with the football media – they pervert the minds of the fans.

It wasn't just affairs at the club that caused me aggravation as Spurs' chairman – the Premier League could be a real drain on my time. Earlier that year, Rick Parry had advised the Premier League that he wished to step down to take up a lucrative job as CEO of Liverpool FC. Barrister Peter Leaver would be appointed CEO of the Premier League, as Rick's replacement. He seconded the services of Sam Chisholm, who'd left BSkyB as a consultant, to advise on the next round of TV negotiations. Together with one of his old colleagues from BSkyB, David Chance, Sam met with Peter Leaver and the then chairman of the Premier League, Sir John Quinton, to discuss the appointment.

The next thing I knew, around March 1998, I was called by David Dein of Arsenal, who was ranting and raving that Leaver and Quinton had done a crazy deal with Chisholm and Chance in relation to the financial arrangements which had been agreed. He couldn't tell me what he had learned, as this would be a breach of confidentiality – apparently, Leaver had insisted that each club chairman had to sign a confidentiality agreement before they could see the terms of the contract with Chisholm and Chance.

Dein informed me that an emergency meeting had been called for all the club chairmen to discuss the contract and I should get down there immediately. When I arrived at the Premier League's HQ, I was greeted by a secretary, who invited me to sign a confidentiality agreement before she handed over the Chisholm and Chance contract. I waited with bated breath, expecting to get a half-inch thick document. Instead, she shoved a single sheet of paper across the desk.

'What's this?' I asked.

'That's *it*,' she replied.

'This is it? This is the contract – a single sheet of paper?'

I could not believe my eyes when I read it. I'd expected to see that a sensible deal had been done with Sam – maybe £200,000 plus some reasonable bonus as and when he pulled off the next deal. Instead, I saw that Chisholm and Chance had the potential of earning up to £50m each for the right deal! No wonder David Dein was ranting; this was outrageous.

Needless to say, the meeting was really heated, with a tirade of abuse hurled across the boardroom at the irresponsible manner in which Leaver and Quinton had conducted the negotiations. It got so heated that at one point one of the chairmen called a halt and suggested that Leaver and Quinton leave the room. Everyone was so shell-shocked over this arrangement that not much sense was spoken at that meeting, save that it was agreed the league would instruct its lawyers to advise them on what actions could be taken to nullify this crazy deal.

There followed a series of emergency meetings, where the club chairmen were given advice from attending lawyers and a barrister. At one of these meetings, I aired my view that we were well and truly stuffed. I explained that in the past one of my Amstrad executives had made a poor arrangement with a third party and, having clapped eyes on it, I'd tried to have it reversed, only to find that under law we didn't have a leg to stand on. With this precedent in mind, I explained that in the case of the league we had even greater problems, as this wasn't some simple executive who'd made the deal with Chisholm and Chance; it was the bloody CEO and chairman!

I must have come across as a bighead, as I was kind of ignored and shouted down. Sam Hammam of Wimbledon and Freddie Fletcher of Newcastle told me that we should leave it to the lawyers. I told them that the lawyers, with all due respect, would just run us up big bills and end up at the same conclusion. I had taken the precaution of looking up the Amstrad case and was able to quote the relevant section in open forum, but the high-flying barrister politely said he was encouraged by what he'd heard from Sir John Quinton and Peter Leaver on this matter and, while he would take into account the precedent I'd quoted, he still wanted to explore other avenues. I told him he should be mindful of not running us up a large bill, which went down like a lead balloon with him and his instructing lawyer sidekicks.

As a realistic person, I knew we had no alternative but to try to do a deal with Sam to get out of this stupid arrangement, but no one was listening.

The club chairmen passed a vote of no confidence in respect of Peter Leaver, resulting in him and Sir John resigning from their posts. There was also talk amongst some of the chairmen that we should take legal action against the pair of them for the irresponsible manner in which they'd handled this deal. Once again, as devil's advocate, I piped up, saying that this was a waste of time. It would cost a fortune to fight in court and in the end we would get lumbered with another bill. And even if we *won*, they could not afford to pay the likely damages, let alone our legal expenses.

Then came the hammer-blow. At another meeting, the barrister advised that Sir John had rethought his position. Both he and Peter Leaver were adamant they had acted in good faith and their reputation was now at stake. To top it all, the barrister started quoting the section of the law that *I* had brought up a week or so earlier, as if he had discovered it there and then!

I couldn't hold back. 'Hold up a minute. With respect to your thousand-pound-per-hour advice, you are now telling us what I said two weeks ago! Are you saying we have no case now?'

'Well, I am not saying you have *no* case,' he replied, 'but it has now become complicated by Sir John's position and I would suggest that before you embark upon what could be a very costly court case, you might wish to see if you can settle with Mr Chisholm and Mr Chance.'

I glared across the table at Freddie Fletcher, who had been the most vociferous over keeping the lawyer engaged on this matter. I screwed up a piece of A4 paper into a ball and threw it at him, and then I did the same to Sam Hammam.

I blurted out, 'Sorry, can I ask the league's secretary what we are paying the lawyers and how much is on the clock? I want it to go on record. I also want to enquire if my comments of two weeks ago were minuted.' The whole outing cost the league the thick end of £200,000. There was a stunned silence, then some sheepish muttering. The legal team left the meeting, never to be seen again.

I know that I may come across as a know-it-all bighead who thinks he's always right – all I can say is that the above is an accurate record of events. Believe me, if you were able to talk to any of the chairmen present at that time, they would endorse every single word.

Dave Richards, ex-chairman of Sheffield Wednesday, was appointed as the new chairman of the Premier League in March 1999. He was tasked, among other things, with sorting out this mess and finding a new CEO. As I was perceived to be a close associate of Sam, it boiled down to me to try to make him see sense and do a reasonable deal. I had countless meetings with Sam and countless phone calls with Dave Richards.

The aggravation we had in the chairmen's meetings was indescribable as we tried to get everyone to allow Dave a clear remit to come up with an amount to attempt settlement. In the end, he did a deal and paid the pair of them off. I can't say how much they got – that was confidential – but I can say it was a lot less than we'd have had to pay them if the contract was played out.

*

I was so heavily engrossed with the football rubbish, I only half listened to one of my Amstrad people, David Hennell, when he tried to convince me to invest our money in an internet service or start up our own. One day, he took me to meet a bunch of nerds located on the top floor of an old building in Soho. The room was full of computer racks – I was looking at an internet service provider (ISP) in its earliest form. David had asked Bill Poel to try to explain to me what this internet service provider stuff was all about, but I didn't really grasp it. It sounded like a bit of a pipe dream to me, with a lot of heavy investment in equipment. Quite honestly, it passed me by.

History tells us that companies like Demon and Freeserve started in the same humble way as the bunch of people I saw in Soho. I am not saying that if I'd listened intently we would have been another AOL, but I *am* sure that if I hadn't been deflected by football, I'd have concentrated a bit more. Who knows? I might have started an ISP business and been able to sell it on, just as Dixons did when they sold Freeserve to the French ISP Wanadoo.

However, I couldn't miss the fact that by 1998-9, the use of email was becoming increasingly popular. Most large companies were using it to communicate, but it wasn't so popular yet with the public – people were frightened off due to technophobia. Bob Watkins and I debated the possibility of creating and selling a special telephone that would enable consumers to send and receive emails. I liked the idea of this phone and believed it would appeal to the man in the street who wanted to venture into the world of email. The other interesting aspect was the business model. Every time an email call was made, we could earn some money by using a special tariff connection. Moreover, as the phone would have a large screen, we could target adverts to consumers at home.

To be honest, during that period, you felt you were being left out or had missed a trick if you didn't have something to do with the internet. Dot-com companies were springing up all over the place and a new breed of young people were coming up with internet ideas, creating 'websites' and promoting various services. Any Hooray Henry with a navy blazer, open-collared white shirt and a pair of jeans – armed with a bottle of Evian and a PowerPoint spreadsheet on an Apple laptop – could walk into a bank and, as long as 'dot com' was part of his new company's name, he could walk out with five million quid's worth of venture funding. It was *that* crazy.

On top of this, the New Amstrad shares were starting to rise, for no reason other than we were in the technology business. We hadn't *done* anything – there were no massive profits. It just goes to show how stupid the stock market can be. Looking back to the days when I'd tried to privatise Old Amstrad – when we really *did* have substantial assets and cash – the share price had lingered around 23p. Yet here we were a few years later, seeing New Amstrad's share price creeping up and up for no reason at all.

No one could understand it. I remember being away in Spain in

November 1999 and Simon was calling me virtually every day. 'Dad, I don't know what's going on – the share price is one pound fifty.'

Half an hour later, he'd call me back. 'It's crazy – the share price is two pounds.'

An hour later: 'I really have no idea what's happening – the shares have hit three quid.'

This went on for a couple of days, until the share price reached a ridiculous level of nearly £4. It actually put a market capitalisation on New Amstrad of over £300m and there was absolutely no rhyme or reason for it.

That November trip to Spain is imprinted on my mind because when we got home to England, I received a very official-looking letter the following Monday. It was from the Queen's equerries, informing me that I was being proposed for a knighthood in the New Year's Honours List. What a fantastic surprise!

I was kind of aware this might happen *someday*, as I was somebody who'd received so much publicity as a businessman in the eighties. I had constantly been involved in backing various government initiatives and in 1997 had engaged in a round-the-country Enterprise Tour at the request of Gordon Brown, the then Chancellor of the Exchequer. This involved visiting virtually every university in the land and speaking to students by way of Q&A sessions. I can't remember how many of these things I did, but I must have spoken to thousands of students during that period. In fact, these days, in other seminars I conduct, members of the audience often say they were at one of my Q&A sessions when they were students. I spoke at the Oxford Union three times and at the Cambridge Union twice. Therefore, I imagined that the Prime Minister, Tony Blair, had put my name forward for a knighthood based upon this work, as well as my contribution to the computer industry. I was to learn later that it was to celebrate, at the end of a millennium, exceptional entrepreneurs who had grown over the past decades. Richard Branson was also awarded a knighthood.

I showed the letter to Ann, who was very excited. I told her we had to keep the thing very quiet – she mustn't tell anyone. The letter stated it was merely to advise me that my name had been put forward for the honour. It invited me to write back and officially accept, but added that even if I did, the knighthood might not be conferred, hence the warning that we should keep the news to ourselves. As you can imagine, Ann and I were frustrated that we couldn't tell people. Obviously we did share the news with the kids and I couldn't resist, when I went into work the next day, popping into Bob Watkins' office and telling him too. As someone who had been with me for over twenty years, I knew he'd be very pleased for me.

On 5 December 1999 we had another great thing to celebrate when my son Daniel got married to Michaela. His father-in-law laid on a great wedding in one of the London hotels and, of course, we invited all our family and friends. By then, Simon had had another son, Matthew, and both he and Nathan were page boys at Daniel's wedding. It was a great day and I was bursting to tell Derek, Daphne and Shirley, as well as Johnnie and Mark Simons, about the knighthood. I pulled them to one side during the evening and spilled the beans. They were all so very excited.

Daniel and Michaela went to South Africa on their honeymoon, then faced a long flight halfway round the world to get to our home in Florida to join the rest of the family to see in the new millennium. You can imagine how jet-lagged they both would be. Certainly, Simon and I could imagine it . . .

I have to admit to having what some might say is a twisted sense of humour, which Simon also seems to share. We had bought the grand-kids an electric dancing model of Father Christmas, one of those things you plug in and it plays a Christmas song and kind of sways from side to side in a dancing action. The kids were fascinated by it. Now Simon and I cooked up a devilish plot. We bought a mains timer switch and connected it to the Father Christmas and a table lamp. We placed the Father Christmas under the lampshade and put them both on a small table in Daniel and Michaela's bedroom. Then we set the timer switch for 3 a.m.

After their epic flight, they arrived at the house totally shattered at around midday. They fought to stay awake, to try to get back into a conventional sleep pattern. When they went upstairs to unpack, Michaela commented how nice the Father Christmas looked in their room. It was hard to keep a straight face, as we all anticipated the timer kicking in at three in the morning, with the light coming on, the music blaring out and Father Christmas dancing.

The next morning, we were all waiting to hear from them. When they came down, they didn't say a word, but after a bit of prompting, they told us how they'd nearly jumped out of their skins and didn't know what had hit them. They got the joke in the end and we had a good laugh. The thought of it still makes Simon and me chuckle, imagining their faces when the light came on and Santa let rip.

It wasn't until 1 January 2000 that everyone and his brother knew I'd been awarded a knighthood. It was obviously a very exciting day and I received lots of congratulatory telegrams and telephone calls. My brother and sisters, though they already knew about it, were particularly delighted to see it confirmed. Their little brother Alan, from the council flat in Clapton, was going to be a knight. I remember reflecting on what my mother and father might have said – it would have been a marvellous thing for them to have seen.

A load of people from the football world congratulated me, David Pleat being one of the first on the phone. John Ireland, with all the efficiency of a corporate lawyer, took it upon himself to send a memo around Tottenham Hotspur Football Club informing all the staff that the chairman Alan Sugar had been knighted and his title in future would be Sir Alan. Up till then I was called Mr Sugar or Mr Chairman.

Unfortunately, his efficiency and correctness backfired. Someone at Tottenham had given the memo to the training ground people and they had passed it on to a tabloid journalist, who spun it as me *insisting* upon how the staff should address me. I asked John why he'd bothered to do it and he quite innocently said he'd thought it was the right and proper thing to do, especially as some of the staff had asked him how they should address me in future. No one at Amstrad had thought of sending out memos about this, as they knew it wouldn't be necessary – most of the staff had called me Alan for years. It was only those that were new who addressed me more formally.

The *Daily Mail*, of course, was not going to write anything positive by way of congratulating me on being a worthy recipient of this honour; instead, they chose to go with the story that I'd got the honour because I was a contributor to the Labour Party – that effectively I'd

bunged them some money to get a knighthood. Certainly, it was true
that over the years I'd made political contributions to both the Conservative Party and the Labour Party, but I've always stated that my
donations were given (prior to elections) to assist in funding the party
in question to promote their policies.

The *Daily Mail*'s negative publicity, together with the tabloid back-
page journalists harping on about my insistence on being called 'Sir
Alan', took the shine off the moment a bit. Regrettably, we live in a
country where you're not really allowed to enjoy success. Nevertheless,
I've always thought the negative stuff is outweighed by the genuine
positive stuff.

The official knighthood ceremony wasn't until June 2000 and it
was a great day. Once again, I was about to meet the Queen. At Buckingham Palace, I was escorted away from my family and taken to an
area where all the people receiving honours were assembled. We were
given some quick training on exactly what we had to do when we
addressed the Queen and practised how you positioned your shoulder
before the Queen knighted you with the sword.

I noticed that the people arriving in front of the Queen would have
a little chat with her. Here I was once again in this embarrassing
situation, thinking to myself, 'What am I going to chat to the Queen
about?'

As I arrived in front of her, I noticed one of her equerries, dressed
in a sort of military uniform, whisper something in her ear. When the
Queen spoke to me, she said, 'Ah, Sir Alan, not only are you known for
your exploits in the computer industry and the wonderful contribution you've made to information technology, but I'm also informed
you are in the football industry, which must be rather interesting?'

I replied, 'It certainly *is* an interesting business. However, it's
sometimes not very rewarding and can also be a little demoralising, in
a similar way that Your Majesty must have felt last night when England was knocked out of Euro 2000. So bearing in mind this terrible
result against Portugal, Your Majesty, perhaps we should move on and
let me say how honoured I am to accept this knighthood.'

Well, at least that was a little bit better than the first time I'd met
her back in 1987. Not bad off-the-cuff stuff.

We had a great time at the lunch afterwards. All my friends were invited, together with the family and some of my oldest and most respected employees. It was a real milestone in my life and a great honour.

A week or so later, Piers Morgan, the then editor of the *Daily Mirror*, invited me to the boardroom at Mirror HQ to have lunch with the executives and some senior columnists. This is something national newspapers do from time to time. During lunch, Piers congratulated me on the knighthood and asked that I explain what actually goes on in the ceremony, in particular what the Queen said to me and what I said to her.

I thought that recounting the real conversation would be boring, so with a serious look on my face and the attention of the guests focused on me, I explained the whole ceremony up to the part when the equerry whispered in the Queen's ear.

Then I said, 'The Queen said, "Sir Alan, apart from your obvious involvement in the world of IT, I understand you are also involved in football?"

'"Yes, Your Majesty, that's true – a strange business, but in view of last night's terrible result for England against Portugal in Euro 2000, I feel on this great occasion the least said the better."'

Then I paused until someone asked, 'What did she say to that?'

'Well, she said, "You're absolutely right, Sir Alan. In my opinion, one should have played Beckham in front of a flat back four as a play-maker, with two wing-backs raiding up and down the flanks."'

There was a stunned silence. I smiled and they all burst out laughing.

*

It had taken about nine months to get it ready, but the email phone was launched on 29 March 2000 at quite a big bash organised by Nick Hewer. On the day, the share price rose to 610p, putting a market capitalisation on the company of £500m. There was no rationale behind the share price rise; we were simply caught up in the internet boom, which had just about peaked out by then. The fact that the email phone was perceived to be a joint venture between Amstrad and

British Telecom attracted a lot of attention in the City on the day, but the rise in the share price was very short-lived. Soon after the launch, the so-called 'dot-com boom' imploded and the Amstrad share price fell rapidly. The penny had dropped: some companies whose values had risen to great heights actually had *no substance* – people had just been dragged in on a whim or a hope.

The business model of the email phone was all about consumers sending emails and us receiving a share of the call charge. On top of this, we were going to sell advertising to display on the screens of the phones, a kind of electronic billboard in consumers' homes. The idea was that we would subsidise the cost of the phones so they'd sell at a low retail price.

Sales of the phone went quite well – over 400,000 were sold. However, some people only realised after purchase that sending emails was not free and we experienced lots of disconnections. Also, the advertising model was not attracting the attention of potential advertisers. It seems we had launched at a time when most advertisers were sick and tired of what they called 'internet advertising'.

The first wave of internet advertising came during the dot-com boom. Everybody thought this was a major breakthrough and advertisers threw a lot of money at advertising on various websites. It turned out to be a disaster and the advertising fraternity pulled away from it very quickly, reverting to conventional media. By the time we launched the email phone, the term 'internet advertising' was like the kiss of death in advertising circles.

I argued with advertising agencies and media buyers that they needed to convince their clients that advertising on the email phone was *not* internet advertising – our screen was like a miniature version of a street hoarding which sat in people's homes. Where else could you *guarantee* consumers would get to see the advert? Despite these arguments, we failed. We had a great technical solution to send targeted adverts to users' screens; we could profile different regions and change the adverts quickly. Yet in spite of all this, the advertisers did not cotton on that we were offering them, in advertising terms, a Trojan horse into consumers' homes. The only company who actually understood the concept was BSkyB, who spent a lot of money on advertising these phones and proved they got new subscribers from it. Yet even with BSkyB's testimony, we still weren't able to convince others.

Bob Watkins also wanted us to embark on developing our own mobile phone. Having spoken to Dancall's former chief engineer, Per Christianson, Bob told me that mobile phone technology had become much simpler now and it would be easy for us develop a phone and get a share of the market.

Bob had seen his return to New Amstrad as a last throw of the dice to be a businessman rather than just an engineer. His first project was the email phone, on which he *did* spend most of his time handling the engineering side. I left him to this mobile phone business on the basis that he would try to replicate what we'd achieved at Dancall.

Around that time, Virgin had decided they would start a mobile phone service. I set up a meeting with Richard Branson and the chief executive of Virgin Mobile to discuss the possibility of us supplying them and as a result they became our first customer. I left the whole thing in Bob's hands, thinking it was a done deal. All he had to do was develop the phone and get it into mass production.

Unfortunately, Bob's assertion about the technology no longer being rocket science turned out to be untrue. Bob had laid on production with a sub-contractor in China and promised them we were going to make millions of these phones, but as time passed, the software was nowhere near finished and there were terrible technical problems.

As a side issue, Margaret Mountford had decided she'd had enough of being a corporate lawyer, working every hour of the day, and wanted a less demanding but interesting challenge. I was eager to get her on the board at New Amstrad, and she joined Jeoff Samson as a non-executive director.

Cracks started to appear on the mobile phone project. Pressure was coming from Margaret and Jeoff to the effect that Bob's adventure was burning money and putting the company in a vulnerable situation. On deeper investigation, it seemed we'd committed over a million pounds for parts with the sub-contractor in the Far East. It was another disaster, which resulted in me having to ask Bob to leave for the third time, which he duly did in September 2001.

It was a crying shame that this man was not satisfied doing what he was best at – engineering. He had this unshakable conviction that he was a businessman. In the early days after bringing him back to New Amstrad, I gave him his head and let him get on with things, as he'd learned a lot about telephones when he worked for Gulu, and he decided we should continue with the traditional Betacom business of selling ordinary fixed-line telephones. For the first couple of years, I went along with his scheme, but it was peanuts selling £5–6 phones to people like Argos and every year the division lost money. I'd made the point to Bob so often – that the effort involved in selling items for a fiver is a waste of time – yet he convinced me to continue with it. After losing money for two seasons I gave him six months to sort it out. Bob finally realised I was right and I managed to sell the division, with the staff included, to the company Alba – a nice, elegant way out. Now it was again left to me to get us out of trouble, this time on the mobile phone venture. It cost us a lot of money to pay off the sub-contractor in the Far East. Fortunately, Richard Branson was okay with the situation and was able to buy his phones from other suppliers. That was the end of our romance with mobile phones.

*

Back at Spurs, George Graham had become something of a silent assassin. He would pretend to be trying to work professionally with me, but at every press conference he would tell the media that the Tottenham team was not capable of winning things, saying that he needed at least three new players. If we bought three players, he would tell the press he needed *another* three players.

I decided, from past experience, to keep my mouth completely shut when questioned by the media about Graham's opinions. Thankfully, some journalists could see that Graham was constantly buying players yet continually saying he still needed more, and it was mildly heart-warming to see the sensible ones picking up on exactly what I was thinking. Nevertheless, Graham sang the same old song at every press conference after he'd lost a match.

I recall one particular game in the League Cup, in December 1999, when we were drawn against Fulham, who were not in the Premier League at the time. It was one of those games that Graham and his squad thought would be a walk in the park. We'd roll over this lower-league team – no problem at all – and march into the next round.

Wrong. We were beaten 3–1. After the match, I was gutted we were out of the cup. As I left the ground, I looked across at Graham and shook my head. He knew I was angry at our defeat. I saw him scuttling away with a bunch of his cronies. Fulham's ground was close to London's King's Road, where all the flash restaurants were, and he was off to dinner with his wife and his friends, including Jeff Powell of the *Daily Mail*.

The following day the most disgusting article, written by Jeff Powell, was published in the *Daily Mail*. The outrageous headline read, 'Why miserly Sugar must come out of his counting house and give George the money.' The article accused me of never investing in the club. What's more, the loss at Fulham was *not* the fault of football genius Graham; no, it was *my* fault because of lack of investment.

I went berserk. I rushed down to the training ground where Graham was in a meeting with some of his staff. I burst through the door and told them to get out. Graham looked at me and said, 'Chairman, we're having an important meeting about tactics.'

I told him I didn't give fuck about tactics and to get them out now. They all jumped up and scurried out. I slammed the article down on the desk in front of Graham and said, 'This is what your mate has written. Did you tell him to write this when you went out to dinner with him?'

Graham said, 'No, Chairman. This is a surprise to me – I haven't seen it. I've been working all morning, I haven't even looked at the papers. I don't know what it's all about – what does it say?'

'You know exactly what it bloody says. It's your friend Jeff Powell protecting your arse. Now, here's a fucking message from me to you to give to him. My lawyers are going to be on to the *Daily Mail* today. If he doesn't retract what he says in the paper, I'm taking him to court. And here's the bad news, George: *you* are going to be called as a witness, simple as that. I will drag you into the witness box, because *this* is a piece of shit. I've had enough stick now from people. And by the way, I've had enough of you telling everyone in press conferences you need six more players.'

Graham could see I was really angry. He reiterated that the article had nothing to do with him.

Now, I want to explain why I reacted so strongly to these types of articles by some of the sports journalists. I'd learned to take the rough with the smooth when it came to the press – it comes with the territory when you put yourself in a goldfish bowl as a high-profile businessman. The financial media bigged me up when I was on the way up in the mid-eighties, then they slagged me off when things started to go wrong. This is par for the course. I think it fair to say that the treatment I received from the UK financial media was 'reasonable and correct reporting' and I never engaged in any arguments or litigation with the UK media over any criticism of me to do with business.

With football, however, it was a different matter. I think one has to look at the quality of some of the football journalists writing for the tabloid newspapers to understand why. Basically, they are glorified fans, in awe of people like Terry Venables, George Graham and Brian Clough. In the eyes of these hacks, the chairmen and directors of football clubs are the devils, while the players and managers are the angels.

Before I alienate the whole of the sports-reporting industry, I will make the point that in some of the serious newspapers there are some great journalists who are balanced and honest – Neil Harman, Patrick Collins and Oliver Holt, for example, and to a certain extent Brian Woolnough. On the other hand, if Harry Harris didn't like somebody, he would criticise them. Fortunately, he trusted me and was very supportive. So much so that sometimes it was a bit cringey and in fact he got himself in bad odour with his contemporaries for being so supportive of this ogre Sugar in the days of the Venables altercations.

I can take fair reporting, but unlike many other chairmen, I wasn't prepared to put up with lies printed about me in the football media. I had taken legal action against newspapers on many occasions. Most never reached court and were settled with damages paid to me and an apology printed in the paper. The system was unfair in that they'd write an article about me which was a pack of lies and it would appear as a back-page headline or a double-page spread, but the apology would be no bigger than a postage stamp, lost in the body of the paper.

During the years I was involved in football, over £800,000 was paid to me in damages, all of which was donated to Great Ormond Street Hospital. The people at Great Ormond Street still joke with me that sadly they haven't seen me being slagged off in the papers lately, a shame as they were looking forward to another donation.

The *Daily Mail*'s in-house lawyer, who had dealt with Alan Watts from Herbert Smith a number of times before on defamation matters, was quite a sensible person. He knew, from the letters Herbert Smith had sent, that Powell was dead in the water. Under normal circumstances, I'm sure he would have agreed to pay some damages and print the usual postage-stamp apology. The *Daily Mail* had coughed up loads of money in the past to compensate for the lies they'd printed about me. These disputes never got as far as court and it wouldn't have surprised me if this time, once again, another piece of medical equipment was going to be winging its way to Great Ormond Street.

However, on this occasion, we received a letter from the *Daily Mail* saying they would *not* be offering an apology or paying any damages and that Jeff Powell stood by his words and would be defending the case. Powell had obviously persuaded his bosses that this matter should be fought, regardless of their lawyer's advice. Powell reckoned I was the kind of person who would threaten to take legal action but would fold before it got to court, because I wouldn't want to stand up and be a witness.

The case took about fifteen months to get to trial. Meanwhile, Graham was shitting himself. He'd never been called to court to be a witness before. I told him I wanted him to provide a witness statement and if he didn't, we'd have to subpoena him. I explained that all he had to put in his witness statement were the facts: that during his management of Tottenham he had purchased more players than he'd ever purchased in his whole managerial career and that he'd spent more money at Tottenham than he'd ever spent at any of the previous clubs he'd managed. He couldn't deny these facts, as they were on the record. Therefore, having taken separate advice from his lawyer, he grudgingly completed his witness statement and signed it.

I guess my wildcat decision to appoint Graham as manager was, to a certain extent, acceptable to the fans, as long as results were coming in. The fans could no longer argue about money, as even the biggest thicko could see that a fortune had been spent since Graham had come in, but he turned out to be useless as far as management was concerned. Fans could now see beyond his so-called reputation, but his pals in the media would never blame Spurs' poor performances on him. Instead, when the results weren't good, there was a groundswell of criticism of *me*. The emphasis changed from me being the horrible man who wouldn't invest any money in the club, to me being the horrible man who'd brought George Graham to the club and ruined it.

After one particularly dismal performance under Graham's management – a cup tie against Birmingham (again a lower-league team), when we got slaughtered 3–1 at home – the fans were frustrated and started chanting for my head. Ann was sitting next to me while the crowd were screaming, 'Sugar out! Sugar out! Sugar out!' This wasn't the first time they'd chanted this, but on this occasion the whole stadium seemed to erupt; it was really frightening.

Karren Brady, Birmingham's managing director, spoke to me after the match, saying how disgusted she was at the way the fans were treating me. She went to the trouble of writing an article in the *Sun* the next day, saying how unreasonable the fans were and how they'd forgotten all I'd done for the club. It was nice of her – she was genuinely upset at what she saw and felt very sorry for Ann too – but her words in the *Sun* fell upon deaf ears, as one would expect.

The company Enic, headed by Daniel Levy, had been in touch with me months earlier to ask if I would sell my shareholding in Spurs. I knew Daniel personally – he was the son of some people who lived in Chigwell and we'd seen him and his brothers grow up. Enic was partly owned by him, but the majority owner was billionaire Joe Lewis, who was originally from England but was now stationed in the Bahamas. Enic had acquired a financial interest in several football clubs throughout Europe, including Poland, Greece and the Czech Republic, as well as Glasgow Rangers. They planned to gain shareholdings in a lot of football clubs, to accomplish a kind of universal marketing and merchandising strategy. I'd rejected their approaches in the past, but this outburst at the Birmingham game was the last straw as far I was concerned. Daniel and Ann had been telling me for ages that I was banging my head against a wall trying to do my best for the club, when instead of thanks, all I got was more and more stick. They were right. Perhaps I was stupid to stay as long as I did.

I contacted Daniel Levy and we struck a deal. He had already acquired some shares in Tottenham and didn't want to hold more than 29.9 per cent or he'd be forced to make an offer for the whole club. He bought enough shares from me to take him to just under this figure, paying me £21.9m and leaving me with a 13 per cent shareholding in Spurs.

There were quite a few twists and turns between the lawyers, the Premier League and the Stock Exchange, but eventually the deal was done. Daniel Levy took over control of the board at Tottenham and I duly resigned. It was kind of a relief to have the whole thing taken off my shoulders, though I was going to continue to be a regular visitor to the Spurs boardroom on match days. I still am.

Coinciding with the sale of Tottenham to Enic in February 2001, the court case against the *Daily Mail* had started. The build-up to the case had seen a really nasty legal battle, with the *Daily Mail*'s lawyers pulling all kinds of stunts and demanding lots of information on me and my companies; really trying to create a lot of trouble. I devoted a great deal of my time assisting Herbert Smith in preparing for this trial – a lot of research needed to be done and we had to be on the ball. Whatever crap they threw at us, we batted back to them immediately. Ultimately, they failed in their efforts to make me back down and call off the trial. It was a horrible period, made worse by the stories running in the tabloids about the upcoming case, but finally we were at court.

On the first day, as my barrister started to read out the accusations made by Jeff Powell against me, a very strange thing happened. I must have been at one of the lowest ebbs in my life – exhausted from fire-fighting the football situation and hyped up from preparing myself for this court case – and I suddenly burst out sobbing! I don't know to this day what came over me. I had *never* cried like that before, not since I was a kid. I imagine I must have looked like I was having a nervous breakdown.

Ann and Nick Hewer, who were in court with me, were stunned. I had to get up and walk out of the courtroom for a few minutes. As the opening of the case continued, inexplicably, I continued to cry at various intervals – I couldn't stop myself. Ann was asking me what was wrong, trying to calm me down and supplying me with tissues out of her handbag.

Eventually, it was time for me to be called to the stand. The *Daily Mail* had employed some smart-arse barrister, whose second-in-command was a female barrister who'd once done some work for me on Venables matters. I pointed out to Alan Watts that this didn't seem right. We'd tried to get certain barristers to work for *us* and they'd told us that they were unable to do so because they'd worked for the *Daily Mail*. So how was this woman, who was privy to lots of information about Tottenham and me from the Venables days, allowed to take up the job as number two in this case? In truth, it was something Alan Watts had overlooked. He kind of waffled, saying there wasn't much we could do about it now.

I must have been in the witness box for two days. This barrister threw every bit of rubbish at me he could find but, in between my crying fits, I was giving him back more than he was giving me, in some cases making him look a real fool when he got his facts wrong. Although the back of the courtroom was full of tabloid journalists, not one positive thing I said was reported – the 'facts' in the next day's papers were always manipulated. Only Harry Harris from the *Daily Mirror* gave an accurate account of what was actually said.

There were a couple of highlights, I recall. The barrister questioned me about the previous season, saying that Tottenham had romanced with relegation and barely scraped through. I pointed out to him that we'd finished fourteenth in the league, which could hardly be described as 'just scraping through'. Despite that, he kept repeating, 'You just scraped through.'

In the end, I turned to the judge and said, 'Your Honour, the jury needs to be given a little maths lesson. This gentleman has repeated six times, to the best of my knowledge, that we "just scraped through", so with your permission, may I demonstrate that he is wrong?'

The judge nodded.

I lifted my hand up and, using my little finger as if to recite, 'This little piggy went to market,' I said, 'Do you see this?' waggling my little finger. 'This is twentieth position in the league and you get relegated.' Then using the next finger, 'And this one is nineteenth position in the league and you also get relegated. And this next finger is eighteenth and you still get relegated. Now, above eighteenth is seventeenth and you *don't* get relegated. And above that is sixteenth and you *certainly* don't get relegated, followed by fifteenth where there's *no chance* of being relegated. And finally we get to fourteenth which is *a mile away* from being relegated.' This lightened up the courtroom and the barrister was made to look a double-barrelled schmock.

When you break for lunch while you're still giving evidence, the law states you must not talk to your lawyers, which was rather frustrating. The *Daily Mail*'s legal team were carefully monitoring me as I walked out of the courtroom, making sure I didn't talk to Alan Watts or make any eye contact with the jury. I felt they would pull any stroke possible to try to get a mistrial, so we religiously stuck to the rules. I waited for Alan Watts and my barrister to leave the area, then I walked out alone.

Being in the witness box for a whole day, certain things come to mind and you suddenly remember something which might be helpful to the case. I remembered something Powell had once written about me, but had no idea how to get hold of it. It played on my mind. There was no Google around in those days, so at 6 a.m. the next morning, I called Piers Morgan. I considered him an associate now that I was writing for his newspaper and I knew, as editor of a national paper, that he'd be on call 24/7. He answered his mobile immediately. I apologised for waking him up and explained that I was engrossed in this court case and needed his help. Could his people search the *Daily Mirror*'s database and find Powell's article for me?

Piers asked, 'Are you okay, mate?' having heard about my crying fits in court. 'It seems you're having a tough time.'

'Yeah, no problem, just very frustrated. If you can find this stuff, it would be a great help.'

'Okay, leave it with me. I'll call you back.'

About fifteen minutes later, he called me back to say his people had located the article and he would fax it to me. He had done me a great favour, as the article showed something that would make Powell look like he'd not been right in his witness statement.

'Brilliant, Piers. That's a great help. I really appreciate it.' This article would come in handy when my barrister got to cross-examine
Powell.

The whole of the *Daily Mail*'s case against me was that I didn't
spend enough money and was not supportive of the club. To bolster
this argument in court that day, the barrister started bringing up matters to do with Blackburn Rovers FC and referred to a glowing
chairman's statement which said how wonderful Jack Walker the
chairman was, and how he'd supported the club so well financially,
how when he took over he managed to put together a team that once
won the Premier League. I pointed out that chairmen's statements are
designed to give a report to the shareholders. The fact that Mr Walker
owned 99 per cent of the shares and therefore owned the football club
meant he was talking to himself! The courtroom burst into laughter –
even the judge couldn't hold back and I heard him stifle a laugh.

Confident that I was in command of the facts, I began to enjoy
myself. I felt the barrister had been poorly prepared by his instructing
solicitors. Clearly they had not accounted for my attention to detail.

On another occasion, when cross-examining me, he said, 'Are you
aware, Sir Alan, that Mr Powell was once consulted by Margaret
Thatcher over the Hillsborough tragedy as part of a team set up
following the disaster? Are you also aware that Mr Powell has won
numerous awards for writing and is a well-respected journalist?'

I replied, 'Are you expecting me and the jury to believe that Mr
Powell had a one-to-one conversation with Margaret Thatcher over
the Hillsborough disaster? Could you clarify to me whether this was a
one-to-one thing? Could you consult and take instructions from your
client and ask for clarification as to whether he was seconded to 10
Downing Street by Mrs Thatcher to sit across the table from her and
discuss the tragedy, or was he just invited to one of those bashes that
are held at Downing Street where two hundred people turn up? Can
we get clarification on that?'

He was stuck at that question, so I pushed him again. 'Well? Was
he one-to-one? Will you please tell the jury if he was consulted one-to-
one by Margaret Thatcher – yes or no?'

'Sir Alan, *I'm* the one asking the questions here, not you.'

'Don't try pulling that stunt on me – *"I am the one asking the questions here not you"* – you just told me that Jeff Powell was consulted by Margaret Thatcher over the Hillsborough disaster. I am asking a fair question which I'm sure the jury will be asking too. Was he consulted one-to-one or was he just there as part of some gathering of people from the football industry?'

'I don't have to answer your questions, Sir Alan. We will come back to that point.'

'What you mean by coming back to that point is that *you don't know*, so it should be accepted that actually Jeff Powell was *not* consulted by Margaret Thatcher. In fact, if I were to speak to Lady Thatcher today, she wouldn't know who the bloody hell Jeff Powell is – right or wrong?'

He refused to answer, but I had made my point very strongly. He went on to say, 'However, one cannot deny, Sir Alan, that Mr Powell is a well-respected journalist who has won many awards.'

'Hold on, hold on one minute. Let's clarify these awards for the benefit of the jury. I don't think he's won a Pulitzer Prize, right? No, of course he hasn't won a Pulitzer Prize. The kinds of awards you're talking about are those given to him by his contemporaries – awards like Best Sportswriter of the Year. Let the jury know that Best Sportswriter of the Year is voted for by the sportswriters themselves. Think of it as an association of thieves admiring who pulled off the best bank job that year. It would be the thieves voting for the best thief. You see, the jury needs to understand the criteria upon which people get voted Best Sportswriter of the Year. It's not for their literary genius – it's based on how the writer has managed to screw someone, turn them over or drop them in the mud; it's based on how they managed to stir up trouble at this or that football club. *That's* the criteria on which Best Sportswriter of the Year is awarded. So let's make it perfectly clear: Powell is no literary genius.'

I was really in full flow, maybe overstepping the mark, and the *Daily Mail* side were in total shock and expecting the judge to shut me down. But what I was saying was true and the judge let me ramble on. At least it made me feel better to get this stuff off my chest.

The barrister then asked me to look at one particular document and pointed out some financial fact on expenditure which, on the face of it, made things look quite bad – it made me look as though I hadn't told the truth over some financial issue. On the face of it – looking at the piece of paper he'd shown me – it seemed the numbers he was showing were right and they were different to the amount I had put in my witness statement. I couldn't understand it. This development resulted in headlines in the next morning's *Daily Mail* saying that Sugar had lied on expenditure. It made me look pretty bad, certainly from a public point of view.

However, Adam Tudor, the assistant lawyer helping Alan Watts, spotted that the document in question was originally *two* pages long – the barrister had shown the court just one page. The other page of the document completely exonerated me from the allegations, showing more expenditure and a total which then agreed with the figure in my witness statement.

I was furious and convinced the *Mail* had done this deliberately. Earlier in the trial they had arranged lots of clips from various newspaper articles pasted in isolation on plain sheets of paper. The words had indeed been spoken by me, but the way they were presented had been taken out of context and that seemed to me to be deliberate. I protested to the judge that this was very misleading. The only other explanation given to me by my lawyers was that maybe someone on the *Mail* team had been incompetent. Whatever the reason, for these accusations to be levelled against me in such circumstances was sick. Given this development, my lawyers were able to confer with me. They told me the bare bones of what they'd discovered and that the next morning, after the *Mail*'s barrister had finished with me, my barrister would get up to rebut the allegations.

That night, Herbert Smith informed the *Daily Mail*'s lawyers that the court had been misled and that the matter would be disclosed the next day. The next morning, the *Mail*'s barrister did not turn up. On the previous day there had been talk of him not feeling well for some reason and, before court started, we were told that he had been taken to hospital, although it was unclear why. Whatever it was, he was not going to be in court when the jury would see the full document and how misleading his cross-examination of me the previous day had been. The *Daily Mail*'s second-in-command, the female barrister, was going to take over and finish the case off.

I was called to the witness box and was cross-examined by my own barrister, who drew the jury's attention to the document which had been discussed the previous day. He then produced the second page of the document. He asked the jury to study the second page and note that it totally exonerated me from the allegations made the previous day. My barrister then invited me to comment on how I felt about this.

I said, 'The jury is made up of ordinary people, similar to me, who don't really understand the legal process. They look at the man standing in the court wearing the wig and gown and assume – as he's a barrister acting on instructions – that everything he is saying is correct.'

Turning to the jury I continued, 'Maybe on your journey here today by bus or tube you saw yesterday's allegations – which have now been exposed as false – printed in the national newspapers ...' I stopped and pointed to the back of the court, '... written by those people there.

'Thankfully, there are times when a bad thing comes to some good, because *you*, the jury, have now seen in full Technicolor – you've seen it all play out in front of your eyes just how these people work. You have seen an untrue accusation made to the court and you've seen that lot back there repeat it in the papers. I couldn't *ask* for any better evidence than that.'

Finally, glaring at Powell, I added, '*That* is the way he works.' Once again, I was getting things off my chest, possibly overstepping the mark, but I was on a roll.

After I'd finished my evidence, I was still furious about what had happened. The next day in court, the *Mail*'s female barrister told the judge (the jury were out of court) that the page had been missed out by 'mistake', because the *Mail*'s team had prepared the trial 'bundles' (what lawyers call files) in a 'tremendous rush' and she apologised. But that didn't explain how the *Mail*'s top QC had been asking me questions based on the incomplete document. Whatever the reason was, the judge was in no doubt that the cross-examination was 'aggravation' – which it certainly was – and that the jury could take this into account when assessing damages.

The *Daily Mail* had tried everything in the book. They'd contacted Gerry Francis to see whether he would give any evidence against me, but he wouldn't – in fact, he didn't want to be involved for either side. The only person they could get to speak out against me was Teddy Sheringham and all he reported were factual matters that didn't add up to anything. It made no sense calling him.

George Graham was shitting himself, thinking I was going to call him as a witness, but my lawyers felt it would be counter-productive. If he were cross-examined about my investments in the club, he could obviously not deny the money I'd spent, but he had this theory that he was only able to buy second-class players because I never provided him with *enough* money to buy first-class players. There was a danger he would come out with this rubbish to try to protect his position, so right up to the eleventh hour we never told him whether he would be called as a witness or not, leaving him plutzing.

I asked Sol Campbell to be a witness; he refused. I asked a few other players; they also refused. They didn't want to be involved. The only person who stood by me was David Pleat. He was prepared to do something unprecedented. You see, the chairman was the enemy and the playing staff would always side against him. It was unacceptable in the football world for an ex-player or ex-manager – someone on that side of the fence – to side with a chairman, let alone stand up in court to support him. Yet David Pleat did. I am sure that, amongst his contemporaries, he was frowned upon at the time. However, all he did was honestly portray events and give his fair comment on the marketplace and how much money I'd invested in the football club. Now, that might not sound a lot, but it took a lot of balls to do what he did – be a witness in such a high-profile case. I think only those closely involved with football will understand what I am saying.

Jeff Powell himself was called to the stand. He started off in a very cocky manner, at one point trying to imitate George Graham's Scottish accent when explaining how friendly he was with him. My barrister tore him apart and brought up past articles he'd written about me, and also my son Daniel, to show that Powell had some vendetta against me and the way Spurs was run. It's important to understand that Venables was also a big pal of Jeff Powell.

At the end of giving evidence, the jury was instructed by the judge that if they found the *Daily Mail* guilty of defaming Sir Alan Sugar, they had various options open to them as far as financial damages were concerned. He read them some examples. In the case of someone sustaining a broken leg, they may be awarded £5,000; a broken ankle may be £4,000; an incapacitation £100,000, and so on. He told the jury he was obliged by law to give them these examples and that when they deliberated, if they felt Sir Alan Sugar was entitled to any damages, they should take these examples into account.

I was obviously not allowed to allude to the fact that any damages I might be awarded would be donated to Great Ormond Street Hospital. This would have tainted the jury and caused a mistrial. While the judge was talking, my thoughts went back to the Western Digital jury, who'd reasoned, 'Why should we award this multi-millionaire anything at all?' However, this time I wasn't interested in the money. I was interested in winning.

The judge sent the jury out at 12.55 p.m., telling them they must start to deliberate *after* lunch, at 2.00 p.m. They came back at 2.05 p.m., having taken just five minutes to find in my favour. They awarded me £100,000 in damages, a massive amount, the maximum awarded in recent times.

Once the jury had announced their verdict, my barrister stood up and informed the court that the £100,000 would immediately be donated to Great Ormond Street Hospital. I looked at the jury and a couple of the people were nodding their heads, as if to say, 'Well done,' while others, I could see, were thinking, 'Bloody hell, if we'd have known *that*, we'd have awarded a million!' I was very emotional when the verdict was read out, as indeed were Ann and David Pleat. We'd all sat through a week's trial, with lots of twists and turns and dirty tricks, and we had come out winners.

The press were hanging about outside, as were the TV cameras. I stepped outside and spoke to the media, telling them I hoped this case would be used as an example in showing the media that there *are* people who will stand up to them. I could afford to finance this long court case, but sadly there aren't too many people who can afford to take them on, so they just have to suffer the media's abuse. I said, 'My victory today is not just for me – it is for them too.'

That little outing must have cost the *Daily Mail* a fortune. They had to pay our costs, as well as damages, on top of whatever they'd paid their barrister and team of lawyers. After the verdict, my lawyers asked the *Daily Mail* for a 'full and frank' explanation of why I had been cross-examined on the incomplete (not the full) document and why no one on their team had pointed out that there was a missing page. As the letter said, we would 'have to draw our own conclusions' if they didn't answer. They didn't give any explanation, but they seemed keen to reach an overall settlement, including our costs. In all the cases I've ever been involved in, I've never seen someone settle up so quickly. The deal included that we wouldn't pursue any of the matters against them raised in the letter. What mattered was that the case was over and I'd been vindicated, all my costs were paid, and Great Ormond Street got £100,000.

A few days later, I was ready to hand over the reins of Tottenham Hotspur to Daniel Levy. At my last game as chairman of the club, I had cause to go down to the dressing room and speak to George Graham, who yet again had been bleating to the press about how bad our squad was and how we needed to boost it with better players.

I pulled him to one side in the medical room and tore him off a strip. I told him to keep his big mouth shut in the future when it came to talking about players in press conferences. From now on, he was not to mention the quality of the players he had and how many players he needed and all that stuff. I stormed out, leaving him standing there.

Enic took over and it didn't surprise me that they wanted Graham out. I think Graham himself wanted out too. Somehow or other, Enic found some justification to chuck him out, but inevitably there was an argument about compensation. Strange – when I severed the services of the managers I'd employed, there were never any rows or arguments over money. The Football Managers' Association used to say that Tottenham Hotspur, under the leadership of Alan Sugar, were very good in dealing with their members. Enic had only been in for a few weeks and were already having aggravation over disposing of Graham.

Some newspaper articles started to appear with stories about the fines that Graham had imposed on his players. These fines were still sitting in a drawer in Graham's office. Like many managers, he would fine players who were late or didn't turn up for training, all that stuff, but he insisted they paid in cash. Normally, fines paid by players go into a pot and at the end of the season the contents are donated to a local hospital or some other worthy charity, which was the case at Tottenham. But now there were some distorted stories in the national newspapers asking why Graham was accumulating the cash in his office drawer. The suggestion was that Spurs had implied he was going to nick the money for himself – which was not true at all. Graham had no intention of taking the money and neither did Spurs accuse him of such.

Who piped up in his defence? Terry Venables, with his headline story, 'Typical Spurs – always accusing people of stealing money.' I decided, as I was leaving, I would have a final swipe at football, so I wrote a double-page spread for the *Daily Mirror* about George Graham's sacking by Tottenham. I highlighted the fact that if Graham felt he had a friend in Terry Venables, I wouldn't like to know who his enemies were. Venables had spouted off in the media that Tottenham were accusing Graham of stealing money, when in fact *no one* from the club had ever made that suggestion. The only one saying this was Venables himself – so with friends like him, you really *didn't* need enemies.

I finished off the article by summing up my time in football. I talked about the Sky TV programme *Soccer Saturday*, broadcast every week during the season, where a panel of four people talked about that day's games. I explained that in football it doesn't matter *what* you do; once you're part of the football mafia, no one will ever say you've done anything wrong. If George Graham were to be seen live on camera taking a kitchen knife and sticking it straight through someone's heart,

Frank McLintock would watch the video and say, 'George is innocent – the man lunged towards him and fell on the knife. If *anyone* is guilty, it must be David Dein, the Arsenal vice chairman.'

Years later, in 2007, Enic bought the balance of my shares in Spurs for £25m, making the total they paid me around £47m.

*

Back in 2001, just after I sold the first chunk of shares, I decided that as Spurs fans didn't value me rescuing their great institution, I'd put some of the money into rescuing another one – the Hackney Empire.

I used to go there as a kid with my mum. It was a famous old theatre located right opposite Morning Lane (where my first secondary school, Joseph Priestley, was). In its heyday, the theatre had hosted people such as Charlie Chaplin, but now the place was going to close, as it was in need of total refurbishment.

The actor and comedian Griff Rhys Jones was doing a great job raising money and getting grants from the Arts Council for this purpose. He was in regular contact with me over the progress of the refurbishment, as I'd made a modest contribution towards it in the past. A few days after I sold Tottenham to Enic, I called Griff and asked him to meet me for tea at the Savoy Hotel in London. I knew they were still struggling and I'd already made up my mind that I was going to use some of the money from Spurs to sort it out. I just needed to understand the extent of what was required before I splashed out. I asked Griff how things were going at the Empire.

'Well, Alan, we've done well to get where we have so far – people have been great – but we're miles away from commissioning a builder.'

'How much do you need to finish the project off?'

'Loads – we need at least another two to three million to do it.'

'Two to three million? Okay, well, now you've got it!'

'What? We've got it? What do you mean, Alan?'

'I mean – *you've got it*. I'll give you the two million and now we'll get on with bringing the Empire back to life.'

'I don't understand, Alan. I'm in shock!'

'Look, mate, this might not mean anything to you, but I've been involved with Tottenham Hotspur for the past ten years. I don't know if you know anything about football, but I rescued the club from near extinction. Tottenham is also a great institution – I was a fan as a kid and I kind of did it for old times' sake. Anyway, to cut a long story, I got a load of stick, so I sold out.'

'Hold on, Alan, I may be in the entertainment industry, but I haven't been living on Mars. *Everyone* knows the flak you've taken over Tottenham, but what's that got to do with the Empire?'

'Well, it's as simple as this, Griff. The Spurs fans' loss will be Hackney's gain. I made some money selling Spurs and I want to throw some into helping the Empire and the people of Hackney. So let's get on with it.'

'I'm flabbergasted, Alan, you've blown me away, I don't know what to say. After years of campaigning and fund-raising, it's finally going to be a reality. It's fantastic!'

A few days later, a big sign went up on the front hoardings of the theatre: 'THANK YOU, SIR ALAN, FOR SAVING THE EMPIRE'.

The issue was picked up by the media, including one of the serial hecklers of me while I was at Spurs, freelance journalist Matthew Norman. Being Jewish *and* a Spurs fan, he felt doubly qualified to comment on me and thought he would have a last swipe. In the past, he'd written sarcastic articles which included allegations that I referred to some of Spurs' black players using a nasty Yiddish expression. He also said I only bought the club to make my father happy on his death bed. All crap. Of course, my lawyers kicked his arse and the papers in question coughed up loads for Great Ormond Street. This time, he suggested that my donation to the Hackney Empire had nothing to do with any philanthropic thoughts, but was a way of me saving tax. The thick prick couldn't even get that right – there were no tax-saving implications at all.

I will finish where I started on this football thing. I'll say it again: I wasted ten years trying to do something great for that football club. Yes, I put Tottenham into a sound financial position, but as far as performance on the pitch was concerned, we did nothing.

Amstrad suffered the most. In those ten years I don't know what I could have turned my hand to, but I'm sure I would have turned my hand to *something* – and I'm absolutely sure the fortunes of Amstrad would have been far better. In fact, after I was free of football and had refocused on New Amstrad, we *did* see our fortunes rise again – and perhaps that tells you something about me.

Am I a one-trick pony? Can I only concentrate on one thing at a time? I guess the answer to that must be yes. It is perhaps because I have to be in *total* control and understand everything about everything – every last nut and bolt.

Football took its toll on me. People say that in the period I was involved in football, I lost my sense of humour – 'What happened to the Alan who used to make us laugh?' The Alan who used to make them laugh went into protective mode. He assumed that everybody who spoke to him was sniping; he looked for the ulterior motive behind every question put to him.

I felt an immediate sense of relief when I left Spurs. For one, the media stopped mentioning me, which was great. I know that Ann and the family were glad that I was able to relax a bit, once all the stress of the constant fire-fighting was over. But it's true to say that the scars remain and to this day I still find it hard to shrug off the feeling that every question has an ulterior motive; I still remain sceptical and untrusting of new people I meet. I have never regained the light-hearted sense of humour I had as a younger man – it's really now just dry sarcasm.

To be fair, these days when I visit the club on match day and take up my seat in the directors' box to watch the team, I come across passionate Spurs fans who still thank me for putting the club on a sound financial footing. There is a certain smugness about some Spurs fans these days, knowing that out of all the Premiership clubs Spurs is one of the most financially stable and well run. In recent times we have seen great clubs like Liverpool and Manchester United turned into a financial mess by their foreign owners. We've also seen irresponsible financial management resulting in clubs like Leeds United being relegated from the Premier League after going into administration and now trying to claw their way back from two divisions below, and, more recently, Portsmouth facing the same struggle.

Daniel Levy, the current chairman, has continued to run Spurs based on the solid foundations I implemented in my reign and has managed to balance competing in the transfer market with keeping the club well insulated from financial danger while turning Spurs into a force to be respected on the pitch. So I guess I can look back and say that I am happy I took the club from the verge of extinction and helped it to move forward to the position it is in today – a club on the verge of success.

On another positive note, my daughter Louise got married to Mark Baron on 5 August 2001. Mark was once a member of the boy band Another Level and had also been brought up in Chigwell. The wedding was a grand affair in the grounds of Bramstons. The ceremony and party were held in a massive marquee and, once again, Simon's sons Nathan and Matthew were page boys. We also had a new addition to the family, Daniel and Michaela's firstborn son, Alex. There were some funny pictures of Alex taken on the day. Michaela, being a typical Jewish mother, was always worried that her baby boy was hungry and the pictures showed little Alex wasn't so little – she had chubbed him up good and proper.

As usual, all our family and friends were at the wedding, as well as people from Amstrad and some from the world of football. In his speech, Mark joked that when he asked me for my daughter's hand in marriage, he saw a look of relief on my face that he'd only seen once before – and that was when I'd finally sold Spurs to Daniel Levy!

18

'I Don't Like Liars, Bullshitters, Cheats and Schmoozers'

Hired on The Apprentice!

2002–6

While I was preoccupied with football, Amstrad's relationship with BSkyB was going down the pan. By the time I came back to Amstrad, I found we'd lost our position as BSkyB's main supplier. Instead, Pace had got their feet well and truly under the table, aided and abetted by their new managing director, Malcolm Miller, who had joined them from Sega. To make matters worse, there was talk of a change in technology from analogue to digital and none of our engineering people had any experience of digital satellite receivers.

The BSkyB situation had been deteriorating for some time. Unbeknown to me, BSkyB had decided once again that they would sell direct and arrange the installations themselves, buying the equipment directly from manufacturers. The only problem was, they weren't buying it from us!

Sam Chisholm had been replaced by a new guy, Mark Booth, and when I looked at Sky's management team it was unrecognisable. A new wave of people had been brought in on the marketing side, younger people who knew nothing of the history between Rupert Murdoch and me, between Sky and Amstrad. When I tried explaining to this new wave of people who I was and what Amstrad and Sky had done in the past, they couldn't have cared less. It didn't occur to them that the existence of BSkyB – and their very jobs – was largely down to Amstrad. That was all history now.

Simon, our sales director, told me, 'They're not interested in listening to stories from the past – we're treated just like any supplier – there's no special relationship going on here any more.'

I called Mark Booth. When Mark took the job, one of the first things he did was meet up with me to have a recap on the past. At the time, he was quite sympathetic to my feelings; now, however, he told me that things had to be handled in 'a more professional way'. They'd now put in layers of management whom he could *not* be seen to undermine.

Some of the technical staff taken on in this new regime were ex-Pace employees who were still very pally with the Pace organisation. It appeared to me that the new regime certainly had a tendency to support and side with Pace. They also enjoyed the hospitality Pace dished out, not to mention flying off to every electronics fair in the world for no reason at all. These jobsworths would use any opportunity to slope off when there was a good junket going.

There's a lesson to learn here. When you are faced with the situation I was, where you actually *know* the top man, what you imagine to be 'playing your trump card' turns out to be administering the kiss of death. You might speak to the boss and try to influence him to override his lower-level management, and this may work once, but after that you've made enemies for life with those managers. Believe me, I tried it. It got to a stage where it was like pouring oil on the fire. The more my people alluded to 'Sir Alan's great relationship with Rupert Murdoch', the more difficult these people would be, particularly those in the technical department.

The problem with BSkyB in those days was a classic example of a company which – how can I put it? – was simply making too much money! There were endless divisions, all with executive heads of department. Each and every time some marketing brain surgeon came up with an idea, a new division was formed or a new feature was incorporated on the product or a new method of procurement was introduced.

One example was the e-auction. Simon explained that we were going to be asked to tender for an order for digital set-top boxes, but this tender was going to be conducted on the internet, the idea being that all the manufacturers go online at the same time and start beating each other up. The BSkyB people would oversee the e-auction, like people watching a dogfight, baiting the manufacturers with comments like, 'Your price is still not good enough – someone else has come up with a better one.'

As the e-auction went on, Simon called me up and told me it was getting stupid. We were being prompted by BSkyB to reduce our price ridiculously. I told him to type in something derisive like, 'We're not playing this space invaders game any more. Goodnight. Call us when you get some common sense,' and we logged off.

Mark Booth had been moved on by then and the new CEO was Tony Ball. He also came to see me when he first got the job and tried to pick up some history. At top management level, I was still respected and a friend of the company. Tony Ball was a reasonable fellow, he spoke my language and wasn't a bullshitter in any way, shape or form. I called him and went straight for the jugular, telling him this new wave of people and their mad ideas were a total and absolute joke. I couldn't stand by any more, sitting there on the periphery, being treated as if we were a piece of shit with all this e-auction bollocks.

I said to him, 'The place is being run by a bunch of Harvard Business School graduates. In the meantime, your so-called best pals, the ones who helped your boss start this business, are being kicked to one side, being asked to piss about playing space invaders with this new cyber-bid scheme.'

My tirade paid off. I had touched a nerve. Tony told me they'd paid some consultancy firm a big fee to initiate this e-auction crap and he'd subsequently canned it. When BSkyB finally dished out orders for that particular period, they had to start from scratch in the conventional way.

I don't know whether I was justified in feeling that I had a right to be a supplier since I'd helped them start the business. I *did* feel they owed me something, but perhaps I'm old-fashioned – *I* was in the habit of remaining loyal to *my* suppliers, but that was an ethic not shared by this new wave of young management. It simply goes to show that in the cruel, hard world of business there is no sentiment.

While all this was going on, Ian Saward had managed to get to grips with developing digital satellite receivers in the traditional Amstrad way. We found a very hungry chip manufacturer, Conexant, who could supply the core chips and, more importantly, would take on most of the rocket-science software development, allowing us to concentrate on the hardware. We developed a win-win situation between Conexant and our own hardware people and were able to develop the digital boxes quickly and recover our position from being behind the pack.

On top of becoming one of the suppliers to BSkyB, we also managed to pull off a deal with Sky Italia, a company owned by News Corporation, to supply them with digital boxes, so things were going quite well on that front.

However, the relationship between BSkyB's middle management and Amstrad was still quite frosty, so much so that we were totally excluded from a brand-new technology, one which would go on to revolutionise the face of digital television. This was the digital PVR (personal video recorder), a set-top box incorporating a hard disk drive which enabled users to record TV programmes. It effectively replaced the VCR.

BSkyB had secretly developed a PVR with Pace – they called it 'Sky+'. Launched in September 2001, it was a great product. Customers could use an on-screen TV guide to choose the programmes they wanted to record. I fully believed the advent of Sky+ was going to change the habits of TV viewers and I said as much during a Q&A with a group of advertising executives at a function hosted by ITV. They invited me along to give my opinion on marketing in general. During the session, I must have upset the hosts because I told the advertising executives, 'If I were you, I'd leave ITV and get a job with the BBC because the writing is on the wall.'

ITV's revenue came from advertising. Why should viewers sit through an hour-long TV show which effectively only provides forty-five minutes of real programming (plus fifteen minutes of adverts) when they can whizz past the adverts and get back to the programme? My comments that day were premature and the audience couldn't understand what I was talking about. They thought I was just being provocative. But anyone who was there and recalls what I said would agree about the effect Sky+ has had on TV advertising. In the United States, advertisers are no longer interested in hearing how many people viewed a particular show; they want to know how many people saw their adverts in the breaks. One of the advantages of digital equipment is its ability to store data inside the box which can be read remotely by the broadcasters, giving them visibility on consumers' viewing habits. Giant companies like Coca-Cola or Gillette in the United States are demanding data to verify that people actually *saw* their adverts and didn't skip through them on their PVRs. Only on the basis of this proof are they prepared to pay for advertising.

When I first saw Sky+, alarm bells started to ring in my head – not because of any concern for the advertising industry, but rather that Amstrad might be kicked out as suppliers to BSkyB. To my mind, it was inevitable that the conventional set-top box would die off and the whole market would change to Sky+.

Ian Saward told me the engineers at BSkyB would not release any technical data to us – their boss had told them Amstrad was not in the frame to be a supplier of PVRs. I suggested we should go ahead and develop the box anyway and once we had it working I'd present it to BSkyB as a fait accompli and hit them with a fantastic price. He explained that while my idea was good, it would be impossible to develop the box unless certain BSkyB contractors would co-operate and give us some of the technical data.

It was time for me to get on the phone again to Tony Ball. Tony was a bit fed up with me pestering him all the time and he told me this approach wasn't doing Amstrad any good inside BSkyB. He said that instead of me crying into my beer, our companies should try to enhance relationships at middle management level.

The good thing about Tony was that we could talk frankly in this kind of way. I laid my cards on the table and told him I understood that he, as head of Sky, had lots of things on his plate and procurement of set-top boxes was probably one of the least important things he had to worry about. I understood him leaving this matter to his management, particularly on the technical front, but I wanted him to know one important fact. I said to him, 'Your procurement people are *not* being fair at all. To be perfectly blunt, they don't like Amstrad simply because we've sung the old "Sugar knows Murdoch" song so many times. On top of this, the Pace people are so far up their arses, it's untrue.'

I won't say it was a row, but Tony didn't like me telling him what I considered to be a few home truths. But he was a fair bloke and, to make a long story short, he instructed his people to release to Amstrad all the technical documentation on Sky+. I told him we'd sign all the non-disclosure agreements he wanted.

I suggested, 'Once we've got the technical information, let us, at our own cost and our own risk, go ahead and develop a product. Then we'll demonstrate it and put in an attractive price.' I rubbed it in a bit more by reminding him that Pace had billed BSkyB for an upfront, non-refundable development fee, which we *wouldn't* be doing. He couldn't turn down my proposition – he really had nothing to lose.

The technical people at Sky were not happy bunnies. They reluctantly handed over the data to Ian, including permission to talk to the Israeli company NDS, who by now had grown from the small firm supplying smartcards into a giant organisation developing the software for Sky+. I won't say our relationship with NDS was bad – I think they were quite professional – but there were no favours coming from them.

Between Ian and myself, we got this project on the road. Ian would brief me daily on the bureaucratic blocking going on with BSkyB and NDS, while I stayed on the periphery, trying to bash these obstacles out of the way. Abe Peled, the boss at NDS, was known to me and I managed to convince him to allocate some engineering people to assist us in developing the Sky+ box. From then on, from a technical point of view, we were at the races. We had the ingredients necessary to at least develop the box, but of course we had no orders. The only way we could get BSkyB's attention was to blow the other manufacturers out of the water from a price point of view.

Pace, with their feet tucked cosily under the table, were charging some outrageous price for the Sky+ box. Ian and I (and our parts buyer) worked diligently on the bill of materials, concentrating on the high-priced core components. There was the main chip, supplied by NEC, and the hard disk drive, supplied by – guess who? – our old friends Seagate.

Interestingly enough, the Seagate management had changed from those we'd locked horns with years before. And just as the new wave of Sky management wasn't interested in my relationship with Rupert Murdoch, the same thing happened at Seagate, but in a positive way – they weren't interested in the fact that we'd kicked their arses for $150m in the past. They were a far more professional organisation than the one we'd engaged with in the mid-eighties and the technology on hard disk drives had been perfected by now.

We got ourselves to the stage where, in the good old-fashioned Amstrad way, we had come up with an amazing bill of material. I asked Simon to find out through his cronies at BSkyB when the next tender for the Sky+ box was coming up. He tipped me the wink that it would be happening in a few weeks' time.

Having got ourselves on the tendering list, we shoved in a blow-them-out-of-the-water price that got BSkyB's attention – around £40 cheaper than Pace's. The French company Thomson had also been taken on by BSkyB as a second supplier and we were £40 cheaper than them as well! This woke BSkyB up to the fact that they were overpaying for Sky+ boxes. Having given them this reality check, you would have thought we'd then receive a pile of orders – not so. Human nature being what it is, BSkyB's engineering people started poking their noses into things. You can imagine what a bunch of dickheads they must have looked to their bosses when we tendered a price of £40 less than they normally paid. They had to justify themselves, so they tried to cloud the issue by saying we had not yet *proved* we could produce this technology to the required quality and that price was not always the criterion upon which you buy merchandise. At the same time, by some magical means, our low price had filtered back to Pace and Thomson and – surprise, surprise – they re-tendered with massive reductions.

Now, if I were Tony Ball, I'd have got hold of these Pace and Thomson people and said to them, 'How come you can suddenly drop your price by forty pounds? What's changed? You've been ripping me off, haven't you?' But, as I've said, Tony was occupied with BSkyB's core business and left these matters in the hands of his middle management. I called Tony a couple of times, telling him he should ignore this smokescreen from his technical people. My persistence paid off and Tony agreed to give us our first order for 200,000 Sky+ units. We were well and truly in the PVR business. We also developed a second version of the Sky+ box which was much smaller physically, cost a lot less, looked more attractive and did five times more, spec-wise.

One thing about the BSkyB organisation is they seem to churn their CEOs quite a lot. By November 2003, Tony Ball was on his way and James Murdoch, one of Rupert's sons, came in to take over the business. James, one of the new young breed of executives, had a completely different style of management to Tony. He placed far more importance on his middle management, which meant my route to solving problems was no more. It was the end of another era.

On the occasions I tried to speak to James, he would never override any of his employees. As far as he was concerned, *they* made the purchasing decisions within the company. In a few of my general conversations with him, I would enquire as to the health of his father and he would politely reply, 'Rupert is very well and sends you his best regards.' It was James's way of saying, 'Yes, Sir Alan, you don't need to remind me about how the company started; I know the story, but now we're moving on.'

I guess I was less useful to Sky when I left the football industry. Prior to that, I was heavily involved in all the Premier League meetings and must have been quite a good ally for them, but now I was totally out of football, I suppose they thought I was no longer an asset. That's a realistic position as far as I am concerned. I can't really complain because business is business and it's human nature to want to deal with today's issues and not look back. Anyway, from then on, it was a case of me keeping my head down and allowing Simon and Ian to be the front men as far as BSkyB was concerned.

With my concentration back on Amstrad, the upturn in business proved to me that when I put my full effort into something, there's a good chance it'll end up successful. History showed that when my attention was deflected by football and the crazy litigation stuff, the fortunes of Amstrad went down the pan. Having reshuffled the management and focused everyone on the digital set-top box business, we were starting to make money – around £20m a year – not to be sneezed at, considering this was the small, renamed Betacom company that had hardly ever made a profit.

Pace was also a public company and when Malcolm Miller arrived as managing director, a new share option scheme was implemented. When the share options kicked in, Malcolm made £8m, and good luck to him.

In comparing Pace and Amstrad, I would say that, from a technical development point of view, they were superior to us in that they had loads of engineers (maybe 200 compared to our 30). However, when it came to buying and component procurement, Pace was clueless, and the same could be said when it came to manufacturing. They used sub-contractors in Romania and Hungary and even attempted to assemble some of the stuff themselves in England, the consequence being that they hardly ever made a profit.

By autumn 2002, Malcolm had seen the writing on the wall, in the same way as he did when he left Amstrad. There was no more big money to be made by him at Pace; it was going in the opposite direction. His contract with Pace was up and so, as he put it, he was free to leave to take up other opportunities, as you do when you realise there's no more cash coming your way. At least he didn't quote the usual 'irreconcilable differences with the board' bollocks that people use in order to piss off when they've copped their dosh.

While he was at Pace, Malcolm and I spoke on and off – just general industry chitchat. He never disclosed to me any of their so-called secrets or pricing. However, he did ask me why, when Amstrad took some of the Sky+ business, we slashed the price by £40. I told him he should know better than anyone that as long as we were meeting our 1.54 profit index, I was a happy bunny. The lower the price, the more orders we would *all* get and, more importantly, BSkyB could subsidise the product so even more consumers would take it up. He moaned about having to come down in price to compete with us and how it forced Pace to lose money.

After leaving Pace, he called me and asked whether he could come and see me at home, to seek my advice on something. He rolled up in a bright-red Ferrari, bought with some of his £8m windfall. It turned out that Malcolm wanted me to give him a reference for the job of president and CEO of the company Raymarine. He was hoping he would get share options and make himself another packet. I was happy to recommend Malcolm – I saw no problem in helping out some of my old people – and he got the job.

Given our long relationship, I didn't expect what happened next. Ann and I and some friends were in Scalini, a restaurant in the West End, when I noticed Malcolm's wife walk past our table. She saw Ann and me, stuck her nose in the air and blanked us completely. To be perfectly honest, Ann and I had never really got on well with this woman. There were always rumours around the firm that she was a bit of a demanding snob and gave Malcolm a lot of grief. In the past, the pair of them had turned down invitations to my fiftieth birthday and other family functions with various excuses, and we'd always thought it was his wife not wishing to come rather than Malcolm. However, on this occasion, Malcolm was also in the restaurant. Later in the evening, he got up with his entourage and walked out. I could see that he knew I was there, yet for some reason or other, he did not come over to my table to say hello. Given our history and the favours he had asked, I was stunned. It seemed to me a blatant snub. That was it! If Miller wanted help or advice in the future he knew where he could stick it. It seemed to me he was being a real selfish shit.

Malcolm did get in touch with Nick Hewer to say I'd misunderstood his behaviour, that really it was pressure from his wife (from whom he was now separated) and that he would like to mend the relationship. Nick, being the nice fellow he is, can sometimes be a bit naïve. I told him, 'Malcolm is off the radar, Nick, forget him. I *know* what happened in that restaurant and, trust me, he was just being Mr Bigshot in front of his pals. He didn't want to come up to someone like me, as it would have been deemed grovelling, which of course it wasn't.'

*

My son Daniel left Spurs shortly after I sold it to Enic and came back to Amshold to run the property business, Amsprop. Up until then, I hadn't fully concentrated on the property side of things. I'd always viewed it as an investment, but boring. However, over the years, it had grown and it was now time to pay more attention to it, so I put Daniel in charge.

So far I've been sharing lots of stories with you about many of the deals I've done. Reading them, you might think I'm stretching the truth a bit or that I've got a big ego. They say gamblers only talk about the bets they won and forget to mention the losses. Let me assure you, no matter how unbelievable some of the stories I've shared may seem, they're all 100 per cent true. Having said that, in the football days, you'd have seen another side of me. There was no shrewdness shown in some of the negotiations for players – I lost my marbles completely in that industry. I was intimidated by managers and fans into making sure we had a constant supply of players. When you're desperate to land players, you do silly things. I could tell you stories about football deals I did where I was legged-over badly. You'd wonder whether you were reading about the same person.

Things didn't always go smoothly in the property business either. Take the building I acquired in Old Park Lane, London, which I wanted simply because it was in such a prime location. According to the estate agent, it was being sold on behalf of some Middle Eastern gentlemen who had owned it for many years. On the ground floor and basement was the Hard Rock Café and there were six separate apartment floors above, each being around 5,000 sq ft. The apartments were totally dilapidated – they hadn't been used for years – but the agent told me that if I were to spend just £2–3m in total on refurbishing them, we could easily sell them for around £2.5–3m *each*. Having been advised by this prestigious firm, and having the hots for this wonderful building, I purchased it on impulse for £12.7m and engaged the services of Igal Yawetz, the architect associated with Spurs.

To fast-track the story, it transpired we needed to spend around £12m in refurbishing the apartments, not the £2–3m the agent suggested. We found the Hard Rock Café was emitting horrible smells cooking their hamburgers, making it unbearable to live in the apartments above. And when the builders finally got on site, they discovered that the whole of the steel frame of the building was rotten. Apparently, there had been an internal water leak for the past ten years which had rusted the steel. We had used a firm of mechanical engineers to survey the building and they'd signed it off, telling us it was okay to buy. Clearly it wasn't.

I instructed one of my staff, Andrew Cohen, together with Alan Watts at Herbert Smith, to try to recover some damages. When we finally settled with this company, we only managed to get about £1m in compensation, as this was the cap they were insured for. In the end, the lawyers got £250,000 and we got the balance. How shrewd is that, eh?

The contractors we employed were also a bunch of monkeys. Halfway through the building works, I received a surprise phone call from the *Sun*, telling me the Hard Rock Café building was on fire! It turned out the builders had left a heater on overnight, which had set fire to a whole section of the building. This put the contract back by about six months and a lot of the work had to be started all over again.

My daughter Louise, who was working for Amsprop at the time, was in charge of furnishing and decorating the apartments, each of which had its own character – we spent a fortune on the finest finishes. At last, we were ready to start marketing the apartments.

The Hooray Henry agent who'd sold me the building still maintained that the apartments would fetch only £2.5–3m each. I reminded this prick that he'd told me it was going to cost £3m max to refurbish the building and I had just spent the thick end of £12m. So if you divide this £12m by the six apartments, they'd already cost me £2m each on refurbishment! I told him that none of the apartments was to be sold for less than £5m. He started quoting me industry statistics on how it would be impossible to achieve £5m – effectively £1,000 per sq ft – and how it had never been achieved, even in Mayfair, the poshest of places.

I suppose the point I'm banging on about is that these agents know sod all. They're only interested in receiving their commission. It seems when they're trying to sell something *to* you, it's the best thing since sliced bread. When they're trying to sell something *for* you, it's the worst thing on the planet. An estate agent has a very simple business. The only thing they have to invest in is an office and some people. They have no stocks, no inventory and they have nothing to sell or buy. They make all their money by taking a commission on recommending properties to buy, or acting as an agent for sellers. Sounds good, right? Sounds good if they knew what they were talking about, but most of them don't.

Say I had a property I wanted to sell for £5m. An agent would charge 1 per cent for selling it and if he did a good job, he'd deserve his £50,000 fee. However, say I insisted on £5.5m, his fee would be £55,000 instead of £50,000. Typically, he'll bullshit me that the best he can do in the marketplace is £5m. All *he* wants is a quick sale – from his point of view £50,000 in hand is better than hanging on dreaming of £55,000. He doesn't care that I want the extra half a million quid.

Their so-called 'research documents' are not worth blowing your nose with. Everything they do is based on events that happened a week before, meaning that if someone sold something for £1m last week, *that* is the basis of their research on how much something comparable is worth today. I explained to the bozo who'd sold us the Mayfair building that we had created 5,000 sq ft apartments – something very special, something you could not normally find in this area of London, so there was nothing to compare it to. I told him it would need a very special buyer to come along with lots of money, who would fall in love with the apartments and buy one, and *that* was whom they should target. If his firm wanted to sell them, he should not waste my time bringing anyone along unless they had north of £5m in their head.

In the meantime, the Hard Rock Café, who had enjoyed occupancy of this building for many years without any interference from the landlord, was starting to realise they weren't dealing with a bunch of idiots in Amsprop. They had to start cleaning up their act and install new equipment in their kitchens to cut down the smells. On top of this, they were playing loud music which, of course, would disturb any residents moving into the new apartments. We advised them that we would have to report the environmental damage they were causing by way of smells and noise to Westminster Council. This resulted in them taking the unprecedented step of buying the first-floor apartment from us to use as offices for the Hard Rock Group. By doing this, they would protect the apartments above from the sound (and to a certain extent the smell). They were not happy bunnies, as you can imagine. They'd been there for years, running their business without any disturbance, then along I come and upset the apple cart. The former Middle Eastern owner had completely ignored the management of this building.

When the first lot of punters started to look at the apartments, the idiot agent put forward offers of £3m and £3.5m, which I summarily rejected, reminding him of what I'd said. Eventually, as I'd predicted, along came a couple who fell in love with the idea of these wonderful 5,000 sq ft apartments, with their exceptional views over Green Park and London. They paid £5.5m for the second floor – just like that, without blinking.

I think a picture now emerges of what total tossers some of these estate agents are. They do not know what they are talking about. In the case of the Hard Rock building, it was only my insistence that I wasn't going to sell any of these apartments for less than £5m that made it happen. And here's the funny part of the story. In the *Estates Gazette*, the estate agents' industry magazine, our agent put out a story about how they'd magnificently achieved the highest sales price for apartments in Mayfair, at over £1,000 per sq ft, taking full credit for their brilliant achievement. If I'd taken their advice, we'd have lost a packet on the building.

People wonder why I have such a low opinion of estate agents. Perhaps now they will understand, as this was just one of *many* experiences I've had with these people. I've come across other estate agents, particularly in the early days, who would sell their grandmothers for 50p. And it is those rogues, I'm afraid to say, who formed my general opinion of certain agents, an opinion which still remains to this day.

Another genius I came across was a so-called expert on the Mayfair retail market. We owned a few buildings in the fashionable Bond Street area and, having acquired one for about £26m, we were on the lookout for others. This genius offered us an inferior building at a massively expensive price. He assured us this was the way the market was.

I said that if that was the way the market was, then the building we'd bought for £26m a year ago would now be worth £43m! I offered him my hand, ready to shake on it.

'Well, bigshot? What about it? Where's the forty-three million? Ours is in a better location in Bond Street than the one you're offering, so come on, Mr Expert, where's the forty-three mil?'

What was his answer?

'No, no, you won't get forty-three million for that building. Every-one knows you only paid twenty-six million for it a year ago.'

You couldn't make it up, could you? I promise you, that's what he said. What a tosser.

We went on to sell all the apartments at the Hard Rock, including the penthouse, which I personally sold to the steel billionaire Lakshmi Mittal for £7.25m.

This episode demonstrates one thing. People who have cash (and don't need to panic to repay a bank) can take their time in the decision-making process. So many of the horror stories in the real estate business come from people who use bank financing to cover the acquisition of buildings and refurbishment. This places them under enormous pressure to sell in order to repay the bank.

I've concluded over the years that there is no science to the real estate market – it just tracks the general economy. If retailers are doing well and business is booming, premises will be taken and high rents will be paid. I've sat through a few peaks and troughs of booms and recessions and seen the value of buildings rise and fall like a yoyo. Over the long haul, buildings in strategic prime positions in high streets and town centres will always maintain their value. Eventually, through one of the cycles of boom and bust, you will have the oppor-tunity to sell at the top of the market or buy at the bottom.

I openly admit that I am no expert in the real estate business. As I've said, I find it a bit boring. However, if it is played correctly, it's a safe place to be. Having said I'm no expert on real estate, I can double-barrel assure you that neither are any of these agents.

*

All through the nineties and well into the new millennium, I had been writing for some of the national newspapers, mainly on business or football. I'd agreed with Piers Morgan, the then editor of the *Daily Mirror*, to do a weekly business column answering questions from readers who were either interested in starting their own businesses or needed advice on their existing ones. And Nick Hewer received lots of requests for me to be a guest on various chat shows or to be involved in some second-rate TV reality or quiz show, all of which I rejected. However, I had given many interviews on TV – on football programmes and *The Money Programme* in the computer days – and while I wasn't an expert, having done it so many times, I'd become experienced in how to deal with it.

In March 2004, a young researcher from the BBC came to Brentwood to talk to me about a reality programme known as *The Apprentice*. The BBC was considering the programme, which had been successful in America. She gave me the bare bones of the format: a leading businessman such as myself would be presented with fourteen candidates, who would be split into two teams each week and given business tasks. Over the course of a twelve-week period, I would eliminate one candidate each week who'd failed to perform well. The researcher had been sent to check out some potential businessmen to head up the programme. I told her I was mildly interested, but needed more detail. She said she'd get back to me and that was the last I heard.

I thought no more of it until I went to Florida at Easter-time. Ann told me that her American friends there were raving about a programme called *The Apprentice*, headed up by Donald Trump. Apparently, it was the biggest hit in America and everyone was talking about it. It kind of rang a bell in my mind and I remembered the young lady from the BBC who'd come to visit me in March. When I spoke to people *I* knew at the tennis club, they also told me how popular *The Apprentice* was and how they always stayed in to watch it.

So I was interested (although surprised) when on returning from Florida after Easter, I was contacted by the television production company Talkback Thames who wanted to talk about – *The Apprentice*. The rights had been bought by Talkback Thames's parent company, Fremantle. Knowing the BBC, it may well be that during their slow deliberations they were gazumped by Fremantle.

The irony was that Talkback Thames, having now acquired the rights to produce *The Apprentice*, entered into an agreement with the BBC for them to broadcast it! To be honest, I wasn't interested in all the politics of who did what, but I *was* interested in doing the show, simply because I'd seen it in America and knew how popular it had become. Additionally, I felt it would be an extension to the work I'd done over the years in promoting enterprise and business to young people.

Nick Hewer got busy and talked to the producer at Talkback Thames, Peter Moore, who said I was one of three or four people they were homing in on. A couple of the other obvious candidates were Philip Green and Stelios Haji-Ioannou. Interestingly, Richard Branson wasn't on their list, as he had agreed to appear in a copycat version of *The Apprentice* in the USA for Fox TV.

I admit, I *really* wanted to do this – no question about it. I told Nick to get to work on Peter Moore. Having seen how successful the show was in America, there was no question of me needing to be persuaded. I also called Philip Green to ask if he had been contacted about this show. He told me he had, but said he didn't have enough time to do all this stuff and wasn't interested. In fact, he said, 'It's much more suited to you.' I think the truth of the matter (and Philip may agree) was that he didn't have much experience in front of a camera. On top of that he was very busy building his booming business and wasn't prepared to allocate any time to the programme.

*

Eventually, I met with Peter Moore, a very slight man about my height with flowing silvery-grey hair, and Daisy Goodwin, who appeared to be his boss at Talkback Thames, for a drink at the Dorchester Hotel. It was the first time they had seen me face to face and after a few niceties, I launched into, 'I've seen this programme in the USA and, quite frankly, I could carry off Trump's role with my eyes closed. I know you don't know me from Adam, but it's a shame you weren't a fly on the wall at some of my board meetings at Amstrad – if you had been, you'd know you need look no further for the right man.'

Peter was really onside because, as a Spurs supporter, he had followed me and seen my so-called brash approach in TV interviews. However, Daisy didn't know me at all and said, 'Well, Alan, as you may know, we're looking at some other options, but it's been very nice meeting you.'

Peter had kind of hinted that to me and told me he was going into bat on my behalf. 'As far as I'm concerned, Sir A [that's what he always called me], *you're* my man. I can see your enthusiasm and you're not afraid to speak your mind. That's what this show will need.'

He set up a meeting for me with the controllers of BBC2. Peter and Daisy also turned up. What I didn't realise at the time was that they were pitching me to the BBC. It obviously worked because a day later Peter told me he was going to make a certain Mr Stelios very upset by telling him he hadn't been chosen.

I was at my house in Spain at the time and suggested his team fly out there, as they needed to start the production planning. We could have a relaxing day discussing the details. Nick Hewer was staying with me at the time and, as he had been so involved in arranging all this, I thought it'd be a good idea if he was also at the meeting.

One of the first things they asked me was who I wanted for my two lieutenants. These two advisers would be tracking the teams of candidates throughout the tasks and would then report their findings to me. I hadn't really thought about who I would have at my side until that moment. I felt it was important, from a credibility point of view, that they were people who had worked with me for a long time and knew how I thought.

Peter said, 'How about Nick Hewer, Sir A? He seems to know you very well. He's been around you for twenty-odd years. He seems the perfect person.' Tanya Shaw, the number two producer of the show, agreed immediately that Nick would be ideal.

'Bloody good idea!' I said. 'Nick, you'll be great, you know everything about me.'

Nick's initial reaction was one of shock. 'No, not me, I'm a PR consultant. No, you'll have to find someone from the business world.'

'Nick, you don't need to know all the ins and outs of business,' I said. 'Plus, you're selling yourself short – you say you don't know, but you *do*. How many deals have you been involved in with me, burning the midnight oil? It's a great idea – you are my number one choice.'

I had to think of a lady to assist me and Margaret Mountford came to mind immediately. She'd been there through most of my deals; she'd helped me float the company back in 1980 and she was now a member of the board at Amstrad. However, she wasn't the type of person you'd expect to participate in a TV programme, so I parked the idea. I told the people I had someone in mind, whom Nick knew, but I needed to talk to her to see if she'd be prepared to do it.

I told Talkback I was so eager to go ahead with this, I would do it for no fee at all. However, if my two advisers were to give up twelve weeks of their time running around doing this programme, they *would* have to be paid. It was the first time I'd seen how money played a big part in the production of television programmes. When I mentioned that Nick required a fee, Talkback started to get a bit hot under the collar. I think they misread my offer of participating free of charge as *desperation* and assumed I would provide two free advisers as well!

I wouldn't say it was a heated debate, but it was certainly a serious one. I needed to put my stake in the ground to show them I wasn't just a telly wannabe, prepared to do anything for them. Sometimes these TV people assume that if someone who's relatively unknown is given the opportunity of being on TV, they'll stop at nothing to get on the box.

It transpired that the BBC, due to some rule or other, insisted I *had* to have a fee, so a figure they'd expect to pay for comparable hosts was put in my contract. I donated the fee to Great Ormond Street Hospital.

Once these boring matters of contracts and money were out of the way, things really started to get exciting. We now had to discuss the tasks we would be setting the candidates. A lot of debate went on to come up with twelve ideas. I have to say that the production team actually *listened* to my ideas. I had learned – in football, for example – that you don't share your ideas with people who are supposed to be experts, like managers, as they don't welcome it. It's the old 'not invented here' syndrome. But here were a bunch of people that took me into the fold and were grateful for my input. There was a good atmosphere of brainstorming, where everyone's ideas were thrown into the pot and the best ones were used, whether they were mine or someone else's. In many cases, somebody came up with the seed of an idea and somebody else went on to enhance it. That's how it should be.

There was also a lot of discussion about the *rules* of the tasks, in anticipation of the candidates arguing the toss on what they could and couldn't do. All this took weeks of to-ing and fro-ing and, to be fair to Talkback, they made me feel part of the team compiling these tasks.

The selection of the candidates, however, was done entirely by Talkback. They placed some advertisements in the national newspapers for people to apply for a business show. Despite the fact that no one had heard of *The Apprentice*, we had thousands of applicants, many of whom just wanted to be on TV. The BBC insisted that when Talkback selected the candidates, the application process had to be done in a fair and democratic way. The recruitment process had to take place nationwide – in London, Birmingham, Manchester and Glasgow – so as to give the whole of the country a chance. This was part of the BBC's strict rules and regulations in accordance with their compliance standards.

I didn't have any input into the final choice of the fourteen candidates – that was all down to Peter Moore and Tanya Shaw. I think they were a bit paranoid in distancing me from this process, but I guess they didn't know me and I can understand them having the wrong impression from what they'd read in the media, particularly the football stuff. I'm sure they thought I was a bit of an interfering, domineering autocrat who would try to take control of every single thing. Little did they know, this was a long way from the truth. I knew nothing about television production – these people were the experts. Having said that, I don't think it would have hurt, as we neared the closing stages of applications, to have shared with me the final fifty or a hundred applicants' CVs. Instead, they were presented to me as a fait accompli and I was shown their pictures a week before we started filming.

This was a really exciting venture and it was something I needed. I'd done the business with Amstrad and I'd romanced the football industry without succeeding (albeit I still made a bit of money), but this was a new voyage in my life.

When we got close to filming, I was introduced to two other senior members of the production team, Dan Adamson and Beth Dicks. Beth was going to be the lady by my side, filming the general visual shots of me they'd use in the makeup of the programme, like the opening scenes or me driving around in my car or on my boat. These shots are normally done in advance, so when they come to edit the final shows, they can slot them in at the appropriate places.

I recall going to Stansted, standing in front of my plane and being given a script of what to say. It was at this point that I realised I hadn't mentioned to Peter or Tanya that I was *not* going to be scripted in any way, shape or form, or told what to say or do!

The script they had given me was difficult for me to rattle off in a natural way. They weren't 'Alan Sugar words' and after an hour of repeatedly trying to record it in a noisy aeroplane hangar, having to stop and start every time a plane took off, I was getting a little frustrated and so was Beth. I reckon she must have been thinking, 'Bloody hell, we've picked a wrong 'un here – he can't string a set of words together.'

This prompted me to speak to Peter and Tanya. I said, 'I think there's been a bit of a misunderstanding here. When I'm talking to the candidates or my advisers, if you think I'm going to work from a script or read out the lines I'm going to say to people, then you've made a serious mistake. I'm sorry not to have thought of mentioning it to you earlier, but there's no way I'd be prepared to do that. I'm not an actor and it will just come across as false. If you want to get the best out of me, you just need me to let rip and do what I want to do.' Peter and Tanya were quite shocked that this is what I had thought.

Peter said, 'We actually chose you *because* you're a motor-mouth. There is no way we're going to script you – you *are* going to be let loose. Do what you want, say what you want. At the end of the day, if *you* don't like some of the things you said, or *we* don't like some of the things you said, it's not a live programme – we'll edit it.'

This assurance came as a great relief to me. From that day, all the things I said out on location and in the general shots were my own words, after I'd got the gist of what the production people wanted me to put across. Luckily, Peter was very pleased with the videos coming back from the location shoots. It was a big risk taking me on and his reputation was on the line. He wouldn't know if he'd made a mistake or not until the candidates turned up for the first time in the boardroom and we got started.

In the meantime, at the end of an Amstrad board meeting, I took Margaret to one side and told her I was going to participate in a TV programme called *The Apprentice*. I gave her a video of the American version to watch and told her I'd be taking on Donald Trump's role in the UK version. Nick Hewer had already accepted the role of one of the advisers; would she consider the other role?

Her immediate reaction was, 'I've never done anything like that before – I wouldn't know what to do. I've never been on television or given an interview. As you know, Alan, I have always kept away from the press and I have always warned you to keep away from the press and keep your mouth shut. I'm not sure whether this is meant for me, but I'll have a look at the video and let you know if I'm interested.'

I didn't want to put too much pressure on her, but asked her to let me know in the next couple of days. Judging by her initial reaction, I wasn't very hopeful she'd go for it. Thinking about it more though, it looked like the dream team. Nick, a very stand-up, posh-speaking, respectable man; Margaret, an eloquent, high-profile ex-City lawyer. Two serious people – and in the middle, this kind of rough diamond, a hard-nosed businessman. What a mixture!

Margaret called me back a day later and said she would do it, so long as it didn't interfere with her other commitments (some non-executive directorships). She felt, as I did, that it was quite an exciting and interesting challenge. Knowing she was onboard, I told Peter and Tanya of my choice. They didn't raise any objection – they too knew that three most unusual characters from different walks of life would be a winning formula for TV.

I was now to meet the fourteen candidates for the first time. Nick, Margaret and I were positioned in the boardroom waiting for them. *They* knew they were going to meet Sir Alan Sugar, but I didn't know who they were. And no one had any idea what I was going to say to them apart from me. Over the weeks of preparation, I'd worked out in my mind the thrust of what I wanted to say to let them know who I was and what I expected. I had it kind of stored in my memory cells, ready for the big day.

As they sat down, I started explaining to them, calmly at first, what the process was about. I would be putting them in teams, sending them out to do various business tasks. One team will win, one team will lose, and someone in the losing team will be fired. At the end of the twelve-week process, there will be one person left who will get a six-figure salaried job with me. So far, so good.

Then I upped the volume and broke into my famous tirade, telling them not to underestimate me – I don't like liars, bullshitters, cheats and schmoozers. I ranted on for what felt like ages but was only a few minutes, then sent them off to a house I'd got for them to live in over the course of the next twelve weeks. I told them I'd be calling them later to set the first task.

The candidates exited the boardroom and were whisked off to the house. Peter and Tanya were absolutely delighted. The cameramen filming the thing found it hard to keep a straight face as they saw how the candidates were in shock. I often wonder now how cameramen manage to keep their mouths shut or not burst out laughing.

I felt pleased at that moment for Peter Moore. He had gambled on me and it was the first time he had seen me in full flow in front of the candidates. As a professional who had made lots of successful television programmes, he must have been relieved. From that moment on, I think he knew he was going to have a big hit on his hands.

It was time to get going on the first task. We'd come up with an easy opener for the candidates – to go to a wholesale flower market to buy flowers, then sell them on the streets. I'd chosen flowers because they are perishable items and in that kind of business there's an art to buying the right amount of stock to make sure that, at the end of a trading day, you don't have any left, as they will decay and be unsaleable. When introducing the task, as an analogy for the flower-selling situation, I asked the candidates to turn up at the printing works of the *Financial Times*. I told them we were there to illustrate that a daily newspaper has to be produced and delivered overnight, put on sale and by the end of the day there should be none left, as there's nothing more useless than yesterday's news. *Their* task was to sell a commodity with a similarly short shelf-life.

Despite my having no input in the selection of candidates, they turned out to be quite a good bunch of people, quite credible and from all walks of life. Some of them were highly qualified. A few were in the business world, while others worked for ordinary organisations. Tim Campbell, for example, worked for London Underground.

Surprisingly, the boys won the first task. There was a brilliant performance from Paul Torrisi, a fiery northerner with Italian blood in him, who turned out to be one of the show's main characters in that series. It was clear from the way the show was going that, apart from the underlying business message, it was great entertainment seeing these characters performing under pressure, getting stressed and arguing with each other.

At the end of the task, I would question the candidates. It wasn't until I was thrown into the deep end that first time that I realised I was talking blind. How could I judge something if I hadn't seen what was going on? Sure, anyone could judge which team had won by selling more items, but to work out which person from the losing team was culpable, I needed Nick and Margaret's feedback. I forced a debate amongst the candidates and asked Nick and Margaret to interject. It went on for ages, as I needed to get a clear picture in my mind of what had happened. From then on, I had a serious debriefing with Nick and Margaret after every task was performed, before the candidates came into the boardroom to face me.

To dispel any rumours, I have to say that I really *don't* get to see what goes on while the candidates are out in the field or at the house. As much as I'd like to be a fly on the wall, the fact is, the footage takes weeks to process and put into a format for viewing. In most cases, I meet up with the candidates the day after the task is completed. As I don't have any footage to view, I have to use my imagination and rely on the feedback from Nick and Margaret.

The candidates would argue with each other in front of me and some would bend the truth for sure. When I picked them up for being less than honest, they were totally shocked at the information I had on them, which was all down to Nick and Margaret – my eyes and ears. I'd also learned a few techniques from the barristers I'd observed during my court cases. I would let the candidates ramble on with their version of events – and, in some cases, bury themselves – then I'd pounce on them with the truth. After a few weeks, they got the plot not to bullshit me.

What became clear was how people would make the most irrational business decisions under pressure. Some of the simple basics of
business were being ignored, such as paying attention to costings,
working out how many items to buy so they didn't get stuck with leftover stock and ensuring that what they were selling made a profit!

It was also quite amazing to see the naïvety of academics who had
never been involved in business or, worse, those who claimed they
were experienced in business. After all, one wasn't asking them to
create a complex business model – it was all simple stuff. It came as a
great shock to me that some people completely ignored simple maths
and hadn't realised their early decisions had left them dead in the
water before they'd even started. Even more fascinating was seeing
how, having explained the errors of their ways throughout the course
of the process, the same mistakes were repeated over and over again.

Eventually, in that first series, the very worthy winner was Tim
Campbell, after a closely run final with Saira Khan. Tim came to work
at Brentwood and got on very well with the staff. He was given a new
project to head up, an electronic face-care system, and he worked with
the engineers to develop both the product and a website to host the
sales.

I have to say that it was time-consuming and gruelling filming the
show. Occasionally it involved working over weekends, which was
sometimes inconvenient to family life. Little did Nick, Margaret and I
know at the time how popular the programme would become. Once
the filming was over, we all went our separate ways and got on with
our own business. I was invited to the editing suite from time to time
to see rough cuts of sections of the programmes. It wasn't until I saw
the footage of the candidates running round in the streets and in
offices and shops did I actually realise what they'd been up to. I was
comforted in most cases that the decisions and criticisms I'd made,
somewhat blindly, were borne out by what had actually gone on.

I was very impressed when I first saw the opening title sequence of
the programme, showing the sweeping views of London and the
Thames, together with the very distinctive music. It was all very exciting stuff. I was told I hadn't seen *anything* yet, as none of it had been
polished. They had hired helicopters to film London, as well as film

crews to capture the candidates driving around in the vans and me riding along in my car.

I was getting an understanding of how a programme is produced. In the case of *The Apprentice*, each one-hour programme has been edited down from over a hundred hours of filming, as the teams go off to separate locations and sometimes split into sub-teams, each with separate crews filming them. Then there's the film of the candidates in the house and the boardroom. There can be up to four sets of crew following them around and six cameras in the boardroom. From that mountain of material, the editors have to make the programme. It was a new world I was experiencing and it was fascinating to watch these talented people cutting and pasting the raw footage to create a one-hour, feature-packed show.

As time went on, I started to see some of the finished films and they were excellent. Peter Moore wouldn't give me copies of them. I think he was worried I might show them to somebody and breach the contract Talkback had with the BBC!

Peter had a bit of a fiery temper and we had a couple of rows. He was one of those temperamental people you'd expect to find in the media industry, the sort who would have a tantrum and walk off the set, so to speak. These artistic people are a bit funny in that way. They're a completely different bunch of people to those I'd come across in business, very touchy and sensitive about their artistic genius.

I wasn't poking my nose into their business – I wouldn't have had a clue what to do with respect to filming and editing – but I used to get very frustrated waiting for the cameras and lighting to be set up. It was all very time-consuming and I would sometimes lose my rag and come out with some verbal tirade. By the back end of the filming, being a quick learner, I was seeing stuff go on which was grossly inefficient and it was winding me up. On one occasion, I think it was while filming the penultimate show, Peter came storming into the boardroom, ranting and raving at me about my objections. I stood up and told him to fuck off, and he could take his fucking TV show and stick it up his arse. I shut the book I had in front of me on the table and walked out, saying, 'I'm going home. That's it. It's over.'

Peter might have got away with losing his rag on shows he'd done in the past, but he'd dropped a real bollock this time. His temper could have cost his company millions of pounds. If I'd walked off, they'd have had no show! At that time, they only had ten shows recorded. He'd have had to explain to his bosses what had gone wrong, and they'd have had to explain it to the BBC. I don't think he'd expected me to react the way I did, but he'd picked a bad time to start on me, as there were some family problems playing on my mind. Also, it was a Sunday and I was supposed to be at a family event, so I was in a foul mood anyway.

After I'd walked off, Nick told me to calm down. He said he understood how frustrated I was, but reminded me of all the work we'd put in up to now and said it would be unprofessional and uncharacteristic of me to storm off. While I was talking to Nick outside the boardroom, James, the senior cameraman, came up and asked me whether I wanted a cup of coffee and to take a break for a few moments. He had a look on his face as if to say, 'I don't blame you for walking off, but all our jobs are on the line here and we'd like you to stay.' Not that he actually said anything – it was just his body language.

Nick and Margaret calmed me down and I went back into the boardroom and finished off the show, but I went home fuming. I phoned Peter the following morning and told him I was a professional and that if I was committed to do something, then I would do it, but I wasn't going to put up with any more of his bloody nonsense. I guess if you asked him for *his* take on that phone call, he'd say that that's what *he* said to *me*. I think it reasonable to say we agreed to disagree.

The BBC didn't have a clue how popular the programme would become. There was no formal press conference, which they'd normally have before launching a new programme. It just went out, with no fanfare, for the first time in February 2005, while I was away on a family holiday, skiing in Courchevel – boys only.

I'd seen the final cut already, but it was interesting to watch my family's reactions. They were glued to the TV, asking me what would happen next. The format was new, so they had no idea, having just seen me for a short time at the beginning of the show, when I would come back into play. They certainly got it when we reached the boardroom scenes.

Ann was at home, as were Louise and Michaela. The show first aired at 9 p.m. on a Wednesday night on BBC2. As soon as it was over, my mobile started ringing. Jeremy Beadle was on the line, telling me the BBC had a massive hit on its hands and how fantastic the show was. A few minutes later, Bill Kenwright, the Everton chairman, called me saying the same thing.

My brother Derek phoned, telling me he was so surprised – he'd known I was doing a television show, but hadn't realised it was going to be anything like this. Ann called me to say that Daphne had phoned her while the show was on, around the time I was telling the candidates, 'I don't like bullshitters . . .' and she'd said to Daphne, 'You haven't seen anything yet. Call back at the end – let me watch the programme.'

They were all tremendously excited, as one would expect from the family when you're on telly. However, in TV terms, the way they gauge success is the viewing figures. Next day, I called Peter Moore and asked him what he thought. He wasn't exactly jumping up and down. He told me it had achieved something like 1.9 million viewers and I detected a tone of disappointment, as if that wasn't good enough. I, of course, couldn't put this in context – I didn't know whether 1.9 million viewers was good or bad. Whatever, Peter didn't seem to think it had set the world alight. The second week's viewing figures went down to something like 1.8 million, but then word must have started getting around, as numbers started to grow and reached around 3.5 million, which I was told was *brilliant* for BBC2.

As the popularity of the programme grew, it was quite interesting to watch the reaction of people when they saw me in the streets. Up till then, I'd been recognised a fair bit because of my involvement in football, with such welcoming greetings as, 'All right, Alan, how's that bleedin' team of yours?' stretching to, 'Oi, Sugar, get your fucking chequebook out, you prick!' All that type of stuff, if you know what I mean. Now people would come up to me, tell me how good the show was, shake my hand and be very polite. Of course you *did* get the odd person who'd make an idiot of themselves by saying, 'You're fired!' and then laughing hysterically while everyone else looked at him as if he was a prat.

I was particularly encouraged to see that many teenagers were inspired by the show. It seemed that everywhere I went I was asked by this young audience to have photos taken with them or sign autographs. I also started to get lots of letters from young people telling me about their business ideas. It was comforting that one of my objectives was bearing fruit.

One of the funny things was the number of women in their forties and fifties who would come over to me and compliment me on the show. It was particularly amusing when they were accompanied by their husbands, who would kind of loiter with false smiles, holding in some kind of inner rage as their wives poured compliments on me. It was embarrassing though, and it got to the stage where I would spot these women out of the corner of my eye and, knowing they were about to pounce, would start a conversation with someone next to me in the hope that they would go away. I couldn't stand that look of resentment from the hubbies. Let me make it clear, these ladies were only expressing their admiration of my business acumen and the way I performed on the show – nothing else. Let's face it – George Clooney I'm not.

The other 'commentators' were men aged between thirty-five and fifty: 'This *Apprentice* is all a load of rubbish. That's not business. That Sugar's talking a load of bollocks.' That was the testosterone speaking and, funnily enough, I would get more of this kind of thing if the chaps' female companions had complimented me.

Being on TV affects different people in different ways. Margaret, for example, claims she hates the fame *The Apprentice* has brought her. I do find it hard to believe, but she insists she does. She doesn't like people recognising her when she's on the tube or the bus, or impertinently coming up to her on the street saying, 'You're that lady from the TV programme.' Nick, on the other hand, accepts recognition with ease. I sometimes joke that he would turn up to the opening of an envelope. 'Only if there's a cheque inside,' he says.

To be honest, I thought it was great being part of such a popular television programme. *The Apprentice* brought me fame and I won't deny that I enjoyed it. However, I feel I managed it quite well and didn't go overboard. I was getting offers for newspaper interviews, invitations to cocktail parties and all that stuff, but I turned most of them down. I did appear on Jonathan Ross's show because I understood it was a BBC request to help promote the series. For the same reason, I did a few press interviews for some of the national newspapers, but that was it. I also turned down all sorts of reality television programmes, panel games and, would you believe, *Strictly Come Dancing*!

Unbelievable – the idiots, thinking I would get involved in that.

19

Luvvies and Darlings

And the End of an Era at Amstrad

2005–7

They're a funny bunch of people in television. They're good at what they do – making programmes – but when they try to be shrewd in business, this mob in the TV industry are useless. For instance, after the success of the first series of *The Apprentice*, everybody knew there would be a second series, yet the BBC's Jane Lush was keeping up the charade that it hadn't been decided yet. She was playing it cool, thinking that if she looked too eager, it would cost them too much money. Quite frankly, as an attempt at bluffing it was a bit pathetic. She reminded me a bit of the David Hyams/Bob Watkins/Ian Saward types – trying to be what they're not.

Finally, the BBC did commission the second series and Nick, Margaret and I signed up again. I was expecting to work with the same team, but a few months later, editorial director Daisy Goodwin left Talkback to set up her own company, Silver River Productions. What's more, Peter Moore and Tanya Shaw decided they didn't want to do *The Apprentice* again and also left.

There is a weird artistic snobbery which exists in this industry. You can understand why an actor (for example Ross Kemp who played the character Grant Mitchell in the popular BBC soap *EastEnders*) might feel he's been typecast and want to further his career by taking on other roles, but these production people take it a stage further – they don't want to be typecast as *producers*. They like to find new challenges to widen their portfolios. In Peter's case, he had been around for a long time and had made lots of films, so I can quite understand that he was working more for enjoyment than financial reward. He wanted to do things he was *interested* in and, as far as *The Apprentice* was concerned, he'd set the mould, done it, bought the T-shirt and it was over – time to move on. And for some reason, Tanya Shaw wanted to do the same.

Dan Adamson, one of the senior assistant producers of the first series, took over the second series, which went well as far as viewing figures were concerned, and there were some great characters. However, I personally felt that this series wasn't as professional and that we were getting too close to a *Big Brother*-type show which concentrates on people arguing. My involvement in *The Apprentice* was only on the basis of there being an underlying business message in every episode.

Meanwhile, the first series had been nominated for a BAFTA, the most prestigious of television awards. The ceremony was held on 7 May and I turned up that night at the Great Room at the Grosvenor House Hotel to find it jam-packed full of TV celebrities and stars. It was a massive event. I went with Ann and, not knowing anyone and feeling a bit shy, we tried to hang back in the reception area for a while until they called people to the tables. Eventually, Daisy Goodwin got hold of us, walked us through the main dining area and started introducing me to people. Gordon Ramsay came up and shook my hand, telling me how wonderful the show was. I met Bruce Forsyth, Jack Dee and loads of others. I didn't understand, in TV terms, what a breakthrough *The Apprentice* had been. Only now did I realise, walking through this grand hall and seeing people looking at me or coming to talk to me, that it was a massively popular show.

We won the BAFTA award for 'Best Feature' that night. Peter Moore dragged me up on to the stage in front of all these people and for once I was dumbstruck. I just hung behind him and let him do the talking. There was a press call for me to have my picture taken with the award and there, queuing up in the press room, was David Jason, the great actor from *Only Fools and Horses*. He shook my hand, telling me what a great programme it was and how he'd enjoyed watching it. I told him, never mind all that, it was an honour for *me* to meet *him* and said how he had entertained me over the years as Del Boy and Inspector Frost. Meeting him was a highlight of the evening.

Ricky Gervais was sitting on another table and waved at me. He was hot at the time with his show *The Office*. I went over to shake his hand and he said, 'I don't know why I waved at you because I don't know you. I guess it was just to say well done.'

You can imagine how a moment like this could *really* go to your head, how it could make you want more and more fame. But in a way, this was no different to having a smash-hit Amstrad product – it was great to be congratulated for my success but, like a hit product, I knew it wouldn't go on for ever. My feet were firmly on the ground and I had no delusions that I was some great TV celebrity.

There is no question that if I had my time over again and was asked to do *The Apprentice*, the answer would be absolutely yes. It's tremendously enjoyable and it signs on to my philosophy of assisting small businesses and young people in promoting enterprise. I have to be thankful to Peter Moore for choosing me as his preferred host.

Lots of people have asked whether *The Apprentice* has assisted me in business. The simple answer is no – not one bit. Why should it? I'm in electronics and real estate. Of course, people want to meet me and want me to come to their offices, sign photographs and things like that, but when we get down to serious business, there is either a good deal to be done or there isn't, irrespective of whether or not I'm on TV.

The demand for me to do more Q&As at schools, universities and charities obviously shot up as a result of the show. Whenever I could, I tried to accommodate them, but it's impossible for me to accept every single invitation – there aren't enough hours in the day or days in the week. However, I did do a Q&A session at Brunel University shortly after they awarded me my *second* honorary doctorate (again a Doctorate of Science) on 12 July 2005. By this time, I was an old hand at ceremonies, so there was no nervousness at all. I gave a small speech which was based on enterprise.

I was now a double doctor and a knight! Bloody hell!

After the second series, Dan Adamson joined Daisy Goodwin's newly formed company, which meant more change. I was surprised Dan had decided to leave, since the second series was very successful in his eyes, which was proved by the viewing figures. I still couldn't quite get my head around these people wanting to flip so quickly, but it was something I'd have to get used to. Lorraine Heggessey, a short and fiery character, had taken the role of CEO of Talkback Thames and she recruited the services of Michele Kurland and Kelly Webb-Lamb.

I'd agreed to do a third series but I was a little disappointed that, effectively, we had to reinvent the wheel. It's important in any working relationship that people get to know each other's ways and having worked with Dan for two years, each of us understood the other's thinking about the different aspects of the show. Now I was faced with a new team of bosses and I'm always concerned that new people will want to make their mark by changing things. It's no different in the business world. When a new person arrives to take over a senior position – perhaps because a company's in trouble or needs new direction – there's always a mass culling of ideas, people and systems to reshape things to the new person's liking.

Ego plays a big part in these things. What's the point of taking over an organisation if outwardly one can't see a distinctive change? But, most of the time, changes aren't necessary and can be counter-productive. When Lord Kalms (Stanley) decided it was time for him to retire and recruit a new chairman, I wrote an article for the *Evening Standard* along the lines of, 'When the new bloke comes in, he shouldn't change things for the sake of change. In other words – if it ain't broke, don't fix it.' Stanley sent me a nice note thanking me for this.

Even in Dan Adamson's days on the second series, suggestions were coming from the production people about changing the way we did things. I argued strongly against this on the 'if it ain't broke, don't fix it' basis. The public aren't stupid. Unless the change is really going to improve things, don't do it – because if it's gimmicky, the public will tune out. Fortunately, after much debate, Dan agreed with me. But here I was again, faced with these two new ladies. It's human nature that they would want to put their stamp on the programme and I would have to go through the whole thing again.

To be perfectly honest, I don't like changes of personnel; I like to deal with people I've built a rapport with. So Lorraine was somewhat nervous introducing Michele and Kelly to me – and I think they were nervous about meeting me. Michele was introduced as the senior producer; Kelly effectively being her number two.

As you might imagine, my opening speech to them was along the lines of, 'When you have something successful in business, you don't change it.' I also told them I'd been keeping my eye on the American market and the Trump programme was going down the pan rapidly, not least because they were overexposing it, running series back to back. In the course of eighteen months, they had run two series and the public were getting sick of it. Not only was it on too much, but they started tinkering with the format, doing stupid things like making the candidates live in the garden if they lost or allowing the winning team leader to be immune from being fired on the next task. It was over-complicated and becoming very tacky. I made it clear I didn't want to be associated with any of this stuff.

The thing about television people is, they're all very polite. Everything is wonderful, everything is marvellous, nothing is ever wrong, it's all fantastic, darling. These two ladies had spent many years in the industry, so they kind of agreed with every single thing I said and I knew it was too good to be true. When that happens, I think, 'At least disagree with me about *something*!'

I reckon, as this was their first meeting with me, somebody must have warned them just to go along with whatever I was saying. People already had a skewed idea of what I was like based on my portrayal in the sports media when I was chairman of Tottenham. This was compounded ten times over by the fact that, on TV, I was shown as a real tough nut in the boardroom, banging my fist on the table and dishing out a load of stick. If this is the only vision you have of Alan Sugar, then you can quite understand how people believe that's exactly what I'm like.

I don't want to give away too many secrets here, but the truth of the matter is that the boardroom scenes are edited to create tension. The actual boardroom sessions can take a couple of hours and there's a lot of banter and jokes, as well as me getting a bit angry, of course. However, a lot of the light-hearted stuff gets cut and you end up seeing fifteen minutes of me banging the table. With that in mind, you can understand the ladies' nervousness about meeting me for the first time.

I spent at least ten minutes of that first meeting with Michele and

Kelly trying to convince them, firstly, that I wasn't the person they'd seen on TV and, secondly, that I liked to get involved in all the details and even put my own suggestions forward. I said that I hoped we could end up with a similar relationship to the one I'd had with Dan Adamson. Once again, in TV luvvy terms, they agreed, telling me they knew exactly how TV works and how I'd obviously been portrayed in a certain way to create tension in the programme.

After watching the second series, my family was starting to get a bit concerned that I was coming across as a table-banging monster. They were even suggesting that I shouldn't do it any more, partly because they felt, as I did, that some of the candidates in the second series were getting close to those you'd expect to see on *Big Brother*, and also because they found themselves having to explain to their friends that I'm not really the brute they see on TV.

The thing is, I *do* fly off the handle in real life – in boardroom situations, or when I get angry with inefficiency, or when things go wrong. And I haven't got the greatest patience in the world. It's a bad trait, I know – it's just that sometimes I see things more clearly than others (though I *thought* I was getting better and more tolerant as I got older). When I look back on my business life and the nucleus of people that have worked for me, it must be some sort of testimony to say that a great many of them have stayed with me for most of their working lives. The average length of service is around twenty years, indeed some of them have been with me for well over thirty years. If I'm such a horrible person, why are they all still there? The truth is, I'm very fair and straightforward. My famous expression is, 'What's on my lung is on my tongue.' Generally I think people like it that way – straight-talking.

Michele and Kelly agreed. 'Yes, that's exactly what *we* want when we do *The Apprentice* – straightforward speaking, right to the point.' Both of them were very excited at the prospect of doing *The Apprentice*, which had now become a hit programme. So much so that Jana Bennett, Director of BBC Vision, decided she would elevate it from BBC2 to BBC1, giving it the same nine o'clock slot on a Wednesday night. Talkback were very pleased about this but, naïvely, I couldn't under-stand what the big deal was. In my opinion, if somebody wants to watch a programme, the fact that it's on BBC2 or BBC1 makes no odds. I couldn't get my head around this at all. If people were followers of *The Apprentice* and the fan base grew by word of mouth, as far as I was concerned, the channel made no difference. Lorraine and Michele were a little surprised at my lack of enthusiasm about the channel flip, but that was down to my lack of experience in these matters.

During preparations for the third series, Michele kept me in the loop, seeking my input, and we had many debates over the way forward. Michele asked me to have a word with people like Andy Devonshire and Mark Saben, two of the guys who had worked on the previous series and had accumulated a lot of experience. We were keen to keep them onboard. Andy is responsible for those fantastic pictures of London in the titles and all the general filming. He orchestrates the boardroom and arranges the close-ups on people's faces when they're talking. Mark went around with the teams and organised the crew when filming out in the field. Andy and Mark, like others in the industry, were also considering alternative opportunities and the idea of having to recruit someone new and start from scratch was unthinkable. I spoke to the two guys and luckily I managed to convince them to stay.

A large proportion of the TV production industry is made up of self-employed people who have contracts. The problem is, they have families to look after and the production of a programme like *The Apprentice* means making themselves available not only for the filming period, but also the editing phase. When all that's done, the harsh reality is that they are 'let go' and have to find themselves some fill-in work elsewhere. What's more, they never know whether a show will be recommissioned. Regrettably, TV companies like the BBC don't tend to commission more than one series at a time. They like to keep their options open, understandably, in case viewing figures start to tumble. And even if a programme is recommissioned, by the time the decision's made, the people who worked on it previously might have taken up – quite justifiably – other work to secure some income.

It's like juggling, trying to tell these guys, 'Hang on, don't take on any other work because negotiations are going on to commission a new series.' It's difficult asking them not to accept assignments elsewhere when, in fact, you have nothing concrete on the table to offer them. In the case of Andy and Mark, I told them that although the new series hadn't been officially commissioned, it was 99.9 per cent sure to go ahead. I asked them to trust me that they *would* be required and not to accept other offers.

The camera crew on *The Apprentice* always consisted of the same guys. That was good because they'd done it before and didn't need retraining. They knew what worked and what didn't work.

TV production is no different from any other form of production. When you have a good product running on a production line, the last thing you want to do is lose your production managers, your production engineers or your quality control managers, because new people have to learn stuff by remaking all the mistakes of the past. New people, by definition, must mean a drop in quality. We could not afford to go through that learning curve again, particularly as we were going on to BBC1, where the quality had to be tip-top and we'd be playing to a different type of audience. The art was keeping the team together.

After months of discussion with Michele and the team, some changes were made for the benefit of the show. We decided we would start off with sixteen candidates instead of fourteen, to give us some flexibility. We'd been very lucky in the past two series that none of the candidates got sick or had some personal issue whereby they had to leave the process. If that had happened, it could have had a devastating effect on the flow of the show. Also, there were occasions in the first two series when I felt like firing more than one person – simply because two of them deserved it – but, conscious of the programme's continuity, I restrained myself to individual firings. With sixteen people, if that situation ever occurred again, I would have the flexibility to do so. In my mind, it was never going to be used as a stunt; I would only use the option if needed. And if I didn't, we'd end up with three or maybe four people in the final. I always made it clear I was never going to compromise the integrity of the show.

Michele decided to change the format a bit. At the end of each programme in the first two series you didn't see the losing team returning to the house – *that* was always shown at the start of the following programme. Michele felt this was an untidy way to start the show and that it would be much cleaner to finish the show with the return home, then start afresh the following week. She made a very good point and we changed it.

In view of the growing popularity of the programme, the number of applicants was around the 20,000 mark. The BBC's compliance policy meant that each and every application had to be treated fairly and dealt with on a regional basis. Michele decided to keep me in the loop as far as candidate selection was concerned and take on board some of my comments about the calibre of people we required. By now, I was very conscious of not letting *The Apprentice* be degraded until it became *Big Brother* on wheels. There was a danger of the wrong type of candidates getting in – people who had no real business acumen, just big mouths, like some of those in the second series.

Of course, we also wanted to make good TV, so the candidates should be vociferous and interesting, but I insisted there had to be a genuine reason for their appointment to the show. People like Philip Green, plus a few of my friends and associates, were commenting that all the candidates seemed to be brain-deads and that they would never employ any of them.

I was concerned that we needed to raise the credibility, but at the same time maintain a balance of good entertainment. What people don't understand is that if you have a bunch of sensible people, take them out of their comfort zone and put them into a competitive environment where they want to succeed, they tend to panic. The panic causes bad decisions and sometimes they make themselves look foolish. I remember telling Philip that he had no idea of the pressure these people were under and, with respect, if I had him, Bill Gates, Richard Branson and Stelios on the programme, woke them up at six in the morning and told them they had to prepare some chickens to sell at a festival on the South Bank – buying the stuff, preparing it, cooking it, selling it and coming out with a profit, all in a few days – *they* would also panic.

Unavoidably, certain candidates *do* slip through the net, getting themselves on the programme because they think they are going to enhance some sort of media career – it's human nature to want to be on television. However, the majority are there for the right reason. Over the first two series I learned how to detect the media wannabees and made sure their time on *The Apprentice* was used to the show's advantage, as far as entertainment was concerned, before their departure.

One shining example of this was James Max from the first series. He was a highly intelligent and successful businessman who had worked in City circles and made a lot of money. However, observing this guy, I could tell he didn't want a job with me – he wanted to be famous on TV.

He lasted until the eleventh show. I let him go on the basis that I didn't think he was there for the right reasons, and I was right. This fellow put himself around the media world so much in his search for a TV career, he started driving people mad. A few days after the final, he was on telly in some kiddies' game show in a field somewhere – just to be on TV. I thought to myself, 'You pathetic man, what are you doing?' I even went to the trouble of meeting with him and told him he was wasting his time. Why should a clever chap like him not use his financial brain to carry on doing what he's best at? But he just had a death wish to be in the media. To be fair he now has his own radio show so I guess he got what he wanted.

He was the only contestant to blab to the press about what he perceived had gone on in the production process. He told people that, in the boardroom, my chair was purposely elevated on a box to make me look taller. This was manna from heaven for some of the media, as you can imagine, but it was a load of rubbish. What the set builders had done was build a frame on the floor into which my chair would fit. As the chair was on wheels, the frame was built to stop it sliding around if I moved while I was being filmed. Besides, as any halfwit would know, office chairs are adjustable, so if I wanted to make my chair higher, I could easily do so; I certainly wouldn't need to put it on a box.

During the selection process, Michele shared with me the information on the last hundred candidates. She showed me their CVs and some very short video clips they'd made at the interview stage and together we discussed the final sixteen. As Michele and the team had seen them and spent time with them, I deferred to their judgement, since it was quite difficult for me to appraise them properly with so little information.

At least Michele was being very fair in giving me visibility. And, I guess, she was covering herself so that I couldn't accuse her or Kelly of lumbering me with a load of brain-dead wannabees. We all agreed that keeping me distanced from the candidates was the best thing to do. The first time I would meet them and speak to them would be in the boardroom on day one. One thing that shone through was how hard Michele and Kelly worked. The amount of hours they put in every day was incredible. They were clearly determined that *The Apprentice* was going to be a big hit in its new BBC1 slot.

The third series went exceptionally well. I did have a few of my usual tantrums about having to be up very early in the morning. I'd leave Bramstons at 5 a.m. to get to a location like Greenwich by 7.30, just to introduce a new task. The traffic would do my head in. By the time I got to the location, I'd be ready to tear someone's head off, considering I'd travelled only eight miles in two and a half hours, just to do three minutes of filming. Nevertheless, we made a very, very good series and the viewing figures were exceptional, way beyond the BBC's expectations. The winner was Simon Ambrose, a Cambridge graduate, who joined our property division and took some exams to qualify as a surveyor. After three years, he chose to leave to try to replicate what he'd learned from us and start his own property business.

It's quite strange when the winner of *The Apprentice* comes to work in the firm. There's a certain resentment from some of the staff when a new person suddenly comes into the fold, especially when it's well publicised that his or her salary, as a prize for winning, is £100,000 per annum. They would have seen the candidate make mistakes in the series and classed him or her as a twit, as so many others do.

Meanwhile, other TV channels had tried pathetically to replicate *The Apprentice* with various knock-off shows. Each and every one of them failed miserably. Even Dan Adamson, now with Daisy's new firm, attempted to make one which went down like a lead balloon. ITV also had a go, recruiting the services of Peter Jones, one of the dragons from *Dragons' Den*, making some bizarre replication of *The Apprentice* that also bombed.

The third series went so well, the BBC took the unprecedented step of commissioning *The Apprentice* for *two* new series. Moreover, they wanted to do a one-off version for Comic Relief, to be shown on the evening of Red Nose Day 2007. They wanted to use a bunch of celebrities instead of ordinary candidates, and pit the men against the women. The idea of *The Celebrity Apprentice* sounded exciting and was a great accolade for the show, and I was told that participation in Comic Relief was a very prestigious thing.

Patrick Uden had been involved with *The Apprentice* since the very first series. His background was as a documentary-maker and without a doubt, he was experienced. However, for some reason best known to her, Lorraine Heggessey put him in charge of *The Celebrity Apprentice*, which was clearly not a documentary. She reasoned that Michele and Kelly were too busy with the main series.

Patrick is a nice, polite man and we get on very well. However, we disagreed tremendously about how *The Celebrity Apprentice* should be run. A lot of professional arguing went on and he went into a mode of, 'I'm in charge and that's how it's going to be,' which, as far as I'm concerned, was a bad attitude to take.

The celebrity apprentices included Cheryl Cole, Maureen Lipman, Ross Kemp, Piers Morgan, Alastair Campbell, Jo Brand, Trinny Woodall (from Trinny and Susannah), the famous actor Rupert Everett and radio broadcaster Danny Baker. Also on the girls' team was Karren Brady. While she wasn't a celebrity, she was well known in the football world as the managing director of Birmingham City FC. The task we arranged was for each team to set up a funfair in the centre of London and invite some celebrity guests. The idea was to make them spend lots of money on the amusements, all of which would go to Comic Relief.

I have to admit that when setting the task in the boardroom, I made the mistake of trying to be funny in front of a bunch of professionals. Instead of sticking to my normal routine – introducing myself and dishing out instructions on the task – I tried to add some humour about each individual. I should have known to stick to what I do best. Sadly, most of my quips went down like lead balloons. When I think about it now, I cringe a little, especially since Richard Curtis and his partner Emma Freud, who run Comic Relief, were looking on in the editing gallery.

It appears I upset Rupert Everett and when the teams went off to the hotels we'd laid on for them, he declared the process wasn't for him. He said that he didn't know anyone whom he felt he could ask for money, he didn't know how to sell and, get this, he felt out of his comfort zone in front of the cameras all the time! I couldn't believe what I was hearing. He's a bloody actor! Being in front of the cameras is what he does for a day job. Apparently, he was nervous about answering my questions in the boardroom because it wasn't scripted. Piers Morgan gave him a load of stick, telling him he was a wimp and had let the side down.

The men's team were now a man short, so we seconded Tim Campbell, the winner of the first year's *Apprentice*.

However, under the leadership of Karren Brady (the only business person among the ladies), her team raised an unbelievable £700,000. I believe they got hold of Philip Green and he generously helped by supplying lots of merchandise. Also, Trinny had some great contacts and got them to donate large sums of money. Between the boys and the girls, over a million pounds was raised for Comic Relief that night.

Piers Morgan was the one I fired for being such a clown and causing so much aggravation for the girls. He kept annoying Cheryl Cole in the boardroom, talking about her husband, Ashley, who had left Piers's beloved Arsenal. Cheryl was getting quite angry and she was quite grateful on occasions when I told Piers to shut up.

Piers had been fired from the *Daily Mirror* and had had to reconstruct his career, writing for newspapers and publishing an autobiography. Now he wanted to get into TV, and this was his first real opportunity. Cheryl Cole, who was famous as a member of the group Girls Aloud, also wanted more varied exposure on TV, which she certainly achieved with *The X-Factor*. In Piers's case, he has gone on to be a great TV celebrity and I continually wind him up that he has me to thank for it. He also owes me a debt of gratitude for coaching him through *The Celebrity Apprentice* in the USA.

Mark Burnett, the owner of *The Apprentice* format, had decided the UK's idea of *The Celebrity Apprentice* should be tried out in America, as the main series had gone down the pan. This turned out to be a good move, as *The Celebrity Apprentice* rejuvenated the format in America and it is now very popular again. In my opinion, Donald Trump is fantastic at the job in America – he is tailor-made for the American market, although when they showed the American version in England, it was greeted rather mildly, which I guess is down to the cultural differences between the two countries.

In the first USA *Celebrity Apprentice* series, Piers Morgan managed to get himself on the show and into the final, where he was up against a very popular country singer that everybody loved. Piers, in his usual way, managed to alienate everyone and his brother on the way up, walking all over them and abusing them. Nevertheless, he got through to the final because his teams won most of the time. The final happened to be broadcast while I was in Florida and Piers phoned me and asked me to come up to New York and be in the audience. I told him I couldn't be bothered to schlap all that way and said I'd watch it on TV. He hummed and hawed a bit. Ann was in the room and I told her, 'It's Piers on the phone. He's in the final and wants a few tips from me.'

'No, I'm not asking you for tips, Alan. I'm just telling you I'm in the final tonight. I was just calling to ask you to come along or tune in and watch it.'

'Don't give me any of that bullshit, Morgan. You're calling me to get some tips, right?'

'Well, if you've got anything, I suppose it might be useful.'

'Piers, tell me something. The programmes up to now have all been pre-recorded, right? But the final, from what I've seen on the TV promotions, is actually going to be broadcast *live* in New York – is that right?'

'Yes, it's going to be live.'

'There's not going to be any pre-recording? They can't cut what you say?'

'Yes, exactly right. Why?'

'Well, it's as simple as this – you've won, mate!'

'What do you mean, *I've won*?'

'Listen to me carefully and I guarantee you'll win.'

'Why? I don't understand what you're saying.'

'Well, if the programme can't be cut because it's live, then what you need to do is to put Mr Trump in such a position that he can't do anything *but* choose you.'

'Right . . . I see what you're saying, but how do I go about doing that?'

'Well, it's very simple. Write this down. Mr Trump will ask you about four or five times to plead to him why you should be *The Celebrity Apprentice* winner and here's what you say: "Mr Trump, people might not like me for the way I've gone about doing this, but let me remind you that at the beginning of this process you told us that we had to go out and make the most amount of money for charity. And that, Mr Trump, is exactly what I've done. When you look at the amount of money *my* teams have won compared to this other fellow's, I did exactly what you asked me to do. Now, Mr Trump, you are a businessman and this is a business programme, so it would be difficult for you to go against your principles. You told me to go and make a load of money, and that's what I did. However, if you are going to choose the winner on a popularity vote then, with the greatest respect, Mr Trump, your credibility will go down the pan."'

'Okay, Piers? You say *that* and I'm telling you, you'll have boxed him right into a corner in front of fifteen million viewers – what's he going to say to that? He is a businessman. He told you to make money. The show's not about picking the nicest personality – it's not a singing contest. You are going to win, son.'

'Well, I'm not sure I'd get away with that.'

'Piers, what can they do to you? They can't shoot you – you're on live TV. They can't edit you, they can't cut you. Just have a drink and get into motor-mouth mode and *do it*. I promise you you'll win.'

That's exactly what he did, and he won! Of course, he will never give me the full credit for that speech and will deny all knowledge of our conversation. He just talks about his supreme superiority – but that's Piers Morgan for you! Trust me, it's true. Let's face it, who would *you* believe? He was a tabloid editor – say no more, right?

*

The first UK *Celebrity Apprentice* was broadcast over the course of two days in March 2007. In my opinion, they kind of messed it up, in that they split the show into three sections, leaving the final boardroom climax right to the end of Comic Relief night, the idea being that viewers would hang on to get the result. I was very disappointed with the programme.

Patrick Uden's vision was that the *celebrities* were the ones the programme should focus on and I should be some kind of benign judge. Not wishing to blow my own trumpet, but part of the success of *The Apprentice*, as most people know, is my interrogation of the candidates. He chopped out all the funny and business-specific dialogue that went on in the boardroom. Knowing so much of this had ended up on the cutting-room floor, as they say in the media world, was very frustrating for me when I saw the programme broadcast. People like Lorraine Heggessey didn't understand – she saw the end-product and thought it was great. If only she'd known how it could have been, she wouldn't have formed that opinion.

Regrettably, with this Comic Relief thing, it's a case of too many cooks spoiling the broth and there were arguments about who had jurisdiction over the programme. Was it the BBC (who normally have the final say)? Was it Talkback Thames? Or was it the Comic Relief team?

Emma Freud has her annual moment of power – one year putting on Comic Relief, the next year Sports Relief. There are so many people sticking their oar in – each contributing their so-called artistic brilliance – that all you get in the end, I'm afraid, is a mess. Patrick threw his lot in with Comic Relief, explaining that it was *their* show and *they'd* decide what went in and what didn't.

I was getting quite angry and agitated. In the end, I told Lorraine and the Comic Relief people that if they ever wanted me to do this again, then as much as I liked Patrick personally, he should not be in the picture because he'd forgotten who he was working for. I would want Talkback to have full editing rights.

The thing is, we *all* gave our time and effort and in the end came up with a show that could have been so much better. It was so frustrating.

*

Shortly after Comic Relief, Ann arranged a sixtieth birthday party for me in a classy Marco Pierre White restaurant in St James's. I invited the whole family, including my seven grandchildren. By then, Louise and Mark had had their second child, Fay, named after my mum, and Daniel and Michaela had had their third child, Rachel.

As usual, I invited some of my staff and business contacts like David Gold and Alan Watts of Herbert Smith. I also invited Nick and Margaret, as well as some of the celebrity apprentices who had appeared on the programme and some of the people who were part of my new TV life.

Michele Kurland had secretly laid on a surprise. Andy Devonshire had taken all the grandkids, lined them up on the famous Millennium Bridge (which the apprentices walk over) and filmed a take-off of *The Apprentice*, which ended with all the kids pointing and saying, 'You're hired!'

It was a great surprise for everyone. I was also surprised that some of the celebrities, including Karren Brady, Cheryl Cole, Maureen Lipman, Danny Baker and Jo Brand bothered to turn up. I went to great pains to let them know that any party of mine was not going to be one of those bashes they read about in the papers, thrown by the likes of Rod Stewart, Elton John or even Philip Green. This was essentially a family affair and they should not expect to be hobnobbing with their show-business contemporaries. And, as it was my family and friends, there was a possibility they might get pestered a little – particularly Cheryl Cole – by the kids! Piers was invited, but made some excuse, like his grandmother had just died. He's got a bad memory for excuses – as I recall, she's died seven times. I'm sure my warning that this wasn't a celebrity-infested bash must have put him off, and he decided he was too busy – most probably having a handsome attack.

Karren Brady had phoned Daniel and asked him what he would suggest as a good present to buy me on behalf of the celebrities. Daniel said I was a bit of a hypochondriac (talk about the pot calling the kettle black!) and as Karren had recently overcome a serious brain tumour, which was detected by having frequent check-ups, they bought me a full body scan at one of those medical centres.

This coincided with a second operation I'd just had to fix my groin because of damage I'd caused over the years playing tennis. The surgeon, Mr Gilmore, known for his expertise in groin repair, had failed two years earlier to remedy the problem – if anything, I was in *more* pain – and I had to go back. *This*, in Daniel's mind, was me being a hypo! All I would say to him was, 'If I live long enough, I'll sit back and watch *you* when you get to my age and see how you get on with all these aches and pains.'

Being virtually out of action for over two years, unable to exercise, my weight crept up by a couple of stones, the type of thing you don't really notice yourself, apart from your clothes getting a bit tight. However, when you see yourself on TV and in the newspapers, you realise you're ballooning up.

Fortunately, the second operation seemed to have fixed the groin. I remember joking with Gilmore when I wrote out his cheque that I'd deliberately make the words differ from the figures, so that when the bank returned it to him, he'd have to phone me and say, 'The cheque came back,' to which I'd reply, 'Yeah, so did my fucking groin.'

He had screwed up the first time round. The second time round, he removed a foreign body and proudly presented it to me in a small plastic container. It was allegedly a 'holding stitch' that had gone wrong and had attracted some kind of a cyst around it. I told him that in *my* business, if I didn't fix something properly the first time, I wouldn't have the audacity to charge again. He laughed, but of course it fell on deaf ears.

*

Due to the perceived success of the Comic Relief version of *The Celebrity Apprentice*, the following year we did one in aid of Sports Relief. Thankfully, this time Michele and her crew were responsible for the production. The girls' team of Clare Balding, Lisa Snowdon, Jacqueline Gold, Kirstie Allsopp and Louise Redknapp took on the boys' team of Phil Tufnell, the MP Lembit Opik, Kelvin MacKenzie, Hardeep Singh Kohli and Nick Hancock.

In the opening boardroom scene, I tried to make the candidates feel at home with a few soft jokes which went down quite well – with the exception of one to Hardeep Singh Kohli. He ended up throwing his toys out of the pram when I asked him if he was related to some customers I had in the early days, the Kohlis, who had a shop in Green Street near West Ham Football Club. I explained that the mother of the family took a liking to me and used to give me some of her chapatis. I told him that after I ate them, they would have a special effect on me when I visited my other customers that day and I could understand why the West Ham song was 'I'm Forever Blowing Bubbles'. I went on to ask why, when he appeared in the celebrity chef show, he didn't cook them and blow away the other contestants. I know it sounds like another lead-balloon joke when you read it on paper – and maybe there's a lesson to be learned here: don't try to be funny in front of professional comedians – but he took exception to this and claimed he was going to walk off the set, accusing me of a racist remark. No one else could see how my remark was racist, but Michele got into a panic. I got hold of him after filming and told him he was being stupid. How could he even *think* that was racist? I'm the last person on this planet to make racist remarks. I told him, 'I'm Jewish, you bloody idiot!' He calmed down and agreed to carry on. He and Kelvin MacKenzie locked horns throughout the show and had some big boardroom bust-ups. At one point, Kohli accused Kelvin of comparing him to Hitler.

The show turned out great, much better than the previous year's – it was very funny. The girls wiped the floor with the boys in a great victory. As the boys' team lost, I had to find a culprit. Complaints about Kohli's performance by the others boxed me into a corner and I fired him. It was a tough thing to do, considering his tantrums, but the right person was fired on the day. After the show, I spoke to Adrian Chiles, who worked with Kohli on his popular programme *The One Show*. He told me Kohli was very sensitive and always made a fuss over the smallest of things.

Funny how things turn out. Kohli accepted a six-month suspension from *The One Show* in July 2009 over some alleged misbehaviour. The person in question never made a formal complaint, but it seemed *The One Show*'s management took the matter very seriously. Kohli was quoted as saying, 'Nobody has accused me of sexual harassment. I recognise I overstepped the mark and have apologised unreservedly.'

Quite frankly, dealing with these egos in the celebrity show was starting to become a headache. We did one more show for Comic Relief the following year and the off-camera arguments – particularly among the girls' team, headed by businesswoman Michelle Mone who rowed with Patsy Palmer (Bianca from *EastEnders*) – were ridiculous. Michele Kurland and the excellent producer Colm Martin were pulling their hair out. The situation was compounded by the fact that Emma Freud poked her nose into my decision on the losing team, which comprised Jonathan Ross, Alan Carr, Jack Dee, Gok Wan and Gerald Ratner. After I sent them out of the boardroom, she wound them up by saying they shouldn't have lost. While the general spirit of the show was meant to be light-hearted, the team, having now been wound up by Freud, were acting in a very belligerent manner. At one point, I thought to myself, 'Here I am doing this for charity, giving up my time after a gruelling twelve weeks filming the real series, and all I'm getting is a load of stick from these people.' It was only my professionalism and the intervention of Colm (who was frustrated watching this near sabotage) that stopped me from getting up and walking out. It was a bloody joke. The production team was fuming because for a moment it looked as though all their hard work in arranging the task and filming it had been scuppered. Thanks to Nick, the situation was calmed down and in the end we managed to round off the final scene and it made a good show.

Afterwards, I went to the studio café, where Emma Freud was sitting with her partner Richard Curtis, and tore her off a strip. I told the pair of them that what she'd done was a cardinal sin in TV production terms and that she should have known better than to poke her nose in. I lost it a bit and asked her if she would storm into an operating theatre and interfere with the surgeon if one of her children were being operated on. She denied interfering, but I advised her to be careful what she was denying, as she'd forgotten that all the celebrities' microphones had been on when she spoke to them and we'd heard every word up in the production gallery. Emma couldn't argue with that. Shades of Gordon Brown during the 2010 election campaign, when a microphone he used when meeting a member of the public was left on after he finished talking to her. The TV company continued recording Gordon and transmitted him calling the person a bigot.

I made it clear this was the last time I was going to do any celebrity

versions of *The Apprentice*. I didn't need the aggravation of all the big
egos flying around.

*

Back at Amstrad, the writing was on the wall. It was getting even
tougher supplying BSkyB and there were stories that Samsung, the
giant Korean manufacturer, was after their business. There was also
talk of new HD (high-definition) products being the way forward
but, as ever, BSkyB's engineering division had excluded us. We were
treated as the poor relations, so to speak.

I had spent my whole life hustling in the electronics industry and
was starting to lose my heart for the fight. As I've mentioned, the
people I was doing business with had changed; they were oblivious to
Amstrad's part in their history. Also, methods of negotiation had
changed from the days when I used to sit round a table with Stanley
Kalms or Sam Chisholm and hammer out a deal. Everything was
becoming far more complex and political.

It was clear to me that Amstrad would eventually be completely
excluded from BSkyB's plans. Even though we were fighting for orders
all the time, Amstrad was still a good and profitable company. However, I knew there was only one way to safeguard its future. I arranged
a meeting with James Murdoch and put a proposition to him, laying
my cards on the table. I told him that most of our £20m profit was
coming from BSkyB. If, hypothetically, BSkyB were to take over
Amstrad, all that margin would flow straight through to *him* and
there'd also be a great opportunity for BSkyB to eventually place all
their orders with Amstrad and ultimately reduce their price. I finished
off by saying, 'I'm now sixty years old. I've got a loyal nucleus of
around a hundred people who rely on me to provide them with
employment. They're a great team of people, but the burden of looking after them for evermore is starting to worry me.'

Then I pulled out what I considered my final trump card. I said
that while I was fully aware that he was in charge of the business, he
just might want to run the idea past his dad and pass him a message
that I wanted to bow out gracefully from the electronics business. I was
keen to emphasise that I wanted a win-win situation for my staff and,

from a commercial point of view, BSkyB would eventually save a fortune on set-top box procurement. If there were any loyalty left in this world, Rupert would understand my position.

From every angle I looked at it, it was a great idea, but to be perfectly frank I didn't feel confident anything would come of it. To my surprise, James called me back a couple of days later to say they were interested and would like to take it a little further. Then he added that he would be discussing it in confidence with the senior executives at BSkyB, to see whether they thought it was a good idea. When I heard this, I thought it would be the kiss of death for the deal.

Robin Crossley was a technical consultant for BSkyB. He'd been there a long time and was quite friendly with me – he was about the only one there who remembered my involvement in the early days. Robin called me to discuss the matter and we had a good chat. He was a straightforward kind of fellow and after a while I felt he was onside. Robin got the rationale behind BSkyB taking over Amstrad and told me he'd recommend it as 'not being a bad idea'.

I don't know to this day whether this was a bit of internal play-acting on James Murdoch's part or whether Rupert had told him do it, but this process was repeated a few times over until all his senior staff had discussed the idea with me. I had several conversations explaining the rationale to people like Brian Sullivan, the marketing director, and Alun Webber, the chief technology man.

Webber saw the logic of it, but was concerned about relying on just one factory. 'What would happen if the factory burnt down?' was the argument. I suggested that there were lots of other sub-contractor factories we could use in China and if it made them happy, we could easily set up a second production line at a completely different location, so that in the event of an earthquake, fire or typhoon, at least one of them would be running. I think that satisfied him in the end.

Eventually, the staff at BSkyB signed on to the idea and they moved on to the due diligence phase, checking Amstrad's financial records and the engineering and development department, as well as visiting the factory to see how we had set everything up. When BSkyB investigated the logistics of how Amstrad purchased its components with such a slim team of people, they were astonished. We were advised that Pace had thirty people in the purchasing department – we had two. We also had just two people in the shipping department. They couldn't believe what a well-oiled machine we were.

It became clear to them how we were able to make the profits we had, compared to the likes of Pace. I explained to Alun Webber that, having spent forty years in the electronics industry, I knew what rang the bells of the component suppliers: quantity. Pace and others would never place an order for large quantities of components to cover a contract given by BSkyB. Instead, they figured that giving out the orders month by month would allow them to continually negotiate the price down. We would do the complete opposite. If BSkyB gave us an order for half a million pieces, we would go and negotiate an irrevocable half-a-million order with all the components suppliers and tell them it was guaranteed. Pace thought they were being clever with their strategy, but clearly they weren't.

Component manufacturers are realistic people. They consider that an order is what they *know* they will have to ship on a firm basis. For example, to them, an order for 50,000 with a promise to buy another 50,000 next month is not worth the paper it's printed on. On the other hand, an Amstrad firm order for 500,000 with a delivery schedule for 50,000 a month over ten months – now that's what rings their bells and that's how we got them to come up with the right price. I told BSkyB that each and every time they released an order to us, we would go into bat in this way with our component manufacturers. I also explained that at the same time we would secure the currency, so we'd not be exposed by any variation of the US dollar against the pound.

All in all, they were very impressed and shortly afterwards I received a call from James Murdoch telling me the due diligence had gone well and there were no serious issues. He would be sending me a letter that day making a firm offer for the company.

The offer was for £130m. As we were both public companies, we had to involve investment bankers, lawyers and accountants to come up with an offer document to be sent to BSkyB's shareholders. The deal duly went through and was consummated by September. It was then that I announced to all the Amstrad staff that BSkyB had successfully acquired the company. As far as I was concerned, I had secured their future. I told them that a new wave of management would be coming in, but I had agreed to stay with the company for at least a year to ensure its smooth and gradual transition.

It was quite a sad day really. It was emotional to finally be giving up the reins of my child, Amstrad. But it was the wise and correct thing to do, as the writing was very, very clearly on the wall. Had I not made that move, I fear Amstrad would have been totally pushed out of BSkyB's plans, resulting in the company going down the pan – not because it wasn't a good company, but because it had no ideas other than set-top boxes.

Plus, I was tired of hustling.

Rupert Murdoch rang me the day after the deal went unconditional. I thought it was a strange phone call. He said, 'Thank you very much, Alan, for the deal.'

I was a bit taken aback. 'What do you mean, Rupert?'

'I just mean, thank you very much. You've done me a great favour and I really appreciate it.'

'No, Rupert, I'm the one who should be thanking *you*. You've done *me* a great favour.'

I think it was his way of letting me know that my little throwaway line to James Murdoch a few months back had been the catalyst to make this deal happen. It was Rupert's final gesture, as payback for the effort I'd contributed to BSkyB's fantastic success story. In the end, good old-fashioned loyalty did kick in.

*

Alun Webber became the managing director of Amstrad and asked me to assist him during the changeover, which of course I did. There were regular meetings held at BSkyB's headquarters in Isleworth. At one particular meeting, when we were discussing products, I expressed my surprise (now I no longer had any axe to grind) at how Amstrad had been excluded from HD products. Now we were all one family, I told them they had nothing to lose by letting me know how much they were paying for HD set-top boxes. I'd already heard a figure through the grapevine and had been shocked. We could produce an HD box for around £70 less!

I said, 'With all due respect, now you've acquired Amstrad, you need to exploit what we're good at. I have to tell you, we could produce this HD box seventy pounds cheaper than you're paying for it.'

There was a stunned silence in the room.

'Seventy pounds?!' he exclaimed. 'How much are we paying?' he asked one of his staff. They told him.

'How can Amstrad do it for seventy pounds less?' There were more bemused looks. 'Are you sure, Sir Alan, you could make them for that price?'

'Brian, I'm not normally wrong. I say again, I have no axe to grind other than the prosperity of Amstrad and BSkyB going forward. Give or take a fiver, we can make them at that price, including all the royalties you have to pay and our labour costs. Everything.'

I continued, 'Remember, Brian, under the old circumstances, Amstrad would be asking you to pay more because we'd need to make *our* profit, but now you own the company, there's no Amstrad margin – *you* get the benefit of the low price.'

Brian was shocked. He immediately initiated a plan whereby Amstrad would produce the HD box and, to this day, they continue to produce large volumes of them. In fact, they have now produced a second-generation unit.

BSkyB got their value out of the Amstrad acquisition. I warned them many times, 'If you keep the team mean and lean and let them be autonomous, you'll reap the benefit. But the day you try to integrate them into the massive BSkyB machine and lose control of who does what and start apportioning the costs of your engineering department to Amstrad's, the whole acquisition is going to be a waste of time. You'll lose sight of the true costs and the benefit of making the stuff yourself.' I don't think they grasped this.

The point I was making was that when you acquire a company, you tend to look into whether there's any duplication. You don't, for example, need two accounts departments or two logistics and delivery departments. Regrettably, after I left, they did carry out a certain degree of rationalisation and some things moved to head office. Not that it's any of my business, but by not keeping Amstrad as a separate entity and putting up with a bit of duplication in certain areas, they would lose sight of the benefit of this great deal.

Having spent so many years in business, there are times when I see things so clearly – both advantages and pitfalls. Very often it isn't a case of knowing what to do; it's knowing what *not* to do. I get frustrated when I see people going down the wrong path despite my advice to the contrary. I've come to the conclusion that it's like telling children not to touch a hot kettle – they will only learn and understand why once they do it. There was no better example of this than when, despite my warning them not to set up production in Romania, they did just that shortly after I sold Amstrad to them. That particular lesson took two years for them to learn and, sadly, everything played out exactly as I'd predicted. I guess I must come over as too heavy-handed or too cocky when I say these things. But it was their misfortune that they chose to ignore me.

Nowadays, the Amstrad name is no longer used. I asked BSkyB's CEO, Jeremy Darroch, whether there was any possibility of letting me have it back, just for old times' sake – maybe my grandchildren might want to do something with it in years to come. Apparently, James Murdoch didn't like the idea. It's a shame, but I can't complain really – *they* bought the company. So I guess the Amstrad name will just die out as one of those old brand names of the past.

*

Simon's position at Amstrad was now redundant. Previously, he'd spent his time handling the sales negotiations with BSkyB, but now there was obviously no need for him to sell to them, as they owned the company. A few months after the acquisition they mutually agreed his departure.

Simon and I shared the frustration over what was deemed to be the failure of the email phone project. The advertising model, which seemed a no-brainer to me, had never caught on. With this in mind, I asked Simon to investigate whether there were any companies available to buy which were active in the up-and-coming digital screen advertising market. Today's technology enables advertisers to send adverts remotely to digital screens via the internet. Many of the electronic screens you see these days – in places like Piccadilly Circus or on the London Underground – display adverts which have been remotely downloaded in this way.

We came across a company, Comtech, who had developed a method of sending data to screens using mobile phone technology. We realised it was possible to build this box of tricks into a screen and thereby send adverts to it.

The problem with digital signage up till then was that if you had a screen, for example in a shopping mall, you would also need some sort of internet phone line connection. Comtech's technology simply relied upon a mobile phone module and a SIM card. As long as there was a mobile signal, data could be sent to the screens, so they could be installed wherever you wanted. This looked an interesting proposition. With this, we could try to capitalise on digital advertising, something we'd given up on too quickly with our email phone.

We acquired a majority shareholding in the company and started to invest heavily in a new design for a fully integrated screen with all the mobile rocket science built in. The objective was to strategically locate these screens where advertisers would be happy to place adverts. We could no longer use the name Amstrad, so we changed the name of this company to Amscreen.

It had been a long time since I'd been involved in anything to do with the advertising industry. I soon realised how, with the advent of the internet and hundreds of new TV channels, things had changed. Newspaper circulations had dropped dramatically – younger people were no longer interested in buying papers to read the news, as there was far easier access to whatever they wanted on the internet. On top of this, advertisers needed more and more convincing that the medium could deliver – they wanted concrete proof it was working. The technology employed at Amscreen enabled us to tell our advertisers how many eyes had seen the advert. It was only on that basis that they were prepared to advertise.

We decided to go into this business in the hope that financial rewards would follow in the long haul. We slowly and systematically placed screens in strategic locations throughout the whole country, choosing places like petrol-station checkouts, where they would be seen by a constant flow of customers. Similarly, in the medical market, our screens were placed in doctors' surgeries, where pharmaceutical companies could advertise to a captive audience.

Two of the winners of *The Apprentice* were assigned to work for this company: Lee McQueen, who won series four, and Yasmina Siadatan, who won series five. Lee was there at the very start of our acquisition of Amscreen and has seen it grow steadily.

The technology opens up a whole new world. Perhaps it will be the next blockbuster event in my business life. It makes tremendous sense. The revenues which can be made from advertising income really stack up, but it was clear to me that a lot of patience would be needed, something I don't have. Therefore I tend to keep myself out of it, occasionally pulling the team together to check they're still on the right lines.

I will have to wait and see where this company goes.

*

Another era came to an end when we moved out of our Brentwood House office block, which we acquired back in 1984. Daniel, now heavily involved in the property business, managed to convince a budget hotel group to take it over, subject to us completely refurbishing it. It's quite strange to see our old headquarters functioning as a hotel and to consider that my offices on the tenth floor are now used as bedrooms. Rumour has it, they charge a little bit extra for the top-floor rooms and have named them 'the Alan Sugar Suites'!

20

'Mum, It's Not Lord Beaverbrook, It's Lord Sugar'

A Journey from Clapton to Clapton

2008–10

Even a seasoned poseur like Piers Morgan said to me, 'I've been to a lot of bashes in my time, but this one's the best.' The mere fact that he didn't mention his dying grandmother when he was invited meant I knew our party would be a success!

In May 2008, Ann and I celebrated our fortieth wedding anniversary with a fantastic party at Bramstons. Tony Page, who had arranged so many of our previous functions, organised it brilliantly. We built a massive marquee which incorporated a stage, a backstage area and artists' dressing rooms.

We invited all our family and friends and acquaintances old and new. All seven of my grandchildren were there as well as former colleagues such as Bob Watkins and David Pleat, and people from the TV world. Bruce Forsyth was the master of ceremonies and the evening started with the famous Jewish-American comedian Jackie Mason, who had the audience in hysterics, particularly when he was insulting me. There was a surprise for Ann when Daniel's oldest son Alex, who was six, went up onto the stage and sang a rendition of the famous Elton John song 'Daniel' – the lyrics were adjusted to reflect his own father's antics. He performed it with great confidence and he brought the house down.

Next on stage was the cast of *Jersey Boys*, who'd come to London the previous year and had been a great hit. I managed to persuade them to appear, even though they'd never played a private function before. Ann must have seen *Jersey Boys* about six times, so I knew she'd appreciate it.

The evening was rounded off by a spectacular performance by Elton John, who arrived by helicopter, landing in the field next to my house. We had tried to keep the celebrity cabaret a secret from the guests, but unfortunately one of the national newspapers got hold of the story and blew it the day before, which was a bit of a shame.

As you can imagine, everybody had a wonderful evening. My old friends Geoff, Steve, Tony and Malcolm were there with their wives – they'd never had the opportunity to see three star acts like this *live*. It was an amazing night and one which people tell me they will never forget. Apart from Piers, maybe – I don't think he saw too much of it. His poor young lady, Celia, had to drag him home, as he was blind drunk. She thanked me for a great evening, then glanced at Piers and shook her head, as if to say, 'Look at him!'

Nick Hewer gave a speech, which was quite humorous. I think he too might have had rather a lot of the superb red wine. In my response speech, I included all the expected clichés one can imagine about being married for forty years. I concluded by saying to all the young people present that there was a lesson to be learned here. 'Look around the room and you'll see my family – *they* are my greatest wealth. The material things youngsters seem to target are meaningless. The biggest achievement in my life, together with Ann, was ensuring our children grew up to be the decent human beings they are. And I'm thankful that we can already see the same culture coming through in our grandchildren.'

*

I had been pestering the BBC for at least two years to consider a junior version of *The Apprentice*, but they'd always claimed they lacked the budget. I don't think the BBC executives believed in it, plus there was a bit of the 'not invented here' syndrome. They'd had great success with the main series and could not really see the benefits of a junior version. The thing is, despite the sophisticated way the BBC and other TV channels measure their audience, I personally thought the biggest

Apprentice audience was kids. I believe in the old adage 'seeing is believing' and while statistical data and all that stuff is great, the fact was that wherever I went, I was (and still am) surrounded by kids between the ages of fourteen and eighteen, wanting their picture taken with me or an autograph. I don't know why they love *The Apprentice* so much. Maybe the authoritative way in which I conduct the show reminds them of being at school, or maybe they just like my straight-forward manner – who knows? Whatever the reason, they certainly are, in my mind, our biggest fans. This is in stark contrast to the people I described earlier as the closet male followers of *The Apprentice*, in the thirty-five to fifty age group. I'm convinced there'll be a big market for plain, brown-paper covers for this book, so that these chaps can dis-guise what they're reading on the plane or the beach.

When the time came to discuss the possibility of a sixth series of *The Apprentice*, Talkback and the BBC could see a slight reluctance on my behalf to do it. Sometimes they mistakenly categorise me with people they deal with on a day-to-day basis who derive their income solely from TV. Such people, quite rightly, are eager to take on more and more work and it's normally the TV company that decides when a programme has reached its sell-by date.

I kind of rolled the dice one more time and told them that for me to be interested in doing another series of *The Apprentice*, I would want to do *The Junior Apprentice*, even if it was just as an experiment. It's fair to say that I did slightly hint that if this were not agreed, then I'd seriously consider whether I wanted to do another senior series. However, I despise any form of commercial blackmail, so I'd therefore like to make it very clear that there were no 'take it or leave it' demands from me, as I wouldn't do that – and neither would the BBC stand for it. After much discussion, the BBC finally agreed to commission a cut-down, six-episode version of *The Junior Apprentice*. One of the things I like about doing *The Apprentice* is that I get to learn how TV works. Getting things done with the BBC, with their strict guidelines, is a bit like taking part in the Grand National. There are so many obstacles to overcome before you have a chance of finishing, let alone winning.

We were in new territory now. I'm sure Michele Kurland and I have become experts on the rules about using kids in a TV production.

There aren't enough pages in this book to explain them all, save to say that the regulations are tortuous – some quite rightly so, but others are a bloody joke, dating back to when they sent kids up chimneys! There were restrictions on the time the kids could be available for filming. If we wanted to go for fourteen- to seventeen-year-olds, permission had to be granted by each kid's local education authority – and you can imagine all these jobsworths chucking their two-pennyworth in. There was a massive debate on what the prize should be and what it would be used for. After checking all the BBC guidelines, we ended up agreeing that the winner would get the benefit of a £25,000 fund for them to draw upon in furthering their careers or business ventures. I would preside over the fund and dish it out as and when required, if the request was appropriate.

Over 28,000 kids applied and the logistics of narrowing them down to a final group were handled with military precision, taking into account BBC guidelines on the need to be fair from a regional point of view. As part of the process we came across parents who, understandably, wanted to know the ins and outs of a duck's arse. Actually, the parents were quite fascinating. On the one hand, some of them were desperate for their little Johnny to be on TV; on the other hand, once their child was put on the shortlist as a contender, the penny dropped with the parents that something might happen and they started putting in all sorts of demands and questions. To take account of this, we chose more contenders for the final batch than we needed, in anticipation of some parents changing their minds and withdrawing their children.

It took *months* before we finally got through all this stuff and selected the prospective ten candidates (five boys and five girls). And we hadn't rolled one bloody camera yet! In light of the grief we had, you can imagine how frustrated I got when trying to explain to the BBC executives how hard it had been to organise, only to get a simple reply like, 'Oh really? That's a shame . . . Anyway, when are you going to start filming?' You get close to whacking them, but that would breach another BBC guideline I expect.

Michele recruited the services of Tom McDonald, who was involved in the third main series and, later, Michael Jochnowitz joined, another person with experience of the main series and who knew the format well. Michele also appointed Sue Davidson, who had experience working at the BBC but was new to the format of *The Apprentice*.

As Margaret Mountford no longer wanted to take part, I recruited Karren Brady, whom I'd known for over sixteen years from my Spurs days. She and I had had some run-ins when she was managing director of Birmingham City – she was the youngest-ever director of a public company and one very shrewd lady. Plus, of course, she'd had a bit of first-hand experience as the girls' team leader on *The Celebrity Apprentice*.

Nick was excited about this new venture and, like me, saw it as a refreshing challenge. But being the worrier he is, he wondered whether he could adapt to dealing with youngsters; whether he'd be able to treat them correctly.

In the end, the final candidates were aged between sixteen and seventeen because the regulations made it untenable to work with under-sixteens, as I'd originally wanted. I was conscious, from certain media coverage, that my reputation of being a bit tough on contestants in the main series would be a major concern to the BBC and the public at large. But having spoken to thousands of kids over the years in my Q&As at schools, I was confident I could pull off the fine balance of care mixed with a bit of authority.

The careful choice of candidates, as well as some great filming and boardroom scenes, produced a massive hit for the BBC. Michele, Tom and Michael worked relentlessly and, once again, were all over it like a rash – as was Andy Devonshire, the man who made the pictures work. During the filming period, there were so many ups and downs, but with a great production team (as well as mentors for the kids), we made a great series. Surprise, surprise, suddenly the BBC executives came out of the woodwork, all claiming this was under *their* watch and what a great idea they'd had!

I have to say I've never enjoyed myself so much as I did making *The Junior Apprentice*. What I got from it was laughter and a sense of pride – and it showed. My idea had really worked but, more to the point, it was heart-warming to see how we'd resurrected some confidence in the young. Through my visits to schools, I've always known that we in Britain *do* have great young people who are resourceful, willing to learn and hard-working – now we were showing the nation! Bloody brilliant stuff. I will follow the future of the class of 2010, to see how their lives pan out. I have the utmost confidence that there are a few Alan Sugars or Richard Bransons amongst them, so watch this space. In fact, Richard very kindly agreed to be one of the 'treats' for a winning team. They were gobsmacked when I said I'd arranged for them to meet him at his house for tea. They had just won a task where they had to make and sell cupcakes, so I suggested, half-jokingly, that they should take him a few samples. They had a ball that day.

I can tell you honestly that each week I struggled to choose the candidate to fire, as they were all so good. And I *really* struggled in the final, when Arjun Rajyagor was crowned the first winner of *The Junior Apprentice*. If nothing else, it was a voyage all ten kids will never forget.

*

Three years earlier, in June 2007, Gordon Brown had been appointed Prime Minister after Tony Blair stepped down. A couple of days later, Gordon called me to say he was about to reshuffle his government advisers and he would value me as a member of his Business Council, together with people such as Richard Branson. Gordon and the Chancellor would meet every three months with the Business Council to discuss what was going on in the marketplace.

It was nice to receive the call and to be thought of in such a way. Gordon and I went back over ten years, to when he first took on the role of Chancellor of the Exchequer. It was he who asked me to embark on my trips around the country, talking to universities, colleges and businesses. Every year during National Enterprise Week (around November), I'd be called to attend all the seminars and sessions. More recently, I had also agreed with Ed Balls, the Education Secretary, that I would embark upon an advertising campaign to promote apprenticeships. As well as making some television adverts, I'd have to go on a roadshow, talking to potential employers about the benefits of apprenticeships.

The Business Council meetings were very interesting, though quite formal. Gordon Brown and the Chancellor would share data on the current economic climate, welcoming any input from its members. Little did anyone know that Gordon had walked straight into a hornets' nest when he became PM. The world was about to explode financially.

I'd seen, in the real estate business, the madness that existed in the markets between about 2004 and 2007. Assets were being sold for ridiculous amounts of money. The tradition of conservative lending from banks had gone out the window and now they were dishing out money with no regard for the value of assets they were funding. It was all well and good lending Fred the butcher £50,000, but the banks viewed their margin on that type of transaction as peanuts. What they wanted to do was lend *billions*, so they could make 2–3 per cent on *that* sort of money. Following such a strategy meant they took amazing risks with some strange characters. A whole new wave of so-called entrepreneurs came to fame in the marketplace and were labelled multi-millionaires, or even billionaires, when in fact they didn't have two bob to rub together. All they had was a good and fast mouth and a bank eager to lend them money.

The American market was racing away in the same fashion. The bubble *had to* burst, and burst it did in the fourth quarter of 2008, the so-called 'credit-crunch' crisis. The Americans had been selling what they called 'junk sub-prime loans' between banks. Trouble was, the banks weren't able to pay each other. Many UK banks had bought the sub-prime rubbish from the Americans and got themselves into big trouble paying up.

Like the rest of the UK, I woke up one morning to see on TV that the bank Northern Rock was in trouble. Rumours were rife in the market that they were near insolvency and people were starting to queue outside the branches to get their money out. It was the nightmare all banks dread. The whole banking system rests on the use of depositors' money to invest elsewhere. Therefore, hypothetically, if every depositor demanded their money back on one particular day, they'd never be able to get it. And this was the scenario being played out at Northern Rock.

I remember turning to Ann and saying, 'This is a disaster! You have no idea what this means. If this bank is allowed to go down and ordinary people lose money, the next thing you'll see is long queues outside Barclays and Lloyds. And if that sort of panic breaks out, the whole banking world will collapse and the ramifications will be unspeakable.'

The government stepped in and propped up Northern Rock and tried to calm the situation, but the people still queued. The crisis was not helped by the media, who gave no support to the government – if anything, they were responsible for instilling *more* panic in the public. Finally, the Chancellor announced that the government was taking over Northern Rock, which meant, in simple terms, that ordinary people's money was secure. *Still* some thickos in the media were casting uncertainty on this move, and still some people queued. This only stopped when the government reiterated, for the umpteenth time, that investors' money *was* secure. Eventually, the penny dropped and the public realised that if anything, the *best* place to put their money now was Northern Rock. In fact, after a while, they had to stop taking deposits, as everyone was running back to them.

It soon became clear that *all* the banks were in trouble. Lloyds, who had been my bankers for over forty-five years, decided to acquire HBOS and, in doing so, they bought a can of worms that nearly brought them down. This resulted in the government having to bail them out, as well as RBS.

Gordon Brown was getting so much stick it was unbelievable. The media were blaming *him* for the disaster. As events unfolded, companies were also collapsing, one by one. The famous Woolworths went into administration, as banks started to recall the loans they'd made to them and others. There were mass redundancies and a general negative feeling in the air. It was recession on a scale we hadn't seen before. Real estate assets started to drop in value. This resulted in all the Champagne Charlies and so-called billionaires walking away, leaving the banks with huge debts and a nightmare to clean up.

When the dust settled after the bomb had dropped, it seemed obvious that the problems had started in America and that, basically, the greed of bankers lay behind the mess. Despite this, as far as everyone in Britain was concerned, Gordon was to blame. I was a bit frustrated for him. His swift action to save Northern Rock and inject money into the other banks to avert a disaster was not recognised by Joe Public. They had no idea what life would have been like had there been a full-blown run on the banks.

Baroness Shriti Vadera had been one of Gordon's advisers for at least ten years while he was Chancellor and she was still by his side now he was PM. She sent me an email passing on thanks for my support and said that my explanation of matters in the media was such that it was really understandable to the man in the street. She called me a few days later to ask me to come in and have a chat with her and Gordon.

During my forty-five years in business, I've had the opportunity to meet the last four prime ministers, and when I say *meet* them, I mean *meet* them – I don't mean going to some bum-rush at Downing Street with hundreds of other people; I mean talk to them seriously about important issues. I'm not so naïve that I can't see that, in some cases, these politicians have their own agendas and will use people like me to help them. But give me a bit of credit when I say that, based on what I've seen over the years, Gordon is one of the most sincere and well-meaning people I've met.

The country as a whole had got used to a showman in Blair, one very much modelled on American politicians. He was a good mouthpiece, a good actor and orator. Gordon, however, was criticised for being dull and indecisive. People had forgotten the history of British politics, which is full of past prime ministers who were deemed to be rather cautious, formal and stuffy people – and were none the worse for it!

When I sat down with Shriti and Gordon, I told them he needed to fight back a bit and not stand for all the criticism. He should tell people that he's a serious thinker, not an actor. Spell it out and don't dodge the issue. I spoke to him as I would a friend or business colleague and I gave him my advice, for what it was worth, without holding back. I think Gordon appreciated that, as most people speaking to the Prime Minster tend to be far more subtle.

I went on to talk to Gordon and Shriti many times after that. I once agreed to interview Gordon for a series of video clips to try to put to him what most people were thinking and give him the chance to express himself to the public in a way they'd not seen before. We made five different films, each about six minutes long. They came out quite well and were published on the *Sun*'s website. You can still see them today on Amshold's YouTube channel at www.youtube.com/amshold

Funnily enough, Piers Morgan, who by now had become a real TV celebrity, copied my idea and interviewed Gordon in one of his chat shows. I called Piers and jibed him over this, saying I'd be watching carefully to check he didn't infringe my copyright, as once again he was learning from the master. Piers, of course, ignored my goading. He said, 'The difference is, *your* one went out on the internet – *mine* will be viewed by millions.' In fact, the BBC and ITV turned down the chance of transmitting my clips, as they saw them as being too much of a party political broadcast. Funny how they changed their minds and let Piers do it, though.

On some occasions, I was asked to get to the Business Council meetings a little earlier or stay behind to have further discussions with Gordon. He was concerned the recession was really hurting the small-to medium-sized enterprises (SMEs) and wanted some ideas. Gordon recognised that I'd been there and done it.

*

It was mid-May 2009 and I was in Spain visiting the town of Ronda. While we were having a coffee in the town, my phone rang. It was Gordon Brown, asking whether I could pop into Number 10 the next day, to talk about stepping up my input in assisting SMEs and pro-moting enterprise to the young. He said that, due to the economic climate, he needed additional advisory skills and wanted to draw me into the camp in a more serious and formal manner.

'Well, Gordon, I'd like to help,' I said, 'but right now I'm up a mountain in Spain, checking out a cycle route. I won't be back till next Monday, so it will have to wait until then.'

'Oh, okay, no problem, Alan. Sorry to bother you. Give my regards to Ann. I'll see you next week – my people will arrange a meeting.'

The following Tuesday, I went to Downing Street to see what Gordon had in mind. My car rolled up at the main gates and, after the usual security checks, I was driven to the front entrance of Number 10.

I have visited Downing Street many times, but never take it for granted – it's a rather special place, particularly the Cabinet Room. On this occasion, I was directed up the staircase and past all the portraits of past prime ministers. Despite being a pilot and good at navigation, I still get lost in the maze of rooms in this building. We met in a rather grand, albeit quite small, anteroom which oozed history. Shriti and Gordon were sitting by a small table waiting for me. They both looked as though they'd been up all night. At the time, I didn't realise the PM was working on Cabinet reshuffle decisions – I now appreciate how these deliberations took their toll. I enquired as to their welfare, particularly Shriti's, and asked, 'Are you okay? You look shattered.'

'Yes, no problem, we've just had a lot to do,' said Shriti.

We got down to business. Gordon wanted to discuss the possibility of me formally joining the government to assist in matters dealing with enterprise and small businesses. He asked if I'd consider taking a role at the DBIS (Department of Business, Innovation and Skills), once known as the DTI and, before that, the Department of Trade.

'Gordon, I'd love to help, but I know that when people like Lord Sainsbury took up government roles, they had to distance themselves from their businesses, placing all their business interests in a blind trust. I would have the same problem. And on top of that, as you know, I'm involved in *The Apprentice*, which is actually on air now. It would be impossible for me, at such short notice, to arrange for my business and TV interests to be reorganised to avoid a conflict of interests.'

I continued, 'Frankly, Gordon, I'm not ready to give up business. I'm eager for my companies to remain profitable and take advice from me. Therefore, with respect, I'd have to turn down any offer of a ministerial position. No matter how prestigious it might sound, it would be impractical.'

Like all good politicians, my words seemed to go straight over his head and he continued to talk about wanting me to be a Minister of Enterprise and enter the House of Lords. Had I accepted, it would have meant representing the government, answering questions on business and enterprise. The questions and answers side of things didn't bother me at all, but I reiterated that it really was impossible for me to accept.

'Gordon, I don't want you to think I'm letting you down in any way – I will do anything to help – but you have to recognise it would be impossible for me to accept a ministerial position.'

'Okay, Alan. Look, please go away and give it some further thought. Talk some more to Shriti tomorrow.'

The following week, on 4 June, I met with Shriti and Gordon again. It was the day Gordon was going to announce his new Cabinet. This time, the meeting was in the garden off the Cabinet Room. It was funny to see all the kids' toys there, but it's where the PM lives with his family during the week, so why should it be any different from any normal home with kids? Gordon kept going on about me being a minister and I reiterated that I couldn't do it. He finally settled on appointing me as a government adviser, an Enterprise Tsar or Enterprise Champion – and at the same time he wanted me to join the House of Lords and take the Labour whip. Appointment to the House of Lords would be no problem as far as conflict of interests was concerned and to be an adviser without any ministerial powers would certainly be acceptable, so I agreed to accept the position.

As I drove away from the rear of Number 10, I received a call from a *Financial Times* journalist asking me what I'd been doing there. The call came no more than two minutes after I had walked out the door! I was a bit short with the journalist and told him it was none of his business. He started firing questions at me such as, 'Are you going to be a minister? Are you going to be part of Gordon's new Cabinet reshuffle?'

I told him again, 'With respect, it's none of your business,' and just hung up the phone. That day, there were some comments on Sky TV about me being at Downing Street, as one of their cameras had been positioned at the rear of Number 10 and had filmed me walking back to my car and being driven away.

That evening, I told Ann what had happened and that there was a possibility that I might be made a lord. She was very excited. It must have been a proud moment for her – after all, she'd known me since she was sixteen and she'd watched me over the past forty-odd years as I worked my way up the ladder through Amstrad and Spurs, then became a knight – and now there was the prospect of me being a lord!

But, as it was just a proposal, we kind of parked the notion until it was formalised.

The day the announcement was due, Friday 5 June, was the day I'd put aside in my diary for filming *The Apprentice: You're Hired!*, a show introduced by Adrian Chiles which featured the two finalists for series five – Yasmina Siadatan and Kate Walsh. I'd also arranged to meet Simon Cowell for lunch.

I turned up at the offices of Talkback Thames around ten in the morning and started to discuss our plans for the day with the production people. It's always a difficult moment when the losing finalist has to turn up again and be filmed in the *You're Hired!* programme. Traditionally, I've always taken time to speak to both the winner and the runner-up, just to put them at ease before their first experience of being on a live show in front of an audience. As you can imagine, the runner-up, Kate, was feeling a bit despondent. She needed a bit of personal attention to help her feel comfortable about performing later in the day.

At around half past ten, all hell broke loose. I had imagined the announcement of my new position would be one of those routine stories, just another small detail largely ignored by the media. Not so! First of all, my BlackBerry started pinging every few seconds (I received around 150 emails and texts that day) and my phone was ringing constantly, with friends and relatives congratulating me on my appointment, journalists wanting to discuss the new position, TV companies asking whether they could interview me, all that stuff.

All this was going on amidst our planning discussions for the *You're Hired* show. Michele Kurland and her team could see it was becoming an untenable situation for me and they agreed to leave me alone for half an hour or so to fill out forms and let the dust settle a bit. It was impossible to concentrate on the show.

Left on my own, the whole thing started to sink in – *I was going to be appointed to the House of Lords!* It began to dawn on me what an amazing honour this was. Rumour has it that when people are about to die, their whole life flashes before them. Well, thankfully I wasn't dying, but I have to say there was a moment when I had one of these flashbacks. I remembered my mum on her deathbed saying, 'Who do you think you are, Lord Beaverbrook?' At that moment, I kind of choked up a little, thinking, 'No, Mum, not Lord Beaverbrook – actually, it's Lord Sugar.' It was a very personal moment and I was glad I was alone. I became quite emotional thinking about how my mum and dad would have felt if they'd still been around.

The story was all over the media. The phone had not stopped ringing and my public relations company, Frank PR, was inundated. I suggested they immediately come and meet me to talk about how to handle things. I hadn't really been given a definitive brief on exactly what I was going to do as a government adviser. There was talk of me having an office in the DBIS and some staff allocated to me, but from there on, I had no idea what was expected of me.

I'd already said to Gordon, 'If you've got visions of me spending five days a week in a nine-to-five in Victoria Street, you've picked the wrong bloke.' I wasn't going to change my lifestyle. I deal with things on a 24/7 basis. It doesn't matter where I am. I could be in Spain or America or up a mountain. I could be at home with my BlackBerry or at my office in Loughton. Wherever I might be, I make more decisions in a minute than some businessmen do in a week stuck at their desks. I can operate anywhere and I certainly *wasn't* taking some desk job.

As I wasn't clear on what I'd be doing, it was quite difficult facing the media, who were asking me *exactly* that question. To be perfectly honest, I didn't know at the time what 'taking the whip' was – I'd just accepted the position with whatever conditions were attached. I trusted that Gordon wouldn't ask me to do something I wasn't happy with.

As I walked out of Talkback's offices, I was caught by Sky Television, who asked for an interview. Embarrassingly, the woman interviewer was asking me what my new job entailed and there was I thinking to myself, 'I don't actually know.' I couldn't really say that live on TV, so I waffled a bit: 'I'm going to be looking after matters to do with small- to medium-sized businesses and trying to assist in the promotion of enterprise.'

I then went off to meet Simon Cowell in a restaurant in Bayswater, where we chatted about the TV business. I don't know whether he was oblivious to what was going on as far as I was concerned, but I found it rather strange that he didn't mention my being offered a peerage. Maybe he didn't know or didn't want to bring it up for some reason or other. He got a phone call from Philip Green at one point and said, 'Hey, Phil, I've got Alan Sugar here – he's actually funnier than you!'

After a nice lunch, we went outside and compared cars. Simon had bought himself exactly the same stretched Rolls-Royce I had and our two drivers were exchanging specifications. His was the same colour as mine, but had a more glitzy interior, as one would expect.

When I arrived back at the studio after lunch, Andrew Bloch and David Fraser from Frank PR told me there was a groundswell of feeling against the appointment coming through from the Conservative Party. They were making noises to the effect that I shouldn't be allowed to be a government adviser and at the same time participate in a BBC television programme. We looked at each other as if to say, 'What's that got to do with the price of cocoa?' I simply didn't understand the logic behind their objections. Nevertheless, my two PR guys said this was the general thrust of the comments coming from the media. The same question kept being thrown at me, as well as at Number 10: 'Now that Lord Sugar is going to be an adviser to the government, will you be asking him to give up his television programme?'

My answer was, 'It's nonsense! What the hell have the two things got to do with each other?'

I had to put my frustration on hold as we got on with preparations for *You're Hired!* Despite trying to focus on this, I was constantly being interrupted by Andrew Bloch telling me he needed my attention. 'I've had the *Daily Mail* on the phone. They're going to press right now with some story that you've agreed to give up *The Apprentice*.'

'Tell them it's a load of rubbish. Tell them we'll be making a statement at the end of the day.'

'They say that's not good enough – their deadline is five o'clock and we won't be done till ten tonight.'

'Andrew, what do you want me to do? I'm in the middle of preparing for the show. We can't deal with this now. Just tell them to go away. Whatever they print, they print – we'll have to deal with it tomorrow.'

'Can't you give me a steer on what I should say to them?'

'Okay, I'm *not* giving up *The Apprentice* – that's for sure. It's not for their ears, but it wasn't part of the discussions with Gordon Brown. So say, "It's a load of rubbish" and tell them they've got their facts wrong.'

'Fine, I'll go away and tell them that. That's all I wanted to know – sorry to have interrupted you.'

Half an hour later, Andrew was back again. 'I'm sorry, but there's this fellow called Jeremy Hunt – apparently he's the Shadow Culture Secretary, the Conservative bloke in charge of media matters. Now *he's* blabbing to the media, telling them he's going to protest to the BBC that your appointment cannot go ahead. He's saying that either the BBC must sack you, or Gordon must rescind your appointment – one of the two. We're being pestered non-stop by the media. What shall we tell them?'

'Tell them Mr Hunt is talking a load of rubbish – it's as simple as that. My participation in *The Apprentice* has nothing at all to do with any government work. Nothing I've said in the past five years in *The Apprentice* is political. I don't go round broadcasting, "I'm supporting this party or I'm supporting that party or I endorse this person but not that person." We've never mentioned anything political in the programme, so what the hell is this nutter talking about?'

'Well, I can't put it in those words, but I get the gist. That's what I'll go and tell them.'

'Fine.'

'I'm really sorry to have interrupted you again.'

In the dressing room allocated to me at the studio, I had the TV tuned to Sky News. Every single person and his brother *and* his dog was criticising my appointment. There was the ginger-haired lady on Sky TV, Kay Burley, standing on the green outside the Houses of Parliament, stopping exiting politicians and asking them what they thought of the appointment.

Give a politician a microphone and they won't stop blabbing. Naturally, she only chose to ask Conservatives or Liberals, so all you heard was indignation. 'How can a man like him be appointed as an adviser to the government? He doesn't know how to deal with people – look at how he talks to them in his television programme. What kind of person is *he* to be appointed in a role dealing with enterprise? It's all wrong – there's a conflict of interests with his BBC show.'

I was getting a load of flak on the TV, all based on the biggest load of rubbish I'd ever heard. I'm surprised they didn't haul out Terry Venables to join in. Indeed, the whole thing was reminiscent of the day I'd fired Venables. But if I'd thought *that* had been bad, these goings-on made it look like an outing to Disney World.

I couldn't believe how it had escalated in such a short time, from half past ten that morning to now, six in the evening. The momentum was growing and growing – all over Alan Sugar. I mean, after all, what the bloody hell had I done? Nothing, other than accept a role as an adviser to the government. Maybe it was a slow news day and I was just unlucky to be the top story.

When Ann turned up at the studio at seven o'clock, just before the recording started, she got a total shock when she saw me. 'What's the matter with you? You look terrible!'

'Terrible? You have no idea what's been going on today. I can't believe it! Anyone would think I've just murdered someone or done something awful. Haven't you been watching the TV?'

'No, I haven't seen anything. I've had a lot of people phoning me, telling me how happy they are you've been appointed to the House of Lords and all that stuff, but no one's said anything else.'

'It's been madness, absolute madness. Watch this,' I said as I switched on the TV. Sky News kept repeating the same old tired story, while the ticker tape at the bottom of the screen was showing people's comments on my appointment. Ann realised why I was looking so bad.

It's hard for me to put into words how much pressure I was under that day. To be fair, my PR people, Andrew and David, were fending off most of the stuff, but they had to keep telling me about the latest developments and how we needed to deflate the swell of adverse publicity.

It was hard, but I had to pull myself together and try to purge all this from my brain. It was time for me to go on stage and do my bit in the *You're Hired!* programme. On top of all this, I knew I had to face the prospect of going to the after-show cocktail party, where hundreds of people would be asking me all kinds of questions, not only relating to *The Apprentice*, but also to that day's big news.

The show had started recording. The panel comprised Ruby Wax, Jonathan Ross and a couple of others. When I'd met them in the gallery, Jonathan congratulated me on my appointment and asked about it. I told him, 'My head's spinning, Jonathan. I'm sorry, mate, I'm not being rude, but I've got to concentrate on the show tonight. We've got to get this away and then, if you've got any time afterwards, we'll have a chat. But right now, the room is spinning round.'

'Fair enough, fair enough. Let's get on with it.'

Adrian Chiles, the show's host, started off by asking me, 'What do I call you? Is it Sir Alan or Lord Sugar?'

I replied, 'Well, one day it'll most probably be Lord Sugar, but for now let's carry on with Sir Alan.' Jonathan cracked a few gags about my appointment, as one would expect, and overall the recording went very well.

I don't think I paid too much attention to Yasmina and Kate that night. It was a shame for them, but it was simply because I had so much buzzing around in my head. I don't think they understood the ramifications of what was going on.

After the recording, I mingled with the guests for a while, my thoughts still churning round. Margaret Mountford was there and I also had to announce that this was the last time she would be in *The Apprentice*, which, though it was sad news, thankfully took a bit of the attention away from me. I told her that I appreciated her participation over the years and explained to everyone that when I'd persuaded her to do the show originally, she'd thought it would be just for one season, yet I'd managed to convince her to do it five times. Now she was adamant that she wanted to get on with her PhD. I thanked her publicly for all her efforts and said we'd all miss her in the future. She got a well-deserved round of applause from the audience.

At the after-show party, Margaret congratulated me on my appointment, as did Nick. I started to fill Nick in on some of the background of what had been going on and, as a PR man, he looked as concerned as I was. He could not believe what I was telling him and he too couldn't understand this nonsense about a conflict of interests. I called together Andrew, David and Nick and, there at the party, we drafted out a one-paragraph statement to be sent out to all the media that night. It stated that my role as enterprise adviser was *not* to be confused with that of a minister. I would not be making any decisions, neither would I be promoting any government policies – I was just there to feed back information from the market to the government. I added that any thoughts of me giving up *The Apprentice* were absolutely unfounded. It was a kind of a 'holding' statement that we hoped would shut everybody down. We agreed we would make no further comment at all. Even at 11 p.m., the newspapers were still ringing up, demanding information.

When I left that night, I slumped in the back of my car with my head still spinning. Ann knew not to talk. We drove home and went to bed.

The next morning, Saturday, the phones were *still* ringing. Andrew and David told me that the media had gone absolutely berserk. Every single national newspaper had allocated front pages and double-page spreads to my appointment. In particular, the serious papers went to town. It was as if all the other ministerial appointments paled into insignificance – they were just focusing on me! They kept quoting Shadow Culture Secretary Jeremy Hunt all the time. The media had hooked into this conflict of interests thing.

It's funny how it is with the media. It reminds me of the incident when Jonathan Ross and Russell Brand played that prank on Andrew Sachs – Manuel in *Fawlty Towers*. Yes, I guess their behaviour was a bit childish but, as often as not, something like that will simply pass by without attracting any attention. For some reason, this time the media got the bit between their teeth and blew it out of all proportion. Of course, mine was a completely different situation, but the media frenzy was exactly the same.

I made the fatal error of reading the papers – it was diabolical! If I'd thought what I'd read about myself in the Venables days was bad, this was much, much worse. What the hell had I let myself in for? I had innocently accepted this position and was obviously very honoured at the prospect of being a lord, but I never imagined it was going to cause so much aggravation.

Earlier in the week, I had taken the precaution of finding out whether this appointment would breach BBC policy. I also asked Alan Watts to read my BBC agreement, to get his view as to whether anything in it would prevent me from being a government adviser.

I'd also spoken with David Jordan, an expert in BBC policy, who discussed the matter with me briefly and also concluded that as long as I was not taking a ministerial role and would not be seen to be promoting any government policies, there was nothing to stop me accepting the appointment. With that in mind, I had accepted.

Now I was stuck between a rock and a hard place. I was not going to give up the offer of being a government adviser and a member of the House of Lords; neither was I going to give up doing *The Apprentice*. Above all, I was not going to be intimidated by the newspapers. I was adamant that the media was not going to bully me into making decisions – I made that perfectly clear to Frank PR. They reiterated to the media that we would be standing by the short statement we'd put out the night before and had no further comment to make.

Not only did the Saturday papers have a field day, the Sundays also went to town. The thing reached such a crescendo that my PR people were contacted by the BBC to see whether I'd be prepared to appear on Andrew Marr's Sunday morning show to talk about my new appointment.

Again, I hadn't really been prepped on what my appointment entailed; neither had I fully understood the workings of the House of Lords. Someone like me, an ordinary person, doesn't know the technicalities of being a Labour peer, or what taking the whip means, so I was somewhat off-guard.

I turned up at the BBC Television Centre at Shepherd's Bush. In the green room, I met Andrew Neil, who was also about to appear on the show, to review the Sunday papers. His welcome to me was, 'Ah, Sir Alan! I've heard of rats leaving the ship – now there's a rat *joining* the ship!'

As there's no love lost between us and having had a bellyful of the crap in the papers, I was angered by his remark. 'What are you banging on about, Andrew?'

'Well, now you're going to join the Labour Party. My God, rats joining the ship!'

'Listen, mate, when it comes to talking about rats, you should be careful – you were once editor of the *Sunday Times*, so it's a case of the pot calling the kettle black. Do me a favour – just watch your bloody mouth because I'm going on *after* you, and I can tell them a few stories about you too, okay?'

I was very angry and he saw from my face that I was serious. He backed down and said, 'I'm only joking, Alan, only joking. What's the matter with you? Did you get out of the wrong side of bed this morning?'

'No, not at all, Andrew. I just don't think that welcome was called for. You could have just said a simple hello.'

'Yeah, yeah, sure. Honestly, I was only joking.'

'Yeah, well, not one of your better ones, Andrew.'

It just so happened that Andrew Neil didn't go near the subject of my appointment in his newspaper review. Neither did the lady who was also there reviewing the newspapers. She had overheard my heated conversation with Andrew, so I imagine she too decided that my appointment was a topic to steer clear of.

Also present was Lord Mandelson, who was there to discuss the Cabinet reshuffle and defend the policies of the government, who were under a lot of pressure over the recession. I spoke to Peter for a while. He seemed quite distant and he didn't congratulate me on my appointment. He did, however, pick up on my comments to Sky Television and told me they weren't very helpful. 'Just take care, Alan – there are some very clever and hard-working people at the DBIS. Don't assume they know nothing about business. Make sure you don't repeat such things today.'

It would have been nice if Mandelson could have given me a few hints and tips on what to say, but he shot off to a separate room. I realise now that he was preparing himself for a very tough, in-depth interview with Andrew Marr. Understandably, he wasn't interested in me at all – he needed to psych himself up.

Andrew Marr seemed a nice fellow from what I'd seen in previous broadcasts and, indeed, he turned out to be a reasonable chap. He asked me lots of questions about my new role and I explained as best as I could what I thought I would be doing, but I was conscious that most people were focusing on my new position conflicting with my role on *The Apprentice*. I was eager to deal with that issue and, sure enough, it came up. At this point, I did a classic Alan Sugar. I wasn't bothered that the programme was going out live – in fact, I was delighted it *was* live because I knew that as long as I didn't swear or rant, they couldn't edit me out.

I said to Andrew, 'I don't know who this Jeremy Hunt fellow is, or what his game is, but I'm absolutely amazed from what I've seen in the national newspapers, both today's and yesterday's, that this story has attracted so much interest. Why are the Conservatives so worried about me? I'm just somebody who's going to advise the government on small- to medium-sized enterprises. Why are they focusing their attention on me and winding the media up? Why are they winding *you* up, Andrew, about all this stuff? What's the big deal?'

'Well, do you not think there's a conflict of interests in that the BBC has given you a programme and now you are going to be a government adviser?'

I reminded him, 'In the five years I've been on *The Apprentice*, there has never been anything in the programme which has had anything at all to do with political matters. We discuss people buying too many chickens or not selling enough flowers – nothing to do with politics. I'm sure the viewers are as baffled as I am as to what all this fuss is about.'

I continued, 'In fact, Andrew, the biggest reality TV show on air is your one! What you do is interrogate people like myself and Gordon Brown and Peter Mandelson, and you fit us into your format. You don't really care who we are; we're just contestants – it's a game for you. If the Labour Party gets voted out next year, you will do the same to Mr Cameron and Mr Hunt. We are nothing to you other than good TV, part of the biggest reality show on earth. Both you and that tubby fellow from Sky, Adam Boulton, stand outside Number 10 and abuse Gordon Brown. Then there's that ginger bird, Kay Burley, who stands on the green outside Parliament looking for people to wind up – it's all part of a big charade, Andrew. In fact, what *you* do is no different to me hosting *The Apprentice*.'

He was a bit shocked at that reaction and stumbled on his words. He didn't know how to argue the point because it was true. It's cheap television to bring politicians and people like me onto the programme to be provocative and argumentative. You have to really ask whether the interviewer himself has any sincere feelings concerning the arguments he's putting forward, or whether he's just being devil's advocate for the sake of TV sensationalism. That was the point I was making.

Every single day the following week, the *Daily Mail* ran an article about me and my appointment. They wheeled out everyone they had, journalists and columnists alike. It was non-stop abuse, far more than I'd ever experienced before.

The media had engineered a situation whereby either Gordon Brown would have to back down on my appointment or I would have to give up my role at the BBC (or the BBC would have to dump me). I stressed to the BBC that we were being manipulated by the media and that I for one would *not* be bullied – I have a loyalty to Gordon Brown and a certain loyalty to them. But the whole thing was maddening because it was total nonsense – it shouldn't have even got to this stage.

I went home after a meeting with the BBC and told Ann that this was growing into a total nightmare and the simplest thing for me would be to tell Gordon I'd have to give up the idea. Despite the fact that I was very honoured to join the House of Lords and all that stuff, I didn't need all this aggravation.

As usual, Ann kind of left it to me. She said, 'It's something *you'll* have to decide, but to turn down the opportunity of being in the House of Lords is a big thing. Surely you should fight your way through this, to make sure it's a good situation for everyone.'

Eventually, after a couple of days' deliberation Gordon Brown must have realised that his announcement of my role as Enterprise Champion and my appointment to the House of Lords was something he couldn't be seen to withdraw. If he thought the media frenzy over the past few days was a nightmare, it would have been nothing compared to the furore had I refused to give up *The Apprentice* and he'd been forced to backtrack on the whole appointment. And in addition, the BBC sent out a press release saying, in effect, 'Sir Alan Sugar, soon to be Lord Sugar, is not going to be removed from his position in *The*

Apprentice. Furthermore, the appointment he accepted as government adviser does not conflict with BBC policies.'

This was like a red rag to a bull to the Conservatives. The Jeremy Hunt fellow wrote a letter of complaint to the Director-General of the BBC. The letter was answered and his complaints rejected. However, he wasn't satisfied with the answer, so he formalised his complaint and wrote to the BBC Trust. The Trust took several weeks to deliberate, but upheld the BBC's executive management decision that I was free to do *The Apprentice*, though in their summary they recommended to the BBC executives that the programmes I was involved with should not be broadcast during a general election period.

Meanwhile, Liberal Democrat peer Lord Oakeshott was interviewed by Channel Four News. This guy's self-appointed purpose in life is to ensure that *the right type of person* joins the House of Lords and he's another of these people you have to operate on to surgically remove the microphone from their hands. He said he didn't think I was a 'fit and proper person' for the Lords, that my companies were based in the Channel Islands and were not paying tax and that I was involved in some scandal with a female member of staff who was suing the company for unfair dismissal. In short, I wasn't a suitable person to be in the House of Lords until these matters were resolved. All a load of bollocks. On another day, Baroness Something-or-other was also interviewed and added her tuppence ha'penny worth. She said she didn't think I was the right calibre of person, as I didn't deal with women properly. Another load of rubbish.

I was furious with this Oakeshott fellow. I had never met the man and he had no right to say these things. I wasn't going to stand by and let these people slag me off, so I wrote to Oakeshott, telling him he was talking a load of rubbish. I warned him that if he didn't immediately take back what he'd said publicly, I'd be putting the matter into my solicitor's hands.

He thought I was bluffing. He said this slagging off was normal in politics – par for the course. I reminded him that I wasn't a politician and he had no right to mouth off about me and mislead the media. He wouldn't back down, so I got Herbert Smith to fire off a letter to him, telling him that unless he retracted the statements he'd made in respect to my companies, I would be taking him to court. He well and truly shitted himself and I'm pleased to say that I made him appoint a firm of lawyers and spend some money in legal fees. Eventually, he wrote me an apology on House of Lords paper. I was planning to put copies of the apology in the pigeon-holes of each of the lords at the House. In the end, I chose not to do that, but it was a useful exercise because word must have got round that I wasn't going to take any shit from anyone. If anybody had something to say about me, it would have to be fair comment and the truth – the minute they overstepped the mark, I was going to whack them. I wanted there to be no doubt about this in people's minds.

Lord Mandelson told me that I shouldn't be so touchy about these things, as it was typical of the sort of sniping that goes on in the media and from opposition MPs and peers. I said, 'I don't care whether *you* put up with this type of stuff; *I* don't have to and, quite honestly, I've got the money to employ lawyers to go after these people.' He conceded that on most occasions when he considered *he* was defamed, the blocking issue was the cost involved in taking people to court. He simply couldn't afford to do it, which I suppose is fair enough in his case.

The House of Lords Appointments Commission duly considered my application and informed me that it had been approved. I now needed to consult with the Garter King of Arms, Sir Peter Gwynn-Jones, and decide what my title would be. My initial thought was that I'd like to be Lord Sugar of Clapton. Sir Peter, who was a really colourful character, said the purpose of calling myself Lord Sugar of Clapton, or Lord Sugar of Hackney, or Lord Sugar of Wherever was really to differentiate me from any other Lord Sugars there might be in the House of Lords, and as I'd be the very first Lord Sugar, I didn't need to add anything. Despite this, I asked to be known as Lord Sugar of Clapton. He told me it was no problem at all, and that is what I am called today.

Some interesting trivia emerged. First of all, I was really being made a baron, but I would be referred to as Lord Sugar. This meant that Ann would be a baroness, but would still be known as Lady Sugar. My children, Simon, Daniel and Louise, are entitled to be known as, for example, the Honourable Simon Sugar. Furthermore, my male children's wives, like Daniel's Michaela, are also entitled to the Honourable title. Sons-in-law, however, like Louise's husband Mark Baron, for some reason are *not* accorded that honour. Mark saw the funny side and said, 'It doesn't bother me – I'm already a Baron.'

My introduction to the House of Lords was quite an interesting voyage. It meant meeting people like Michael Pownall, the chief clerk, who briefed me on all the rules and regulations. He also asked me about expenses and whether I'd be taking them. I told him, 'Absolutely not!' I viewed this as entering a hornets' nest. I certainly didn't need the money, I had no real expenses to claim and, even if I did, I could imagine the scrutiny it would attract. He explained that I was entitled to an attendance fee every time I was at the Lords, but I could picture the scenario where I'd pop in briefly (as I often do, to meet someone), then have some media sniper picking up on the fact that the clerk had logged me in for the whole day and I was claiming taxpayers' money when I was only there for ten minutes . . . No, thank you very much! There was no way I was going to be exposed to that.

The ennoblement was on 20 July 2009. I took the opportunity of inviting the whole family and some friends to lunch at the House of Lords' River Restaurant and then to watch me being sworn in. I'd have to dress up in ceremonial robes and be sponsored by two other peers, Baroness Vadera and Lord Davis, who would walk me into the chamber. I would read out my pledge to the House, then leave the chamber after shaking the hand of the Lady Speaker.

At the lunch, my grandson Nathan, then sixteen, proposed a toast to the Queen and Nick Hewer, as usual, made a little speech. When I stood up to speak to my family and friends, I was overcome with the moment and started to feel a bit emotional, thinking of my mum and dad. I mentioned that it was a shame they weren't there and that was nearly enough to bring a tear to my eyes again.

My brother-in-law Harold Regal, with a mischievous glint in his eye, couldn't resist saying, 'Not bad, Alan – better than being a dustman, I guess.' It was the last time I heard Harold's lifelong joke about me being a dustman, as sadly he had been diagnosed with terminal cancer earlier in the year and he passed away a few months later.

In between hosting the lunch and dressing up in my robes, I'd arranged for photographs to be taken with me and the family. Louise told me that when we went into the chamber to have photographs taken with my robes on, Derek was very touched, seeing his little brother standing there in the House of Lords, all dressed up.

Then it was time for the ceremony and most of my guests were escorted to the gallery to watch it. Ann, being a new peer's wife, was allowed to go into the main chamber. We had arranged wheelchairs for Harold and my father-in-law Johnnie, who by now, at the age of eighty-seven, was becoming frail. They were positioned at the entrance of the chamber, watching as the very formal procession of me and the others passed by. I was nervous and didn't know what to expect and, when I glimpsed these two men, who had known me for so many years, out of the corner of my eye as we turned into the grand entrance of the main chamber, again my life kind of flashed in front of me and I started to choke up a bit. As I walked by, Johnnie called out, 'Good luck, Alan.' He kind of looked me up and down in my robes and if I didn't know any better, I'd say it was a look that said, 'All right, you've made your point – you *are* good enough for my daughter.'

In the end, the ceremony, which lasted no more than five minutes, was a piece of cake and I ended up wondering what all the fuss was about.

Once the ceremony was over, to consummate the fact that I was now a member of the House of Lords, protocol dictated that I had to de-robe, then come back into the chamber and sit down on the benches to listen to ten minutes or so of the debate. I was then able to go out again and meet the family and friends to wish them farewell. Ann and I went straight from the House of Lords to Stansted airport, as we were flying to Spain for a couple of weeks' holiday.

As we left London and I reflected on the great day, I tuned into Sky News on my car's TV to see them mention that it was on *this* day, exactly forty years ago – 20 July 1969 – that Apollo 11 had landed on the moon. I could clearly remember standing in Rex Radio, an electrical retailer in Kilburn, watching the moon-landing on one of the black-and-white TVs in the shop. Back then, the thought of Alan

Sugar landing in the House of Lords would have seemed equally miraculous.

*

Prior to my formal introduction to the House of Lords, I'd visited the DBIS and was introduced by Shriti Vadera to the two members of staff who would be assisting me, Paul Hadley and Richard Callard. Both of them were a great help in bedding me into Civil Service ways. Part of the deal agreed with the BBC was that I should not have my own office with my name on the door – pathetic, I know. However, I *was* allowed a desk and the use of a computer.

I started to get to grips with the areas in which I could be useful, mainly to do with the Business Link Centres the government ran. These are organisations where they have experts, gurus, mentors, call them what you will, that small businesses can approach to ask for advice. I didn't want to form any opinions too quickly, but I did initially wonder why, if these mentors were so good at dishing out advice, they were working in some government department. Why weren't they out working for themselves?

I agreed to embark on a round-Britain trip to look at some of these Business Link Centres, just to get an idea of what they do. I'd listen in at their call centres, talk to some of their business advisers and meet the companies they were advising. I wanted to get a flavour of what was going on.

It certainly opened my eyes to what was available for small businesses. I quickly realised that these Business Link Centres were indeed very useful, if a little over-staffed. Obviously they weren't there to give people business ideas; they were there to support and advise businesses on questions they had about matters like VAT, import and export, how to collect money from their customers, how they should approach banks, how to prepare business models and spreadsheets, all that type of stuff. The people seeking advice would have to have the seed of an idea themselves. They couldn't jump out of bed one Monday morning, phone up a Business Link Centre and say, 'Hello, I'd like to be in business, please. I fancy running an airline or being a dotcom millionaire – can you tell me what to do?' Believe it or not, the

Business Link Centres *did* get naïve calls like this, so first and foremost we needed to make sure we projected the Centres in such a way that people understood exactly what they were there for and did not have unrealistic expectations.

Paul and Richard had also arranged a fashion parade of the banks for me, as I wanted to find out whether they really were helping small-to medium-sized businesses. Clearly the banks had been beaten up badly as a result of the irresponsible lending which had led to the recent financial disaster and the subsequent injection of money from the government. They were obviously very nervous and now, when they lent money, they were making doubly sure their risks were min-imised. In tightening their belts, there were some genuine stories of small businesses being squeezed – their overdrafts were being taken away, or renegotiated, or changed into long-term loans. It was true that some of the banks *had* taken liberties, but by the time I arrived on the scene and got stuck into the details, I discovered that this poor treatment had been for a short period of time, following the banking disaster, when, as one would expect, the banks went into protective mode.

I also noticed a wave of complaints which, in my opinion, were unreasonable. Some companies were hooking on to the fact that the banks wouldn't lend them money and accusing them of stunting the growth of their businesses. When I examined some of these busi-nesses, I agreed with the banks – I too wouldn't have lent them a penny. In fact, no one in their right mind would have! In some cases, these businesses were virtually bankrupt – they were simply hiding behind this fashionable trend of blaming the banks.

Throughout the rest of the year, I embarked upon a series of seminars around the country, visiting major towns like Manchester, Nottingham and Bristol. We invited audiences of around 800 people each day over two sessions, the idea simply being that I would answer people's questions, giving them some advice on what they could do about their businesses. Most of the time, this went very well. However, in Manchester a gentleman said he had visited three banks and they'd each turned him down. In my long answer to him, I told him that while I wasn't directing my reply to him personally, I wanted to take the opportunity to dispel the current rumour that banks weren't lending to people. I pointed out that there are many companies which don't *deserve* to be loaned money and that people were making excuses about banks to cover up the inadequacies of their businesses.

Unbeknown to me, a *Daily Mail* sniper was in the audience. I had taken the precaution of ensuring all my seminars were recorded, in anticipation of one of these journalists slipping in. I was fully prepared to take them to task if they wrote a pack of lies. In this case, the *Daily Mail*, as usual, decided to take my words out of context, resulting in a front-page headline stating that I had said, 'Eighty per cent of small businesses in this country are not worth lending money to.' It was an outrageous distortion of the truth. What I'd actually said was that we had sampled a small number of cases where businesses had been turned down for loans and that 80 per cent of *those* cases were justified in not being lent a penny – a completely different scenario. Nevertheless, they ran the lie on their front page and predictably it caused uproar amongst organisations such as the Federation of Small Businesses. It escalated into questions being asked in the House of Lords and in the House of Commons.

For the Conservatives, this was manna from heaven. There were questions to the ministers about whether 'Lord Sugar speaks on behalf of the government'. I was a bit disappointed that the ministers answering those questions hadn't been fully briefed that the newspaper had lied. If they *had* been, the simple answer would have been, 'We have read what has been printed in the newspaper and we assume that your questions arise from that. Our simple answer is that it's a pack of lies. There is a recording of Lord Sugar's seminars and we can verify that he did not say that and, therefore, we have nothing to answer.'

Instead, it appeared to me that they also believed what they had read and were somewhat embarrassed trying to answer questions thrown at them by the opposition – a ridiculous scenario. I protested heavily, through Paul and Richard, that in future, having gone to all the trouble of recording these seminars, they should ensure that ministers' staff were briefed in a much better way and should consult with them first when asked questions about my activities.

The only consolation was that the *Daily Mail* was so far up David

Cameron's arse at the time that I guess any sensible person reading its coverage of me over the preceding months would have realised how totally biased they were. They'd gone so dramatically over the top in hounding me that normal and sane people must have been thinking to themselves, 'What *is* all this Alan Sugar stuff they're always banging on about? They're going a bit crazy.' I would say – and I think the rest of Fleet Street would say – that they made complete idiots of themselves.

When I compare the hostile media coverage of my entry into the political world with what I experienced in the football days, *this* type of sniping was different. In the football days, it was conducted by thick idiots who wrote for the tabloids; the snipers here were at a higher intellectual level.

Paul and Richard were bombarded with questions under the Freedom of Information Act about everything I was doing. All these enquiries came from the opposition offices. They must have had loads of people sitting there dreaming up all kinds of questions and hoping for an answer which revealed some juicy story they could hand over to the media. Here's an example: 'What computer equipment does Lord Sugar have available to him? Does he have a BlackBerry supplied by the department? If so, please supply a list of all contacts contained in the BlackBerry.'

Bloody joke! They were told to piss off, as my BlackBerry is my own.

On 25 November 2009, the matter of enterprise and business was being discussed as part of the follow-on from the Queen's opening of Parliament, which had taken place a week or so earlier – an amazing spectacle, as you can imagine. I decided to attend this for the first time, just to see what goes on. The chamber was filled with peers and the Queen read out her charter for the year – essentially what she wanted her government to do. As is traditional, the whole thing was broadcast. At one point, the cameras focused on me – the new boy on the block. The *Daily Mail* took the opportunity of taking a still frame from part of the video. At one stage, I must have looked around as if I were lost and they printed that picture with a headline saying I had been ostracised by all the other peers – a total joke.

In general, the people I've met so far in the House of Lords are a delightful bunch. There are, of course, the inevitable snobs who look down their noses at me as if I'm not entitled to be there. In general, however, the people I've come across and spoken to are very polite – irrespective of what party they support – and most certainly the staff and all the executives running the Lords are exceptional in the service they provide. They all make you feel very comfortable, right down to the post-room clerks, the doormen and the restaurant and bar staff. I quite enjoy my little banter with the man in the document office, who happens to be a Chelsea supporter. Every week we exchange views about how our respective teams have done. It is a great institution and, without a shadow of a doubt, it's a tremendous honour to be a member of it.

I decided that when entering a place like this, it's important not to sling your weight around. There are people in the Lords who have been there for years. Some are extremely eloquent and highly intelligent speakers who are very interesting to listen to. Clearly, before I ever got anywhere near that stage I would need to do a lot of learning. There is nothing worse than a new boy coming in, shooting his mouth off and making a fool of himself. I was determined that was not going to happen.

There is only one way to earn respect, and that is by being judged on what you say and what you do. I made my maiden speech on 25 November. It lasted no more than eight minutes and was well received by the House, though I was a bit nervous until I got into my flow. In the first six months of being in the House of Lords, I quickly learned what to say and what not to say. It was pointless talking to the media any more.

I also came across, on a day-to-day basis, some of the people appointed to Gordon Brown's Business Council. You can see from the look on some of their faces that they didn't think my appointment to the House of Lords or as Enterprise Adviser was a clever idea. In the same way as I've described the husbands of the women who compliment me on my performance in *The Apprentice*, these people have a false smile and tend to just tolerate me. They think I'm a wanker because they've formed an opinion of me either from what they've seen on TV or what they've read in the papers.

Maybe they're simply jealous. I am not a schmoozer – I'm not prepared to suck up to these people just to get their admiration, and I
certainly don't have to justify myself to them. Let's face it, many of
them have simply worked for companies all their lives, or are glorified
civil servants – ex-lawyers and accountants. At the end of the day, like
it or not, I'm Alan Sugar, worth a few hundred million quid from sheer
hard graft. Having said all that, there are some fine people on the Business Council, one of them being Richard Branson, who grew up in the
same era as me. He's a man to be admired and I like to think there is
some mutual respect between the two of us.

*

Due to my commitments, I stayed in the UK until late December 2009,
before going to Florida for Christmas. Ann went ahead of me, a week
or so earlier. When I arrived, I could see a rather pained and worried
look on her face. She told me that while I was on my flight she'd heard
that her father had been taken ill with symptoms that didn't look
too clever. In the past year or so, Ann had told me and the kids that
she was concerned about the decline in Johnnie's health. He'd lost
his appetite and was getting thinner. And, to make matters worse, it
seemed he was losing his marbles a bit, constantly repeating himself
and asking the same questions over and over again.

Johnnie was a very stubborn man. He'd visited the hospital for a
check-up a year or so earlier and was advised to have a series of tests
to investigate some things they were concerned about. However, he
refused any further medical examination, his principle being, 'If you
look, you will find.' Ann was very frustrated with this, but he would
not change his ways. But this new episode frightened him and his wife
Minnie, so he agreed to let Ann's brother Mark and my daughter
Louise (who thankfully were in the UK) arrange immediate medical
consultations.

Sadly, Johnnie was diagnosed with terminal cancer and given only
a few months to live. He was a very difficult man and in his younger
days he had little regard for other people's ways. Even in later life, his
wife Minnie, and to a certain extent Ann, danced around him so that
everything he wanted was laid on and organised for him. This medical

stuff threw a real spanner in the works, and Ann and Mark decided to keep the severity of his situation hidden from him – they both agreed there was no way he could handle it. In fact, Minnie didn't want to accept the reality that he had only months to live.

As the weeks went by and Johnnie got weaker, the whole family witnessed the most terrible sight of this once very forceful, powerful and opinionated man wither away until, sadly, he died on 3 April 2010 at the age of eighty-eight. Having seen his deterioration, at least her father's death did not come as a shock to Ann, but even so she was very upset when the actual moment came.

Johnnie died right in the middle of the Jewish festival of Pesach. In terms of Jewish law, if ever there *is* a good time to leave this earth, it's *not* during a festival. I knew that, in keeping with Jewish tradition, Johnnie would have wanted to be buried as soon as possible. So out of respect for his deeply held beliefs and his love of his religion, I wanted to arrange this for him. I will keep this very short and simply say that I had him in the ground within twenty-two hours of his death. You would not believe the twists and turns it took to achieve this – considering it was a festival – save to say it would have made a tough *Apprentice* task.

We only got confirmation at 12.30 p.m. on 4 April that the funeral would be at 4 p.m. *that day*, so it was amazing to see the number of people who turned up. Not just the extended family, but members of the community from both Chigwell and Southend.

The traditional shiva was held at my home and hundreds of people came to pay their respects. One touching moment was when my nephew read out a lovely eulogy to his grandfather which encapsulated everyone's thoughts.

Johnnie was a proud and honest man, even if his values sometimes seemed crazy. Apart from his religion, his main love was his family, and this love was reciprocated by all of them. As I said to Minnie, 'He died a wealthy man, with all the love and respect he got from his two children, five grandchildren and eleven great-grandchildren.'

I really believe that, compared to materialistic wealth, I would take what he had anytime.

*

In May 2010 Labour lost the general election and that brought an end to my role as government adviser. Having worked with Gordon Brown since 1997, it felt like the end of an era seeing him leave office as Prime Minister. Like most people, I was touched to see the pictures of him leaving Downing Street with his family. I waited a week or so and spoke to Gordon to see how he was getting on, as he had taken a battering in the past months. He was in surprisingly fine spirits and thanked me for the assistance and support I had given him over the past thirteen years. He followed that up by writing a very kind note to Ann and myself.

Britain entered a new era in the political world with a coalition government formed between the Conservative and the Liberal Democrat parties. I found this marriage quite funny, inasmuch as I had witnessed them in the House of Lords tearing strips off each other in the past. I guess it's a case of watch this space.

It sometimes occurs to me that I'm getting close to the age most people retire but I'm not ready to sit back and relax – not as long as there are new challenges out there to spark my enthusiasm. I am sure there will be more to tell one day but this is the end of my story for now. It describes my long and eventful journey from Clapton to Clapton. That's Lord Sugar of Clapton – not Lord Beaverbrook!

Acknowledgements

I'd like to thank Ivor Spital, my longest serving employee, who has worked with me for many years, for all his research into the archives and his input on my text; Michele Kurland, Nick Hewer and Alan Watts for reading an early draft and giving me their helpful suggestions; Mark Bateman for reminding me that some good came out of my years at Spurs. And above all, my wife and children for encouraging me throughout the writing of this book.

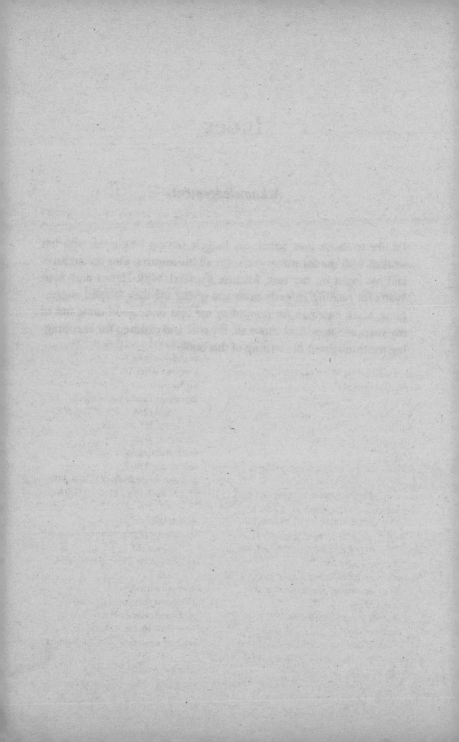

Index

Picture Credits